Lecture Notes in Computer Science 1892

Edited by G. Goos, J. Hartmanis and J. van Leeuwen

Springer

Berlin
Heidelberg
New York
Barcelona
Hong Kong
London
Milan
Paris
Singapore
Tokyo

Peter Brusilovsky   Oliviero Stock
Carlo Strapparava (Eds.)

Adaptive Hypermedia and Adaptive Web-Based Systems

International Conference, AH 2000
Trento, Italy, August 28-30, 2000
Proceedings

 Springer

Series Editors

Gerhard Goos, Karlsruhe University, Germany
Juris Hartmanis, Cornell University, NY, USA
Jan van Leeuwen, Utrecht University, The Netherlands

Volume Editors

Peter Brusilovsky
University of Pittsburgh, School of Information Sciences
135 N. Belleﬁeld Avenue, Pittsburgh, PA 15260, USA
E-mail: peterb@mail.sis.pitt.edu

Oliviero Stock
Carlo Strapparava
ITC-irst, I-38050 Povo Trento, Italy
E-mail: {stock, strappa}@irst.itc.it

Cataloging-in-Publication Data applied for

Die Deutsche Bibliothek - CIP-Einheitsaufnahme

Adaptive hypermedia and adaptive Web based systems : international
conference ; proceedings / AH 2000, Trento, Italy, August 28 - 30,
2000. Peter Brusilovsky ... (ed.). - Berlin ; Heidelberg ; New York ;
Barcelona ; Hong Kong ; London ; Milan ; Paris ; Singapore ; Tokyo :
Springer, 2000
    (Lecture notes in computer science ; Vol. 1892)
    ISBN 3-540-67910-3

CR Subject Classiﬁcation (1998): H.5.4, H.4, H.5., H.3

ISSN 0302-9743
ISBN 3-540-67910-3 Springer-Verlag Berlin Heidelberg New York

Springer-Verlag Berlin Heidelberg New York
a member of BertelsmannSpringer Science+Business Media GmbH
© Springer-Verlag Berlin Heidelberg 2000
Printed in Germany

Typesetting: Camera-ready by author, data conversion by Boller Mediendesign
Printed on acid-free paper   SPIN: 10722531   06/3142   5 4 3 2 1 0

Preface

Web-based application systems, as well as other complex hypermedia systems with a large variety of users, suffer from an inability to satisfy heterogeneous needs. A Web course presents the same static explanation of a concept to students with widely differing knowledge of the subject. A Web bookstore offers the same selection of bestsellers to customers with different reading preferences. A Web museum offers the same "guided tour" and the same narration to visitors with very different goals and interests. A remedy for the negative effects of the traditional "one-size-fits-all" approach is to enhance a system's ability to adapt its own behavior to the goals, tasks, interests, and other features of individual users. Starting in the 1990s, many research teams began to investigate ways of modeling features of the users of hypermedia systems. This has led to a number of interesting adaptation techniques and adaptive hypermedia systems. The Web, with its clear demand for personalization, served as a real booster for this research area, providing both a challenge and an attractive platform.

The International Conference on Adaptive Hypermedia and Adaptive Web-based Systems has continued and joined together two successful workshop series: the Workshops on Adaptive Hypertext and Hypermedia and the Workshops on Adaptive Systems and User Modeling on the World Wide Web previously held in conjunction with such international conferences as User Modeling, ACM Hypertext, and World Wide Web Conference. These workshops were so well-received by the international community that the organizers decided to proceed with a separate conference in the year 2000.

Due to its interdisciplinary nature, the conference has attracted a large number of submissions from researchers with very different backgrounds such as hypertext, user modeling, machine learning, natural language generation, information retrieval, intelligent tutoring systems, cognitive science, and Web-based education. Continuing the tradition of earlier workshops, AH 2000 provided a forum in which researchers and practitioners with different backgrounds could exchange their complementary insights. Overall AH 2000 embodied 4 invited talks, 22 full-paper presentations (selected from 55 submitted), 31 short-paper presentations, and 4 presentations at the Doctoral Consortium. With the exception of some of the invited talks, all presented papers can be found in these proceedings.

The logistics involved in organizing the first full conference of this kind were not trivial. The help from many people and organizations was important to make the conference and the proceedings reach fruition. ITC-irst was glad to host the first European attempt to put together researchers of this field in a conference devoted to this topic. The European Commission sponsorship was very important. We gratefully acknowledge it and consider it a sign of the strategic relevance of this theme. We thank the Program Committee members and the external reviewers for their excellent job in reviewing the unexpectedly large number of submissions. We gratefully acknowledge the help from AH 2000 cooperative societies - AI*IA Associazione Italiana per l'Intelligenza Artificiale, Association for Computing Machinery and its Special Interest Groups SIGART, SIGCHI, SIGIR, and SIGWEB, International Artificial Intelligence in Education Society, and User Modeling Inc. All of them have helped us to deliver the information about AH 2000 to a large number of researchers worldwide. Finally, we are thankful to IJCAI for providing a "conference seeding grant" that has enabled a number of students to attend AH 2000 and to Kluwer Academic Publishers (the publisher of User Modeling and User-Adapted Interaction) for supporting the best paper award.

June 2000

Peter Brusilovsky
Oliviero Stock
Carlo Strapparava

Organization

AH 2000 was organized by ITC-irst Trento, Italy and sponsored by the European Commission: High Level Scientific Conference Program.

General Chair

Oliviero Stock (ITC-irst Trento, Italy)

Program Chair

Peter Brusilovsky (Carnegie Mellon University, USA)

Local Organization Chair

Carlo Strapparava (ITC-irst Trento, Italy)

Doctoral Consortium Chairs

Liliana Ardissono (University of Torino, Italy)
Vittorio Scarano (University of Salerno, Italy)

Program Committee

Marko Balabanovic (InsightMarket.com, UK)
Paul De Bra (Eindhoven University of Technology, The Netherlands)
Dayne Freitag (Just Research, USA)
Wendy Hall (University of Southampton, UK)
Kristina Hook (HUMLE - Swedish Institute of Computer Science, Sweden)
Lewis Johnson (University of Southern California, USA)
Paul Maglio (IBM Almaden Research Center, USA)
Alessandro Micarelli (University of Rome 3, Italy)
Maria Milosavljevic (Dynamic Multimedia Pty Ltd, Australia)
Johanna Moore (University of Edinburgh, UK)
Marc Nanard (LIRMM, France)
Wolfgang Nejdl (University of Hannover, Germany)
Jon Oberlander (University of Edinburgh, UK)
Carlo Tasso (University of Udine, Italy)
Julita Vassileva (University of Saskatchewan, Canada)
Massimo Zancanaro (ITC-irst Trento, Italy)

External Reviewers

Curtis Carver	Mizue Kayama	Pilar Rodríguez
Brian Davison	Eva Millán	Mia Stern
John Eklund	Duncan Mullier	Carlo Strapparava
Miguel Encarnação	Tom Murray	Ross Wilkinson
Serge Garlatti	Estrella Pulido	
Akihiro Kashihara	Riccardo Rizzo	

Co-sponsors

International Joint Conference on Artificial Intelligence
Kluwer Academic Publishers

Cooperating Societies

AI*IA Associazione Italiana per l'Intelligenza Artificiale
Association for Computing Machinery and its Special Interest Groups SIGART,
SIGCHI, SIGIR, and SIGWEB
The International Artificial Intelligence in Education Society
User Modeling Inc.

Table of Contents

Invited Papers

Enhancing Adaptive Hypermedia Presentation Systems by Lifelike
Synthetic Characters 1
  E. André

Full Papers

Dynamic Generation of Adaptive Web Catalogs 5
  L. Ardissono and A. Goy

An Intelligent Tutor for a Web-Based Chess Course 17
  A. Baena, M.-V. Belmonte, and L. Mandow

Adapting Web-Based Information to the Needs of Patients with Cancer ... 27
  D. Bental, A. Cawsey, J. Pearson, and R. Jones

Group User Models for Personalized Hyperlink Recommendations 38
  J. Bollen

Adaptive Navigation Support and Adaptive Collaboration Support in
WebDL 51
  J. G. Boticario, E. Gaudioso, and F. Hernandez

Case-Based User Profiling for Content Personalisation 62
  K. Bradley, R. Rafter, and B. Smyth

Providing Tailored (Context-Aware) Information to City Visitors 73
  K. Cheverst, N. Davies, K. Mitchell, and P. Smith

Adding Adaptive Features to Virtual Reality Interfaces for E-Commerce .. 86
  L. Chittaro and R. Ranon

WAPing the Web: Content Personalisation for WAP-Enabled Devices..... 98
  P. Cotter and B. Smyth

Extendible Adaptive Hypermedia Courseware: Integrating Different Courses
and Web Material 109
  N. Henze and W. Nejdl

Logically Optimal Curriculum Sequences for Adaptive Hypermedia
Systems 121
  R. Hübscher

Towards Zero-Input Personalization: Referrer-Based Page Prediction 133
    N. Kushmerick, J. McKee, and F. Toolan

LiveInfo: Adapting Web Experience by Customization and Annotation 144
    P. P. Maglio and S. Farrell

Adaptivity for Conceptual and Narrative Flow in Hyperbooks:
The MetaLinks System 155
    T. Murray, T. Shen, J. Piemonte, C. Condit, and J. Thibedeau

The MacroNode Approach: Mediating Between Adaptive and Dynamic
Hypermedia 167
    E. Not and M. Zancanaro

ECHOES: An Immersive Training Experience 179
    G. O'Hare, K. Sewell, A. Murphy, and T. Delahunty

A Connectionist Approach for Supporting Personalized Learning in a
Web-Based Learning Environment 189
    K. A. Papanikolaou, G. D. Magoulas, and M. Grigoriadou

Adaptive Hypertext Design Environments: Putting Principles into
Practice 202
    D. Petrelli, D. Baggio, and G. Pezzulo

ECSAIWeb: A Web-Based Authoring System to Create Adaptive Learning
Systems 214
    C. Sanrach and M. Grandbastien

Adaptive Content in an Online Lecture System 227
    M. K. Stern and B. P. Woolf

A Web-Based Soctratic Tutor for Tree Recognition 239
    M. Trella, R. Conejo, and E. Guzmán

Adaptation Control in Adaptive Hypermedia Systems 250
    H. Wu, P. De Bra, A. Aerts, and G.-J. Houben

Short Papers

An Agent-Based Approach to Adaptive Hypermedia Using a Link Service . 260
    C. Bailey and W. Hall

Adaptive Testing by Test++ 264
    M. Barra, G. Palmieri, S. Napolitano, V. Scarano, and L. Zitarosa

What Does the User Want to Know About Web Resources? A User Model
for Metadata 268
    D. Bental, A. Cawsey, P. McAndrew, and B. Eddy

Web Information Retrieval for Designing Distance Hypermedia Courses ... 272
    A. Boitel and D. Leclet

Formative Evaluation of Adaptive CALLware: A Case Study 276
    L. Calvi

How Adaptivity Affects the Development of TANGOW Web-Based
Courses 280
    R. M. Carro, E. Pulido, and P. Rodríguez

An Adaptive Web Content Delivery System 284
    J. Chen, Y. Yang, and H. Zhang

Knowledge Computing Method for Enhancing the Effectiveness of a WWW
Distance Education System 289
    A. Cristea and T. Okamoto

Interface Adaptation to Style of User-Computer Interaction 293
    M. Dimitrova, D. Boyadjiev, and N. Butorin

Adaptation and Generation in a Web-Based Lisp Tutor 297
    I. Fernández-Anta, E. Millán, and J.-L. Pérez-de-la-Cruz

Collaborative Maintenance in ULYSSES 301
    M. A. Ferrario, K. Waters, and B. Smyth

An Adaptive Open Hypermedia System on the Web 305
    G. Fulantelli, R. Rizzo, M. Arrigo, and R. Corrao

Towards an Adaptive Learners' Dictionary 311
    J. Gamper and J. Knapp

Concept Filtering and Spatial Filtering in an Adaptive Information
System 315
    S. Garlatti and S. Iksal

Analysing Web Search Logs to Determine Session Boundaries for
User-Oriented Learning 319
    A. Göker and D. He

Learning User Profiles in NAUTILUS................................ 323
    M. Gori, M. Maggini, E. Martinelli, and F. Scarselli

Lexical Chaining for Web-Based Retrieval of Breaking News............. 327
    P. Hatch, N. Stokes, and J. Carthy

Designing for Social Navigation of Food Recipes 331
    K. Höök, J. Laaksolahti, M. Svensson, and A. Waern

A Study Comparing the Use of Shaded Text and Adaptive Navigational
Support in Adaptive Hypermedia 335
    J. Hothi, W. Hall, and T. Sly

Layered Evaluation of Adaptive Applications and Services............... 343
    C. Karagiannidis and D. G. Sampson

Exploratory Activity Support Based on a Semantic Feature Map 347
    M. Kayama, T. Okamoto, and A. I. Cristea

Adaptivity in AHMED 351
    J. Kurhila and E. Sutinen

An Adaptive Document Generation Based on Matrix of Contents 355
    M. Laroussi, Pr. M. Ben Ahmed, and M. Marinilli

Logical Dimensions for the Information Provided by a Virtual Guide 359
    L. Marucci and F. Paternò

Automated Collaborative Filtering Applications for Online Recruitment
Services... 363
    R. Rafter, K. Bradley, and B. Smyth

ConTexts: Adaptable Hypermedia.................................... 369
    m. c. schraefel

Coherence in Modularly Composed Adaptive Learning Documents 375
    C. Seeberg, A. Steinacker, and R. Steinmetz

ACE - Adaptive Courseware Environment............................ 380
    M. Specht

The Adaptive University Calendar 384
    M. Stede and S. Koch

Sense-Based User Modelling for Web Sites 388
    C. Strapparava, B. Magnini, and A. Stefani

Generating Personal Travel Guides from Discourse Plans................ 392
    R. Wilkinson, S. Lu, F. Paradis, C. Paris, S. Wan, and M. Wu

Doctoral Consortium Papers

Distributed Systems for Group Adaptivity on the Web.................. 396
    M. Barra

Open Multimedia Environment to Retrieve and Organise Documents:
An Adaptive Web-Based IR System in the Field of Textile and Clothing
Industry 403
    C. Chesi and F. Rizzo

Researching Adaptive Instruction 409
    J. E. Gilbert and C. Y. Han

A Modular Approach for User Modelling 415
    I. Torre

Author Index 421

Enhancing Adaptive Hypermedia Presentation Systems by Lifelike Synthetic Characters

Elisabeth André

DFKI GmbH, Stuhlsatzenhausweg 3, D-66123 Saarbrücken, Germany,
andre@dfki.de

Rapid growth of competition in the electronic market place will boost the demand for new innovative communication styles to attract web users. With the advent of web browsers that are able to execute programs embedded in web pages, the use of animated characters for the presentation of information over the web has become possible. Instead of surfing the web on their own, users can join a tour, ask the lifelike character for assistance or even delegate a complex search task to it.

Over the past few years, we developed a number of personalized information assistants that facilitate user access to the Web [2] by providing orientation assistance in a dynamically expanding navigation space. These assistants are characterized by their ability to retrieve relevant information, reorganize it, encode it in different media (such as text, graphics, and animation), and present it to the user as a multimedia presentation.

The screen shot in Fig. 1 shows one of our applications, which is a personalized travel agent. Suppose the user wants to travel to Hamburg and is starting a query for typical travelling information. To comply with the user's request, the system retrieves information about Hamburg from various web servers, e.g. a weather, a restaurant and a hotel server, selects relevant units, restructures them and uses an animated character to present them to the user. The novelty of our approach is that the presentation scripts for the character and the hyperlinks between the single presentation parts are not stored in advance but generated automatically from pre-authored documents fragments and items stored in a knowledge base. For a restricted domain, we are even able to combine information units retrieved from different sources and combine them into a single presentation item. For example, the address entry of a hotel is used as input for another web search in order to generate a map display on which the hotel can be located.

Though a number of similarities may exist, our presentation agents are not just animated icons in the interface. Rather, their behavior follows the equation:

$$Persona\ behavior := directives + self\text{-}behavior$$

By *directives* we understand a set of tasks which can be forwarded to a character for execution. To accomplish these tasks, the character relies on gestures that: express

P. Brusilovsky, O. Stock, C. Strapparava (Eds.): AH 2000, LNCS 1892, pp. 1-4, 2000.

emotions (e.g., approval or disapproval), convey the communicative function of a presentation act (e.g., warn, recommend or dissuade), support referential acts (e.g., look at an object and point at it), regulate the interaction between the character and the user (e.g., establishing eye contact with the user during communication) and indicate that the character is speaking. We use the term *presentation script* to refer to a temporally ordered set of directives.

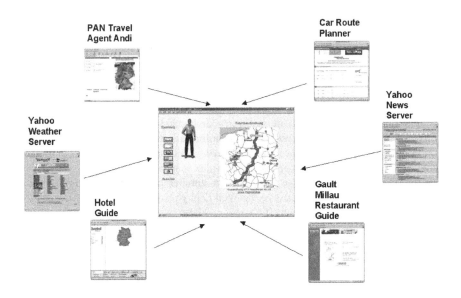

Fig. 1. Personalized Travel Agent.

While a script is an external behavior determinant that is specified outside the character, our characters also have an internal behavior determinant resulting in what we call a *self behavior*. A character's self behavior comprises not only gestures that are necessary to execute the script, but also navigation acts, idle time gestures, and immediate reactions to events occurring in the user interface.

Since the manual scripting of agent behaviors is tedious, error-prone and for time-critical applications often unfeasible, we aimed at the automation of the authoring approach. Based on our previous work on multimedia presentation design [1], we utilize a hierarchical planner for the automated decomposition of high-level presentation tasks into scripts which will be executed by the presentation agent [2]. To flexibly tailor presentations to the specific needs of an individual user, we allow for the specification of generation parameters (e.g., "verbal utterances should be in English", or "the presentation must not exceed five minutes"). Consequently a number of presentation variants can be generated for one and the same piece of information, but different settings of presentation parameters. Furthermore, we allow the user to flexibly choose between different navigation paths through a presentation. That is, the course of a presentation changes at runtime depending on user interactions.

To facilitate the integration of animated agents into web interfaces, DFKI has developed a toolkit called PET (Persona-Enabling Toolkit). PET provides an XML-based language for the specification of Persona commands within conventional HTML-pages. These extended HTML-pages are then automatically transformed into a down-loadable Java-based runtime environment which drives the presentation on standard web browsers. PET may be used in two different ways. First of all, it can be used by a human author for the production of multimedia presentations which include a lifelike character. Second, we have the option to automate the complete authoring process by making use of our presentation planning component to generate web pages that include the necessary PET-commands.

In the talk, the approach will be illustrated by means of several academic and industrial projects currently being carried out at DFKI GmbH.

Part of this research was supported by the German Ministry for Education, Science, Research and Technology (BMBF) under contract 01 IW 806 and by the European Community under the contracts ERB 4061 PL 97-0808 and EP-29335. The talk is based on work by the following people (in alphabetical order): Steve Allen, Elisabeth André, Stephan Baldes, Patrick Gebhard, Bernhard Kirsch, Thomas Kleinbauer, Martin Klesen, Jochen Müller, Susanne van Mulken, Stefan Neurohr, Peter Rist, Thomas Rist, Ralph Schäfer and Wolfgang Wahlster.

References

1. André, E., and Rist, T. (1995). Generating coherent presentations employing textual and visual material. *Artificial Intelligence Review,* Special Issue on the Integration of Natural Language and Vision Processing 9(2–3):147–165.
2. André, E., Rist, T. and Müller, J. (1999). Employing AI Methods to Control the Behavior of Animated Interface Agents. *Applied Artificial Intelligence* 13:415-448.
3. André, E., Rist, T. and Müller, J. (1998). Guiding the User through Dynamically Generated Hypermedia Presentations with a Life-Like Presentation Agent. In: Proceedings of the 1998 International Conference on *Intelligent User Interfaces*, pp. 21-28, New York: ACM Press.
4. André, E., Rist, T. and Müller, J. (1998). Integrating Reactive and Scripted Behaviors in a Life-Like Presentation Agent. In: Proceedings of the Second International Conference on *Autonomous Agents* (Agents '98), pp. 261-268, New York: ACM Press.
5. André, E. Rist, T. and J. Müller (1998). WebPersona: A Life-Like Presentation Agent for the World-Wide Web. *Knowledge-Based Systems*, 11(1):25-36, 1998.
6. André, E. and Rist, T. (2000). Presenting through Performing: On the Use of Multiple Life-Like Characters in Knowledge-Based Presentation Systems. In: Proceedings of the 1998 International Conference on *Intelligent User Interfaces*, pp. 1-8, New York: ACM Press.
7. André, E., Rist, T. , van Mulken, S., Klesen, M. and Baldes, S. (2000). The Automated Design of Believable Dialogues for Animated Presentation Teams. In: Cassell et al. (eds.): *Embodied Conversational Agents*, 220-255, Cambridge, MA: MIT Press.

8.   van Mulken, S., André, E. and Müller, J. (1998). The Persona Effect: How Substantial is it? In: Proc. of *HCI'98*, Sheffield, pp. 53-66.

9.   van Mulken, S., André, E. and Müller, J. (1999). An empirical study on the trustworthiness of lifelike interface agents. In H.-J. Bullinger and J. Ziegler, eds., *Human-Computer Interaction* (Proc. of HCI-International 1999), 152–156. Mahwah, New Jersey: Lawrence Erlbaum Associates.

Dynamic Generation of Adaptive Web Catalogs*

Liliana Ardissono and Anna Goy

Dip. Informatica, Università di Torino, Corso Svizzera 185, I-10149 Torino, Italy
{liliana,goy}@di.unito.it

Abstract. This paper describes the techniques used to dynamically generate personalized Web catalog pages in a prototype toolkit for the creation of adaptive Web stores. We focus on the integration of personalization strategies for selecting the layout and content of the catalog pages, with Natural Language Generation techniques, used to dynamically produce the descriptions of products, tailored to the individual user.

1 Introduction

With the increasing popularity of e-commerce, the development of adaptive Web catalogs has become a central issue. Several commercial tools for the creation of on-line stores tailor the interaction to the customer by suggesting goods on the basis of her/his preferences; however, they adopt quite simple, if any, techniques for personalizing the presentation of items. Most Web catalogs fail to provide the information relevant to the customer's interests and, especially in technical sales domains, challenge her/him with very complex descriptions. Finally, the internal organization of the catalogs unavoidably reflects the designer's view of the sales domain, which can hardly correspond to the customer's one, making it difficult for the user to find the products (s)he needs. In this scenario, the quality of Web stores could be enhanced by dynamically generating personalized catalogs during the interaction with the customer.

The personalization of the presentation style concerns several aspects, including the customization of the page layout and of the media used in the presentation (e.g., see [11,13]), the inclusion of targeted advertisements, and so forth. In this paper, we present the strategies exploited to dynamically generate personalized catalogs in SETA, a prototype toolkit for the creation of adaptive Web stores developed at the CS Department of the University of Torino [2]. In [3], we described the strategies used to handle the user models and personalize the selection of the information to be presented. Here, we focus on two main issues: a) enhancing the accessibility of Web catalogs by providing the user with information about their organization; b) generating rich presentations, where different types of information about products are conveyed in structured descriptions.

---

* This work extends the SETA system, developed in the "Cantieri Multimediali" initiative funded by Telecom Italia. In particular, we thank Cristina Barbero for her contribution to the design and implementation of the NLG module described in this paper.

P. Brusilovsky, O. Stock, C. Strapparava (Eds.): AH 2000, LNCS 1892, pp. 5–16, 2000.

The Web store catalogs generated by SETA are organized as two-level hypertexts: the first level includes pages sketching the main characteristics of the product categories; the second level includes pages describing in detail the items available for each product category. Although the transparency of the catalog could be further improved by providing extra information, such as a map of the store, the separate presentation of product categories and individual items helps the user to recognize whether a product category is relevant to her/his needs as soon as (s)he visits the related page, without inspecting the available items.

SETA exploits template-based Natural Language Generation (NLG) to dynamically generate the descriptions of the product categories and their items: in the descriptions, the system merges different types of information about features and properties of the presented goods. This approach reduces the amount of pre-compiled information to be defined at configuration time: in fact, the NLG module used to generate the product descriptions retrieves the data about products from a single internal information source and supports the generation of text in different languages as well as the production of alternative descriptions of items, tailored to different user characteristics.

2   Adaptivity Issues

In the adaptive hypermedia research, different techniques have been used to develop systems tailoring the interaction style and the information they present to the user's individual characteristics. A major distinction has been made between the personalization of the link level, i.e., the navigation structure, and the personalization of the content level, i.e., the information to be presented [7]. Some researchers, like [8], have focused on the dynamic adaptation of the hypertextual structure to users with different backgrounds. Others, like [16], [17], [12], [9] and [10] have focused on the dynamic generation of text tailored to the user. Some recent applications are also focused on the generation of personalized presentations exploiting life-like characters [1].

Although, as mentioned in section 1, e-commerce has strong adaptivity demands, it constraints the potentialities of adaptive hypermedia in several ways. For instance, from the viewpoint of the customer, Web stores must be accessible via standard equipments, such as a personal computer, a (usually not very fast) Internet connection and a Web browser. Moreover, the time needed to browse the catalog and find the needed products must be as short as possible, and the run-time efficiency of the system is essential.

A further constraint arises in the development of Web store shells, which must satisfy the requirements of the store designer, possibly reducing the overhead in the configuration of a new Web store. There is a trade-off between developing systems characterized by powerful capabilities in the generation of pages, but typically requiring a very detailed description of the domain-dependent knowledge, and the need to configure such systems on new sales domains with a limited effort.

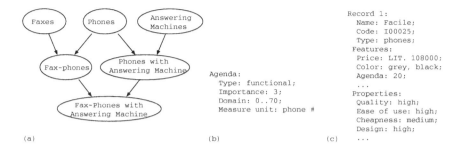

Fig. 1. (a) Portion of the Product Taxonomy. (b) Representation of a feature (c) Representation of an item.

The use of sophisticated page generation techniques, including for instance complex NLG engines, supports the development of extremely flexible systems, but can be problematic for two main reasons: first of all, these techniques may sensibly slow down such systems during the interaction with the customer. Second, the definition of very detailed domain ontologies and large linguistic resources, such as lexicons and grammars, challenges the store designers and threats the exploitation of shells in different domains.

In our work, we have focused on the selection of the type and quality of the presented information, because this aspect is essential to adapt Web catalogs to heterogeneous customers and help them to efficiently get the needed information. To this extent, a dynamic generation of the descriptions presented in the Web catalog is essential. However, to support the configurability of our system, we used template-based generation techniques, therefore avoiding the need for large lexicons, syntactic knowledge bases, and so on. Moreover, we have exploited relatively simple personalization and generation techniques, with a limited impact on aspects such as the system's accessibility, its speed during the interactions, and the overhead in the creation of new Web stores. For example, we have not exploited complex multimedia solutions (as, for instance, VR applications), or high-quality graphics that can dramatically slow down the system.

3   The Knowledge about Products

SETA retrieves the (domain-dependent) information about the product categories, their features and the relations among products from the Product Taxonomy. This is a declarative knowledge base which the system uses to reason about products and exploits to provide a rational organization of the hypertextual catalog. Moreover, the system gets the information about the items available for a product category from a Products Database (DB).

Representation of product categories. The Product Taxonomy (see Fig. 1.(a)) is a conceptual representation of products: its roots describe the general product categories (e.g., phones, faxes, etc.) and have subclasses representing more complex products (e.g., fax-phones, fax-phones with answering machine, etc.); see [4] for details. Each node of the Product Taxonomy defines the features of a product category, specifying the range of values they can take.

This taxonomy is organized as a multiple-inheritance network to handle the description of features in an compact way. In the first version of SETA, this taxonomy was handcrafted, but we have recently developed a tool which creates it automatically, given the definition of the items in the Products DB.

The features of products are structured entities, characterized as follows:

- *Type*: the features concern different aspects of products and we have characterized them in an abstract way, by defining the following feature types:
  - *Functionalities* are basic facilities representing the purposes for which a product has been designed; e.g., phones support vocal communication, while faxes are designed to transmit documents.
  - *Technical features* concern technical details; e.g., the resolution of a fax.
  - *Functional features* include minor facilities offered by the product; e.g., the agendas offered by phones.
  - *Aesthetic features* concern aesthetic aspects, such as color and size.
  - *Generic features* include information not belonging to the previous types, such as the price.
- *Importance*: this slot specifies to which degree the feature represents a mandatory piece of information in the description of a product.[1]
- *Domain*: this slot represents the range of values that a feature can take.
- *Measure unit*: this slot characterizes the type of information which the feature values refer to.

For instance, Fig. 1.(b) shows the "agenda" which is an important functional feature and takes values in the [0..70] range: the values represent the maximum number of phone numbers which can be stored.

Representation of items. The items of a product category are described in the Products DB, which reports the values of their features and properties. As described in [4], the properties are qualitative evaluations of items and can take three scalar values: "low", "medium, "high". For instance, Fig. 1.(c) sketches the description of the "Facile" phone. This item costs Lit. 108.000 and is available in the gray or black colors; it has an agenda to store up to 20 phone numbers; it is a high-quality, very easy to use phone; it is not very expensive and has a very good design.

4   Structure of the Web Catalog

The Web catalog is a two-level hypertext and includes pages describing product categories and pages presenting the individual items of a category.

---

[1] The importance recalls the "salience" of features introduced in [14] and is used to describe the store designer's viewpoint on the relevance of a feature, in contrast to the possibly different customer's interests. For instance, a feature might be essential to the product description, extremely trendy, or other.

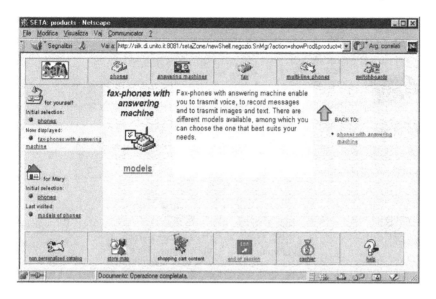

Fig. 2. A page describing the fax-phones with answering machine category.

Product pages. These pages represent the higher level of the hypertext and enable the user to browse the catalog without analyzing the individual items.

A product page is organized in areas displaying the contextual information (leftmost part of the page), the navigation buttons (upper and right parts), the control buttons (lower bar) and the description of the product category (central part). This description specifies the functionalities offered by the product items: e.g., fax-phones with answering machine enable the user to transmit voice, record messages and transmit images and text; see Fig. 2. The description is dynamically generated when the related page has to be displayed, by extracting the functionalities of the product category (defined in the Product Taxonomy as features of type "functionality") and applying a template-based NLG technique to produce the NL sentence; see section 5.

A product page also offers the links to access the pages describing other product categories related to the current one. The Product Taxonomy represents the skeleton of the hypertext: at the beginning of the interaction, the user enters the catalog by selecting some of the main product categories. Then, (s)he can visit pages presenting more complex products, by following hypertextual links corresponding to the possible paths in the taxonomy. Fig. 2 shows a page describing the "Fax-phones with answering machine" category, which the user has reached by visiting the page describing "phones" ("Initial selection" slot) and moving down to the more complex products: "phones with answering machine", "fax-phones with answering machine".

Pages describing items. Given a product page, the user can inspect the items belonging to the related category by following the "models" link, which enables

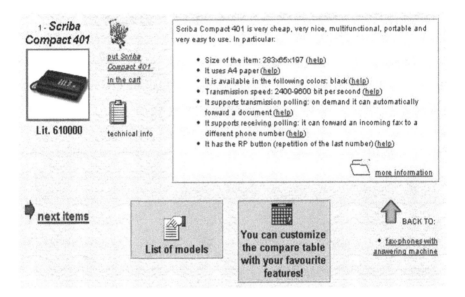

Fig. 3. A page describing a fax-phone with answering machine.

her/him to visit the pages in the lower level of the hypertext. These pages are similar to the product pages, except for the central area, which reports a detailed description of the items. Fig. 3 shows a portion of a page presenting the "Scriba Compact 401" item: the "next items" link allows the user to inspect the other available items, while the "BACK TO" link enables her/him to go back to the product page presenting the product category (higher level of the hypertext).

The description of an item specifies its properties and features. In particular, the definition of the features in the Products Taxonomy is exploited to select the information to be described, while the specific values of both properties and features are retrieved from the record of the item in the Products DB. In order to tailor these descriptions to the user, a Personalization Rule Manager sorts the features on the basis of their relevance to the user's interests and their intrinsic importance to the presentation of the item. Then, it decides how many features should be displayed in the page, on the basis of the user's receptivity. The features falling out of the limit are linked by means of the "more information" link. Finally, template-based NLG techniques are exploited to generate different linguistic descriptions, on the basis of the user's expertise level: simpler descriptions are produced for non-expert users, while more technical ones are provided to experts; see [3].

5 Dynamic Generation of Personalized Web Pages

Fig. 4 shows the architecture of the part of SETA devoted to the generation of the Web pages. The dotted boxes represent agents; the plain ones are sub-

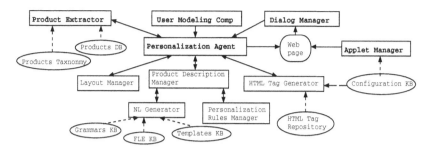

Fig. 4. Part of the SETA architecture devoted to generate the Web store pages.

modules of the Personalization Agent, which generates the Web store pages; the ovals represent knowledge bases and databases.

The Personalization Agent is invoked to produce a page by the Dialog Manager, which handles the logical interaction with the user, deciding at each step which type of page has to be produced next. When the Personalization Agent is invoked, it gets from the Product Extractor the data about products and items; moreover, it gets from the User Modeling Component (which handles dynamic user models [5]) the data about the user's characteristics; then, it generates the pages by applying its customization strategies [3].

The Web pages include standard HTML, produced by the Personalization Agent, and Java applets, provided by the Applet Manager. The Personalization Agent invokes specialized modules which apply different strategies to customize the layout and content of a page. Then, it generates the page by composing the results of their processing. In particular:

- it gets the page layout (background, fonts, etc.) from the Layout Manager;
- it gets the personalized description of the features and properties of products and items from the Product Description Manager;
- it provides these data to the HTML Tag Generator which generates the code for the requested page, by accessing a HTML Tag repository.

We focus on the activity of the Product Description Manager, which generates the NL descriptions of products and items: the selection of the information to be presented (i.e., the sorted feature list) is performed by the Personalization Rule Manager according to the rules described in [3]. Then, the generation of the linguistic description is performed by the NL Generator, which produces the sentences by exploiting the following knowledge sources:

- the Templates KB, storing the templates of the NL sentences;
- the Grammar KB, specifying the (language dependent) syntax of the expressions filling the slots of the templates: this grammar is used to select, for instance, the agreement rules for articles and the connectors;
- the Feature Linguistic Expressions (FLE) KB, mapping the internal codes of products, items, features, properties, and of their values, to linguistic expressions.

While the templates only depend on the selected language (e.g., Italian or English) and can be exploited in different domains, the other two knowledge sources depend on both the language and the sales domain; thus, they have to be configured by the store designer for the specific Web store instance.

The NL Generator exploits JTg2, a small and flexible text generation engine developed by DFKI and CELI, which, basically, produces (complex) strings receiving as input a (complex) object. This engine can be plugged in a NLG component thanks to a straightforward interface to external modules. In the following, we will not describe the engine itself,[2] but we will focus on the strategies we implemented for the generation of the product descriptions in SETA.

Generation of the descriptions of products (product pages).
The NL Generator produces these descriptions by exploiting generic templates and filling their slots with the linguistic expressions of the functionalities offered by the product categories. Such expressions are generated on the basis of the rules defined in the Grammar KB: each rule has an optional applicability test, specifying the contexts where the rule can be applied. These tests are used to represent context-dependent information: as we will see, they are essential to directly feed the NL Generator with the data to be described when the descriptions have to be generated.

For example, consider the first part of the description in Fig. 2: "Fax-phones with answering machine enable you to transmit voice, to record messages and to transmit images and text". The sentence is generated using the template:

$< product\_name >$ enable you to $< functionality\_list >$

The NL Generator fills the first slot with the name of the product category, retrieved from the FLE KB: "Fax-phones with answering machine". For the Italian version, it also selects the appropriate article (the plural feminine "Le" or the masculine "I"), depending on the gender of the name.

Given the list of functionalities offered by the product category, the second slot of the template is filled by exploiting the grammar rules which determine the introduction of the appropriate commas and the coordinating particle "and" to link the last functionality:

funct(w:3) = ""	*{if there are no functionalities left}*
funct(w:2) = altFun	*{if we are describing the last functionality}*
funct(w:1) = altFun + <u>cong</u> + funct	*{if there are only two functionalities left}*
funct(w:0) = altFun + <u>comma</u> + funct	*{otherwise}*

In the rules, "funct" and "altFun" are non-terminal symbols, while "cong" and "comma" are terminal ones. Each rule has an associated weight, shown in brackets: rules with a higher weight are evaluated before the other ones. The applicability tests are shown in italics.

The NL expression of each individual functionality is generated by applying rules such as the following ones:

altFun(w:0) = memoF	*{if memoF is top of of functionality stack}*
altFun(w:0) = voiceF	*{if voiceF is at top of functionality stack}*

---

[2] For more information, see http://www.celi.it/english/tecnologia/tecLing.html.

where "memoF" and "voiceF" are non-terminal symbols, each one associated to a functionality. The NL Generator handles the list of functionalities supplied by the Product Extractor as a stack: it pops the element at the top of the stack and applies the related grammar rule, until the stack is empty. The applicability tests of these rules are used to trigger the rule associated to the top functionality and disable all the other ones. If the rule of a functionality F applies, the NL form is generated, by retrieving the linguistic expression for F from the FLE KB, and F is deleted from the stack.

Generation of the descriptions of items.
The descriptions of items include a presentation of their properties, a list of feature descriptions and an optional "more features" link. Since the properties represent a more general evaluation of the item, the paragraph presenting such properties is linked to the list of feature descriptions by means of the expression "In particular:". Currently, this is the only template expression at the discourse-level and all the rest of the generation process concerns the sentence-level.

The generation of the **property descriptions** is similar to that of the functionalities, but must include the property values. Each property is expressed by means of an adjective or a simple expression: e.g., the ("cheapness") "ease of use" is described by ("cheap") "easy to use". The ("low", "medium" or "high") property value associated to the item is added as a modifier of the adjective: for the English language, "high" is mapped to "very", "low" to "little" and "medium" to the null string.

The **feature descriptions** are generated by examining the customized feature list supplied by the Personalization Rule Manager: similar to the previous cases, the NL Generator handles the feature list as a stack, popping each feature and applying the related grammar rule to produce the NL description, until the stack is empty. Each description includes an optional template, the linguistic expression of the feature and of its values and, in some cases, the measure unit. A grammar rule is associated to each feature defined in the Product Taxonomy; e.g., the description of the "agenda" is generated by exploiting the rule:

agenda = templ + agDescr + agVal + agMeas   {*if agenda is top of feature stack*}

which supports the generation of sentences like "It enables you to store up to 20 phone numbers", where "It enables you to" is the template, "store up to" is the linguistic description, "20" the value and "phone numbers" the measure unit.

Alternative rules can be introduced to support the generation of different (e.g., simple, or technical) feature descriptions, on the basis of the user's domain expertise [3]: the applicability tests of the rules will refer to the user's knowledge level. For instance, the following rules can be defined to support the generation of alternative descriptions of the "agenda" feature:

agDescr = agDescrL   {*if the user expertise level is low*}
agDescr = agDescrM   {*if the user expertise level is medium*}
agDescr = agDescrH   {*if the user expertise level is high*}

where "agDescrL/M/H" define the feature "agenda" in natural language at different technicality levels (e.g., agDescrH = "store up to"; agDescrL = "directly select up to"). This mechanism supports a high flexibility in the generation of sentences: e.g., alternative templates, tailored to different knowledge levels, could be defined as well, by expanding the "templ" part in different ways; for instance, "It enables you to", or "A device is offered to".

6   Evaluation of SETA

The current interface of SETA, its interaction style and its functionalities are the result of several revisions, which we have done thanks to the comments and suggestions of about 120 users involved in a subjective evaluation of our telecommunication prototype. The selected users belong to rather heterogeneous groups, including people with different age, backgrounds, job and education level.

During the experiments, we let the users free to browse the catalog, with the only requirement that, before closing the session, they had to select the item which they would have liked to purchase, out of all the items of a certain product category (specified before starting the experiment, e.g., phones or faxes). We also asked them to make comments on the type and amount of information about products provided by the system and on the quality of the linguistic descriptions.

One of the main results of this evaluation concerns the overall structure of the hypertextual catalog: in the first version of SETA, some users had problems in finding the navigation path which led them to the desired products. In order to improve the clarity of the catalog, we have structured the interface of the Web store as the two-level hypertext described in Section 4. This revision greatly improved the interaction with the users, because they could quickly search the catalog for the products offering the needed functionalities, skipping the descriptions of the items belonging to the other categories.

Another major finding concerned the description of items, which proved to be suited to users with very different levels of expertise, thanks to the adaptation of its linguistic style and to the presence of descriptions concerning both features and properties. All the users appreciated the schematic presentation of the features, based on the use of bullets, which clearly separate each feature from the other ones. Moreover, we noticed that the users' domain expertise influenced the way how they analyze the various items to select the preferred one. More specifically:

- expert users focus on the descriptions of the features offered by the presented item and rely on that information to evaluate the various items, looking at the description of the properties in rare cases;
- novice users strongly rely on the description of the properties of items and confirm that such information helps them in the selection of items.

The tests also confirmed that the use of buttons to ask for particularly technical or complex information is very useful to reduce the overhead on novice or little receptive users. In particular, these users appreciated the fact that the system focuses the presentation on the most relevant features, linking the other ones as "more information", or "technical information", so that the presented information is reduced, in their case, to the essential data.

7   Conclusions

We have described the techniques used in SETA to dynamically generate an adaptive hypertext representing a Web store. Such techniques are embedded in a shell supporting the construction of new Web stores [2]. The dynamic generation of the catalog, based on data retrieved from declarative knowledge sources (e.g., Product Taxonomy and Products DB) represents an improvement with respect to previous approaches, such as [18] and [6], where multiple versions of the catalog existed and the system selected the one to be displayed. In fact, we don't need to store redundant information about the content of pages. Moreover, the product descriptions are adapted to the user at the granularity level of their features.

The specification of the knowledge about products has a strong impact on the personalization of catalogs. For instance, a detailed representation of the domain concepts and of their features, such as the one adopted in [15] supports the exploitation of powerful techniques to describe and compare products to one another. However, it requires the definition of hierarchies for specifying not only the relations among products, but also those among the product features (e.g., to identify more general / specific features, etc.). In contrast, a flat representation of the knowledge about products, such as the one exploited in several information filtering systems [19], can be easily applied, but does not support the generation of structured presentations. In our work, we have adopted a knowledge-intensive approach to the description of the knowledge about products, in order to support effective personalization strategies. However, we have simplified the definition of the product features to enhance the configurability of the system.

In particular, the catalog structure of SETA is based on a taxonomic organization of products which provides the user with a rational navigation space. Furthermore, the classification of features in types supports the use of personalization rules, based on such types, for generating product descriptions in different domains, without requiring the introduction of complex knowledge bases. Although we defined feature types relevant to a technical sales domain, new types can be added with a modest effort. Finally, we have exploited flexible (template-based) NLG techniques, enabling the system to dynamically produce product descriptions, tailored to the individual users, in an efficient way.

Most of the applications using NLG to tailor documents to the reader require a module for dealing with discourse structure. As product descriptions used in an e-commerce interface must support a fast and efficient interaction with the user, we have not yet included a discourse planning component in the NLG module of our current prototype, e.g., like those described in [15], or in [10]. However, we think that a simple discourse planning component could improve the item descriptions to provide an explanation of the way how the item features support certain properties; for instance, in the case of phones, the ease of use relies on the availability of particular "fast access" keys. We are also improving the generation of the property descriptions themselves: in particular, we would like to filter out the properties irrelevant to the user and focus on the most important ones, on the basis of her/his preferences.

References

1. E. André and T. Rist. Presenting through performing: on the use of multiple lifelike characters in knowledge-based presentation systems. In *Proc. 2000 Int. Conf. on Intelligent User Interfaces (IUI'00)*, pages 1–8, New Orleans, Louisiana, 2000.
2. L. Ardissono, C. Barbero, A. Goy, and G. Petrone. An agent architecture for personalized web stores. In *Proc. 3rd Int. Conf. on Autonomous Agents (Agents '99)*, pages 182–189, Seattle, WA, 1999.
3. L. Ardissono and A. Goy. Tailoring the interaction with users in electronic shops. In *Proc. 7th Int. Conf. on User Modeling*, pages 35–44, Banff, Canada, 1999.
4. L. Ardissono, A. Goy, R. Meo, G. Petrone, L. Console, L. Lesmo, C. Simone, and P. Torasso. A configurable system for the construction of adaptive virtual stores. *World Wide Web*, 2(3):143–159, 1999.
5. L. Ardissono and P. Torasso. Dynamic user modeling in a web store shell. In *Proc. 14th Conf. ECAI*, to appear, Berlin, 2000.
6. C. Boyle and A.O. Encarnacion. Metadoc: An adaptive hypertext reading system. *User Modeling and User-Adapted Interaction*, 4(4):1–19, 1994.
7. P. Brusilovsky. Methods and techniques of adaptive hypermedia. *User Modeling and User-Adapted Interaction*, 6(2-3):87–129, 1996.
8. L. Calvi. Multifunctional (hyper)books: a cognitive perspective (on the user's side). In *Proc. workshop "Adaptive Systems and User Modeling on the World Wide Web"*, pages 23–30, Chia, Italy, 1997, http://www.cs.usask.ca/UM99/w4.shtml.
9. R. Dale, S.J. Green, M. Milosavljevic, and C. Paris. Dynamic document delivery: Generating natural language texts on demand. In *Proc. 9th Int. Conf. and Workshop on Database and Expert Systems Applications (DEXA'98)*, Vienna, 1998.
10. B.N. De Carolis. Introducing reactivity in adaptive hypertext generation. In *Proc. 13th Conf. ECAI*, Brighton, UK, 1998.
11. J. Fink, A. Kobsa, and A. Nill. Adaptable and adaptive information for all users, including disabled and elderly people. *New review of Hypermedia and Multimedia*, 4:163–188, 1998.
12. G. Hirst, C. DiMarco, E. Hovy, and K. Parsons. Authoring and generating health-education documents that are tailored to the needs of the individual patient. In *Proc. 6th Conf. on User Modeling*, pages 107–118, Chia, Italy, 1997, http://www.cs.usask.ca/UM99/w4.shtml.
13. T. Joerding. Intelligent multimedia presentations in the web: Fun without annoyance. In *Proc. of the 7th World Wide Web Conference (WWW7)*, Brisbane, Australia, 1998.
14. K.F. McCoy. Generating context-sensitive responses to object-related misconceptions. *Artificial Intelligence*, 41:157–195, 1989.
15. M. Milosavljevic. *The automatic generation of comparison in descriptions of entities*. PhD thesis, Macquarie University, 1999.
16. M. Milosavljevic, A. Tulloch, and R. Dale. Text generation in a dynamic hypertext environment. In *Proc. 19th Australasian Computer Science Conference (ACSC'96)*, pages 417–426, Melbourne, 1996.
17. A. Ndiaye and A. Jameson. Predictive role taking in dialog: global anticipation feedback based on transmutability. In *Proc. 5th Int. Conf. on User Modeling*, pages 137–144, Kailua-Kona, Hawaii, 1996.
18. H. Popp and D. Lödel. Fuzzy techniques and user modeling in sales assistants. *User Modeling and User-Adapted Interaction*, 6:349–370, 1996.
19. P. Resnick and H.R. Varian, editors. *Special Issue on Recommender Systems*, volume 40. Communications of the ACM, 1997.

An Intelligent Tutor for a Web-Based Chess Course

Antonio Baena, María-Victoria Belmonte, and Lawrence Mandow

Dpto. Lenguajes y Ciencias de la Computación, Universidad de Málaga
Campus de Teatinos, P.O.B. 4114, 29080, Málaga, Spain
{mavi,lawrence}@lcc.uma.es

Abstract. Web-based intelligent tutoring systems try to fill the gap between human teachers and printed textbooks as distance learning aids. Actually, intelligent tutoring systems research is concerned with the development of computer tools that show adaptive capabilities in the domain of tutoring, where the student's progress is autonomously monitored and guided according to some tutoring strategy. This paper provides details on the analysis, design and implementation of such a system. STIA (**S**istema **T**utor en **I**nternet de **A**jedrez) is a fully implemented Web-based tool developed to provide adaptive guidance and help while learning chess basics. In STIA the task of the tutor is to guide the student efficiently through the course material, according to the tutoring strategy defined by the course authors. This is achieved in two ways. First, it imposes limits on the portion of course material the students can access. This prevents them from getting lost in a flood of information. Second, the tutor evaluates each student's knowledge through a set of problems, and according to result recommends reviewing theory, solving more problems or advancing through the course.

1 Introduction

Courses are a common way to organize teaching at a high level. For each course and context, teachers decide what concepts will be taught, at what depth, and in what order, devise or select detailed examples for those concepts that are expected to raise more questions, and prepare an evaluation scheme to monitor the students' progress and understanding. In new courses most decisions can be based on the teacher's previous understanding of the course contents. Otherwise, these are frequently motivated by the teacher's previous experience in classrooms. In any case, they are certainly open to changes and improvements during the course itself.

Occasionally, teachers summarize their knowledge about a certain subject and how it should be taught, and write it down in the form of textbooks. Of course, textbooks can never be full substitutes for teachers. Students always have different background knowledge, attitudes, preferences and prejudices. Nobody can be sure where doubts will arise. Teachers are sensitive to this information and use it dynamically to attain their goals. On the other hand, books need to carry static compromises that range from giving too much detail and boring students, to giving too much for granted about students' knowledge, what is usually bad for their motivation. Books do not allow for much flexibility in this sense, except for brief notes like those found in prefaces that

P. Brusilovsky, O. Stock, C. Strapparava (Eds.): AH 2000, LNCS 1892, pp. 17-26, 2000.

explain how the book should be used. In contrast, web based text books can be used by students in a more dynamic way. Systems like ELM-ART [1] or TEA [2] are based in a free navigation style, that is, suggest the recommended topic or action, but do not force the student to take it. The Interbook system [3] can be used to develop web-based text books with a minimum effort.

In recent times, the technologies of the World-Wide-Web (WWW) and Artificial Intelligence (AI) have made possible the idea of developing Web-based tutoring systems like ELM-ART [1] and ILESA [4], where the student's progress is autonomously monitored and guided according to some tutoring strategy. While these technologies are independent, their combination has caught the imagination of a growing community of researchers.

Many people find that the *hypermedia documents* used in the WWW are specially fit for didactic purposes. It is easy to locate concepts and get to them. Links to related concepts can be established. Sounds, graphics, and animations can be integrated with text. Contents can be revised and changed and are immediately available to readers.

AI, on the other hand, is concerned with the development of systems that display some degree of *intelligence*. In this field, the term intelligence has come to mean a kind of measure of how an agent (e.g. a person, an animal, or a robot) is able to adapt its behaviour in a changing environment in order to achieve its goals, whatever these may be. Thus, AI concepts and methodologies offer the opportunity to develop intelligent tutoring systems (ITS) capable of evaluating a student and guiding him/her efficiently through a course material and on a personal basis. ITS research is concerned with the development of computer tools that show adaptive capabilities in the domain of tutoring [5]. Therefore, it is also definitely linked to educational science research.

In short, Web-based ITS try to fill the gap between human teachers and printed textbooks as distance learning aids. This paper provides details on the analysis, design and implementation of such a system. STIA (**S**istema **T**utor en **I**nternet de **A**jedrez) is a fully implemented Web-based tool developed to provide adaptive guidance and help while learning chess basics.

While there are several good chess tutorials on the Web, they are not capable of tutoring actions according to the level of their users. STIA is „intelligent" in the sense that guidance and help should be given on a personal basis to each of its users or students. The system has been implemented in C and JAVA, which allows the inclusion of animations and problems that reinforce the interactive nature of the tutor.

In STIA the task of the tutor is to guide the student efficiently through the course material according to the tutoring strategy defined by the course authors. This is achieved in two ways. First, it imposes limits on the portion of course material the students can access. This prevents them from getting lost in a flood of information [6] [7]. Furthermore, the tutor evaluates each student's knowledge through a set of problems, and according to result recommends reviewing theory, solving more problems or advancing through the course.

The paper is organized as follows. First, the course design is described, including the tutoring strategy. Section 3 presents the system architecture developed to support the course. Section 4 briefly illustrates two sample sessions with the tutor. Then some important implementation details are discussed. Finally, conclusions and future works are outlined.

2 Course Contents and Tutoring Methodology

Surely, the most important part in any ITS is the course itself. This is developed by one or more persons (the teachers), who design the course contents and tutoring methodology. This includes the course objectives, the concepts to be taught, their relationships, the order in which they should be presented to the student, the examples and the evaluation methodology. These features define to a great extent the requirements of the future system.

2.1 A Basic Chess Course

The game of chess can be very complex. Therefore the course was limited initially to beginners learning basic concepts like piece movement, notation, and simple checkmates. This set of basic rules and concepts should allow a beginner to start playing (though almost surely in a rather naive way, given the amount of sophistication that can be reached even in local chess tournaments), which is the stated objective of the course.

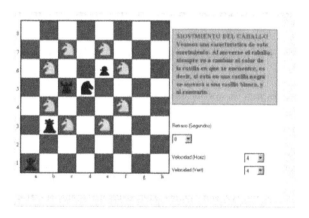

Fig. 1. Theory page: This page illustrates the legal movements of the knight using an animated example

The chess course in STIA was designed in part according to the Curriculum Theory [8], which structures the domain in lessons and prerequisite relationships between them. Some amount of flexibility was introduced in the curriculum sequence to prevent users with previous knowledge to go again through concepts they already know. At a high level concepts have been arranged in three different levels according to their difficulty. When the student starts his/her first session, he/she is asked about his/her previous knowledge of chess, and STIA lets him/her proceed to the appropriate level. The three levels are,

1. Basic concepts: intended for students that are taking their very first steps in chess. These include the description of the chessboard and the different pieces with their legal movements.
2. Game goals: At this level the student can start to play for the first time. The concepts included here are the initial location of pieces, advanced movements like *to castle the king*, and possible game outcomes like *draw*, *stalemate*, and *checkmate*. Additionally, the student is taught basic movement notation, which is not strictly necessary for a beginner's play, but is a useful support for concepts in the next level.
3. Basic checkmates: which show how to succeed in some common game situations, where only a few pieces are involved.

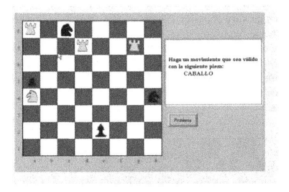

Fig. 2. Theory page: this page shows an interactive chessboard where the student can move pieces using the mouse, and is informed of good and bad movements

The course explains seventeen different chess concepts. All are described textually and illustrated graphically with the help of computer animations. The student is encouraged to gain practical experience with them through sets of practice problems available on request. Attractive Web pages have been designed for all concepts. For example, to illustrate basic piece movements, animated chessboards show legal movements (figure 1). Practice problems are provided in the form of interactive chessboards where the student can move pieces using the mouse and is informed of good and bad movements (figure 2).

A detailed description of the course contents is well beyond the scope of this paper. Probably the best reference to the course contents is the course itself, which is currently available at http://www.lcc.uma.es/stia/index.html (in Spanish).

2.2 Tutoring the Chess Course

STIA incorporates a tutor that evaluates the student's knowledge and provides him with just the portion of material deemed adequate for his current understanding of chess. At any time, the student should move freely only through the portion of material that has been made available to him. To make this guidance possible, the tutor uses two kinds of knowledge:

▢ Knowledge about the curriculum structure. This is based in prerequisite constraints that establish how concepts are organized so that the learning process is clear, easy, and effective. It is the skeleton of the course contents described above.
▢ Knowledge about the student, particularly about his understanding of the chess concepts explained in the course

It is through these two kinds of knowledge that the tutor is able to adapt its guiding actions for each particular student. While knowledge about curriculum structure is available a priori, knowledge about each student is gained dynamically during the course through interaction. The main adaptation capability of the system is the navigation. The same pages of the tutorial provide different navigation possibilities, customized navigation links and buttons, depending on the student's profile (page variants).

The evaluation methodology defines how knowledge about the student is to be gained and recorded. Two options were considered in STIA for evaluation: multiple choice tests or interactive problems (figure 3). The latter option was selected since it provided more motivation for students trying to learn how to play a game, which is in line with the course objectives. However, this requires a more complex evaluation scheme and more programming effort.

Evaluation criteria vary for each problem, but most include elapsed time, help requests, as well as answer accuracy. These results are in a 0-10 score. A minimum number of problems need to be solved for each concept, and an average score equal or better than five is needed before the student is allowed to proceed to the next concept. The student may receive at request some help or the problem's solution with associated penalties in the final score. The simpler problems can be solved with a single movement, while advanced ones call for several movements.

Fig. 3. Evaluation pages: these pages contain interactive problems, which are used to evaluate the student's knowledge. Evaluation criteria include elapsed time, help request and answer accuracy

Problems for the same concept are sorted according to difficulty. Once a student has read about all concepts in a level and has been evaluated satisfactorily in them, he can proceed to the next level (figure 4).

The student's interactions with the tutor may be: join the course, log into the system, navigate freely through theory, navigate through theory following tutor advises, request problems, request help, and send back problem solutions.

The tutor's interactions with the student may be: ask the student to review theory and grant or deny access to course material (evaluation problems and theory pages).

It is important to note that the intelligent tutor does not know anything about chess. It is not a 'chess expert' in any sense. What the tutor knows about is how to monitor and guide a student's progress through some course material. It knows about the elements that make up the course: concepts and the relationships between them, problems, evaluation, and students' scores and progresses.

3 System Architecture

A software architecture has been developed to support the course and the tutoring actions described in the previous section. The main components of STIA are shown in figure 5 and described below,

▫ **Course material**. STIA appears to the student as an hyper-document written in HTML language. The hyper-document is made up of nodes (or information pages), and links between them. There are three different kinds of pages:

1. Theory pages. These introduce new concepts using animated examples and interactive chessboards, but are never used to evaluate the student's knowledge.
2. Evaluation pages. These are used to evaluate the student's understanding of concepts already visited. Each one contains a different problem.
3. Special pages. These are needed for additional interaction with the student (log-in page, welcome page, evaluation results page, and so on).

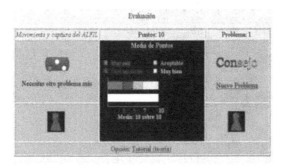

Fig. 4. Evaluation page: in this page the tutor evaluates the student's knowledge through a set of problems, and according to result recommends reviewing theory, solving more problems or advancing through the course

- **User interface**. Since the course material is composed of hyper-documents, the interface can be any standard Web navigator (like Netscape or Internet Explorer).
- **Didactic module**. This is the core component in the tutor that decides about the „intelligent" tutoring actions. The didactic module uses two knowledge structures to reach decisions,

1. The **curriculum structure**, which has a great influence in the system's flexibility and adaptability. The curriculum organizes the tutorial contents in concepts, taking into account: 1) its order in the learning process and, 2) the prerequisite relationships between them. This arrangement of the concepts is basically linear, but still leaves some room to provide adaptation and flexibility of the curriculum to the student's profile (knowledge and capabilities).

   In this sense, and in order to prevent students with previous knowledge to go again through concepts already known, they are asked to establish their knowledge level of chess when their first session with the tutorial is started. STIA provides three different possibilities: beginner, medium and expert. The curriculum structure is used decide the order in which the student will enter to the different parts of the course (basic concepts, game goals and basic checkmates), and his/her freedom or guidance degree in the concepts learning process, depending on the selected knowledge level and the concepts' arrangement above mentioned.

2. The **student model**. The student model is an overlay over the domain knowledge (for a description of overlay student models see [9]). The information stored is: (1) Profile: the access level granted to the student; (2) Domain knowledge: a record of the concepts the student is believed to have learned; (3) History: a records of the problems that were solved by the student and the score reached.

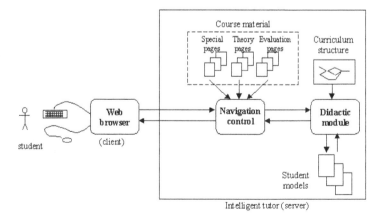

Fig. 5. System architecture

The student is advised to proceed to a new concept or to evaluation pages on the basis of simple checks with the curriculum structure and his own model. When the curriculum is linear there is not much room for adaptability. However, if the curriculum has a rich structure, more room is available for adaptation to each student's preference and capabilities.

The most complex decisions taken by the tutor involve the evaluation of the student. In STIA problems are selected according to different criteria for each course level. These include student's current knowledge, the number of problems already presented on the same concept, and estimated problem difficulty. Therefore, different problems may be presented to different students and in different orders, and care is taken not to present the same problem twice to the same student.

Finally, the didactic module provides the customized navigation links that are to be included in each student's pages depending on his model.

▢ **Navigation control**: This module carries out two important functions, communicate the students with the tutor, and deliver the customized course material requested by students. Therefore, this module executes the tutoring actions suggested by the didactic module.

4 Typical Tutoring Sessions

A new student. Before a new student can join the course, the system's log-in page requests her name, a new password, and information regarding her previous knowledge of chess (her profile). The didactic module through navigation control receives this information. A new student model is created, and access level is granted according to profile. Then a welcome page is returned that lets the student proceed to an adequate course page.

A session with a known student. Let's assume a different student wants to continue her course. After typing her name and password at the log-in page, the system recovers her model and sends back a welcome page which contains a link to the most advanced concept reached in previous sessions.

The student may navigate freely through already visited theory pages. These are customized with a „return" button that will take her right back to her most advanced theory page. Problem pages for known concepts are no longer available since the student was already evaluated for them.

After examining and practicing with the new concept (figures 1,2), she can request a problem page (figure 3). Then the system selects an associated problem according to the student's model. Once she receives the problem page, the system records a temporary 0 score, thus encouraging her to send back the answer (whatever it is, it can never be worse than 0).

Depending on the evaluation results and the student's model, the system sends back a page displaying the student's average and some advice in the form of a customized link (go through to next concept, solve a new problem, or go back to theory) (figure 4).

5 Implementation Details

This section describes some of the techniques used to turn the architecture described previously into a working reality. There are two common ways to associate programs with HTML documents: CGI programs and JAVA applets. Both have been used in STIA to solve different problems.

Perhaps the main problem in the development of a guided Web-based tool is the fact that the Web itself is based on the idea of unguided navigation. Thus special control mechanisms need to be devised.

This problem is solved in STIA with the navigation control module (NC). It is a CGI program written in C that is run on the server and communicates with the user's navigator. Course pages are not full HTML pages, but HTML templates that contain special STIA marks or keywords. Before pages are sent to the student, the NC module checks the student's knowledge through the didactic module and replaces these keywords with customized navigation links and buttons. Thus, the same pages provide different navigation possibilities depending on the student's model current status (page variants).

All navigation links and buttons are actually calls to the same NC CGI program that include the necessary parameters needed to recover, build, and send back the requested pages (page name, an internal student ID, and so on).

The didactic module itself is another program written in C run on the server that keeps each student model in a separate file (a student database could be used instead).

A different problem arises from the decision to include interactive practice and evaluation problems in the course. Both are built as JAVA applets, and are therefore run on the client's computer. The difference between them is that the former is not intended for evaluation purposes. Evaluation problems include help, mistake explanation, solutions and evaluation criteria. After the applet calculates the score, it is sent back encrypted to the tutor. Navigation control de-encrypts before sending it to the tutor. Each problem is a different JAVA applet. This is a heavy programming task, but the course is much more attractive, since there are very different kinds of problems. Some applets include a simple code that plays with the user in problems related to basic checkmates.

The use of illustrative animations, on the other hand, does not pose a special problem, since they can be easily included as GIF files.

6 Conclusions and Future Works

Intelligent tutors can be built to serve the specific tutoring needs of Web-based courses. This paper describes the main features of such a system: course and tutoring strategy design, system architecture, and Web-related implementation details.

The course takes advantage of the possibilities offered by Web-based documents (like navigation links, animations, and interactive JAVA applets) to make the course more attractive, enjoyable and effective. Furthermore, the course provides additional capabilities not available in traditional textbooks or Web-based chess tutorials. These include help and guidance through the course on the basis of each student's knowledge and progress. Customized tutoring actions involve course material sequencing and adapted evaluation.

Regarding future work, some aspects in STIA that can be improved have already been identified. Current trends in education consider evaluation as a process where both the student and the teacher are evaluated. A student's mistake reflects, in an important sense, a teacher's misjudgment that requires some reflection. The student models, recorded by STIA, provide an important feedback on the difficulties found by students during the course. In this sense, an important research direction is to improve the didactic module reasoning capabilities, taking this information into account.

References

1. Weber, G., & Spechlt, M.: User modeling and Adaptive Navigation Support in WWW-based Tutoring Systems. In: Proceedings of the 6th International Conference on User Modelling UM'97 Vienna, New York: Springer Wien New York (1997)
2. Belmonte, M.V., Berbel, J., & Conejo, R.: TEA: An Agrarian Economics Instructor System. European Journal of Engineering Education, Vol.22, No. 4, pp. 389-399 (1997)
3. Brusilovsky, P., Schwartz, E., & Weber, G.: A Tool for Developing Hypermedia-based ITS on WWW. In: Proceedings of Workshop on Architectures and Methods for Designing Cost Effective and Reusable ITS at the 3rd International Conference on Intelligent Tutoring Systems (1996)
4. López, J. M., Millán, E., Pérez J.L., & Triguero F.: ILESA: A web-based Intelligent Learning Environment for the Simplex Algorithm. In: Proceedings of the 3rd International Conference on Computer Aided Learning and Instruction in Science and Engineering CALISCE'98 (1998)
5. Shute, V. J.: Intelligent Tutoring Systems: Past, Present and Future. In D. Jonassen (ed), Handbook of Research on Educational Communications and Technology. Scholastic Publications (1995)
6. Thuring, M., Hannemann, J. & Haake, J.: Hypermedia and cognition: designing for comprehension. Communications of the ACM, 38, pp.57-66 (1995)
7. Isakowitz, T., Sthor, E. & Balasubramanian, P.: RMM: a methodology for structured hypermedia design. Communications of the ACM, 38, pp. 34-44 (1995)
8. Lesgold, A.: Towards a theory of curriculum for use in designing intelligent instructional systems. In: Mandl, H., Lesgold, A. (eds.): Learning Issues for Intelligent Systems. Berlin, Springer-Verlag (1988)
9. VanLehn, K.: Student Modelling. In M. C. Polson, & J. J. Richardson (eds.), Foundations of Intelligent Tutoring Systems. Hillsdale, NJ: Lawrence Erlbaum Associates Publishers (1988)

Adapting Web-Based Information
to the Needs of Patients with Cancer

Diana Bental[1], Alison Cawsey[1], Janne Pearson[2], and Ray Jones[2]

[1] Dept of Computing and Electrical Engineering, Heriot-Watt University, Edinburgh
EH14 4AS, UK
{alison, diana}@cee.hw.ac.uk
http://www.cee.hw.ac.uk/~diana/patinfo/index.html

[2] Department of Public Health, University of Glasgow, 1 Lilybank Gardens, Glasgow
G12 8RZ, UK
j.pearson@clinmed.gla.ac.uk, r.b.jones@udcf.gla.ac.uk

Abstract. Good patient education can help to reduce health service
costs and improve the quality of life of people with chronic or terminal
conditions. Adapting educational materials to the patients' needs and interests can make them more effective. Computer-based techniques make
this adaptation more feasible.

In this paper we describe a theoretically motivated framework for the
provision of computer-based information for cancer patients, and the
computational techniques used to implement it. Our goal is to develop
an interactive hypertext system which could provide patients with the
right information at the right time, avoiding some of the need to search
through the copious literature available.

The paper describes how we use an explicit model of relevance to select
and present information that is adapted at different levels to the situational and process-based aspects of the patient's illness and treatment.

1 Introduction

Good patient education can help to reduce health service costs and improve
the quality of life of people with chronic or terminal conditions. Computers
can be used effectively to complement more traditional means of information
giving, such as personal contact, posters and leaflets, and public access health
information kiosks are widely accepted.

Studies in health promotion suggest that educational materials have a higher
impact when they are adapted to the individual patient (e.g. [17]). The effects of
adaptation have been demonstrated convincingly for written materials (e.g. in
smoking cessation [18]), and there is also some evidence that tailoring of interactive computer-based presentations would have similar benefits in areas such
as decision aids for cancer patients [16]. Other work on personalised computer-
based patient education is summarised in [3].

A wide range of health information exists on the World Wide Web. For example OncoLink, the University of Pennsylvania Cancer Center Resource[1], offers

---

[1] URL: http://cancer.med.upenn.edu/

P. Brusilovsky, O. Stock, C. Strapparava (Eds.): AH 2000, LNCS 1892, pp. 27–37, 2000.
© Springer-Verlag Berlin Heidelberg 2000

extensive information about cancer, with information for professionals and researchers as well as the general public. The variety and quantity of information in these sites make them potentially overwhelming. A few health information Web sites do provide some minimal tailoring (for example, Storksite[2] offers readers a bulletin for each week of their pregnancy) but these sites do not have an explicit model of relevance. Our goal is to develop a model which could provide patients with relevant information at the right time, avoiding some of the need to search through the copious literature available. While not all patients will want this facility, we believe that it may be especially valuable for patients who have difficulty conducting a literature search.

In earlier research [2,6], we used techniques from adaptive hypermedia [5] and natural language generation [13] in a hypertext system which presented patients with information from their own medical record and explained the terms used in a personalised way. Simple medical information was encoded formally in terms of object hierarchies that describe illnesses, treatments and tests. A small collection of general rules generated the text to describe different objects. The rules also generated hyperlinks, so that the reader could access explanations of other terms used in the text. Pages of hypertext and links were generated on demand, as the user selected each page.

In this early research, personalisation was achieved in three ways. The information was automatically organised round the patient's own medical record, so that information relevant to the patient was most readily available. It also provided the patient with summaries of *their* particular treatments, e.g. "You are taking X twice a day". Finally, a dialogue history allowed the system to refer back to items that were already explained. This system was evaluated on a small scale with patients from a diabetes clinic, who found that it gave useful and appropriate information [2]. A simplified version of this system was also used to tailor information for cancer patients, and a randomised trial demonstrated that patients preferred this system to one that provided general information only [6].

The adaptation in this early cancer system was very simple; we did not have any specific theoretical framework motivating the approach. The tailoring was also quite fine-grained. Information was selected at the level of individual sentences, phrases and even words. In the rest of this paper, we describe subsequent research in which the essential developments are: a theoretically motivated framework for the provision of information; tailoring at a coarser grain in which whole paragraphs of information can be selected or rejected; and an architecture which applies filters to select the most relevant information for the patient.

2   A Process Model of Cancer Patients' Information Needs

Cancer patients' need for information varies according to their situation and disposition, as well as the process of illness and treatment. Cancers are of many

---

[2] URL: `http://www.storksite.com/`

types, with different severities, courses of illness and courses of treatment, and patients need information that is relevant to their own situation. These are *situational* variations. Different individuals respond differently to the stress of cancer. Some respond by avoiding information while others seek information and wish to take an active role in decision making. These are *dispositional* needs. Patients also need different information at different stages of their illness and treatment, for both practical and psychological reasons. Patients have different practical concerns at different times, such as choosing a treatment [16], or caring for themselves on leaving hospital [10]. The patients' psychological needs also change, affecting their ability to deal with information and their priorities for information [12,8]. These are *process-based* variations. Meanwhile socioeconomic differences (such as gender and education) seem to make comparatively little difference to patients' desire for information (e.g. [10]).

Cancer puts patients through an identifiable series of psychological stages [9]. These process-based stages affect the types of interactions (one-to-one or group) and the types of supporting media (e.g. booklets, audio-visual material, tutorial programs) that are most likely to be useful. For example, when patients are first coming to terms with very shocking situations, such as at first diagnosis or relapse, they need short explanations of key information. Once misconceptions take hold, they may be difficult to correct and cause great anxiety.

Coping Theory [7] offers an underlying explanation of what type of information is likely to be relevant and acceptable to the patient. Patients use information to cope with the threat or harm posed by illness, and therefore the information offered must help them to cope with the most immediate and most severe threat. Patients are unlikely to attend to less relevant material until they have assimilated the most relevant information. Several studies of cancer patients' information needs have been based on this theory. In particular, information for cancer patients can be divided into four categories [8]):

Disease concerns This category covers information about diagnosis, tests, treatments and prognosis, including survival.

Personal concerns The impact of the disease and treatments on the patients' physical well-being and ability to function; psychological well-being; job or career; and long-term plans or goals.

Family concerns The physical, emotional and financial impact on the family, and communicating with them about the cancer.

Social concerns Communicating with friends about the cancer; maintaining friendships and membership of social groups; the need to make contact with medical staff and to make friends with other patients and their families.

A similar hierarchy of information has needs has been identified and successfully used in the Migraine system [4] which informs migraine patients. For cancer patients, we explicitly add the dimension of time and process–based needs. Cancer patients value different types of information at different stages. During the initial distress, disbelief and shock which results from pre-diagnostic symptoms and diagnosis, life-and-death concerns are paramount. Patients may be unable to absorb much information and they may use denial as coping strategy. Following this initial shock and up to the end of the initial treatment period, patients generally start to adapt to their illness and begin to be able to absorb more information. During these early stages, informed consent to treatment may be required. Once treatment is finished, coping strategies can be taught and social relationships become more important, while other issues such as work and finance, sexuality, and fears may also be explored [9]. However, information about their disease and treatments remains important to many patients, and they appreciate re-iteration of this information even when it is no longer of critical importance [12].

3 A Preliminary Investigation

The research outlined above provides us with a framework for categorising information for cancer patients, and suggests how we may assess the likely relevance of different types of information at different time points. This does not, however, translate straightforwardly into the development of a tailored computer system. We must both develop very specific rules from the general guidelines suggested above, and also deal with the specific characteristics of interacting with a computer.

To obtain some early feedback on the feasibility of a process-based approach and to inform the design of the automated system, a preliminary investigation was undertaken with patients from a major cancer centre[3]. Prototype systems were developed, all of which tailored information to the patient's medical record and some of which also tailored information to the time point in the patients' illness and treatment. The information in these prototypes was hand tailored by the researcher.

Patients with breast and prostate cancer who had taken part in an earlier study on personalised information [11] (which was not time-based) were invited to take part in this study. Due to difficulties in getting patients to participate and the time needed to hand tailor the information, only nine patients were able to take part in this study. All nine participants tried out the prototypes and then completed a feedback questionnaire. They were asked about whether they found the prototypes easy to use and which of the systems they preferred.

None of the patients assessed any of the systems as difficult to use. Four of the patients declared they would prefer to have relevant information selected for them on a time basis, while four would have preferred to have had all the information available at once and make their own selection (the ninth patient expressed no preference).

From this preliminary investigation, we can conclude that a time-based presentation was likely to be feasible and usable by patients, and that enough patients valued the time-based presentation to make further investigation worthwhile. The numbers taking part were too small to draw any firm conclusions

---

[3] The Beatson Oncology Centre, Glasgow

about users' preferences for presentation methods, but the feedback from this study influenced the design of our subsequent architecture.

4   A Time-Based Architecture Which Models Patients' Information Needs

In this section, we describe: the representation of information about the patient; the representation of information about cancer; and the text planning methods which adapt the presentation to the patient at each of the different levels. Our implementation used an object-oriented extension of Prolog, and we use (a simplified version of) this notation in the following figures and examples.

4.1   Representing Information About the Patient

In our present work we focus on the type of cancer, the stage and severity of cancer and the treatments being undergone. Other information such as specific symptoms and side effects of treatment encountered may also be included. We expect that this type of information would be available in advanced computerised medical records systems. We have encoded this medical information using the Read medical code system [15], in which e.g. B46 is prostate cancer, B34 is breast cancer. In our earlier work, we used a static representation of the patient record – a list of Read codes with dates of diagnoses, treatments etc. attached, as described in [2]. In this work we extend the representation so as to distinguish the patient's place in the "cancer process".

The process is represented by a timeline, that is, a sequence of time frames. Each time frame represents the patient's current position in the process. Cancer treatments often extend over time and have multiple parts that may overlap. A typical timeline might contain frames such as: at diagnosis; before chemotherapy; during chemotherapy; after chemotherapy and before radiotherapy; during radiotherapy; at follow up.

Our implementation uses a modified version of the interval calculus [1], in which the events are treatments, tests and diagnoses. Events can have a start date, a stop date and a duration. We have the following relationships between events: *at*, *before*, *after*, and *during*. These relationships describe the timeline for each patient's illness and therapy (Figure 1). A time frame describes the patient's situation during a period when all of these relationships to events are unchanged.

In each time frame, different issues are explored and they are explored to different depths. For example, in the frame immediately after diagnosis, the diagnosis is explored in detail while treatment options are explained only in overview, and follow-up care is not raised as an issue at all; and in the following frame diagnosis is summarised while treatment is explored in detail. The following sections describe the representations that we use to allow this, and the way in which they are used.

frame(frame_1, at, B46)	At a diagnosis of prostate cancer
frame(frame_2, before, 59)	Before radiotherapy ...
frame(frame_2, before, 52)	... and X-ray
frame(frame_2, before, 7B36)	... and surgery

Fig. 1. Patient data: Fragment of a timeline

4.2   Representing the Cancer Information

Information about cancer is represented at two levels: the *issues* or topics that might interest the user; and the *texts* which inform the user about each issue. When a user selects an issue, the response will be made up of one or more texts. Each text is independent chunk of information, usually consisting of one or more sentences. Issues and texts are annotated with information about when they are relevant.

- the psychological category of information being conveyed;
- the time when this information is most likely to be relevant;
- the type of illness, test, treatment etc. to which it is relevant.

Issues Each issue corresponds roughly to a question or a heading which refers to some paragraphs of explanatory text (Figure 2). Each issue is classified into one of five psychological information categories: diagnosis, treatment, personal, family and social. For example, issues in the "treatment" category include "Which treatments are available?" and "What are the side effects of treatment?" Each issue is also annotated with information about when it is relevant (using the *before*, *after*, and *during* relationships), and the type of illness and treatment (using the same Read code system as is used in the patient's medical record).

```
which_treatment_issue :: super(issue),
    category(treatment),
    relevant_time(at, B),
    title('Which treatments are available?'),
    texts(which_treatment_texts),
    plan(which_treatment_plan)
```

Fig. 2. Example of the representation for issues

The issues themselves are quite general, while the text that is displayed for each issue may vary considerably according to the individual. Each issue therefore points to a *set* of texts in a database.

```
which_treatment_texts :: super(text),
    issue(which_treatment)
which_treatment_prostate :: super(which_treatment_texts),
    code(B46), level(overview),
    text('There are many choices of treatment for prostate cancer.
        This depends on a number of different factors. ...')
which_treatment_breast :: super(which_treatment_texts),
    code(B34), level(overview),
    text('Surgery, radiotherapy, hormone therapy and chemotherapy
        may be used alone, or in combination, to treat breast
        cancer. ...')
```

Fig. 3. The representation for texts: hierarchical example

Texts Each text is an independent paragraph. Texts and issues are both annotated with the situations in which they apply — by illnesses, treatments and locations in the body. The annotations for texts are often more specific than those for issues, so that only a subset of possible texts for each issue is chosen for a given patient. Texts are made specific in two ways. First, the Read code system is hierarchical, so that the issue (Figure 2) "Which treatments are available?" is annotated B, meaning that it is relevant to *all* cancers, while the texts (Figure 3) are annotated B34 (relevant to breast cancer only) or B46 (for patients with prostate cancer).

Second, in order to facilitate text planning, texts may also contain additional annotations which describe more properties of the situation in which that text is likely to be relevant. Figure 4 shows an example for side effects texts.

```
side_effect_01 :: super(side_effect_text),
    code(radiotherapy),
    treatment_location(body),
    effect_location(blood),
    text('Radiotherapy can sometimes affect the cells which
        produce your blood. If this is thought likely in
        your case you will have regular blood tests ...')
```

Fig. 4. The representation for texts: additional properties example

Texts also exist at different levels of detail. We offer two levels at present: an overview text for an issue, or texts which offer fuller details. Each text is annotated with the level of detail which it represents. Overview text is presented before the other texts for that issue, and if the patient does not need (or wish) to explore the issue in depth then it may be the only text that is presented (see Section 4.3).

4.3   Adapting the Presentation

We consider two layers of adaptation: deciding which issues to present, and deciding how to present the information for each issue.

Adapting the List of Issues An issue is only presented to the user if it is relevant to that time frame and to the patient's specific illness and treatment. In a given time frame, the relationships and codes in the time frame are matched to those in all the issues, so as to identify the relevant issues. The list of relevant issues is sorted according to their psychological category, and the categories are presented to the user in a fixed order. An example of the output is shown in Figure 5.

Following diagnosis, you may want information on the following topics:

Diagnosis What is my diagnosis?
                What is the medical name of my illness?
                Will it spread anywhere else?
                What does "positive lymph nodes" mean?

Treatment What treatments are there?

Personal   How am I going to cope with this?
                What about my job?
                What does the future hold now?

Family   Talking to the family
                Talking to the children
                Are my family at risk?

Social   What about my friends?
                What about my social life?
                How can I talk about this?

Fig. 5. Example front page for issues in the first time frame. The questions are all issues, which are links to information pages. Subsequent time frames also contain links back to previous frames

In principle the relevance of the different categories (i.e. diagnosis, treatment, personal, family and social) might vary for different patients or change over time, and so our architecture permits re-ordering, but the literature suggests that their relative importance remains fairly constant [12]. To allow for individual variations in interest, psychological categories are used only for sorting and not for selection.

Each issue may also be linked directly to other relevant issues. This facility is provided in the form of a static list of links stored with each issue. Whenever the text for an issue is presented, this "See also" list is also presented. If the patient chooses to follow such a link, then the resulting text is filtered (as usual) to suit the current time frame. These embedded links offer access to information that may be of interest but are not necessarily assumed to be of immediate interest.

Adapting the Texts When the user chooses an issue, suitable texts are selected according to the patient's illness and treatment. These selections are made with the patient's record and the text annotations shown in Figures 3 and 4. Issues are all selected and sorted according to a single set of criteria (described in Section 4.3 above), but the texts for different issues may be selected and sorted in different ways. For most issues, the texts only need to be filtered according to their main Read codes (e.g. only texts which refer to the patient's own illness and treatments are used), but some issues require more complex combinations of filtering and sorting in order to present relevant information in a coherent order. We therefore specify a *text plan* for use with each issue, which selects the texts and groups similar texts together in order to provide a coherent page. Issues can share the same (standard) text plan so the loss of generality is not excessive, and we have the flexibility to add extra plans wherever it is worthwhile to gain extra coherence.

```
Text_Plan(side_effects)
    input(SideFXTexts) -- Set of texts to describe side effects
    input(TreatmentCodes) -- Read codes for patient's treatments

    -- Filter by the (treatment) code and location
    constrain_texts(SideFXTexts, TreatmentCodes, by_codes)
    constrain_texts(SideFXTexts, TreatmentCodes, by_treatment_location)

    -- Sort them by code and location
    sort_texts(SideFXTexts, TreatmentCodes, by_code)
    sort_texts(SideFXTexts, TreatmentCodes, by_treatment_location)
    sort_texts(SideFXTexts, TreatmentCodes, by_effect_location)
```

Fig. 6. Part of a complex text plan: for side effects

For example, a complex text plan is needed for the issue "What are the side effects of treatment?". There are many different treatments and their side effects may affect many different parts of the body. Each patient may undergo several different kinds of treatment, treatments may overlap and some side effects may remain after a treatment has finished. The location of the treatment and the location of the side effect are described by properties in each of the side effects texts (Figure 4). The text plan for side effects specifies that texts are first filtered (and, for multiple treatments, grouped together) according to the type and location of the treatment(s). Then the texts for each treatment are grouped according to the part of the body where the side effects occur. The parts of the text plan which perform these operations are shown in Figure 6. Time is also taken into account: full details are presented for current treatments, overviews only for previous or planned treatments (not shown).

Most of the texts are made up of pre-stored sentences, but some of the texts also contain personal information from the patient's medical record, such as the patient's own diagnostic, staging and treatment information. Sentences which are based on patients' individual data need to be generated at run–time, and we use the same methods for this as our earlier research [2,6].

5   Evaluation and Discussion

This system was made available on the World Wide Web, and feedback solicited from a number of groups of people including readers of cancer newsgroups (who may themselves be patients) and members of an electronic mailing list for experts in health informatics and public health. We created some example patients to provide exemplars of the kind of tailoring that can be done by the system. The demonstration system contained complete sets of issues for sample patients' time frames, but the text for many of these issues was incomplete and we did not put much emphasis on surface presentation techniques such as graphics, fonts and screen layout. More than 100 people used the system while the demonstration was available, with 18 returning questionnaires. Feedback was generally positive (6 felt that the system was better than non-tailored resources, 12 were unsure) and most critical comments were on the detailed content and presentation.

We have so far applied our approach to information within a local site in which we can annotate texts according to our model. As information extraction techniques improve and web resources are increasingly being annotated with standardised metadata, it is becoming feasible to select information from appropriate web resources according to psychological models of their relevance. The techniques described here might also eventually be applied to users who are searching for relevant medical information among many web sites. Where psychological models of readers' information needs exist, these models may provide a useful complement to existing information filtering techniques [14].

We have considered the practicality of the techniques we have developed. The model of the likely information needs of cancer patients is theoretically based, but the way the model is realised is computationally quite simple. The psychological basis for the design and the explicit model of relevance enables us to create useful personalised information without a great computational overhead.

6   Acknowledgments

This work was supported by EPSRC grant GR/K55271.

References

1. Allen, J.: Maintaining Knowledge About Temporal Intervals. Communications of the ACM. **26** (1983) 832–843
2. Binsted, K., Cawsey, A., Jones, R.: Generating Personalised Information Using the Medical Record. Artificial Intelligence in Medicine: Proceedings of AIME 95, Springer Verlag, Berlin (1995) 29–41.
3. Bental, D., Cawsey, A., Jones, R.: Patient Information Systems that Tailor to the Individual. Patient Education and Counselling. **36** (1999) 171–180
4. Buchanan, B., Moore, J., Forsythe, D., Carenini, G., Ohlsson, S., and Banks, G. An Intelligent Interactive System for Delivering Individualized Information to Patients. Artificial Intelligence in Medicine **7** (1995) 117–154.
5. Brusilovsky, P. Methods and Techniques of Adaptive Hypermedia. User Modeling and User-Adapted Interaction. **6** (1995) 87–129
6. Cawsey, A., Pearson, J., Jones, R.: The Evaluation of a Personalised Information System for Patients with Cancer. User Modeling and User-Adapted Interaction. **10** (2000)
7. Cohen, F., Lazarus, R.S.: Coping With the Stresses of Illness. In: Stone, G., Cohen F., Adler, N. (eds.): Health Psychology. Jossey-Bass, (1970) 217–254.
8. Derdiarian, A.: Information Needs of Recently Diagnosed Cancer Patients: A Theoretical Framework. Part I. Cancer Nursing. **10** (1987) 107–115
9. Fredette, S.L.: A Model for Improving Cancer Patient Education. Cancer Nursing. **13** (1990) 207–215
10. Galloway, S.C., Graydon, J.E.: Uncertainty, Symptom Distress, and Information Needs After Surgery for Cancer of the Colon. Cancer Nursing. **19** (1996) 112–117
11. Jones, R., Pearson, J., McGregor, S., Cawsey, A.J., Barrett, A., Craig, N., Atkinson, J.M., Harper Gilmour, W., McEwen, J.: Randomised trial of personalised computer based information for cancer patients. British Medical Journal **319** (1999) 1241–1247
12. Luker, K.A., Beaver, K., Leinster, S.J., Owens, R.G.: Information Needs and Sources of Information for Women With Breast-Cancer: A Follow-Up Study. Journal of Advanced Nursing. **23** (1996) 487–495
13. Milosavljevic, M., Oberlander, J.: Dynamic Hypertext Catalogues: Helping Users to Help Themselves. Proceedings of the 9th ACM Conference on Hypertext and Hypermedia, Pittsburgh, PA, USA (1998) 20–24
14. Oard, D.: The State of the Art in Text Filtering. User Modeling and User-Adapted Interaction. **7** (1997) 141–178
15. Read, J.: Coding and Classification in Health and Medical Care Systems. Proceedings of the Second Hong Kong (Asia-Pacific) Medical Informatics Conference. Hong Kong Society of Medical Informatics Ltd, Hong Kong (1993) 175–180
16. Schapira, M.M., Meade, C., Matzinger, A.B.: Enhanced Decision Making: the Use of a Videotape Decision-Aid for Patients with Prostate Cancer. Patient Education and Counselling. **30** (1997) 119–127
17. Skinner, C.S., Strecher, V.J., Hospers, H.: Physicians' Recommendations for Mammography: Do Tailored Messages Make a Difference? American Journal of Public Health. **84**:1 (1994) 43–49
18. Velicer, W.F, Prochaska, J.D.: An Expert System Intervention for Smoking Cessation. Patient Education and Counselling. **36** (1999) 119–129

Group User Models for Personalized Hyperlink Recommendations

Johan Bollen

Los Alamos National Laboratory,
Computer Research and Applications group (CIC3)
Los Alamos, NM (USA)
jbollen@lanl.gov

Abstract. This paper presents a system that combines adaptive hypertext linking based on group link preferences with an implicit navigation-based mechanism for personalized link recommendations. A methodology using three Hebbian-style learning rules changes hyperlink weights according to users' overlapping navigation paths and causes a hypertext system's link structure to converge to a valid group user model. A spreading activation recommendation system generates navigation path based recommendations for individual users. Both systems are linked, thereby combining both personal user interests and established group link preferences. An on-line application for the Los Alamos National Laboratory Research Library is presented.

1 Introduction

1.1 Adaptive Hypertext and Hypermedia

The domain of Adaptive Hypertext and Hypermedia (AH) has focussed on enabling hypertext systems to cope with highly diverse user demands by personalizing the system's interface, content and structure[5]. A number of different approaches to this complex problem have been proposed, most based on the notion that particular user characteristics can be measured and used to personalize the behavior of a given hypermedia system. Brusilovsky (1998) [4] provides an excellent review of the state of the art.

An overview paper by Eklund (1998) [7], however, shows the relatively low level of empirical support for the effectiveness of a large number of (educational) AH systems. This clearly relates to the complexity of the task at hand, but also reveals a number of persistent problems for the domain of AH. First, although personalization could solve a large number of human-hypertext interaction problems, in many cases individuals do not hold the requisite knowledge to solve certain retrieval problems. This knowledge might, on the other hand, be collectively present. For example, a user searching for information, within a domain he or she is quite unfamilar with, may benefit more from the aggregated knowledge of other users that are familiar with the domain than from a personalized interface. In other words, personalization could in many cases be improved

P. Brusilovsky, O. Stock, C. Strapparava (Eds.): AH 2000, LNCS 1892, pp. 38–50, 2000.
© Springer-Verlag Berlin Heidelberg 2000

by involving group knowledge[18]. Second, both user information needs and personal characteristics are highly unstable and complex factors, raising the issue of measurement validity. Even though some AH systems claim to be based on measurements of some of these factors, it is often difficult to demonstrate that these measurements are actually valid ones [20]. An AH approach that focusses on stable and relatively simple user factors is required. Third, factors such as a user's information need, personal background, knowledge level, retrieval strategies, the system's hyperlink structure, etc. can all be expected to interact strongly [16]. AH systems will only with great difficulty be able to base their adaptivity on effectively isolating any of these factors.

1.2   The Interaction Perspective

The mentioned problems associated with the implementation and evaluation of AH systems have prompted the development of the presented system which addresses the above described issues: how can we agregate the collective knowledge of a group of users and use it to improve and personalize the experience of individual users? The approach that I have taken is based on the following methodologies:

1. a methodology to transform hyperlink structure into a group user model
2. page relatedness measures from simple recordings of user retrieval paths (sequences of retrieved hypertext pages)
3. guided user navigation by spreading activation recommendations

The system based on these methodologies will use a hypertext system's network structure to store the aggregation of users' collective knowledge on a given domain (that I will refer to as the group user model). Hypertext network structure will be updated according to simple measurements of user retrieval patterns (hyperlink traversal counts). Individual user interests will be derived from users' individual retrieval paths. A spreading activation system will, based on an interaction between individual retrieval paths and group user model determined network structure, generate personalized hyperlink recommendations.

1.3   Related Research

Group User Models and Domain Knowledge The presented system is based on the construction of models of users' collective domain knowledge, similar to previous research on group user models. In [14] Kaplan et al. argue that hypertext systems can be seen as semantic networks and can thus be represented by associative matrices whose elements indicate the strength of relation (link weights) between information topics in the network. As values in a matrix, these link weights can conveniently be updated according to user feedback, thereby allowing a hypertext system to adapt its structure to user feedback by simply changing matrix elements. When used by groups of users, the *HYPERFLEX* system presented in [14] will gradually evolve from an author-defined hyperlink structure into a model of any group of users' collective knowledge (i.e the group user model), represented by a concept similarity matrix. Encarnacao(1997) [8] provides another demonstration of how a multi-level adaptive hypermedia system can use associative graphs of action events to model collective user knowledge. A formal analysis and generalization of the concept of representing hypertext networks as semantic networks or associative matrices was presented in [9].

A major advantage of the use of associative matrices for group user model representation is that it allows relatively simple and quantitative measures such as hyperlink traversal frequencies to be used to generate the matrices' values. There exists strong empirical support for the position that user retrieval behavior (as e.g. expressed in hyperlink traversal frequencies) is stable across groups of users and shaped by relatively stable characteristics of a given group of users [12][19]. The use of group user models represented by associative matrices thereby induces the use of more quantitative and reliable measures of user characteristics (and for this application, measures of their aggregated knowledge).

Individual Preferences and Navigation Paths Although group user models can be developed for any group of users (the set of WWW users, local experts and even individuals) and have strong implications for the organization of hypertext network structure, they need to be combined with individual short-term preferences in order to provide a personalization of services. Otherwise all users would simply be faced with the same group-defined hyperlink structure. The presented system uses an implicit approach where an individual's retrieval path through the hypertext system (i.e. a set of n previously retrieved pages) is used to assess an individual's interests. Personalized link recommendations can then be generated based on this retrieval history and the system's adaptive group user model (hyperlink structure).

This approach is similar to the Letizia [15] and WebWatcher [13] systems. In the Letizia system a user's past retrieval path is used to pro-actively search the pages within a static hypertext system and offer the user recommendations to pages that might be of interest. The WebWatcher system combines hypertext link updating by keyword annotation with retrieval based recommendations based on a user's individual retrieval path.

1.4   Paper Structure

The following sections will outline the basic components and functionality of the in this paper presented system. First, the adaptive hyperlinking component that re-organizes network structure towards a group user model will briefly be described, followed by an introduction to the principle of using spreading activation for personalized link recommendations. Finally, the paper concludes by presenting a recently implemented system that combines both methodologies into a system that uses collectively shaped hypertext network structure and individual retrieval paths for personalized link recommendations.

2   Hypertext Linking from User Mental Models

2.1   Adaptive Hyperlinks

In 1996 and 1997 I set up a number of experiments with an adaptive hypertext methodology that will from now on be refered to as @ApWeb. The methodology uses a set of three learning rules that dynamically change a network's link structure according to overlapping user retrieval paths. These networks have been shown to converge to a stable and valid representation of the group user model (i.e. the collective domain knowledge of its users). A full account can be found in [2], but this section will repeat the most important parts of the set-up.

The notion of representing a hypertext network as a directed graph is extended with the concept of weighted hyperlinks; each hyperlink in the network is associated with a weight expressing the degree of associative relation between two hypertext pages. A hypertext network is then represented by a directed, weighed graph $G = (V, E)$ where the set of hypertext pages $V = \{v_0, v_1, \ldots, v_n\}$ and $E = V \times V$. A weight function is defined over all pairs of hypertext pages $(v_i, v_j) \in E$ so that $W : E \to \mathcal{R}_0^+$. The weights that are thus defined over all pairs of hypertext pages can be stored in a $n \times n$ matrix M, whose elements $w_{i,j}$ correspond to $W(v_i, v_j)$. If we denote each sequence of three visited pages in a user's navigation path as $P = (v_i, v_j, v_k)$, then, for each retrieval sequence, three Hebbian-style learning rules [10] are executed: Frequency, Symmetry and Transitivity, each respectively associated with a reward r_{freq}, r_{symm} and r_{trans}. The algorithm to update hyperlink weights based on these learning rules can then be formalized as follows. While the hypertext network is being browsed by a group of users, at each link request t (or iteration of the algorithm):

Frequency $W(v_i, v_j)_t = W(v_i, v_j)_{t-1} + r_{\text{freq}}$ and $W(v_j, v_k)_t = W(v_j, v_k)_{t-1} + r_{\text{freq}}$
   This learning rule reinforces connections between two nodes that have been retrieved concurrently.
Symmetry $W(v_i, v_j)_t = W(v_j, v_i)_{t-1} + r_{\text{symm}}$, and $W(v_j, v_k)_t = W(v_k, v_j)_{t-1} + r_{symm}$
   This learning rule reinforces a partially symmetric, associative relation among two pages consequently visited in a website.
Transitivity $W(v_i, v_k)_t = W(v_j, v_k)_{t-1} + r_{trans}$,
   This rule attempts to bridge connections by reinforcing a transitive associative relation in any set of three consequently visited nodes.

By the actions of these learning rules, a group of users will, by their overlapping patterns of navigation activity, selectively reinforce specific network connections. Matrix M's values will gradually change, and with it the hyperlink structure of the weighted hypertext network it represents.

2.2   Initializing a Network of Journal Relations

The Los Alamos National Laboratory (LANL) Research Library is consistently moving a growing part of its journal collection to an electronic database that researchers can access from their desktops. A large part of its local collection of

9804 journals is now available in a digital format, and can be downloaded from the library's website. An initial "virtual" hypertext network was generated, by the @ApWeb methodology, for the local electronic journal database (SciSearch) from a web log based simulation of user retrieval behavior in the following manner.

The library's journal database is accessible from the LANL website and extensive web logs are available. We used a part of the web log that was registered in February 1999 and contained 31992 user requests. Each record in the log contained the user's IP number, time of the request, requested article (SICI number), an indication of whether or not the request succeeded, and the number of bytes transferred.

Since every HTTP request registered in the log also carried a time stamp, it was possible to temporally trace the retrieval sequences of individual users and reconstruct their retrieval paths. A new log was created that contained these user retrieval paths. Only requests to download an actual paper (not its abstract or meta-data) were used, since this was considered the most reliable indication of a user's true interests in the item. Furthermore, rather than constructing actual article relations, we aimed to construct journal relations based on the journals in which retrieved articles appeared. This information could be derived from an article's SICI number, i.e. a unique identifier for every article in the database that contains the ISSN number of the journal in which it appeared. For every user we thus derived a retrieval sequence of journals rather than articles. This decision was made to allow for later cross-validation of our data with journal citation records. In addition, IP numbers were anonymized to user ID numbers (for reasons of privacy), only successful requests were retained and the byte count was removed. Table 1 shows a section of the transformed log.

userID	data	time	ISSN	SICI
USER139	07/Dec/1998	16:56:25	0003-6951	1996;0003-6951()72:25<3338:>
USER139	18/Dec/1998	17:24:12	0039-6028	1996;0039-6028()360:1/3<180:>
USER140	27/Apr/1998	14:45:50	0039-6028	1996;0039-6028()358<96:>
USER140	27/Apr/1998	14:46:09	0039-6028	1996;0039-6028()358<96:>
USER141	03/Mar/1998	09:04:24	0921-4526	0921-4526()230<794:>
USER141	03/Mar/1998	09:05:48	0921-4526	0921-4526()230<576:>

Table 1. An example of the transformed SciSearch Web log used to reconstruct user navigation.

The Research Library's web logs were then split up into individual retrieval paths that were fed into the above described @ApWeb methodology, as shown in fig. 1, simulating actual user interactions with the system. This is a departure from our previous experiments, since the network of hyperlinks is not being generated interactively in a process where users shape the network by their navigation patterns and network structure shapes new user navigation behavior. Rather, we see this process as a way of creating an acceptable initial network that can then later be refined by the previously mentioned interactive @ApWeb methodology.

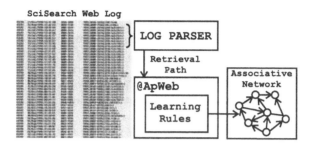

Fig. 1. Constructing a network of journal titles from the LANL Research Library web logs

A well-connected network of 472 journal titles [1] (average of 12.78 non-zero edges per nodes) and their weighted associations was generated based on this data and setup. Table 2 shows a section of the generated journal association matrix.

		Linked journal													
Linking journal		01	02	03	04	05	06	07	08	09	10	11	12	13	14	15
ADV COLLOID INTERFAC	01	0	0	0	0	0	0	0	0	0	0	0	0	0	0	0
ADVAN MATH	02	0	0	1.5	0	0	0	0	0	1.5	0	0	0	0	0	0
ANALYT CHIM	03	0	0.3	0	6.9	0	0	0	1	0	1.2	0	0	0	0	0
ANALYT BIOC	04	0	0	19.6	0	0	0.6	0	1	0	2.1	0	0	0	0	0
ANIMAL BEHAVIOUR	05	0	0	0	0	0	0	0	0	0	0	0	0	0	0	0
ANN PHYS-NEW YORK	06	0	0	0	3	0	0	0	0.6	0	0	0.3	0	0	0	0
APPLIED ACOUSTICS	07	0	0	0	0	0	0	0	0	0	0	0	0	0	0	0
APPL PHYS LETT	08	0	0	0.3	0.3	0	2.5	0	0	0	0	0	0	0	0	0
ARCH RATION MECH AN	09	0	0.3	0	0	0	0	0	0	0	0	0	0	0	0	0
ARCH BIOCHEM BIOPHYS	10	0	0	5.5	10.5	0	0	0	0	0	0	0	0	0	0	0
ARTIF INTELL	11	0	0	0	0	0	1.5	0	0	0	0	0	0	0	0	0
ASTRONOM J	12	0	0	0	0	0	0	0	0	0	0	0	0	0	0.3	0
PUBL ASTRON SOC JPN	13	0	0	0	0	0	0	0	0	0	0	0	0	0	0	0
ASTRON ASTROPHYS	14	0	0	0	0	0	0	0	0	0	0	1.5	0	0	0.9	
ASTROPHYSICAL JOURNAL	15	0	0	0	0	0	0	0	0	0	0	0	0	0	4.5	0

Table 2. Sample of generated journal relations matrix.

---

[1] This network could only contain journal titles that were actually retrieved within the registered web log

3   Interactive Recommendations by Spreading Activation

3.1   Spreading Activation (SA)

The technique of spreading activation assumes that information stored in human memory is represented by a distributed, associative network in which the most strongly associated memory items have strongest connections [11][1]. Retrieval by spreading activation is initiated by activating a set of cue nodes which associatively express the meaning of the items to be retrieved. Activation energy spreads out from the cue nodes to all other related nodes, modulated by the network connection weights. Nodes that achieve an activation value above a given threshold are considered retrieval results.

Apart from being a well established model of retrieval from human memory, SA can be simulated and applied to associative networks for IR applications. Spreading activation for hypertext IR has a number of strong advantages over traditional IR techniques as shown and argued in [17][6][3] . First, SA uses network structure for retrieval and does not rely on explicit query keyword matching against page text. This feature avoids a number of persistent problems with polysemy and synonymy in traditional IR; retrieval is not dependent on exact keyword matches. In addition, user queries can consist of a list of activated nodes; a feature allowing the nodes in a user's retrieval path to be used as queries, rather than a user-provided list of keywords. Second, the nature of SA is such that, in an associative network, returned items match the combined "meaning" of the query items, thereby allowing a descriptive manner of querying. For example, given adequate network structure a SA query such as *"water fuel"* could return pages on *"hydrological engineering"* or *"hydrogen combustion"*, rather than a set of pages that merely contain both query keywords.

3.2   Simulating Spreading Activation

Simulating retrieval by SA implies two representations: one for the associative structure of the network of hypertext pages, i.e. an associative network, and one representing the (initial) activation state of the network, i.e the query.

Let the set of n network nodes or documents be $V = \{v_0, v_1, \ldots, v_n\}$. Every pair of nodes (v_i, v_j) is connected by a hyperlink, associated with a link weight of w_{ij}. The structure of this network will then be represented by the n by n matrix M whose elements w_{ij} correspond to the weight of the link between the nodes v_i and v_j. The activation state of the network at time t will be represented by the vector a_t the elements $0 \leq a_i \leq 1$ of which indicate the activation value of each node v_i. The initial activation state a_0 will express how the SA system was queried for retrieval.

Computationally, spreading activation can then be simulated as an iterative process in which the matrix M is multiplied by the activation vector A_t, starting with a_0. For every node v_i, the resulting activation would then be $a_i = \sum_{j=0}^{n} a_j w_{ij}$, i.e. the weighted sum of the activations of all nodes connecting to v_i. At each iteration the resulting vector $A_{t+1} = MA_t$ is fed back into the multiplication. After a given number of iterations a list of network nodes that achieved highest activation values can be returned as the results for the query expressed by a_0.

3.3 Spreading Activation and Adaptive Linking for Hypertext

A spreading activation system making use of the above described algorithm was implemented for the network of weighted journal links generated by the in section 2.2 described @ApWeb technique. The system was set up in the form of a Java Servlet, accessible from the LANL library servers. The servlet used three modules. The first module contained a coupled list of journal titles and network node labels (ISSN numbers), and received either a list of user-provided keywords (to start interaction) or a user's retrieval path (up to 5 last retrieved nodes). An initial activation vector a_0 was generated by simply matching keywords to this stored list. Activation values for network nodes corresponded to the number of matches found. For example, a query consisting of "cell" and "biochem", would result in an activation value of 1 for the journal of "**cell**ular immunology" while the journal "internation journal of **biochem**istry & **cell** biology" would receive an initial activation energy of 2. The activation value of all non-matching network nodes would be set to zero. This matching process could be used to activate specific journals by specifying their entire title or ISSN number, a feature that made it possible for the system to, after the initial user provided keyword query, use the set of network nodes in the user's retrieval path.

The second module applied the SA algorithm to this initial activation vector and returned an ordered list of spreading activation results, i.e. network nodes achieving highest activation values over all iterations of the algorithm.

The third module would translate the returned set of network nodes to a human-readable hypertext page that the LANL server would return to the client.

This spreading activation system was connected to the @ApWeb system for the same network of journal titles. A user request would first be redirected to the @ApWeb system that would change network structure according to the user's navigation path as described in section 2.1. The request would then be passed on to the spreading activation module that generated a list of recommended hyperlinks and returned it to the user. The user could then select a request for a hyperlink which would again be redirected to both the @ApWeb system and the spreading activation module, and so on.

Fig.2 shows a graphical representation of the system and outlines how the library database's web log was used to generate a virtual hypertext network of journal titles (1). The spreading activation system was then connected to the @ApWeb system and the virtual network to provide an actual hypertext interface that users could navigate (2).

3.4 Interface

A user interaction would start with the user formulating a query consisting of a set of keywords that would associatively describe the nature of the desired jour-

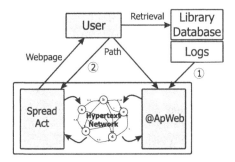

Fig. 2. Structure of combined recommendation and @ApWeb system

nal, e.g. "information processing security" for journals on encryption technology.
[2] A hypertext page consisting of the user's retrieval path, a list of hyperlinks
for all direct keyword matches and recommended connections for that position
in the network would be generated. Two types of hyperlinks would be available for each recommended item: browse-links and retrieval-links. By selecting
the browse-link for a given journal, the user would issue a request to the system which would followingly return a hypertext page for the selected journal.
The selected journal would furthermore be added to the user's navigation path
and refine the generated spreading activation recommendations. Selecting the
"retrieval"-link, on the other hand, would terminate the hypertext navigation
process and take the user to the actual library page for that journal where they
could download its articles. [3]

4   Results

4.1   A User Session

The following section will describe a user session with a prototype of the system
that was registered during our recent tests with the system. Figure 3 shows a
screen dump of the spreading activation output page for an initial query consisting of one single keyword: "earth". This vague description of the user's information needs resulted in a wide range of recommendations. The result page first
showed hyperlinks to journals whose titles directly matched this keyword, and
were thus activated in the inital activation vector for the spreading activation
module of the system. This list contained items such as "Earth and Planetary
Science" and "Earthscience Reviews". Below that list the page displayed all

---

[2] This feature was implemented to allow user to start the interaction with the system
since users at the start of their session have not established a retrieval path. All
following interaction with the system would consist of actual hypertext navigation.

[3] This feature was implemented to leave the functionality of the existing library
database undisturbed while still allowing users to interact with its content

spreading activation recommended hyperlinks to journals such as: "Journal of Atmospheric and Solarterrestrial Physics", "Topology" and "Astronomical Journal". These items covered a wide range of possible interpretations of the user's interest as expressed by the single keyword "earth". Although none of these actually match the provided keyword "earth", they are almost all strongly related to matters concerning the earth. This demonstrates the capability of the SA methodology to assess the meaning of a query without having to resort to actual keyword matches (except those to generate the initial activation vector).

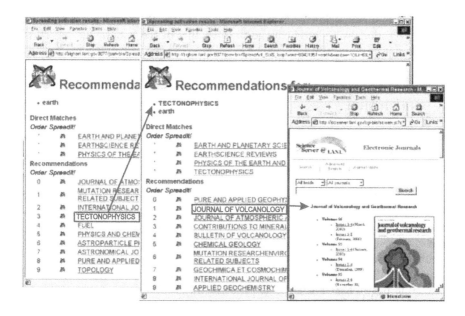

Fig. 3. A user first requests recommendations for the keyword *earth*, refines this search by browsing to the *tectonophysics* page and finally retrieves the library web page for the *Journal of Vulcanology and Geothermal Research.*

This user was apparently more interested in "earth"-tectonics than atmospheric science and topology, and selected the browse-hyperlink associated with the "Tectonophysics" journal, as is shown in fig. 3. This selection was added to the retrieval path and generated new hyperlink recommendations for "earth" and "Tectonophysics" combined. The results of this search are shown in the righthand side of table 3. A whole new list of recommended journals had been generated to reflect the addition of "Tectonophysics" in the user query such as "Pure and Applied Geophysics" followed by "Journal of Vulcanology and Geothermal Research", "Journal of Atmospheric and Solarterrestrial physics" and "Contributions to Mineralogy and Petrology". These new recommendations all clearly corresponded to the new "tectonic" quality of the query and indicated that the spreading activation module had successfully estimated the user's information need from his navigation path. The addition of the new selected item to the user's path had refined the initial "earth" query.

This user was in fact interested in the "Journal of Vulcanology and Geothermal Research". By clicking on this item's retrieval-hyperlink she was taken to the LANL library's electronic version of that journal where specific articles of interest could be downloaded, as is shown in fig. 3. This completed the user's session with the system. Other users will go through a similar interactive, navigation process whereby the generated recommendation are continuously improved by the addition of new items to the user's retrieval path. The overlapping patterns of their selections will slowly change the structure of the underlying hypertext network, which in its turn will change (and improve) the recommendations that are generated for each individual user.

5   Conclusion

Although this recently developed system has not yet been subjected to rigorous user tests, it does show the viability of a number of concepts that were outlined in the introduction of this paper. First, the system shows how the previously developed @ApWeb methodology can be used to initialize a group model of user knowledge by generating adaptive hyperlinks for unstructured information resources like a library database. The system also demonstrates how spreading activation retrieval can be used to generate personalized link recommendations from group structured hypertext and individual retrieval paths. By doing so, it combines the know-how of the entire group of users stored in network link structure with the interests of an individual user implicitly expressed in their navigation paths. Last but not least, the system's structure is continuously updated by individual user hyperlink selections, implementing further refinement of the initial hypertext network structure. Therefore, even if the system is bootstrapped with inaccurate data (inaccurate or incomplete), network structure will still gradually improve and adapt to users' actual selections.

A number of issues still have to be addressed. First, extensive user tests need to determine whether this system allows users to more efficiently retrieve the items for which they are looking than other systems like human or database generated hypertext networks. Second, the system has been applied to journal relations which might not be the ideal testground for an adaptive hypertext system. An application for an existing website has recently been implemented and is at present undergoing user tests. Third, the adaptivity of the system warrants a special investigation. How fast does network structure change from the initial log based structure? In what respect do the initial network structure and later adapted versions differ? Future research will focus on this important issue.

References

[1] John R. Anderson. A spreading activation theory of memory. *Journal of Verbal Leaning and Verbal Behaviour*, 22:261–295, 1983.

[2] Johan Bollen and Francis Heylighen. A system to restructure hypertext networks into valid user models. *The new review of Hypermedia and Multimedia*, 4:189–213, 1998.

[3] Johan Bollen, Herbert Vandesompel, and Luis M. Rocha. Mining associative relations from website logs and their application to context-dependent retrieval using spreading activation. In *Proceedings of the Workshop on Organizing Webspaces (ACM-DL99)*, Berkeley, California, 1999. in preparation.

[4] P. Brusilovsky, A. Kobsa, and J. Vassileva, editors. *Adaptive Hypertext and Hypermedia Systems*. Kluwer Academic Publishers, Dordrecht, The Netherlands, 1998.

[5] Peter Brusilovsky. Methods and techniques of adaptive hypermedia. *User Modeling and User-Adapted Interaction*, 6(2–3):87–129, 1996.

[6] Fabio Crestani. Application of spreading activation techniques in information retrieval. *Artificial Intelligence Review*, 11(6):453–582, 1997.

[7] John Eklund. The value of adaptivity in hypermedia learning environments: a short review of empirical evidence. In Peter Brusilovksy and Paul de Bra, editors, *Proceedings of the 2nd Workshop on Adaptive Hypertext and Hypermedia (Hypertext 98)*, pages 13–21, Pittsburgh, USA, June 1998.

[8] L. Miguel Encarnacao. Multi-level user support through adaptive hypermedia: A highly application-independent help component. In *IUI'97*, pages 187–194, Orlando, FL, 1997.

[9] Jonathan Furner, David Ellis, and Peter Willett. The representation and comparison of hypertext structures using graphs. In Maristella Agosti and Alan F. Smeaton, editors, *Information Retrieval and Hypertext*, pages 75–96. Kluwer Academic Publishers, Dordrecht, 1996.

[10] Donald O. Hebb. *The Organization of Behavior*. John Wiley, New York, 1949.

[11] G. Hinton and J.R. Anderson. *Parallel Models of Associative Memory*. Hillsdale Publishers, New Jersey, 1981.

[12] Bernardo A. Huberman, Peter L. T. Pirolli, James E. Pitkow, and Rajan M. Lukose. Strong regularities in world wide web surfing. *Science*, 280(5360):95–97, April 3 1998.

[13] T. Joachims, D. Freitag, and T. Mitchell. Webwatcher: A tour guide for the world wide web. In *Fifteenth International Joint Conference on Artificial Intelligence (IJCAI-97)*, 1997.

[14] C. Kaplan, J. Fenwick, and J. Chen. Adaptive hypertext navigation based on user goals and context. *User Models and User Adapted Interaction*, 3(2):193–220, 1993.

[15] H. Lieberman. Letizia: An agent that assists web browsing. In *Proceedings of the International Joint Conference on Artificial Intelligence*, Montreal, August 1995.

[16] Gary Marchionini. *Information Seeking in Electronic Environments*. Cambridge University Press, Cambridge, UK, 1995.

[17] Peter Pirolli, James Pitkow, and Ramana Rao. Silk from a sow's ear: Extracting usable structure from the web. In *Proceedings of CHI'96 (ACM), Human Factors in Computing Systems*, Vancouver, Canada, April 1996. ACM.

[18] Luis M. Rocha and Johan Bollen. Biologically motivated distributed designs for adaptive knowledge management. In I.Cohen and L. Segel, editors, *Design*

Principles for the Immune System and other Distributed Autonomous Systems. Oxford University Press, Oxford, In Press, 2000.

[19] Stuart Schechter, Murali Krishnan, and Michael D. Smith. Using path profiles to predict HTTP requests. *Computer Networks and ISDN Systems*, 30:457–467, 1998.

[20] A. Tricot, E. Puigserver, D. Berdugo, and M. Diallo. The validity of rational criteria for the interpretation of user-hypertext interaction. *Interacting with Computers*, 12:23–36, 1999.

Adaptive Navigation Support and Adaptive Collaboration Support in WebDL

Jesus G. Boticario, Elena Gaudioso, and Felix Hernandez

Dpto. de Inteligencia Artificial
Universidad Nacional de Educacion a Distancia
Senda del Rey, 9; Madrid, Spain
{jgb,elena,felixh}@dia.uned.es

Abstract. This article presents adaptive navigation support and adaptive collaboration support tasks in WebDL, an interactive system for focusing teaching on student performance and resolving problems detected in Internet use for distance learning. This adaptation is done through user model acquisition from the student data available and interaction with the system. WebDL combines techniques used in intelligent tutoring systems, adaptive hypermedia programs and learning apprentice systems for software personalization.

1 Introduction

An educational web site offers a wide variety of sources of information and communication services to meet students' needs thereby enabling them to take an active part in the teaching process. Despite the obvious advantages of this approach, there are however two main difficulties. Firstly, every individual has specific needs that differentiate them. Secondly, the restrictive nature of a web site map's preconceived static and general structure for meeting any need at any moment (depending on the level of experience in the use of the resources offered on the Web) is not suitable for the changing needs of students with different needs, tastes and preferences. The latter inevitably affect the choice of sources of information used (study guides, indexes, glossaries, guided navigation of the course syllabus, complementary activities, etc.) and the use of alternative communication channels (newsgroups, mailing lists, shared workspaces ...).

Bearing in mind these difficulties, and other related ones, we are constructing WebDL, an interactive system that personalizes and adapts all the sources of information and communication channels available on the web to meet individual needs and preferences as and when they arise. The adaptation is done by presenting different structured resources every single moment on the screen in a variety of ways and it also includes, whenever appropriate, advice on using the material available. This approach is therefore wider than the one usually adopted by adaptive educational systems, where adaptation and tutoring tasks focus on access to course contents [11, 5].

We have thus constructed a multiagent architecture, WebDL, which is designed to adapt to user needs [2] and is based on a combination of techniques

P. Brusilovsky, O. Stock, C. Strapparava (Eds.): AH 2000, LNCS 1892, pp. 51–61, 2000.
© Springer-Verlag Berlin Heidelberg 2000

applied in intelligent tutoring systems (ITS) [16], adaptive hypermedia programs (AH) [4] and learning apprentice systems [7]. It falls into the category of so-called Web-based Adaptive Educational Systems [5]. With the learning apprentice approach the initial knowledge base is expanded in order to reduce the effort required for user decision-making (adaptive hypermedia).

The objective of this article is to present the adaptive navigation and adaptive collaboration supports in WebDL. We describe the system's architecture, its components and its current learning tasks. Taking this description as a starting point, we then focus on the adaptive navigation support and adaptive collaboration support tasks.

2   WebDL Architecture

WebDL consists of a Web server that allows students to access the system, a database and a core implemented using a multiagent architecture.

The Web server that we are using, CL-HTTP [8], allows us to construct functions that compute responses to incoming HTTP requests, and to emulate CGIs functionality.

To accelerate system response a database is used that stores the elements learnt and deemed to be most reliable.

The WebDL core [3] is implemented in terms of a multiagent decision approach and is organized as follows (see Figure 3). Two main components are involved: user interaction and the adaptive module. The former is implemented by the *interface agent* and is in charge of the organized presentation of the different types of material. This module provides a single, integrated response to the user.

The adaptive module consists of the following agents: user model agent, user modeling agent, material agent, pedagogical agent, contact agent, service identification agent, service model agent, service modeling agent and coordinator agent.

The first four provide basic ITS functionality. The next four are useful for identifying, by *collaborative filtering*, the system services of interest to users with similar profiles.

Each one of these agents has their own knowledge base with the entities that they control together with their respective relations. The agents that perform learning tasks are able to extend their knowledge base dynamically adding new entities and changing the existing ones as the user interacts with the system (they adjust to what have been called *learning apprentice systems*). All the entities contained in the aforementioned knowledge bases are represented via THEO [9], a framework for learning and problem solving.

A brief description follows of each of the agents highlighted above.

- **Interface Agent**

  It has two main functions: to gather student requests and forward them to the coordinator agent and to construct pages finally presented to a student;

these pages are constructed according to the coordinator agent's response and design rules defined in its knowledge base. For example: "IF (preferred-text-only preferences-id-user) THEN (take-only-alt ¡image¿ ¡page-html¿)" (in section 3.2 a more detailed description is given of how rules are used and represented in WebDL). This rule tells the interface agent how to project an image in accordance with student interface preferences (if a student prefers HTML pages with just text, then the agent only shows the text defining the image (in HTML code it corresponds to the ALT property of the images)). To obtain these preferences a student is asked to complete a form, and using these data the entity for defining specific user preferences is built in the interface agent database as shown in Figure 1.

```
(preferences-anonymous *novalue*
    (id-user anonymous)
    (colors-code RGB)
    (links-color (0 0 238))
    (visited-links-color (85 26 139))
    (active-links-color (255 0 0))
    (backg-color (255 255 255))
    (frames No)
    (preferred-text-only Yes)
... )
```

Fig. 1. Example of the entity defining *anonymous* user preferences

– **Coordinator Agent**
   It is responsible for gathering the interface agent request and forwarding the student request to the agents involved in the request. When the coordinator agent finally receives the response from the rest of the agents it constructs one response to send to the interface agent. In order to construct this response, this agent creates a special entity, **advice**, for each request in its knowledge base, where other agent responses to the request are stored. These requests are saved in their respective attributes as shown in Figure 2. These attributes are described in more detail in section 3.
– **User Model Agent and Service Model Agent**
   The user model and service model agents are responsible for acquiring, saving and managing all the WebDL user or service information. They collaborate with the other agents to provide them with data that might be necessary for their tasks (personal data ...).
– **Material Agent**
   The material agent is responsible for gathering and managing all the Web-site material, for example, definition of HTML pages, exercises, ...
– **Pedagogical Agent**
   The pedagogical agent is responsible for personalizing teaching to connecting students; it is the equivalent of the pedagogical module of an intelligent

```
(advice *novalue*
    (id-user anonymous)
    (id-request 10-03-00-69555)
    (page-html-associated int-4-5.html)
    (next-link-advised section4)
    (contact-media-preferred e-mail)
    (cmp-exer-acs e-mail)
    (contact *novalue*)
 ... )
```

Fig. 2. Definition of the entity advice

tutoring system. So far it provides adaptive guidance to the student via
adaptive navigation support through the course material.

- **Contact Agent**
  The contact agent is responsible for cooperation and communication among
  students and with the professors. It thus uses the user model, student and
  professor contributions, data about the users that are connected at every
  single moment, etc ... This agent will be described in more detail in section 3.3.
- **Service Identification Agent**
  The service identification agent selects the services of interest to a significant
  number of users through *clustering* techniques; the intention here is for the
  system to learn the characteristics determining which services may be of
  interest to a given user.
- **User Modeling Agent** and **Service Modeling Agent**
  These agents are responsible for learning each system user model and service
  model (see advisor agent description).
- **Advisor Agent**
  In order to achieve good user personalization, we have chosen heterogeneous
  agents that combine the solutions learned with different biases corresponding
  to different machine learning methods (C5.0[12], Naive Bayes[14], Progol[10],
  Backpropagation[13], Tilde[1] and Autoclass[6]). It is thus possible to apply
  different approaches to different tasks and clarify which option is the most
  appropriate for each instance.
  To implement this combination, a special type of agent has been introduced:
  the advisor agent. Several advisor agents learn the competence range of each
  of the other agents. A task is only distributed to those agents that have been
  proved to be competent in it. We thereby aim to establish a gradual process
  of agent specialization with concrete architectures for specific problems.
  Competence region learning is done by reinforcement, accounting each modeling option agreement or disagreement with the right or wrong solution.
  So, for example, if the contact-media-preferred, learnt by the agent user
  modeling C5.0 is newsgroup and if this agent were chosen by the advisor
  agent as the best learnt one up to now, then the system would return the
  newsgroup value. The interface agent would then convert this into an access

option to a newsgroup related to an element previously selected on the web screen. If we test that a user chooses this newsgroup, this action is converted into a positive reinforcement on this modeling agent, otherwise it is a negative reinforcement.

Concerning system functionality, two fundamental learning tasks are carried out: one when the different modeling agents infer a certain value of their corresponding models; another when the advisor agents learn the degree of competence of the corresponding modeling agents, once system interaction with a user has finished.

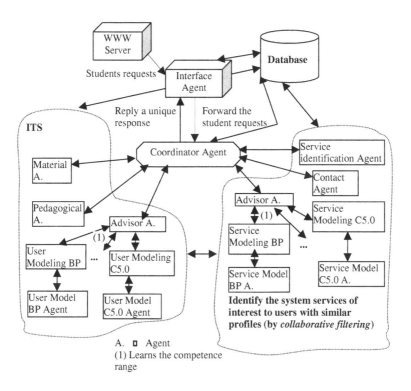

Fig. 3. System's general architecture

3   Adaptive Navigation Support and Adaptive Collaboration Support in WebDL

In this section we are going to describe how WebDL performs the adaptive navigation support [4] and adaptive collaboration support [5] tasks to personalize student access to the course web-site.

3.1   User Interaction

The user interface has two different working areas when the advice cannot be integrated into the information shown (e.g., the upper part displays an access to a newsgroup while the lower part shows another news group or a related mailing list; see Figure 4) or when the advisory information is contextual and does not directly affect the information shown (e.g., the upper part shows the course syllabus, and the lower part shows courses with related syllabuses). Otherwise, the system constructs the page together with the system's recommendations, adding annotations, highlighting or hiding parts of the document, changing the order of the document's elements, etc.

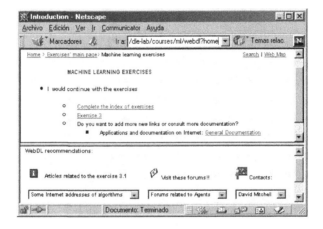

Fig. 4. WebDL's screen with two working areas

When students connect to WebDL, there is an initial page dynamically generated in accordance with their user model and earlier interactions. If it is the first time that students have connected, a user model is created with a default value on which the initial page is constructed.

Thereafter students can interact with the system in the same way as they would do with a static Web site, while WebDL is saving the user access traces.

The system content pages are defined beforehand by the professor via THEO. The coordinator agent takes these pages and sends them to the interface agent together with the entity advice described earlier.

The requests the interface agent receives are as follows:

`http://hostname/webdl/webdl?computed+<id-user>+<page-name>`

Where the attribute `computed` indicates that the page must be constructed dynamically, the attribute `id-user` identifies the student connecting and the last parameter `<page-name>` indicates the page requested by a student.

When a student requests one of the subject-exercise-pages, the coordinator agent forwards the request to the agents that can give a response. In the example we give, the coordinator agent forwards the request to the material, pedagogical and contact agents.

We are going to exemplify the adaptive navigation support and adaptive collaboration support tasks that allow WebDL to assist students with the subject exercises.

3.2 Adaptive Navigation Support

WebDL guides students through the subject-exercise contents via adaptive link annotation. Other adaptive navigation support techniques are not used (direct guidance, sorting, hiding, ... [4]) given the eminently practical character of the subject presented.

In this instance, the pedagogical agent performs the adaptive navigation support task, which consists of guiding students through Web contents via link annotations. For this the pedagogical agent represents the content pages as shown in Figure 5. The attributes **title** and **source-int** define the title and the path to the file containing the page constructed beforehand by a professor.

```
(int-4-5.html *novalue*
    (id-user anonymous)
    (title "Introduction to the exercise 4-5 ")
    (links-opc (("Dif" "Differences between algorithms"
            "DifCBR.html" "Look at the diferences!!")
        ... ))
    (source-int "intro-4-5-txt.html")
    (annotations-allowed yes)
    (next-link-advised *novalue*
            (all.prolog.clauses (
            ((next-link-advised ?r ?value):-
                    (id-user ?r ?user)
                    (eval (visited-page '?user "tutorial.html") nil)
                    (eval "DIF" ?value))
            ... ))))
```

Fig. 5. Representation in THEO of the problem statement of one of the subject exercises

The attribute **next-link-advised** is the one that determines which link is going to advise the pedagogical agent. This attribute is calculated using a rule defined in the knowledge base as shown in Figure 5; the syntax is similar to PROLOG logical programming language rules. It considers whether a user has already visited the tutorial page and if so, the link advised is "differences between algorithms". The professor defines the possible links to be recommended in the attribute **links-opc**. These links are defined using a list of values where the link identifier is defined, which will be used after in the rule (in the example: "DIF"), the text appearing in the link (in the example: "Differences between algorithms"), the link destination (in the example: "DifCBR.html") and the text, icon, ... appearing as a link annotation to indicate it as a recommended link (in the example: "Look at the differences!!"). The professor can thus justify why this is the advised link. Figure 6 shows a system screen with a recommended link.

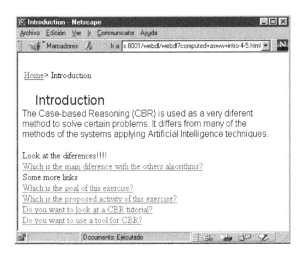

Fig. 6. System screen with an advised link

3.3   Adaptive Collaboration Support

In WebDL we distinguish different kinds of collaboration between students and professors (see [15] for related work): collaboration via public annotations in the exercises (up to now this is the one that has been implemented), collaboration via synchronous communications of the people connected at a specific moment (chats, ...), and collaboration via the setting up of workgroups based on student similarities.

The contact agent is the one that provides the coordinator agent with the recommendations, which may help the student to communicate and cooperate with other students or with the professors. For this, the contact agent constructs the entity, `contact`, which will then be part of the coordinator agent's entity `advice` (see Figure 2). The entity `contact` contains the following attributes: `annotations` (it contains the list of annotations done by other students and which may be of interest), `newsgroups` and `mailing lists` (newsgroups and mailing lists which may be of interest), `fellows` (indicates the students who can help you for a specific exercise), and `fellows-online` (indicates the students connected at the same time and who can help you).

We are going to look at how the contact agent determines the annotations that may be of interest to a specific student.

The students in WebDL can do annotations on the course pages following the link included on all the pages where annotations are allowed. Professors can indicate that they do not allow students to annote a specific page using the attribute **annotations-allowed** (see Figure 5).

If this attribute has the value **yes**, then on the page in front of students a link appears which allows them to do a specific annotation on this page (using an HTML form). This annotation is kept in the contact agent's knowledge base together with identification of the user who has done it, the main topic of the annotation, etc ... (See Figure 7)

```
(annotation *novalue*
    (author DavidS)
    (page-id int-4-5.html)
    (topics (cbr))
    (text "I think this is a very
        important exercise for the exam")
    ... )
```

Fig. 7. Representation in THEO of public annotations in WebDL

When students request an annoted page, the contact agent determines which annotations may be of interest, in accordance with the attribute **topics** of the entity **annotation** and the attribute **interest-items** of the student model (if the interests coincide, the annotation is shown) and depending on the student who has done the annotation (if both students have similar characteristics, then the contact agent shows the annotation)(see Figure 8).

4   Conclusions

In this paper we have described how are performed the adaptive navigation support and adaptive collaboration support tasks in WebDL, an interactive system that personalizes and adapts all the sources of information and communication channels available on the web to meet individual needs and preferences as and when they arise.

To attain these objectives student modeling is based on the application of a set of machine learning techniques from the a priori student data available and their interaction with the system. WebDL provides a multiagent architecture capable of reusing the system components so that the representation of the application domain (course material) can be substituted and thus used for the teaching of another course.

Currently, the basic architecture of the system has been implemented and it has been applied to the access to the course material of the machine learning

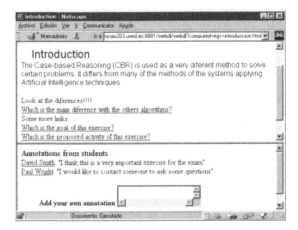

Fig. 8. WebDL screen with advised annotations

course of the Computer Science degree at the Spanish National Distance Learning University (UNED). The system tasks which have been implemented to the moment are: curriculum sequencing (of the course material), adaptive collaboration support (of the course practical exercises) and adaptive navigation support (for every page constructed by the system).

Acknowledgements

The authors would like to acknowledge the helpful comments of Anita Haney, arising in the course of her language revision of this article. We also thank the entire Artificial Intelligence Department for providing support for this project. We would like to express our deep gratitude to professor Tom Mitchell at Carnegie Mellon University for providing THEO for research purposes.

References

[1] H. Blockeel and L.D. Raedt. Top-down induction of logical decision trees. In *Proceedings of the 9th Dutch Conference on Artificial Intelligence NAIC97*, 1997.

[2] Jesus G. Boticario and Elena Gaudioso. Towards personalized distance learning on the web. In J. Mira and J.V. Sanchez-Andres, editors, *Foundations and Tools for Neural Modeling*, number 1607 in Lecture Notes in Computer Science, pages 740–749. Springer Verlag, 1999.

[3] Jesus G. Boticario and Elena Gaudioso. A multiagent architecture for a web-based adaptive educaticon system. In Seth Rogers and Wayne Iba, editors, *Adaptive User Interfaces, Papers from the 2000 AAAI Spring Symposium, TR SS-00-01*, pages 24–27. AAAI Press, March 2000.

[4] Peter Brusilovsky. Methods and techniques of adaptive hypermedia. In *User Modeling and User-Adapted Interaction*, pages 87–129. Kluwer academic publishers, 1996.

[5] Peter Brusilovsky. Adaptive educational systems on the world-wide-web: A review of available technologies. In *Proceedings of Workshop WWW-Based Tutoring at Fourth International Conference on ITS (ITS'98)*, San Antonio, TX, August 1998. MIT Press.

[6] P. Cheesman, J. Stutz, R. Hanson, and W. Taylor. *Autoclass III*. Rsearch Institute for Advanced Computer Science, NASA Ames Research Center, 1990.

[7] L. Dent, J. G. Boticario, J. McDermott, T. M. Mitchell, and D. T. Zabowski. A personal learning apprentice. In *Proceedings of the Tenth National Conference on Artificial Intelligence*, pages 96–103, San Jose, CA, 1992. MIT Press.

[8] John C. Mallery. A common lisp hypermedia server. In *Proceedings of The First International Conference on The World-Wide Web*, Geneva: CERN, 1994.

[9] Tom M. Mitchell, John Allen, Prasad Chalasani, John Cheng, Oren Etzioni, Marc Ringuette, and Jeffrey C. Schlimmer. Theo: A framework for self-improving systems. In K. VanLehn, editor, *Architectures for Intelligence*. Erlbaum, Hillsdale, NJ, 1990.

[10] S. Muggleton. Inverse entailment and progol. *New Gen. Comput.*, 13:245–286, 1995.

[11] K. Nakabayashi. An intelligent tutoring system on the www supporting ubteractive simulation environments with a multimedia viewer control mechanism. In *Proceedings of WebNet96*, page 366, San Francisco, CA, October 1996. World Conference of the Web Society.

[12] Ross Quinlan. *C5.0 Data Mining Tool*. www.rulequest.com, 1997.

[13] D. E. Rumelhart, G. E. Hinton, and R. J. Williams. Learning internal representations by error propagation. In D. E. Rumelhart and J. L. McClelland, editors, *Parallel Distributed Processing: Explorations in the Microstucture of Cognition*. MIT Press, Cambridge, MA, 1986.

[14] J. Smith. *Decision Analysis, A Bayesian Approach*. Chapman and Hall, 1988.

[15] J. Vassileva, J. Greer, G. McCalla, R. Deters, D.Zapata, C. Mudgal, and S.Grant. A multi-agent approach to the design of peer-help environments. In S.P. Lajoie and M. Vivet, editors, *Proceedings of the International Conference on Artificial Intelligence in Education*, volume 50 of *Frontiers in Artificial Intelligence and Applications*, pages 38–45, Le Mans, France, July 1999. IOS Press. Available on-line at: http://julita.usask.ca/Texte/AIED'99.zip.

[16] Gerhard Weber and Marcus Specht. User modeling and adaptive navigation support in www-based tutoring systems. In *Proceedings of the Sixth International Conference on User Modeling*, pages 289–300, Chia Laguna, Sardinia, Italy, June 1997.

Case-Based User Profiling for Content Personalisation

Keith Bradley , Rachael Rafter & Barry Smyth

Smart Media Institute
Department of Computer Science
University College Dublin
Belfield, Dublin 4, Ireland

{Keith.Bradley, Rachael.Rafter, Barry.Smyth}@ucd.ie

Abstract. As it stands the Internet's "one size fits all" approach to information retrieval presents the average user with a serious information overload problem. Adaptive hypermedia systems can provide a solution to this problem by learning about the implicit and explicit preferences of individual users and using this information to personalise information retrieval processes. We describe and evaluate a two-stage personalised information retrieval system that combines a server-side similarity-based retrieval component with a client-side case-based personalisation component. We argue that this combination has a number of benefits in terms of personalisation accuracy, computational cost, flexibility, security and privacy.

1 Introduction

The Internet currently consists of approximately 800 million pages of information across more than 8 million web sites, and there are over 200 million regular users from all walks of life with varying degrees of computer literacy and a wide range of interests and preferences. Retrieving the right information for a particular user is one of the most difficult information retrieval tasks imaginable. It is made more difficult because a typical Internet user is unlikely to provide a well-specified search query to a search engine. Many search queries contain only two or three search terms for example, and the inevitable result is that the user is swamped with a deluge of irrelevant retrieval results.

Recent work in the areas of adaptive hypermedia, content personalisation and user profiling(e.g. [1,2,5,6]) has presented a number of potential solutions to this problem by automatically learning about the likes and dislikes of individual users in order to personalise information retrieval for each user. For example, by constructing a detailed profile on a user it may be possible to supplement that user's search queries with additional relevant search terms, or it may be possible to filter the retrieval results to weed our irrelevant hits.

In this paper we describe part of the work carried out in the CASPER (Case-Based Profiling for Electronic Recruitment) project [3,10,11]. Very briefly, the aim of CASPER is to build a more intelligent search engine for use in specialised Internet information retrieval applications – specifically, our application test-bed is the

P. Brusilovsky, O. Stock, C. Strapparava (Eds.): AH 2000, LNCS 1892, pp. 62-72, 2000.

JobFinder web site (www.jobfinder.ie), which specialises in the provision of job listings. Several approaches to this problem were examined in the CASPER project with a view to discovering synergies between the methods. Rafter et al., in this volume, discuss a different but complimentary approach that uses Automatic Collaborative Filtering to also provide a job recommendation facility for CASPER. The focus of that work is on providing a query-less content-free filtering service, whereas in this paper we focus on a content-based search service.

Here we describe and evaluate a two-stage personalised job case retrieval system (CASPER PCR) that combines a server-side similarity-based retrieval component with a client-side case-based personalisation component. We argue that this combination benefits from superior cost, flexibility, and privacy characteristics.

2   Related Work

Recently a number of successful adaptive hypermedia systems have appeared under a number of headings including "personalised systems", "recommender systems", and "information butlers". Many share a common goal: to learn about the implicit preferences of individual users and to use this information to serve these users better.

PIMA is a client-side, content-based recommender system that monitors a user's actions in an application environment such as MS Word and suggests relevant resources from the Web to aid the user in their current task [4]. As the user works the PIMA client builds a summary of the current page using standard content-based information retrieval techniques. This information then forms the basis of queries that are submitted to various web-based resources such as search engines. PIMA is essentially a reactive system and does not maintain persistent profiles of the user. In other words profile information is lost at the end of a session.

Both Personal Web Watcher (PWW) [9] and Letizia [8] are content-based systems that recommend web-page hyperlinks by comparing them with a history of previous pages visited by the user. Letizia uses the unused time when the user is actually reading a web page to search the adjoining hyperlinks. The user's profile is composed of keywords extracted from the various pages visited. PWW uses an offline period to generate a bag of words style profile for each of the pages visited during the previous browsing session. Hyperlinks on new pages can then be compared to this profile and graded accordingly.

GroupLens [7] is a server-side recommendation engine for Usenet news. A user's profile is created by recording the user's explicit ratings of various articles. Automatic collaborative filtering is then used to statistically compare one user's likes and dislikes with another user and to recommend articles from other similar users profiles.

PTV is a personalised TV listings service, providing users with personalised TV guides based on their learned viewing preferences [12,13]. It employs a hybrid recommendation strategy using both content-based and collaborative methods. Its server uses explicit user gradings on various programmes, channels, and viewing times to build a profile.

CASPER's PCR component shares many of the same motivations and objectives as the above systems. Like GroupLens and PTV, CASPER maintains long-term user profile and like PIMA, PWW and Letizia it implements a client-side personalisation policy. Like PIMA, PWW, Letizia and PTV, our system uses a content-based approach to personalisation, while these systems use unstructured keyword-type profiles, CASPER PCR uses a structured case-base profile representation.

3   Case-Based User Profiling for Content Personalisation

JobFinder is an award-winning Irish recruitment site that provides conventional search engine functionality over a dynamic recruitment database. Its reliance on exact-match retrieval functionality introduces many problems for the average job-hunter. For example, a JobFinder user might specify that they are looking for a software development job with a salary of £25k. However, the reality is that they may actually be looking for a permanent C++ or Java software development job, with a salary in the region of £25k (preferably greater), in the Dublin or Wicklow area. In other words, the supplied query is usually only a very small part of the equation. Furthermore, as it stands, two users with the same queries will receive the same search results even though they may both have very different personal preferences – a second user, looking for a "software development job in the region of £25k", may actually be looking for a Visual Basic job in Cork, and not want to see information on Dublin, C++ or Java jobs.

This makes JobFinder an excellent test-bed for a more sophisticated approach to information retrieval, and the aim of the CASPER project is to assess the potential impact of artificial intelligence and content personalisation techniques in a JobFinder setting. Specifically, in the remainder of this paper we will describe and evaluate a two-step personalised retrieval engine designed to improve the precision of JobFinder's searches.

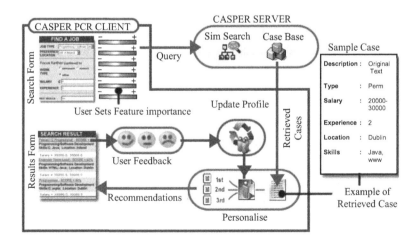

Fig. 1. Overview of the two-stage retrieval process in CASPER PCR

3.1 CASPER Personalised Retrieval Architecture

Fig. 1 outlines the architecture of CASPER's personalised case retrieval engine. When a user enters a new search query, a server-side similarity-based search engine is used to select a set of similar job cases (see Section 3.2). However, unlike a traditional search engine, CASPER does not return these results to the user directly. Instead, they are processed on the user's machine by the *personalisation client*. Personalisation is essentially a post-processing retrieval task where the result-set is compared to a user profile in order to filter-out irrelevant jobs (see Section 3.3). Each user profile is simply a set of graded jobs that the user has viewed (and graded) in the past as part of the normal JobFinder functionality. The final result of a retrieval session is a set of jobs that are not only relevant to the user's search query but that are also appropriate given the preference encoded within the user's profile.

3.2   Stage 1: Similarity-Based Retrieval

The first stage of the CASPER PRC system is equivalent to a traditional search-engine in the sense that it takes a user's query and compares it to job cases in the job case-base to identify the best matches. However, unlike a traditional search engine, this process is based on a similarity-based retrieval technique rather than on an exact-match technique. This means that relevant jobs can be identified even though they share no features with the original user query.

Each job case is made up of a fixed set of features such as job type, salary, key skills, minimum experience etc. And during retrieval the user's search query or *target query* is compared on a feature by feature basis to each of the job cases. The similarity metric shown in (1) is used to compute the similarity between each job case and the target query, based on the similarity of corresponding features; this metric is a fairly standard weighted-sum metric.

$$Sim(t, j) \square \sum_{i \square 1}^{n} similarity(t_i, j_i) * w_i . \tag{1}$$

The key to the success of this similarity-based approach is the ability to accurately estimate the similarity between individual features of a job case and target query. Each case will contain different types of features; for example, the minimum experience feature is a numeric feature while key skills contains symbolic values. We have defined a range of different feature similarity metrics to handle each of the different case features. For example, numeric features can be handled using a simple distance function; although some numeric features (for example salary) may use a more sophisticated asymmetric distance function to account for certain types of biases (for example most users are happy to accept jobs with higher salaries than they asked for, but the reverse is not always true).

Symbolic features are more difficult to handle. In CASPER we have defined a domain ontology in which symbolic features are represented as concept trees, and symbolic feature similarity is based on subsumption relationships and on the distances between nodes in these trees; see Fig. 2(a). For example, CASPER PCR performs two types of similarity-based matching using concept trees. The first type is called *subsumption matching* (see Fig. 2(b)) and allows for different granularities of abstraction to be used in a search query. For example in Fig. 2(b) the user has submitted a query for OOP or Object Oriented Programming based jobs. Any job containing a concept that is a descendant of OOP in the tree is taken to be an exact match. This is logical since all descendants of OOP in the tree are object oriented programming skills.

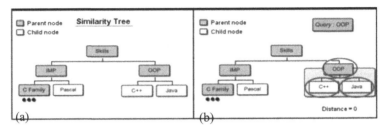

Fig. 2. (a): A concept tree: this tree shows the domain knowledge available for job skills (b): Subsumption Matching: descendants of a node are taken as exact matches for that node

The second type of concept similarity method is based on *concept proximity* as shown in Fig. 3(a) and Fig. 3(b). In other words, the closer two concepts are in the tree the more similar they are. As an example in Fig. 3(a) the distance between C++ and Java is 2. These concepts are therefore taken to be quite similar. Distance is measured in terms of the number of inter nodal edges or links between the two concepts. By contrast the similarity between Java and Pascal is judged to be quite low as shown in Fig. 3(b) since there are four edges between them.

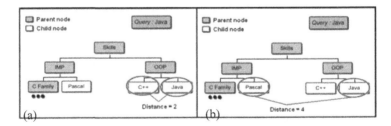

Fig. 3. (a): Proximity Matching: the skills of C++ and Java were taken to be conceptually quite similar (b): Proximity Matching: in this case Pascal and Java were deemed less similar

It is quite possible for concepts to recur within a given concept tree, that is, for a concept to have multiple parents. The final similarity score is then taken to be the best similarity score from all of the permutations of candidate / target available.

3.3   Stage 2: Result Personalisation

As it stands CASPER's similarity-based retrieval engine allows job cases to be retrieved on the basis of a fluid feature-based similarity assessment procedure borrowed from the case-based reasoning community. However, as it stands this retrieval approach is still ignorant of the implicit need of individual users, and therefore retrieval results are not personalised for individual users.

This motivates the need for the second stage of retrieval, which is capable of personalising the retrieval results from the client-side. Before describing how this personalisation process works, let us first talk briefly about CASPER's user profiling functionality.

As users interact with the JobFinder system they are presented with various jobs and a number of useful options. For example, users can apply for jobs online, they can submit their resume to the relevant contact point, or they can e-mail themselves a copy of the job for their files. As part of the CASPER project we have explored various techniques for monitoring this type of user activity and for converting it into useful user profiles [10,11]. The upshot of this is that user profiles are available for each JobFinder user and these profiles contain a record of which jobs a user has liked and which jobs they have not liked.

The client-side personalisation technique views the personalisation task as a classification problem. In other words, personalising the retrieval results amounts to classifying each individual retrieved job as either relevant or not relevant. To do this we propose a nearest-neighbour type classification algorithm that uses the graded job cases in a target user's profile as training data. Each profile case serves as a training example with the job grade (liked or disliked / good or bad) serving as the example classification.

In order to classify a candidate retrieved job we compare it to each profile job case, using the similarity metric defined earlier, to locate the k nearest profile jobs; the value of k is usually a low odd number and needs to be set experimentally for the classification domain in question. A judgement about the job's relevance can then be based on the classifications of these nearest neighbours. For example, one simple strategy is to take the majority classification of the nearest neighbours; according to this strategy, the candidate job shown in Fig. 4 would be classified as 'good' or relevant (with k=5).

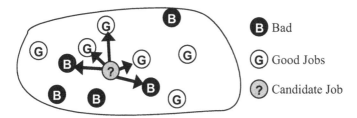

Fig. 4. Client-side personalisation is viewed as a classification problem and implemented with a k nearest-neighbour classification algorithm.

$$Rel(\,j,P\,) = 1\;if\;\sum_{p\,=\,knn(\,j,P\,)} Sim(\,j_i,p\,).classification(\,p\,) \geq 0,\; = 1\;otherwise\,. \tag{2}$$

Instead of the simple majority classification strategy, CASPER PCR uses a weighted-similarity metric whereby the similarity of a profile case to the retrieval candidate determines how much influence that case has in the overall classification, as shown in (2). The relevance of a candidate job j to user profile P is the sum of the product of the similarity values of the k nearest-neighbours to j by their class value (+1 indicates that the user liked the job and −1 indicates that they disliked it).

4   Experimental Evaluation

Of course ultimately the important question to be asked about CASPER's approach is does it work? Does it produce retrieval results that are more relevant to a given user than JobFinder's conventional retrieval engine? Does it produce personalised results that reflect a user's implicit preferences? In this section we describe some preliminary experiments, carried out on real users, to evaluate the effectiveness of the personalisation side of CASPER PCR.

4.1   Set-Up

Eleven subjects were selected for this experiment, all of them postgraduate students and staff members in the Department of Computer Science at University College Dublin. In addition a subset of 58 jobs (from a database of 3800 jobs) were chosen as the basis for user profiles for the subjects. These jobs were selected because they provided a good cross-section of employment characteristics. Each subject was asked to grade each of the 58 jobs as relevant or not relevant to provide the raw data for the 10 user profiles.

4.2   Experiment 1

The aim of this experiment is to evaluate the impact of k (the number of nearest neighbours used in the classification process) on the classification/personalisation accuracy (this is equivalent to the precision of the filtered result set). We used a leave-one-out method to compute the overall personalisation accuracy for each profile for different values of k (1 – 15). That is, for each profile and value of k, we classified each profile job using the remaining 57 profile jobs, and compared the predicted classification (relevant or not relevant) to the actual known classification as provided by the user during the initial grading process. The personalisation accuracy for a given user is the percentage of correct classifications over the set of 58 jobs. For each value of k, this produces 10 personalisation accuracy values, which are averaged to produce a mean accuracy over all profiles for this value of k.

The results are presented in Fig. 5 as a graph of mean classification accuracy versus k. The results show that as k increases so too does the classification accuracy, up to a point. The maximum accuracy tends to be obtained at around the k=11 or k=13 mark. This behaviour is to be expected as nearest-neighbour algorithms are known to be adversely affected by training noise for low values of k. Our user profiles are known to contain a lot of noise in the sense that users are often inconsistent in their grading of jobs, and hence we would expect improved performance from higher values of k.

All of the jobs presented to the users were obtained from a query submitted to the first stage retrieval engine. We therefore chose to use the number of jobs liked by the user from this initial query as our baseline. Since we are looking at the average accuracy for each value of k across all users, we averaged this base measure for all users to give the baseline shown in Fig. 5. This baseline therefore corresponds to the average accuracy of the first stage retrieval system.

In general the results are very positive, showing a personalisation accuracy of over 70% for reasonable values of k and relatively small profiles. In fact, it is particularly positive given the high degree of noise in the profile data. The personalisation system consistently outperforms the first stage retrieval when taken on its own by a significant margin.

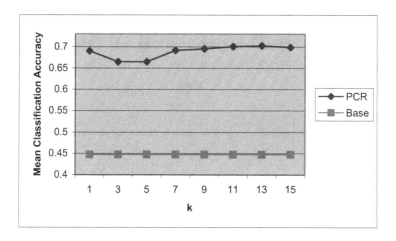

Fig 5. Mean personalisation/classification accuracy across all users for varying values of k.

4.3   Experiment 2

The aim of this next experiment is to examine the personalisation accuracy for different individual users at a given value of k. In this case we chose k=13, since this value returned the highest overall accuracy. The personalisation accuracy for k=13 was calculated using the same method described above and the results are shown in Fig. 6 for each of the 10 users.

In general the results are positive although there is a high degree of variation between individual users. Overall, 8 out of the 10 users benefit from a personalisation accuracy in excess of 60%. However, for one user (6) the reported accuracy was only 57%; this users were found to have a very noisy profile with many inconsistencies apparent in the way that the original jobs were graded.

Again we used the number of jobs liked by the user out of the original query as a baseline. Clearly in almost all cases the personalisation engine achieved better results and indeed achieved significant improvements in over half of those tested.

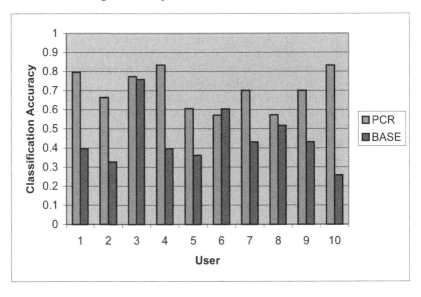

Fig 6. Mean personalisation/classification accuracy for all users at k = 13.

5   Discussion

CASPER's PCR approach to client-side personalisation brings with it a number of potentially significant advantages. First and foremost is the fact that the computational load is transferred from the server-side to the client side, and this brings with it the potential for greatly improved overall response times.

However, possibly the most important benefit has to do with the privacy and security issues. CASPER PCR does not require server-side access to user profiles, and unlike collaborative personalisation techniques [7,12,13], there is no need to access the profiles of other users. This means that an individual user can benefit from personalisation safe in the knowledge that her profile has never left her client machine; this is especially important in any personalised applications that may involve the collection of sensitive personal data, for example, medical data or financial data. This advantage is not available with many other personalisation techniques and is becoming more and more critical in the context of promised privacy legislation for e-commerce and Internet systems.

Finally, although we have described the CASPER PCR approach in the context of the JobFinder domain, there is of course no reason why the approach could not be applied to a range of other information retrieval domain. In fact, we would suggest that any existing search engine technology could benefit from CASPER's client-side personalisation strategy, assuming that suitable user profiles are available or can be collected.

6   Conclusions

We have motivated the need for personalised information retrieval systems and described one particular implementation in the form of CASPER PCR. This technique works as a two stage process: stage one performing a similarity-based server-side retrieval, and stage two performing a content-based filtering of the retrieval results with respect to a store user profile. Our evaluation demonstrates the technique to be effective.

We have argued that this combination of server-side search and client-side personalisation offers a number of important advantages over many existing approaches, not the least of which are the advantages pertaining to user privacy and security issues. The benefit, from a users point of view, of hiding valuable and private profile data from a remote server cannot be understated, and in the future may even a critical feature for the universal adoption of personalisation technology. We believe that this positions our work well as a realistic, practical and safe personalisation technology for the future.

7   References

1 Balabanovic M, Shoham Y.: FAB: Content-Based Collaborative Recommender. Communications of the ACM 1997; 40:3:66-72.
2 Billsus D & Pazzani M.: Learning Collaborative Information Filters. In: Proceedings of the International Conference on Machine Learning. Morgan Kaufmann, Madison, Wisc. 1998
3 Bradley, K., Rafter, R., and Smyth, B.: Personalised Case Retrieval. In: Proceedings of the 10th Irish Conference on Artificial Intelligence and Cognitive Science, Cork, Ireland. (1999)
4 Budzik, J., Hammond, K. J., Marlow, C., and Scheinkman, A: Anticipating Information Needs: Everyday Applications as Interfaces to Internet Information Sources. In Proceedings of the 1998 World Conference on the WWW, Internet, and Intranet. AACE Press, (1998)
5 Goldberg D, Nichols D, Oki B M, Terry D.: Using Collaborative Filtering to Weave an Information Tapestry. Communications of the ACM 1992; 35: 12: 61-70
6 Kay J.: Vive la Difference! Individualised Interaction with Users. In: Proceedings IJCAI '95, Montréal, Canada, (1995), 978-984
7 Konstan J.A, Miller B.N., Maltz D, Herlocker J.L., Gordon L.R., Riedl J: Group Lens: Applying Collaborative Filtering to Usenet News. Communications of the ACM, 40(3) (1997) 77-87
8 Liebermann, H.:Letizia: An agent that assists web browsing. In: Proceedings 14th International Conference Artificial intelligence (IJCAI) (1995)

9   Mladenic, D.: Personal WebWatcher: Implementation and Design. Technical Report IJS-DP-7472, Department of Intelligent Systems, J.Stefan Institute, Slovenia (1996)
10 Rafter R., Bradley K., Smyth B.: Passive Profiling and Collaborative Recommendation. In: Proceedings of the 10th Irish Conference on Artificial Intelligence and Cognitive Science, Cork, Ireland, September.(1999)
11 Rafter R., Bradley K., Smyth B.: Personalised Retrieval For Online Recruitment Services. In: Proceedings of the 22nd Annual Colloquium on IR Research, Cambridge, UK, (2000)
12 Smyth B & Cotter P.: Surfing the Digital Wave: Generating Personalised Television Guides using Collaborative, Case-based Recommendation. In: Proceedings of the 3rd International Conference on Case-based Reasoning, Munich, Germany, (1999)
13 Smyth B & Cotter P.: Sky's the Limit: A Personalised TV Listings Service for the Digital Age. In: Proceedings of the 19th SGES International Conference on Knowledge-Based and Applied Artificial Intelligence (ES99). Cambridge, UK, (1999)

Providing Tailored (Context-Aware) Information to City Visitors

Keith Cheverst, Nigel Davies, Keith Mitchell, and Paul Smith

Distributed Multimedia Research Group,
Department of Computing,
Lancaster University,
Lancaster, LA1 4YR.
e-mail: kc,nigel,mitchelk,smithp@comp.lancs.ac.uk

Abstract. The GUIDE system has been developed in order to provide city visitors with an intelligent and context-aware tourist guide. The system has been deployed in the city of Lancaster and integrates the use of hand-held personal computing technologies, wireless communications, context-awareness and adaptive hypermedia. This paper focuses on the role of adaptive hypermedia within the GUIDE system and the techniques used to tailor or adapt the presentation of web-based information. The context used by GUIDE includes the visitor's personal context, e.g. the visitor's current location and personal profile, and the environmental context, e.g. the opening times of the city's attractions. Following a field trial based evaluation, in which positive feedback was received, the system is now publicly available to visitors who wish to explore the city.

1   Introduction

The GUIDE project [4][6] has been developed to provide city visitors with up-to-date and context-aware [2] information whilst they explore a city using handheld GUIDE units. The use of adaptive hypermedia is fundamental to GUIDE in that web-based information is presented to visitors in a way that is tailored to both the visitor's personal context (including her location and profile) and the environmental context.

The most important piece of personal context that is used to tailor or constrain the information presented to the visitor is the visitor's current location. However, other examples of personal context used by GUIDE include: the visitor's profile (e.g. the visitor's interests and preferred reading language) and the set of attractions already visited that day. This latter piece of context enables pages of information to reflect those attractions that the visitor has already seen. For example, if a visitor makes a return visit to an attraction then the information presented should reflect this fact, e.g. by welcoming the visitor back. Oberlander [13] uses the term coherence to describe the tailoring of information in this way. Examples of environmental context utilised by the system include: the time of day, and the opening times of attractions. This type of context is of particular relevance to GUIDE when the system is instructed to create a tailored tour and navigate a visitor around the city.

P. Brusilovsky, O. Stock, C. Strapparava (Eds.): AH 2000, LNCS 1892, pp. 73-85, 2000.
◻ Springer-Verlag Berlin Heidelberg 2000

The requirement to tailor the information presented to visitors was identified following a comprehensive requirements capture process [4] involving Lancaster's Tourist Information Centre or TIC. This process also identified the need to support dynamic information, e.g. changes to the normal opening/closing times of attractions or the daily specials menu of the city's cafés. The requirements capture also identified the need to provide visitors with sufficient flexibility to explore, and learn about, a city in their own preferred way. For example, some visitors prefer to play a passive role when exploring a new city, e.g. following a guided tour; while others may choose a more active role by using guidebooks or street maps. It was also thought important that visitors should be able to control their pace of interaction with the system, e.g. being able to interrupt a tour in order to take a coffee break.

The structure of the remainder of this paper is as follows. An overview of the GUIDE system is presented in section two. Section three describes some of the ways in which contextual information is obtained in GUIDE. Following this, section four details our approach towards modelling contextual information. Next, section five describes the techniques employed for generating information tailored to the current context. Section six briefly describes the acceptance of the system by city visitors while section seven describes related and future work. Finally, in section eight, we present some concluding remarks.

2   The Guide System

2.1   The GUIDE End-System

We considered a range of devices for use as the GUIDE end-system including Windows CE based machines and other PDAs, such as the Apple Newton. After much deliberation, we chose the Fujitsu TeamPad 7600 [7] (see figure 1) as the end-system.

Fig. 1. The GUIDE end-system.

The TeamPad measures 213x153x15mm, weighs 850g and features a transflective screen, which enables the display to be readable even in direct sunlight. The relatively powerful Pentium 166 MMX processor driving the Teampad is well-matched to the computationally intensive task of generating and updating tailored tours (as described in section 2.3.2) based on both the visitor's and the environmental context.

We have found the unit to have a battery life of approximately two hours (driving a wireless networking card). Although this period of battery life has been suitable for evaluation purposes, the ideal GUIDE unit would clearly require substantially longer battery life. During an initial evaluation of the system, the reaction of visitors to the chosen GUIDE unit was very positive. In general, visitors did not want a viewable display area any smaller than that available on the TeamPad. However, some visitors did suggest that a slightly thinner and lighter unit would have been preferable.

2.2   The User Interface to GUIDE

The user interface to GUIDE (as illustrated in figure 2) is based around a modified browser metaphor. This decision was made for two reasons. Firstly, the metaphor seemed appropriate for presenting (and supporting the navigation of) the required structure of information, i.e. the notion of following hypertext links in order to access greater levels of detailed information. Secondly, the browser metaphor was based on the growing acceptance of the web and the increasing familiarity of the metaphor as a tool for interacting with a large and heterogeneous information space. We hoped that positive transfer from the use of common web browsers would help make the system both easy to use and easy to learn for users with previous web experience. However, we also wanted to ascertain the extent to which the basic metaphor would prove appropriate in supporting the additional functionality required by GUIDE.

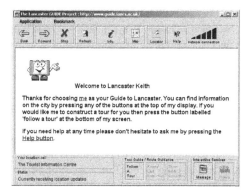

Fig. 2. The user interface to GUIDE.

We had considered incorporating a multimodal user interface into the GUIDE system, e.g. one in which information and navigation instructions could be delivered to the user using speech output [12]. However, we had reservations about this approach based on the fact that GUIDE is designed for outdoor use and Lancaster has its fair share of traffic noise. We were concerned that visitors might be distracted when crossing roads if the system chose that time to deliver some information. Following on from this point, in general we have reservations about the effective bandwidth of voice for information transfer and the extent to which visitors could control the pace of information delivery with a speech-based system.

2.3   GUIDE Functionality

The GUIDE system provides city visitors with a wide range of functionality [4][6]. However, in terms of utilising adaptive hypermedia, the two most relevant elements of functionality are: providing the visitor with access to context-aware information, and creating a tailored tour of the city and navigating the visitor through this tour.

Providing Access to (Context-Aware) Information. The visitor can use GUIDE to retrieve information about the city and its attractions, and this retrieval process can be simplified or constrained by utilising the current context, e.g. the visitor's location or the opening times of nearby attractions. In order to retrieve information the visitor simply has to tap the 'Info' button and this causes a set of choices to be presented in the form of hypertext links. It is important to note that not all the options are location-aware, i.e. offer information based on the visitor's current location. For example, the visitor is given the option to search for information using a keyword search facility if he or she is not interested in accessing information regarding their current locale.

An earlier version of the system did not offer this facility and, in effect, restricted the scope of information available to a visitor to that closely related to the visitor's location. An expert walkthrough of the system [4] revealed that constraining a visitor's access to information based on their current location needs to be done with great care. It can be very frustrating for visitors when the particular piece of information that they require cannot be accessed because the system designers did not consider it to be of sufficient 'relevance' to warrant inclusion in the page associated with that locale. This anecdote highlights the need for designers of context-aware systems to be careful not to overly constrain the information provided by the system based on current context.

Creating a Tailored Tour of the City. To create a tour of the city the visitor is initially asked to select from a list the attractions that she wishes to be included in the tour.

The system takes both personal and environmental context into account when creating a tailored tour (and navigating the visitor through the tour). For example, the system utilises the opening and closing times of the requested attractions, the optimum time to visit an attraction (e.g. avoiding opening time if there is often a queue), the distance between attractions and the most aesthetic route between them.

Once created, the system breaks the tour down into a number of stages. The visitor can then request GUIDE to navigate them from one attraction to the next by clicking on the 'show next instruction' button. It is important to note that the recommended ordering of the tour can change dynamically. This can occur when a visitor stays at a location longer than anticipated or if one of the attractions announces that it will close early. The system regularly calculates whether or not the current order for visiting the remaining attractions is appropriate, given current time constraints.

The visitor can either agree to be taken to the next attraction recommended by GUIDE or override this recommendation by selecting a different attraction to be the next destination. The system provides this choice in order to prevent behaving in an overly authoritarian manner. It does, after all, seem quite reasonable to allow a visitor to delay their current tour and get directions to the nearest café instead.

Fig. 3. The presentation of navigation information.

In addition to the description, the visitor is presented with information about their current location, i.e. the gateway to the castle, and a hypertext link is available should the visitor wish to find out further information on this attraction (see figure 3).

The visitor can also choose to view the navigation instruction as an annotated map. At an early stage in the project we discussed whether or not the system should present maps because of the apparent sufficiency of providing succinct location-aware directions. However, from early field-trials [4] it soon became apparent that a significant portion of visitors wanted to view a map at some point in their visit.

3   Obtaining Contextual Information

This section described the two basic approaches adopted by GUIDE in order to obtain context. The first involves the use of a cell-based wireless communications infrastructure whilst the second involves requesting information from the visitor.

3.1   The Cell-Based Wireless Communications Infrastructure

The GUIDE system is engineered using a high-bandwidth cell-based wireless networking infrastructure [6] and this network has a dual role:

- It is used to broadcast dynamic and contextual information to GUIDE units.
- It is used to provide course grained positioning information to GUIDE units.

The wireless network is based on Lucent Technologies' 802.11 compliant ORiNOCO system. The version used by GUIDE offers a maximum bandwidth of 2 Mbps per cell. Each cell provides wireless communications coverage to a selected area of the city and has associated *cell-servers* with local storage and processing that effectively act as a proxy cache to the central GUIDE web server. Currently, six communication cells have been deployed within the city covering the major tourist attractions. Although, the range of ORiNOCO is approximately 200m in free space, ORiNOCO signals have poor propagation characteristics through buildings and, therefore, by the strategic positioning of cell-servers, we have been able to create relatively small cells offering reasonably accurate position information.

A visitor interacts with his or her GUIDE unit through a local web browser embedded within the GUIDE application. In effect, all HTTP requests are processed by a local web proxy, which may, in turn, need to interact with other objects in order to service the request. This aspect of the GUIDE system is described in detail in [6].

3.2   Interacting with the Visitor

Obtaining the Visitor's Preferences. In order to use GUIDE a visitor is asked to enter certain personal details as shown in figure 4. Examples of such details include the visitor's name, their interests and preferred reading language. The specific interests currently supported by the system are: architecture, maritime and history.

Fig. 4. Obtaining the visitor's preferences.

Once entered, this information is stored locally on the visitor's GUIDE unit using a special 'visitor-profile' object. Although the visitor is currently asked to specify their interests in absolute terms, i.e. yes or no, the visitor-profile object is designed to record visitor interests as values with a range of between 0 and 100. Associated with the visitor-profile object is the 'visitor-context' object and this is used to store contextual information related to the visitor, e.g. her current location. Both of these objects can be queried through the use of special GUIDE tags (section 5).

It important to note that the information stored in the visitor-profile object is currently static. However, in the future we intend to investigate the potential for making this information more dynamic. In more detail, we intend to trace the visitor's page requests and update the visitor-profile object appropriately. For example, if the visitor makes a number of requests for pages that we have tagged as having a strong historic relevance, then the visitor's 'history' interest rating can be increased.

Using the Visitor's Assistance to Solve Location Problems. When visitors do leave cell coverage and up-to-date positioning information becomes unavailable, the GUIDE system tries to locate the visitor by establishing a form of partnership between itself and the visitor. In more detail, the visitor is shown a series of thumbnail pictures showing attractions in the vicinity of the visitor's last known location. Hopefully, the visitor is then able to recognise and select one of the pictures in order to enable the GUIDE system to ascertain the visitor's location within the city.

4   Modeling Contextual Information

The GUIDE system utilises a purpose built information model (as illustrated in figure 5) to store and represent the following four distinct types of information:

i)   information that can be tailored to reflect the current context, e.g. 'it is raining' and 'the user is outside the castle and has an interest in history'.

ii)   geographic information, which can be either expressed in geographic terms (e.g. 'location a is at co-ordinates x,y') or symbolic terms (e.g. 'the Cottage Museum is in the Castle Hill area').

iii)   hypertext information, which can be either global (i.e. internet based) such as the world-wide-web, or stored locally.

iv)   active components, which are capable of storing state (such as a visitor's preferences) and of performing specific actions.

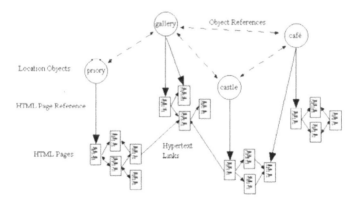

Fig. 5. The GUIDE information model.

Although each particular information type has been successfully modelled, no models could be found that were capable of handling the full complement of information types described above [6].

The information model that we have developed for GUIDE is based on the integration of an active object model with a hypertext information model. The model contains two distinct object types: navigation point objects and location objects. Navigation point objects represent waypoints between location objects and are required in order to support the construction of tour guides. Alternatively, location objects actually represent attractions in the city and are the fundamental building blocks of our model. One example of a location object used in the information model is Lancaster Castle. This object has state representing its physical location within the city, opening times, and links to other nearby locations. Location objects also support methods to enable state information to be accessed and modified. For example, the 'ProvideDescription' method is designed to return a handle to information about the location object based on the visitor's profile. For example, if the visitor required information in German then this method would return a handle to information on the castle presented in German.

The information model allows geographical information to be represented by creating relationships between objects. These relationships can have attributes (weights) assigned to them to denote, for example, the distance between two objects by a variety of means of transport. Using this representation, other objects can traverse relationships in order to determine optimal routes between attractions.

The effort required for populating the information model with information for a city should not be underestimated; nearly eight person months were invested entering the details required for the hundred or so location and navigation objects required to model a key tourist area within Lancaster. Although tools have been developed for semi-automating the task of producing an appropriate information model for any city, the job of producing an information model for a large city, such as New York, would be an engineering task in itself. Furthermore, the computational complexity of calculating a tailored tour based on an information model with thousands of objects would require significantly increased processing power on the local client. One alternative to increasing local processing power would be to generate the tour at the server and then transmit the graph representing the tour to the client.

5   The Use of Context to Generate Adaptive Hypermedia

In order to allow hypertext pages to reference the object model we enable the authors of hypertext pages to augment their pages with tags that control the display of the information (see examples below). These tags take the form of special instructions that are able to query location object and the visitor's profile. A selection of the tags currently supported and in use by GUIDE are described below:

<GUIDETAG INSERT POSITION>

This tag can be used to dynamically insert a tourist's location into a page. So, if a tourist followed a link and asked 'tell me about the area in which I am located' the resulting page could include this tag to inform the visitor of their location.

<GUIDETAG INTEREST ((HISTORY > 50) AND (ARCHITECTURE > 50))

This tag enables the application to tailor pages based on a visitor's expressed interests. In more detail and using the above example, prior to rendering the current page, the system would check the values stored in the visitor-profile object representing the visitor's interest ratings in bath history and architecture. If the two ratings were both found to be greater than 50 then the information enclosed within the INTEREST tag would be deemed sufficiently relevant and therefore displayed.

<GUIDETAG INSERT NEIGHBOURS>

This tag enables the dynamic generation of pages containing attractions that are within close proximity to the visitor and is used by GUIDE for generating the 'nearby attractions' page (see figure 6). In more detail, once the page containing this tag has been retrieved from the unit's local cache or from a cell-server, a special purpose software filter is used to process it and replace the tag with the appropriate html code.

Fig. 6. The dynamically created 'nearby attractions' page.

Generating the 'nearby attractions' page further highlighted the difficulty of successfully pre-empting the user's goal. In more detail, the list of nearby attractions is sorted in such a way that those attractions that are open, and have not already been visited, are placed higher up the list. The assumption is made that the visitor is more likely to be interested in attractions that are open and that have not already been visited. However, an earlier version of the system constrained the output by removing all closed attractions from the presented list. When evaluating the system, we found that this constraint frustrated some visitors who were interested in visiting the regardless of whether the attraction was open or closed; they simply wished to view the architecture of the building.

6   The Evaluation of GUIDE

Our evaluation of the GUIDE system involved two distinct phases: an expert walkthrough of the system and a field trial. A more detailed discussion of the evaluation and its results can be found in [4]. The main objective of our evaluation was to focus on the quality of the visitor's experience [8], as opposed to studying absolute performance times for accessing specific pieces of information.

During the field trial part of the evaluation, we felt acutely aware of impinging on the leisure time of tourists. For this reason, we asked visitors to use the system as they wished, rather than performing some predefined series of tasks. Our method for evaluation was based on direct observation, with visitors encouraged to use a talk-aloud protocol. In addition, we maintained a time-stamped log of the user's interaction with the system. A semi-structured interview was conducted following each session in order to obtain the visitor's subjective opinion of using GUIDE.

Over a period of approximately four weeks, 60 people volunteered to use the system. The profile of the visitors varied widely in terms of age, gender and web experience. Regarding the provision of tailored information, the vast majority of visitors (including those with no previous web experience) expressed the opinion that the context-aware navigation and information retrieval mechanisms provided by the system were both useful and reassuring, and stated that they enjoyed using GUIDE to explore the city. Indeed, the vast majority of visitors said that they were prepared to trust the information presented by the system, including the navigation instructions. Investigating this issue further revealed that the reputation of the source providing the GUIDE units, i.e. the TIC, contributed significantly to the visitor's trust. However, a number of visitors suggested that their level of trust was not constant but varied with the apparent accuracy of the information presented. In addition, a significant number of visitors expressed some concern about the potential for inadvertently missing certain pieces of information associated with a particular attraction because of the 'automated' way in which some of the information was retrieved.

7   Related and Future Work

The GUIDE project builds upon the work of earlier location-aware tourist guides such as the Cyberguide project [10]. This system can be viewed as the first in a series of location-aware 'City Guide' applications, such as [9] and [11]. However, the GUIDE system differs from the typical location-aware tourist guide application in that it is actually available for public use. Furthermore, reaching this stage has been the culmination of a number of distinct research efforts, including: requirements capture, the design and deployment of a cell-based wireless communications infrastructure, developing and populating an information model to represent context-aware information, user interface design and system evaluation.

In common with GUIDE, the HIPS (Hyper-Interaction within Physical Space) project [1][12] is also concerned with enriching the experience of visitors by presenting up-to-date tailored information. HIPs is also addressing the many human factors issues that arise from the design and evaluation of mobile adaptive hypermedia based systems.

Comprehensive research into the development and evaluation of an adaptive hypermedia system to present 'intelligent labels' to museum visitors has been carried through the auspicious of the ILEX project [5][13]. The group's Intelligent Labelling Explorer (ILEX) is capable of generating tailored information based on the visitor's profile, including their expertise, age and what they have seen previously.

Staying within the museum domain, Twidale [14] has conducted research into the nature of a docents' work in museums and is currently investigating the notion of a cyberdocent. This agent will make use of advanced technologies, such as wireless communications and PDAs, in order to enrich the experience of visitors to a museum.

The fact that GUIDE is currently installed in Lancaster, provides a rare opportunity to conduct further research into the suitability of existing techniques and methodologies for the appropriate design and evaluation of mobile, context-aware, interactive systems. In particular, we hope to experiment with future versions of GUIDE to find ways in which the highly adaptive nature of the system can be squared with the fundamental design principle of ensuring predictability. It is hoped, this work will add to existing research in this area, such as that undertaken by Hook [8], Oberlander [13] and Cox [5].

8   Discussion and Concluding Remarks

This paper has described the use of adaptive hypermedia in the GUIDE system. The system presents city visitors with web-based information, tailored to reflect both the visitor's personal context and also the environmental context. Contextual information is obtained via a cell-based wireless communications infrastructure and also from interaction with the user.

Underpinning the GUIDE system is an information model that combines the event-based aspects of context-aware models with the geographic functions commonly associated with geographic information systems (GIS). Crucially, this model enables the creation of objects that can respond to events and, therefore, adapt their behaviour to reflect the current context. The information model also provides access points into a collection of web pages whose presentation can be tailored dynamically through the use of special GUIDE tags. These tags enable the information model to be interrogated at run-time, e.g. to retrieve the set of location objects representing attractions within close proximity to the visitor. In order to generate a 'Nearby Attractions' page, each object from this set can then be instructed to return a description, which is, in effect, a packet of hypermedia information.

In general, system's that can adapt appropriately to context have the capability to reduce the quantity (or increase the quality) of information output by the system [16]. In addition, context can be used to reduce the complexity of the user's task specification [3]. These capabilities are crucial when one considers the next generation of interactive systems that will be inherently complex but will need to have 'Information Appliance' like simplicity of use.

Through our evaluation of the GUIDE system, we found that city visitors expressed a high level of acceptance and trust for the 'intelligent' information provided by the system. However, we also discovered that designers should take great care when trying to pre-empt what information should be regarded as relevant (and therefore presented) to the visitor given a certain context, e.g. the user's location.

References

1. Broadbent, J., Marti, P.: Location Aware Mobile Interactive Guides: usability issues. In: Proceedings of the Fourth International Conference on Hypermedia and Interactivity in Museums (ICHIM97), Paris (1997)
2. Brown, P.J.: The stick-e document: a framework for creating context-aware applications. In: Proceedings of EP'96, Palo Alto U.S. (1996) 259-272
3. Cheverst, K., Davies, N., Mitchell, K., Efstratiou C.: Using Context as a Crystal Ball: Rewards and Pitfalls. In: Proceedings of the workshop on Situated Interaction in Ubiquitous Computing. CHI'2000, Hague Netherlands (2000) 12-16. Available at: http://www.teco.edu/chi2000ws/proceedings.html
4. Cheverst, K., Davies, N., Mitchell K., Friday, A.: Developing a Context-aware Electronic Tourist Guide: Some Issues and Experiences. In: Proceedings of CHI'2000, ACM Press, Hague Netherlands (2000) 17-24
5. Cox, R., O'Donnell, M., Oberlander, J.: Dynamic versus static hypermedia in museum education: an evaluation of ILEX, the intelligent labelling explorer. In: Proceedings of the Artificial Intelligence in Education conference, Le Mans (1999)
6. Davies, N., Mitchell, K., Cheverst, K., Friday, A.: Caches in the Air: Disseminating Tourist Information in the Guide System. In: Proceedings of the 2nd IEEE Workshop on Mobile Computing Systems and Applications, New Orleans (1999) 11-19
7. Fujitsu TeamPad 7600 Technical Page. Available at: http://www.fjicl.com/TeamPad/teampad76.htm (1999)
8. Hook, K., Svensson, R.: Evaluating Adaptive Navigation Support. In: Proceedings of Workshop on Personalised and Social Navigation in Information Space, Stockholm (1998) 119-128
9. Kreller, B., Carrega, D., Shankar, J., Salmon, P., Bottger, S., Kassing, T.: A Mobile Aware City Guide Application. In: Proceedings of ACTS Mobile Communications Summit, Rhodes (1998) 60-65
10. Long, S., Kooper, R., Abowd, G.D., Atkeson, C.G.: Rapid Prototyping of Mobile Context-Aware Applications: The Cyberguide Case Study. In: Proceedings of the 2nd ACM International Conference on Mobile Computing, ACM Press, Rye NY (1996)
11. Montelius, J., Danne, A.: An outdoors location-aware information-system. In: Proceedings of the Workshop on Personalised and Social Navigation in Information Space, Stockholm (1998) 168-173
12. Not, E., Petrelli, D., Stock, O., Strapparava, C., Zancanaro, M.: Person-oriented guided visit in a physical museum. In: Proceedings of the Fourth International Conference on Hypermedia and Interactivity in Museums (ICHIM97), Paris (1997)
13. Oberlander J., Mellish C., O'Donnell, M.: Exploring a gallery with intelligent labels. In: Proceedings of the Fourth International Conference on Hypermedia and Interactivity in Museums (ICHIM97), Paris (1997)
14. Rayward, W.B., Twidale, M.B.: From Docent to Cyberdocent: Education and Guidance in the Virtual Museum. Technical Report ISRN UIUCLIS--1999/8+CSCW. To appear in: Archives and Museum Informatics (1999) Available at: http://www.lis.uiuc.edu/~twidale/pubs/docents.html

15. Reeves, B., Nass, C.: The Media Equation: How People Treat Computers, Television, and New Media Like Real People and Places, Cambridge Press, ISBN: 1575860538. (1997)
16. Schmidt, A.: Implicit human-computer interaction through context. In: Proceedings of the 2nd Workshop on Human Computer Interaction with Mobile Devices, Edinburgh (1999) 23-27. Available at: http://www.dcs.gla.ac.uk/mobile99/papers/schmidt.pdf

Adding Adaptive Features to
Virtual Reality Interfaces for E-Commerce

Luca Chittaro and Roberto Ranon

Department of Mathematics and Computer Science
University of Udine
via delle Scienze 206, 33100 Udine, ITALY
+39 0432 558450
chittaro@dimi.uniud.it

Abstract. Virtual Reality (VR) interfaces to e-commerce sites have recently begun to appear on the Internet, promising to make the e-shopping experience more natural, attractive, and fun for customers. Adaptivity is an important issue for these VR applications, because it would make them suitable for the 1-to-1 e-commerce strategies towards which sellers are increasingly driven. It is thus surprising that the introduction of adaptive features in VR stores remains a completely unexplored issue. This paper begins to face the problem, presenting and discussing ADVIRT, a first prototype of an adaptive VR store. In ADVIRT, a set of personalization rules exploits a model of the customer to adapt features of the VR store such as: (i) the display of different products in the store (e.g., shelf space, display spots, banners, audio advertising), (ii) the navigation aids available to the customer, (iii) the store layout, organization, and look.

1   Introduction

One of the recent research trends in e-commerce is to provide Web sites with a Virtual Reality (VR) interface that allows the customer to interact with the e-commerce service through a 3D representation of a store that supports natural actions such as walking, looking around, and picking up products from shelves. Although almost all e-commerce sites on the Internet use traditional 2D interfaces based on menus and links, a growing number of sites are deploying VR interfaces[1] to attract customers. A VR interface can bring relevant benefits, if properly designed: (i) it is closer to the real-world shopping experience, and thus more familiar to the customer, (ii) it supports customer's natural shopping actions, (iii) it can satisfy the needs of customers who have an emotional style of buying, by providing a more immersive, interactive, and visually attractive experience, (iv) it can even satisfy social needs, by allowing customers to meet and interact with people (e.g., other customers or salespeople).

Although the idea is promising and can lead to more natural, attractive, and fun e-commerce sites, VR stores have to face major challenges in order to gain wide

---

[1]   Some examples are @mart at www.activeworlds.com, Cybertown Shopping Mall at www.cybertown.com, Giftworld at www.leap.to/euro/enter.html.

P. Brusilovsky, O. Stock, C. Strapparava (Eds.): AH 2000, LNCS 1892, pp. 86-97, 2000.

customer and seller acceptance. The first challenge is usability: guidelines for designing usable e-commerce sites (e.g., [10]) do not deal with VR stores, and usability studies of e-commerce sites in the literature (e.g., [11]) have considered only traditional 2D interfaces. The second challenge is the suitability of VR stores for the 1-to-1 e-commerce strategies towards which sellers are increasingly driven. From this point of view, it is surprising that the introduction of adaptive features in VR stores is a completely unexplored issue in the literature.

In our research, we focus both on how to design usable VR stores, and how to obtain a personalized user interaction with them. In the following, we first briefly sketch our approach to VR store usability, then we discuss in detail how we are adding adaptive features for 1-to-1 e-commerce to our VR store.

2   Designing Usable VR Stores

In our approach, we tackle the problem of designing usable VR stores from two synergistic directions: (i) designing usable environments by following selected guidelines from real-world stores (e.g., store layout, signs, product positions,...), and (ii) exploiting the virtual nature of the store by providing users with empowerments (unavailable in real-world stores) to augment their navigation capabilities.

2.1   Store Design

To identify a proper set of design guidelines, we are proceeding as follows: (i) acquiring the guidelines used in real-world stores (extensive experience is available on the topic, and can be acquired through specialized literature and expert interviews), (ii) identifying the VR counterparts of real-world guidelines (some might be directly translated, some need adaptation, and some can be impossible to translate, e.g. those concerning scents), (iii) identifying the proper implementation choices to adequately apply the guidelines in VR, (iv) evaluating the effectiveness on users (a guideline which has been proven to work in real stores does not necessarily work in virtual ones). For example, we have determined with a between-groups experiment that the "massification" guideline adopted in real-world stores (i.e., increasing the number of items displayed for the same product to increase its visibility and sales) positively transfers to VR stores [5].

2.2   User Empowerments

Simply taking traditional VR navigation aids (such as electronic maps) and including them in the VR store is not the best solution, because it does not take into account seller needs. For example, when it comes to product finding, one seller priority (both in traditional and electronic commerce) is to achieve the best compromise between two (often conflicting) goals: (i) allow the customer to find the desired products quickly and easily, and (ii) make the customer take a look also at other products while on his/her way to the desired ones. The second goal is essential for sellers to increase sales. It is indeed well-known that a substantial part of purchases are not planned in advance before entering a store, but occur as an impulsive response to seeing the product (impulse purchase). Moreover, sellers are also typically interested in increasing the likelihood that *specific* products are seen by the customer according to their merchandising strategies (e.g., Christmas' gifts in December, products being heavily advertised in the media, special offers,...).

In [4], we proposed a navigation aid for e-commerce that takes into account the above mentioned merchandising considerations. The aid is based on 3D animated representations of products (called *Walking Products*, *WPs* for short) that move through the store and go to the place where the corresponding type of products is. A customer in a VR store sees a number of WPs wandering around (see Figures 1 and 2): if (s)he is looking for a specific type of products, (s)he has just to follow any WP of that type and will be quickly and easily lead to the desired destination. The specific path followed by the WP to accompany the customer to his/her destination takes also into account the merchandising strategy of the store. If the customer wants to stop along the way and take a look at other products, (s)he can count on the fact that WPs will be always available to lead him/her to the original destination.

WPs have several advantages over the navigation aids adopted in current VR stores, i.e., signs and maps. Signs do not give a detailed enough indication of product location, while maps impose on the customer a translation effort from their exocentric perspective to his/her egocentric one. On the contrary, WPs: (i) support product finding in a easy, natural way: one has just to follow the WP as (s)he would do with a friend or a salesperson in a real store; (ii) increase the number of products seen by the customer, especially those which are relevant for current merchandising strategies, (iii) convey the feeling of a "living" place and contribute to satisfy the need for interactive experiences typical of emotional customers.

A more thorough presentation of the WP aid is provided in [4]. In one of the following subsections, we will instead extend the WP idea to the context of the adaptive VR store.

3   ADVIRT: The Adaptive VR Store

While increasing and guaranteeing usability is one of the current top priorities for VR e-commerce sites, one has to take into account that an increasing competitive factor among Internet sellers is the possibility of offering personalized services to each customer (1-to-1 E-commerce). Some research effort is being devoted to this need, but is limited to traditional 2D sites. In this Section, we first briefly survey related work on building customer profiles for adaptive e-commerce, then we present in detail our ADVIRT (Adaptive VIrtual Reality sTore) prototype, which is able to personalize a VR store using the profile of the customer who is visiting it. The type of stores we focus on are department stores, selling many different product categories.

3.1   Related Work on Adaptive E-Commerce

Techniques to build customer profiles in e-commerce have been recently proposed in the user modeling literature. In particular, the approach by [1] combines *form filling* with *stereotyping*: it asks the customer to fill a form about herself, and then assigns him/her a stereotyped profile by matching the form data with a database containing an hierarchical taxonomy of stereotypes clustering the properties of homogeneous customer groups. A different approach is adopted in [7,8]: the system tries to tailor future presentations of products by *monitoring past customer choices* in terms of kind of medium presentation chosen (e.g., text, graphics, video,…), downloading time (e.g., does the customer interrupt downloading of pictures?), and content (e.g., time spent by the customer on specific presentation elements).

As we will show in the following, we build customer profiles by using a combination of the three above mentioned techniques. No research instead exists on exploiting customer profiles for adapting a VR store, so the approach we discuss represents a first attempt at tackling the problem.

3.2   Acquisition of Customer Profiles in ADVIRT

Our approach to building the customer profile mixes three different techniques:
-   Have the buyer fill an initial form that asks for typical information (such as buyer's gender and year of birth), and some specific information (such as product categories of interest among the list of categories available in the store). Since only a limited amount of information can be acquired in this way (customers might not be able or might not like neither to fill large forms, nor to provide some personal details and preferences), the approach we follow is to present the customer with a limited number of fields to fill and to let him/her decide which fields (s)he is willing to fill (if the customer does not provide information about his/her interests, it can be derived by using the other two techniques).
-   Exploit demographic profiles (available on the market) that give detailed and readily available information on the different categories of buyers, and can be used to make predictions about consumer interests (e.g., a customer in the 16-24 age range is very likely to be interested in the latest models of cellular phones), preferences (e.g., if the above mentioned customer is female, she is very likely to prefer cellular phones with a stylish and colorful design), and behavior (e.g., a customer who is more than 65 years old is very unlikely to change often his/her cellular phone because new models have appeared).
-   Dynamically update the model by considering data (e.g., purchases made, number of visits,…) recorded on past visits to the VR store.

These three techniques complement each other, allowing one to obtain a more complete customer model. In the following, we present the detailed information we acquire, specifying which techniques are employed for each type of data.

3.3   Contents of Customer Profiles in ADVIRT

The information contained in the customer models of our prototype is organized in three parts: (i) biosketch, (ii) consumer aspects, (iii) interaction aspects.

Biosketch

The information contained in the biosketch part of the customer profile concerns typical information about the customer (i.e., *gender*, *year of birth*, *occupation*, and *level of education*). The primary way to get the information for the biosketch is by having the customer fill the corresponding fields in the above mentioned initial form.

Consumer Aspects

The information contained in the consumer aspects part aims at characterizing the customer with attributes directly related to purchases and shopping behavior.

During each visit to the VR store, the following four kinds of time-stamped data are recorded by monitoring customer actions:

- *Seen Products*. While the customer wanders around the store, (s)he voluntarily or involuntarily looks at the products which fall in her field of view. We keep a record of which products have been seen by the customer. Unlike 2D e-commerce sites, where it is often assumed that every product in a downloaded page has been seen, a 3D environment allows one to track better what products the customer is seeing, by verifying that two conditions hold: (i) the customer has to be near enough to the product in the 3D space, and (ii) the virtual head of the customer must be oriented towards the product.
- *Clicked Products*. When the customer wants to know more about a product, (s)he clicks on it to get the product description. We keep a record of which products have been clicked by the customer.
- *Cart Products*. The product description allows the customer to put the product in the shopping cart for a possible later purchase. We keep a record of which products have been put in the shopping cart.
- *Purchased Products*. If a product in the cart is later purchased, we record the event, and keep track of which products have been purchased.

In particular, the above described data allow one to obtain a precise quantitative measurement of which brands, product categories, specific products, price categories, and special offers have been respectively seen, clicked, put in the shopping cart or purchased by the customer.

Another information contained in this part of the model is the *product interest ranking*, which tries to list product categories in the order that is more relevant to the customer. An initial ranking is determined in two different ways: (i) the initial form allows the customer to fill fields about his/her products of interests: if (s)he chooses to do it, the information is used to initialize the ranking, (ii) if the customer does not provide product interests in the form, the system tries to predict them by using a demographic profile. Regardless of the quality of the initialization, product interests will be continuously updated by exploiting some of the data described above, i.e. each purchase, cart insertion, and click at a product increases (with different weights) the level of interest in the product category.

Finally, this part contains preferences on *preferred music genres*, if the customer has agreed to enter them in the initial form.

Interaction Aspects

The information contained in the interaction aspects part aims at characterizing the customer with attributes directly related to his/her preferences and behavior in using the interface to the e-commerce site. It contains information about the preferred *type of interface* (2D or 3D), the preferred store organization features (*size, style, assistance*), *number of visits* (i.e., the number of times the customer has used the interface), and if (s)he likes *background music* (if she likes music, the music played is possibly chosen according to the *preferred music genres* in the consumer aspects part). At present, the *number of times* information is automatically recorded, while the other data are acquired by graphically showing different possibilities to the user in the initial session (e.g., to determine the preferences about *size* and *style* of the store, the user can click on thumbnails representing different kinds of stores).

More advanced possibilities are at study (e.g., to switch the state of *background music*, and to determine *music genres* preferences, an interactive 3D jukebox can be included in the store). We are also considering recording the average speed at which the customer is able to move in the virtual world to get an estimate of his/her 3D navigation ability and tailor the animation of navigation aids to it.

3.4   Creating a Personalized VR Store in ADVIRT

The adaptation of the appearance and content of the VR store depends on three sources of information: (i) the customer profile, (ii) current merchandising strategies (e.g., promoting special offers) of the seller, and (iii) current products in the seller's catalog. The adaptation is performed by *personalization rules* which influence the parameters describing the state of the VR store. A simple example is the direct association between the user preferences about *size* and *style* of the store and specific 3D models for the virtual building.

We now discuss in detail the personalization rules mechanism using a more complex example concerning the exploitation of the customer profile to change product exposure in the VR store. The level of exposure of each product can vary the product visibility and attractiveness, e.g. by increasing its space in the store or adding banners advertising it. We call ExposureLevel(X) the parameter which represents the level of exposure for product X. The value of ExposureLevel(X) is determined by four more specific parameters:

- ShelfSpace(X) indicates the space assigned to product X on the shelf. It can take four different values: higher values make X more visible to the customer, increasing ExposureLevel(X). The products in the Figures 1 and 2 show different possible allocations of shelf space.
- DisplaySpot(X) is false if product X is displayed only on its shelf (together with other products of its category), while it is true if product X is displayed also in a separate display spot in a prominent place.
- Banner(X) is true if there is a banner advertising product X in the store.

- `AudioMessage(X)` is true if audio advertisements for the product are played.
- `WP(X)` is true if there is a WP representing product `x` in the store.

Fig. 1. A first adaptation of ADVIRT.

Fig. 2. A second adaptation of ADVIRT.

A true value for any of the last four boolean parameters increases `ExposureLevel(X)`. Personalization rules first suggest changes to exposure level by asserting increase or decrease goals for specific products. Then, they focus on achieving those goals, by changing one or more of the above described parameters, according to the availability of store resources (e.g., if a shelf is full, shelf space for products in it cannot be increased).

We now examine some examples of personalization rules, and how they relate to the information recorded in the customer model. Suppose that a product x has never been seen by the customer, or that changes in the *product interest ranking* show an increasing attention towards the product. In both cases, a seller would like to increase the exposure of the product (in the first case, to give the customer the opportunity of seeing the product; in the second case, to better match customer interests). The rules that implement the two cases can be expressed as follows (seen(X) is the recorded number of times a product has been seen, ProductInterest(X) is the rank in the *product interest ranking*, NumberOfVisits is the number of times the user has visited the store):

```
IF seen(X)=0 AND NumberOfVisits>3 THEN goal(IncreaseExposureLevel(X))
IF increasing(ProductInterest(X)) THEN goal(IncreaseExposureLevel(X))
```

The following rule considers the case when the purchase of a specific product x is an indicator of a likely future interest for related products, e.g., if a customer buys a computer and has never purchased a printer, s(he) could be soon interested in a printer. In this case, the rule dynamically updates the user model (purchased(X) is the recorded number of times a product has been purchased, lastVisit extracts the value of data considering only the last visit to the store, and RelatedProduct(X,Y) relates products exploiting associations provided by the seller):

```
IF lastVisit(purchased(X))>0 AND RelatedProduct(X,Y)
AND purchased(Y)=0 THEN increase(ProductInterest(X))
```

As an effect of the increasing product interest, the second rule examined above will then suggest an increase in the exposure level of related products which have not been purchased yet. Note that the RelatedProduct relation cannot be used transitively, because this could lead to uneffective merchandising strategies, e.g. an ink cartridge is obviously related to a printer, and a printer is obviously related to a computer, but it does not make sense to increase the exposure level of ink cartridges if a customer has purchased a computer but not a printer.

In general, to prevent an excessive number of changes to the store from one session to another (which would confuse the user), a limit is imposed on their number for any given session. In this way, the experience of returning to a virtual store is not too different from the familiar experience of returning to a known real-world store: (i) the store layout, organization, and style remain essentially the same (these parameters are indeed under user control, and are not changed autonomously by ADVIRT unless the user explicitly modifies its preferences about *dimensions* and *style*), and (ii) a limited number of changes concern what products are displayed, and how the attention of the customer towards those products is sought.

A limit is also imposed on the maximum value that ExposureLevel(X) can take for any given x, in order to avoid overexposure of products, which would have a negative effect on the customer.

In the following, we provide an overview of all the features which can be personalized in ADVIRT.

Type of Interface

While a VR interface can be appealing to customers who have an emotional style of buying, and useful for customers who are not expert in using search tools, it must also be clearly said that it is definitely not suited for some other categories of customers. For example, the customer could be very experienced in the use of computers and prefer to use an advanced search engine, or (s)he can be a rational customer who prefers to see plain text tables of product features, or (s)he can be using a very slow computer which does not support graphics at a reasonable speed. We thus believe that a VR store should be provided in addition to a more traditional interface to an e-commerce site. The preferred *type of interface* information in the customer profile is used to choose which interface (2D or 3D) is started[2]. The following personalization features we discuss refer to the 3D interface.

Store Layout, Organization, and Look

The preferred *dimensions* and *style* information provided by the customer are used to choose store layout and look of the 3D representation of the store. For example, the stores in Figures 1 and 2 show two different sizes and styles available. In this way, the customer can visit a VR store which is closer to the ones (s)he chooses in the real world (or safely experiment with stores she would like to try in the real world, but avoids, e.g. for emotional reasons such as fear of judgement).

As described in detail in a previous section, the organization of the store (product placement, product space, banners) is dynamically personalized.

Set of WPs

The navigation aid we have previously presented (WPs) is tailored to the customer profile. A first basic choice is about WPs presence or absence in the virtual store. This choice is left to the customer and stored in the *assistance* field of the customer profile (presence is the default, but can be changed at any moment by the customer). The specific WPs shown in the virtual store are chosen by personalization rules, to increase the exposure level of specific products. For example, the two stores in the Figures contain significantly different sets of WPs. Adding this adaptive dimension to the WP navigation aid allows it to gain the following benefits which were not available in its non adaptive version described in [4]:

Dynamical WP set. Since the choice of WPs is affected by the evolution of the customer profile, the members of the set of WPs change over time. This allows one to: (i) save store space and rendering resources which would be wasted by less interesting WPs, (ii) introduce in the set new WPs which can attract the customer

---

[2] An additional possibility would be to offer also a third (hybrid) solution, exploiting the 2D approach for product finding and the 3D approach for product display and examination.

towards potentially promising purchases, (iii) create a continuously evolving environment that keeps customers' attention alive (a static environment could easily become boring after some visits for customers with an emotional style of buying).

WPs as tailored hypermedia links. The customer has been given the possibility to automatically run to the proper shelf by clicking on the corresponding WP. In this case, since the products displayed by some WPs correspond to the products the customer purchases more frequently, WPs partially act also as a "favorites" list of products which can quickly lead to product purchase.

Features of WP animation could be also adapted to user profile. For example, it would be possible to vary WPs speed (e.g., slow for the first visits, then progressively faster; or, as we are planning, adapted to the measured movement ability of the customer in 3D space), and WPs paths (e.g., dynamically determining them according to the parts of the store that are more likely to interest the customer, and the locations of products which the seller wants to promote).

Audio

In the case of store background music, unlike real stores, we have the possibility to choose genres according to the customer's *preferred music genres* data.

Background music can be interrupted by voice messages as in real stores (e.g., advertising a special offer), if the AudioMessage(X) is set by personalization rules. Unlike real stores, the chosen voice messages can be targeted to the specific customer, both in the promoted product, in the type of voice, and in the choice of words (e.g., a teenager and a elder customer prefer very different kinds of message style, voice, and emphasis).

4   Implementing Adaptive VR Stores

A good discussion of the different modules needed by an architecture for traditional adaptive e-commerce sites is provided in [2]. In this section, we briefly add some considerations on the further technical needs imposed by the implementation of an adaptive VR store.

First, there is the need of a language for describing the 3D scenes that could be easily supported by the customer's browser. Although proprietary technologies are being proposed by some companies, VRML is the only language whose plug-in has already been distributed in tens of millions of free copies, and is regulated by an international ISO/IEC standard [6]. We thus considered the choice of VRML as mandatory for delivering 3D content on the Web.

Second, since VRML is mainly a 3D scene description language, it does not offer sufficient programming capabilities. When, as in our case, there is the need for controlling the virtual world with non trivial programs, the more natural choice is to integrate VRML with Java. For a brief and clear introduction on how the two languages can support each other to provide both interactive 3D graphics and complete programming capabilities, we refer the reader to [3].

Third, architectures like the one described in [2] need to be augmented with additional modules devoted to take personalization decisions about 3D content (as already seen in previous sections) and to implement them by properly assembling different 3D models into a single virtual store and tailoring their attributes. This second task is performed by a *VR Store Creator* module. At the beginning of each ADVIRT session, this module considers: (i) the preferences of the customer about store style, size, music, assistance, and (ii) the changes decided by personalization rules. Then, it implements them by assembling a proper VRML world. The VRML file does not change during the same session to avoid the need for multiple downloads (and resulting waiting times). Decisions for future adaptations will be taken off-line after the session has ended, and will affect the VRML world in the next session.

5   Conclusions and Future Work

This paper has examined the current features and mentioned the short term ones of our adaptive VR store. A more long term goal is to explore the possibility of significantly extending the abilities of WPs, enriching them with further user assistance functionalities besides that of leading customers to specific parts of the store. These extended animated characters would be closer to store assistants, capable for example of addressing simple customer questions, taking the customer to any product shelf, and then performing product presentations. Some issues in adding animated presentation characters to a Web interface are discussed in [9].

A recent trend in 3D e-commerce sites is to allow customers to meet and interact in VR stores to satisfy their social needs and build a sense of community. We intend to investigate the impact of this possibility on ADVIRT: it is indeed interesting to note that adding this social dimension can conflict with personalization aspects, limiting the possibilities of 1-to-1 e-commerce. For example, if multiple users have to walk together and interact in the same VR store, the customization of the several features mentioned in this paper cannot target anymore the specific profile of a single customer. Trying to find the best compromise which maximizes the match with the different user profiles can be a possible solution, but it would not be easy to implement, considering that the set of customers in the stores would continuously change.

References

1. Ardissono L., Goy A.: Tailoring the interaction with users in electronic shops. In: Proc. of UM99: 7th International Conference on User Modeling. Springer Verlag (1999) 35-44.
2. Ardissono L., Goy A., Meo R., Petrone G., Console L., Lesmo L., Simone C., Torasso P.: A configurable system for the construction of adaptive virtual stores. World Wide Web Journal **2** (1999) 143-159
3. Brutzman, D.: The Virtual Reality Modeling Language and Java. Communications of the ACM **41** 6 (1998) 57-64
4. Chittaro L., Coppola P.: Animated Products as a Navigation Aid for E-commerce. In: Proc. of the CHI2000 Conference on Human Factors in Computing Systems, Extended Abstracts Volume. ACM Press, New York (2000) 107-108

5. Chittaro L., Coppola P., Ranon R.: New Directions for the Design of Virtual Reality Stores on the Web, in preparation (2000)
6. International Standard ISO/IEC 14772-1:1997: The Virtual Reality Modeling Language. (1997) http://www.vrml.org/Specifications/VRML97/
7. Joerding T.: User Modeling for Electronic Catalogs and Shopping Malls in the World Wide Web. In: Proc. of the 1st Workshop on Adaptive Systems and User Modeling on the WWW (1997) http://fit.gmd.de/UM97/Joerdung.html
8. Joerding T.: A Temporary User Modeling Approach for Adaptive Shopping on the Web. In: Proc. of the 2nd Workshop on Adaptive Systems and User Modeling on the WWW (1999) http://wwwis.win.tue.nl/asum99/joerding/joerding.html
9. Rist T., André E., Muller J.: Adding Animated Presentation Agents to the Interface. In: Proc. of the IUI97 Conference on Intelligent User Interfaces, (1997) ACM Press 79-86
10. Serco Ltd.: How to Design a customer friendly on-line store. (1999) www.usability.serco.com/pdfs/guidelines.pdf
11. Tilson R., Dong J., Martin S., Kieke E.: Factors and Principles Affecting the Usability of Four E-commerce Sites. In: Proc. of the 4th Conference on Human Factors and the Web (1998) www.research.att.com/conf/hfweb/index.html

WAP*ing* the Web:
Content Personalisation for WAP-Enabled Devices

Paul Cotter and Barry Smyth

Smart Media Institute,
Department of Computer Science, University College Dublin,
Belfield, Dublin 4, Ireland
{Paul.Cotter, Barry.Smyth}@ucd.ie

Abstract. Content personalisation technologies may hold the key to solving the information overload problem associated with the Internet, by facilitating the development of information services that are customised for the needs of individual users. For example, PTV is an award-winning, Web-based personalised television listings service capable of learning about the viewing habits of individual users and of generating personalised TV guides for these users. This paper describes how PTV has been recently adapted for use on the new generation of WAP-enabled Internet devices such as mobile phones - the need for content personalisation is even more acute on WAP devices due to their restricted presentation capabilities.

1   Introduction

The information overload problem is almost synonymous with the Internet as it is increasingly difficult for users to locate the right information at the right time. If anything this problem is exacerbated by the new generation of WAP-enabled devices, such as mobile phones - if our desktop PCs have opened a doorway to the Internet, then the limitations of the current generation of WAP phones (reduced screen-size, memory, and bandwidth) can offer only keyhole access to Internet content.

Personalisation methods may hold the key to solving the information overload problem by customising the delivery and presentation of relevant information for individual users. In this paper we focus on the issues involved in developing personalised information systems for WAP-enabled devices. We present a case-study in the form of PTV (www.ptv.ie), a popular Web-based personalised television listings service with over 15,000 registered users, which has been recently adapted for use as a WAP service; we will refer to this new WAP system as PTV Mobile.

2   The WAP World

If we believe the 'hype' the new generation of WAP-enabled mobile phones will usher in a new era of the information age as they offer near-universal access

P. Brusilovsky, O. Stock, C. Strapparava (Eds.): AH 2000, LNCS 1892, pp. 98–108, 2000.
© Springer-Verlag Berlin Heidelberg 2000

to Internet content. To a large extent this is true, but at the same time we rarely hear about the significant problems associated with these new devices, problems such as screen size, memory capacity, and bandwidth. For example, the display size of a typical WAP phone is only 95x65 pixels (the popular Nokia 7110 handset), to provide an effective viewing area that is 1/80th that of our normal PC displays. Current WAP phones have about 1.4Kb of available RAM which greatly limits the amount of information that they can store, and increases the number of server requests needed in a typical session. Finally, the current bandwidth available for WAP devices is only 9.6Kbps compared to 33-56Kbps for normal modem connections.

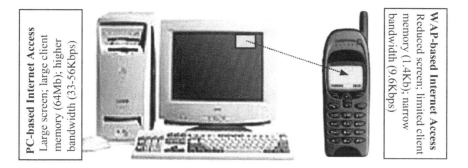

Fig. 1. Traditional PC *vs.* WAP Internet Access.

These limitations do not mean that WAP phones are useless as an Internet device, far from it, but it does mean that traditional information services, services that have been designed and influenced by the conventional modes of Internet access, may not translate effectively onto the WAP platform.

The information overload problem associated with conventional Internet access is exacerbated by the display and bandwidth restrictions of current WAP technology, and hence there is an even greater motivation to develop services that are personalised for the needs of individual users. In short, we argue that the marriage between WAP technology and content personalisation technology is a necessity rather than a luxury.

3   PTV - A Personalised TV Listings Service

With the arrival of new cable and satellite television services, and the next generation of digital TV systems, we will soon be faced with an unprecedented level of programme choice (upwards of 200 channels and 4000 programmes per day). Navigating through this space constitutes a new information overload problem, and it will become increasingly difficult to find out what relevant programmes are showing on a given day. The digital TV vendors are aware of these issues, and their current solution is the Electronic Programme Guide (EPG), providing users with on-screen access to online TV listings. However, simply providing an electronic equivalent of the paper-based TV guide is not a scalable solution to the problem. For example, a typical EPG can cover a 90-minute timeslot for 5 to 10 channels in a single screen. This means that even a relatively modest line-up of 70 channels will occupy 10 screens of information for each 90-minute slot, or 160 screens for each viewing day.

The PTV project is motivated by the belief that a genuine solution to this information overload problem requires an understanding of the viewing preferences of users to enable EPG's to adapt information for individuals, filtering out irrelevant programme content, and transforming the space of viewing options from an intractable cast of thousands to a manageable few. In this section we describe PTV and explain how it combines user profiling and content recommendation techniques to generate personalised TV guides for individual users.

3.1 The PTV System Architecture

PTV is designed as a client-server system with the heart of the system residing with its server-side components, which handle all the main information processing functions such as user registration and authentication, user profiling, guide compilation, and the all-important programme recommendation and grading (see Fig. 2). The system consists of three main sources of domain knowledge.

The **schedule database** contains TV listings for all supported channels. Each listing entry includes details such as the programme name, the viewing channel, the start and end time, and typically some text describing the programme in question. The schedule database is constructed automatically from electronic schedule resources.

The **profile database** contains a profile for each registered user. Each profile encodes the TV preferences of a given user, listing channel information, preferred viewing times, programme and subject preferences, etc.

The **programme case-base** contains the programme content descriptions (programme cases). Each entry describes a particular programme using features such as the programme title, genre information, the creator and director, cast or presenters, the country of origin, and the language; an example programme case for the comedy 'Friends' is shown in Fig. 2.

The **recommender component** (see Fig. 2) is the intelligent core of PTV. Its job is to use user profile information to select new programmes for recommendation to a user as part of their personalised TV guide. In Sections 3.3 we will explain in detail how PTV uses a hybrid recommendation approach that combines content-based and collaborative recommendation strategies. Once the recommender has selected programmes that are relevant to the target user, the guide compiler and guide translator components produce a personalised guide according to a given day's viewing schedules and for the required client platform (HTML for the Web or WML for WAP devices).

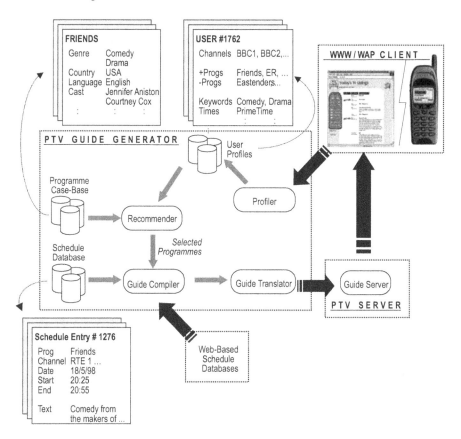

Fig. 2. The PTV Architecture.

3.2   User Profiling

The success of PTV depends ultimately on the quality of its personalised guides, and this depends largely on the quality of the user profiles and their ability to represent the viewing preferences of users [5, 6, 9]. In PTV each user profile contains two types of information: domain preferences and programme preferences (see Fig. 2). The former describe general user preferences such as a list of available TV channels, preferred viewing times, subject keywords and genre preferences, and guide format preferences. Programme preferences are represented as two lists of programme titles, a positive list containing programmes that the user has liked in the past, and a negative list containing programmes that the user has disliked.

Profiles are constructed in two ways. Users can manually update their profiles by specifying viewing preferences directly. However, while manual profile editing has its advantages (usually in terms of profile accuracy) it is a burden for the users. In particular, we have found that users are happy to provide fairly complete domain preferences but tend to provide only limited programme preferences. For this reason, PTV includes a profile update facility that is driven by direct user feedback by rating programme recommendations as they use the system (see Section 4.2). PTV's profiler uses this information to automatically alter a user's profile to reflect new programme preferences as well as channel and viewing time preferences (see also 11]).

3.3   Collaborative, Content-Based Programme Recommendation

Ultimately in PTV, personalising a given user's TV guide boils down to recommending the right programmes for that user given their various viewing preferences. PTV harnesses two complementary recommendation strategies, content-based recommendation and collaborative recommendation.

Content-based recommendation has its roots in information retrieval. The basic philosophy is to recommend items that are similar to those items that the user has liked in the past; see also [1, 4, 11]. For PTV, this means recommending programmes that are similar to the programmes in a user's positive programme list and dissimilar to those in the negative programme list. PTV's programme case-base has already been outlined (Section 3.1) and an example case is shown in Fig. 2. Each case is described as a set of features and the similarity between two cases can be defined as the weighted-sum of the similarity between corresponding case features. However, there is no direct means of computing the similarity between a case and a user profile, as user profiles are not described as a set of case features. Instead each raw user profile is converted into a feature-based representation called a profile schema. Basically, the profile schema corresponds to a content summary of the programme preferences contained in a user profile, encoded in the same features as the programme cases. The similarity between a profile and a given programme case can then be computed using the standard weighted-sum similarity metric as shown in Equation 1; where $f_i^{Schema(u)}$ and f_i^p are the ith features of the schema and the programme case respectively.

This technique produces a ranked list of programme recommendations, where the similarity between a given programme and the target profile scheme corresponds to the estimated quality of the recommendation; programmes that are very similar to the target profile are judged to be good recommendations. The best r content-based recommendations are selected as candidates for the user's personalised guide.

$$PrgSim(Schema(u), c) = \sum_i w_i \bullet sim(f_i^{Schema(u)}, f_i^c) \tag{1}$$

An important problem with content-based methods is the knowledge engineering effort required to develop case representations and similarity models. Moreover, because content-based methods make recommendations based on item similarity, the newly recommended items tend to be similar to the past items leading to reduced diversity. In the TV domain this can result in recommendation lists that are narrow in scope; for example, if a user's positive programme list contains mostly comedies then the content-based recommendation strategy will tend to recommend more comedies.

Collaborative recommendation methods, such as automated collaborated filtering, are a recent alternative to pure content-based techniques. Instead of recommending programmes that are similar to the ones that the user has liked in the past, they recommend programmes that other similar users have liked [1, 2, 3, 7, 8, 10]. In PTV user similarity is computed by using the graded difference metric shown in Equation 2; where $p(u)$ and $p(u')$ are the rated programmes in each user's profile, and $r(p_i^u)$ is the rating assigned of programme p_i in profile u. The possible grades range from -2 to +2 and missing programmes are given a default grade of 0. Of course this is just one possible similarity technique that has proved useful in PTV, and any number of techniques could have been used, for example statistical correlation techniques such as Pearson's correlation coefficient (see eg., [2, 10]).

Once PTV has selected k similar profiles for a given target user, a recommendation list is formed from the programmes in these similar profiles that are absent from the target profile. This list is then ranked and the top r programmes are selected for recommendation. The ranking metric is shown in Equation 3; U is the subset of k nearest profiles to the target that contain a programme p. This metric biases programmes according to their frequency in the similar profiles and the similarity of their recommending user. In this way popular programmes that are suggested by very similar users tend to be recommended.

$$PrfSim(u, u') = \frac{\sum_{p(u) \cup p(u')} |r(p_i^u) - r(p_i^{u'})|}{4 \bullet |p(u) \cup p(u')|}$$
(2)

$$PrgRank(p, u) = \sum_{u' \in U} Prf Sim(u, u')$$
(3)

Collaborative recommendation is a powerful technique that solves many of the problems associated with content-based methods. For example, there is no need for content descriptions or sophisticated case similarity metrics. In fact, high quality recommendations, that would ordinarily demand a rich content representation, are possible. Moreover, recommendation diversity is maintained as relevant items that are dissimilar to the items in a user profile can be suggested. However, collaborative recommendation does suffer from some important shortcomings. First, there is a startup cost associated with gathering enough profile information to make accurate user similarity measurements. There is also a latency problem in that new items will not be recommended until these items have found their way into sufficiently many user profiles. This is particularly problematic in the TV domain because new and one-off programmes occur regularly and do need to be considered for recommendation even though these programmes will not have made it into any user profiles.

PTV benefits from a combined recommendation technique using both content-based and collaborative recommendation. For a given user, a selection of programmes is suggested, which includes some that are produced through content-based recommendation (including new or one-off programmes) while others are produced by collaborative recommendation. Guide diversity is improved through the use of collaborative recommendation and the latency problem can be solved by using content-based methods to recommend relevant new or one-off programmes

4   PTV Mobile

In the previous section we described the form and function of PTV, focusing on the underlying personalisation technology, which can be used to compile personalised TV guides that will ultimately be delivered to a range of target clients including, traditional desktop PC browsers, WAP phones, or WebTV clients. Once a personalised guide has been compiled by the personalisation engine the guide translator converts it into a suitable target format such as HTML or WML. This section will outline the modifications necessary to customise PTV to generate WML content for WAP devices. A short PTV Mobile demonstration will also be described.

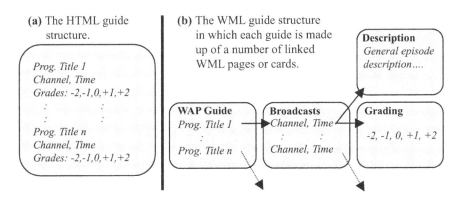

Fig. 3. The PTV guide structure for Web and WAP clients.

4.1   From Web to WAP

In the Web-based version of PTV each user request results in the retrieval of a single HTML page, for example, the user preferences page or a personalised guide page. In contrast, because of the screen and memory limitations associated with

WAP devices, each PTV Mobile request can result in the retrieval of multiple WML pages (actually multiple WML cards as part of a single deck). Thus, the majority of the effort required in converting PTV from the Web to WAP is concerned with defining a suitable WML format for the PTV guides, and we have found that the same core personalisation technology can be used to drive the new WAP system. For example, the Web-based PTV guide page is formatted to contain programme title, description, channel, time, and grading information as part of a single HTML page. This is not feasible with WAP phones because of the limited screen space available. Instead, a WAP guide is made up of the following individual page units (cards): a guide page listing relevant programme titles; a programme page for each relevant programme that lists the channel and viewing time information for each broadcast of that programme; a description page for each programme broadcast; and a grading page to allow the user to grade a particular broadcast (see Fig. 3).

4.2   System Demonstration

Once a user has logged on to PTV Mobile they are presented with the main menu screen (Fig. 4(a)), which provides option links to their personalised guides, their preferences, as well as a whole range of TV information such as the top ten programmes, what's on now and next, etc. At any stage a user may view or edit their preferences including channels preferences, viewing times, preferred programmes, and keyword preferences, as shown in Fig. 4(b).

A subset of the screens making up a single personalised WAP guide is shown in Fig. 4(c). Unlike the Web-based version of PTV, where each guide is viewed as a single HTML page, the WAP version presents each guide as a collection of WML pages (cards) as discussed above. The main guide page lists programmes by title only, and by selecting a title the user can receive information about the various channel and viewing times for a given programme. In addition, each programme can be graded by the user as shown in Fig. 4(c).

5   Evaluation

Ultimately the success of the PTV Mobile system will depend on the quality of its programme recommendations, and as such on the appropriateness or relevance of its personalised TV guides. PTV Mobile is powered by the PTV personalisation engine and this technology has been extensively evaluated in the past as part of a series of comprehensive live user trials - although these results are taken from the Web-based PTV we believe that they are equally valid in the context of the new WAP-based version, since the same personalisation technology is driving both systems.

5.1   Overall Precision

To measure the precision of the personalised guides produced by the PTV per-sonalisation engine we carried out a comprehensive user study in the first half of

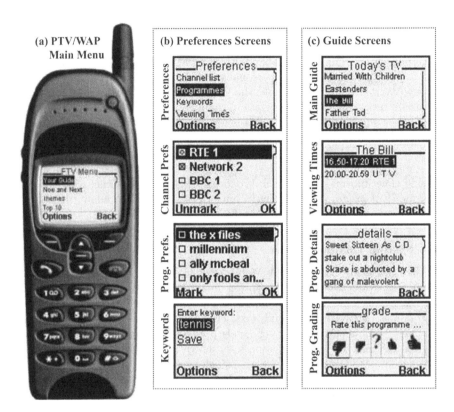

Fig. 4. (a) The PTV Mobile main menu; (b) the preferences screens; (c) a part of a personalised guide including viewing times, programme description, and grading screens.

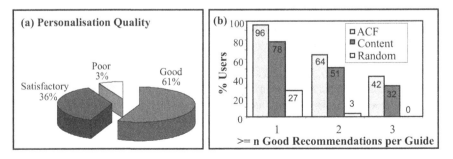

Fig. 5. (a) Overall guide precision / personalisation quality. (b) Relative guide precision.

1999, where regular and new users of the Web-based PTV system were asked to evaluate the system in terms of guide precision, ease of use, and speed of service. The guide precision results are of interest here. In total 310 PTV users were included in the evaluation, and in terms of guide quality (precision) they were asked to rate the appropriateness of their personalised guides. The results are presented in Fig. 5, and are clearly extremely positive. The average personalised guide contained between 10 and 15 programmes and critically, 97

5.2 Relative Precision

This experiment was carried out to evaluate the relative precision of the collaborative and content-based recommendation strategies used in PTV. The PTV grading logs for a one month period were analysed to examine the user gradings associated with programmes that were recommended by each recommendation technique. Specifically, we measured how often a given recommendation methods produced at least 1, 2, and 3 good recommendations (that is, recommendations that were subsequently graded as positive by users) in a single guide. We also included the results for a naive random recommendation strategy to serve as a benchmark.

The results in Fig. 5(b) show that collaborative recommendation consistently out-performs the content-based strategy. For example, the collaborative strategy produces at least one good recommendation per guide in 98% of the guides produced, compared to 77% for the content-based recommendation strategy. Both of these techniques are significantly better than the random benchmark.

6 Conclusions

Adaptive hypermedia technologies may provide a solution to the information overload problem by automatically learning about the information needs of individual users, in order to customise the delivery of the right content to the right user at the right time. PTV is one example of a successful personalised information service, operating in the domain of TV listings. As a Web service PTV has attracted over 15,000 users(nearly 5% of the Irish Internet users population) and in this paper we have focused on how PTV has been recently adapted for use on WAP-enabled devices such as mobile phones, devices where, we argue, the information overload problem becomes more acute and thus, where content personalisation information services such as PTV become even more necessary. We have described the form and function of PTV/WAP and evaluated its core personalisation engine. These results indicate that high quality personalised guides are being produced and we have every confidence that PTV/WAP will prove as successful and popular on WAP as PTV has on the Web.

References

[1] Balabanovic, M. and Shoham,Y.: *Fab: Content-based collaborative recommender.*, Communications of the ACM **40** (1997), no. 3, 66–72.

[2] Billsus, D. and Pazzani, M.J.: *Learning collaborative Information Filters*, Proceedings of the International Conference on Machine Learning, 1998.

[3] Goldberg, D. Nichols, D. Oki, B.M. and Terry, D.: *Using collaborative filtering to weave an information tapestry*, Communications of the ACM **35** (1992), no. 12, 61–70.

[4] Hammond, K.J., Burke, K.J. and Schmitt, K.: *A case-based approach to knowledge navigation*, ch. A Case-Based Approach to Knowledge Navigation, pp. 125–136, MIT Press, 1996.

[5] Jennings, A. and Higuchi, H.: *A user model neural network for a personal news service*, User Modeling and User-Adapted Information **3** (1993), no. 1, 1–25.

[6] Kay, J.: *Vive la Difference! Individualised Interaction with Users*, Proceedings of the 14th International Joint Conference on Artificial Intelligence (Chris Mellish, ed.), Morgan Kaufmann, 1995, pp. 978–984.

[7] Konstan, J.A., Miller, B.N., Maltz, D., Herlocker, J.L., Gordan, L.R. and Riedl, J.: *Grouplens: Applying collaborative filtering to usenet news*, Communications of the ACM **40** (1997), no. 3, 77–87.

[8] Maltz, D. and Ehrlich, K.: *Pointing the Way: Active Collaborative Filtering*, Proceedings of the ACM Conference on Human Factors in Computing Systems , ACM Press, 1995, pp. 202–209.

[9] Perkowitz, M. and Etzioni, O.: *Adaptive Web Sites: An AI Challenge.* , Proceedings of the 15th International Joint Conference on Artificial Intelligence, 1997.

[10] Shardanand, U. and Maes, P.: *Social Information Filtering:Algorithms for Automating 'Word of Mouth'*, Proceedings of the ACM Conference on Human Factors in Computing Systems , ACM Press, 1995, pp. 210–217.

[11] Smyth, B. and Cotter, P.: *Surfing the Digital Wave: Generating Personalised TV Listings using Collaborative, Case-Based Recommendation*, Case-Based Reasoning Research and Development. Lecture Notes in Artificial Intelligence (Klaus Dieter Althoff, Ralph Bergmann, and L.Karl Branting, eds.), Springer Verlag, 1999, pp. 561–571.

Extendible Adaptive Hypermedia Courseware: Integrating Different Courses and Web Material

Nicola Henze and Wolfgang Nejdl

Institut für Technische Informatik
Rechnergestützte Wissensverarbeitung
University of Hannover
Appelstraße 4, D-30167, Germany
{henze, nejdl}@kbs.uni-hannover.de
http://www.kbs.uni-hannover.de

Abstract. Adaptive hypermedia courseware benefits from being distributed over the Web: content can always be kept up-to-date, discussions and interactions between instructors and learners can be supported, new courses can easily be distributed to the students. Nevertheless, adaptive hypermedia systems are - even in the web content - still stand-alone systems as long as they lack the ability to integrate and adapt information from arbitrary places in the web.

In this paper, we discuss the integration of hypermedia courses and web material into existing, adaptive hypermedia courses. We show a possible solution which we have used for an undergraduate course about Java programming. We then discuss this solution as well as advantages and problems, and identify several research issues which have still to be solved for adapting distributed course materials.

Keywords: Open adaptive hypermedia systems, educational hypermedia systems

1   Introduction

While the delivery of instruction, courses and tutorial help is often managed over the web, existing adaptive hypermedia systems have so far neglected the issue of integrating Web material directly into their courses, though most courses can strongly benefit from integrating additional materials into the curriculum. Additional material can provide alternative views or explanations of a topic, it can relate to background information, or it can show further developments.

Within our KBS Hyperbook project [12], we are working on concepts and techniques for building adaptive hypermedia systems which are *open*, e.g which are able to integrate distributed information resources. In this paper, we will discuss advantages and problems of creating such an open, adaptive hypermedia system. We discuss our approach for building an open courseware system and show how we used it to implement an undergraduate course about Java programming. We then discuss advantages and problems of our current system and

P. Brusilovsky, O. Stock, C. Strapparava (Eds.): AH 2000, LNCS 1892, pp. 109–120, 2000.

identify several research issues which have still to be solved for adapting such distributed course materials.

2   Modeling a Course by Using a Hyperbook

In our KBS Hyperbook project [12] we are working on a tool for modeling, organizing and maintaining adaptive, open hypermedia systems on the WWW. The adaptive component of the hyperbook personalizes information according to the user's needs, goals and knowledge [8, 9]. For a comparison of the KBS Hyperbook system in the context of adaptive hypermedia systems, we refer to the more thorough discussions in [1, 7]. In this paper we concentrate on the aspect of extendibility of such a system, and how different course material can be included and adapted in one integrated system, an aspect not explicitly present in existing systems.

Explicit modeling of structure and contents is important for building reusable, extendible hypermedia applications. The KBS Hyperbook system structures and displays hypertext materials based on a conceptual model. This conceptual model describes courses, different kinds of materials (such as projects, examples, portfolios, HTML pages) and the integration of other information from the World Wide Web. In this section, we first describe the basic structure of our current conceptual model, consisting of different courses and lectures (section 2.1) and then describe the basic *content map* which we use for indexing course material material (section 2.2).

2.1   Modeling the Basic Structure

The conceptual model depicted in Figure 1 contains an entity *course* which represents a real course given at some university or at other institutions, and is related to various other entities structuring the course. The concepts belonging to this basic structure are highlighted in figure 1 with light grey.

Each course consists of several *lectures*, which themselves consist of some sequence of *text units*. Several courses can belong to one *course group* (figure 1), this course group integrates different courses on the same topic. Currently, our hyperbook system contains one course group, a CS1 course (Computer Science 1, an introductory course to Java programming). In the last semester (1999 / 2000), we held this course in Hannover for undergraduate students of electrical and computer engineering. A second course, using much of the same material, was given at the University of Bozen, Italy, with our participation. Both CS1 courses are modeled as courses, and belong to the course group "CS1".

Each course has its *glossary* and a number of *areas* which structure the application domain. Embedding projects and project portfolios in our course materials is an important part of our teaching concept [10]. To model this integration, each course is related to *projects* (figure 1). These projects can be the *actual projects* of the current course, or they can be *former projects*, which give examples of projects performed by students of previous courses and contain

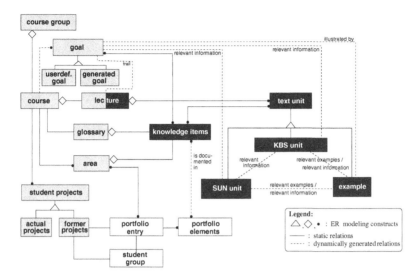

Fig. 1. Conceptual model of the Java hyperbook, course related modeling is highlighted in light grey, modeling of different information resources is highlighted in dark grey

the corresponding project portfolios (see section 3.2). To support goal-oriented learning, students can define their own learning goals (*user defined goals*) or can request new reasonable goals from the hyperbook (*generated goals*). For the selection and the support of goals in KBS Hyperbooks, see [9, 7].

Figure 2 gives an example of the CS1 course given in winter semester 1999 / 2000. The relations mentioned above from a course to other concepts are displayed as links in the left frame. The picture shows specific lectures of this course, current student projects, the different areas of this course, examples of former projects, reference to the next reasonable learning goal, and the reference to the lecture group.

The so far described conceptual model is a proposal for modeling courses, lectures, and for the integration of different course materials into a group of hyperbooks on the same topic. Authors of hyperbooks can of course define their own conceptual model for presentation of their courses. The KBS hyperbook system generates on base of some conceptual model the particular hyperbooks.

2.2   Enabling Adaptation: Indexing Material

To relate the different types of text units, to support student's goals, or to provide guidance (i.e. to enable the different adaptation features of the KBS Hyperbook system), we index the course materials which is contained in or should be integrated into the hyperbook. In our conceptual model, we can see the index concepts (called *knowledge items*), and their relations to the glossary,

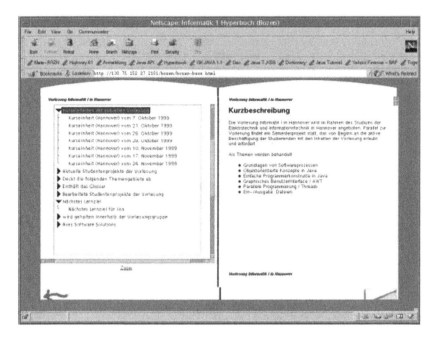

Fig. 2. Example for a course modeled in the KBS Hyperbook system

areas, portfolios, goals, and text units (see the relations between the concept *knowledge item* and other concepts in figure 1). Each of these concepts is indexed with a set of such knowledge items. The origin of an information resource is not relevant for indexing, only the content defines the index. We assume that any information resource which should be displayed in our hyperbook is contained on some HTML page. We can therefore define a *content map* which represents the index for an information resource:

Definition 1 (Content Map). *Let* $\mathcal{S} \neq \emptyset$ *be the set of all knowledge items, and let* $\mathcal{H}$ *be a set of HTML pages. Then*

$$I : \mathcal{H} \to \mathcal{P}(\mathcal{S}) \backslash \{\emptyset\} \qquad (1)$$

is the content map, which gives for each information resource in $\mathcal{H}$ *the index of this HTML page, e.g. the set of knowledge items describing its content.*

Currently, our content map is built manually by the author of that information resource. We use knowledge items for indexing each kind of information material, which, as we will see in the next section, can originate from our local file-system or can be located anywhere in the WWW. This kind of indexing is different to other indexing concepts in student and user modeling. In many other adaptive hypermedia systems, dependencies like prerequisites or outcomes are directly modeled within the information resources themselves (see for example

[3, 13, 4, 11]). For a review on indexing strategies in adaptive web-based systems see [2]. In our system we separate knowledge and knowledge dependencies from the actual information, as we model learning dependencies solely on the set of knowledge items of a hyperbook. The connection between the student modeling component and the hyperbook system is provided by the content map (see definition 1), which maps each information resource to a set of knowledge items. This separation allows easier integration of additional resources on the same topic than an integrated approach which directly models outcome and income with the information resource.

3   Integrating Additional Information Resources

Calling the KBS Hyperbook system an open hypermedia system means, that is able to integrate different sources of materials. On the one hand, it is easily able to refer to and integrate single information resources located anywhere in the web. This will be discussed in section 3.1, where we also show, how we integrated different material in our hyperbook for the Hannover and Bozen courses. In section 3.2 we show how we enlarge the conceptual model to integrate the results of student work, especially the results of the projects they have worked on while learning with the hyperbook.

If the material to be integrated is structured already, integration is still possible but with more difficulties as we discuss in the last part of this paper.

3.1   Integrating *Text Units*

Each lecture consists of a sequence of *text units* which are used by the teacher during the lecture (see dark grey-colored concepts in figure 1). A text unit can be a *KBS Unit*, which is an information page on our local file-system. It can be an *example*, which illustrates the use of some concept. As the KBS Hyperbook system allows to integrate arbitrary WWW pages, text units can also be information pages located elsewhere, in our case in the online SUN Tutorial, the pages of which are modelled by the concept *Sun Unit*. If we want to integrate additional information resources, we model them as additional subclasses of *text unit* in our conceptual model.

In our current Java programming hyperbook system we integrate pages from the Sun Java Tutorial [5] into the hyperbook. The Sun Java Tutorial is freely available on the internet and thus very suited for being integrated into the learning material of the Java hyperbook.

For each type of text units, links to related information are computed by the hyperbook system. For example, from a KBS Unit, links to relevant examples are computed, as well as links to relevant Sun Units, which give alternative descriptions of these concepts. The computation of relevant information is done by selecting those information pages whose index (by means of the content map) is not disjunct to the index of the current page. Thus in the current state of our development we select an information page P_2 as relevant for page P_1 whenever at least one concept of $I(P_1)$ is also contained in $I(P_2)$. This criterion can be refined for calculating graduation of relevance: Two pages P_1, P_2 with $I(P_1) = I(P_2)$ contain information on the same topics and therefor fall into the category "alternative views" for each other. Whereas if $|I(P_1) \cap I(P_2)| < |I(P_1)|$, P_2 will explain only some aspects of the content of P_1. If in addition $|I(P_1) \cap I(P_2)| < |I(P_2)|$, P_2 contains further information which is not directly related to P_1, in case of $|I(P_1) \cap I(P_2)| = |I(P_2)|$, P_2 describes some aspects of P_1 without further references.

In figure 3, we see on the right hand side the (local KBS) page about methods from the hyperbook library. The use of methods can be studied in the example of the student group "BugFix" (uppermost link on the left hand side), and the Sun Java Tutorial contributes many links to relevant information pages. As the KBS Unit "Methoden" is contained in a specific lecture, we also display the link to this lecture.

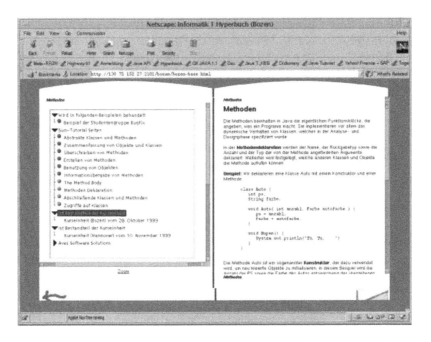

Fig. 3. KBS Unit "Methoden" with links to examples, Sun Units and to the two lectures where it occurs.

In figure 4, we see the integration of a Sun Unit into the hyperbook. The page itself is displayed in the same manner as the local pages. We stream such pages without any modifications into the hyperbook. That means that the hyperbook's functionality is then to display this integrated page as a normal web browser would display it. However, the hyperbook gives the frame for viewing the information and shows the user the actual context in the hyperbook and thus in his curriculum. Even links contained on these integrated information pages remain valid. If a user clicks on such a link, the corresponding page will be displayed in the same way while the left frame in the hyperbook itself will still show the actual context in the hyperbook from which this page was accessible for the particular user. For the Sun Unit seen in figure 4, a link to an example as well as to a KBS Unit is computed; these links remain unchanged in the left frame of the hyperbook when the user browses the Sun Unit itself.

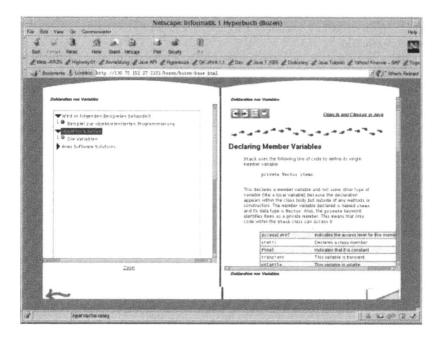

Fig. 4. Example of the integration of Sun Units in the KBS Hyperbook system

All information resources are equal in the sense that they only need to be indexed to be integrated in a particular hyperbook, as described in the previous section 2.2. This implies on the one hand that arbitrary information found in the internet can be integrated in a hyperbook. On the other hand all integrated pages can be fully adapted to the needs of an individual user: We can propose programming examples described on additional WWW pages, compute reading sequences which contain both local and Web material, calculate the educational state of WWW pages according to the student's actual knowledge state, etc. In the current paper, we will not further describe the functionality of the adaptation component and refer to [8, 12].

This makes clear, that the use of a separate knowledge model makes the hyperbook system robust against changes and extendible. If we add additional information pages or change contents, we only have to (re-)index these pages accordingly. No further work has to be spent on updating other material, as it would be necessary if knowledge, and thus reading or learning dependencies, would have been coded in the material itself.

3.2   Integrating Student Projects: *Portfolios*

In order to support project-based learning as described for example in [10], our conceptual model contains the concept *portfolio* (see figure 1). As discussed in [6], assessment based on portfolios realizes the idea that project results can be used to represent and to assess what topics / concepts a student has successfully applied or learned.

Thus, a portfolio can be modeled by relations between project results (portfolio elements) and those topics / knowledge items which have been used for these parts. In our conceptual model, this is expressed by a relationship between portfolio elements and knowledge items (see figure 1).

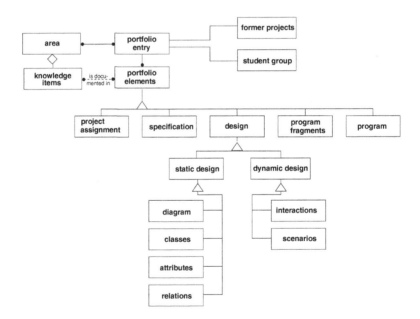

Fig. 5. Schematic view of the portfolio concepts

The portfolio elements represent the different different parts of a student project. In figure 5 we see the different kinds of portfolio elements for our CS1 course. This hierarchy mirrors the simplified software modeling process we use in our CS1 course. Important portfolio elements are the specification written by the students, an object oriented design proposal consisting of several subdocuments, documentation of the implementation, and the program code itself. The program code is broken down into different program fragments, each showing the use of some specific concept of the application domain.

To help the students define their own portfolios, we propose a list of knowledge items for the domain of Java as a programming language, plus some knowledge items related to software engineering. There are some KIs which are mandatory for our student portfolios (for example the scenarios and interactions from the dynamic design phase of a project), and a lot of other optional KIs. The students can use a subset of these optional KIs for representing their work in the portfolio individually.

A subset of KIs contained in the portfolio can be seen in the following list. KIs marked with an asterisk must be referenced in a student's portfolio, other KIs are optional. As an area consists of several KIs, we are able to easily integrate the portfolios and portfolio elements into the hyperbook. Thus, we define both the basic structure of student projects as well as their connection to the remainder of the course material.

```
object oriented design            user interface
 *specification                    event model
  static design                     *event source
    *classes                        *event listener
    *attributes                    adapter
    *relations                     *events
    ...                              action event
                                     text event
                                     ...
```

An important part of a portfolio is also the presentation of the students who have worked on the project. Therefore the student's homepages are also integrated in the hyperbook (see relation between the concepts *student group* and *portfolio* in figure 1).

4   Research Issues for Distributed Adaptive Systems

In the previous sections, we have discussed our current system, which is able to refer to external information resources and can adapt these additional information resources to the user's knowledge, goals and preferences. The system makes no difference between local and distributed materials, its adaptation functionality applies equally well to internal and external data.

The approach we have described is based on describing the content of data by relating it to index entries in a content map. Knowledge or learning dependencies are separated from content and are contained in an extra model. This approach allowed us to integrate the Sun Java Tutorial into our hyperbook about Java programming, and to integrate student projects into the learning materials. While investigating and implementing our approach, we have come up with some challenges for further research in this area which we discuss in the following sections.

Learning Dependencies - always the same? In the hyperbook system, we store learning dependencies in a separate model: the knowledge model. This model contains the prerequisite knowledge required to understand some concept, as well as the resulting knowledge. It does not refer to a certain teaching strategy. Nevertheless, assumptions about the sequencing of the learning material are encoded in this knowledge model. This can be made clear for our course on Java programming. While this area is well structured, the kind of learning an instructor has in mind while designing his material is implicitly given in the way he defines the knowledge model: If the focus is on object orientation, the author usually starts with explaining the ideas of object orientation without referring to any required (pre-) knowledge. However, if the instructor is coming from a structured programming background, he usually introduces object oriented language constructs after discussing structured programming constructs. In this case, information material describing object oriented programming concepts requires previous knowledge about structured programming.

Thus, even if we separate knowledge dependencies from content, we have to deal with the problem, that knowledge, or, in the educational area, learning dependencies are not the same for every instructor, but still depend on the content used in a specific course. Modeling these dependencies explicitly helps us in comparing and integrating these different teaching strategies. In subsequent work, we will probably switch to using several knowledge models in parallel, to allow the integration of course materials which use different assumptions about learning dependencies.

Generating Reading Sequences Curriculum sequencing is an important adaptational functionality in hypermedia systems. In case of our *open* hypermedia system, we have sometimes to deal with too much information: The same knowledge is made available by different resources, in our case on local Hannover KBS pages or on SUN Tutorial pages or on pages belonging to our Bozen course. Take, for example, that we have two HTML pages H_1 and H_2 with $I(H_1) = \{X_1, X_2, X_3\}$ and $I(H_2) = \{X_1, X_2, X_4\}$. (Recall that $I(H)$ denotes the index of resource H.) If the system infers that X_1 should be contained in the reading sequence, which of these HTML pages should be selected, which should be skipped? In such cases, the knowledge dependencies - maybe from different knowledge models - as well as the whole reading sequence has to be considered to make an appropriate choice. In the current state of the KBS Hyperbook system, we do not compute reading sequences with content from different origins. Instead, we are generating separate trails, through the local material itself (Hannover and Bozen pages are largely homogeneous) or through the Sun Tutorial.

Integration of Structured vs. Unstructured Materials Our open hypermedia system has to integrate both structured and unstructured materials. In this paper, we have proposed a solution for integrating material by taking it as "stand alone information". We have not used the context and structure, in which these pages are embedded (e.g. that the SUN Java Tutorial uses trails with a hierarchic structure of information elements). In cases where the information in the SUN

Java Tutorial is more detailed than our own local KBS pages, these leads to references to a whole lot of SUN Tutorial pages, without making the hierarchic structure of this additional information apparent.

A possible solution for the integration of such structured material can be preselection. In this way, we can for example filter according to depth of information and reference only pages, which are on the same level. Thus, more detailed pages from the SUN Java Tutorial are available only from a top level page, which is referenced from the appropriate KBS page, and not directly linked to the KBS page itself. Also, the additional hierarchy available can be displayed similar to a table of contents for some area. The advantage in this approach is, that the structure of the hypermedia system this page originates from, will be presented to the user by the page itself. Drawbacks are the existence of two different structures (though the second structure can sometimes be seen as a direct extension of the first, less detailed structure).

In the case of integrating project portfolios, what is still missing are explanations of why certain portfolio elements are relevant to a specific topic / knowledge item. When the portfolio is used during an exam, and the student can explain this relationship and why he uses a specific portfolio element to illustrate a certain topic, this is ok. However, if the portfolio elements are used as part of the learning materials without any additional explanations provided, it is sometimes very difficult to use the referenced program fragment as a stand alone example for a specific topic.

Reuse and Integration of Indices As adaptive hypermedia systems are becoming more common, reuse and integration of indices from different courses on the same topic becomes an interesting issue. Currently, two courses developed at CTE (Carnegie Technology Education) cover several overlapping areas with our CS1 course, and they also use indexing similar to our content map (though with additional relations) [2]. Using a comparison of these content maps and the topics contained within them currently seems to us a good starting point for exploring the issues involved in integrating and reusing content maps from different courses but overlapping areas, and even might lead to standardized content maps for different areas, possibly with different learning dependencies.

Furthermore, as the meta data in our hyperbook system are largely compatible with the RDF standard for Web annotation, it would be interesting to come up with standardized means of reuse and exchange of those content maps, giving distributed adaptive hypermedia systems really access to the full content of the Web (at least to those parts which are relevant and also are annotated with appropriate metadata information).

References

[1] P. Brusilovsky. Adaptive and intelligent technologies for web-based education. *KI-Themenheft*, 4, 1999.

[2] P. Brusilovsky. Course sequencing for static courses? Applying ITS techniques in large-scale web-based education. In *Proceedings of the fifth International Conference on Intelligent Tutoring Systems ITS 2000*, Montreal, Canada, 2000.

[3] P. Brusilovsky, E. Schwarz, and G. Weber. ELM-ART: An intelligent tutoring system on world wide web. In C. Frasson, G. Gauthier, and A. Lesgold, editors, *Intelligent Tutoring Systems (Lecture Notes in Computer Science, Vol. 1086)*, pages 261–269, Berlin, 1996. Springer.

[4] L. Calvi and P. de Bra. Improving the usability of hypertext courseware through adaptive linking. In *The Eighth ACM International Hypertext Conference*, Southampton, UK, April 1997.

[5] M. Campione and K. Wallrath. *The Java Tutorial*. Addison Wesley, 2nd edition, 1999. http://www.javasoft.com/docs/books/tutorial/index.html.

[6] R. A. Duschl and D. H. Gitomer. Epistemological perspectives on conceptual change: Implications for educational practice. *Journal of Research in Science Teaching*, 26(9):839–858, 1991.

[7] N. Henze. *Adaptive Hyperbooks: Adpatation for Project-Based Learning Resources*. PhD thesis, University of Hannover, 2000.

[8] N. Henze and W. Nejdl. Adaptivity in the KBS hyperbook system. In *2nd Workshop on Adaptive Systems and User Modeling on the WWW*, Toronto, Canada, May 1999.

[9] N. Henze and W. Nejdl. Bayesian modeling for adaptive hypermedia systems. In *ABIS 99, 7. GI-Workshop Adaptivität und Benutzermodellierung in interaktiven Softwaresystemen*, Magdeburg, Sept. 1999.

[10] N. Henze, W. Nejdl, and M. Wolpers. Modeling constructivist teaching functionality and structure in the KBS hyperbook system. In *CSCL'99: Computer Supported Collaborative Learning*, Standford, USA, Dec. 1999.

[11] J. Kay and R. Kummerfeld. An individualised course for the C programming language. In *Proc. of the 2nd International World Wide Web Conference*, Chicago, USA, Oktober 1994.

[12] W. Nejdl, M. Wolpers, and C. Capelle. The RDF Schema Specification Revisited. In *Workshop Modellierung 2000*, St. Goar, Germany, 2000.

[13] G. Weber and M. Specht. User modeling and adaptive navigation support in WWW-based tutoring systems. In *Proceedings of the Sixth International Conference on User Modeling, UM97*, Sardinia, Italy, 1997.

Logically Optimal Curriculum Sequences for Adaptive Hypermedia Systems

Roland Hübscher

107 Dunstan Hall, Department of Computer Science and Software Engineering
Auburn University, Auburn, AL 36849-5347, U.S.A.
roland@eng.auburn.edu

Abstract. Curriculum sequencing is an important technique used in many adaptive hypermedia systems. When following one of the possible page sequences, visiting some pages may become redundant, because its content has been covered already by another page. Using disjunctive and conjunctive prerequisites instead of partial orders to describe the many possible sequences, *logical redundancy* between pages can be computed on the fly without burdening the teaching model with that task [1]. Although the general case of finding all redundant pages is NP-Complete [2] and thus, intractable unless P = NP, a large subset can be located efficiently in realtime. The advantage of separating out logical redundancy, the advantage of using conjunctive and disjunctive prerequisites, and the algorithms to find redundant pages are discussed. An interesting characteristic of the presented approach is that it can be used together with a wide variety of user and teaching models.

1 Introduction

The goal of curriculum sequencing is to provide a student with an optimal path through the material to be learned and tasks to be executed, e.g., practicing a skill or answering questions [3]. Since every student has different prior knowledge, preferences, and often different learning goals, providing individualized curriculum sequences for each student using adaptive hypermedia is a promising approach.

But what is an optimal path? In an educational adaptive hypermedia system, an optimal path maximizes a combination of the student's understanding of the material and the efficiency of learning the material. However, it makes more sense to attempt to suggest a few good paths instead of an optimal one, because the latter does not exist. It should then be left to the learner to select whichever one of the, possibly many, paths that are expected to lead to effective learning for this student. Otherwise, the hypermedia looses its big advantage of being freely explorable, providing at least somewhat of an authentic learning experience to the student [4]. However, providing a hypermedia system with a link structure that allows the user to choose between good paths could result in redundant visits to certain pages and thus, in a suboptimal curriculum sequence. This situation cannot be avoided if a wide variety of learners need to be supported.

P. Brusilovsky, O. Stock, C. Strapparava (Eds.): AH 2000, LNCS 1892, pp. 121–132, 2000.

Different examples, different kinds of representations, different modalities, etc. can be used for explaining the same concepts in slightly different ways which means that not everybody ought to have to look at everything everybody else does.

For instance, assume that in one sequence concept A needs to be studied before concept X. In another sequence, we want the student, again for pedagogical reasons, to read about concept B before X. Looking at the bigger picture, we realize that either A or B ought to be studied before X. Thus, once the learner understands A, he or she can ignore B, as it has become redundant with respect to the goal of understanding X. However, as we will see later, the general case is not as simple as this trivial example may imply.

A guiding principle for our approach is that the space the user may explore is maximized, i.e., we want to constrain the user's choice as little as possible. However, navigation support should scaffold [5] the user to take the best paths with respect to the user's interest and current understanding of the domain, the domain itself, and the underlying pedagogical framework. In short, we are interested in effectively supporting scaffolded exploration.

In this paper, we study how we can find logically optimal paths in hypermedia systems that adaptively provide many good curriculum sequences. Curriculum sequencing is used as a technical term, although most of the time this sequencing, or adaptive ordering [6], is applied to smaller parts, like courses. Logically optimal paths do not contain pages that are redundant based on logical, and not on pedagogical, grounds. Sometimes, one explicitly wants to be redundant to some degree, e.g., an issue should be covered by at least two examples. Such situations can also be described by the presented formalism. We show that generally all redundancy cannot be detected in realtime, however, a large subset can be found efficiently by the presented algorithms.

2   Sequencing with Prerequisites

The material to be learned and tasks to be executed, from now on simply called "units," need to be ordered for each learner dependent on the teaching method employed and the model the system has of the student. The resulting structure describing all the sequences can be represented as a directed acyclic and-or graph where the vertices are the units and the edges are prerequisites between the units. This graph is called a *prerequisite graph*. Note that we use the term "prerequisite" not in a strictly pedagogical sense, i.e., we do not claim that organizing a course simply using prerequisites is appropriate. We simply call the temporal constraints between the units prerequisites. However, we claim that most pedagogically interesting organizations of the units can formally be reduced to a prerequisite graph.

One might argue that a simple partial-order representation of the units is just as expressive. Although this is true in principle, the size of the partial-order graph would be exponentially larger than the prerequisite graph as will become clear below.

A prerequisite is either a conjunctive or a disjunctive. A conjunctive prerequisite $u_1 \wedge u_2 \wedge \ldots \wedge u_n \Rightarrow u$ asserts that all of the units $u_1, u_2, \ldots, u_n$ need to be "visited" by the student before unit u may be visited. Instead of "visited" we could also say "learned," "seen," "understood," etc., depending on the specific design of the adaptive hypermedia system and the teaching method adopted. This is independent of our concept of logically optimal paths. Similarly, a disjunctive prerequisite $u_1 \vee u_2 \vee \ldots \vee u_n \Rightarrow u$ asserts that at least one of the units $u_1, u_2, \ldots, u_n$ needs to be visited by the student before unit u.

We are currently designing a language that allows course designers to describe teaching methods that can be translated into the prerequisite formalism introduced here. The following few simple examples will provide an idea of where this language is going.

Assume that x and y are some knowledge units, for instance, a concept or a topic consisting of several knowledge units. Sometimes, for instance in Problem-Based Learning [7, 8], it is preferable to have the students find out that they have a need to learn certain prerequisites. So, one would like to talk first about y and only then about x. The rule

if x is required to understand y **then** $y \Rightarrow x$

says that prerequisites (in the pedagogical, not formal, sense) should be visited *after* what they are prerequisite for. This example makes it explicit that we use the prerequisites in the formal sense as a way to order the units. However, how prerequisites in the pedagogical sense are used depends on the teaching method used.

The following rule results in a top-down organization of part-whole hierarchies since it says that one should learn about the whole before learning about its parts.

if y is part of x **then** $x \Rightarrow y$

And finally, the last rule says that related issues should be visited in parallel to the main topic: If x is strongly related to y, then x is visited while visiting y. This rule only makes sense if x and y are more complex hypermedia structures than a single page. Then we can refer to the start and the beginning units of those structures and use our prerequisites again. Virtual units introduced below can be used as special start and end units if necessary.

if x is strongly related to y **then** $\text{start}(y) \Rightarrow \text{start}(x)$
if x is strongly related to y **then** $\text{end}(x) \Rightarrow \text{end}(y)$

In order to make the simple formalism of conjunctive and disjunctive prerequisites a bit more expressive, we introduce the notion of *virtual units*. A virtual unit does not exist for the student, however it is an element in the prerequisite graph. This allows us to have prerequisites with nested conjunctions and disjunctions like the following one requiring the learner to visit exactly two of the three units u_1, u_2, u_3 before visiting u:

$$(u_1 \wedge u_2) \vee (u_1 \wedge u_3) \vee (u_2 \wedge u_3) \Rightarrow u$$

This constraint can be implemented with the following four prerequisites introducing three virtual units v_1, v_2, and v_3:

$$u_1 \wedge u_2 \quad \Rightarrow v_1$$
$$u_1 \wedge u_3 \quad \Rightarrow v_2$$
$$u_2 \wedge u_3 \quad \Rightarrow v_3$$
$$v_1 \vee v_2 \vee v_3 \Rightarrow u$$

At each moment, a set of units is called the *goal*. The goal is what the user tries to learn. For instance, for class notes the goal is quite constant for a semester, namely covering a certain minimal set of topics. For a manual, though, the goal may change whenever the user is accessing the manual.

We do not plan to add negations to the formalism because that would result in non-monotonic behavior, i.e., units that used to be accessible to the user are suddenly not accessible anymore. This would violate our guiding principle that the space the user may explore is maximized, i.e., that the user's choices are constrained as little as possible. Furthermore, we believe that this would cause even more potential usability problems than the appearance of new links as is common in adaptive hypermedia [9]. However, we do not have any empirical evidence for the negative effect of non-monotonic adaptive hypermedia as of yet.

2.1 Disjunctions Add Complexity

As will be shown below, disjunctive prerequisites come in handy in some situations. However, adding disjunctions causes problems, because they add degrees of freedom. If both, u_1 and u_2 are required for u, then the user has no choice, and adding more conditions $u_3, \ldots, u_k$ does not add any new choices. There is one way to get to u: Visit all units $u_1, \ldots, u_k$ in the prerequisite. However, if we have a disjunctive constraint $u_1 \vee u_2 \vee \ldots \vee u_n \Rightarrow u$ there are $2^n - 1$ subsets of $u_1, u_2, \ldots, u_n$ that can be visited before visiting u. So disjunctions add an exponential amount of choice. Thus, if the representation with disjunctive and conjunctive prerequisites would be replaced by a partial-order representation as in other adaptive hypermedia systems[3, 10], the size of the partial-order graph would increase exponentially.

That does not seem to be a serious problem, though, because as soon as a disjunct u_i in the above prerequisite gets visited, all the other $u_j, j \neq i$, are redundant because u may be visited now. However, some of the units u_j may be involved in some other prerequisites and have to be visited for other reasons than just enabling u to be visited. And what's worse, this is not a local phenomenon: These other units may be far away in the graph. The algorithm described later will solve this problem.

2.2 Using Prerequisites to Order Units

We claim that the use of conjunctive and disjunctive prerequisites with virtual units is powerful enough to describe a large class of dependencies in adaptive hypermedia systems. An interesting characteristic of this approach is that it is relatively independent of the underlying teaching methods and user model. Thus, it can be used with a wide variety of user models and teaching methods [1]. All the model needs to output is the set of units that can be considered visited (or learned, seen, etc.).

Providing just one of many effective sequences to the user would be the wrong approach, since that would get rid of most of the benefits of having *hyper*media in the first place. Providing conjunctive prerequisites is very close to providing one sequence only. Furthermore, separating the pedagogical and the logical characteristics of the dependencies makes it more clear what the semantics of the user model and teaching method are. Finally, adding disjunctions allows one to nicely describe certain dependencies that are quite important in an educational setting.

Disjunctive prerequisites are useful if there is redundant material in the hypermedia system supporting diverse set of learners. For instance, the same concept can and often should be described in different ways, using different representations, different modes of presentation, etc., [11, 12]. However, the student should have the freedom to select the most appropriate one (from the set of "good" ones). This relationship can then be described with a disjunction. Of course, one might argue that the adaptive system should provide the appropriate representation and mode. However, that is pushing adaptiveness too far. Sometimes a system can safely make a good choice, but taking all the decisions away from the learner is a misguided approach.

Another example use of disjunctions is if one wants to make sure that a student sees the use of a certain concept or feature, say of a programming language, in at least two examples. This constraint can be easily expressed as a disjunction of conjunctions. Letting e_i be the examples and t be the topic to cover, we can express this constraint as follows.

$$(e_1 \wedge e_2) \vee (e_1 \wedge e_3) \vee \cdot \vee (e_1 \wedge e_n) \vee \cdot \vee (e_{n-1} \wedge e_n) \Rightarrow t$$

A similar example where disjunctions come in handy is where the instructor has several illustrating examples to explain an issue in the lecture notes. He wants to select just one example and make sure he is not going over other, redundant examples. Conjunctions alone cannot express such a relationship easily. Again, let e_i be the examples and t be the topic to cover. Then, we can express the instructor's approach in subtly different ways. If the example needs to be covered *before* the topic then this is expressed as follows.

$$e_1 \vee e_2 \vee \cdots \vee e_n \Rightarrow t$$

If the instructor want to make sure at least one example is used to illustrate the topic *at any time*, then we introduce two virtual units v_1 and v_2 and describe the organization as follows.

$$e_1 \vee e_2 \vee \cdots \vee e_n \Rightarrow v_1$$
$$t \wedge v_1 \qquad \Rightarrow v_2$$

Of course, one could implement this prerequisite in some ad-hoc fashion, but that tends to be a bad idea in the long run and complexity will show its ugly face in some form sooner or later.

3   Redundant Units

As mentioned earlier, without disjunctions, there is no need to deal with redundant units, because, sooner or later, all units will be necessary. However, as soon as disjunctions are added, things are getting more complicated. Let's look at a few small examples.

Example 1: There is one disjunctive prerequisite, such that at least one of A or B must be visited before X is visited.

$$A \vee B \Rightarrow X$$

Assume we want to visit X. As soon as A is visited, X may be visited next. Since X is now enabled, i.e., can be visited, there is no need to visit B, since it does not enable something of any value. We say that visiting A makes B *redundant* (via X). Similarly, visiting B first makes A redundant.

Example 2: We extend the first example by adding B as prerequisite for a new unit Y and our new goal is Z.

$$
\begin{aligned}
A \vee B &\Rightarrow X \\
B \quad\ &\Rightarrow Y \\
X \wedge Y &\Rightarrow Z
\end{aligned}
$$

In this case, visiting A does not make B redundant, because B is still needed to enable Y to be visited. It also becomes clear that visiting A is actually inefficient. B needs to be visited independently of whether A is visited or not. Thus, A is redundant before any of the units has been visited, because B is *required* and, sooner or later, will be visited.

Example 3: A slightly different situation arises in the final example.

$$
\begin{aligned}
A \wedge B &\Rightarrow X \\
B \wedge C &\Rightarrow Y \\
X \vee Y &\Rightarrow Z
\end{aligned}
$$

Here, we have the case where B is required, although there is only a disjunctive prerequisite for the goal Z.

These examples show that some units may become redundant due to other units being visited and some units are redundant simply due to the structure of the prerequisite graph and the goal unit. They also show that these decisions cannot be made locally.

3.1   Formalizing Redundancy

Before redundancy of units can be formalized, a few terms need to be defined.

unit   A unit is the smallest description of some concept, method, etc. Without loss of generality for our discussion, it can be thought of as a web page.

goal   A goal is a set of units that the user wants to visit, but might not be able to right now, because it is not enabled yet.

virtual unit   A virtual unit is a unit that exists in the prerequisite graph in order to express the necessary prerequisites (e.g., a disjunction of conjunctions), however, it is invisible to the user, i.e., it does not represent an actual page.

visited unit   A unit is visited if the concept the unit describes is assumed to be known by the user. Only enabled units may be visited. When and why a concept is assumed to be known depends on the user model. For simplicity reasons, without sacrificing any generality, we assume that the user visiting a page means he or she has actually learned its content.

enabled unit   A unit is enabled if all of its prerequisites are satisfied. If the prerequisite is a conjunction, then all of its prerequisite units need to be visited. If it is a disjunctive prerequisite, then at least one of the units needs to be visited.

redundant unit   A unit is redundant if it has not been visited, and visiting it does not enable any unit at any time in the future. A more formal description follows below.

In a simple web-based adaptive hypermedia system (WHAM, see section 3.4) where we employed the described adaptive algorithm, we used three types of hyperlinks: recommended links displayed in bold blue; redundant links displayed in purple; and forbidden links which were plain text, i.e., not links. Recommended links pointed to enabled, non-redundant units. No links (or forbidden links) were made to units that were not enabled. Redundant links pointed to enabled, redundant units.

Redundant units can then be defined as follows. Let $P = \{u_1, u_2, \ldots, u_k\}$ be the set of units representing the prerequisite units of $P \Rightarrow u$. A *future-enabled* unit is a unit that is enabled assuming that all required units have been visited in addition to those units the user actually has visited. Then we can recursively define a redundant unit u as follows, where "$\rightarrow$" stands for the material implication:

$$\text{redundant}(u) \equiv \forall P'.(u \in P') \wedge (P' \Rightarrow u') \rightarrow \text{redundant}(u') \vee \text{futureEnabled}(u')$$

That is, u is redundant if all units u' for which u is a prerequisite are either redundant, or enabled or will be enabled for sure in the future. An efficient algorithm to find most, but not necessarily all, of these redundant units will be presented below.

3.2 Complexity of Finding Redundant Units

Finding enabled units is easy, and therefore, finding disabled units is easy. The real difficulty in a computational sense lies in finding the redundant units as we will see in a moment.

The input to the problem of finding redundant units are the prerequisite graph $G = (V, E)$, the goal unit g, and the set of visited units U. We assume that there is only one goal unit. If there are more than one, say $u_1, \ldots, u_n$ then we simply introduce a new, virtual unit g and a conjunctive prerequisite $u_1 \wedge \ldots \wedge u_n \Rightarrow g$. The graph's vertices V is the set of units in the graph, and the directed edges E are between the prerequisites of a unit and the unit.

Unfortunately, finding out whether a unit is required is NP-complete as can be seen as follows. Let $v(u)$ stand for "unit u has been visited." Let F be a set of formulas in propositional logic as follows. For each conjunctive prerequisite $u_1 \wedge \ldots \wedge u_k \Rightarrow u$ add $v(u) \rightarrow v(u_1) \wedge \ldots \wedge v(u_k)$ to F because u can only have been visited if all $u_1, \ldots, u_k$ have been visited. Similarly, for each disjunctive prerequisite $u_1 \vee \ldots \vee u_k \Rightarrow u$ add $v(u) \rightarrow v(u_1) \vee \ldots \vee v(u_k)$ to F. Then, to show that u is required one has to show that $F \cup \{g\} \vdash u$. This is equivalent to the satisfiability problem which is known to be NP-complete [2]. Thus, we cannot expect to find an efficient algorithm that finds all required units.

Although this is bad news, all hope is not lost. If the graph and the goal are constant, then finding the required units can be done off-line. For instance, for class notes the goal can be assumed to be constant for the whole semester, namely cover a certain minimal set of topics. However, for a manual where the goal changes very often, solving an NP-complete problem in realtime is not feasible. Although finding required units is hard, finding only those redundant units as a function of enabled, but not future-enabled, units can be done efficiently.

3.3 Finding Most Redundant Units

Now that it is clear that we cannot find all redundant units on the fly, we look at a simpler version of the problem that will result in an algorithm that is correct but not complete, i.e., it will find only redundant units but possibly not all. However, the same algorithm can be used to find all redundant units if all required units are known.

Finding Redundancy-Propagating Paths The prerequisite graph G is initialized independently of the user's actions and goals, i.e., the initialization is only dependent on the prerequisites. Once the graph is initialized, redundant units can be efficiently computed while the user is visiting pages.

A unit u was earlier defined to be redundant if $\forall P'. u \in P' \wedge P' \Rightarrow u' \rightarrow$ redundant$(u') \vee$ futureEnabled(u'). Note that "futureEnabled" may have to be replaced with "enabled" depending on whether the required units have been computed or not. Checking each enabled unit recursively to find out whether it is redundant or not would be prohibitively expensive.

Therefore, we devised an algorithm that allows redundancy to be propagated from visited towards non-visited units, which is computationally much cheaper. This requires the system to find the so-called *redundancy-propagating paths* in the prerequisite graph $G = (V, E)$ as follows. (We say that a vertex "represents a conjunct/disjunct" if it is part of a conjunctive/disjunctive prerequisite.)

for each vertex v in reverse topological order **do**
    // *i.e., ordered such that if there is a path from v' to v'',*
    // *then v'' must appear before v' in the topological order*
    $c(v) \leftarrow |\text{tokens}(v)|$
    for each v_i, where $(v_i, v) \in E$ **do**
        $\text{tokens}(v_i) \leftarrow \text{tokens}(v_i) \cup \text{tokens}(v)$
        if (v_i, v) represents a conjunct **then**
            $t \leftarrow$ new unique token
            $\text{tokens}(v_i) \leftarrow \text{tokens}(v_i) \cup \{t\}$
        end if
    end for each
    // *the set* $\text{tokens}(v)$ *can now safely be deleted*
end for each

The algorithm generates a unique token for each conjunct in a prerequisite and propagates it away from the goal. Each vertex v then counts how many different tokens arrive which is the number, denoted as $c(v)$, of different conjuncts it is involved in. Then, an edge (v_i, v_j) is redundancy propagating (rp) from v_j to v_i, if the following condition holds:

$$rp(v_i, v_j) = \begin{cases} \textbf{true} & \text{if } (v_i, v_j) \text{ represents a conjunct} \wedge c(v_i) = c(v_j) + 1 \\ \textbf{true} & \text{if } (v_i, v_j) \text{ represents a disjunct} \wedge c(v_i) = c(v_j) \\ \textbf{false} & \text{otherwise} \end{cases}$$

The time complexity of this algorithm is $O(|V|^2)$ which is fast enough since it has to be run only once for a given set of prerequisites and is independent of the goals. Note that it is also independent of knowing the required units.

Propagating Redundancy Once the user starts using the hypermedia system, all new redundant units need to be found each time a unit is visited. Thus, this algorithm needs to be very efficient to be useful.

We define a procedure *visit*(v) that is called for a vertex when it is visited. Of course, only enabled vertices can be visited. Procedure *visit*(v) checks whether visiting v resulted in another unit becoming enabled. If so, procedure *propagate* defined below will find the redundant units.

procedure visit(v):
    $\text{visited}(v) \leftarrow \textbf{true}$
    for each v_i, where $(v, v_i) \in E$ **do**
        // *one step forward*

```
    if enabled(v_i) then
        // start from v_i and propagate redundancy backwards
        propagate(v_i)
    end if
end for each
end procedure
```

Procedure *propagate* finds redundant units by searching backwards along the redundancy-propagating paths only. Note that we only have to call *propagate* if visiting v caused v_i to become enabled, but not if it was already enabled before v was visited. We omit this code here for simplicity.

```
procedure propagate(v):
    if not redundant(v) and not visited(v) then
        for each v_i, where (v_i, v) ∈ V do
            if rp(v_i, v) then
                // we only propagate along the redundancy-propagating paths
                propagate(v_i)
                redundant(v_i) ← true
            end if
        end for each
    end if
end procedure
```

Worst time complexity is $O(|V|)$. However, this is irrelevant for any practical system. Since each vertex can become redundant only once and the user will need to visit $O(|V|)$ vertices, the expected time complexity is roughly constant as informal testing has shown.

3.4   Implementation for the World Wide Web

We have implemented these algorithms in WHAM (Web-based Hypermedia for Adaptive Manuals) using a simple user model, that stores which pages the user believes to understand and which not. Initially, we want to use this prototype to study the following issues: does the distinction between recommended, redundant, and forbidden links support scaffolded exploration effectively; is the continuously changing interface (links may come and go) a source of serious usability problems or not; are very simple user models good enough for many situations, or do we need indeed advanced cognitive models to provide useful navigation support.

In WHAM, the above algorithms are implemented using Java applets accessing a relational database storing the prerequisite graph including the count c for each node used to compute whether a link is redundancy propagating. The algorithms needed to be modified to work for large web sites. Computing the redundancy-propagating paths requires all nodes to be visited in topological order. Since there may be very many nodes to be visited when traversing the prerequisite graph, an iterative version of topological sort is used. The **visit** and the **propagate** functions are currently implemented recursively since they are not expected to traverse many edges of the prerequisite graph. All the data structures are implemented as tables in a relational data base (we use MySQL as relational database together with Apache as web server). The transformation of above rather simple looking algorithms into an efficient iterative, database-oriented version was not as straight forward as we expected.

The result is an efficient and scalable set of Java applets that can be used in various ways by adaptive hypermedia systems that implement different kinds of pedagogical models and different kinds of user models.

4   Conclusions

A large class of curriculum sequences can be described with conjunctive and disjunctive prerequisites. Using disjunctions implies that some of the content is redundant. By separating out logical redundancy from the pedagogical rules, we can simplify those rules and focus on the pedagogical issues more. However, using disjunctions comes, as so often, with a price to pay. Finding redundant units, or pages, is not easy, and to find all redundant units may be prohibitively expensive.

We have presented an algorithm that initializes the prerequisite graph, so that all redundant units that are only dependent on visited, but not on required, units can be found efficiently. If there is enough time to compute all the required units, for instance, if the goal is not going to change while the user is using the system, then the algorithm is complete, i.e., it will find all redundant units.

References

[1] Paul De Bra, Geert-Jan Houben, and Hongjing Wu. Aham: a dexter-based reference model for adaptive hypermedia. In *Proceedings of the 10th ACM Conference on Hypertext and Hypermedia*, pages 147–156, 1999.

[2] Michael R. Garey and David S. Johnson. *Computers and Intractability: A Guide to the Theory of NP-Completeness*. W. H. Freeman and Company, New York, NY, 1979.

[3] Peter Brusilovsky. Adaptive educational systems on the world-wide-web: A review of available technologies. In *4th International Conference in Intelligent Tutoring Systems*, San Antonio, TX, 1998.

[4] Joseph Petraglia. *Reality by Design: The Rhetoric and Technology of Authenticity in Education*. Lawrence Erlbaum Associates, Mahwah, NJ, 1998.

[5] Roland Hübscher, Sadhana Puntambekar, and Mark Guzdial. A scaffolded learning environment supporting learning and design activities. In *AERA*, Chicago, 1997.

[6] Peter Brusilovsky. *Methods and Techniques of Adaptive Hypermedia*, volume 6, pages 87–129. Kluwer Academic Publishers, 1996.

[7] Howard S. Barrows. *How to Design a Problem Based Curriculum for the Preclinical Years*. Springer Verlag, New York, NY, 1985.

[8] Roland Hübscher, Cindy E. Hmelo, N. Hari Narayanan, Mark Guzdial, and Janet L. Kolodner. McBAGEL: A shared and structured electronic workspace for problem-based learning. In *Second International Conference on the Learning Sciences*, Evanston, IL, 1996.

[9] Kristina Höök. Evaluating the utility and usability of an adaptive hypermedia system. In *Proceedings of 1997 International Conference on Intelligent User Interfaces*, Orlando, FL, 1997. ACM.

[10] Nicola Henze and Wolfgang Nejdl. Adaptivity in the kbs hyperbook system. In *Second Workshop on Adaptive Systems and User Modeling on the World Wide Web*, 1999.

[11] Juan E. Gilbert and C. Y. Han. Adapting instruction in search of 'a significant difference'. *Journal of Network and Computer Applications*, 22, 1999.

[12] Rand J. Spiro, Paul J. Feltovich, Michael J. Jacobson, and Richard L. Coulson. Cognitive flexibility, constructivism, and hypertext: Random access instruction for advanced knowledge acquisition in ill-structured domains. *Educational Technology*, May 1991:24–33, 1991.

Towards Zero-Input Personalization: Referrer-Based Page Prediction

Nicholas Kushmerick[1], James McKee[2], and Fergus Toolan[1]

[1] Computer Science Department, University College Dublin, Ireland;
nick@ucd.ie
[2] PredictPoint.com, Seattle, Washington, USA

Abstract. Most web services take a "one size fits all" approach: all visitors see the same generic content, formatted in the same generic manner. But of course each visitor has her own information needs and preferences. In contrast to most personalization systems, we are interested in how effective personalization can be with zero additional user input or feedback. This paper describes *PWW*, an extensible suite of tools for personalizing web sites, and introduces *RBPR*, a novel zero-input recommendation technique. RBPR uses information about a visitor's browsing context (specifically, the referrer URL provided by HTTP) to suggest pages that might be relevant to the visitor's underlying information need. Empirical results for an actual web site demonstrate that RBPR makes useful suggestions even though it places no additional burden on web visitors.

1 Introduction

Most web services take a "one size fits all" approach: all visitors see the same generic content, formatted in the same generic manner. But of course every visitor has their own needs and preferences. Consider visitors to a computer science department web site: a student might want course materials; a prospective student might want application information; an employer might want lists of graduating students; a journalist might want general background information about the field of computer science. Personalized information services—delivering the right information, at the right time, in the right format—represent the Holy Grail of web design.

Personalized content requires access to a representation visitors' information needs and preferences. Much recent personalization research requires that visitors explicitly describe their interests. Content-based systems (e.g. [5, 2]) require that users explicitly provide a model of what they are looking for, such as a list of query terms. Collaborative or social filtering systems (e.g. [8, 10]) require that users rate items. While user-interface design can simplify the process of providing such information (e.g., [1]), a natural question arises: *Can personalization be effective with no explicit visitor input?*

Web personalization can take many forms, from client-side browsing assistants that help users find interesting web sites, to server-side tools for augmenting an existing web site with personalization features, or automatically generating

P. Brusilovsky, O. Stock, C. Strapparava (Eds.): AH 2000, LNCS 1892, pp. 133–143, 2000.

personalized web views. We focus on the intermediate goal of suggesting pages within a web site that that visitors will find relevant or interesting. Specifically, in this paper, we (1) describe *PWW*, a suite of personalization tools for rapidly adding personalization features to an existing web site; and (2) use PWW to investigate *referrer-based page recommendation*, a novel zero-input recommendation technique.

The intuition behind referrer-based page recommendation is as follows. When a visitor arrives at a web site, she carries with her a rich browsing context that can illuminate her ultimate information needs and preferences. For example, suppose a visitor arrives at a computer science department web by selecting a hyperlink on a page that contains word such as `course`, `degree` and `application`. A referrer-based page recommendation system would notice that this *referrer page* shares many words with web pages presenting information for prospective students. On the other hand, if the referring page contains terms such as `project` and `grant`, the recommendation system would suggest pages related to the department's research, since such pages would contain these terms. Referrer-based page recommendation uses information retrieval techniques to suggest pages based on their similarity to the visitor's referrer page. The main advantage of referrer-based recommendation over alternative approaches is that it imposes no additional burden on site visitors. Finally, we observe that page prediction has uses beyond personalization. For example, such predictions can be used by browsers to improve caching, and by servers to prefetch requests.

The remainder of this paper is organization as follows. In Section 2, we formalize our approach to web personalization and describe the PWW system. In Section 3, we describe our main technical contribution, the referrer-based page recommendation technique. We then empirically demonstrate that this technique makes useful suggestions, even though no explicit user input is needed (Section 4). We conclude with a discussion of related work (Section 5), and a summary of our contributions and future plans (Section 6).

2   Personalizing Web Sites

Our personalization research is aimed at building server-side tools that help visitors to a particular web site find interesting or relevant web pages. Specifically, we assume that visitors browsing through the site have some particular *information need* or goal, and we seek to provide assistance that is tailored or customized to that need.

Our ultimate goal is to customize both layout and content based on a visitor's information needs. In the current implementation, PWW tackles one aspect of this personalization process: PWW suggests which of a site's web pages are likely to be relevant. The recommendations are displayed in a personalization frame; the original web site is left intact and displayed in its own frame.

As described in the introduction, recommender systems usually require that a visitor states her information need, either explicitly (in the case of content-based filtering) or implicitly (in the case of collaborative filtering). As an alternative, we are interested in *inferring* a visitor's information need. To do so, we exploit the fact that visitors do not simply read isolated web pages, but rather browsing is an interactive process that generates a rich *browsing context*. Our zero-input personalization techniques attempt to infer a visitors information needs from this browsing context.

We formalize our intuitions below, but for now we can informally state the page recommendation process as follows: given some representation C of a visitors browsing context, and her current web location U, we want to compute a set $R(C, U) = [R_1, R_2, \ldots]$ of personalized URL recommendations.

PWW operates by repeatedly offering personalized suggestions to each visitor. When the visitor requests page U, PWW detects her context C, and then displays page U as rendered by the original web site, as well as a separate frame listing the recommendations $R(C, U)$. The visitor then selects a new hyperlink U'—either one of the links on page U or some recommendations in the list $R(C, U)$. As a result of this additional browsing activity, the visitor's context becomes updated to C' and the process repeats, with page U' being displayed together with recommendations $R(C', U')$.

This high-level problem statement encompasses a vast space of approaches to personalization. PWW is an extensible suite of tools for incorporating recommendation techniques that can be described in this manner into existing web sites. Because PWW is extensible, we see it as a research platform for both developing new recommendation techniques, and for comparing existing techniques. We have used PWW to develop our novel referrer-based page recommendation technique, and are currently adding collaborative filtering techniques to PWW.

In the next section, we describe referrer-based recommendation in detail, but first we show how PWW has been used to enhance the UCD/CS web site; see Figure 1. Suppose a visitor is interested in Kushmerick's AdEater system that learns to remove advertisements from web pages. To find a description of this research, the visitor might reasonably submit the query terms "kushmerick adeater" to a search engine such as Lycos; see Figure 1(a). Note that Lycos' search results include a hyperlink to page describing Kushmerick's research. When selected, this hyperlink leads to the page shown in Figure 1(b). The main frame of this page is the original web page as it would be rendered without PWW. PWW occupies the small frame at the bottom of the page. As we describe in the next section, PWW uses referrer-based page recommendation to suggest a small set of pages within the UCD/CS web. These suggestions are displayed in the menu in the lower-left corner of Figure 1(b). Note that PWW's top-ranking suggestion describes the AdEater project. (The other suggestions, while not strictly relevant, involve related research projects and lecture materials.) Note that PWW's suggestions are personalized (different visitors get different recommendations based on their browsing context), and require no user input (the visitor need not explicitly tell PWW anything about her needs and preferences).

PWW has been fully implemented as a distributed collection of Java servlets and applets, and Javascript. Visitors are individuated and tracked with cookies, and requests to the UCD/CS web are passed through PWW. PWW replaces the

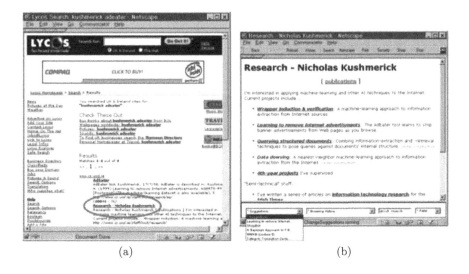

(a)   (b)

Fig. 1. A visitor clicks on an external hyperlink into the UCD/CS web (a), and PWW provides personalized suggestions for other UCD/CS pages that might be relevant (b).

original page with the two-frame page as shown in Figure 1(b), and then invokes the recommendation module to create the suggestion menus. PWW currently uses referrer-based page recommendation, and we are currently implementing a collaborative filtering module.

3   Referrer-Based Page Recommendation

Referrer-based page recommendation (RBPR) is a URL recommendation algorithm as defined in the previous section: the input is a representation of the visitor's browsing context C and the visitor's current URL U, and the output is a ranked list of suggested URLs, $R(C, U)$.

The intuition underlying RBPR is as follows. Suppose you are searching for Alon Levy's work on data integration, so you decide to submit the the query "alon levy data integration" to a search engine. The output from this query will probably include (among many others) a hyperlink to Levy's home page in the University of Washington Department of Computer Science & Engineering (UW/CS&E) web, www.cs.washington.edu/homes/alon. If you decide to select this link, then a personalized version of the UW/CS&E web might suggest you go to data.cs.washington.edu/integration/tukwila, which describes Levy's Tukwila data integration system. (A particularly confident personalization system might even override your request for Levy's home page and take you directly to its top suggestion.)

How does PWW use your browsing context to infer that you are interested in Tukwila? The page you were looking at when you requested Levy's home page (called the *referrer URL*, in HTTP parlance) contains numerous terms—data, integration, names other researchers, etc.—that provide valuable clues about your "true" information need. RBPR uses the terms from the referrer URL as query against the entire UW/CS&E web, and then suggests the K highest-ranking pages (we call K the *retrieval window*, and use $K = 5$ in the implementation).

RBPR assumes that document that rank highly with respect to this query are likely to be relevant to the visitor's "true" information need. In terms of the model described earlier, the browsing context C comprises the referrer URL, and RBPR is a technique for inferring a visitor's true information need from the context C. Specifically, RBPR assumes that the visitor's true information need can be characterized by a list of query terms, and RBPR guesses these terms by examining the page containing the hyperlink that lead the visitor to the site.

Since the referrer URL is standard HTTP header, the RBPR algorithm can be implemented entirely on the server. We have explored two techniques for constructing the query terms from the referrer URL. First, the URL itself often contains relevant terms. For example, the Levy example above the referrer URL might be www.metacrawler.com/crawler?general=alon+levy+data+integration. In this first "URL only" mode, RBPR simply removes punctuation from the referrer URL, and uses the resulting terms as the referrer query. Alternatively, in "referrer contents" mode, RBPR extracts the query terms from the actual contents of the referrer URL.

"URL only" mode has the advantage of being very fast, since RBPR can start generating suggestions as soon as the original HTTP request arrives. The disadvantage is that some referrer URLs do not contain indicative terms. Furthermore, "URL only" mode is well suited to searchable web indices, but some search engines use POST rather than GET forms, and the search terms are simply not available in the HTTP request. However, we find that "URL only" mode is appropriate not just for search engine output, but also for static pages. For example, www.rulequest.com/see5-examples.html contains a hyperlink to Kushmerick's home page, because it mentions the AdEater system as one application of the C4.5 machine learning algorithm. Presumably a visitor to UCD/CS selecting this hyperlink would be interested in the AdEater description rather than the home page. Fortunately for "URL only" mode, the referrer query and the AdEater page both contain the term rulequest.

"Referrer contents" mode has the advantage of being more accurate, but RBPR can not generate suggestions until the referrer URL has been retrieved. In an attempt to get the best of both worlds, the PWW generates an initial preliminary set of recommendations using "URL only" mode, and displays them for the visitor. In parallel, RBPR operates in "referrer contents" mode. The initial recommendations are invisibly replaced when the final recommendations have been computed.

RBPR uses standard information retrieval term-vector techniques for identifying pages relevant to the referrer query terms. In an off-line indexing phase, RBPR indexes the entire web site to which PWW applies.

In the next section, we empirically demonstrate that RBPR makes reasonably useful recommendations, despite the fact that RBPR requires no explicit input about a visitor's information needs. Before describing our experiments, we first observe that there are certainly situations in which RBPR does not work. Though standard, clients might not provide the Referrer HTTP header, either because it is undefined (e.g., the visitor directs their browser at a URL directly rather than selecting a hyperlink) or to maintain privacy. Furthermore, it is easy to envision counterexamples that directly contradict RBPR's heuristic assumption that a visitor's information needs can be approximated by the referrer terms. For example, in the Levy example, the `metacrawler` term extracted in "URL only" mode could lead RBPR to incorrectly suggest Selberg and Etzioni's work on meta-searching [9], which is also described in the UW/CS&E web.

4   Evaluation

Despite these complications and subtleties, our experiments demonstrate that referrer-based page recommendation represents interesting progress toward the goal of zero-input personalization.

Before we can describe our experiments, we must first define how we measure the performance of PWW. We are interested in a numeric measure of how "useful" are PWW's recommendations. Ideally, PWW's first recommendation would be a page that satisfies their information need. Unfortunately, without intrusive intervention, we can know neither a visitor's true information need, nor whether any particular page they they saw satisfied that need. That is, we have no way to determine whether a visitor gave up in frustration after browsing though several hyperlinks, or found exactly what they were looking for and left satisfied.

Our evaluation metric is therefore based not on whether visitors' information needs are satisfied, but rather whether RBPR would speed visitors' navigation through the site. Specifically, we will measure the fraction of selected hyperlinks that are "anticipated" by RBPR in a previous recommendation. For visitors that exit the site with their information need satisfied, optimizing navigation time is equivalent to optimizing search for a "goal" page. For visitors that leave the site dissatisfied, we expect that visitors would prefer to reach this decision as soon as possible.

More precisely, consider a scenario in which a visitor enters a PWW-enabled web site from page U_0 by selecting a hyperlink to U_1 (so that the referrer is U_0), and then goes on to request pages U_2, U_3, and so on, leaving the site after visiting URL U_N. PWW first calculates the best K recommendations $R(U_0, U_1) = [R^1, R^2, \ldots, R^K]$, where K is the retrieval window. Then, when the user requests page U_i, the page is displayed along with these K suggestions. Note that all recommendations are based on the first referrer URL, since that is most likely to contain useful hints regarding the visitor's true interests.

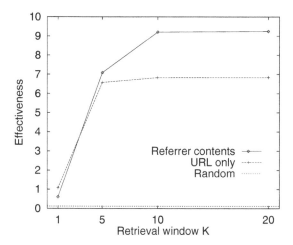

Fig. 2. Empirical results: percentage of useful suggestions as a function of the retrieval window K.

To evaluate RBPR, we are interested in how many recommendations are eventually selected by the visitor. Each such overlap represents an opportunity for PWW to recommend a shorter trajectory through the site. Specifically, the performance of PWW for a single visitor is measured in terms of *effectiveness*, the fraction of URLs that were both recommended by PWW and visited by the user:

$$\text{effectiveness}_{\text{PWW}} = \frac{|\{1 \leq i \leq N : U_i \in [R^1, R^2, ..., R^K]\}|}{N}$$

To evaluate PWW for a series of visitors we average this per-visitor effectiveness.

We evaluated RBPR using access logs from actual visitors to an independently maintained web site. The Music Machines site [`machines.hyperreal.org`] contains 4227 pages about electronic musical instruments. These access logs to this site have been used by Mike Perkowitz and Oren Etzioni in their research on adaptive web sites [6, 7]. (This dataset is *not* a standard server log; Perkowitz and Etzioni used cookies and heuristics to partition the accesses according to individual visitors.)

We evaluated three RBPR in the two modes, and measured the effectiveness of RBPR as a function of the retrieval window K; we varied K from 1 to 20.

Our results are shown in Figure 2. Performance is poor with $K = 1$, though since Music Machines contains more than four thousand pages performance is still well above chance. As K reaches 20, performance asymptotically reaches 9.3% for the "referrer content" mode, and 6.8% for "URL only" mode. Our choice of $K = 5$ is justified by these data: for $K > 5$, the increase in performance is probably outweighed by the fact that visitors must examine long lists of recommendations.

While RBPR's best performance of about 9% is hardly earth-shattering, recall that these recommendations do not require the visitor to assist PWW in any way. Visitors do not have to express their interests in terms of query terms, and they do not need to rate web pages during browsing. Furthermore, note that because the contents of the referrer URLs or Music Machines itself might have changed substantially in the two years since the dataset was gathered, our experiments probably underestimates PWW's performance on live data.

We observe that hyperlink recommendation is notoriously difficult. For example, [2] report that WebWatcher makes useful recommendations about 43% of the time based on an explicit statement of the visitors interests, while expert human performance on this task is about 48%. We do not claim that RBPR outperforms alternative page recommendation algorithms, but rather that it represents evidence that zero-input personalization can be effective.

Joachims et al also report that randomly guessing URLs is effective about 22% of the time, and thus WebWatcher is 1.95 times more useful than random guessing. Note that WebWatcher recommends one of the current page's URLs, while PWW recommends URLs from the entire Web site. Suppose PWW is deployed on a web site containing W pages, and a visitor examines N of these pages during her visit. PWW tries to guess which pages the user will visit, and thus the probability of guessing correctly is N/W. PWW makes K suggestions per page, so over the course of the N pages visited PWW makes KN suggestions. If we define $\Pr[i]$ to be the probability of making exactly i useful suggestions, then effectiveness of random guessing is:

$$\text{effectiveness}_{\text{random}} = \sum_{i=1}^{KN} \frac{i}{KN} \Pr[i].$$

$\Pr[i]$ obeys a Binomial distribution, where the probability of success (making a useful recommendation) is N/W:

$$\Pr[i] = (N/W)^i (1 - N/W)^{KN-i} \binom{KN}{i}.$$

In our experiments, $K = 5$ and $W = 4227$. If visitors examine $N = 5$ pages, then we have effectiveness$_{\text{random}} = 0.12\%$, making PWW $\frac{9.3}{0.12} = 77$ times more effective than random guessing.

5   Related Work

Most work on automatic personalization requires some form of user input. Content-based systems (e.g. [5, 2]) require that users describe what they are looking for; when applied to web recommendation this corresponds either to lists of query terms, or to page ratings from which query terms are derived automatically. Collaborative or social filtering systems (e.g. [8, 10]) require that users explicitly rate items, such as clicking a "thumbs up/down" button. There has also been some informal attempts to sidestep explicit user input by measuring quantities thought to be correlated with interest [1].

Three recent systems are based on a zero-input customization model: Letizia [4], Footprints [11], and Conceptual Cluster Mining [7].

Letizia is a browsing assistant that finds relevant web pages by searching in the neighborhood of the current page for pages that are similar to recently-visited pages. PWW and Letizia provide complementary functionality. As a server-specific enhancement, PWW is designed to assist all visitors to a particular site; as a client-side browsing assistant, Letizia helps a particular user wherever they may be in hyperspace. One more substantial difference is that Letizia can not offer suggestions until it has observed at least one request/response cycle, which is arguably when the visitor needs the most assistance. In contrast, PWW provides recommendations in all responses, and it's first set of recommendations are likely to be the most helpful. Letizia is the most similar to PWW of the systems described in this section, but [4] does not evaluate Letizia experimentally and so the two can not be empirically compared.

Neither Footprints nor Conceptual Cluster Mining are aimed at web personalization, but rather *optimization* (to use the terminology in [6]): based on an analysis of *all* user accesses, these systems make these modifications available to *any* subsequent visitor. Footprints identifies hyperlink paths that are frequently traversed, and suggests these paths to visitors. While some paths will inevitably be suboptimal, the intent is that eventually a set of useful paths will naturally emerge. Conceptual Cluster Mining involves automatically builds new *index pages* that contain hyperlinks to sets of documents that past visitors often tended to access together.

These systems represent interesting progress in self-adaptive web sites, but PWW and other personalization systems offer complementary services. While some "personalized" recommendations may be so useful as to merit displaying them to all visitors, we expect that other specialized recommendations will be relevant only to relatively few visitors. One possibility is a hybrid approach that mines lists of personalized recommendations rather than the server logs.

6   Conclusions

We are motivated by the problem of one-size-fits-all web design. Any non-trivial web attracts a variety of different visitors, and could therefore serve those visitors better if the information were tailored to their tastes and preferences.

This sort of automatic personalization is an ambitious goal, so (in common with much on-going research) we have focused on the more modest goal of recommending hyperlinks. We have focused specifically on how effective such recommendations can be when provided with no feedback or input from the user. We have describe a novel technique, referrer-based page recommendation, that makes effective recommendations over 9% of the time, quite respectable given the very little knowledge it has of visitors. RBPR estimates a visitor's information need based on his browsing context (specifically, his HTTP referrer URL), and uses standard information retrieval techniques to identify relevant pages. We are currently extending PWW is several ways. We are interested in personalizing both web *content* and *layout*. Doing so will require a structured model of the web site's content; we are investigating the use of information extraction techniques (e.g., [3]) to extract such structure. Using one page of browsing context is clearly inadequate in some cases. We are considering ways to incorporate additional evidence about a visitor's information needs while maintaining the zero-input constraint. Unfortunately, such extensions will require client-side cooperation, and we may find that the requirement to download additional software outweighs the benefits of better predictions. RBPR does not use any form of query term selection, but the information retrieval community has investigated this issue at length. While RBPR's performance could probably be improved substantially, we are currently investigating how to combine its recommendations with other techniques, such as collaborative filtering. As Joachims et al observe for WebWatcher [2], we expect that there is no single best recommendation technique, and so the most fruitful approach is to integrate the suggestions from multiple techniques. Finally, we are exploring the privacy issues related to web personalization. While PWW guarantees visitors' anonymity and uses only information available to any HTTP server, we observe that web users tend to react uncomfortably when "intelligent" user interfaces start behaving in unexpected ways.

Acknowledgements. This research was funded in part by grant N00014-00-1-0021 from the US Office of Naval Research, and grant ST/1999/071 from Enterprise Ireland.

References

[1] M. Balbanovic. An interface for learning multi-topic user profiles from implicit feedback. In *Proc. AAAI-98 Workshop on Recommender Systems*, 1998.

[2] T. Joachims, D. Feitag, and T. Mitchell. WebWatcher: A tour guide for the world wide web. In *Proc. 15th Int. Joint Conf. AI*, pages 770–777, 1997.

[3] N. Kushmerick, D. Weld, and R. Doorenbos. Wrapper Induction for Information Extraction. In *Proc. 15th Int. Joint Conf. AI*, pages 729–35, 1997.

[4] H. Lieberman. Letizia: An agent that assists web browsing. In *Proc. 14th Int. Joint Conf. AI*, pages 924–929, 1995.

[5] M. Pazzani, J. Muramatsu, and D. Billsus. Syskill & Webert: Identifying interesting web sites. In *Proc. 13th Nat. Conf. Artificial Intelligence*, pages 54–61, 1996.

[6] M. Perkowitz and O. Etzioni. Adaptive web sites: an AI challenge. In *Proc. 15th Int. Joint Conf. AI*, pages 16–23, 1997.

[7] M. Perkowitz and O. Etzioni. Adaptive web sites: Conceptual cluster mining. In *Proc. 16th Int. Joint Conf. AI*, pages 264–269, 1999.

[8] P. Resnick, I. Neophytos, S. Mitesh, P. Bergstrom, and J. Reidl. GroupLens: An open architecture for collaborative filtering of netnews. In *Proc 1994 Conf. Computer Supported Cooperative Work*, pages 175–186, 1994.

[9] E. Selberg and O. Etzioni.   Multi-service search and comparison using the metacrawler. In *Proc. 4th World Wide Web Conf.*, pages 195–208, 1995.

[10] U. Sharanand and P. Maes. Social information filtering: Algorithms for automating "word of mouth". In *Proc. 1995 Conf. Human Factors and Computing Systems*, pages 210–217, 1995.

[11] A. Wexelblat and P. Maes. Footprints: History-rich tools for information foraging. In *Proc. Conf. Human Factors and Computing Systems*, pages 270–277, 1999.

LiveInfo: Adapting Web Experience by Customization and Annotation

Paul P. Maglio and Stephen Farrell

IBM Almaden Research Center
650 Harry Road
San Jose, California 95120
{pmaglio,sfarrell}@almaden.ibm.com
http://www.almaden.ibm.com/cs/people/{pmaglio,sfarrell}

Abstract. Intermediaries are perfectly suited to customizing and annotating web pages, as they can stand in the flow of data between web browser and web server, monitoring user behavior and modifying page markup. In this paper, we present LiveInfo, an intermediary-based framework for customizing and annotating web pages. LiveInfo breaks customization and annotation into four steps: (a) splitting streaming data into useful chunks, (b) identifying meaningful patterns of chunks, (c) merging together overlapping patterns, and (d) adding markup to customize and annotate. Each of these steps is easily replaced or configured, making it simple to adapt web experience by customization and annotation.

1 Introduction

The World Wide Web (WWW) presents users with a particular view of information — the view that the information authors built into it. Systems for adapting the web to individual users or to groups of users can present different views of the available information. Many approaches for adapting the web are targeted at applications such as education, modifying what links appear on pages based on a user's skill [1,2]. Other approaches adapt web pages to a user's history of interaction with the web by adding links to pages that have been repeatedly visited [3,4]. A system for adapting web pages is a special case of an *attentive system* [5], as adapting web pages involves monitoring what web users see and modifying what web users see, effectively paying attention to what users do to attend to users' information needs. *Intermediaries* are particularly well-suited to adapting web pages, as they sit between an information consumer and an information producer, monitoring and modifying data that flow between them [6,7].

In this paper, we outline an intermediary-based approach for adapting a web user's experience through customization and annotation. In what follows, we first discuss intermediary computation in general, and then describe LiveInfo, our intermediary-based scheme for web page adaptation by customization and annotation.

P. Brusilovsky, O. Stock, C. Strapparava (Eds.): AH 2000, LNCS 1892, pp. 144–154, 2000.

2   Intermediaries

Intermediaries are a general class of computational entities that act on data flowing along an information stream [6,7]. In general, intermediaries sit along a data flow, possibly affecting the data that flow from some origin to some destination. In the case of TCP/IP computer networks, the abstract concept "intermediary" might be instantiated as a hypertext transfer protocol (HTTP) proxy server, which provides a specific point on the communication stream for adding function. Many other application-layer protocols support the addition of intermediary computation, including simple mail transfer protocol (SMTP), which can incorporate mail exchangers at specific points along the flow, and network news transfer protocol (NNTP), which involves peer-to-peer information transfer and so servers themselves can act as intermediaries.

At a low level, there are a variety of ways in which an intermediary might affect the flow of data (see Figure 1). In the simplest case, an intermediary might tunnel data through without having any effect on the data at all. Another basic intermediary function is filtering, which preserves the essential structure of the origin data, but removes or adds information to the stream. An intermediary can replace the origin data with data from a different source, or it can merge data from several different sources.

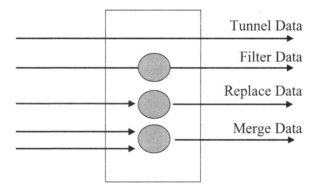

Fig. 1. An intermediary can perform many operations on data flowing through it.

At a higher level, an intermediary can perform a variety of functions. For HTTP streams, for instance, intermediary computation (e.g., by an HTTP proxy server) might be used to (a) customize content based on history of interaction of individual users [3,4], (b) annotate content with traffic lights to indicate network delay [3,8], (c) add awareness and interaction to enable collaboration with other users [9,10], (d) transcode data from one image type to another [11,12], (e) cache content, and (f) aggregate content from several sources. Thus, we distinguish six broad applications of intermediary computation: customization, annotation, collaboration, transcoding, caching, and aggregation. More precisely, we distinguish these intermediary functions by the kinds of information they take into account when performing their transformations. Customization takes into account information about the user or the user's environment when modifying data on the stream, for instance, adding links the user often visits. Annotation takes into account information about the world outside the user or user's environment, for instance, by determining link speed. Collaboration takes into account information about other users, for instance, what web page they are currently visiting. Transcoding takes into account information about the data's input and desired output format, for instance, transforming a JPEG to a GIF image. Caching takes into account when data were last stored or last changed. Aggregation takes into account a second data stream, for instance, merging results from several engines into a single page.

2.1   Customization and Annotation

Here, we focus on customization and annotation. As noted, these are distinguished from other sorts of intermediary functions by what the intermediary process takes into account. Customization uses information about the user to tailor the data flowing along the stream. For instance, the way many web-based shopping sites automatically fill out forms based on stored user profiles is a kind of customization (such as, Yahoo! Shopping[1]). In adaptive hypertext, one common customization is to incrementally add links to pages based on a student's familiarity with a course, for example, allowing the student access to more advanced material only after the student has a certain amount of experience with less advanced material (e.g., [1]). In the case of automatic form-filling, the web is customized based on an explicit profile provided by the user. In the case of adaptive courseware, pages are customized based on a model of the user gathered implicitly from user activities (see also [2]).

Annotation relies on information about the world outside the user to tailor data flowing along the stream. For instance, many web systems have been constructed to annotate hyperlinks on web pages with visual indications of how popular or well-traveled the link is (e.g., [13,14]). Others have used auditory annotations to convey a link's popularity [15] or how long it takes to download [16]. Still others have annotated links to network news articles with ratings [17] or links to search results with visual indications of relevance along certain dimensions [18]. In all cases, annotations are derived from information about the document, its history of use, its server, and so on.

Of course, customization and annotation can be combined by an intermediary process that takes account of both information about the user and information about the world outside the user when tailoring the data stream. Taken together, customization and annotation can do more than the two taken independently,

---

[1] http://shopping.yahoo.com/

as annotations can be customized and customizations can be annotated. For instance, adaptive courseware might customize pages to users' abilities, removing and adding text and links as appropriate, and then added links might be annotated with information about the difficultly of the linked-to material (cf. [2]), resulting in annotated customization.

2.2 Web Intermediaries (WBI)

The Web Intermediaries (WBI) Development Kit[2] is an implemented Java framework for adding intermediary functions to the WWW [6,7,3]. WBI is a programmable proxy server designed for easy development and deployment of intermediary applications. Using WBI, intermediary applications are constructed from four basic building blocks: request editors, generators, document editors, and monitors. We refer to these collectively as MEGs, for Monitors, Editors, Generators. Monitors observe transactions without affecting them. Editors modify outgoing requests or incoming documents. Generators produce documents in response to requests. WBI dynamically constructs a data path through the various MEGs for each transaction. To configure the route for a particular request, WBI has a rule associated with each MEG that specifies a boolean condition indicating whether the MEG should be involved in a transaction based on header information about the request or response. An application (WBI plugin) is composed of a number of MEGs that operate in concert to produce a new function.

One way WBI can customize web pages is by adding links to pages frequently visited by a particular user [4]. Because web users rely on routines and standard behaviors to access information, WBI's "Short Cuts" plugin adds links to pages that a user routinely visits shortly after visiting the current page. This plugin uses a monitor to build up a database of pages that a user visits, and a document editor to add links when there are pages in the database that the user habitually visits within some number of links from the current page.

One way WBI can annotate web pages is by adding extra information about the hyperlinks on a page, such as the speed of downloading information from a particular site [3]. WBI's "Traffic Lights" plugin uses a document editor to add green, yellow, and red images next to hyperlinks to inform the user that responses from the server on the other end of that link is fast, slower, or slowest. It turns out that people can effectively use these traffic images to help themselves decide which links to follow [8].

3 LiveInfo Framework

LiveInfo is a WBI plugin for customizing and annotating hypertext markup language (HTML) data. It provides a mechanism for transforming "interesting" words or phrases into visually distinct hyperlinks. When followed, these LiveInfo links pop up a non-disruptive, floating window that contains more information

---

[2] http://www.almaden.ibm.com/cs/wbi/

about the hyperlinked word or phrase. In one example, an IBM employee's name appearing in a web page from the `ibm.com` domain is transformed into a hyperlink with a pale blue background. When clicked, this link will pop up summary data for that person from the IBM-internal directory, including phone number, email address, and so on (see Figure 2).

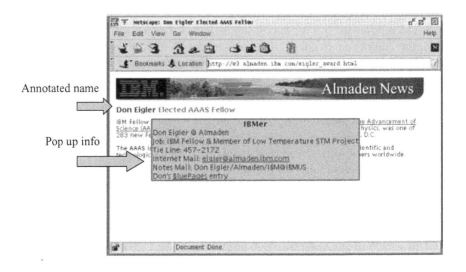

Fig. 2. Web page showing annotation of IBM employee name, and a pop up window showing employee data.

Annotating web pages with hyperlinks is not new (see GuruNet[3], flyswat[4] and Wordbot[5]), but such previous systems were inflexible. For example, GuruNet and flyswat are tied to browser-specific plugins as well as proprietary and non-extensible content sources. By contrast, LiveInfo was designed to be client-neutral and to allow content to be extended. This flexibility is achieved with an open, pluggable architecture built on the WBI application programming interface (API)[6]. In particular, the logic for recognizing and annotating items in a document can be loaded and unloaded dynamically, allowing a user or organization to select and create custom data analyzers and annotaters.

---

[3] http://www.gurunet.com/
[4] http://www.flyswat.com/
[5] http://www.wordbot.com/
[6] http://www.almaden.ibm.com/cs/wbi/doc/

3.1 Architecture and Implementation

LiveInfo's annotation process is broken down into four steps: chunking, analyzing, coalescing, and marking up. Each of these steps constitutes a pluggable component of the LiveInfo framework (see Figure 3). LiveInfo first breaks the incoming data stream into potentially useful pieces or chunks (e.g., words, phrases, or paragraphs). These chunks are then analyzed to find relevant items (e.g., employee names or phone numbers). Overlapping items are then merged (or coalesced) so that the document can be annotated and reconstructed. Finally, markup is added to the document based on items that have been identified.

More precisely, processing in LiveInfo proceeds as follows: First, an HTML document is split into discrete chunks based on the policy implemented in the **Chunker**. Second, **Analyzers** are run to find interesting items within the chunks (e.g., names are identified). **Analyzers** also associate metadata with items. In this case, metadata for an item include the item's type and a key that can be used for subsequent lookups. The third step, the **Coalescer**, resolves overlapping items by merging them into either a single item or groups of items. Finally, the **Markupper** combines chunks with markup based on the items and their metadata, and eventually the results are written onto the output stream.

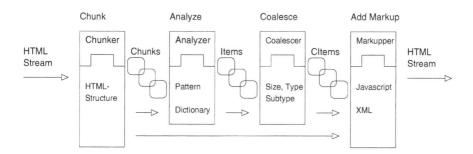

Fig. 3. Flow of processing in LiveInfo plugin.

Our design of the LiveInfo framework was motivated by concern for performance and flexibility. Performance is essential because LiveInfo modifies the data stream before returning to the user. To minimize response times, LiveInfo (a) uses streaming rather than buffering of the data source, (b) communicates with components through simple method calls, and (c) analyzes data in chunks rather than term-by-term.

There are two dimensions of flexibility that our design addresses. First, we wanted to allow programmers to create (and allow users to choose) different algorithms for recognizing which terms and phrases are interesting. Second, we wanted to experiment with various solutions to the following three problems: (a) how to break up the document into meaningful blocks or chunks, (b) how to produce a well-formed document in the case of overlapping items, (c) how to create an appropriate user experience. The four steps chosen—chunking, analyzing, coalescing, and marking up—allow us to try out different solutions to these problems rapidly and independently of one another.

We now discuss each of the four pluggable components in turn.

Chunker. The `Chunker` sits in the data stream, transforming bytes that flow past it into "chunks" of data. Each chunk consists of a plain text portion, the corresponding node from the document structure tree, and an association between the two. The `Analyzers` will process the plain text portion, and the `Markupper` will ultimately combine the results of the `Analyzers`, the parsed document node, and the association between the text and the node to construct the modified document.

The simplest `Chunker` implementation flattens the parsed document tree and returns chunks representing the text between HTML tags. This approach is susceptible to producing chunks that are too large (e.g., a large document with little or no markup) or too small (e.g., a single sentence which contains several tags, such as `<b>...</b>`). If chunks are too large, space-efficiency might suffer, buffering the entire document in the worst case. If chunks are too small, meaningful sets of terms (e.g., an address) might be split into multiple chunks, precluding proper analysis. For example, one might write `19 <b>Bridge</b> Road` to emphasize the word "Bridge" in an address. An `Analyzer` might recognize "19 Bridge Road" as a street address, but will not be able to infer the same meaning from the three separate strings "19", "Bridge" and "Road".

A better approach might be to divide the document based on grammatical structures, such as sentences and paragraphs. This technique is likely to preserve meaningful term constructs (e.g., a date, address, name), as well as provide a reasonable upper-bound on chunk size (e.g., the algorithm might count n paragraphs, sentences, or words).

Analyzer. `Analyzers` do the interesting work of finding useful terms or phrases within text. HTML markup is fully abstracted away from the analysis code: analyzers are passed plain, untagged text, and later stages of the LiveInfo process are responsible for reconstructing the markup. This design makes it easier to use text analysis engines that may not have been designed with HTML data in mind. Any text analysis engine (e.g., [19]) can be plugged into LiveInfo by writing a wrapper for it that implements the `Analyzer` interface. `Analyzers` return their result as a list of `Items` that contains the extents (where the item begins and where the item ends) and metadata for each interesting portion of text.

Two useful specializations of the `Analyzer` interface are (a) pattern matching and (b) multi-term dictionary. Generic code was written to simplify the writing these sorts of analyzers. For pattern matching, a regular expression library detects items such as phone numbers, uniform resource locators (URLs), email addresses, currency, and so on. Regular expression matching can also be used to minimize the frequency of expensive operations. For example, our name recognition algorithm for the employee directory example comprises three steps: (a) the regular expression engine searches for pairs of capitalized words, possibly separated by a single capitalized letter and a period; (b) the first name is compared against a list of known first names or the first and last name are compared against a list of known non-name words; and (c) an LDAP query is issued to confirm that the discovered pair of names is in fact in the directory.

An alternative to the pattern-matching specialization is the multi-term dictionary. In contrast to a dynamic lookup scheme that relies on regular expressions, the multi-term dictionary provides a way of building a set of key words and phrases into the `Analyzer`.

Coalescer. The `Coalescer` implements the policy for handling overlapping items. The problem with overlapping items is that only a single item can be annotated or customized at a time. If several items overlap, it is not clear which of the items should be treated as distinct. For example, the following string contains overlapping items,

> `...send a note to Stephen Farrell/Almaden/IBM and...`

including the name "Stephen Farrell", the Lotus Notes address "Stephen Farrell/Almaden/IBM", and the stock symbol "IBM". Note that the first two are the same kind of thing: a person. Given a choice, the user might prefer the more specific match. However, the "IBM" symbol is a different kind of thing, and the fact that it is located within another recognized item (a Lotus Notes address) should not prevent the user from learning more about it.

There are several ways to handle overlapping items. The first might be called "exclude-on-overlap", in which a particular item dominates, presumably based upon some prioritizing scheme or by the size of the match. The problem with this approach is that the information gathered by the other items is lost. Another possibility is "retain-overlaps", in which all of the items are retained and the work is passed to the next step of the process. One flaw of this approach is that the resulting structure will not be a tree in the case of strict overlaps, and thus the resulting document will be invalid. Another concern is that it is difficult to represent the overlaps to the user; one might imagine blending colors or hatch patterns.

Another approach, "coalesce-on-overlap", merges all of the overlapping items and their metadata into a single, coalesced item. This approach retains all of the information while at the same time ensuring a proper tree structure. There are still some problems, however. In the case of "Stephen Farrell" and "Stephen Farrell/Almaden/IBM", the user is handed both person identifiers, and in this case one is definitely better than the other (as there are many Stephen Farrells at IBM). Another problem is the case of the largest item being much larger than the contained item. For example, if a whole paragraph of one hundred words is matched as well as several individual words within that paragraph, then the position of the words within the paragraph is lost.

A good policy might be a hybrid of exclude-on-overlap and coalesce-on-overlap: If overlapping items are from the same analyzer (i.e., are the same kind of thing), the one with the largest extents is chosen. If items are from separate analyzers, they are coalesced. In the current example, this means that of the two items recognized by the Bluepages analyzer, the name "Stephen Farrell" is discarded, but the Notes address is retained. Because the stock symbol "IBM" came from a different analyzer, it is added to the coalesced item and can be shown as another menu item in the user interface.

Markupper. The `Markupper` is responsible for generating `begin` and `end` tags for each interesting item or coalesced set of items the system has encountered, as well as for combining these tags with the original parsed document to produce a well-formed result. To generate appropriate `begin` and `end` tags, a `Markupper` implementation might use XML to produce machine readable content, or Javascript to produce a floating-window user interface. To create the document written onto the output stream, the `Markupper` merges the tags it has added with the original parsed document nodes. Because overlaps can occur between recognized items and original document markup, the `Markupper` must be prepared to split tags. For example, the HTML construct `<b>not Stephen</b> Farrell, but...` might become `<b>not</b> <liveinfo...><b>Stephen</b> Farrell</liveinfo>, but...`

If the `Markupper` produces a user interface that relies on a Javascript-based interface like that shown in Figure 2, it must also provide a WBI generator to render the contents of the floating window. As this content is only generated on demand, this step can be more expensive than the initial annotation of the document. In this case, the contents of the corporate directory entry can be displayed.

3.2 Customization and Annotation

The LiveInfo framework can be used to customize or annotate web pages. The corporate directory plugin (shown in Figure 2) is an example of annotating web pages with information from the outside world, namely employee data. Another example of annotation would be a LiveInfo plugin that turns ordinary words on web pages into hyperlinks that point to their definitions as found in some web-based dictionary. In this case, the `DictionaryAnalyzer` would use a list of all terms found in some external dictionary, and the `Markupper` would add links to this external definition to fill the pop up window with the definition.

The same approach can be used to customize web pages, for instance, by relying on a user's explicitly created profile when adding annotations to a page. In this case, the user might create a list of words or phrases that he or she is particularly interested in noticing on web pages. The `Analyzer` would use this list as its basis for discovering terms, and the `Markupper` might simply highlight these terms in a bright color. Another example of using LiveInfo to customize web experience relies on analyzing term-frequencies of words encountered on pages the user regularly visits. In this case, the `Analyzer` might use as input high frequency terms, and the `Markupper` would link these terms to previously encountered pages with similar term-frequency distributions.

The LiveInfo framework can also be used to customize annotations. For example, any of the annotations schemes we have described, such as the corporate directory or the dictionary, can be customized so that the user can select how the annotations are displayed. Our examples have focused on inline annotations, but a user may prefer to see these in a pop up window or in the header or footer of the page. In this way, users can customize how annotations are presented.

4   Summary

Customization and annotation are two broad methods for adapting web pages beyond the structure and information that was designed or authored into them. Intermediary-based computation provides one clear approach to adapting web pages in these ways. In this paper, we have presented the LiveInfo framework, an intermediary-based approach to web page customization and annotation. LiveInfo breaks the process into four easily replaceable steps: (a) splitting the input data into chunks, (b) identifying patterns of chunks, (c) merging overlapping patterns, and (d) adding markup that customizes and annotates.

Acknowledgments

Thanks to Rob Barrett, Steve Ihde, and Jörg Meyer for all manner of practical and philosophical support. Thanks to Andreas Dieberger for helpful conversations on this topic. Thanks to Teenie Matlock and three anonymous reviewers for many helpful comments on a draft of this paper.

References

1. DeBra, P., and Calvi, L. Towards a generic adaptive hypermedia system. In *Proceedings of the Second Workshop on Adaptive Hypertext and Hypermedia* (1998), pp. 5–11.
2. Brusilovsky, P. Methods and techniques for adaptive hypermedia. *User-Modeling and User-Adpatped Interaction 6* (1996).
3. Barrett, R., Maglio, P. P., and Kellem, D. C. How to personalize the web. In *Proceedings of the Conference on Human Factors in Computer Systems (CHI '97)* (New York, NY, 1997), ACM Press.
4. Maglio, P. P., and Barrett, R. How to build modeling agents to support web searchers. In *Proceedings of the Sixth International Conference on User Modeling* (New York, NY, 1997), Springer Wien.
5. Maglio, P. P., Barrett, R., and Campbell, C. S.and Selker, T. Suitor: An attentive information system. In *Proceedings of the International Conference on Intelligent User Interfaces 2000* (New Orleans, LA, 2000), ACM Press.
6. Barrett, R., and Maglio, P. P. Intermediaries: New places for producing and manipulating web content. In *Proceedings of the Seventh International World Wide Web Conference (WWW7)* (1998).
7. Barrett, R., and Maglio, P. P. Intermediaries: An approach to manipulating information streams. *IBM Systems Journal 38* (1999), 629–641.

8. Campbell, C. S., and Maglio, P. P. Facilitating navigation in information spaces: Road signs on the world wide web. *International Journal of Human-Computer Studies 50* (1999), 309–327.

9. Maglio, P. P., and Barrett, R. Adaptive communities and web places. In *Second Workshop on Adaptive Hypertext and Hypermedia* (1998), P. Brusilovsky and P. DeBra, Eds.

10. Maglio, P. P., and Barrett, R. Webplaces: Adding people to the web. In *Poster Proceedings of the Eighth International World Wide Web Conference* (1999).

11. Fox, A., and Brewer, E. A. Reducing www latency and bandwidth requirements by real-time distillation. In *Proceedings of the Fifth International World Wide Web Conference (WWW5)* (1996).

12. Ihde, S., Maglio, P. P., Meyer, J., and Barrett, R. Intermediary-based transcoding framework. In *Poster Proceedings of of the Ninth International World Wide Web Conference* (2000).

13. Dieberger, A., and Lonnqvist, P. Visualizing interaction history on a collaborative web server. In *Hypertext 2000* (San Anotnio, TX, 2000), ACM Press.

14. Wexelblat, A., and Maes, P. Footprints: History-rich tools for information foraging. In *Proceedings of the Conference on Human Factors in Computing Systems (CHI '99)* (Pittsburgh, PA, 1999), ACM Press, pp. 270–277.

15. Dieberger, A. A sonification enhanced navigation tool for history-enriched information spaces. In *International Conference on Auditory Displays (ICAD '2000)* (2000).

16. Albers, M., and Bergman, E. The audible web: Auditory enhancements for mosaic. In *CHI'95 - Conference Companion* (Denver, CO, 1995), ACM Press, pp. 318–319.

17. Konstan, J. A., Miller, B. N., Maltz, D., Herlocker, J. L., Gordon, L. R., and Riedl, J. Grouplens: Applying collaborative filtering to usenet news. *Communications of the ACM 40* (1997), 77–87.

18. Hearst, M. A. Tilebars: Visualization of term distribution information in full text information access. In *Proceedings of the Conference on Human Factors in Computing Systems (CHI '95)* (Denver, CO, 1995), ACM Press, pp. 59–66.

19. Boguraev, B., and Kennedy, C. Applications of term identification technology: Domain description and content characterization. *Natural Language Engineering 1* (1998), 1–28.

Adaptivity for Conceptual and Narrative Flow in Hyperbooks: The MetaLinks System [§]

Tom Murray [1]
Tina Shen [1]
Janette Piemonte [2]
Chris Condit [2]
Jason Thibedeau [1]

[1] Computer Science Department, [2] Department of Geosciences, [3] School of Education
University of Massachusetts, Amherst, MA
tmurray@cs.umass.edu, www.cs.umass.edu/~tmurray, (413) 559-5433

Abstract: In this paper we discuss MetaLinks, a framework and authoring tool for web-based adaptive hyper-books. We focus on how features of the system address the problem issues of disorientation, cognitive overload, discontinuous flow (poor narrative flow or poor conceptual flow), and content non-readiness.

1 The Tension Between the Linear vs. Associative Natures of Electronic Books

Innovations in computing have been altering the way that we author, access, and use information for several decades. Technologies such as hypermedia are blurring the distinctions between textbooks, reference books, and databases, and are introducing new forms of documents that are combinations of and extensions to these traditional forms. Specifically, three technological innovations are behind our reconceptualization of "the book" and related artifacts: the random access provided by hypermedia links and database storage, the universal access provided by the internet, and the computer's ability to customize content for each reader and situation. These innovations have allowed the creation of electronic textbooks, hypermedia documents, highly useable data bases, and web sites (terms not exclusive of one another). All of these forms typically contain hyper-linking and searching features that allow the user to immediately access any part (or many parts) of the information space from any other part. The various forms *differ* in where they fall along the spectrum of text-like narrative to database-like non-narrative information. The focus of this research is on quasi-narrative content authored for instructional or illustrative purposes.

[§] This work was supported by the Office of Naval Research ASSERT grant no. ONR/N00014-97-1-0815, and the National Science Foundation's CCD program grant no. NSF DUE-9652993. We would like to thank Saunders College Publishing for the use of content from their introductory geology text book [1].

P. Brusilovsky, O. Stock, C. Strapparava (Eds.): AH 2000, LNCS 1892, pp. 155-166, 2000.

It has become common belief that it is of little use to convert a textbook into electronic form without taking advantage of the hypermedia and interactivity afforded by the new medium. The "electronic page turner" is an underachieving artifact, a poor application of the technology and ignorant of its potential. Electronic books (or "hyper-books") can correctly be called a subset of hypermedia. Our working definition of hypermedia is the standard notion of chunks of content (nodes) with hyperlinks between them [2]. What distinguishes electronic textbooks from other forms of hypermedia, including the world-wide web (WWW)? Unlike heterogeneous multi-authored collections of documents like the WWW, electronic textbooks are designed (authored) with a coherent purpose in mind.[1] They constitute a cohesive information space or narrative space with a particular structure, focussing on a conscripted subject area. Electronic textbooks are designed for the purpose of learning or studying a subject area, unlike fictional or entertainment hypermedia. Our concern is with any electronic document that has these properties. Also, though interactivity and feedback are key aspects of digital technology as applied to educational material, our discussion is limited to the more passive reading, searching, and browsing of educational material. Though reading and browsing are mundane activities compared to the possibilities inherent to electronic learning environments such as intelligent tutors and simulations, there are important issues related to these limited activities. Reading and browsing currently comprise most of the time spent in educational multimedia and in educational uses of the WWW.

Though this definition of electronic textbooks is simple, it highlights two aspects whose divergent implications lead to our research issues: the purposeful structuring of the material for multiple uses, and its educational or informative purpose. Hyper-books consist of quasi-independent units of material (pages) linked in ways which allow multiple uses and perspectives. In addition, hyper-books are not just reference collections of information or knowledge, they are designed to move or encourage a learner along a path toward increased understanding. It is desirable for the learner's experience to have felicity in both narrative flow and conceptual flow. Flow implies linear motion. The interplay between the necessarily linear acts of reading and learning, and the associative (non-linear) nature of both electronic mediums and human memory, provides a tension that is at the heart of our research concerns. Luckin et al. ([3], page 1) observes that "the very nature of the medium...also results in a deconstruction of the narrative which is normally present in [instructional] media...The narrative can be suspended or altered and may thwart of confuse our expectations."

A number of benefits have been identified in the shift from traditional to electronic books. Hyper-books can be authored to contain alternative structures, content, and navigation paths that emphasize different goals, skill levels, or perspectives ([4] [5] [6]) . Learners have the ability to navigate through the content in ways that match their goals, interests, and learning styles. The learning experience can be more learner-centered and interactive, as learners actively create their learning trajectories in ways not easily done with traditional books.

Both the potential benefits and the known difficulties with hyper-books have lead researchers to implement a number of adaptive and intelligent software features

---

[1] Of course hyper-books exist *on* the WWW. But here WWW refers to heterogeneous, organically structured collections of documents.

([2] [7]). *Adaptive* hypermedia documents are composed "on the fly," so that the content, style, and/or sequencing of the pages is customized to the needs of the particular learner and situation ([8] [9] [10]). As mentioned, several potential problems arise in the shift from traditional to electronic books, essentially stemming from the ability to link (or "jump" or "go") from one "location" to another, and related to the tension between the linear/narrative and non-linear/associative natures of hyper-books. Research has substantively documented the existence of three problems for which adaptivity might provide a solution: disorientation, cognitive overload, and discontinuous flow ([2] [3] [11] [12] [13]). **Disorientation** refers to users not knowing where they are, where they have been, or how to get to where they want to go in hypermedia space. **Cognitive overload** refers to users being overwhelmed or confused by the options available to them in multi-path, multi-tool environments such as hypermedia documents. We separate the problem of discontinuous flow into two issues: narrative flow and conceptual flow. **Narrative flow** refers to the didactic or dialogical flow of the text itself. **Conceptual flow** refers to the flow of ideas or concepts.[2] To this list of issues we add **content readiness**, which is the traditional intelligent tutoring systems goal of tailoring content so that the student is neither bored because it is too easy, nor overwhelmed because it is too difficult (i.e. remaining within the learner's "zone of proximal development").[3]

In this paper we will describe the MetaLinks system, an adaptive hyper-book architecture, web server, and authoring tool (see [14] for a more detailed description of the architecture). We will describe how the adaptive and non-adaptive features of MetaLinks relate to the problems of disorientation, cognitive overload, discontinuous flow (poor narrative flow or poor conceptual flow), and content non-readiness. We have used the MetaLinks framework to author a web based hyper-book called Tectonica Interactive in the domain of introductory geology. Tectonica Interactive, with approximately 400 pages and 500 graphics, has undergone three rounds of formative evaluation [15]. Figure 1 shows a page from Tectonica Interactive.

Learner's goals in navigating through hypermedia material vary along a spectrum from convergent or "finding" goals through divergent or "exploratory" goals [16] [17]. MetaLinks contains tools that support both types of user goals, but was designed specifically to support behavior called inquiry-based, discovery, or exploratory. Exploratory navigation is appropriate for open-ended questions and/or learning in ill-structured domains in which the richness of the content suggests multiple themes, perspectives, or learning paths [5]. Also, inquiry-based learning methods involve initial stages of articulating and refining the driving question and then exploring potential sources of information before narrowing down an information search [18]. Both convergent and exploratory navigation behaviors can result in disorientation, cognitive overload, discontinuous flow, and content non-

---

[2] To clarify the difference, one could imagine a text with a good conceptual flow which was poorly written and choppy, thus having poor narrative flow. Similarly one could imagine text that seemed to read very smoothly but did not make rational sense, or in which prerequisite concepts were not introduced sufficiently for understanding the text, and thus the text has poor conceptual flow.
[3] Conceptual flow and content readiness are closely related since adapting for both involves reasoning with topic difficulties and prerequisites.

readiness, but these problems are more severe for exploratory learning behaviors because they tend to be less systematic and direct by nature.

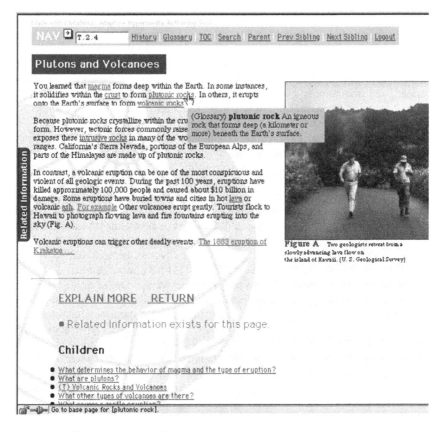

Figure 1: Tectonica Interactive page T.2.4, with a picture showing two geologists running from a lava flow.

2 MetaLinks System Description

MetaLinks content is stored in a relational database (using web-enabled FileMaker Pro) and requires only a web browser for delivery (we make heavy use of JavaScript and Dynamic HTML in the implementation).[4] Because a MetaLinks hyper-book's content and all of its navigation tools are created and web-delivered on the fly, and since we maintain a record of every student action (including page visits and tool use), we have complete flexibility to adapt the content and its sequencing for each user. To address the problem issues described above we considered a number of

---

[4] To author a MetaLinks document, only FileMaker (available cross-platform) is needed (plus any graphics programs needed to prepare figures).

software features: Adaptive navigation support using history-based and prerequisite-based link annotation (similar to [8]); Adaptive content, (using methods similar to [19] [10]); Adaptive sequencing (as in [20]); Adaptive navigation maps (as in [21]); and Coached inquiry (supporting learner goals of broadening, breadth and coverage, completeness, efficiency, and readiness, using path analysis methods similar to those used in [22]). Our initial implementation is aimed at providing powerful user interface tools, with very modest adaptivity and intelligence. We want to leave the locus of control and locus of intelligence with the user as much as possible, and supplement with machine control or intelligence if a need is demonstrated.

MetaLinks has a "full-featured" user interface. Our primary grant funding is through a curriculum development grant that requires us to aim toward creating web-based Earth Science software that is usable and useful in high school and introductory college classrooms. We include many software features for reasons of usability or because users might expect some features based on their use of other web-based software or web sites. Also, early observations (see [23]) indicated that students had quite a variety of styles and needs, and that a similar variety of features was needed. The software has a full range of features because of these pragmatic goals, even though the inclusion of these features was not directly relevant to our main research questions, and their inclusion made it more difficult to analyze the data. Test subjects were familiarized with the following navigation and orientation tools/features, and data was collected about the use of each item in this "MetaLinks Navigation and Orientation Feature List" (see Murray et al. 1999 for a description of the software architecture).

- Table of Contents (TOC), Graphical TOC, Search
- Custom Depth Control (Explain More, Next Page/Return buttons)
- Go to parent, Go to child, Go to next/prev sibling, Direct to page number
- Glossary, Glossary base page
- Annotated History
- Go to Related Page (with a variety of typed links, as explained below)

In addition to the navigation and orientation features above, MetaLinks pages are adapted using features called stretch-text and narrative smoothing. Below we explain those features that are relevant to the issues of disorientation, cognitive overload, discontinuous flow, and content readiness. Following this description we will highlight which features are adaptive (vs. passive or canned).

1. **Annotated Table of Contents**. Content in MetaLinks hyper-books has a primarily hierarchical organization. The **disorientation** issue is addressed by providing a hierarchical TOC page that shows where students have visited, and where the current page is ("you are here"). In addition each page lists its "children" pages at the bottom. Pages are also numbered to show their place in the hierarchy, for example 4.5.6.2 is a sibling of 4.5.6.3. We have also implemented a "pictorial table of contents" feature that allows the use of an "image map" with hot spots to show a graphical portrayal of a section of the hyper-book.

2. **Stretch Text**. Non-essential text and graphics such as examples and footnotes can be hidden inside "stretch text" (really "stretch media"). Stretch text is colored green, and when the user passes the mouse over stretch text the hidden text (or graphics) pops up adjacent to the green text, and disappears when the mouse is moved away from the green text. We also use stretch-text to imbed the glossary definitions of all glossary terms (see Figure 1). Using this method the user can choose whether to see additional detail. It serves the same function as adaptive content (Brusilovsky 1998) but lets the learner decide what will appear. This feature addresses the **content readiness** issue. It also helps with the **cognitive overload** issue by reducing the amount of content visible on the page.

3. **Glossary base pages**. The terse definitions that pop up in the stretch text of glossary terms may not be enough to alleviate the learner's ignorance about a concept. If the user *clicks* on a glossary term they navigate to its "base page," which is the page in the hyper-book that best explains that concept. This feature addresses the **content readiness** issue. It also addresses the **conceptual flow** issues by allowing learners to easily learn about prerequisite concepts. Base pages also address the cognitive overload issue by anchoring starting points for exploration.

4. **Horizontal reading**. The default narrative flow (a linear navigation path for which the reading or organization of the content is most natural or perspicuous) in MetaLinks hyper-books differs from text books and other hyper-books -- it is breadth-first rather than depth-first, and organized for "horizontal reading." The default "next" page is the sibling page. Thus the default is to continue reading at the same level of generality. The children of any page cover the material at greater depth. Horizontal reading addresses the **narrative flow** issue in providing a framework in which the author can add more depth to any topic without having to rewrite the narrative. In contrast, in normal books adding more depth requires, in effect, inserting pages into the narrative.

5. **Custom Depth Control**. Horizontal reading sets the stage for an innovation called "custom depth control," which addresses the problem of **cognitive overload.** It has been shown that some users of hyper-books are overwhelmed by the navigation options and are happy to navigate by limiting their navigation to pressing the Next and Back buttons [20]. We call such users "two-button users." Custom depth control is a simple technique which gives two-button users (and all users) much greater control while not significantly increasing the complexity of the interaction (it still involves only two buttons). In MetaLinks the Next and Back buttons in traditional hyper-books are replaced with Explain More and Next buttons. "Next" goes to the next page which, as explained above, continues at the same level of generality. "Explain More" begins a path across the children of the current page. When the last child in a sibling sequence is reached the Next button becomes a Return button, and the user is returned to the parent page where they originally pressed the Explain More button.[5] Thus, the user has continuous control over whether they want to continue at the same level or delve into more detail on the current topic.

---

[5] Actually, Explain More pushes the children of the current page onto an agenda mechanism and Next pops the top item from the agenda. The agenda mechanism allows the user to go off on tangential paths and return to where they left off, for instance mid-way through viewing a sibling sequence.

6. **Narrative smoothing**. We have a simple but elegant partial solution to the **narrative flow** problem. Each page has associated with it an "intro text" paragraph. This paragraph eases the reader into the subject of the page, giving a little background or introduction. If the user jumps to that page in a non-standard way, the intro-text is pre-pended to the main text of the page. As explained above, MetaLinks is unusual in that the standard flow of text is breadth first.

7. **Typed Non-hierarchical Links**. As mentioned, the primary organizational structure for MetaLinks hyper-books is the hierarchy, as reified by the TOC. However, hierarchies do not capture the conceptual richness of most domains. Each concept is related to others in numerous ways. There are multiple perspectives on the material, suggesting multiple learning paths. From a given topic or page the most useful or interesting next topic will differ for different learners. MetaLinks includes (non-hierarchical) links called Related Links in addition to the hierarchical child and parent links between pages. Each page has a set of Related Links to other pages. These links are "typed" or categorized to indicate the type of relationship they represent. The authoring tool provides a list of possible link types, but the author can create her own types for each hyper-book or domain. Here are some of the approximately 20 link types we use in Techtonica Interactive: Where in the world?, Are scientists sure?, Famous catastrophes!, Historical Background, How is it measured? Related Links address the issue of **Conceptual Flow**. They allow the learner to maintain a path through the material that matches their curiosity and inquiry goals. Figure 2 shows the Related Links, group by link type, that appear in a pop-out menu.

8. **Annotated History**. The typed links allow us to provide an "annotated navigation history" that helps with the "where have I been?" **disorientation** issue. The list of visited links is annotated with the type of link, i.e. the "reason" they went there. This makes it easier for users to go back to where they left off after going down one or a series of tangents to their main exploration goal. They can visually see the difference between going to a "next" page, vs. diving down for more information, vs. jumping off on a tangential link. When they want to go "back to where I was" they may want to retrace to the last tangent or perhaps recover their path back at an earlier tangent, and the annotated navigation history provides information that allows them to make such decisions.

9. **Inquisitory Page Titles**. To support our goal of inquiry based and exploratory navigation, MetaLinks pages have an in inquisitory title in addition to the regular title. For example the page T.2.1.1.1, titled "Earth's Layers: The Crust," has a question title "What are the properties of the earth's crust?". Another page with a related link to T.2.1.1.1 will have "What are the properties of the crust?" as the link text (see Figure 2 for inquisitory links). As mentioned above, the typed links anticipate prototypical questions that might arise in the reader's mind, and add conceptual structure to the information space. Using inquisitory titles gives the navigational interaction a conversational feeling, adding to the **Narrative Flow** of the experience. Upon navigating to a page that addressees one question, new links answering new questions are available, giving the interaction a feeling of a question and answer dialog.

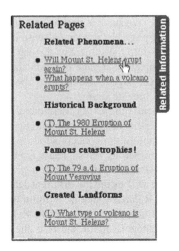

Figure 2: The Related Links pop-out menu for Page T.2.4.

The following table summarizes how the features relate to the issues:

	Disorien- tation	Cognitv. overload	Narrative flow	Con.Flow/ readiness
Annotated TOC	√			
Stretch text		√		√
Gloss. base pages		√		√
Horizontal reading			√	
Custom depth		√		
Narrat. smoothing			√	
Related links				√
Annotated history	√			
Inquisitory pg title			√	

Table 1: Features vs. Hypermedia issues

3 Relation to Previous Work

Our solutions to the issues of cognitive overload and disorientation are not particularly innovative, as they are variations of techniques seen elsewhere. The main contributions of this architecture include horizontal reading, custom depth control, narrative smoothing, and annotated history. It is important to note that one of the primary contributions of this work, one that is not the focus of this paper, is the authoring tool. We provide a highly usable graphical interface for authoring all aspects of MetaLinks books, and tools which automate many features (such as the creation of the TOC and glossary links). Our representational framework has been purposefully limited to features which can be easily portrayed in the GUI and authored by anyone with minimal training (one hour). All of the features mentioned above come practically "for free" when the author enters the text and graphics, and defines links between pages.

Innovative features of MetaLinks were described above, and here we relate MetaLinks to other systems. Using typed links that structure the information space according to a fixed set of common issues, questions, or themes, was inspired by ASK systems ([4]). Such conceptual structuring of the information space aides both user and author in creating a mental model of the semantic space with appropriate expectations for how things can be related. The use of inquisitory page titles for adding a conversational feeling to navigation was inspired by the inquisitory link types used in ASK systems[6]. ASK systems are not adaptive however, and have no user history or model.

The MetaLinks design was also influenced by the designs of InterBook and Elm-ART. We have a similar goal of helping students find an optimal path through content (i.e. maximize conceptual flow). MetaLinks maintains a user history but makes no inferences about student knowledge, and thus does not contain a working "student model." Actually, we have implemented a mechanism similar to InterBook's ([8]) which uses glossary concepts with prerequisite links as a domain model/concept network, and we have the ability to create an overlay student model using this network. However, unlike InterBook, for the time being we have decided not to include user tasks or quizzes in our hyperbooks, and thus the only information we have about the user is the navigation history. Because we have typed links, our navigation history tells us something about *why* a user navigated as well as *where* she navigated to and how long she spent on each page. We feel that this gives us substantially more information about the user. However, it is still not enough to make sufficiently confident inferences about the user to create an overlay model of user "knowledge." Thus, we currently annotate pages according to whether they have been visited, but not whether they are "known" or "ready to be learned." We side with the InterBook notion of giving users information and choices about where (and why) they can/should navigate, rather than automatically sequencing pages for them. In our tests so far we have found that making glossary definition pop-ups and links to glossary base pages allows users to acquire background and prerequisite information as needed.

MetaLinks seems to be the only hypermedia system (adaptive or not) to have a full featured GUI authoring system. InterBook addresses authoring by allowing tagged text to be imported from word processing files. The AHA system ([10]) addresses authoring by using and HTML-compatible mark-up language for specifying prerequisite and content requirement relationships through Boolean expressions. This makes authoring more powerful but it does not include an authoring tool, and thus does not make authoring easier. AHA also allows authors to adapt the content of each page to include or not include information based on the users knowledge level. In MetaLinks we decided to use pop-up stretch text to give the user a choice to see additional or parenthetical information, rather than have the system make that choice.

---

[6] However, MetaLinks is not based on a database of indexed expert story segments, which is central to ASK systems.

4 Conclusions Regarding Adaptivity

Several of the features mentioned above involve adaptivity. Adaptivity here is defined by those features that adapt to the user, content type, or navigation history. The TOC is annotated to show which pages have been visited. Each page also has an indication of whether it has been visited before. The narrative smoothing feature adds the introductory paragraph to pages conditioned upon whether the navigation path was "horizontal." The function and availability of the Explain More, Next, and Return buttons changes based on whether the user chooses custom depth control or jumps to a tangential page. Pages links are shown using the page title or the "question title," based on the type of link. The links in the annotated history page are annotated with the link types, or "reasons" why the page was visited.[7] We have also implemented a perquisite overlay structure, using the glossary terms as a concept map. Our intention was to use this to indicate "learned" and "ready to learn" pages as in the InterBook system (Brusilovsky et al 1996). But we felt that just the page visitation data (our system does not yet include quizzes or interrogative interactions) was insufficient to infer concept knowledge, and we are looking for evidence to support the need for this feature.

As mentioned, we took a conservative approach to adaptivity and intelligence, by implementing a moderately adaptive version of the software and testing it for the need for more sophistication. Our formative evaluation (described in [15]) involved 19 subjects, and data was collected from navigation traces, a questionnaire, focus group discussions, and think-aloud interviews. What we discovered was that the current set of features, which leave the locus of control and intelligence solidly with the student, in general avoid all of these potential problem issues of disorientation, cognitive overload, discontinuous flow (poor narrative flow or poor conceptual flow), and content non-readiness. Learners responded positively to questions regarding the usability and usefulness of MetaLinks. 90% said they would prefer using the hyper-book to a text book. No individual feature stood out as being confusing, but the Related (non-hierarchical) Links and the Custom Depth Control features did not get as much use as we had intended. At this point we have not found any strong evidence for the need of additional adaptivity or intelligence. These results are very limited, due to the small sample size and the particular nature of the geology hyperbook and the tasks given. We are not generalizing to say that additional intelligence is not needed in other contexts, but we do wish to use out results to advocate for testing more minimalist versions of software before adding additional sophistication. This work supports the notion that good interface design and passive but powerful user features can sometimes provide the benefits that are ascribed to more sophisticated or intelligent features (which can be more presumptive, controlling, or intrusive than passive features). A corollary to this notion, which we did not test but has been proven out in numerous projects, is that no matter how intelligent or sophisticated educational software is, inadequacies in the interface or usability of the software will

---

[7] We intend to use this to implement an "adaptive back button" feature which infers what a student means when they want to "return from where they left off."

surely overshadow the benefits of the intelligence.[8]   We by no means intend to indicate that sophisticated modeling and intelligence is of no benefit, but rather that non-intelligent, yet full-featured, base-line software should be developed and evaluated before adding intelligence, in order to determine the most effective applications of intelligence.

References

[1] Thompson, G.R. & Turk, J.T. (1997). Modern Physical Geology, Second Edition.. Saunders Publishing Co: Philadelphia, PA.

[2] Conklin, J. (1987). Hypertext: An Introduction and Survey. IEEE Computer, September 1987, pp. 17-41.

[3] Luckin, R., Plowman, L., Laurillard, D. Straforld, M., & Taylor, J. (1998). Scaffolding Learners' Constructions of Narrative. *Proceedings of Int. Conf. of the Learning Sciences*, 19988.

[4] Ferguson, W., Bareiss, R., Birnbaum, L, & Osgood, R. (1992). ASK Systems: an approach to the realization of story-based teachers. *J. of the Learning Sciences* 2(1), pp. 95-134.

[5] Spiro, R.J. & Jehng, J.C. (1990).   Cognitive Flexibility and Hypertext: Theory and Technology for the Nonlinear and Multidimensional Traversal of Complex Subject Matter. In D. Nix & R. Sprio (Eds.) *Cognition, Education, and Multimedia*. Erlbaum, 1990.

[6] Cleary, C. & Bareiss, R. (1996). Practical Methods for Automatically Generating Typed Links. *In Proc. of the Seventh ACM Conference on Hypertext*, Washington, DC, March 16-20, 1996.

[7] Brusilovsky, P. (1998). Methods and Techniques of Adaptive Hypermedia. In P. Brusilovsky, A. Kobsa, and J. Vassileva (Eds), *Adaptive Hypertext and Hypermedia*, Chapter 1, pages 1-44, Kluwer Academic Publishers, The Netherlands.

[8] Brusilovsky, P., Schwartz, E., & Weber, G. (1996). A Tool for Developing Adaptive Electronic Textbooks on the WWW. *Proc. of WebNet-96*, AACE.

[9] Vassileva, J. (1994). A Practical Architecture for User Modeling in a Hypermedia-Based Information System. In *4th International Conference on User Modeling*, pages 115-120, Hyannis, MA, 1994.

[10] De Bra, P. & Calvi, L. (1998). AHA: a generic adaptive hypermedia system. Proceedings of he 2nd Workshop on Adaptive Hypertext and Hypermedia, Hypertext '98, Pittsburgh, June, 1998.
http://www.contrib.andrew.cmu.edu/~plb/HT98_workshop/

[11] Beasley, R.E. & Waugh, M.L (1995). Cognitive mapping architectures and hypermedia disorientation: An empirical study. J. of Educational Multimedia and Hypermedia 4(2/3), pp. 239-255.

[12] Plowman, L., Luckin, R., Laurillard, D. Straforld, M., & Taylor, J. (1998). Designing Multimedia for Learning: Narrative Guidance and Narrative Construction. Draft paper available from the authors.

[13] Stanton, N.A. & Baber, C (1994). The Myth of navigating in hypertext: How a "bandwagon" has lost its course! J. of Educational Multimedia and Hypermedia, 3(3/4), pp. 235-249.

---

[8] In a similar way, educational technology researchers are finding that the pragmatic issues of getting software working in classrooms often overshadows the particular technological innovation being introduced.

[14] Murray, T., Condit, C., Piemonte, J., Shen, T.,& Khan, S. (1999). MetaLinks—A Framework and Authoring Tool for Adaptive Hypermedia. Proceedings of AIED-99, pp. 744-746.

[15] Murray, T., Condit, C., Piemonte, J., Shen, T.,& Khan, S. (2000). Evaluating the Need for Intelligence in an Adaptive Hypermedia System. In Frasson & Gautheir (Eds.), *Proceedings of Intelligent Tutoring Systems 2000*, Springer-Verlag:New York.

[16] McAleese, R. (1989). Navigation and Browsing in Hypertext. Chapter 2 in R. McAleese *Hypertext: Theory Into Action.*. Norwood NJ: Ablex Publ.

[17] Heller, R. (1990). The Role of Hypermedia in Education: A look at the research Issues. J. of Research on Computing in Education, Vol 22, pp. 431-441.

[18] Wallace, R.M., Kuperman, J., Krajcik, J. & Soloway, Elliot (2000).Science on the Web: Students Online in a Sixth Grade Classroom. JLS 9(1) 75-104.

[19] Stern, M., & Woolf, B.P. (1998). Curriculum Sequencing in a Web-Based Tutor. In the Proceedings of Intelligent Tutoring Systems-98.

[20] Brusilovsky, P. & Eklund, J. (1998). A study of user model based link annotation in educational hypermedia. J. of Universal Computer Science, vol. 4, no. 4, pp. 429-448.

[21] Verhoeven, A. & Waarendorf, K. (1999). External Navigation Control and Guidance for Learning with Spatial Hypermedia. J. of Interactive Media in Education 99(1).

[22] Suthers, D. & Weiner, A. (1995). Groupware for developing critical discussion skills. CSCL '95, Computer Supported Collaborative Learning, Bloomington, Indiana, October 1995.

[23] Khan, S., Murray, T., & Piemonte, J., (2000). Qualitative Hypermedia Evaluation Methods. A paper presented at the Eastern Educational Research Association, Clearwater, FL.

The MacroNode Approach: Mediating Between Adaptive and Dynamic Hypermedia

Elena Not and Massimo Zancanaro

ITC-irst
Panté di Povo 38050 Trento Italy
{not,zancana}@irst.itc.it

Abstract. In this paper, we discuss an approach that tries to blur the distinction between *adaptive* hypermedia and *dynamic* NLG-based hypermedia. The approach aims at finding an optimal trade-off between resource reuse and flexibility: existing atomic pieces of data are collected and properly annotated; at the interaction time, the system dynamically builds the nodes of the hypermedia composing different pieces together. The proposed annotation formalism is illustrated and a rule-based system to compose hypermedia nodes exploiting different knowledge sources is presented. Finally, the advantages of this approach with respect to adaptation and dynamic generation are discussed.

1 Introduction

In the literature, a distinction is made between *adaptive* and *dynamic* hypermedia. The former exist prior to their use and a user model is employed to hide part of the structure (or to highlight another part) to better support a particular user in the exploration of the content. Fully dynamic hypermedia, instead, do not exist until the very moment in which a user explores them: they are dynamically created on the fly using automatic text generation techniques ([10], [3]). The benefits and the drawbacks of both approaches have been largely discussed elsewhere (among others, [2]). In this paper, we propose an approach that tries to blur that distinction aiming at finding an optimal trade-off between resource reuse and flexibility[1]: existing atomic pieces of data are collected and properly annotated[2] and the system dynamically builds a node of the hypermedia composing different pieces together. Discourse strategies and linguistic rules borrowed from the field of Natural Language Generation (NLG) are exploited to reuse existing texts/audio/images introducing flexible content selection and organization and control over the linguistic realization.

The MacroNode formalism presented in this paper is intended to supply a conceptual tool to segment a repository of data into units of content and to annotate each of them ([9]). For each unit, the annotation encompasses the description of the information

---

[1] The MacroNode Approach presented in this paper has been developed within the HyperAudio project ([8]) and the HIPS European project ([1]).

[2] Porting to extremes the idea of annotating canned text mentioned in [5].

P. Brusilovsky, O. Stock, C. Strapparava (Eds.): AH 2000, LNCS 1892, pp. 167–178, 2000.

contained, the relations with other units and the different ways in which the unit can be presented to the user. In our formalism, an atomic piece of data is called a *macronode* and, for textual information, it typically corresponds to a paragraph. Indeed, a macronode can represent data in different media, for example text, audio, images, or a combination of these.

At the interaction time, the annotated data is processed by a Composer Engine, a rule-based system which encodes the strategies to dynamically assemble flexible hypermedia presentations from macronodes. The rules can make reference to external knowledge resources, like the user model, the domain model, and so on and work to guarantee that the composed message displays (i) a coherent rhetorical structure, (ii) a topic flow compatible with discourse and interaction context, (iii) cross-references to material already presented and to user interests and (iv) a linguistic realization emphasizing cohesion.

As an example of the flexibility that can be achieved using the MacroNode approach, let us compare the two sample texts below generated by the HIPS system, in a scenario where the hypermedia is integrated in a portable electronic guide to a museum. The two texts provide a description of the same painting for two different users. Example 1 is a description built using an «elaboration» strategy: there are a lot of details and the description is quite long. Example 2 is a description built using a «comparison» strategy: the text is rather short and the description is mainly given by comparison with another fresco. You can note the slightly different beginning to the two presentations («This is the great fresco...» and «In front of you, you can admire the great fresco ...») depending on two different realizations of the same macronode.

Example 1: «elaboration-based» description of the La Maestà	Example 2: «comparison-based» description of the La Maestà
This is the great fresco La Maesta`, depicted by Simone Martini in 1315. La Maesta` was the first decoration piece of Palazzo Pubblico, therefore it acquired through the centuries a particular value for	*In front of you, you can admire the great fresco La Maesta`, depicted by Simone Martini in 1315. The fresco is located in the main part of the hall, the central point that gave the orientation of the Sala del Mappamondo. On the contrary the*
Sienese population. It's not surprising that the very first decoration of Palazzo Pubblico (the site of political power) was a religious artwork. Only four years before, in fact, the 'Fabbrica del Duomo' the other civic power of Siena influenced by the bishop, commissioned the famous 'Maestà' to Duccio di Boninsegna. The traditional spirit of competition between the two great 'factories' of the city demanded an adequate reply	*Guidoriccio fresco, on the opposite side of the room, was a sort of great 'poster', glorifying the power of the Siena Republic. It was a sort of historical documentation more than an artwork to be judged for its artistic value*

2 Representing Content Potential: The MacroNode Formalism

As mentioned above, in the MacroNode formalism information presentations are built concatenating material selected from a repository of information units (possibly derived from an existing multimedia database) which is designed so that its contents and its structure can be used in an adaptive way. The information unit is the *macronode*. Figure 1 graphically shows the information included in a sample macronode.

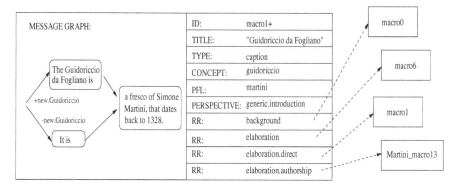

Fig. 1. Sketch of the contents of a sample macronode for the artwork «Guidoriccio da Fogliano»

Each macronode is a data structure consisting of several fields:

▫ The ID field is a unique identifier for identifying the macronode in the macronode repository.

▫ The TITLE field is a string that may be used as mnemonics for the macronode and possibly as title of a presentation.

▫ The TYPE field has to be filled by a keyword chosen from a given list. It describes the status of the content of the macronode with respect to other macronodes describing the same entities (that is, *caption* for the main information about an object, *additional_info* for other less relevant information, *welcome* for short messages describing minimal information on an object; see below).

▫ The CONCEPT field is filled by the entity which represents the *focus* of the information unit, that is the entity which the information unit is centrally about. For example, a macronode describing an artwork in a museum has the artwork as focus. The CONCEPT entity must be an instance of the `concept` category in the domain taxonomy (see below).

▫ The PFL (Potential Focus List) field is possibly filled by a list of other entities which are focal in the text and could become the focus of the following discourse. For example, in a macronode discussing an artwork in relation to its author, the author is a candidate for a possible focus shift in the following discourse. Each entity in the PFL must be an instance of the `concept` category in the domain taxonomy (see below).

▫ The PERSPECTIVE field describes how the content of a macronode is expressed (that is, from an anecdotal/historical/generic point of view). The filler of this slot has to be an entity chosen from the instances of the `perspective` category in the domain taxonomy (see below).

▫ The RR field states the rhetorical relations between this macronode and the others. The field may have multiple values, each one in the following form: [RR *relation id*] where *relation* is a rhetorical relation (see below) and *id* is the identifier of a macronode.

❑ The GRAPH field has to be filled with a graph of message nodes. Each message node is an atomic piece of data (an audio file, a text file or an image). The links in the graph are augmented with conditions. Each path through the graph represents a way of expressing the content of the macronode.

In summary, TYPE, CONCEPT, PFL, and PERSPECTIVE describe the content of the macronode, RR describes the relations among the macronode and the other macronodes in the repository and GRAPH represents the different ways in which the content of the macronode can be realized. A graphical design environment, the MacroNodeEditor, has been developed to support the user in authoring macronodes. The tool also provides testing facilities that allow, at authoring time, an easy verification of how macronodes' contents could be «glued» together. For more details on this environment, see [11].

In the following subsections we describe in more detail the most crucial aspects of the annotation required by the MacroNode formalism to allow the dynamic composition of flexible hypermedia.

2.1 The Domain Taxonomy

Entities selected to specify CONCEPT, PFL and PERSPECTIVE of a macronode have to be classified under a domain taxonomy. The taxonomy is organized hierarchically and is divided in two main sub-hierarchies: concept and perspective (see figure 2).

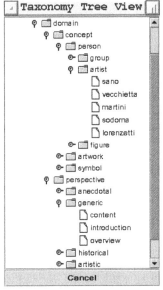

The concept hierarchy contains the main types for the objects of the domain (in the HIPS domain: person, artwork and symbol). The perspective node is the concept which groups together the instances which fill the PERSPECTIVE field of macronodes. In the HIPS domain they are currently: anecdotal, generic, historical, and artistic.

The taxonomy supports the reasoning processes of the Composer Engine and has to be manually authored for each different application domain. However, this authoring task is simpler than authoring of ontologies for deep generation systems, given that the MacroNode approach requires less representation details about the content of the message units, and no semantics and syntactic structures are built from scratch. In the HIPS project, the ontology is built using a simple feature formalism that allows expressing ISA relations as a tree.

Fig. 2. Sketch of the domain taxonomy hierarchy

2.2 The Message Type

The purpose of the TYPE field is to describe the way in which a macronode talks about its content. For some purposes, in fact, knowing what the macronode is about (i.e. its focal entities) is not sufficient; for example, in ordering a set of macronodes talking about the same artwork it is useful to distinguish between macronodes containing essential information from those reporting ancillary information.

In more formal terms, the notion of message TYPE is inspired to the theory of global text structuring from System Functional Linguistics called *Generic Structure Theory* ([4]). According to Halliday and Hasan, every text has a structure (expressing how the sequence of topics/discourse elements evolve) and classes of texts (i.e. genres) can be characterized by a common *Generic Structure Potential* (GSP). The GSP of a genre specifies which elements are obligatory and which optional in the text structure, what the preferred ordering of elements is and so on. For example, in the museum domain, the description of an artwork for a first-time visitor typically contains a short object introduction, followed by a bulk of essential information and possible deviations with background or elaborating information, whose presence and length might be decided according to the visitor's interests or interaction history. The macronode's TYPE names the macronode's function as structural element within a GSP. For example, the macronode in figure 1 has TYPE *caption* to indicate that it reports essential information for the related artwork. The discourse rules used by the Composer Engine check macronodes' TYPE to guarantee that sequences of macronodes respect GSP directives for text structuring.

Each genre is characterized by its own GSP(s) and, through force of circumstances, is characterized by a different set of genre-dependent message TYPEs (e.g., the structural elements for narrative texts are different from those for museum labels). In the application domain of the HIPS project, for example, we extended the classification proposed in [12] that identifies message types for the museum setting, and we consider, among others, the following types:

- **introductory labels**: descriptions of exhibition goal and extent;
- **welcome messages**: indication of what the visitor is currently looking at;
- **captions**: object descriptions; when they are heard in front of the object, they contain visual, concrete information and make use of deictic language;
- **additional information to captions**: information related to objects (for example, general descriptions, anecdotes or similar); they are meant to elaborate information in caption messages;
- **linked information:** similar to the previous item, but in this case the macronode does not contain any further rhetorical link, nor can be presented alone, since it contains complex references to the content of a previous macronode.

2.3 Rhetorical Links

The rhetorical links used to connect macronodes to each other express which (and how) information units can be composed together to instantiate a text in the given genre. A rhetorical link specifies the coherence relation existing between two portions of discourse, e.g. whether text span B describes the event that caused state A to occur

(CAUSE rhetorical relation), or whether text span B provides background information useful for interpreting the assertion in text span A (BACKGROUND relation).

As a starting point for the identification of a set of relevant rhetorical relations, we take as a reference the work by Mann and Thompson ([6]). In HIPS, we exploit a set of basic relations considered as the most relevant for our application task:

□ **elaboration**: when text span B provides more details for what is discussed in text span A; an additional domain-dependent refinement of the elaboration relation (elaboration.authorship, elaboration.direct, elaboration.indirect, elaboration.repre-sented) was introduced to capture different ways to add details to an artwork description.

□ **background**: when text span B provides information useful for interpreting the assertion in text span A;

□ **comparison**: when text span B compares the object/concept described in A with another relevant object/concept;

□ **navigation**: when text span B provides suggestions about where to go/what to look at next.

Figure 3 shows a sample fragment of macronode net, where rhetorical links signal the coherence relations between different macronodes.

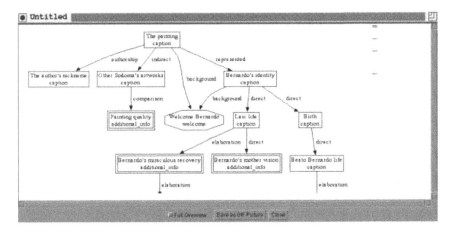

Fig. 3. A sample portion of macronode network displaying the rhetorical links (view provided by the MacroNodeEditor Tool)

2.4 The Message Graph

The basic idea behind the message graph is that the same content can be realized in different ways depending on the discourse and interaction context, and usually these alternatives can be simply obtained by adding or skipping some small sentence parts. In a macronode, the content is divided into small parts (sometimes as small as a pronoun) and these parts are linked in a directed acyclic graph; each path in the graph is a possible realization of the content of the macronode. In HIPS, the nodes of the graph can be audio files, text files, and images. Each arc in the graph is labeled with a condition over the discourse context that describes the situations for which the two connected nodes can be played together in sequence. Figure 4 shows the internal content structure of a sample macronode: for clarity, the transcription of the audio files is shown inside the nodes.

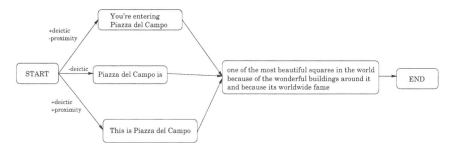

Fig. 4. The internal structure of a sample macronode (the message graph).

The macronode audio file network in Figure 4 can be instantiated in the following messages, where the same description of Piazza del Campo is adjusted taking into account the visitor's position:

- when the visitor is in front of the object being described (so the feature deictic is selected) but he is not close to it (feature proximity not selected): *«You are entering Piazza del Campo, one of the most beautiful squares in the world because of the wonderful buildings around it and because its worldwide fame»*
- when the visitor is in front of the object being described (so the feature deictic is selected) and close to it (feature proximity selected): *«This is Piazza del Campo, one of the most beautiful squares in the world because of the wonderful buildings around it and because its worldwide fame »*;
- when the visitor is not in front of the object described (so the feature deictic is not selected): *«Piazza del Campo is one of the most beautiful squares in the world because of the wonderful buildings around it and because its worldwide fame».*

3 Composing Macronodes

The MacroNode formalism has been designed with the purpose of building a new kind of flexible hypermedia systems which can overcome the limitations of the current adaptive hypermedia and the difficulties/costs of the dynamic hypermedia. The emphasis has been put in developing a formalism allowing a proper annotation of data which can then be used both to reason on the *semantic structure* of the ongoing presentation and to adjust its *surface form* (e.g. its linguistic realization).

When deciding what information to include in the presentation and the most suitable discourse structure, the system takes into account different knowledge sources about the user and the interaction. Discourse rules are encoded to avoid the presentation of already known information, to choose the kind of information on which the user's interest is high (for example, weighting the different perspectives), to present new information when the user goes back to a previous topic.

Moreover, rules checking the rhetorical links between macronodes guarantee the global coherence of a presentation, controlling for example the length of an elaboration chain or the inclusion of background information to clarify a topic, and so on.

New discourse rules can easily be written and added to the system, since a declarative programming style was adopted to emphasize flexibility and extensibility. In the following section, the working of the Composer Engine is introduced in more detail.

3.1 The Composer Engine

The Composer Engine is the module that, at each step, builds a presentation (which corresponds to a node in an hypermedia) accessing the macronodes repository, the user model and the other knowledge sources. The output of the module is a Presentation Structure in the following form:

❏ **user**: the user for which the presentation has been composed;

❏ **title**: the title of the presentation (usually the title of the main macronode);

❏ **content**: an ordered list of macronodes that compose the presentation (for each macronode, a particular path in the message graph is specified);

❏ **links**: a list of macronodes that can be used to generate follow-up presentations.

The Composer Engine can be activated either specifying the object to be presented or the macronode to start with. The main part of the Composer Engine is a rule-based engine with three clusters of rules: the first cluster (*select_starting*) aims at the selection of the main macronode given the object to talk about (of course, this step is skipped if the module is activated specifying the starting macronode); the second cluster (*traversal_repository*) specifies how to traverse the macronode repository following the rhetorical relations to collect other macronodes to enrich the content of the current presentation; while the third cluster (*collect_followup*) specifies the rules to select hyperlinks to further information.

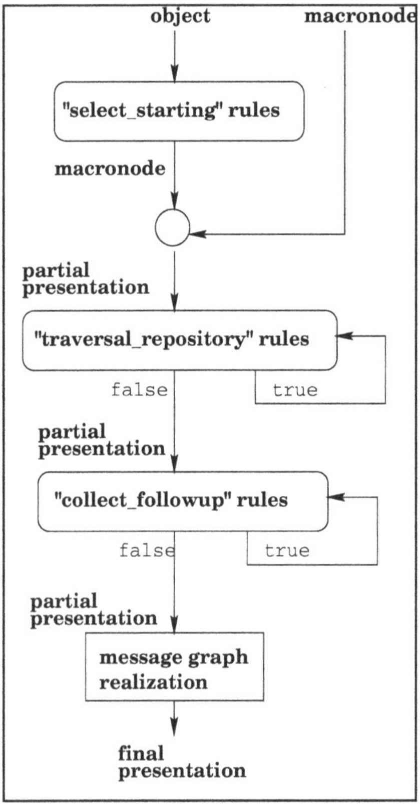

Fig. 5. The Composer Engine

Each rule of a cluster is composed by a condition (written in a declarative language that resembles Prolog) and an output variable. When the condition is true, the value of the output variable is returned and the cluster succeeds[3]. If the conditions of all rules are not satisfied, the cluster fails. Figure 5 shows how the three clusters are applied.

```
defRule background_1 link_traversal
    inputVars: [ Id MN Pres]
                # Id: user ID
                # MN: macronode that originated the current
                    presentation #
                # Pres: current presentation
    conditions: [
            !um_last_presentation(Id,LastPres)
                # there is no previous presentation #
            presentation(Pres,macronodes,MNList)
                # get the macronodes of current presentation #
            head(MNList,StartMN)
                # consider the first macronode of current
                    presentation #
            macronode(StartMN,ttype,Type)
                # get its message type #
            !equal(top.macronode.ttype.welcome,Type)
                # verify that it is not a welcome #
            macronode_rr(MN,top.macronode.rr.background,MNs)
                # get background material for macronode MN  #
            head(MNs,WelcomeMN)
                # take the first macronode of this background
                    material (it's a welcome) #
            head(MNList,WelcomeMN)
                # add it in front of the current presentation
            equal(WelcomeMN,Out)
            ]
    priority: 0
    outputVar: Out
endRule
```

Fig. 6. Example of a rule

The *select_starting* is run once, the output is the starting macronode. A partial presentation is then built using the starting macronode as the content (and its title as the presentation title). The *traversal_repository* cluster is then run with the partial

---

[3] It is also possible to run a cluster in a *inclusive* modality, where the results of all applicable rules are collected. At present, all the clusters are run in a *exclusive* modality.

presentation as input. This cluster is repeatedly run until it fails: at each step, a new macronode is selected and added to the presentation. Note that the starting macronode is not necessarily the first macronode in the content list: figure 6 shows an example of rule to add a welcome macronode before a caption.

When the *traversal_repository* cluster cannot be applied any longer, the content field of the presentation structure is considered complete. The last cluster of rules, the *collect_followup* cluster, is then run to collect the list of macronodes that can be used to generate follow-up presentations related to the current one. Note that in this implementation, the links to further information do not have anchors inside the presentation content. This was an explicit choice due to the fact that the macronode formalism has been mainly used to produce audio-based presentations coupled with links displayed on a screen. An extension of the MacroNode formalism and the engine to deal with anchored link is in progress.

Finally, for each macronode selected to be played, a path in the message graph is selected, checking the conditions against the *Discourse Context*. Recalling that the message graph encodes only surface variations of the same content, this last step of the presentation composition ensures the *cohesion* of the current presentation while the former ensured its *coherence*.

```
defRule perspective_caption select_starting
    inputVars: [ Id Exhibits ]
    conditions: [

                    length(Exhibits,1)
                    head(Exhibits,Exhibit)
                    um_preferred_perspective(Id,Perspective)
                    macronodes(NULL,concept,Exhibit,MNs)
                    macronodes(MNs,perspective,Perspective,MNs)
                    macronodes(MNs,ttype,top.macronode.ttype.caption,MNs)
                    um_not_already_heard(Id,MNs,MNs)
                    head(MNs,MN)
                    equal(Out,MN)

                    ]
    priority: 1
    outputVar: Out
endRule
```

Fig. 7. A rule that exploits the user model

3.2 A Note on User Modeling

At present, the user model encompasses different information about the user:
- a history of already presented macronodes
- a history of visited locations

□   an estimated level of interest for each concept in the taxonomy
□   a classification of the visiting behavior (only for HIPS, see [7]).

The information represented in the user model are accessed by appropriate tests in the discourse rules. For example, in figure 7 is depicted one of the rules used to select the starting macronode of a presentation: here the user model is accessed to get the visitor's preferred perspective (using the test *um_preferred_perspective*); a macronode with the selected perspective and type caption is then extracted from the repository, provided that it has not been already heard (using another test on the user model: *um_not_already_heard*).

4 Conclusion

The approach discussed in this paper aims at providing a conceptual tool to segment existing information repositories into units of content which, once properly annotated, allow the dynamic composition of flexible hypermedia. The approach tries to blur the distinction between *adaptive* hypermedia and *dynamic* NLG-based hypermedia by finding a trade-off between resource reuse and flexibility. The table below summarizes a comparison among the three approaches.

	Adaptive hypermedia	Macronode-based hypermedia	Dynamic hypermedia using NLG
Pages generated on demand	no	yes	yes
Reuse of existing information	substantial	substantial	limited
Adaptation to user	limited content adaptation	enhanced content adaptation	sophisticated content adaptation
Granularity of adaptation	page	inter- and intra-macronode	sentence/phrase
Cohesion assurance	no	partial	yes

The scalability of the MacroNode approach has yet to be proved. However, preliminary results are encouraging: we started with the HyperAudio domain encompassing 50 macronodes and easily ported the formalism to the HIPS domain, with a net of more than 170 macronodes. In a new project on the Ercolano archaeological site in Italy we expect to have more than 1000. The MacroNodeEditor Tool already proved very useful in facilitating authors. Other semi-automatic authoring tools (e.g., to support text chunking) will facilitate scalability.

Acknowledgements

We wish to acknowledge the contribution of all the members of the HyperAudio team, and in particular Daniela Petrelli and Carlo Strapparava (ITC-irst), to the development of the ideas presented in this paper. Many thanks to the partners of the HIPS consortium and in particular to Mick O'Donnell (Univ. of Edinburgh) for the fruitful discussions which helped refine the macronode formalism.

References

1. Benelli, G., Bianchi, A., Marti, P., Not, E., Sennati D.: HIPS: Hyper-Interaction within the Physical Space. In Proceedings of IEEE Multimedia System '99, International Conference on Multimedia Computing and Systems, Firenze (1999)
2. Dale, R., Oberlander, J., Milosavljevic, M., Knott, A.: Integrating Natural Language Generation and Hypertext to produce Dynamic Documents. In Interacting with Computers **11**(2) (1998) 109-135
3. De Carolis, B., De Rosis, F., Andreoli, C., Cavallo, V., De Cicco, M.L.: The Dynamic Generation of Hypertext Guidelines, In The New Review of Hypermedia and Multimedia **4** (1998) 67-88
4. Halliday, M.A.K., Hasan, R.: Language, context and text: Aspects of language in a social-semiotic perspective. Deaking University Press (1985)
5. Knott, A., Mellish, C., Oberlander, J., O'Donnell, M.: Sources of Flexibility in Dynamic Hypertext Generation. In Proceedings of the 8th International Workshop on Natural Language Generation, Herstmonceaux, Sussex, UK (1996)
6. Mann, W.C., Thompson, S.: Rhetorical Structure Theory: A Theory of Text Organization, In: L. Polanyi (ed.): The Structure of Discourse, Ablex Publishing Corporation (1987)
7. Marti, P., Rizzo, A., Petroni, L., Tozzi, G., Diligenti, M.: Adapting the museum: a non-intrusive user modelling approach. In Proceedings of UM99, Banff (1999)
8. Not, E., Petrelli, D., Sarini, M., Stock, O., Strapparava, C., Zancanaro, M.: Hypernavigation in the Physical Space: Adapting Presentations to the User and to the Situational Context. In The New Review of Hypermedia and Multimedia **4** (1998) 33-45
9. Not, E., Zancanaro, M.: Content Adaptation for Audio-based Hypertexts in Physical Environments. In Proceedings of the second Workshop on Adaptive Hypertext and Hypermedia, held in conjunction with Hypertext '98, Pittsburgh (1998)
10. Oberlander, J., O'Donnell, M., Knott, A., Mellish, C.: Conversation in the museum: experiments in dynamic hypermedia with the intelligent labelling explorer. In The New Review of Hypermedia and Multimedia **4** (1998) 11-32
11. Petrelli, D., Baggio, D., Pezzulo, G.: Authors, Adaptive Hypertexts, and Readers: Supoorting the Work of Authors for User's Sake. This volume.
12. Serrell, B.: Exhibit Labels. An Interpretative Approach. Altamira Press (1996)

ECHOES: An Immersive Training Experience

Gregory O'Hare, Katherine Sewell, Aidan Murphy, Thomas Delahunty

Practice and Research in Intelligent Systems & Media (PRISM) Laboratory,
Department of Computer Science
University College Dublin
Belfield,Dublin 4,Ireland
+353 1 7062472
Gregory.OHare@ucd.ie

Abstract. The main objective of the ECHOES[1] project is to build a distributed, adaptive, dynamic environment for educating and supporting technicians in the use and maintenance of complex industrial artefacts. To pursue this objective, Web Based Training, Virtual Reality and Multi-Agent Systems are synthesised within the ECHOES environment. Users co-exist within the virtual environment and with time social cohesion emerges yielding a virtual community. User profiling techniques facilitate adaptive courseware presentation.

1 Introduction

This paper presents the ECHOES (EduCational Hypermedia OnlinE System) System, a multi-user immersive training environment hosted across the internet delivered using multi-agent techniques. ECHOES addresses the maintenance of complex industrial artefacts specifically radar components. The ECHOES environment seeks to provide a *comfort zone* which engineers will visit and revisit throughout the lifetime of their career. This environment provides a single world within which information relating to repair and diagnostic procedures can be placed.

ECHOES enables user immersion, within a virtual three dimensional world together with the virtual community which utilises this space. Two parallel world depictions are catered for, namely a two dimensional and three dimensional view. The former will be invoked where user technology or preferences dictates. Users become part of a community, however the individuality of each user is still preserved. User profiling techniques enables personalisation of the user experience providing for example courseware delivery mindful of individual achievement to date.

The remainder of this paper reviews the research landscape and describes the ECHOES system.

---

[1] ECHOES (European Project Number MM1006) is partially funded by the Information Technologies, Telematics Application and Leonardo da Vinci programmes in the framework of Educational Multimedia Task Force.

P. Brusilovsky, O. Stock, C. Strapparava (Eds.): AH 2000, LNCS 1892, pp. 179-188, 2000.

2   Background Research

Multi-user environments, multi-agent systems and web-based training are the three technologies that combine to give us the ECHOES Collaborative Virtual Environment. Stand alone virtual worlds that support only one user have limited appeal to users and are restricted in their ability to perform as an effective training environment. Multi-user environments are required in which users may interact and collaborate as part of a virtual community. Research in this area includes investigations of the architectures required to support such environments. The Living Worlds Group [1] part of the Web 3D consortium define a conceptual framework and specify a set of interfaces to support the creation and evolution of multi-user applications based on Virtual Reality Modelling Language (VRML). One such architecture is MASSIVE-3 [2], developed at the University of Nottingham. MASSIVE-3 delivers a distributed multi-user virtual reality system based on a client server architecture, together with support for real-time audio communication between users and dynamic modification of virtual worlds. In contrast DIVE [3] uses multicast, which is based on peer-to-peer communications without the use of servers. NPSNET [4] uses an object and event based approach to implement its environment where virtual worlds consist of objects that interact with each other by broadcasting a series of events. A number of *off the shelf* multi-user servers are now available [5]. These include servers such as Deep-Matrix[6] and Blaxxun Community Server [7].

User embodiment is central to effective Collaborative Virtual Environments (CVE). The Humanoid Animation Group [8] has developed a specification for VRML avatars. Part of this specification deals with avatar animation. Gestures or facial expressions can be an important means of nonverbal communication within virtual worlds [9][10]. The use of user embodiment, through avatars, in virtual environments provides a richer communication metaphor, providing perception, locating and identification of other users.

Adaptive hypermedia has been delivered in a two dimensional context through the use of agent technologies. Patient Advocate [11] was designed to be an intelligent assistant for patient-centred health care. The system has to provide a user interface according to the users' needs, expertise and abilities, and contains a monitoring and consulting agent to guide user toward a reasonable explanation or solution. Based on the RETSINA multi-agent infrastructure [12] have developed an implementation for information retrieval and analysis in support of decision-making for aircraft maintenance and repair. The system uses 3 agents: a form agent, a history agent and a manuals agent. RoboTA [13] is an architecture for a colony of distributed agents aimed at supporting instructional tasks. It provides software coaches in educational environments to supplement the restricted amount of time instructors can spend with their students. To date multi-agent systems have been used rarely in the delivery of adaptive virtual environments. Notable among these is the Steve agent [14]. One particular implementation of this architecture is to provide training for navy personnel in the operation and maintenance of HPAC (High Pressure Air Compressors) on board ships. Steve offers advice, answers questions and demonstrates tasks all within an environment that is shared with students using Head-Mounted Displays (HMD). The architecture used by Steve incorporates *Partial Order Planning* [15]. Another such system is that of VETAF (Virtual Emergency Task Force) system [16], which introduces the use of intelligent agents into collaborative virtual environments as a future conferencing system.

The ECHOES Training Environment comprises a collaborative virtual environment, with user embodiment and an agent-oriented architecture design. ECHOES adopts the client-server approach of the MASSIVE [2] and DeepMatrix [6] systems. The user embodiments provided within ECHOES provide the means for the user to feel part of the virtual community and the ability to personalise the avatars further enhances the capability to recognize colleagues. The agents within the system provide the user with an adaptive interface to ECHOES by dynamically personalising the world view. User monitoring facilities provide the system with a relevant profile of the user's abilities and preferences. Systems such as VETAF [16] and Steve [14] attempt to provide similar intelligence to their virtual environments, but they lack the completeness of the ECHOES system which also provides individually tailored courseware, trouble-shooting facilities for the technician in the field (similar to [12]), and a virtual library, as well as the more common chat and whiteboard facilities.

3   ECHOES Motivation

The primary motivation for the ECHOES system is to provide technicians and trainees with an intuitive, useable and enjoyable interface to access the information they require. To this end, the provision of the ECHOES system can be defined as a set of goals, which are:

❑ To strengthen the idea of a connected, collaborative virtual community.
❑ To deliver the core functionality through the adoption of a multi-agent paradigm.
❑ To provide a personalised and contextualised training experience.

Our approach seeks to enhance the user experience by presenting a familiar environment that in many ways mirrors the real world to which they are accustomed. Personalisation of the immersive environment augments user interaction through careful manipulation of a users personal view.

In pursuit of these objectives, it was decided to firstly view the overall system in terms of a group of interacting components, each charged with providing one of the core ECHOES services. Secondly, component decomposition to a set of collaborating agents was achieved, before finally determining the precise functional responsibilities of each agent. These components consist of the *Co-Inhabited Virtual Training Environment (CVTE)*, User Profile Management, Diagnostic Support, Training and CSCW. The ECHOES components can be divided into two disparate layers; the CVTE and User Profile Management are primarily charged with providing an adaptive user interface, while the Training, CSCW and Diagnostic Support components form a service layer.

In the remainder of this paper we convey a picture of how the ECHOES environment provides a collaborative virtual community, before proceeding to outline how adaptability is incorporated into the training experience through the adoption of a multi-agent paradigm.

4   Agent Oriented Design

Much research work has been commissioned on Multi-Agent Systems (MAS) and Distributed Artificial Intelligence (DAI) [17][18]. In the delivery of computationally tractable models of deliberative reasoning, one approach that has gained wide acceptance is to represent the properties of an agent using mental attitudes such as belief, desire, and intention. In this terminology, an agent can be identified as having: a set of beliefs about its environment and about itself; a set of desires which are computational states which it wants to maintain, and a set of intentions which are computational states which the agent is trying to achieve. Multi-agent architectures that are based on these concepts are referred to as BDI-architectures (Belief-Desire-Intention) [19][20][21]. The tool we commission to deliver the ECHOES agents is Agent Factory (described in §4.1) which is a member of the class of systems that embraces the BDI philosophy [19].

4.1   Agent Factory

In essence, Agent Factory [22][23] is a tool that facilitates the rapid prototyping of intelligent agents. One of the key Agent Factory components is a generic agent model. The agent is the base computational unit of Agent Factory whose mental state is comprised of a set of beliefs. This mental state is augmented by a set of commitment rules that define specific conditions for the adoption of particular commitments.

Central to the future directed behaviour of agents within Agent Factory, is the adoption of commitments. Currently blind and single-minded commitment management regimes are supported. The adoption of commitments is determined by logical conditions expressed as commitment rules.

4.2   Commitments & Commitment Rules

Commitments are pledges, made by an agent to undertake a specific course of action at some future point in time. Agents can make pledges about both actions and beliefs, and these commitments may be conditional [18]. Within Agent Factory, commitments are of the form:

COM <agent-name><time><action><persistence-condition>

Figure 1: EBNF Structure of Commitments.

Once an agent has decided to perform some behaviour, it needs to be able to represent that decision. This representation is in the form of commitments. Essentially, a commitment is comprised of: an agent name (to whom the commitment was made), a time (when the commitment was made), and a capability name (what was committed to). On completion of the action which has been committed to, the commitment is dropped.

If an agent is to adopt commitments, some form of rule is required to describe this adoption process. Within Agent Factory a set of commitment rules associated with each agent encode the criteria which must pertain in order that a given commitment be adopted [18]. The structure of the commitment rules is described in Figure 2.

```
<commitment-rule> ::= <belief-sentence> => <commitment>
<belief-sentence> ::= < belief > {< operator >< belief >}
```

Figure 2: EBNF Structure of Commitment Rules and Beliefs.

5   ECHOES Architecture

At a purely functional level, the ECHOES system consists of a group of cooperating agents that:

- Respond to user interaction.
- Manage and control access to services and ensure consistency of data stores.
- Provide personalisation through user-tracking and dynamic user profiling.

Figure 3 depicts an agent level view of the ECHOES Architecture. The architecture is presented as a number of layers, where all of the agents in each layer are tasked with specific roles. These layers deal with presentation, system management and system services. The ECHOES environment delivers two primary representations of the information space, those of 2D or 3D. Contingent upon user preferences and hardware capabilities, the Interface Agent will select the appropriate view.

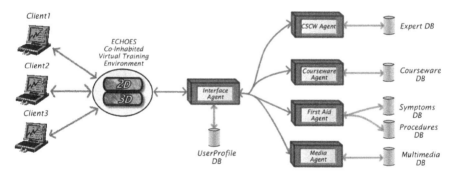

Figure 3: ECHOES Agent Architecture

It is the task of the Interface Agent to present the CVTE to the user, subject to their personal requirements. This agent must also manage user requests and user profiling, as well as make decisions on what other services it will need to employ to satisfy user requests. The tasks of the remaining agents – the CSCW Agent, the Courseware Agent, the First Aid Agent and the Media Agent are to manage the resources for which they are responsible. Their secondary roles are to provide a set of services upon which the Interface Agent may call on in response to the commitments it has accepted on behalf of its clients.

6   ECHOES Agents

To deliver this agent-oriented system a specific agent development tool, Agent Factory (See §4.1) has been utilized to fabricate the agents contained within the ECHOES system. The rest of our discussion will examine the adaptive hypermedia properties of two agents described in §5, namely the Interface Agent and the Courseware Delivery Agent.

6.1 The Interface Agent

The role of the Interface Agent is to deal solely with user interaction, and to pass requests onwards to the correct service. To provide this level of service further decomposition into a group of agents is performed, each assigned a specific function, or service that it must provide. In essence, the Interface Agent can be sub-divided into three functional subsets, which are:

- To listen for, analyse and forward on requests to the appropriate agent;
- To accept service data and format it in a presentable manner for the user;
- To manage user sessions and user-tracking;

Figure 4 outlines the functional composition and interrelationships between this grouping of agents. Each of these agents handles part, or all of the requirements as previously outlined. The numbers within the diagram highlight the ordering in which events within the Interface Agent occur, which are referenced in subsequent sections.

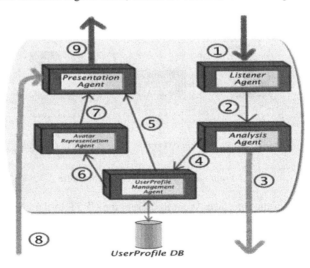

Figure 4: The Interface Agent.

Listener Agent: gathers information about particular users behaviour within the virtual world. The data captured when the user interacts with the ECHOES virtual space (1) will typically contain details of navigation paths through the activation of *proximity sensors*, time spent in different VRML *rooms* through the activation of *time sensors* and user activities through the activation of *touch sensors.*

Analysis Agent: makes rational inferences based on the information provided by the Listener Agent (2,3). The pivotal task is taking the quantative raw data and converting this into added value qualitative data. A weighting algorithm is applied to user interaction history data in order to extract relevant features which are then used to characterise the users perceived preferences.   The user profile represents the addition of added value to the raw user information (4).

UserProfile Management Agent: delivers a multi-user capability by providing user management, session management and event management. User-tracking capabilities are achieved by recording all user events and keeping consistent, concise and recent information on all aspects of user involvement and interaction within the ECHOES CVTE. The inclusion of this agent within the Interface Agent abstracts away multi-user requirements from the underlying service-oriented architecture. This reduces system complexity thus simplifying the underlying architecture, making it easier to both maintain and extend.

Avatar Representation Agent: controls and manages all aspects of avatar representation and interaction within the 3D embodiment of the CVTE. Avatars provide a sense of immersion in both the *virtual world* and the *virtual community* by enabling a user to perceive, identify and locate other members within the environment.

An avatar selection page enables users to customize an avatar form, of their choosing, which will subsequently be used to embody the user within the virtual world. Component parts of this avatar are stored as URLs within the user profile. Once inside the ECHOES world the user's location information (translation and orientation) is updated every time they move. This is achieved by remotely invoking methods (*setTranslation, setOrientation*), using Java Romote Method Invokation (RMI), which updates the user profile (6). This information along with the URLs for the face and body are then used to display the avatar in the world of other users. This avatar is dynamically created using a *CreateFromString* method from the External Authoring Interface (EAI). The EAI allows the VRML browser window to communicate with an applet on the same page. The avatar representation agent implements a client server architecture. Clients obtain location information for their avatar via the EAI and in turn communicate this to the server (7). Each client will thus have it's own copy of the virtual world. To monitor events in the virtual world we created an object called an *AvatarObserver*. This *AvatarObserver* monitors a connection to the server for any information on changes in location or orientation of the other clients. If changes have occurred it will move the avatars representing those clients to their new locations. The *AvatarObserver* will also monitor the orientation and translation of it's own avatar and when a change occurs it will instruct the server to inform all the other clients of this event.

Presentation Agent: provides a contextualised and personalised training environment. As can be seen from Figure 5 below, the CVTE can have two presentation forms, a 2D web-based environment, or a 3D immersive environment. Each of these states must concurrently provide a set of users with consistent, personalised views of the ECHOES system. Therefore the role of this agent is to take raw ECHOES data (8), and through cooperation with the UserProfile Management Agent (5), provide context, perspective and personalisation of each individual's view (9), regardless of their form. This agent's primary objective is to ensure a co-habitation of ECHOES environments by 2D and 3D users, whilst managing consistent world content.

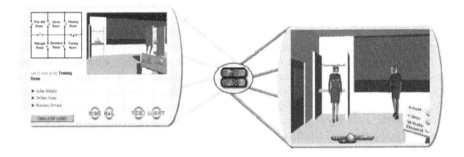

Figure 5: Correlation of 2D and 3D Environments.

ECHOES social cohesion is fostered by effective inter-user communication. Each avatar is provided with a Personal Digital Assistant (PDA), which hosts functions including mail, chat, shared whiteboard and other CSCW capabilities.

6.2   Courseware Delivery Agent

One of the major goals of the ECHOES system is to provide individually tailored courseware to users in order to enhance their learning experience. This personalised courseware is rendered by a Courseware Delivery Agent. The purpose of the Courseware Delivery Agent (CDA) is to manage the presentation of courseware to the user. Courseware is personalised to meet the needs of individual users based on previous expertise and other relevant information stored in the user profile. The user requests courseware and transparent to the user the CDA interrogates the UserProfile Database and Courseware Database, and, based on this decides on the most appropriate module of courseware to present to the user. Elements affecting this decision-making process include previously viewed courseware, associated test scores, and the user's overall level of expertise.

As described in §4.2, the agents in the ECHOES system make their decisions based on a set of beliefs and a set of commitment rules. The CDA is an instantiation of this particular agent structure and hence contains such beliefs and commitment rules.

The CDA provides the decision-making machinery for courseware delivery. Commitment rules encode delivery criteria, examples are contained in Figure 6.

```
BEL(UserN = novice) AND BEL(score (UserN,MCQTestN,>60)) AND
  BEL(completed(UserN,ModuleN))

  ◻ COM (course_del_agent,NOW,present (ModuleN+1,UserN),
        NOT(completed(UserN,ModuleN+1)))


BEL (UserN=novice) AND BEL (completed (UserN,ModuleN)) AND BEL
  (next(ModuleN, ModuleN+3)

  ◻ COM courseware_del_agent, NOW,present(ModuleN+3,UserN),
        NOT (completed(UserN,ModuleN+3))
```

Figure 6: Example Commitment Rules for CDA.

An aggregation of such rules provides a mechanism for selecting the appropriate Blocks or Modules of courseware for presentation to the user. The Courseware Delivery Agent evaluates all the commitment rules and identifies the possible set of commitment rules that evaluate to true. It achieves this by inspecting its mental state. It looks at its belief set to ascertain if any commitment rule evaluates to true, and then adds this to the commitment set. A commitment set is a time ordered set of commitments. Once the internal clock gets to integer N, the Courseware Delivery Agent honours commitments whose timestamp delivery is that of the current time. In the context of the examples shown above, this would mean that we would present ModuleN+1 to UserN at the time when the other conditions held true, and not at some future time.

7   Conclusions

This paper has presented the ECHOES system, which provides a collaborative, adaptive virtual training environment. ECHOES supports multiple simultaneous users, who are encouraged to become part of a virtual community. Personalisation of the training environment is provided by comprehensive user-tracking and individual user profiling. The overall objective of ECHOES is to provide a co-inhabited training space that is intuitive, comprehensive and practical. This system has been delivered through the medium of VRML and system intelligence provided through a collection of intelligent collaborative agents.

8   Acknowledgements

We would like to acknowledge the contribution made by our ECHOES project partners, namely Alenia Marconi Systems, University of Siena and Sogitec Industries.

9   References

1. http://www.vrml.org/WorkingGroups/living-worlds/
2. http://www.crg.cs.nott.ac.uk/research/systems/MASSIVE-3/
3. Carlsson, C., Hagsand, *DIVE– A Multi-User Virtual Reality System.* Proceedings of IEEE Virtual Reality Annual International Simposium (VRAIS'93),Seattle,Washington, Sept1993., pp 394-400.
4. Monahan, J.G., Pratt, D.R., Wilson, K.P., Zyda, M.J. *NPSNET: Constructing a 3D World*, Proc. 1992 Symposium on Interactive 3D Graphics (Mar 1992) pp147-156.
5. http://www.web3d.org/vrml/mu.htm
6. Reitmayr, G., Carroll, S., Reitemeyer, A., Wagner, M.G., *DeepMatrix–An Open Technology Based Virtual Environment System.* Whitepaper on DeepMatrix System, (October 30, 1998) .http://www.geometrek.com/
7. http://www.blaxxun.com/products/server/index.html
8. http://ece.uwaterloo.ca/~h-anim/
9. Capin, T.K., Magnenat-Thalmann, N., Pandzic, I.S., Thalmann, D. Vuillieme, A.G. *Non-verbal Communication Interface for Collaborative Virtual Environments*, The Virtual Reality Journal, Springer, (1999 Vol. 4), pp.49-59.
10. Capin, T.K., Magnenat-Thalmann, N., Pandzic, I.S., Thalmann, D. *Realistic Avatars and Autonomous Virtual Humans in: VLNET Networked Virtual Environments*, Virtual Worlds in the Internet IEEE Computer Society Press, (1998), pp.157-174.
11. Miksch, S., Cheng, K. Hayes-Roth, B., *An Intelligent Assistant for Patient Health Care.* Agents '97, Marina del Rey, CA, USA.
12. Sherory, O., Sycara, K., Sukthankar, G., Mukherjee, V., *Agent Aided Aircraft Maintenance.* Autonomous Agents '99, Seattle, WA, USA.
13. Forbus, K.D., Kuehne, S.E., *RoboTA : An agent colony architecture for supporting education.* Autonomous Agents 98, Minneapolis, MN, USA.
14. Johnson, L., Rickel, J. Stiles, R., Munro, A. *Integrating Pedagogical Agents into Virtual Environments* MIT Press Journal Presence (7(6) Dec 98)
15. Weld,D.S., 1994.*An introduction to least commitment planning.* AI Magazine, 15(4):27-61
16. Peters, R., Graeff, A., Paul,C., *Integrating Agents into Virtual Worlds* .NPIV '97, Las Vegas, Nevada, USA.
17. Durfee, E.H., Lesser, V.R., Corkhill, D.D., Trends in co-operative distributed problem solving, IEEE: Knowl. Data Eng. 11(1), (1989) pp63-8.
18. O'Hare, G.M.P., Jennings, N.R. *Foundations of Distributed Artificial Intelligence*, Sixth Generation Computer Series, Wiley Interscience Publishers, New York, 1996.
19. Rao, A.S. and Georgeff, M.P., *Modelling Rational Agents within a BDI Architecture*, Prin. of Knowl. Rep. & Reas., San Mateo, CA., (1991)
20. Jennings, N.R. *Specification and implementation of a Belief-Desire joint intention architecture for collaborative problem solving.* Int. Jour. of Intel. and Co-op. Info. Sys. Vol. II no3, (1993).
21. Wooldridge, M., Jennings, N. R. *Intelligent Agents: Theory and Practice*, Knowledge engineering review, (October 1994).
22. Collier, R. *The realisation of Agent Factory: An environment for the rapid prototyping of intelligent agents*, M.Phil., Univ. of Manchester, (1996).
23. O'Hare, G.M.P., Abbas, S. *Commitment Manipulation within Agent Factory*, Proceedings of DIMAS '95, Cracow, Poland, (22-24 Nov. 1995).

A Connectionist Approach for Supporting Personalized Learning in a Web-Based Learning Environment

Kyparisia A. Papanikolaou[1], George D. Magoulas[2], and Maria Grigoriadou[1]

[1] Department of Informatics, University of Athens, T.Y.P.A. Buildings,
GR-15784 Athens, Greece
{spap,gregor}@di.uoa.gr
[2] Department of Information Systems and Computing, Brunel University,
Uxbridge UB8 3PH, United Kingdom
George.Magoulas@brunel.ac.uk

Abstract. The paper investigates the use of computational intelligence for adaptive lesson presentation in a Web-based learning environment. A specialized connectionist architecture is developed and a formulation of the planning strategy retrieval in the context of the network dynamics is proposed to select the content of the lesson in a goal-oriented way of 'teaching'. The educational material of the course is stored in a connectionist-based distributed information storage system that provides capabilities for optimal selection of the educational material according to the knowledge needs, abilities and preferences of each learner. Low-level tests of the system have been performed to investigate how the connectionist architecture and the learner model function together to create an operational learning environment. Preliminary experiments indicate that personalized content delivery is provided in an educational effective way.

1 Introduction

An important characteristic of a Web-based Learning Environment (LE) in order to succeed to its educational potential is the opportunities it offers for personalized learning. It is well known that the appropriate match of the learners to the learning experience significantly affects their achievement [3], as the order and the manner in which topics are treated can produce very different learning experiences [16]. A recently proposed approach, which aims to accommodate diversity in student learning needs, abilities and preferred style of learning, is the adaptive LE [2]. Towards this direction, this paper investigates the use of methods from computational intelligence to support adaptation in a LE and focuses on the domain model and the lesson generation process that influence the educational effectiveness of personalized learning. A connectionist-based structure for representing domain knowledge and facilitating a goal-oriented way of 'teaching' is proposed. The interactions between the connectionist architecture and the learner assessment procedure, as well as the role undertaken by the learner in the lesson generation process are described. Experiments and performance results are reported to evaluate the proposed approach.

P. Brusilovsky, O. Stock, C. Strapparava (Eds.): AH 2000, LNCS 1892, pp. 189-201, 2000.

2 Goal-Oriented Connectionist Knowledge Representation

A main issue in the development of an educational system capable to support pedagogical decisions, is the domain knowledge to include multiple curricular viewpoints
on the same knowledge [16]. To this end, a layered curriculum representation has
been suggested with each layer providing a different type of pedagogical information
[6]. This distributed approach to subject matter representation emphasizes the notion
of lesson rather than that of model as a reservoir of domain knowledge, [16], and
formulates the basis of the three-layer connectionist architecture which is proposed in
this section for representing domain knowledge (see Fig. 1).

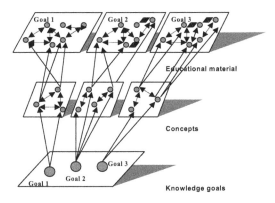

Fig. 1. The connectionist-based structure of the domain knowledge of a course.

In the first layer of the connectionist architecture the *knowledge goals* are defined.
Each goal is related to a subset of *concepts* of the domain knowledge that is located at
the second layer. Assigning qualitative characterizations provides interrelation among
the different concepts of a knowledge goal. The *most important* among them, named
outcome concepts, should be fully explained in the HTML pages using text, images,
examples, exercises and so on. Others, named *prerequisite concepts*, are *less important but essential* for the learner to understand the outcome concepts of a goal. Finally,
there are concepts related to specific outcome concepts, named *related concepts*,
which are *moderately important* for the selected goal and they just complement the
presentation of the goal.

Table 1. Knowledge goal 'LAN topology' (13 concepts). Each row contains an outcome concept followed by its prerequisite and related concepts.

No	Outcome concepts	Prerequisite concepts	Related concepts
1	LAN topology	Network nodes, Types of connections, LAN	Transmission means
2	Bus topology	Multidrop connection	Ethernet
3	Star topology	Point to point connection, polling	
4	Ring topology	Error rate	

Table 1, above, presents a knowledge goal with its associated concepts, referred on the chapter *Computer Networks* of a course entitled '*Introduction to Computer Science and Telecommunications*', offered by the Department of Informatics, University of Athens [15]. Note that the order of the outcome concepts corresponds to their sequencing in the lesson. Other examples of knowledge goals for this chapter: Transmission means, ISO Architecture, Internet services, etc.

The third layer of the connectionist architecture consists of different types of *educational material* related to each concept of a knowledge goal, i.e. text, videos, simulations, examples, exercises and etc., named *knowledge modules*. The description of the knowledge modules is based on the ARIADNE recommendation for educational metadata [1]. Metadata specify the attributes that fully and adequately describe each knowledge module of the educational material. In Table 2, a part of knowledge module description is presented using three types of descriptors: *(i) general information* on the resource itself, *(ii) semantics* of the resource, and *(iii) pedagogical attributes*. Following the above-mentioned description: *(i)* the *different types* of the educational material can be denoted by altering the values of the Pedagogical attributes' fields *{Doc_Format, Interactivity_Level}, (ii)* the different *learning outcomes* of each knowledge module are related to the values of the Pedagogical attributes' field *{Difficulty_Level}, (iii)* the *concepts* that are presented by each knowledge module are defined in the fields *{Main_Concepts, Other_Concepts}* of the Semantics of the resource, and *(iv)* the *knowledge goal* that is related to each knowledge module is defined in the field *{Sub-discipline}* of the Semantics of the resource.

Table 2. A sample of the metadata information of the knowledge module {Ed12} of the goal 'LAN topology'. It is a text-type module presenting the outcome concept 'Ring topology'

General Information	Semantics of the resource	Pedagogical attributes
Identifier: Ed12	*Discipline*:	*End User Type*: 'Learner'
Title: 'Ring topology'	'Computer Networks'	*Document Type*: 'Expositive'
Authors: 'K. Papanikolaou'	*Sub-discipline*:	*Doc. Format*: 'Text'
Date: '09/01/1999'	'LAN topology'	*Usage Remarks*:
Language: 'GR'	*Main Concept*:	*Didactical Context*:
Publisher:	'Ring topology'	'University level'
'Dept. of Informatics,	*Main Concept Synonyms*:	Course Level:
University of Athens.'	*Other Concepts*:	*Difficulty Level*: 'Low'
Sources: 'Computer Networks',		*Interactivity Level*: 'Low'
A.S.Tanenbaum, 1992, 2nd Ed.		*Semantic Density*: 'High'
		Pedagogical Duration: 20

The proposed three-layer connectionist architecture allows to generate the content of a lesson from knowledge modules based on a goal-oriented way of 'teaching', which is supposed to be more adequate to adults who are motivated to learn a specific knowledge goal. Thus, a generated lesson should include: *(i)* complete presentation of the outcome concepts, *(ii)* links to brief presentations of the prerequisite concepts, and *(iii)* links to the related concepts in a glossary.

2.1 The Connectionist Implementation

In this subsection, a technical description of the connectionist architecture is presented. Each knowledge goal in the first layer is associated with its corresponding concepts in the second layer (see Fig. 1), where each concept corresponds to a single Concept Node (CN) of a dynamic associative memory, named Relationships Storage Network (RSN). An RSN is described by:

$$\mathbf{x}(k \, \square \, 1) \, \square \, sat(\mathbf{T}\mathbf{x}(k) \, \square \, \mathbf{I}), \tag{1}$$

where $\mathbf{x}$ is a real n-dimensional vector with components $x_i, i=1,...,n$, which denotes the state or activity of the i-th concept node; $\mathbf{T}$ is a $n \, \square \, n$ symmetric weight matrix with real components $T(i,j)$; $\mathbf{I}$ is a constant vector with real components $I(i)$ representing external inputs; sat is the saturation activation function ($sat(t) = 1$, if $t \, \square \, 1$; $sat(t) = -1$, if $t \, \square \, -1$; $sat(t) = t$ otherwise). The class of systems described by Eq. (1) retains the basic structure of the Hopfield model [4], but possesses some special features as will be explained below (see [9] for another application of the RSN).

Training each RSN is performed off-line using groups of patterns that establish relationships among the concepts of a knowledge goal and are defined by an n-dimensional vector $\mathbf{x}$: $\{\square 1,1\}^n \, \square \, \square \square \square \, (x_1, x_2, ..., x_n) \square \, \square \, ^n \, | x_i \, \square \, \{\square 1,1\}, \, \square \, 1 \square \, i \square \, n\square$. These groups of m patterns are generated in accordance with particular strategies for planning the content of the lesson, i.e. for selecting the appropriate concepts to be presented to the learner. For example, the human instructional designer of the course [15] may define the following strategies: *(i) Strategy A.* Learner has successfully studied all the prerequisite concepts of a knowledge goal. Then, in order to achieve this goal, s/he has to study only the outcome and the related concepts, *(ii) Strategy B.* Learner has successfully studied several prerequisite or related concepts of a knowledge goal. Then, in order to achieve this goal, s/he has to study the entire outcome concepts and the rest of the prerequisite and related concepts, and *(iii) Strategy C.* Learner 'has failed' in a number of outcome concepts. Then in order to achieve this goal, s/he has to study only these outcome concepts and their prerequisite and related ones. The overall strategy that guides the interaction of the system with the learner supposes (or implies) that a learner achieves a knowledge goal when s/he studies successfully all the outcome concepts of this goal.

A storage algorithm that utilizes the *eigenstructure method* [8] is used for specifying the appropriate $\mathbf{T}$ and $\mathbf{I}$ parameter values that guarantee that patterns of concepts' combinations are stored as equilibrium points of the RSN (see [8] for a description of the algorithm). When two or more concepts are active in a pattern, i.e. the corresponding components of the pattern are $\{1\}$, this indicates that a relationship among these concepts has to be established. Relationships among concepts are represented by the network parameters (the matrix $\mathbf{T}$ and vector $\mathbf{I}$). Note that during operation, the node inputs, which formulate the initial states of the nodes, are supplied after evaluating the learner's knowledge on the concepts of a knowledge goal. The patterns provided at the input of the network are created according to the level of understanding of the learner on the concepts of the specified goal (see [7][11] for details on the assessment procedure). Depending on the pattern applied to the input, the state vector of the RSN is forced to move toward a stored pattern, i.e. an equilibrium point. Thus, the

RSN performs associate inference depending on the input pattern and, unlike the general use of an associative memory, it operates synchronously: *(i)* it updates the states of its nodes simultaneously, and *(ii)* the input pattern is kept unchanged until convergence of the network (see [8] for details on the network operation).

It is worth noticing the advantages of the proposed method for designing the RSN over alternative methods, such as the outer product method [4], or the projection learning rule [12]. For example, the outer product method does not guarantee that networks will store all desired vectors as equilibrium points. In addition, experience has shown that the storage ability of networks designed by the outer product method is up to $0.15n$, where n denotes the order of the network [4]. On the other hand, the eigenstructure method possesses the following features: *(i)* the designed networks have the ability to store more patterns than corresponding discrete-time networks designed by other methods, *(ii)* all the desired patterns are stored as asymptotically stable equilibrium points, and *(iii)* guidelines are provided for reducing the number of spurious states and for estimating the extent of the domains of attraction for the stored patterns. Comparative results among several design methods for this Hopfield-type class of systems, described by Eq. (1), have been reported in [8].

2.2 The Educational Material

Several RSNs construct the third layer, each one corresponding to a different knowledge goal (see Fig.1 – the layer of educational material). RSNs function in this layer is analogous to the storage of information in an associative memory [5]. An associative memory is able to recall a full set of the information of the memory when the network is excited with a sufficiently large portion of this information. Note that in conventional forms of information storage, such as dictionaries or telephone catalogues, the only way to access information is by the address of the place where it is stored, usually called the 'key', e.g. *Id* field in Table 3.

Table 3. A sample of the educational material of the goal 'LAN topology'. Each line describes a knowledge module of the goal.

Id	M_concept	Other_concept	Dif_level	Doc_format	Inter_level
Ed1	LAN topology		01	Text	Low
Ed2	-‖-		01	Example	Low
Ed3	-‖-		02	Exercise	Low
Ed4	-‖-		02	Exercise	Medium
....	....	....	......	....	......
Ed12	Ring topology		01	Text	Low
Ed13	-‖-	{Star, Bus} Top.	01	Example	Medium
Ed14	-‖-		03	Exercise	Medium

Note that Table 3 shows how the information about the educational material, i.e. the knowledge modules, of the goal 'LAN topology' might be stored in a conventional information system. Following [1], the different columns of Table 3: *Id* (identifier) is a unique identifier for the resource; *M-concept* (main concept) is the main concept that is covered by the educational resource; *Other_concepts* is a list of domain concepts, other than the main concept, that is covered by the resource; *Dif_level* (difficulty level) denotes how hard is for the typical user to work through the resource; scale adopted {01, 02, 03}; *Doc_format* (document format) is a field that takes value from a list whose content depends on the doc type, i.e. {text, exercise, example, simulation, case study}; *Inter_level* (interactivity level) is the level of activity between the resource and the end-user, i.e. {low, medium, high}. Obviously, multiple classes of information should be developed, so that the educational material presenting a concept of the subject matter takes into consideration different learning styles. Furthermore, multiple levels of difficulty should be introduced aiming at different learning outcomes, so that the different learners' educational needs are fulfilled.

In order to store the information shown in Table 3 in a distributed connectionist network, such as the RSN, the different instances of the features {Identifier, M_concept/Other__concept, Doc_format, Dif_level and Inter_Level} need to be represented as nodes of the network. For example, each of the different instances of the M_concept feature, i.e. the outcome concepts of the knowledge goal 'LAN topology': {Net topology, Bus topology, Star topology, Ring topology}, is represented by a single node and so on (see Fig. 2, description A).

In each RSN, a memory is formed by setting up a link between two nodes corresponding to the same knowledge module. Thus, in order to store all the information about a knowledge module, e.g. {Ed2}, positive links between all the possible pairwise combinations in the different feature-areas will be set during the training phase (see Fig. 2, description B). To this end, the RSN is trained off-line using patterns that establish relationships among the different instances of the feature-areas for each knowledge module of the goal and are defined on $\{□1,1\}^n$. The groups of patterns that are stored to the network are generated in accordance to the knowledge modules of the educational material, as shown in Table 3.

During RSN's operation, the state vector of the network is forced by the pattern applied to the input to excite or inhibit certain links between the different instances of the feature-areas and, thus, satisfy the constraints that the input pattern poses; for example, deliver educational material of certain format and difficulty level, etc.. Actually, what is retrieved is the information, which corresponds to the most active node(s) once this flow of activity has established. Thus, the RSN's input pattern assigns values on the features of the educational material and it can be seen as setting constraints on the final state that the network can settle into. Following this approach, the system's response to the selection of a knowledge goal will be different under different conditions, i.e. input patterns. It is worth noting that, the RSNs operate as distributed information storage systems providing capabilities such as: *(i)* retrieval on the basis of partial information, and *(ii)* fault tolerance. For example, a full set of information regarding a knowledge module can be easily retrieved from the content-addressable database (RSN) by simply providing partial information about it, such as the name of the main concept related to it, the difficulty level etc. (see Table 3). Therefore, the connectionist approach to a content-addressable database provides the learner/educator/system with an effective way of retrieving data for different uses, such as *(i)* the evaluation of the level of understanding of the learner through the construction of tests that correspond to certain concepts and level of difficulty, or *(ii)* the generation of a lesson that meets the learner's needs according to his/her level of understanding and preferences.

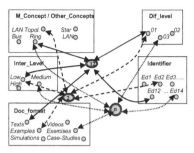

Fig. 2. The architecture of an RSN of the third layer that stores information about the educational material of a knowledge goal, i.e. about its different knowledge modules. (A) Each area represents a certain feature of the knowledge modules with the nodes within an area representing possible instances. (B) The information about a knowledge module, e.g. the 13th knowledge module corresponding to the 13th line in Table 3, is represented by setting up excitatory connections between the facts that are known about it. In this figure, this is done by setting up a knowledge module node (the gray nodes in the middle of the figure, e.g. '2' corresponds to the 2nd, '12' corresponds to the 12th and 'n' to the 14th knowledge module) and linking this to all the instance nodes that represent its properties in Table 3. This form of representation is used for illustration purposes, as it reduces the number of connections required to set up the model and makes the operation of the model easier to follow. The excitatory connections necessary to represent all the information about 3 knowledge modules of the knowledge goal 'LAN topology' have been entered, for illustration purpose, using three different line types.

3 Implementing Personalized Learning

Didactic decisions are made by references to the evaluation of the learner's knowledge / preferences and to the domain knowledge. They are responsible for deciding how to sequence knowledge in order to achieve the instructional goals of the learning environment and they are concerned with both the content and the delivery of instruction [13]. Therefore, the lesson generation process is realized in two stages: *(i) planning the content*, that is, selecting the appropriate concepts of the lesson by making use of learner's background knowledge and educational needs, and *(ii) planning the delivery* of the educational material. The planning of delivery is responsible for the optimal selection of the educational material. Note that the development of the educational material, in this approach, is of major importance, as it should address different educational needs, learning styles and capabilities.

As shown in Fig. 3 below, the Learner's Evaluation module influences the operation of the connectionist architecture. Following the learner evaluation procedure described in [7][11], six categories are used to classify the level of understanding of the learner with respect to each concept of the selected goal: {*EI, I, RI, RS, AS, S*} = {*Extremely Insufficient, Insufficient, Rather Insufficient, Rather Sufficient, Almost Suffi-*

cient, Sufficient}. This scale has been experimentally found to provide evaluation results closer to human teachers' evaluation performance, when compared with previous work in the area [13].

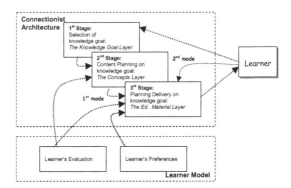

Fig. 3. Diagram of the interactions for the lesson generation process. The input of the 3rd Stage can be formulated either by the system (1st mode) or by the learner (2nd mode)

Note that, when the learner's knowledge with respect to a concept is characterized as *Extremely Insufficient*, a value of approximately 1 is assigned to the corresponding component of the input pattern, which means that the learner *certainly* has to study this concept. On the other hand, a value of approximately 0.1 is assigned when the learner's knowledge on a concept is evaluated as *Sufficient*. The magnitude of the assigned value depends on the importance of the concept in achieving the knowledge goal and on the concept's characterization (outcome, related, prerequisite). For example, the degree of membership of the learner's knowledge on the outcome concept *LAN topology* in each of the 6 above-mentioned categories is given by the set:

$$\mu(x)\square\{1|\,1\square 0.99|\,2\square 0.89|\,3\square 0.69|\,4\square 0.49|\,5\square 0.2|\,6\},$$

where an integer value 1,2, ...,6 is mapped to a linguistic term {*EI, I, RI, RS, AS, S*} and the symbols '|' and '+' are used only as syntactical constructors. Similarly, the set

$$\mu(x)\square\{0.97|\,1\square 0.87|\,2\square 0.67|\,3\square 0.37|\,4\square 0.27|\,5\square 0.1|\,6\}$$

is an example of learner's knowledge on the related concept *Transmission means*

The results of the evaluation formulate the input patterns of the RSN of the second layer and thus affect the content planning process for the selected knowledge goal. Note that different strategies for planning the content are implemented by means of the dynamics of the RSN. As mentioned in Sect. 2.1: a *strategy* is stored in the RSN, as a collection of *m* patterns defined on $\{\square 1,1\}^n$. The results of the Learner's Evaluation module are further used to specify the difficulty_level feature, which is a part of the input pattern of the third layer. To simplify the practical implementation, the following conventions are used: educational material of difficulty level {01} should be selected for learners characterized *EI* or *I* with respect to a specific concept; educational material of difficulty level {02} should be presented to learners characterized *RS* or *RI*. Finally, learners characterized as *AS* are supported by educational material of difficulty level {03}. Additionally, the output of the second layer, i.e. the concepts that the learner has to see next, specifies the Main_concept/Other_concept feature, which is another part of the input pattern of the third layer. The learner's preferences, which are provided by the Learner Preferences module, formulate several parts of the input pattern of the third layer, such as the inter_level, and the doc_format.

The proposed approach supports two modes of personalized learning: (*i*) the learner selects a knowledge goal in Stage 1 of Fig. 3 and the system generates a lesson of difficulty level {01}. Next, the learner studies the educational material provided and submits the included tests. During the learner-system interaction, the Learner's Evaluation and Learner Preferences modules evaluate or keep data about the learner performance and preferences and estimate his/her level of understanding, preferences, learning style, etc. The results of the evaluation procedure influence the lesson generation process that takes place, as previously described (see also Fig. 3 – the 1st mode of personalized learning), in Stages 2 and 3 and help the educational environment to generate a lesson according to learner's knowledge needs, abilities and preferences. Alternatively, end-user modifiability can be supported: (*ii*) the learner by-passes the Learner Evaluation and guides the lesson generation process by selecting the concepts to be included in the lesson and the different features of the educational material, i.e. the input pattern of the 3rd layer (see Fig. 3 – the 2nd mode of personalized learning). During this type of lesson generation the Learner's Evaluation module is only used to keep a record of the learner's attitude and performance.

4 Experiments

The proposed connectionist model has been tested under various learner performances on the chapter *'Computer Networks'* of the Web-based course *'Introduction to Computer Science and Telecommunications'* [15]. In this chapter adult learners have to study 25 knowledge goals, each one containing 10-26 concepts. The response of the system has been evaluated by teachers-experts in *Computer Networks* and has been characterised as predictable, reliable and educationally effective.

4.1 Planning the Content: Selecting Concepts for Presentation

The content planning process is realized by the 2nd Stage of the connectionist architecture (see Fig. 3) and is mainly affected by the selection of the knowledge goal by the learner in the 1st Stage, and the estimations of the Learner's Evaluation module. Depending on the knowledge goal, the input pattern of the corresponding RSN is formulated and the final state vector of the network (the nodes' activities) determines the concepts that need to be included in the generated lesson. In the example described below, the learner has selected the goal 'LAN topology' and his/her performance with respect to the various concepts s/he already studied has been evaluated as 'Rather Sufficient' with respect to the outcome concepts {LAN_topology, Star_topology} and to the prerequisite concept 'LAN', and 'Almost Sufficient' with respect to the rest of the prerequisites and related concepts.

In Fig. 4 below, it is shown that the activity of the concept node that represents the prerequisite concept *Transmission means*, i.e. related to the outcome *LAN topology*, goes to –1, which means that the node is deactivated and this concept will not be presented. On the other hand, the activity level of the concept *LAN*, which is a prerequisite to the outcome *LAN topology*, goes to +1 and thus it will be presented. Note that, the nodes' activity level at cycle=0, when transformed to the interval $(0,1)$, is related to the result of the learner's knowledge evaluation procedure. For example, the learner has been evaluated as '0.27|Almost Sufficient' on the concept *Transmission means* (cf. with this concept's set in Sect. 3). Similarly, the concept nodes *LAN topology* and *Star topology* are activated since the learner has been evaluated as '0.69|Rather Sufficient' and '0.68|Rather Sufficient' respectively. Thus, following the recalled planning strategy B, the generated lesson includes all the concepts of the knowledge goal apart from the successfully studied prerequisite and related ones. The performance of the system with 40 learner profiles has been significantly high, almost reaching 100%. Similar performance on planning the content of a lesson has been achieved in the experiments reported in [7][10].

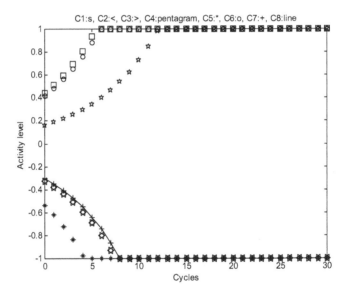

Fig. 4. Example of Strategy B: LAN topology (C1): square; Network nodes (C2): left-triangle; Types of connections (C3): right-triangle; LAN (C4): pentagram; Transmission means (C5): star; Star topology (C6): o-mark; Point to point connection (C7): +-mark; Polling (C8): line

4.2 Planning the Delivery: Selecting the Educational Material for Presentation

The planning of delivery is based on the results of the recall operation of the RSN in the third layer. RSNs input patterns consist of three parts: *(i)* the output of the 2nd Stage, *(ii)* the estimations of the Learner's Evaluation module that suggests the appropriate difficulty level of the educational material, and *(iii)* the output of the Learner's Preferences module that provides information with respect to the type, format and interactivity level of the educational material. In addition, the relevant importance for each of the selected concepts on achieving a knowledge goal is considered, as at this stage of implementation only outcome concepts are represented in the third layer. The selection of specific knowledge modules for different educational uses, such as lesson generation or learner assessment, is obtained by means of the retrieval of the educational material using specific parts of the information that describes it, which formulates the input pattern of the RSN. The following examples illustrate this approach.

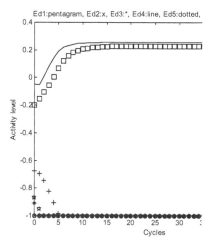

Fig. 5. Example of 3rd layer operation with target the generation of a lesson

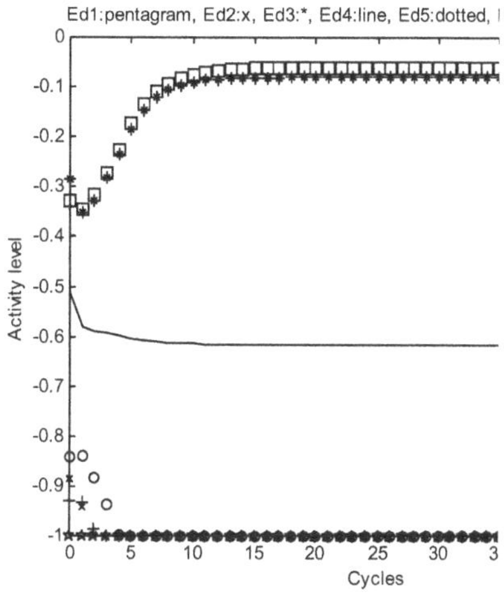

Fig. 6. Example of 3rd layer operation with target the learner assessment

    In the first case, the target is to generate a lesson suitable to the learner needs and preferences. Expanding the example described in Sect. 4.1, planning the delivery has to do with selecting the appropriate educational material for presenting the outcome concepts {LAN_topology, Star_topology}. This process is guided by the results of the Learner's Evaluation module concerning the level of difficulty of the knowledge modules to be presented, and of the Learner's Preferences module concerning their type and/or format. As the learner's level of understanding on these concepts has been evaluated as {RS}, the corresponding level of difficulty should be {02} (see Sect. 3), while it is estimated that learner should be motivated to undertake a more active role (Medium interactivity). Note that in Figs. 5 and 6 the knowledge modules of the concepts LAN topology and Star topology are: {Ed1, Ed2, Ed3, Ed4, Ed5} and {Ed9, Ed10, Ed11} respectively. The RSN, taking this input pattern, results after some cycles in activating the nodes: {Ed4} (line in Fig. 5) and {Ed11} (square in Fig. 5). Actually, these are the only knowledge modules of the two concepts that satisfy the above-mentioned constraints (cf. with their features in Table 3); {Ed3} is a knowledge module of type 'Exercise', but it is not activated since its *Interactivity level* is Low.

In the second case, the target is to assess the learner on the concepts {LAN_topology, Star_topology}, i.e. to construct an assessment test of difficulty level {02}. The RSN, taking this input pattern, results in activating the knowledge modules {Ed3} {Ed4} and {Ed11} (see Fig. 6). Actually, these are the only knowledge modules that satisfy the above constraints (cf. with their features in Table 3). The RSN performed retrieval on the basis of partial information and achieved an overall performance of 90% in 40 different input conditions. Performance mainly depends on the size of the partial information provided to the network.

5 Conclusions

This paper has described some important parts of a personalized learning environment, how they are designed and interact. A formulation of the planning strategy retrieval for generating the content of a lesson in the context of the dynamics of the connectionist network has been proposed. This approach seems to accommodate the goal of improving learners' learning process by matching the lesson to their level of understanding and educational needs. At the same time the system has the potential to provide learners with control over the lesson generation process, in the sense of learner's preferences. It also supports end-user modifiability offering opportunities to the learner to intervene on the selection of the educational material by defining the values of the different features of the educational material.

References

1. ARIADNE project. URL address: http://ariadne.unil.ch, accessed January 2000
2. Brusilovsky, P.: Methods and Techniques of Adaptive Hypermedia. User Modeling and User-Adapted Interaction, Vol.6. Kluwer Academic Publ. Netherlands (1996) 87-129
3. Ellis, R.: Individual learner differences. In: Ellis, R. (ed.): The study of second language acquisition. Oxford: Oxford University Press (1994) 471-527
4. Hopfield, J.J.: Neural Networks and physical systems with emergent collective computational abilities. In: Proc. Nat. Acad. Sciences, Vol.79, Apr. (1982) 2554-2558
5. Kohonen, T.: Self-Organization and Associative Memory. Springer-Verlag, Berlin (1988)
6. Lesgold, A.M., Bona, J.G., Ivill, J.M., Bowen, A.: Toward a theory of curriculum for use in designing intelligent instructional systems. In: Mandl, H., Lesgold, A.M. (eds.): Learning Issues for Intelligent Tutoring Systems. Springer-Verlag, New York (1987)
7. Magoulas, G.D., Papanikolaou, K., Grigoriadou, M.: Towards a computationally intelligent lesson adaptation for a distance learning course. In Proc. of the 11th Int. Conf. on Tools with Artificial Intelligence, Chicago (1999), IEEE Computer Society Press 5-12
8. Michel, A., Si, Y., Yen, G.: Analysis and Synthesis of a Class of Discrete-time Neural Networks Described on Hypercubes. IEEE Tr. Neural Networks, Vol. 2. (1991) 2-46

9. Michos, S. E., Magoulas, G. D., Fakotakis, N.: A hybrid knowledge representation model in a natural language interface to MS-DOS. In: Proc. of the 7th IEEE Int. Conf. on Tools with Artificial Intelligence (1995), IEEE Computer Society Press 480-483
10. Papanikolaou, K.A., Magoulas, G.D., Grigoriadou M.: A Connectionist Approach for Adaptive Lesson Presentation in a Distance Learning Course. In: Proc. of Int. Joint Conf. on Neural Networks, Washington (1999), IEEE Catalog: 99CH36339C, paper #679
11. Papanikolaou, K. A., Magoulas, G. D., Grigoriadou, M.: Computational intelligence in adaptive educational hypermedia. In: Proc. Int. J. Conf. on Neur. Net., Como, Italy (2000)
12. Personnaz, L., Guyon, I., Dreyfus, G.: Collective computational properties of neural networks: New learning mechanisms. In: Phys. Rev., A, Vol.34, Nov. (1986) 4217-4228
13. Stathacopoulou, R., Magoulas, G.D., Grigoriadou, M.: Neural network-based fuzzy modeling of the learner in intelligent tutoring systems. In: Proc. of the Int. Joint Conf. on Neural Networks, Washington (1999), IEEE Catalog: 99CH36339C, paper #680
14. Wasson, B.: PEPE: A computational framework for a content planner. In: Dijstra, S.A., Krammer, H.P.M., van Merrienboer, J.J.G. (eds.): Instructional Models in Computer-based learning environments. NATO ASI Series F, Vol. 104. Springer-Verlag, NY, (1992)
15. DIUoA: *Introduction to Computer Science and Telecommunications*, Distance Learning Course, Department of Informatics, Univ. of Athens. URL: http://hermes.di.uoa.gr
16. Wenger, E: AI and Tutoring Systems. Computational and Cognitive Approaches to the Communication Knowledge. M. Kaufmann Publishers, Inc., California (1987) 20

Adaptive Hypertext Design Environments: Putting Principles into Practice

Daniela Petrelli, Daniele Baggio, and Giovanni Pezzulo

ITC-Irst
I-38050 Povo - Trento, Italy
{petrelli,baggio,pezzulo}@irst.itc.it

Abstract. This paper discusses the design of a tool for authoring adaptive hypertext. First we describe the task of adaptive hypertext design. The network editing task as well as the testing phase are explored showing the importance of a design environment for authors and developers of hypertext adaptive systems. Then the required support such environment has to provide are presented. Finally we describe how principles can be translated into practice by illustrating the implementation of a design environment for developing and testing a very flexible adaptive hypertext.

1 Introduction

In standard hypertext there are two playing actors: the author and the reader. What the author composes, the reader receives. Pages, links and net structure are the author's responsibility. Instead in adaptive hypertext applications, an "autonomous" entity enters into play between the author and the reader. Such entity, the system, tailors the final page by interpreting the data the author wrote. In principle, this could bring uncertainty, in practice this simply complicates the scenario. As a matter of fact, given a specific set of conditions (the context in which the user action takes place), the behavior of the system is fixed: given a context the system behaves always in the same way.

Designing standard hypertexts means in general to re-organize pre-existing information in a structured way. In adaptive hypertext, besides creating a structure there is the not trivial task of enriching it with decorations (on nodes and links) that allow the system to dynamically select (or hide) the parts that will compose the final page. When editing "standard" hypertext, authors are in full control of the final result, whereas when editing adaptive hypertext they can not directly see by themselves what the result of their work is, i.e. what content and links the page presented to the user will include. In this scenario, a support to foresee the result is mandatory if the author is not an expert of the adaptive system. This is the purpose of a tool for adaptive hypertext design: make it possible for authors to do their work being experts in the domain and not in the adaptive system.

In this paper, we discuss the most crucial issues of editing adaptive hypertexts and present a design environment that was developed to support authoring and testing of a

P. Brusilovsky, O. Stock, C. Strapparava (Eds.): AH 2000, LNCS 1892, pp. 202-213, 2000.

flexible hypermedia. Such environment was developed within the HIPS project[1] [1]. HIPS aims at developing a portable electronic guide that dynamically composes presentation taking into account a mixed context of physical model and user models[2]. The original flexible hypermedia used is based on the concept of *macronode*, a piece of information (of whatever combination of media) that describes a single concept in a certain way; macronodes are connected by typed links (see [9] this proceedings for a full description). The MacroNodeEditor (MNE) was built for supporting the development and testing of macronode networks.

2   Adaptive Hypertext Design Task: Which Support?

Authoring is a crucial task in adaptive hypertext (AH). As it is well known [3], an adaptive hypertext system consist of a hypertext and a user model. It is adaptive in the sense that it adapts the hypertext by using the model. The quality of the output depends on both the quality of the user model and its adaptation methods. But these are system requirements (architectural matters). From the point of view of the development of new applications, the quality of data (hypertext) becomes crucial. The presentation effectiveness of AH depends on the careful and precise work of authors: selecting a certain content or hiding some links cannot be done if authors fail in properly marking either of them. As a consequence, authoring has to be properly supported.

As stated by J. Nanard and M. Nanard (in [7]), hypertext design activity does not consist simply in following some formal technique; it is a recursive process with backtracking and erratic switching among thinking, production, reorganization, modification, and evaluation. In their view, "hypertext design environments should support both formal tools for reasoning and experimental feedback for checking design choices." A design environment has to give formal support in the early steps, while support for testing is valuable when the hypertext structure is almost consolidated.

Formal tools or methods are essential when the focus is on elicitation of concepts and on the general organization of the hypertext network. A model to follow speeds up the start up process: a formal description and a suggested sequence of steps are of great help. Formal design models have been proposed and used in non-adaptive hypertext (as the HDM - Hypertext Design Model [5]). A general, common, formal model has not yet been proposed for adaptive hypertext. Nevertheless it is important for each system intended to leave the lab for the applicative world to develop a proper model of itself easily understandable by non-technical but nonetheless professional users. It really does not matter if the model for AH design is a formal one, a collection of useful patterns, a set of rules, or a mix of them [2,8]. In our view, what really matters is that the model has to be effective in supporting the initial design stage: the

---

[1] HIPS is a EC founded project in the Esprit i3 initiative. Partners are: University of Siena (coordinator, Italy), Alcatel-SIETTE (Italy), CB&J (France), GMD (Germany), ITC-Irst (Italy), SINTEF (Norway), University College Dublin (Eire), University of Edinburgh (Scotland).

[2] HIPS allows also the user to mark with spots space and objects.

problem of how to communicate to authors the concept of run-time composition has to be carefully considered because this is the core of adaptive systems. Thus the goal of the formal definition is to let authors clearly know what are their best options: what type of content has to be considered persistent and which is optional, when and how it is better to use one or the other of them, how to categorize the links, and so on.

Supports for testing are equally important. For non-adaptive hypertext "testing" means to see the appearance of the structure under construction as presented to the user, in a word, its look-and-feel[3]. In our opinion, testing an AH has a broader sense: it includes also testing the final selection the system will perform at run time. So the goals are two: testing the content and evaluating the appearance. They can be profitably separated since they require different subjects (authors vs. users), set up (the design environment vs. the final system), and methods (lab evaluation vs. in-the-field evaluation). The evaluation of the look-and-feel (the appearance) can be postponed until the data structure (the content) is optimal. Thus, the first goal of the testing phase is to create the best network given the adaptation methods available, or possibly to realize the best synergy between data and adaptation methods allowing authoring of both. Here we focus only on this evaluation step. In this case, the testing means to be able to simulate all the conditions that the system will use at run time. In other words, it has to be possible to compose a kind of snapshot of the context that could plausibly occur at run time and then run the adaptive engine on the AH authored so far.

3   Adaptive Hypertext Design Environments: Some Principles

Support authors of AH with editing and testing facilities requires creating a sophisticated environment composed of pieces of the adaptive system and simulated parts. In this section, we discuss the main issues involved in developing such environments. A tool we realized to support authoring flexible hypermedia is used as example.

3.1 Supports for Conceptualization and Editing

Authors must have enough knowledge to predict the type of presentation the system will compose on the bases of the current net and context conditions and have to inherit part of the control over the adaptive system. Only this knowledge allows finding out what has to be modified when a problem occur (i.e. bad output). Thus authors' understanding of the system is the first goal. In the concept elicitation phase, help is given by formal methods (an analytic description of both structure and process) as well as by other less demanding supports: golden rules, patterns and templates can be effective in making the adaptive mechanism easily understandable.

In the design environment we implemented, the MacroNodeEditor (MNE), formal tools are a simplified version of the formalism, a set of design rules, and templates.

---

[3] In human-computer interaction "look and feel" denotes the concrete sensory experience of using an artifact -what the user looks at, feels, and hears while using it.

Each of them serves to a different purpose and all of them are essential parts of the user manual:

□   **formalism**: the formal model provides a systematic and motivated analysis of the structure and how it is used by the system. As support to the design phase, the essential part of the macronode formalism is coupled with a set of examples to clarify the function of each item in the marker set in order to let authors assimilate the type of annotation required. This is fundamental, since authors maintain a strong decision power that affects system effectiveness. For example, the granularity of a macronode is totally under author responsibility: it might be one phrase or a long paragraph. Authors have to decide what is the most appropriate depending on the situation (type of user, function of the text, content).

□   **rules**: a set of design rules supports a better understanding of the formalism as well as a fast start up phase. They are valuable in the early steps of data structuring, when, for example, text has to be split into pieces that have to be properly classified. MNE has rules for composing groups of nodes out of split text (e.g. how to identify macronode chains) and others at the level of the single macronode (e.g. how to mark a node of type "direction"). Some these rules can be encoded in the tool as automatic checking of the correctness of the net under construction.

□   **templates**: templates are an empty, prototypical scaffolds defined as the most representative of certain desired data configurations[4]. Templates are fundamental to support adaptive mechanism understanding: test sections can be described on the bases of templates showing the effect changes in the net have on results. Different templates were defined in MNE to capture the ideal shape of sub-networks devoted to describe objects of museum domain, such as halls, collections, and artworks. The implicit purpose is to push as much as possible authors to fit the best structure for a certain goal. Of course, authors can autonomously decide to modify the template, to use it only partially or to ignore it completely, but they have to bear in mind that the suggested one is optimal for the adaptive methods.

The design environment has to complement the described formal tools with editing facilities. As a matter of fact providing only the theory does not guarantee authors to be able to easily and effectively come to optimal data organization or succeed in properly marking. Moreover the finer the adaptation is the richer annotations must be. Authoring task ranges from introducing tags into HTML files (as in AHA [4]) to build a knowledge base for complex fact-representation (as in ILEX [10]). While writing annotated HTML files can be done using standard text editors [6], editing more sophisticated structures requires ad-hoc tools. MNE provides graphical editing facilities discussed in 4.1.

---

[4] This idea of templates is different from the one expressed in [8]. We consider only the content and completely ignore the layout of the final page. Secondly, our constructive mechanisms are in the adaptive methods and not in the templates. Finally our templates concern only optimization of data annotation respect to adaptivity, something that is not relevant for standard hypertext.

3.2 Supports for Testing

The second important phase in AH design task is testing. An essential feature of a design environment is to give authors the possibility of evaluating the current network against the final adaptive system: they will learn how it works by testing. Therefore the design environment has to include modules coming from the adaptive system. Which ones are appropriate to import depends on the purpose of the final design environment. If the final goal is to better support the composition of data structures, then it is probably enough to include the adaptive core and the data management. Another perspective is to use the design environment as test-bench for the adaptive system itself. In this case, the user model module has to be included too in order to monitor its evolution while the interaction is going on. While in the first case the focus is on the data optimization, in the second the main purpose is to test adaptive modules in an extensive and easy way. The design environment will of course reflect these different purpose and the different users, i.e. authors vs. developers.

Modules of the adaptive system that do not need to be tested or that are insignificant in respect to the adaptive mechanism can be simulated through an appropriate graphical interface in the design environment. Authors will be required to set the current condition of the simulated modules by clicking on it (see user models simulation in MNE described below and in 4.2).

As an example, let consider the architecture of the HIPS system against the one of the MNE (Figure 1). In general, HIPS analyses both visitor's movements and explicit selections and, when appropriate, reacts by dynamically creating presentations. A presentation is composed by: i) an audio message (derived by the content of a set of selected macronodes), ii) an image relevant for the described object, and iii) a set of links related to other macronodes. To create a presentation, HIPS traverses the macronode network (recorded in the Macronode Repository) and decides which nodes will be part of the presentation by taking into account a mixed context of physical model (the Physical Organization Knowledge Base) and user models (Visitors Models and Interaction History in figure).

Testing the AH of HIPS means to apply the adaptive core, the Composer Engine, to the net under construction held in the Macronode Repository. Therefore both modules are included in the MNE without making any modification.

Since the Composer Engine evaluates the current context, it is necessary to simulate the work of the modules that contribute to it, namely the Interaction History, the Physical Organization Knowledge Base, and the Visitor Models. The Interaction History (the sequence of visitor's stops and presentations heard) was simulated collecting the output of test sections, while the Visitor Models values were directly set by authors at the interface.

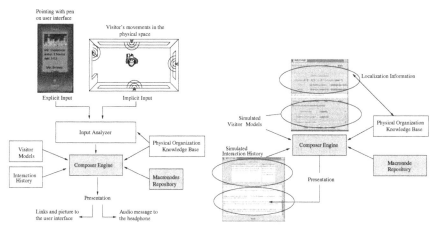

Fig. 1. A simplified view of the HIPS architecture (left) compared with the on of MNE (right). The boxes in gray are the data structure (the hypermedia) and the adaptive core, essential parts of the testing. MNE panels are presented and discussed in the next section.

The Physical Organization Knowledge Base (POKB) was not essential, but it was of great help in setting the physical context: given a certain position in the space it automatically sets many variables such as the current room and area the visitor is in, and the exhibits in sight. So the POKB was included in the MNE for the only purpose of helping in the task of setting the current context.

The Visitor Models were simulated at the interface level since the focus was on the correctness of macronodes networks with respect to the adaptive mechanisms[5]. Nevertheless, these modules can be easily interfaced with the environment since the functional interfaces were not changed at all: they run in the same way in HIPS and in MNE. In this way, MNE will become a full test-bed allowing for both user model and adaptation testing.

The MNE was intended as a tool for supporting macronode networks composition. As a consequence, modules like the localization subsystem and the user interface were not considered relevant, thus they were not included nor simulated. Leaving out the user interface might sound strange. However, since the same adaptive core is used to generate web pages as well as HIPS screens, there is not a single appearance of the hypertext, so look-and-feel evaluation was left for a specific user evaluation section.

4 A Closer Look at the MacroNodeEditor

Properly defined tools accommodate task sharing between users and systems. In AH design, tasks humans have to be in charge of are: selection, classification and marking

---

[5] Visitor Models (namely Visiting Style and User Model Application) are under other HIPS partners responsibility.

of contents and relations; run testing and judge the result. The system has to support: data organization and overviews, abstraction from internal format, network consistence checking, and test-revise cycle.

4.1   Abstraction, Views, and Editing

One of the duties of a tool for authors is to hidden the syntactic details of the system internal formalism. MNE realizes a high level abstraction from the data internal form. Very briefly, a macronode is an annotated unit composed of (i) a marker set that has the purpose of fully describe (ii) the content part. Marker items are among the others ([9] in this proceedings reports an exhaustive description):

- **type** to express the role the node has in the broader view of a potential presentation; e.g. *welcome* marks an introduction, *caption* marks a primary information, *additional* and *liked* signals secondary and ancillary contents and *direction* indicates orientation information towards other related objects;
- **concept** to describe what the node is about, e.g. an artwork, the person portrayed, the author;
- **perspective** to make clear the particular view over the concept, its flavor, e.g. generic, artistic, historical, anecdotal;
- **rhetorical relations** to connect macronodes by explicitly showing text relations.

The marker set is used by the system at run time for deciding, on the basis of the current context, which macronodes will compose the presentation. Figure 2-left shows the panel used to compose the marker set.

The content of a certain macronode is a bulk of information that can be presented in different circumstances changing only partially its form. How the content is realized depends on the current value of the discourse context. The discourse context contains both the communicative context (the world around speaker and hearer) and the textual context (the text that surrounds a certain utterance). A reference to an object in the physical space like "*this is* the great fresco La Maestà" concerns the communicative context since a correct interpretation is given only merging the utterance with the environment. An example of co-textualization occurs when a pronoun substitutes the subject like in "*It* is one of the absolute masterpiece of the European gothic painting.": the comprehension of this sentence requires to know the previous utterance. To realize such a different form of the same content, the text is split into steps that are points of choice. Each step has mutually exclusive messages each activated by features. Features refer to each variable of the discourse context (Figure 2-right displays the panel used to edit macronodes steps).

The macronode model is an articulated formalism that supports very flexible adaptations, but that requires a careful annotation. To avoid mistakes, typing is never required (authors can add in the message panel personal comments as they see fit, which are never used by the system). The filling-in is done by properly selecting the desired item out of displayed lists. For example adding a *concept* means selecting it from the 'concept tree' displayed when the corresponding *add* button is pressed.

Fig. 2. A macronode as presented by MNE: the marker set on the left, the content on the right.

A tool for editing hypertext has to support personal data organization and view over the hundreds nodes that easily populate the net. MNE supports data organization allowing recording into many files: authors can focus only on part of the network by opening just some files (through the browser in Figure 3 left). Views and overviews on data are supported by displaying essential information in the browser and in the graph. The macronode type is visually coded by a shape and is coupled with the title at the browser level. The graph has the main purpose of showing relations among nodes; node content is summarized by the shape (the macronode *type*), by the title and by other user chosen slots (*concept* and *perspective* in the figure). Thus the essential part of the macronode formalism is used consistently throughout the whole tool.

Fig. 3. The MNE browser (left) and the graph viewer (right).

Another support for data organization are templates (introduced in section 3), i.e. skeletons for organizing data in a new design process. A template is defined for each of the relevant items of the domain. The one for exhibits is illustrated in Figure 4. It suggests to provide a short object introduction (*welcome* node in the figure), a bulks of essential information for each flavor (*captions* with generic, historical, artistic or anecdotal *perspective*), and possible deviations with elaborating information (*additional* and *linked* nodes).

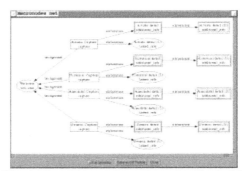

Fig. 4. The exhibit template as instantiated by the MNE.

This configuration is optimal since the more diverse the information is the richer the final presentation will be. In fact the Interest Models (one of the HIPS Visitor Models) allow the adaptive mechanism to choose at run time the most appropriate content; thus the user interested in art will receive artistic descriptions, while for curious visitors an anecdotal perspective is preferred. Moreover chains of macronodes (connected *additional* nodes following a *caption*) will allow to vary the presentation length depending on the Visiting Style (an estimation of user's attitude towards the exhibition, part of HIPS Visitor Models).

4.2   Test-Revise Cycle

The design environment has to adequately support typical user actions at testing time, such as simple check, quick identification of problems, and immediate revision. For this purpose MNE provides the author with a couple of panels to set the hypothetical context, run the system and collect the produced output (Figure 5); these panels are integrated with the previously discussed editing ones.

The test panel, on the left in Figure 5, allows setting context conditions on which HIPS adaptive methods are applied. Very briefly HIPS uses clusters of rules applied in sequence to detect the exhibit on sight, select the most salient macronode (the one to start with), collect the macronodes that follow, and finally select the related macronodes to be presented as links (a wider description of the mechanism is reported in [9]). Through the test panel the author sets the current context for the next run.

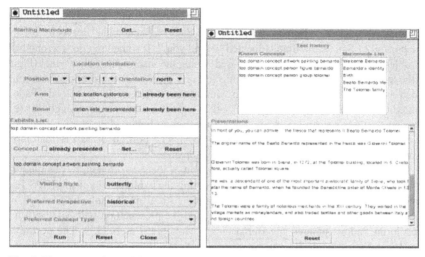

Fig. 5. The two panels used during testing for setting the context and presenting the output.

The upper part, *Starting Macronode*, can be used to skip the first step to make a very punctual evaluation since it allows setting the macronode to start with. The area below is the *Location Area* that represents the physical context. Filling is done by MNE (through the POKB) that, as visitor's *Position* and *Orientation* change, automatically updates the *Area* and the *Room*, displays the *Exhibits* on sight, and sets the *Concept* of the presentation to the default value (first object in the *Exhibits* list). The last section simulates the current user models values (*Visiting Style, Preferred Perspective, Preferred Concept*).

The author sets the context and runs the adaptive engine by clicking on the interface. The test outputs are recorded in the output panel (Figure 5 right). In its upper part, the list of *Known Concepts* and the list of *Macronodes* heard is displayed. Together with the sequence of positions, these two lists simulate the Interaction History, the last important component of the context. This mechanism allows articulated tests that emulate a sequence of interactions by a hypothetical user.

The test-revise cycle is very fast: the context is set by few clicks and the result of the adaptive process is immediately displayed; if the output is not satisfactory, the author just turns attention to the editing facilities for updating, switching then back for another test turn. Generally the problems that can occur are few and with practice it is easy to identify the key points. Let us consider some examples. By setting the variables in the Location Area the visitor is supposed facing the fresco of the Bernardinian Monogram. Since only three nodes are available on this artwork, the system selects all of them: a *welcome* and a *caption* to introduce the painting and a *direction* node towards the portrait of San Bernardino. If the system fails in selecting one of the macronodes, then a missing link can be supposed. A look at the editing graph (Figure 3) will easily confirm the hypothesys.

Supposing the selection succeeded, then the output should be[6]: "This is the Bernardinian Monogram + Batista di Niccolo da Padova painted the fresco in 1425. + The portrait of San Bernardino is located behind you.". If something goes wrong here, a problem at the step level can be supposed. Using the macronode editor panel (Figure 2) the author can see if a step is missing (e.g. no breaks for the pronoun was introduced as in "This is the Bernardinian Monogram + Batista di Niccolo da Padova painted the Bernardinian Monogram in 1425."), or if a feature was wrongly set (e.g. ignoring the user's position as in "This is the Bernardinian Monogram + Batista di Niccolo da Padova painted the fresco in 1425. + The portrait of San Bernardino is located on the opposite wall of the Sala del Mappamondo.").

It is also possible to check all the other output of the same content by changing the setting in the test panel. A visitor who is browsing the exhibition by using HIPS floor map is simulated by setting a different Location Area but leaving the Concept unchanged. Then the *welcome* node is ignored and the presentation will be: "Batista di Niccolo da Padova painted the Bernardinian Monogram in 1425. + The portrait of San Bernardino is located on the opposite wall.". Note that no pronoun as well as no reference to the physical space is used here.

Through MNE it is possible to simulate sequences of interactions, i.e. a full tour. Suppose that the visitor is in the middle of a tour (previous runs) and already saw the portrait of San Bernardino: "This is the Bernardinian Monogram + Batista di Niccolo da Padova painted the fresco in 1425. + You already saw the portrait of San Bernardino on the opposite wall."

Finally another different form is realized when the visitor is coming back later to the same object. Only the *welcome* is proposed since no other new information are available: "You are back to the Bernardinian Monogram."

Conclusions

The need for an environment for supporting the design of adaptive hypertexts was discussed. This task is crucial when sophisticated AH have to be written. From our experience such a type of environments are valuable also for testing extensively the behavior of an adaptive system against the possible context conditions. It helps in checking if adaptation methods were correctly stated and to verify the quality of the adaptive process thus providing designers with a full control over the system.

An improvement will allow authoring the adaptive methods in an easy way. This of course would mean to think the adaptive system as an architecture for producing adaptive applications. Authors could then be in full control of the final production by tuning adaptive methods and data.

---

[6] In these examples '+' shows the connection between macronodes, while text in box emphasizes the steps regulated by features.

References

1. G.Benelli, A. Bianchi, P. Marti, E. Not and D. Sennati. HIPS: Hyper-Interaction within the Physical Space. *IEEE Multimedia Systems '99*, Firenze, 1999.
2. M. Bernstein. Patterns of Hypertext. *HyperText'98*. 21-29, Pittsburgh PA, 1998.
3. P. Brusilovsky. Methods and techniques of adaptive hypermedia. *User Modeling and User Adapted Interaction*. 87-129, v 6, n 2/3, 1996.
4. P. De Bra, L. Calvi. AHA! An open Adaptive Hypermedia Architecture. *The New Review of Hypermedia and Multimedia*. 115-140, v.4, 1998.
5. F. Garzotto, L. Mainetti and P. Paolini. Hypermedia Design, Analysis, and Evaluation Issues. *Communication of the ACM.*, 74-86, v 38, n.8, 1995.
6. K. A. Lemone. Issues in Authoring Adaptive Hypertext on the Web. *2nd Workshop on Adaptive Hypertext and Hypermedia,* in conj. with HyperText'98, 85-86, Pittsburgh PA, 1998.
7. J. Nanard, and M. Nanard. Hypertext Design Environments and the Hypertext Design Process. *Communication of the ACM*, 49-56, v 38, n.8, 1995.
8. M. Nanard, J. Nanard, and P. Kahn. Pushing Reuse in Hipermedia Design: Golden Rules, Design Patterns and Constructive Templates. *HyperText'98*. 11-20, Pittsburgh PA, 1998.
9. E. Not and M. Zancanaro. The MacroNode Approach: mediating between adaptive and dynamic hypermedia. *AH2000 (this proceedings)*.
10. J. Oberlander, M. O'Donnell, C. Mellish, A. Knott. Conversation in the museum: experiments in dynamic hypermedia with the intelligent labelling explorer. *The New Review of Hypermedia and Multimedia*. 11-32, v.4, 1998.

ECSAIWeb: A Web-Based Authoring System to Create Adaptive Learning Systems

Charun Sanrach and Monique Grandbastien

Equipe Informatique et Formation
Bâtiment LORIA – Campus Scientifique
B.P.239, 54500 Vandoeuvre lés Nancy, France
{Charun.Sanrach, Monique.Grandbastien}@loria.fr

Abstract. ECSAIWeb is a variant of ECSAI, an environment for designing intelligent tutoring systems. The tutoring knowledge contained in a tutor agent designed to run in a non-networked environment is reused and updated for the World Wide Web. We concentrate on a flexible architecture that allows teachers or authors to modify and add their knowledge in the domain. We apply adaptive techniques: adaptive presentations and adaptive navigation to present the domain knowledge to learners.

1 Introduction

The World Wide Web is becoming an important tool to increase the possibility for delivering on-line learning courses. The advantages of this tool are clear: classroom independence and platform independence. The users, in any place of the world, can access to a learning centre with any kind of Internet-connected computers.

On the one hand, [9] point out that hypertext allows instructional designers to create documents with embedded links to provide learners with opportunities to follow sequences that can be predetermined according to individualised needs of the learners. However, one of the hypertext disadvantages in instruction is the following: it is nearly impossible to predetermine strictly a link for all students because we cannot predetermine exactly how or at what point in the sequence a student can and will enter an instructional environment or leave it.

On the other hand, one of the most important characteristics of some existing advanced learning environment is their ability to evaluate the knowledge acquisition and retention rate of their users, and to adapt to their needs. Consequently, it is not surprising that many systems have been moving into the World Wide Web, they shifted from an individual delivery system to collective distribution. For example Ritter passed from PATAlgebratutor to PAT Online [10], we have MANIC [12] to allow teacher-author to take some existing courses and to convert them to on-line courses. Generally, most systems support only the learners without supporting enough the teachers. This means that most systems don't allow these teachers who are the best teachers in the domain in any part of the world to add their knowledge in the system.

P. Brusilovsky, O. Stock, C. Strapparava (Eds.): AH 2000, LNCS 1892, pp. 214-226, 2000.
☐ Springer-Verlag Berlin Heidelberg 2000

In this context our objectives are the following: First, we aim at producing an environment for designing courses for the Web starting from the existing environment ECSAI [5]. Then we aim at studying the process of adaptation of the environment on the one hand and of teaching materials on the other hand, we also aim at drawing the possible benefits introduced by the use of the Web. Lastly, we hope to propose some recommendations usable for the authors who have to adapt existing courses or environments.

In this article we describe ECSAIWeb, an environment for designing learning systems for the Web. The second section presents the underlying principles, the dynamic creation of a learning path starting from a universe of learning units and the subjacent models. The functions available in the author mode and in the student mode are the subject of the third section. Finally, we compare the functions established in our system with those, which are proposed in several widespread platforms.

2   Environment for Designing Learning Systems for the Web

A majority of intelligent tutoring systems do not allow teachers - authors to add their knowledge in the system. In certain cases the author part is limited to the instructional designers, in other cases it is difficult for teachers to understand the underlying models and to manage to enrich the contents indeed.

2.1   An Environment Opens to the Author

E. Gavignet proposed in ECSAI [5], a generator of learning systems open to teachers bringing their teaching materials. ECSAI relies on a set of physical learning units provided by teachers. This set is represented within the system in a model from which ECSAI proposes learning paths according to the learning objectives of each learner. We took again the principles of ECSAI to build ECSAIWeb. We preserve a set of independent units, domain model and the generation of a learning path dynamically adapted to the learner. We introduce the adaptive techniques [2] related to the use of navigators (annotation, hiding, etc). The authors also have increased possibilities remote updating of teaching materials.

2.2   Models of ECSAIWeb

Faculties of opening to the teachers and of adapting to the students rely mainly on the used models, in particular on the domain models and the user models. We describe in this section the domain models used in ECSAIWeb and the student model is present thereafter.

2.2.1 Domain Models
The simplest form of domain model is a set of domain concepts. For the concepts to be taught, our system proposes the idea of evaluation items [5], [6] and [8]. A list of concepts can be associated easily with pedagogical objectives and evaluation

processes. Of course, the learning units may deal with many concepts, but only the evaluation items are included in the domain model. By concepts we mean elementary pieces of knowledge for the given domain. Depending on the domain and the application area, concepts can represent bigger or smaller pieces of domain knowledge.

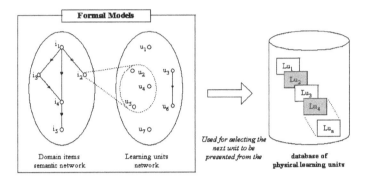

Fig. 1. The co-operation between several formal models and a database of learning units in ECSAIWeb

A more advanced form of the domain model is a network with nodes corresponding to domain concepts and with links reflecting relationships between concepts. We use two types of relationships. The first type represents the hierarchical organisation of the domain. The second type represents pedagogical constraints for example «*item i1 must be learned before item i2*». This type of network represents the domain structure to be taught in ECSAIWeb (Fig 1). The same domain model provides also a structure for the representation of the student's knowledge about the taught subject. For each concept of the domain model, the knowledge model of an individual student records a certain value, which is an evaluation of the student's knowledge level about this concept. This type of model, which is called an overlay model, is powerful and flexible: it can measure independently the student's knowledge of different topics.

2.2.2 Universe of Logical Learning Units

In this model, a learning unit is presented by its description. A description of unit includes three parts, represented on Fig 2. Firstly, prerequisites or preconditions including constraints, which must be satisfied in order to carry out the unit. Secondly, the contents are composed of several parameters: identifier, type, referenced items, filename, title and number of pages. And thirdly, the post-actions describe the changes to be carried out in the student model when the unit is finished and other actions, which the system will carry out. These descriptions of units allow the construction of learning units' network, represented in the right hand side of the formal models of Fig 1. With the models provided by the teacher in our example, the unit U3 precedes obligatorily the unit U6 (represented the *access-directly-to* link).

Pre-conditions	Contents	Post-actions
Antecedent unit : none Pre-require : Item i7 : tokens = 0, 0 Item i8 : tokens = 0, 0	Label : U9 Type : Presentation Items used : i9 Title : Conductance and Conductivity Filename : pi1090 Pages : 6	Knowledge level : Item i9 : tokens = +0, +0 (depending on the result) Access-directly-to : none

Fig. 2. A learning unit description

2.2.3 Base of Physical Learning Units

The physical learning units provided by the teachers can have very diverse forms, simple presentations, animations, tests by QMC, exercises to be solved, etc and thus allow the use of existing modules. However we propose to privilege the principle of the hypermedia on-line handbooks to represent the human in presenting concepts to the students. We will describe in the third section the functions available for creating the physical learning units.

2.3   Dynamic Presentation of Teaching Materials

The teaching materials can be presented in a static and in a dynamic way. In the static way, the presentation of teaching materials is fixed once for all and is thus always the same. In the dynamic way, the presentation of teaching materials can vary according to the used models: domain model and student model that we will describe this later in the section 3.2.1.

3   Implementation of ECSAIWeb

ECSAI was initially written in C for PCs, it was entirely rewritten in Perl and was adapted for the Web environment. The keys of this version are an independence of platform, an independence of domain and the adaptability of the contents. This system is composed of two environments: the authoring environment and the learning environment.

3.1   Authoring Environment

This environment is employed by authors to define the pedagogical objectives, the universe of learning units (course materials), and includes tools to check pedagogical objectives and to simulate the learning path. To develop pedagogical materials, we chose the electric circuit analysis for the directed current as a test domain. We propose a course development process in 5 steps: definition of the evaluation items, determination of the pedagogical objectives, description of the learning universe, edition of physical learning units, and validation of the coherence of the learning universe. Steps 1, 2 and 3 are dealing with the models, step 4 is about Web-based module design, and step 5 is about checking consistency and adequacy between the models and the database. Our environment offers tools to help the teacher-authors to create easily their course on the Web according to this process.

3.1.1 Definition of the Evaluation Items

The first phase of the development is to define the evaluation items. They represent the domain concepts. In the current version, the order of the items in the list is important because the learning environment will employ this criterion among others to choose the next unit to be presented. These items are always accompanied with two values. These values represent the aptitudes of the student, which will be called "competence" related to the evaluation items. The first value is a quantitative value, called total measurement. It lets us know if the item was the subject of any presentation during the learning sequence. The second is a qualitative value, called acquisition degree. This value specifies the way in which the student controls the ability to apply or the know-how related to an item. The acquisition degree is in fact a couple of integers, depending on the student's knowledge level and which are updated at the end of execution of each exercise. The first of them corresponds to the application - restitution aspect and the other corresponds to the manipulation - utilisation aspect.

3.1.2 Determination of the Pedagogical Objectives

The pedagogical objectives describe the knowledge level that the student must approach. Each objective is represented by a set of items. The learning environment uses pedagogical objectives to select the next activity for the learner. The determination of the pedagogical objectives constitutes a central part of the definition of the learning system and it is made in an interactive way like shown on Fig 3 (right screen).

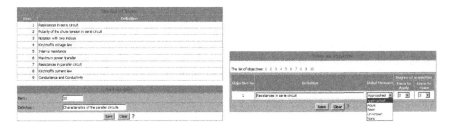

Fig. 3. Definition of the evaluation items (on the left) and of the pedagogical objectives (on the right)

3.1.3 Description of the Logical Learning Units

The data entry of the various elements composing a learning logical unit (pre-conditions, contents and post-conditions) is also controlled by the system. Fig. 4 shows how the teachers or the instructional designer can regulate parameters for the unit U9. This unit is of presentation type. It is associated with concept i9 and linked to the physical learning unit pi1090 that includes 6 pages.

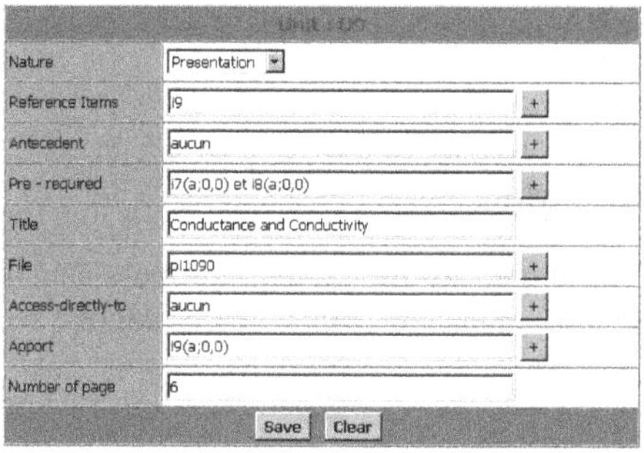

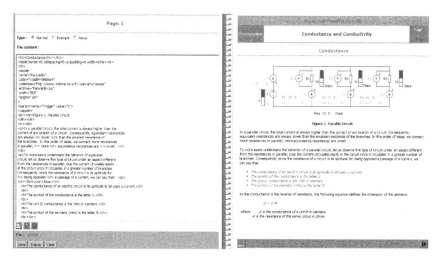

Fig. 4. Description of the logical learning unit U9

3.1.4 Edition of the Physical Learning Units

For editing the physical learning units, we propose frameworks that allow authors to create various types of units. The physical learning units are divided into 2 categories according to their nature: presentation and exercise. Fig 5, on the left-hand side shows how to edit a presentation unit with recall type and on the right hand side presents the result page that will be displayed to the student.

Fig. 5. Edition of unit U9 (left hand) and the result page (right hand).

3.1.5 Validation of the Coherence of the Learning Universe

The possible inconsistencies inside the learning universe or between it and the pedagogical objectives are detected and presented to the author who can reconsider a particular point and introduce modifications. Moreover, this method is also used to assure that a student does not get lost in the hyperspace and to verify that all pedagogical objectives can be archived. So this step is a mandatory one to continue the system design.

3.2   Learning Environment

After the student was identified by the system, he must choose a learning method, either free mode or guided mode. In both modes, adaptive techniques are used in order to fulfil student's needs as much as possible.

3.2.1 Adaptation of Learning Materials

In this section we aim at characterising two complementary aspects in the presentation of learning material: contents itself and navigation. Navigation presents the list of paths which can be borrowed by a learner, how to traverse the learning universe or the set of the activities to be realised in the course.

The learning materials can be presented in a static way and in a dynamic way. When the presentation is dynamic, we will distinguish the following concepts relating to this point. Firstly, an *Adaptive Contents*, the information displayed in the user's screen can vary dynamically and automatically according to predefined criteria such as for example the rate of success to exercises, the time spent on a section, etc. Secondly, an *Adapted Contents* means that students follow a same course with different profiles to obtain different formations. Thirdly, an *Adaptive Navigation*, the set of activities, which can be carried out starting from one point of the course, is calculated dynamically according to predefined criteria. And finally, an *Adapted Navigation*, just like the contents, the path to be traversed in the subject can vary according to the learner's profile.

In addition, navigation can be of two types: *forced* and *free or open* navigation. Forced navigation in a course can completely be controlled by the system or not. A linear navigation is a typical example of strict control of navigation: the data elements are then presented the ones following the others as the pages of a book, which we turn. In the case of free or open navigation, the learner is free to pass from one node to the other without any constraint coming from the system.

In our system, we employed the adaptive contents and the adaptive navigation: forced navigation and half-open navigation with using an adaptive annotation technique [2] in both modes: free mode and guided mode. The adaptive annotation means that the system employs visual selections like icons, font, and colours, which are dynamically calculated by using the individual student model to show the type and the teaching role of each link.

3.2.2 Free Mode

In the free mode, the student chooses the subject from a menu. Then the system proposes a predetermined list of pedagogical objectives. For each chosen pedagogical objective, the system determines the learning units to present. To follow each unit, a list of concepts associated with this unit is given but the system will propose only the units, which contain at least the selected objective, known concepts and the required concepts (or pre-requisite list). The units are ordered according to the nature of unit, first the presentation then the exercise. As the student is progressing through the unit, an adaptive menu reminds him what has been activated, with which results and what remains to be done as represented in Fig 6. The navigation used in this mode is half-open navigation that the decision made from both the student and the system. The student chooses the pedagogical objective to learn, so the system finds in domain model the learning unit according to the student's needs.

3.2.3 Guided Mode

In the guided mode, the system proposes a menu, which is the list of subjects. When the student has selected the subject, the system takes the hand and generates the learning path for each student. The system decides the next unit to present by using the parameters of the current unit, the student model and additional criteria.

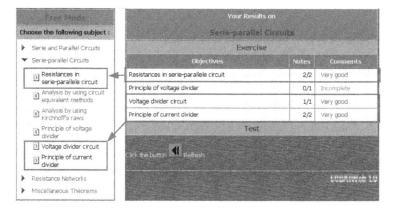

Fig. 6. Adaptive navigation for student X (on the left) compared to the result (on the right).

After the current unit is accomplished, the student model is updated according to post-actions in the unit, and the next unit to be presented is calculated. These units constitute the nodes of a semantic network whose arcs are created during learning to supplement the network and to form the learning universe. This characteristic confers a dynamic learning aspect since the orientation of learner is carried out in real time according to its progression. The system creates links between current unit and candidate units. Then the system selects one of the candidate units by applying the additional criteria. The system stops when all of pedagogical objectives are achieved or when no other unit can be carried out. Fig 7 shows the candidate units after execution of U1, so several types of links are employed to bind the current unit to candidate units, which can be selected as the next unit. In this case we employed forced navigation to show only the next unit.

For a more detailed description of the algorithm for calculating dynamic links, the reader can refer to [5].

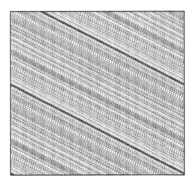

Fig. 7. Links between current unit (dark) and candidate units (clear) for student X

3.2.4 Multiple-Layered Overlay Student Model

The student model in our system is related to the declaratory conceptual domain knowledge. It can be presented as a "multiple-layered overlay model" within the meaning of [14]. We explain now how the multiple-layered model allows the adaptive annotation. Firstly, a concept is annotated as "*already studied*" if the exercises related to this concept were solved successfully. Secondly, the concept can be annotated as "*implied*" if the concept is not already studied but it is deduced as learned through another concept. Thirdly, the concept is annotated as "*indicated as known by the student*" if the student would mark this concept as known and if there is no independent information that the concept is "already studied" or "implied". Fourthly, the concept is annotated as "*ready and suggested to be visited*" if it is not assigned with one of the first three cases and all pre-requisites with this concept are satisfied. Finally fifthly, a concept is annotated as "*not ready to be visited*" if no previous case apply.

The current version of ECSAIWeb employs only three cases: "*already studied*", "*ready and suggested to be visited*" and "*not ready to be visited*". In free mode, if the student can solve successfully the exercises corresponding to the chosen pedagogical objective, then we mark this objective as "*already studied*", otherwise we mark it as "*not ready to be visited*". In guided mode, the next unit to be visited is computed dynamically according to the general learning goal and the learning state of the concepts. The next suggested unit would belong to the concept that is not assigned to one of the first three cases and that is the next one ready to be learned.

4   Comparison with Existing Systems

There currently exist many platforms for developing and distributing courses on the Web, for example non-adaptive or less adaptive systems like WebCT [7], and adaptive systems like InterBook [3], and ACE [11]. We use the criteria of CEDITI [4] study that produces an interesting comparative study of WEDS (Web-based Education Delivery System) system. We use the two following criteria: entities generated by the platforms and functions offered to the various users to compare ECSAIWeb with the systems mentioned above.

4.1 Entities Generated by the Platform

Several types of entities are taken into account by the WEDS. We distinguish the entities playing a primordial role in the distributed learning environments. But we will detail only objects that constitute teaching material.

4.1.1 The Teaching Materials

All four systems handle various types of materials in order to constitute teaching materials for learners. These teaching materials are thus the raison of being of the WEDS. Among these materials in general handled by the systems, we find courses, learning units, smaller entities (concept, themes, notions), exercises and evaluation, resources and syntheses. We also find in WebCT the following complementary objects: a glossary, an index, helps and a library, in InterBook a glossary. This criterion thus makes it possible to establish the nature of the objects which constitute teaching materials generated by the WEDS.

All the exploitable formats by the Web navigator can be used to carry out teaching material: indeed, the access to ECSAIWeb is done through standard Web navigator since the Web approach was privileged at the beginning of the project. In our system, we add special tags to mark physical learning units such as the tag PRESENTATION or QUESTION, and other tags to classify categories of presentation or question. We add the same tags in the formal model the logical learning units. InterBook uses the structure of the document through the use of headers to tell the system which concepts stand behind each section. ACE system divides the learning materials into several categories such as an introduction, texts, playgrounds, examples, tests, and summary. The special formats can thus be also used when plug-in is exploited by the navigator used on the station of learners.

4.1.2 Presentation of Objects

All of four environments chose the dynamic presentation of contents. In WebCT, the contents of a course can be adapted for a learner from a class, by the tutor. InterBook uses the domain model as a basis for structuring the content of an adaptive electronic textbook (ET), which uses the student model to adapt its behaviour to each particular user. The contents in ACE can be adapted depending on rules defined with each teaching strategy on each concept. ECSAIWeb exploits the static presentation corresponding to the number of pages of a learning unit which is fixed for all and then the dynamic presentation (adapted contents) of a sequence of learning units.

The possibilities of navigation in WebCT, which exploit opened navigation, allow constantly learners to reach freely the table of contents. InterBook and ACE exploit half-open navigation that allows constantly learners to reach freely the table of contents. Of course this type of navigation requires some handling because learners themselves never have a complete and simultaneous view of all the learning units. ECSAIWeb exploits two types of navigation. Static navigation to indicate the next page in the set of pages of the learning unit. Dynamic navigation: forced navigation to indicate the next learning unit calculated by the system, precisely in the guided mode, half-open navigation in free mode and open navigation for the table of contents.

4.2   Functions Offered to the Users

This criterion deals with the various services that we can obtain from a WEDS. We chose to organise them according to the roles played by the various users. In this part we will describe the point of view of learners and the authors.

4.2.1 Learners Viewpoint
The learner is at the heart of any WEDS. The criteria of description and/or comparison related to the range of tools and the possibilities offered by its learning environment are examined in this section. The course followed through WEDS leaves in general a great degree of freedom to learners on the time schedule. A table of contents is available to access to teaching materials for any course integrated into the seven systems. In an optional way, in the pages of the course we find buttons of navigation (back/next/up to the higher level) and hyperlinks between the pages of the course and the table of contents. The presentation of the content, in all systems, is dynamic in the sense that these tables are folded up and unfolded automatically according to the section of the consulted course or by means of a small mobile cursor which points on the consulted section. In other words, the support with navigation can reflect or not the learner's progression in the course or give a visual indication on the localisation in the course of consulted information. The four systems visualise the learner's progression through assessments, which are the personal assessments of the pedagogical objectives, practical work and the obtained notes. Moreover WebCT exploit also personal assessments of the used tools (banner page, contents, posted articles, reading articles, etc) and the comparative assessments of the obtained notes.

4.2.2 Authors Viewpoint
The role of the author relates to the creation of contents: it is a question of integrating into the WEDS, the multimedia version of the objects, which constitute pedagogical materials. The construction of the contents, its integration under the WEDS as well as the creation of a course is done typically during the same phase. Nevertheless, the development of the contents of the teaching objects "*pages*" can be made outside the WEDS and be integrated afterwards. Lack of authoring tool gives some difficulties to create or modify the content of learning unit.

WebCT offer tools for developing the contents such as tools for editing the pedagogical objectives, practical works, the contents of library and glossary and tools for integrating the external objects to it. InterBook use the regular way of structuring an MS Word file. It uses a pre-defined header text style then involves concept-based annotation of ET. ACE offers an editor that the author can define a curriculum structure, enrich the learning units with learning materials, specify relations between the learning units, and specify the instructional parameters. ECSAIWeb offers tools for defining the evaluation items, pedagogical objectives, logical learning units, tools for creating or modifying the physical learning units, and tools for checking the universe of learning units.

5   Conclusion

This system, like many systems based on the Web, provides a good illustration of the flexibility of the architecture. This architecture allowed us to redirect the tutoring knowledge contained in a tutor agent designed to run in a non-networked environment and to use it on the World Wide Web. However, the system would draw benefit from a better interaction. The use of the Perl programs for interfaces would allow the kind of interaction realised in this version, but the system was still blocked by the potential delay to send messages between the tool and the translator through internet. A more satisfactory solution but in the long term would be to re-write some components in Java likes the AIDS [13] and AlgeBrain [1]. This would allow a fast interaction between all the segments of the system. The strong point of this system is authoring mode, which allows the teacher-authors to modify and add the contents of physical units without modifying the links in the learning universe. Another advantage is that we can reuse physical units in the same subject or in related subjects.

Distance learning and the lifelong learning take an increasing importance. Environments for collaboration supported by computers receive a growing interest from the researchers. New models and architectures are necessary to be applied to such environments including or understanding the human companions as well as software agents. We are currently extending ECSAIWeb to include collaborative and co-operative supported learning.

6   References

1. Alpert, S.R., Singley, M.K. and Fairweather, P.G.(1999). Deploying Intelligent Tutors on the Web: An architecture and an example. International Journal of Artificial Intelligence in Education, 10, pp. 183-197.
2. Brusilovsky, P. (1997). Efficient Technique for Adaptive Hypermedia. In C. Nicholas and J. Mayfield(eds.): Intelligent hypertext: Advanced Techniques for World Wide Web. Lecture Notes in Computer Science n°1326, Berlin: Springer Verlag, pp. 12-30. http://www.contrib.andrew.cmu.edu/~plb/papers/EffTech.ps
3. Brusilovsky, P., Eklund, J., and Schwarz, E. (1998) Web-based education for all: A tool for developing adaptive courseware. Computer Networks and ISDN Systems (Seventh International World Wide Web Conference), 30 (1-7), pp291-300. Brisbane, Australia. http://www7.scu.edu.au/programme/fullpapers/1893/com1893.html
4. CEDITI, http://www.cediti.be/weds
5. Gavignet, E. (1991). Environnement de conception de système d'apprentissage: une modélisation de la connaissance pédagogique. Thèse de l'université de Nancy I.
6. Gavignet, E. (1994). Instructional Expertise in ECSAI. In *Proceedings of International Conference CALISCE'94*, Dessales J.L.ed., TELECOM Paris, France.
7. Goldberg, M.W, Salari, S. and Swoboda, P. (1996) World Wide Web – Course Tool: An Environment for Building WWW-Based Courses. In *Proceedings of Fifth International World Wide Web Conference*. Paris, France. Journal of Computer Networks and ISDN Systems, Volume 28, issues 7–11, p. 1219.
8. Grandbastien, M. (1999) Teaching Expertise is at the Core of ITS Research. International Journal of Artificial Intelligence in Education, 10, pp 335-349.

9. Hites, J.M. and Ewing, K. (1996) Designing and Implementing Instruction on the World Wide Web: A Case Study. In *Proceedings of ISPI'96, International Society for Performance and Instruction*, Texas, USA. http://lrs.stcloudstate.edu/ispi/proceeding.html

10. Ritter, S. (1997). PAT Online: A model-tracing tutor on the World Wide Web. In *Proceedings of the workshop "Intelligent Educational Systems on the World Wide Web" of AI-ED 97*. Kobe, Japan.
    http://www.contrib.andrew.cmu.edu/plb/AIED97_workshop/Ritter/Ritter.html

11. Specht, M. ACE (Adaptive Courseware Environment).
    http://129.26.167.17:8080/pub_html/html/NRHM/NRHM.html

12. Stern, M. K. (1997) The Difficulties in the Web-Based Tutoring, and Some Possible Solutions. In *Proceedings of the workshop "Intelligent Educational Systems on the World Wide Web" of AI-ED 97*. Kobe, Japan.
    http://www.contrib.andrew.cmu.edu/plb/AIED97_workshop/Stern.html

13. Warendorf, K. and Tan, C. (1997). AIDS – An Animated Data Structure Intelligent Tutoring System or Putting an Interactive Tutor on the WWW. In *Proceedings of the workshop "Intelligent Educational Systems on the World Wide Web" of AI-ED 97*. Kobe, Japan.
    http://www.contrib.andrew.cmu.edu/plb/AIED97_workshop/Warendorf/Warendorf.html

14. Weber, G. (1999) Adaptive Learning Systems in the World Wide Web. In J. Kay (Eds.), User modeling: Proceedings of the Seventh International Conference, UM99. Wien: Springer-Verlag, pp. 371-378.

Adaptive Content in an Online Lecture System

Mia K. Stern and Beverly Park Woolf

Center for Knowledge Communication
Department of Computer Science
University of Massachusetts, Amherst
U.S.A.
{stern,bev}@cs.umass.edu
http://www.cs.umass.edu/~ckc

Abstract. This paper discusses techniques for adapting the content in an online lecture system for a specific user. A two pass method is used: 1) determine the appropriate level of difficulty for the student and 2) consider the student's learning style preferences. A simple grading scheme is used to determine the student's knowledge and a Naïve Bayes Classifier is used to reason about the student's preferences in terms of explanations, examples, and graphics. A technique for gathering and using population data is also discussed.

1 Introduction

The World Wide Web, as it currently exists, is not very adaptable to user-specific needs and wants. Although this is changing with web-assistants like personal shoppers, the technology is still moving very slowly.

On the other hand, adaptive hypermedia systems [3] not specifically web based, do claim to be adaptive and adaptable. These systems are able to provide adaptive navigation (help guide the user through the hyperspace) and adaptive content (actually change the content of the pages according to some kind of user model).

Adaptive content can take on many different forms. One technique is to have a hard coded page that has some conditional text, or *fragments*. This text is included if a certain condition is met. The AHA system [5] uses such a technique. Another technique is hotword adaptation, such as that done in KN-AHS [6]. How the hotword is presented is based on whether the student is familiar with the concept. Another technique is *stretchtext*, which allows certain parts of the page to be opened or closed. Specifically, this technique allows a keyword or phrase to be clicked on by the user, and that action provides more information about that phrase. This information is not shown until the user requests it. MetaDoc [2] is an example of a system that uses this technique.

This paper focuses on adaptive content, specifically for instructional on-line material (see [11] for a discussion of our adaptive navigation techniques). De Bra [4] claims that no web-based adaptive hypermedia system is capable of implementing stretchtext. In this paper, we present MANIC, a web-based system that does implement a kind of stretchtext. A two pass approach is used to determine what to show and what to hide. The first considers the student's level of understanding and thus tries to present information that is not too hard nor too easy. The second analyzes the way students like to learn, and incorporates students' preferences.

P. Brusilovsky, O. Stock, C. Strapparava (Eds.): AH 2000, LNCS 1892, pp. 227–238, 2000.

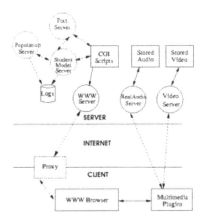

Fig. 1. MANIC system architecture

The rest of the paper is organized as follows. The MANIC structure, including the architecture and the domain organization, which allows for adaptive content, is described. Reasoning about what pieces of stretchtext to include is then discussed. How the user model is updated based on the user's actions is then described. We then describe how population data can be used to increase the accuracy of the tutor. We conclude with a discussion of the techniques presented and of future work.

2   Introduction to MANIC

MANIC is a web-based instructional system which provides lecture-based material [10][11]. Each course consists of "slides" which the instructor of the course designs and audio from the lecture. Although the initial versions of MANIC used static slides [9], i.e. the content was the same for every student, the current version does not. Rather, the slides are constructed dynamically based on a student model. How those slides are dynamically constructed is the main focus of this paper.

2.1   MANIC System Architecture

Because the system models and reasons about actions taken by the students, an architecture is needed that can record each action in a permanent record. Furthermore, the student's state must be kept in memory, rather than being rebuilt each time an action is made. In this section, we discuss how our architecture accomplishes these tasks.

The architecture consists of □ve parts: the client, the HTTP server, the port server, the student model servers, and the population server (see Figure 1). In this section, we discuss the □rst four parts of the architecture.

The client consists of a web browser (Netscape Navigator is the preferred browser) and a control applet that allows the student to traverse the course material. The applet contains buttons such as "next" and "table of contents."

The HTTP server uses Common Gateway Interface (CGI) scripts to interact with the port server and with the student model servers. The port server controls the creation of the student model servers; one server is created for each student using the system. When a student ▢rst logs on to the system, the port server is contacted to choose a port and to spawn a student model server on that designated port.

The main communication link is between the HTTP server and the student model servers. The HTTP server uses "cookies" to maintain state with a given client. The cookie stores the student's name, the server's IP address, and the port on which the student's server is listening.

Every action taken by the student is ▢rst reported to a CGI script. This CGI script contacts the student model server with the action taken (e.g. start topic) and any other pertinent info (e.g. the name of the topic to start).

The student model servers are the elements of the system that perform all of the "reasoning" and dynamic construction of course content. These servers run continuously, thus maintaining state. It is for this reason that this architecture was chosen; we did not want to have to rebuild state each time the HTTP server was contacted.

The student model server performs different actions depending on the message received from the HTTP server. The messages include "display the next slide" or "hide some stretchtext." Each time the student makes an action, his student model server is connected both to log that action and to generate the content as a consequence of the action. All of the HTML that the student eventually sees is generated dynamically by his student model server. The CGI scripts simply output this HTML without alteration.

2.2   Domain Organization

The domain for the lecture course is organized as a semantic network of topics, linked together by descriptive links, such as prerequisite, corequisite, remedial, etc. In [11] we describe how the system selects topics for the student to study.

Each topic itself is the root of a tree of subtopics, which are also topics. The leaves of these trees are *content objects* - either pieces of text or pictures. The trees are structured so that the leftmost and rightmost sets of children are content objects and the middle children are subtopics. However, it is possible that one or two of these sets of children may not exist for a given topic. A topic is presented by performing a depth-▢rst traversal of its tree. Therefore, the same basic information teaching a topic is presented to all students. However, the presentation of the content objects can be altered, which allows for the adaptation of the course. More or less supplemental information can be included, based on the student model.

Adaptation is accomplished through *concepts*, which can also be thought of as keywords. Each concept is a collection of related content objects which describe that concept. Whenever one of these keywords appears in a leaf content object, the tutor decides whether to include any of the content objects associated with that keyword. How the tutor makes this decision will be discussed in section 3.

The technique being used is called *stretchtext* [3]. The technique is modi▢ed by allowing graphics, as well as text, to be used as supplemental information. Furthermore, the keyword that is being "stretched" is not actually removed; rather the supplemental material is added after the sentence in which the keyword appears. We color code the

Table 1. Features in MANIC

Features	Values
Media Type	Graphic, Text
Instructional Type	Explanation, Example, Description, Deonition, Analogy
Abstractness	Abstract, Concrete
Place in topic	Beginning, End
Place in concept	Beginning, Middle, End
Wanted	Yes, No

keyword and the supplemental information so the student knows which supplemental material goes with which keyword (see Figure 2 for a pictorial example).

When a supplemental content object is shown to the user, a link is given allowing the user to hide that information. Similarly, if an object is not shown, the user is given the option of revealing the information. Thus, decisions made by the tutor are changeable by the student, and these student actions help the tutor "learn" to make better decisions.

The adaptive content in MANIC is a recursive process. When a content object is chosen to be used as stretchtext, the text of that content object itself may contain other concepts. Therefore, those concepts must themselves be analyzed to determine if content objects from that concept should be included as stretchtext.

As a result of the adaptive content, slide breaks are no longer static. The tutor dynamically decides where the slide breaks should occur, based on how much supplemental information needs to be shown. The tutor constructs a slide by adding content objects until the length of the slide is around 25 lines (or one screen, without scrolling, using 12pt font). When this length is reached, the tutor forces a slide break.

3   Reasoning about Additional Information

A two pass method is used to determine what supplemental information should be given to each student. The ørst determines, from a concept, what content objects are at the correct "hardness" or level of difoculty (LOD), taking into consideration how much a student knows about a concept. The second determines what the student wants, and takes into consideration how the student likes to learn. There are enough content objects within a concept that the student can be presented just those objects that are appropriate for his mastery level and learning style.

3.1   Determining Correct Level of Difoculty

Supplemental content objects have a "level of difoculty" ranging from 0 to 3 (corresponding to easiest, easy, medium, and hard), which describes how hard they are to understand. This level of difoculty measurement is important for being able to adapt the content based on the student's knowledge.

When deciding what supplemental content objects are at the correct level of difo-culty, the tutor must analyze how well it thinks the student knows the concept. Each concept has four different mastery values, one for each level of difficulty. These mastery values are determined by a pretest. Thus students with differing abilities start the course with different a priori mastery values.

To decide which content objects are at the correct level of difficulty, the tutor simply determines the highest level of difficulty the student has mastered. A level of difficulty is said to be mastered if its score is greater than 0.85 (on a 0 to 1 scale). The tutor then chooses those content objects that are one level of difficulty higher than the student's highest mastered level of difficulty. Of course, if the student has not mastered level 0, then level 0 is chosen as the correct level of difficulty. Also, if level 3 is mastered, then level 3 is the chosen level of difficulty.

3.2 Reasoning about What a Student Wants

The goal in MANIC is to provide a presentation that reflects the student's preferred learning style without him having to take many actions to change the presentation to reflect his preferences. The tutor attempts to learn the student's preferences by observing his interactions with the system.

Content objects at the same level of difficulty have different qualities that the tutor can differentiate between in order to adapt the content on an individual basis. For example, one student may prefer pictures over textual explanations. Another may like concrete, graphical examples early in a concept presentation but prefer more abstract textual descriptions later on. Yet another student may prefer the opposite ordering. The tutor uses these qualities, or *features* to choose what a student wants to see. The features the tutor uses are given in Table 1. The features were chosen by domain experts and take into consideration different ways students can learn.

Some features are set a priori, such as *media type, instructional type,* and *abstractness.* However, *place in topic* and *place in concept* are computed as the object is being considered. The place in topic refers to whether it is in the leftmost or rightmost set of children of a topic. The place in concept refers to how many times the concept has been shown. If it is less than one third of the possible times it could be shown, it is at the beginning. If it is between one third and two third, it is in the middle. Otherwise, it is at the end. These two features are used to reflect the ordering preferences of the student. The *wanted* feature is what is being predicted.

The tutor "learns" what a student's preferences are via machine learning. To do this, a Naïve Bayes Classifier [8] is used as the machine learning technique. A Naïve Bayes Classifier applies to certain kinds of problems where each instance x can be described by a conjunction of attribute values and where the target function $f(x)$ can take on any value from a finite set V. The list of sets of attribute values and its corresponding category are given to the machine learner, and these constitute the training set (or *example space* in MANIC terminology). When a new example is presented, a value for the target function can be predicted based on the training instances. The learner chooses the value for the target function that has the highest probability, based on the training set.

The formula for the Naïve Bayes Classifier is, given attribute values $< a_1, ..., a_n >$:

$$v_{NB} = \operatorname*{argmax}_{v_j \in V} P(v_j) \prod_i P(a_i|v_j). \tag{1}$$

A Naïve Bayes Classifier is the chosen learning method because it is fast and has been proven to be very accurate for user modeling tasks [1]. It also works well with little data [7], which is a consideration with a user modeling application. We want the machine learner to be able to start learning about the student after very few interactions.

Since the goal of the adaptive content is to provide a presentation that does not require any changes by the student, the Naïve Bayes Classifier is used to predict if an object will be wanted or not, based on the other features of that object. Those objects that are predicted to be wanted will be shown to the user, while the others will not be shown.

In order to determine which content objects to show, the tutor first groups all content objects at the correct level of difficulty, as described in the last section, with the same features into a *feature class*. If these objects are shown, they will be shown as a group, in order to simplify the interface for the student. Using this grouping technique, the student does not have to ask, for example, to see all abstract picture examples at level of difficulty 2 to find the one he wants.[1]

After this grouping has been done, the tutor examines each content object in question, and uses the Naïve Bayes Classifier to predict if the object will be *wanted*. The Naïve Bayes Classifier works by essentially comparing the features of the current content object to the features of content objects in its example space. The example space consists of content objects that, in the past, were either wanted or not wanted by the student. Section 4.2 describes how the tutor determines if an object was in fact wanted or not.

3.3   An Example

Let us now consider an example of how the MANIC adaptive content engine works. For the sake of this example, we will consider a student who has the example space given in Table 2. The student also has the following mastery levels on the concept *switch*: Level 0 = 0.92, Level 1 = 0.46, Level 2 = 0.33, Level 3 = 0.1

While planning the next slide, the system comes across the text object that consists of the phrase "a set of computers and/or switches connected by communication links." In this phrase, the word "switch" refers to the concept *switch*. Therefore, the system must decide what content objects that are associated with that concept to include for the student. The possible content object features are given in Table 3.

The first pass of the algorithm determines which content objects are at the correct level of difficulty. Based on the algorithm given in section 3.1, the correct level of difficulty is 1. Therefore, Switch3 can be eliminated, but both Switch1 and Switch2 are at the correct level of difficulty. The system then uses the Naïve Bayes Classifier to determine if either of those objects is *wanted*.

The Naïve Bayes Classifier uses the following formulas to determine if an object is wanted or not. The value x in our application is either *Yes* or *No*.

---

[1] For the remainder of this paper, however, we will use the term content object when referring to feature classes. All the objects in a feature class can be considered to be combined into one content object.

Table 2. A sample example space

Instructional Type	Media Type	Place in Topic	Place in Concept	Abstractness	Wanted
Example	Picture	Beginning	Beginning	Abstract	Yes
Definition	Picture	Beginning	End	Concrete	Yes
Definition	Picture	End	End	Concrete	Yes
Description	Picture	Beginning	Beginning	Concrete	Yes
Explanation	Text	Beginning	Middle	Abstract	Yes
Definition	Picture	End	Middle	Abstract	No
Description	Text	End	Middle	Abstract	No
Explanation	Text	End	End	Abstract	No
Example	Text	Beginning	Beginning	Concrete	No

Table 3. Content objects in concept *switch*

Name	Instructional Type	Media Type	Place in Topic	Place in Concept	Abstractness	LOD
Switch1	Explanation	Text	Beginning	Beginning	Concrete	1
Switch2	Description	Text	Beginning	Beginning	Abstract	1
Switch3	Explanation	Text	Beginning	Beginning	Abstract	2

$$P(Wanted = x) * P(InstructionalType = Definition|Wanted = x)$$
$$* P(MediaType = Picture|Wanted = x)$$
$$* P(PlaceinTopic = End|Wanted = x) \qquad (2)$$
$$* P(PlaceinConcept = Middle|Wanted = x)$$
$$* P(Abstractness = Abstract|Wanted = x).$$

Therefore, when evaluating whether Switch1 or Switch2 should be shown, the tutor performs the following calculations:

- The probability that Switch1 is wanted is $\frac{5}{9} * \frac{1}{5} * \frac{1}{5} * \frac{4}{5} * \frac{2}{5} * \frac{3}{5} = 0.004266$

- The probability that Switch1 is not wanted is $\frac{4}{9} * \frac{1}{4} * \frac{3}{4} * \frac{1}{4} * \frac{1}{4} * \frac{1}{4} = 0.0013$

Normalizing these values, we get $P(Switch1\ Wanted = Yes) = \frac{0.004266}{0.004266+0.0013} =$ 0.7664 and $P(Switch1\ Wanted = No) = \frac{0.0013}{0.004266+0.0013} = 0.23356$. Therefore, Switch1 would be shown. Similarly:

- The probability that Switch2 is wanted is $\frac{5}{9} * \frac{1}{5} * \frac{1}{5} * \frac{4}{5} * \frac{2}{5} * \frac{2}{5} = 0.002844$

- The probability that Switch2 is not wanted is $\frac{4}{9} * \frac{1}{4} * \frac{3}{4} * \frac{1}{4} * \frac{1}{4} * \frac{3}{4} = 0.0039$

Normalizing these values, we get $P(Switch2\ Wanted=Yes)=0.42136$ and $P(Switch2\ Wanted = No) = 0.57863$. Therefore, Switch2 would not be shown. Figure 2 illustrates what the slide would look like to the student, given that only Switch1 was chosen to be shown. There are links to hide Switch1 and to show Switch2 and Switch3.

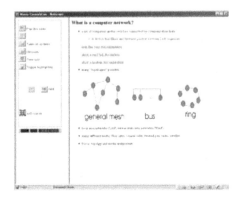

Fig. 2. Sample slide generated by MANIC

4   Grading a Concept

This section discusses how a concept is graded, based on what content objects the student has either seen or not seen.

4.1   Mastery Level

For each content object the student has seen, the mastered values of the associated concept are updated for each level of difficulty. For example, say a student sees a text object of level of difficulty 2. This fact affects the probability that each level of difficulty is mastered. Specifically, there is considerably more evidence that the student has mastered levels of difficulty 0 and 1, some evidence that level of difficulty 2 is mastered, but little evidence that level of difficulty 3 is mastered. Thus all four level of difficulty values need to be updated.

We also consider how much time the student spent studying the object. This measure is used even though time is an inherently inexact measure. However, we feel that it is sufficient for our purposes. The goal is to judge a student's ability partially by the way he studies the material. If he is spending not enough time, he may not be able to learn the material well enough. If he is spending too much time, he may not be comprehending what he is studying.

In order to apply this scheme, we need to determine how much time is too little, how much is optimal, and how much is too much (this terminology refers most accurately to how much time the student should study an object of the same level of difficulty as the level he should be studying, as decided by the tutor). "Optimal" time to spend studying a content object is calculated in a general way. The author of the course decides how much time per line the student should spend studying an object. This value is then multiplied by the number of lines in the object (the author also supplies the approximate number of lines for pictures). The tutor observes how much time has passed since an object was first shown to when it is no longer shown, either due to changing slides or asking to have the object hidden. It then compares this time to the optimal time. If it is

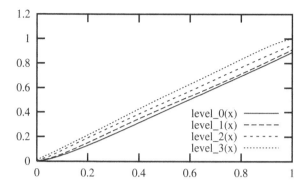

Fig. 3. Regression equations for updating the level 2 mastery when objects seen for too much time

1/3 less than the optimal time, then it is considered to be not enough time. If it is 1/3 more than the optimal time, it is too much time. Otherwise, it is the optimal time.

We use regression equations to determine the how the concept grades should be updated. Each regression equation determines a new value for the probability that the level is mastered, based on the old value. Furthermore, each equation is responsible for calculating new values for a single level of difﬁculty and for a single event. For example, to update the student's level 0 mastery, equations are needed that represent whether a level 0 , 1, 2, or 3 object was seen and whether too little time, optimal time, or too much time was spent on the object. Thus for each level to update, a total of 48 equations are needed: 16 for too little time, 16 for optimal time, and 16 for too much time. Figure 3 shows the regression equations used to update the level 2 mastery values for too much time spent.

The general plan for updating concept grades is based on both the level of difﬁculty of the content objects viewed and the time spent studying those objects. To update the level of difﬁculty x mastery score, the system asks whether the level of difﬁculty is:

- greater than or equal to x. In this case, the score is increased more when the optimal time is spent on the object and increased less when the object is seen for too little or too much time
- less than x. In this case, the score is decreased some for an object seen for not enough time, more for an object seen for optimal time, and even more for an object seen for too much time.

The reasoning for the ﬁrst rule is that if the student sees something harder than what he has mastered, he should be rewarded for that. The reasoning for the second rule is that if the student sees something easier than what he has mastered, the tutor has misjudged his knowledge. However, if he only brieﬂy looks at the object, he should not be penalized the same as if he had studied the object for a longer time.

The regression equations were obtained using the help of an expert in the subject. An expert was asked, given prior values, what the next values should be under the various circumstances. For example, if the student's level 0 mastery value is x, and a level 2 object has been seen for the optimal time, what should the student's new level 0 mastery be? For each such circumstance, the expert provided 5 pre- post-action pairs. We then used polynomial regression to ▢t a curve to those points.

4.2   Wanted or Not Wanted

In section 3.2, we discussed how the Na▢ve Bayes Classi▢er predicts whether an object is wanted or not. In this section, we discuss how the actual wanted values of content objects are determined.

When a student leaves a slide, either to see another slide or to take a quiz, the tutor analyzes which supplemental content objects were shown and which were hidden. Objects which were shown were either originally shown and not hidden or originally hidden and asked to be shown. Objects that were hidden either remain hidden the whole time or were shown and then hidden by the user.

Those objects that were shown are considered *wanted*, while those that were hidden are considered *not wanted*. The tutor sets the *wanted* feature value of the objects to *Yes* if they were shown and to *No* if they were hidden. These objects are then added to the example space of the Na▢ve Bayes Classi▢er, thus increasing the size of the training set.

We do not want to penalize the student for not viewing objects that are at the "wrong" level of dif▢culty. Therefore, objects that were at a level of dif▢culty other than the one chosen by the tutor that were not seen are *not* added to the feature space. However, if the student elects to see objects at a different level of dif▢culty, those objects are considered wanted, and are therefore added to the example space with their *wanted* feature value set to *Yes*.

It is important to note that the Na▢ve Bayes Classi▢er initially predicts the *wanted* value, but it is not that prediction that is added to the example space. Rather, it is the actual value of the student's desires that is added to the example space. It is this growing example space that the classi▢er will use for future predictions.

5   Population Server

One of the bene▢ts of a web-based system is the ability to gather and analyze data from all users of the system. This data can be used to improve a machine learning system for a number of reasons. First, a student may not see a diverse enough set of objects for the predictions to be accurate. However, if other students have a similar pattern of behavior as this student, and they have seen a wider array of objects, their models can be used to predict objects for this student. Second, there may be no discernible pattern based on a student's examples alone. A pattern may emerge, though, when comparing this student's examples to other students who have already used the system.

The goal of using population data is to improve the accuracy of predictions. To do this, *population example spaces* are created and maintained by the population server (see Figure 1). These spaces can be composed of examples from more than one student.

When a student logs on for a session, the ▢rst 10 objects he encounters are collected and classi▢ed using the population example spaces. Whichever population space has the highest accuracy rate (i.e. it classified the objects the same category as they actually were) above a certain threshold (75%) is returned as the space to use for this student. If no space qualifies, the user's own space is used. This returned space is then used by the Naïve Bayes Classifier during the user's session.

At the end of the session, all of the user's examples from that session are classified using the existing population spaces. If there is a space that has a high accuracy above the threshold, the student's examples are merged into that space, and the population example space is grown. If not, then a new population example space is created from this user's examples. It is in this way that new population spaces are created.

6   Conclusions

In this paper we have presented techniques for adaptive content in a web-based adaptive hypermedia system. The technique we use has two passes: the first determines the correct level of difficulty of the content and the second considers the student's learning style preferences. The first pass ensures that the material is not too hard nor too easy. We use mastery scores to make this determination. These mastery scores are then updated based on what supplemental material the student has seen and for how much time.

However, our current method for using time as a measure of understanding does not take into consideration individual differences in learning. For example, some students may read slower than others, but still comprehend just as much. Others may need more time studying pictures than reading text. Our future work will include designing the tutor to "learn" appropriate optimal time values for each individual student interacting with each kind of object.

The second pass of the algorithm ensures that the student will like the presentation, and will thus learn better from it. We use a Naïve Bayes Classifier to learn the student's preferences by watching which supplemental objects he shows or hides. We also use population data to improve the accuracy of the predictions.

The system currently in use is for Unix network programming. However, the techniques we have discussed are not domain specific and could therefore be applied to any other lecture style course. We will in the future be applying these techniques to other courses from many different areas of study.

Acknowledgements

This material is based upon work supported by the National Science Foundation under Grant No. #DUE-9813654 and also by NSF/Darpa and Apple Computer Technology Reinvestment Award (CDA 9408607). Any opinions, findings, and conclusions or recommendations expressed in this material are those of the author(s) and do not necessarily reflect the views of the National Science Foundation. This material is also supported by a University of Massachusetts graduate fellowship.

References

[1] D. Billsus and M. Pazzani. Learning Probabilistic User Models. In *Proceedings of the Workshop on Machine Learning for User Models, Sixth International Conference on User Modeling*, Chia Laguna, Sardinia, June 1997.

[2] C. Boyle and A.O. Encarnacion. MetaDoc: an Adaptive Hypertext Reading System. In P. Brusilovsky, A. Kobsa, and J. Vassileva, editors, *Adaptive Hypertext and Hypermedia*, chapter 3, pages 71–89. Kluwer Academic Publishers, The Netherlands, 1998.

[3] P. Brusilovsky. Methods and Techniques of Adaptive Hypermedia. *User Modeling and User-Adapted Interaction*, 6:87–129, 1996.

[4] P. De Bra. Design Issues in Adaptive Hypermedia Application Development. In *Proceedings of the Second Workshop on Adaptive Systems and User Modeling on the World Wide Web*, Banff, Canada, June 1999.

[5] P. De Bra and L. Calvi. Creating Adaptive Hyperdocuments for and on the Web. In *Proceedings of Webnet*, pages 189–201, 1997.

[6] A. Kobsa, D. Müller, and A. Nill. KN-AHS: An Adpative Hypertext Klient of the User Modelling System BGP-MS. In *4th International Conference on User Modeling*, pages 31–36, Hyannis, MA, 1994.

[7] P. Langley, W. Iba, and K. Thompson. An Analysis of Bayesian Classiﬁers. In *Proceedings of the Tenth Conference on Artiﬁcial Intelligence*, San Jose, CA, 1992. AAAI Press.

[8] T. Mitchell. *Machine Learning*, chapter 6, pages 177–179. WCB McGraw-Hill, Boston, MA, 1997.

[9] M. Stern, J. Steinberg, H.I. Lee, J. Padhye, and J. Kurose. MANIC: Multimedia Asynchronous Networked Individualized Courseware. In *Educational Media and Hypermedia*, 1997.

[10] M. Stern, B.P. Woolf, and J. F. Kurose. Intelligence on the Web? In *Artiﬁcial Intelligence in Education*, 1997.

[11] M. K. Stern and B. P. Woolf. Curriculum Sequencing in a Web-Based Tutor. In *Proceedings of Intelligent Tutoring Systems*, San Antonio, Texas, August 1998.

A Web-Based Socratic Tutor for Trees Recognition

Mónica Trella, Ricardo Conejo, Eduardo Guzmán

Dpto. Lenguajes y Ciencias de la Computación, E.T.S.I. Informática,
Universidad de Málaga, Málaga 29071, Spain.
{trella, conejo, guzman}@lcc.uma.es

Abstract. Socratic dialogues has been widely uses as a way of implement an ITS. The idea behind it is that the teaching and learning process should be based upon a personal reflection that can be obtained posing the right question on a guided dialogue. This methodology assumes that the knowledge acquisition is a discovering process in which both the teacher and the student plays an active role. This tutorial strategy has been developed as a part of a web based ITS architecture for declarative domains and it has been applied to the botanical domain. In this paper we describe this component, the knowledge representation that support it and the web interface used.

1 Introduction

This work arose as a part of the **TREE** project (**TR**aining of European **E**nvironmental trainers and technicians in order to disseminate multinational skills between European countries). The TREE project was included in the EU Leonardo da Vinci Program, and its main goal was the development of an ITS for the classification and identification of different European forestry species. Together with the ITS the TREE project covered the development of a Knowledge Base about the forestry domain [1], an Expert System and an Adaptive Tests Generation System [2]. Each one of these components has an independent Web-based interface that allows the whole system to be used as a learning tool or as an independent consultation tool.

The idea of creating a generic ITS architecture for declarative domains arose parallel to the TREE ITS development. This architecture, which will be briefly described in the next section, has among other modules a set of tutorial components that are tasks that a student can do to learn something (to read a text, make a summary, take a test...).

The goal of this paper is to describe one of those components: the Socratic Tutor. Socratic teaching consists of maintaining a dialogue with the student by asking him questions about the subject domain (forestry morphology in the case of the TREE Tutor). If the student fails, the system will infer the possible causes of this wrong answer so it will assist the student in teaching the correct solution by himself.

Socratic dialogues has been widely uses as a way of implement an ITS. Back in the early days of ITS, the idea of teaching by using a Socratic dialogue was first used by Collins and Stevens in the classical system WHY [3] and also by Brown and Burton in BLOCK [4]. The idea behind the Socratic dialogue strategy is that the teaching and learning process should be based upon a personal reflection that can be obtained

P. Brusilovsky, O. Stock, C. Strapparava (Eds.): AH 2000, LNCS 1892, pp. 239-249, 2000.

posing the right question on a guided dialogue. The Socratic method assumes that the knowledge acquisition is a discovering process in which both the teacher and the student plays an active role. These features are especially interesting for web-based tutorials because a web session can be conceptually thought as a kind of dialogue.

The following dialogue is a very trivial example of this tutorial methodology in the domain of botany. It is supposed to be held between a botany professor and a student during a field visit:

S> *Could you tell me what is this tree?*
P> *I think you already know it, what do you think it is?*
S> *Isn't it a birch?*
P> *No, no, this tree has a conic crown and a birch doesn't.*
S> *All right, I didn't notice that, so it should be a cypress.*
P> *No, it isn't it. Have you noted that the arrangement of leaves in this tree is helicoidal and the cypresses have them opposite?*
S> *is that a fir?*
P> *You're right! It is Abies pinsapo, you may also note that it has cones, dark bark,....*

Note that the professor do not give the answer to the student directly, because he thinks it is something that has been explained sometime before, instead of that he poses an initial open question just to know how much the student knows. After the initial answer the professor already knows that the student hasn't the faintest idea of what it is the tree is. But instead of giving him the answer right away, he gives the student a valuable hint, he points out that the questioned tree has a conic crown, that is something evident, but that has been possibly ignored by the student. He also fails the question, but now the answer can be considered better because both are *Gimnospermae*. The professor happily impressed by the progress made, gives more data to the student, he indicates the main differences between the cypress and the fir. Finally the student solves the question partially. The professor considers enough the answer and gives to the student the rest of the information.

One of the main problems in Socratic tutors has been the knowledge representation. This is, the component that allows the tutor to pose the right question to the student. Most systems deal with non-finite domains, that is, they can not assume that the tutor has all the answer beforehand. They normally use IF-THEN rules and tactical metarules to guide the dialogue and keep it coherent [5]. Another classical problem in Socratic dialogue systems is the natural language interaction. In our case we are dealing with a large (but finite), number of species and with a large (but finite) number of attributes, and we avoid the natural language problem by using a form-based dialogue. The problem that remains is the knowledge representation and the inference mechanism that implements the tutorial strategy. The tutorial knowledge itself has been elicited from heuristic expertise of a human tutor in the domain.

In the following section we describe the general architecture in which the Socratic tutor is embedded. After that, the structure and the behavior of the Socratic tutor are described and a brief example is presented.

2   ITS Architecture

During his academic life, a student must learn many domains in different knowledge areas as geography, natural sciences, biology, language etc. A generic architecture to build Web based ITSs to teach this sort of domains has been designed (*see* Fig. 1).

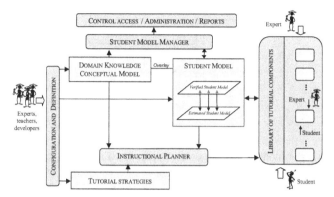

Fig. 1. Generic ITS architecture for declarative domains.

In order to place the Socratic Tutor into this architecture a general view of it is given below.

In this architecture there are some modules that contain data and knowledge and another functional modules that use this information to carry out their tasks.

The firsts ones are:

❑ *Conceptual Domain Model*, a description of the domain to be taught,

❑ *Student Knowledge*, a sub-set of the domain model representing what the student knows,

❑ *Historical Student Record,* that stores all the information of student sessions (number of sessions, session duration, connection address, sessions trace, pages visited, etc.),

❑ *Tutorial Strategies*, a set of rules and session configuration parameters given by the ITS designer.

The functional systems modules are:

❑ *Definition and Configuration module*, that is formed by a set of tools that allow to the experts and teachers to define the Conceptual Domain Model and the Tutorial Strategies,

❑ *Student Model Manager*, that actualizes the Student Model depending on the student's actions results,

❑ *Access Control / Administration / Reports*, that manages the student system access (login, passwords, the courses that he/she is allowed to connect to, etc.), all the administrative tasks and makes reports about the students,

❑ *Instruction Planner*, that takes the tutorial decisions during the learning process. It must to decide depending on the Student Model state wich is the next tutorial goal (what domain concepts would the student learn now) and then the best tutorial strategy to teach this to a particular student. The Instruction Planner is the module that brings to the ITS the capability of adapting the learning to each student,

☐ *Tutorial Components Library*, that implements a set of tasks that a student can do as a part of the tutorial/learning process. All the components have the structure shown in Fig 2.

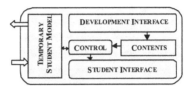

Fig. 2. Tutorial Component structure.

The *Control* is the module in charge of carrying out the component task interacting with the student through the *Student Interface* using the partial knowledge included by the teachers through the *Development Interface*. The nature of the *Contents* module information will depend on the specific component task. For example, a *test* component will contain questions; a *reading-text* component will have HTML pages, etc. All components in the *Component Library* have its own development and student interfaces that are designed to be used through Internet.

The instruction is based upon a main cycle that can be repeated: The *Instruction Planner* first selects a set of concepts to be learned and then it selects the way of teaching them by choosing a *Tutorial Component* in the Library. When the component is selected, the part of the *Student Model* related with the tutorial goal designed by the *Instruction Planner* is copied to the component *Temporary Student Model*, that will evolve with the student's actions. When the student finished his task inside the component, the *Student Model Manager* actualizes the *Student Model* with the contents of the *Temporary Student Model*.

3   Socratic Tutor

The *Socratic Tutor* is a *Tutorial Component* that teaches by posing a problem to the student and, by maintaining a dialogue, guides him towards the correct solution. This component has been designed to teach declarative domains organized hierarchically as for example the botanical domain taxonomy of the TREE ITS (*see* Fig. 4).

The Tutorial Components in a tutorial session are selected by the planner based on the current state of the student model. The planner should identify the students needs and configures a partial tutorial goal. Then it selects the most appropriate tutorial strategy to achieve that goal taking into account student's background. From the Socratic Tutor point of view, the tutorial goal is just to teach the student how to differentiate between two sets of concepts (*A* and *B*) of the same level in the hierarchy. Selecting these sets concerns to the *Instruction Planner* that has access to the global student model.

3.1   Operating Schema of the Socratic Tutor

A session with the Socratic Tutor is divided in several proposals. Each of them will finish in a determined state that is stored by the Tutor. Each time a student finishes a proposal, the Tutor analyses his trajectory and decides if the session in the Socratic Tutor has to finish or must continue with another proposal. In the section bellow, we have represented a proposal example. The tutorial knowledge that guides the Socratic dialogue of a single proposal is represented by a finite state automaton. The input alphabet of this automaton is taken from student possible answers:

- **r**: right answer,
- **f** : failure,
- **f+**: failure more serious than the previous failure, that is, the failure has been increased,
f-: failure less serious than the previous failure, that is, the failure has been decreased,
- **f=**: failure with the same importance than the previous failure,
- **u**: unknown

The system proposal starts in the state 1 asking the student to recognize a concept (*what is that...?*) by presenting a photo or an image, and progress according to the Fig. 3 diagram depending on the student answer. Each proposal finishes with one of the following states: *Bi* or *M*, where *Bi* indicates passing the proposal successfully by doing *i* failures and *M* not passing.

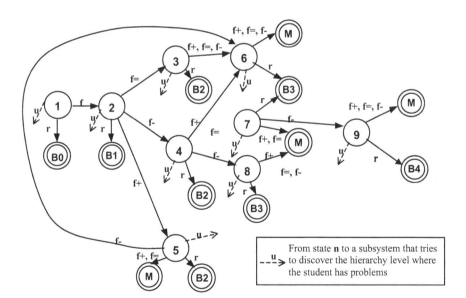

Fig. 3. State diagram in the Socratic Tutor.

The initial question is reformulated each time that the student fails, including a new hint to help him to obtain the right answer. This hint takes into account the wrong answer given. The proposal continues until the student finds out the right answer or the instruction is considered unfruitful.

The system gives more opportunities and help to the student that is decreasing his failures because that means that the student is improving with the Tutor hints, so is probably that he/she reaches the right solution. Whereas if the student increase his failures the system detects that the student is not learning and must give him the opportunity to start another proposal at which he/she would learn better.

Two criterions have been established to classify the student's error into $f+$, $f-$, or $f=$:

1. The main goal of a Socratic Tutor proposal is that the student differentiates between sets of concepts (of the same level in the hierarchy): A and B. C represents the rest of concepts in the knowledge base. So the first criterion to classify the error is the set to which the students answer belongs to. Let us suppose that the proposal concept is $A_j \in A$. Then the possible failures ordered from greater to minor are: $B_i \in B$, $C_i \in C$ and $A_i \in A$.

2. The second criterion of error classification is the domain hierarchy. A student error will decrease if the hierarchy level of the first predecessor non-coincident of the proposal and student response is lower than the one in the previous error. (It is not the same to confuse one concept with another with the same parent in the hierarchy that to confuse it with another that has a completely different predecessor.)

A proposal starts when the system presents to the student a photo or an image of one element of the input sets. From that moment, the Tutor analyzes the student answers and acts in consequence. The Tutor has some tasks that are common to all the states represented in the Fig. 3:

1. Finding non-coincident predecessors of the proposal and the student answer.
2. Extracting the list of differences to be presented to the student as a hint.
3. Finding two photos or images that show as many differences of the list as possible.
4. If there are some features in the list of differences that can not be shown, the Tutor will remove them from the list.

The amount of help is increased each time a student makes an error. As the tutorial goal is learning to distinguish two set elements, the hints given to students are the list of differences between the right answer and the student answer.

The differences are classified in two categories: the important differences (those that are necessaries to differentiate two concepts, clearly observable and substantially significant); and the additional differences (those that are not key features in order to distinguish them but can help in this task).

The hints presented to the student start with the important differences of the higher pair of nodes non-coincident in the hierarchy and advance in two ways: first going down in the hierarchy and then adding additional differences to the list.

Until now we have considered that the student answers the proposal question, but it can occur that the student is not be sure of the answer and he decides not to give any answer. Then the system takes the input *unknown* and tries to discover why the student doesn't know the answer; that is, it tries to find out the hierarchy level in which he has confused. In TREE example (Fig. 4), if the proposal is a species, the system will try to check if the student is not sure about the division, the family or the gender of this specie. This task will be carried out by a subsystem. In order to do that, this subsystem would propose to the student a new question that asks for a simpler task, that is, select among classes in a higher level of the hierarchy. It will ask the students to choose a class that is the predecessor of the proposal question concept. If the student fails then the error level of the student has been detected and a hint to repair can be presented. The subsystem can follow two strategies: (1) Top-Down, asking first for the highest level in the hierarchy and going on with the following levels. For instance, if the proposal level is species, it will ask the student to choose among the highest level. So the next question will be to select among the divisions (Angiosperme/Gimnosperme) of the species in the question, and then the family and finally the gender. (2) Bottom-Up, asking first for the level immediately superior to the proposal level. Following with the example above, the subsystem will ask first for the gender, then for the family and finally for the division.

3.2   Tutor Sessions

A session is composed by several proposals. Each proposal presents to the student a concept of any set of the tutorial goal (A_i $\square$ A or B_i $\square$ B). During a session the same proposal will be presented to he student in order to confirm the previous results. The session finalization criterion will be *maximum numbers of proposals* for any possible finalization state (M or Bi). These factors will be configurable by the teachers and are the following:

□ Maximum number total of proposal presented to the student.
□ Maximum number of consecutive proposals finished in the state M.
□ Maximum number of consecutive proposals finished in the state $B0$.
□ Maximum number of equals proposals (about the same domain concept) finished in the state Bi ($i > 0$).

The finalization criterion is local to the Socratic Tutor, which is just a component of a complex system. The role of the finalization criterion is to decide whether or not this instruction is being useful to the student. In the worst case, the objective previously decided by the *Instruction Planner* might be too difficult, or perhaps the teaching style is not well suited for him. The Socratic Tutor estimates the fulfillment of the goal and passes this information to the *Student Model Manager* that modifies the *Global Student Model* and lets the *Instruction Planner* to act accordingly. The next task proposed to the student may be any other component of the system.

4   Proposal Example

In what follows we will use the TREE tutor and its hierarchically structured domain as an example, in order to make the explanations clearer.

The forestry species domain is structured hierarchically in several levels: divisions, classes, families, genera, and species. We have developed a knowledge acquisition tool for domain experts to complete the domain *Knowledge Base* (*KB*) through a web-interface [1]. Fig. 4. shows a partial view of the domain hierarchical structure. Each node in the hierarchy has its own set of attributes that describes it.

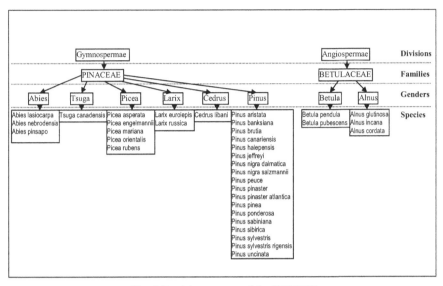

Fig. 4. Partial taxonomy of the TREE KB

In the example of the forestry domain, we can say that a student has learned the European trees if he is able to recognize any given specie from a set of photographs. In order to help in this task, the Domain Model contains the main *differences* and *similarities* between the nodes in the hierarchy. All the differences are extracted automatically of the KB and the botanical experts mark those that are more helpful to differentiate two species. To complete the Domain Model there are a set of photographs that are introduced by experts through the Web interface. Each photo has associated information about what is pictured in it.

A session with the Socratic Tutor is divided in several proposals. In order to explain the interaction between the system and the student, we are going to develop a tutorial proposal example with the Socratic Tutor. Let us suppose that the tutorial goal is that the student distinguishes the sets of genera $A = \{Abies\}$ and $B = \{Betula\}$. The partial taxonomy corresponding to those genera is shown in the Fig. 4.

The goal of this tutor is to teach by practicing with photos. The system will show a photo to the student and he/she will have to classify the genera in the photo.

In the example in the Fig. 5, the Tutor asks the student for the genera *Abies* and he/she answers *Betula*. The first time the student fails (*state 2* in Fig. 3), the Tutor looks for the first non-coincident predecessors between the proposal and the answer, and makes the list of important differences between both. In the example, the non-coincident predecessors of the pair *Abies-Betula* (proposal-student answer) are divisions, *Gimnospermae-Angiospermae* and families, *Pinaceae-Betulaceae* (*see* Fig. 4). So the system presents to the student the main differences between the divisions (first non-coincident predecessors) *Gimnospermae* and *Angiospermae* (*see* table 1).

The next student answer is *Cupressus* and the system must determine if the student failure has been increased or decreased with regard to the previous error. The first criterion was the set to which the students answer belongs to. Both failures are genera of the same set ($C = \{All\ the\ genera\ in\ the\ KB\} - A - B$), so the system analyzes the

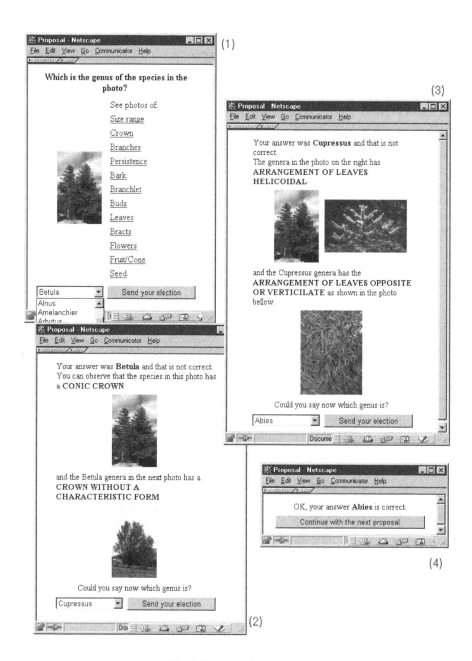

Fig. 5. Example of a proposal

second criterion: the domain hierarchy. In the first failure, the genera *Abies* and *Betula* are from a different division. In the next failure the genera *Abies* and *Cuppressus* are from the same division (*Gimnospermae*) but from different families (*Pinaceae* and *Cuppresaceae* respectively), so the system concludes that the failure has been decreased. The next system action is to decide the hints to be presented and go to the state 4.

The hints advance in two ways during the proposal: first going down in the hierarchy and then adding additional differences to the list. As the hierarchy level of the failure has changed the system presents to the student the main differences between the families *Pinaceae* and *Cuppresaceae*. The next answer is correct so the system progress to the final state B2. If the student would answer another *Cuppressus* species instead of giving the correct answer, the system would present the additional differences between the families *Cuppresaceae* and *Pinaceae*. If the student makes the same mistake again, the system would present the main differences between the genera *Abies* and *Cupressus*.

Table 1. Differences between *Gimnospermae* and *Angiospermae*

IMPORTANT DIFFERENCES	
IT HAS FRUIT OR HAS NOT REAL FRUIT	
It has cone, strobilus or aril	It has real fruit
CROWN TYPE	
Conic crown	Without a characteristic form
FLOWER'S PERIANTH	
Flower without perianth	Flower with petaloid perianth
	Flower with sepaloid perianth
	Flower with calyx and with corolla
ADDITIONAL DIFFERENCES	
APPEARENCE OF FLOWERS	
Not apparent flowers, hardly visible	Apparent flowers, easily visible

Table 2. Differences between *Pinaceae* and Cuppresaceae

IMPORTANT DIFFERENCES	
FLOWER'S PERIANTH	
Helicoidal	Opposite
	Verticillate

5   Conclusions

There are several tasks that have to be done as a part of an instructional process. The instruction over the Internet requires that all of these tasks would have a web interface. We can benefit from the web structure if we could design each component separately. To make it possible a new architecture has been proposed. This architecture is modular and has a library of tutorial components that can be generic (used for any domain as for example test component, reading-text component...) or designed specifically for a particular domain.

In this paper we have described one of these particular components: the Socratic Tutor. This component is based on the Socratic methodology where the teaching and learning process are based upon the personal reflection that can be obtained posing the right question on a guided dialogue. A finite state automaton conducts the Socratic dialogue. This tactical knowledge representation can be easily defined and/or redefined by the human domain experts. This component have been developed for the TREE ITS, that teaches to recognize different European forestry species. The morphological botanical domain is a hierarchically structured domain, the Socratic component can be reused for domains of similar features.

The Socratic Tutor has been completely designed and now we are taking care of the implementation phase. New research lines are open to study the impact that this dialogue has on the student general performance, and to automatic learn while teaching what are the hits that better solve the student impasse.

6   References

1. Trella, M., Conejo, R., Bueno, D. A Web tool to help teaching morphology botany of European forestry species In: ICCE'99 (7th International Conference on Computers in Education).
2. Ríos, Millán, Trella, Pérez de la Cruz, Conejo. Internet based evaluation system. Lajoie,S, Vivet,M. (eds.) ARTIFICIAL INTELLIGENCE IN EDUCATION, IOS Press, Amsterdam, 1999.
3. Stevens, A.L., Collins, A.: The goal structure of a Socratic tutor. Proceedings of the National ACM Conference. Seattle, Washington. Association for Computing Machinery, New York. (1977) 256-263.
4. Brown, J.S., Burton, R.R.: A paradigmatic example of an artificially intelligent instructional system. Int. Jrnl of Man-Machine Studies, vol. 10. (1978) 323-339
5. Woolf, B.P., McDonald, D.D.: Context-dependent transitions in tutoring discourse. Proceedings of the National Conference on Artificial Intelligence. Austin, Texas. (1984) 355-361.

Adaptation Control in Adaptive Hypermedia Systems

Hongjing Wu, Paul De Bra, Ad Aerts, Geert-Jan Houben

Department of Computing Science
Eindhoven University of Technology
PO Box 513, 5600 MB Eindhoven
the Netherlands
phone: +31 40 2472733
fax: +31 40 2463992
{hongjing,debra,wsinatma,houben}@win.tue.nl

Abstract. A hypermedia application offers its users a lot of freedom to navigate through a large hyperspace, described by a *domain model*. Adaptive hypermedia systems (AHS) aim at overcoming possible navigation and comprehension problems by providing adaptive navigation support and adaptive content. The adaptation is based on a *user model* that represents relevant aspects about the user. In this paper, we concentrate on the *adaptation engine* (AE) that is responsible for performing the adaptation according to the *adaptation rules* specified in the *adaptation model*. We analyze the dependencies between the authoring process and the functionality of the adaptation engine. From this we conclude how the authoring process can be simplified by a more powerful AE. In particular, a well-designed AE should be *general purpose* (i.e., not application domain specific) and should guarantee that the interpretation of the rules is deterministic, always terminates and produces the results desired by the author.

Keywords: adaptive hypermedia, user modeling, adaptive presentation, adaptive navigation, hypermedia reference model, adaptation rules.

1. Introduction

Hypermedia systems (including the Web) are becoming increasingly popular as tools for user-driven access to information. They typically offer users a lot of freedom to navigate through a large hyperspace. Unfortunately, this rich link structure of the hypermedia applications causes some serious usability problems:

◻ A typical hypermedia system presents the same links on a page to all users. To eliminate *navigation problems* the system should offer each user (some) personalized links or navigation tools (such as a table of contents or a map). The system should thereby take into account what the user read before, and possibly what the user's interests are.

◻ Navigation in ways the author did not anticipate also causes *comprehension problems* for the user: for every page the author makes an assumption about what foreknowledge the user has when accessing that page. However, this is an impossible authoring task because there are more ways to reach a page than any (human) author can foresee. A page is always presented in the same way. This may result

P. Brusilovsky, O. Stock, C. Strapparava (Eds.): AH 2000, LNCS 1892, pp. 250-259, 2000.

in users visiting pages containing redundant information and pages that they cannot fully understand because they lack some expected foreknowledge.

Adaptive hypermedia systems (or AHS for short) aim at overcoming these problems by providing *adaptive navigation support* and *adaptive content*. The adaptation (or personalization) is based on a *user model* that represents relevant aspects of the user such as preferences, knowledge and interests. The system gathers information about the user by observing the use of the application, and in particular by observing the *browsing* behavior of the user.

Many adaptive hypermedia systems exist to date. The majority of them are used in educational applications, but some are used, for example, for on-line information systems or information retrieval systems. An overview of systems, methods and techniques for adaptive hypermedia can be found in [B96]. We have developed a reference model for the architecture of adaptive hypermedia applications: AHAM (for **A**daptive **H**ypermedia **A**pplication **M**odel) [DHW99], which is an extension of the Dexter hypermedia reference model [HS90, HS94]. AHAM acknowledges that doing "useful" and "usable" adaptation in a given application depends on three factors:

- The application must be based on a *domain model*, describing how the information content of the application or "hyper-document" is structured (using concept).
- The system must construct and maintain a fine-grained *user model* that represents a user's preferences, knowledge, goals, navigation history and other relevant aspects.
- The system must be able to adapt the presentation (of both content and link structure) to the reading and navigation style the user prefers and to the user's knowledge level. In order to do so the author must provide an *adaptation model* consisting of *adaptation rules*. An AHS itself may offer built-in rules for common adaptation aspects. This reduces the author's task of providing such rules.

The division into a *domain model* (DM), *user model* (UM) and *adaptation model* (AM) provides a clear separation of concerns when developing an adaptive hypermedia application. The main shortcoming in many current AHS is that these three factors or components are not clearly separated [WHD00].

In this paper we focus on the *adaptation engine* (AE) that provides the implementation dependent aspects of AHAM. We divide the adaptive control in AHS into two levels, the author level and the system level. On the author level an author writes *adaptation rules*; on the system level the system designers build an *adaptation engine* (AE) to apply the rules. These two parts work together to control the adaptation in the AHS. In this paper we consider three main design goals for the AE:

- Authoring should be simplified as much as possible. The author should not have to include in the adaptation rules any aspects that a (smart) AE can handle automatically. The author should take care of the domain dependent aspects, and the AE should take care of the domain independent aspects.
- The interpretation (or execution) of adaptation rules by the AE should always terminate. Furthermore, the adaptation should not cause noticeable delays.
- The interpretation of the adaptation rules by the AE should be deterministic.

This paper is organized as follows. In Section 2 we briefly recall the AHAM reference model for adaptive hypermedia applications and propose two general constraints on (generic) adaptation rules. In Section 3 we define some terms and discuss system transition issues. In Section 4 we discuss termination and determinism of the AE, and ways to make authoring easier by making the AE smarter. Section 5 presents our conclusions and short-term research agenda.

2. AHAM, a Dexter-Based Reference Model

In hypermedia applications the emphasis is always on the information nodes and on the link structure connecting these nodes. The Dexter model [HS90,HS94] captures this in what it calls the Storage Layer. It represents a *domain model* DM, i.e. the author's view on the application domain expressed in terms of concepts (and content). In adaptive hypermedia applications the central role of DM is shared with a *user model* UM. UM represents the relationship between the user and the domain model by keeping track of how much the user knows about each of the concepts in the application domain.

In order to perform adaptation based on DM and UM an author needs to specify how the user's knowledge influences the presentation of the information from DM. In AHAM [DHW99], this is done by means of an *adaptation model* (AM) consisting of *adaptation rules*. ([DHW99] uses slightly different terms.) An adaptation engine (AE) uses these rules to manipulate link anchors (from the Dexter model's *anchoring*) and to generate what the Dexter model calls the *presentation specifications*. In this section we only present the elements of AHAM that we will need in the following sections when we discuss the implementation aspects of the AHAM.

2.1 The Domain Model

The domain model of an adaptive hypermedia application consists of *concepts* and *concept relationships*. Concepts are objects with a unique object identifier, and a structure that includes attribute-value pairs and link anchors. (The remainder of the structure is not relevant for this paper.)

A *concept* represents an abstract information item from the application domain. It can be either an *atomic concept* or a *composite concept*.

◻ An *atomic concept* corresponds to a fragment of information. It is primitive in the model (and can thus not be adapted). Its attribute and anchor values belong to the "Within-component layer" and are thus implementation dependent and not described in the model.

◻ A *composite concept* has a sequence of children (sub-concepts) and a constructor function that describes how the children belong together. The children of a composite concept are either all atomic concepts or all composite concepts. A composite concept with (only) atomic children is called a *page*.

The composite concept hierarchy must be a DAG (directed acyclic graph). Also, every atomic concept must be included in some composite concept. Figure 1 illustrates a part of a concept hierarchy.

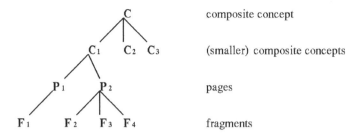

Fig. 1. : Part of a concept hierarchy.

A *concept relationship* is an object (with a unique identifier and attribute-value pairs) that relates a sequence of two or more concepts. Each concept relationship has a type. The most common type is the hypertext **link**. In AHAM we consider other types of relationships as well, which play a role in the adaptation, e.g. the type **prerequisite**. When a concept C_1 is a prerequisite for C_2 it means that the user should read C_1 before C_2. It does not mean that there must be a link from C_1 to C_2. It only means that the system somehow takes into account that reading about C_2 is not desired before some (enough) knowledge about C_1 has been acquired. Through link adaptation the "desirability" of a link will be made clear to the user.

The atomic concepts, composite concepts and concept relationships together form the *domain model* DM of an adaptive hypermedia application.

2.2 The User Model

A user model consists of named entities for which we store a number of attribute-value pairs. For each user the AHS maintains a *table-like structure*, in which for each concept in the DM the attribute values for that concept are stored. Because of the relationships between *abstract* concepts and *concrete* content elements like fragments and pages, a user model may contain other attributes than simply a *knowledge level* (typical in educational applications). For instance, the user model may also store information about what a user has actually read about a concept or whether a concept is considered relevant for the user. Concepts can furthermore be used (some might say abused) to represent other user aspects such as preferences, goals, background, hyperspace experience, or a (stereotypical) classification like student, employee, visitor, etc. For the AHS or the AHAM model the true meaning of concepts is irrelevant.

In the sequel we will always consider UM as being the user model for a single user. In this paper we do not discuss adaptation to group behavior.

2.3 The Adaptation (Teaching) Model

The adaptation of the information content of a hyper-document and of the link structure is based on a set of *adaptation rules*. A rule is typically of the form:

    if <condition> then <action>.

Here condition may specify the occurrence of an external event, such as "page access" (or "click" for short), conjugated with Boolean expressions referring to attribute-values from the DM or UM. The action may be an update to an attribute-value in UM, or be an assignment to a presentation specification for an object: it may specify that a fragment will be shown, or that a link should be treated as being desirable. For example, consider the rule:

if access(C) and F IN C.children and F.relevant = true then F.pres := show.

This rule specifies that when a page concept C is accessed (by clicking on a link to this page) and that page contains a fragment F that is relevant for the user, then that fragment should become visible in the presentation of the page. The consequence of this rule is that all relevant fragments of this page will be shown to the user. Instead of hiding undesired fragments the AHS may gray them out, as described in [HH98].

Adaptation rules form the connection between DM, UM and the presentation (specification) to be generated, and their syntax is AHS-dependent. In fact, in many AHS a number of rules will be hard-coded into the system and not visible or accessible to authors. We partition the rules into four groups according to the adaptation "steps" to which they belong. These steps are IU (initialize user model), UU-Pre (update user model before generating the page), GA (generate adaptation), and UU-Post (update user model after generating the page). The rules in these groups are applied in the order specified. [WHD99]

In a *generic adaptation rule* (bound) variables are used that represent concepts and concept relationships. A *specific adaptation rule* uses concrete concepts from DM instead of variables. Other than that both types of rules look the same. Specific rules always take precedence over generic ones. The syntax of the permissible rules depends on the AHS and is irrelevant for this paper.

The *adaptation model* AM of an AHS is the set of (generic and specific) adaptation rules.

2.4 The Adaptation Engine

An AHS does not only have a domain model, user model and adaptation model, but also an *adaptation engine*, which is a software environment that performs the following functions:

◻ It offers generic page selectors and constructors. For each composite concept the constructor is used to determine which page to display when the user follows a link to that composite concept. For each page the constructor is used for building the adaptive presentation of that page.

◻ It optionally offers a (very simple programming) language for describing new page selectors and constructors. For instance, in AHA [DC98] a page constructor consists of simple commands for the conditional inclusion of fragments.

◻ It performs adaptation by executing the page selectors and constructors. This means selecting a page, selecting fragments, organizing and presenting them in a specific way, etc. It also means performing adaptation to links by manipulating link anchors depending on the state of the link (like enabled, disabled and hidden.).

◻ It updates the user model (instance) each time the user visits a page. It does so by triggering the necessary adaptation rules in UU-pre or UU-post. The engine will thus set some attribute values for each atomic concept of displayed fragments of a page, of the page as a whole and possibly of some other (composite) concepts as well (all depending on the adaptation rules).

The adaptation engine thus provides the implementation-dependent aspects, while DM, UM, and AM describe the information and adaptation at the conceptual, implementation independent level. An *adaptive hypermedia application* is a 4-tuple (DM, UM, AM, AE), where DM is a domain model, UM is a user model, AM is an adaptation model, and AE is an adaptation engine. The challenge, of course, is to design an AE that is not specific to a particular application, but that can handle a wide range of hypermedia applications.

2.5 General Constraints

Performance is a frequently neglected aspect of adaptive hypermedia applications. However, when the execution of the adaptation rules takes a long time there will be a very noticeable delay between the click on a link anchor and the appearance of the link destination page. An easy way to ensure fast response is to require all adaptation rules to be mutually independent. This means that all rules are triggered by an event (such as a "click") and the result of a rule cannot be a trigger for other rules. This is a severe restriction. For instance, it does not allow "knowledge" to be propagated bottom-up through the concept hierarchy automatically.

In this paper we explicitly allow cascades of rule executions. The purpose is to lighten the burden on the author of the adaptive application. For instance, we allow an author to specify that in Figure 1 reading page P_1 or P_2 contributes 50% towards the knowledge of C_1 and that C_1 contributes e.g. 40% towards the knowledge of C. When the user accesses P_1 an adaptation rule will set the knowledge of P_1 to 100%. This rule will trigger another rule (instance) that adds 50% to the knowledge of C_1 and this will trigger yet another rule (instance) that will add 20% (or 40% of 50%) to the knowledge of C. The (current version of the) AHA system for instance allows such cascades of rules. It will be obvious that this recursive definition of user model updates is easier for an author than specifying explicitly that reading P_1 contributes 50% to C_1 and 20% to C, and that reading P_2 also contributes 50% to C_1 and also 20% to C. (It is easier when the author need not explicitly specify directly for each page how much reading that page contributes towards the knowledge of C.)

While we allow cascading rule execution we do propose the following restrictions on the propagation between rules:

□ If the <condition> and <action> of a rule contain an attribute of the same concept then the <condition> must include an *event*. The propagation of attribute values within one concept and without an event indicates bad design and is forbidden.

□ If the <condition> and <action> of a *generic* adaptation rule contain different concepts, then the <condition> must also include a *concept relationship* linking these concepts. Thus, propagation of user model updates between different concepts is only allowed through concept relationships.

An example of a rule that illustrates and satisfies the first constraint (for page P) is:

    if *access*(P) and P.ready-to-read = true then P.knowledge := 'known'.

The update to the knowledge (attribute) of P depends on the ready-to-read attribute of the same P, and therefore must be triggered by an event such as *access*(P).

An example of a rule that illustrates the second constraint is:

if ◻ P', prerequisite(P', P): P'.knowledge = 'known' then P.ready-to-read := true

3. System Transitions

In this section we describe how an AHS works using triggers and rules. However, this does not imply that only rule and trigger based AHS's can be described in AHAM. Triggers and rules are just our means for describing the system behavior.

An *event* in the system means that something outside the system triggers the system to change its state. The user or external programs can only observe the following:

$$UM_s \xrightarrow{\text{event}} UM_f$$

Here UM_s and UM_f are two states of the system. In general these states must differ in at least one attribute value. UM_s is the *start-state* and UM_f is the *final-state*. "Inside" the AHS the transition is, for instance, realized by sequentially executing a number of rules:

$$UM_s \xrightarrow{R_1} UM_2 \xrightarrow{R_2} \dots UM_i \xrightarrow{R_i} \dots \xrightarrow{R_m} UM_f$$

Here R_i is an instance of a generic or a specific rule, i is in [1..m], m must be finite. Thus, internally the system applies a finite sequence of rules (or actually rule instances) to arrive at UM_f. Each step in this transition is called an *update*. When an event occurs, it triggers some rules that deal with that event. These rules will change some values in the UM, and these changes will propagate to other rules. The order in which rules are applied is called the *execution order*.

When a rule's condition changes from false to true, it becomes an *active rule*. The system only executes active rules in the transition. After execution of an active rule, that rule becomes inactive. The execution of a rule may make other inactive rules become active. If there is no active rule anymore, then the transition *terminates*. In Section 4.1 we will consider the detection of potential infinite loops that would cause a transition to never terminate.

Apart from termination of a transition, also the predictability of its final state is an issue. If the execution order of the rules doesn't affect the final state, we call the transition an *order independent transition* (OIT). If the execution order does affect the final state, we call this transition an *order dependent transition* (ODT). Order dependent transitions are not desirable because they make the result (the final state) unpredictable. Order-dependence arises, when there is a choice as to which rule to execute first. For instance, an event may activate more than one rule. In the sequential procedure presented above, we select one rule and execute it. This will produce a new (intermediate) state of the UM in which some other rules may have become active. In the course of the process of rule execution more rules may become active, but also some active rules may become inactive because other rule executions have made their condition become false again. The final result may also depend on the order in which subsequent updates of the same concept attribute take place. To provide a deterministic AE behavior, we have to resolve the order dependence. This issue is dealt with in Section 4.2.

4. Issues in Building the AE

As indicated in the introduction, we consider three design goals. We try to make the burden on the author lighter by providing *simple rules*, while at the same time providing an adaptation engine that generates *predictable* results and that executes rules in such a way that *termination* is guaranteed.

4.1 Termination

There are different ways to ensure that a transition terminates. One way is to write rules in such a way that infinite (triggering) loops are impossible and that long (deep) recursions are avoided. In order to ensure that the rules are written in this way one needs the authoring tool to check for potential (direct or indirect) loops each time an author adds rules to the AM. The added rule can either be rejected or the system may simply warn the author and give advice on how to break the loop in the rules. Whether a rule may lead to infinite loops also depends on whether the concept relationships used in the rule are allowed to be cyclic or not. E.g., link relationships can be cyclic, whereas prerequisite relationships must not be cyclic.

Another way is to have an adaptation engine (AE) that ensures that the transition will stop after some time, even when the rule definitions (together with cycles in DM) cause loops. This approach is easier for the author, because the author need not know or be informed about (potential) loops. There are three easy (and also simplistic) ways to make an AE ensure termination of transitions:

1. The system changes the attribute value of a concept at most once in one transition. Because UM has only a finite number of concepts and each concept a finite number of attributes, the number of possible update steps that do not change a previously updated attribute value is finite. Unfortunately this method inhibits some possibly interesting ways to update the UM. For example, if concept A contributes knowledge towards B and C, and B and C both contribute (a possibly different amount of) knowledge towards D, D's knowledge value can only be updated in a predictable way if knowledge propagation from B and from C are both allowed to happen during one transition. One can easily come up with similar examples using concept relationships instead of the concept hierarchy, and also leading to "premature" termination of parts of a transition.

2. Each rule instance (either an instance of a generic rule or a specific rule) is executed at most once in one transition. A generic rule may be used several times, but with different bindings of its (concept) variables to actual concepts. This method again guarantees termination. In the above example the knowledge value of D can be updated twice because both updates are different rule instances. Unfortunately, if in this example D also contributes knowledge to E, the resulting two knowledge contributions cannot both be propagated to E because that would be done through the same rule instance.

3. The AE can make use of properties of the value domain for each attribute (of concepts) to determine whether repeated updates to a concept or repeated execution of the same rule instance are potential sources of infinite loops. The AE of the AHA system for instance allows repeated monotonic updates to a concept's knowledge value. This poses no danger because the value domain consists of integers between 0 and 100. (All monotonic update loops terminate when the value reaches 100 or 0, depending on whether the value monotonically increases or decreases.)

The first two methods can be modified so that they allow not one but a larger (fixed or variable) number of updates or instances of rules to be executed. This may eliminate some of the negative side effects, but it also slows the AE down in case of an infinite loop that must be terminated. The third method is preferable, but for some value domains it may be difficult to come up with a property that provides a good basis for terminating potential infinite loops. More research on termination is needed, but research on active databases has already shown that termination quickly becomes undecidable.

4.2 Determinism

A single event may activate several rules, and each rule execution may activate some more rules. In the sequential model we presented in Section 3, active rules are executed one by one. The order in which rule instances are executed may influence the final result UM_f. Also, when a potential infinite loop is cut short by one of the methods described in Section 4.1, the order in which rules are executed may influence which rules are executed and which rules are discarded. The problem of non-deterministic results is a direct consequence of our desire to make authoring easier. The easiest way to guarantee deterministic behavior of AE is to define the rule language in such a way that the author has to indicate *when* a rule must be executed, and not only *under which conditions* a rule may be executed. We have chosen an intermediate approach: the author must assign rules to the four categories IU, UU-pre, GA and UU-post, but within each category the author does not indicate execution order.

While we do not have a general solution, an AE can find out potential sources of non-determinism by searching for conflicting user model updates that result from active rules. For instance, consider the following three rules:

if access(A) and A.ready-to-read = true then A.knowledge := 'known'.
if A.knowledge = 'known' and prerequisite(A,B) then B.ready-to-read := true.
if A.knowledge = 'known' and inhibit(A,B) then B.ready-to-read := false.

What these rules actually imply is that there cannot simultaneously be a prerequisite and an inhibit relationship between A and B. If these relationships would exist however then whether B.ready-to-read becomes true or false depends on the order in which the rules are executed. A smart authoring tool can detect that the rules have a conflicting outcome, and thus warn the author of the error in either the given relationships or the supplied rules. There may be cases where conflicting updates are not easily detected during the authoring phase. Such undesirable, ambiguous situations can still be detected by the AE, by not simply executing rules but by first examining all active rules and checking them for a conflicting outcome. What is needed then is a conflict resolution strategy that must be specified by the author or the system and that can be used to eliminate the conflict. Once all conflicts between the active rules have been resolved, the order of execution is not important any more and the transition terminates in a well-determined state. In the case of the prerequisite and inhibit relationships one might for instance state that prerequisites take precedence and that in case of conflict the rule for the inhibit relationship is not executed. In the case of a conflicting generic and specific rule, the specific rule always has precedence.

5. Conclusion and Future Work

We have analyzed several ways to build an AE that is deterministic and produces results in an acceptable number of steps. A viable approach is to assign adaptation rules to groups and specify some general precedence relationships, which will constitute the AE default behavior. This will leave a number of situations in which the author has to provide some mechanism of choice for the order dependent transitions. An attractive option appears to be the collective application of all rules that are active in a particular state and provide a conflict resolution strategy. This way, we can build general AE's that provide a clear separation of responsibilities between the system and the author. The input of the author will, of course, always be required and is best put in the form of overruling general AE behavior with specific, domain dependent choices.

The next research step is to experiment with the various design alternatives for the AE, and to design an appropriate rule language for the author to write the application. The rule language should provide a general way to specify rules for desirable application behavior.

References

[B96] Brusilovsky, P., "Methods and Techniques of Adaptive Hypermedia". User Modeling and User-Adapted Interaction, 6, pp. 87-129, 1996. (Reprinted in Adaptive Hypertext and Hypermedia, Kluwer Academic Publishers, pp. 1-43, 1998.)

[DC98] De Bra, P., Calvi, L., "AHA! An open Adaptive Hypermedia Architecture". The New Review of Hypermedia and Multimedia, pp. 115-139, 1998.

[DHW99] De Bra, P., Houben, G.J., Wu, H., "AHAM: A Dexter-based Reference Model for Adaptive Hypermedia". Proceedings of ACM Hypertext'99, Darmstadt, pp. 147-156, 1999.

[HS90] Halasz, F., Schwartz, M., "The Dexter Reference Model". Proceedings of the NIST Hypertext Standardization Workshop, pp. 95-133, 1990.

[HS94] Halasz, F., Schwartz, M., "The Dexter Hypertext Reference Model". Communications of the ACM, Vol. 37, nr. 2, pp. 30-39, 1994.

[HH98] Hothi, J., Hall, W., "An Evaluation of Adapted Hypermedia Techniques Using Static User Modeling", Proceedings of the Second Workshop on Adaptive Hypertext and Hypermedia, pp. 45-50, 1998.

[PDS99] Pilar da Silva, D., "Concepts and documents for adaptive educational hypermedia: a model and a prototype", Proceedings of the Second Workshop on Adaptive Hypertext and Hypermedia, Pittsburgh, pp. 33-40, 1998.

[WHD99] Wu, H., Houben, G.J., De Bra, P., "Authoring Support for Adaptive Hypermedia", Proceedings ED-MEDIA'99, Seattle, pp. 364-369, 1999.

[WHD00] Wu, H., Houben, G.J., De Bra, P., "Supporting User Adaptation in Adaptive Hypermedia Applications", Proceedings InfWet2000. Rotterdam, the Netherlands.

An Agent-Based Approach to Adaptive Hypermedia Using a Link Service

Christopher Bailey, Wendy Hall

IAM Intelligence Agents Multimedia Research Group
Department of Electronics and Computer Science,
University of Southampton, Southampton, UK.
{cpb99r, wh}@ecs.soton.ac.uk

Abstract. This paper describes an approach to adaptive hypermedia by incorporating linkbases into an agent-based system (PAADS). The agents are built on top of an agent framework developed at Southampton University. Personal agents keep a local user model and provide adaptive navigation support. This is accomplished by extracting keywords found in the user model and through the user's browsing history, and by then replacing occurrences of those words with URL's supplied by a linkbase agent. A third agent provides the ability to query these user models through a web browser.

1. Introduction

The term *Adaptive Hypermedia* means personalizing a user's browsing experience. There are a number of different methods for providing this adaptivity in existing hypermedia systems. Brusilovsky [2] describes two main types: adaptive presentation, which means changing the information conveyed on individual pages, and adaptive navigation support where the appearance and order of the links are manipulated to influence a user when they come to select the next page to visit. To facilitate these techniques, a user model is kept by the system, which contains simple personal information, and any concepts and goals the user has acquired while browsing.

Agent technologies can be used to create adaptive systems as they are quickly becoming popular as a means of building modular systems. It is their inherent flexibility that makes them ideal components for multi-disciplinary tasks. In the IAM research group we have designed our own multi agent system, SoFar (Southampton Framework for Agent Research) [5], which is a Java-implemented platform designed for rapid agent development. These agents communicate using a pre-defined set of methods (performatives, such as *inform*, *subscribe* and *request*) that can be invoked on any agent. To aid communication between agents, SoFar incorporates the idea of using ontologies (the semantic structure of data) [7], as a means of specifying particular data domains. Mobility is also provided by SoFar, allowing agents to migrate to new platforms as and when they desire.

The work described in this paper involves introducing the concept of linkbases to this agent domain to provide adaptive hypermedia. A (distributed) linkbase is a means of separating link information from the body of a hypermedia document. Linkbases, first developed as part of the Microcosm system [4], allow authors to manage web sites with greater efficiency. These links reside in a database where they can be maintained by a link service, such as the DLS [3], which provides link functionality to

P. Brusilovsky, O. Stock, C. Strapparava (Eds.): AH 2000, LNCS 1892, pp. 260-263, 2000.

other programs. The following system uses such a linkbase to add links to the web page that match a user model. One advantage of such a technique is that the structure of the existing web page is left unaltered and the user just sees more links to sites they are interested in.

2. PAADS Implementation

For this work, a collection of agents have been built on top of SoFar that all recognize a pre-defined group of ontologies. PAADS (Personal Agent information Acquisition and Delivery System) is a web-centred approach, written entirely in Java 2, to record user details, provide adaptive navigation support to users and present this information to others who can query the data. The system is shown in Fig. 1.

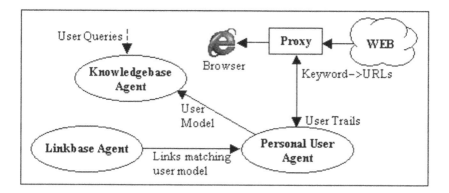

Fig. 1. A diagram showing the interaction between agents in PAADS. The user's agent supplies keyword & URL pairs from the linkbase agent to the proxy. The user model is sent to the knowledge base agent and can be accessed through user queries

2.1 The Agents

There are three types of agents running in PAADS. There are Personal User Agents, Knowledgebase Agents and Linkbase Agents, each of which has a specific purpose. The Personal User and Knowledgebase agents are *active* agents - they interact with other agents in the system to accomplish their goals, whereas the Linkbase agent is *passive* - it supplies services to other agents but has no goal itself.

Personal User Agent. In principle, Personal User agents follow a single user, accumulating information about their interests and expertise and storing this data in a user model. At present, this model is simply made up of key value pairs entered manually by the user. Agents also add keywords to the model that have been extracted from web pages visited by the user. This model is then sent to the Knowledge Base Agent.

Knowledgebase Agent. The Knowledgebase agent acts as a central repository for data accumulated by personal agents. The knowledge base agent provides an interface to this data allowing other users to query the information via a web browser. The agent can respond to questions such as *"Who is J. Bloggs?"* or *"Who can help me with my Java program?"*

Linkbase Agent. Acting as a distributed link service, the linkbase agent maintains a local linkbase and provides performatives to other agents allowing them to query the linkbase and add or remove links. At present, the Linkbase Agent only responds to requests from Personal Agents for URLs. The linkbase used by this agent conforms to the XML standard set out by the DLS [3], where a link is defined with, amongst other things, a type, a destination URL, keyword(s) and the title of the web page.

Users can enter data directly into their personal agent, or allow their agent to acquire knowledge about them implicitly. This is achieved by recording the user's trails (or paths) as they browse through the WWW and then keywords are extracted from these web pages. A frequency count is performed and the highest occurring words are stored in the user model as an *interests* field. PAADS provides a web interface giving the user a view of all the data acquired about them and allowing them to configure their agent. To provide adaptive navigation support for the user, the personal agent requests links from the linkbase agent that match the keywords found in the user model. The linkbase agent returns a set of matching links, which are then sent to a proxy. This proxy replaces all occurrences of the keywords in a web document with the corresponding URL's. Two different methods of presenting the links have been implemented. The keyword can either become a link or have the links, if there are more then one, tagged onto the end of it (e.g. a standard style, or a bibliographic [x,y] style).

3. Conclusions and Future Work

Due to the dynamic nature of agents, PAADS continues to work even if some or all of the agents are unable to be found. This makes PAADS fault tolerant, and the web front end allows it to be easily configured by users. Personal agents can refine their user models over time so that as the user moves around the web, the agent slowly gains more information about their interests, which is then fed back to provide more personalized link adaptivity. A further advantage is that the adaptivity does not destroy the original structure of the web page as links are only ever added. This means well designed web sites will remain intact and the user benefits from both their structure and the additional links PAADS provide.

However, more work needs to be done to improve the control and presentation of the links. Because there could be several URL's associated with a given keyword, the system would benefit from weighting each URL. This would give the agent a means of selecting one URL over all the others, or allow the links to be presented in an ordered list based on some criteria (adaptive link sorting). The next step is to build a more advanced learning algorithm into the system. Any improvements to automate acquisition of the user model would be beneficial to the user; reducing the time they spend interacting with the personal agent, thereby freeing them up to focus on their own tasks. This could be done by extending the link definition to calculate the frequency of page hits or include ratings for web pages. From this new information, favourite pages (bookmarks) could be inferred by the agent and thereby given stronger weights.

This agent-based approach to the provision of distributed link services and adaptive navigation support is a good example of how agent technology can be applied to new areas. The linkbase agent can offer its services not just to these personal agents but also to any agents interested in link manipulation. Although not implemented at the moment, more linkbases need to be introduced to give the agents a better choice when finding relevant URL's. Examples could include general linkbases for a wide range of topics, linkbases that cover a specific domain (such as a corporate web site, or a technical subject) and individual user linkbases formed from a user's web trails.

Finally, by giving personal agents the ability to query other agents, possible links could be suggested to the user by comparing their trails against those of other users, creating a trail-based recommender system [1,6].

This work shows that agent technology is a viable means of providing adaptive navigation support. Maintaining separate linkbases allows greater flexibility for adaptive hypermedia systems and intergration with the personal user agents provides an ideal platform for future experimentation.

References

1. Balabanović, M. and Shohom, Y. Content-Based, Callaborative Recommendation. In Communications of the ACM, Vol 40, No. 3. March (1997)
2. Brusilovsky, P. Methods and techniques of adaptive hypermedia. From User Modeling and User Adapted Interaction. Vol 6, No 2-3, (1996) 87-129
3. Carr, L., De Roure, D., Hall, W. and Hill, G. The Distributed Link Service: A Tool for Publishers, Authors and Readers from World Wide Web Journal 1(1), O'Reilly & Associates (1995) 647-656
4. Hall, W., Davis, H., Hutchings, G. Rethinking Hypermedia : The Microcosm Approach (Electronic Publishing Series , No 4). Kluwer Academic Pub; ISBN: 0792396790 (1996)
5. Moreau, L., Gibbins, N., De Roure, D., El-Beltagy, S., Hall, W., Hughes, G., Joyce, D., Kim, S., Michaelides, D., Millard, D., Reich, S., Tansley, R. and Weal, M. An Agent Framework for Distributed Information Management. In The Fifth International Conference and Exhibition on The Practical Application of Intelligent Agents and Multi-Agents, Manchester, UK (2000)
6. Pikrakis, A., Bitsikas, T., Sfakianakis, S., Hatzopoulos, M., De Roure, D., Hall, W., Reich, S., Hill, G., Stairmand, M. MEMOIR - Software Agents for Finding Similar Users by Trails Nwana, H. S. and Ndumu, D. T. (eds), PAAM98 - The Third International Conference and Exhibition on The Practical Application of Intelligent Agents and Multi-Agents. London, UK. March (1998) 453-466
7. Huhnd, M., N. and Singh, M., P. Ontologies for Agents. In the IEEE Internet Computing, Vol. 1, No. 6, November/December (1997) http://computer.org/internet/

Adaptive Testing by Test++

Maria Barra, Giuseppina Palmieri, Simona Napolitano*, Vittorio Scarano, and
Luca Zitarosa

Dipartimento di Informatica ed Applicazioni "R.M. Capocelli"
Università di Salerno
Baronissi (Salerno), 84081, Italy
{marbar,palmieri,vitsca}@unisa.it

Abstract. We present the adaptive features of Test++, an adaptive
system for training and teaching on the Internet. The system integrates
an adaptive training environment for personalized training and a cooperative environment for exams both accessible via Internet and a standard
Java-enabled browser.

1 Introduction

The World Wide Web [1] explosion has strongly influenced everyday life of almost
everybody in the industrialized world. Particularly it changed many things for
people that, in a way or in another, are involved in the educational field. In fact,
WWW now is able to efficiently deliver true *e-learning* to user by a variety of
tools to support [7,8], integrate [6] and, sometimes, substitute the traditional
methodologies used in schools of any kind [5,10].

Adaptive hypermedia [2,3] is one of the most effective disciplines to help
tailor e-learning to each student's needs. Techniques for adaptive hypermedia,
that were developed for local systems before the advent of WWW, have proven
themselves extremely useful to provide an interactive and personal environment.
Several systems are developed in Computer Adaptive Tests (CATs) and Item
Response Theory fields (see [4] for comprehensive survey and [9] for SIETTE, an
Intelligent Evaluation System). Their goal, in general, is to accurately estimate
students knowledge by user-tailored systems.

We describe, here, the adaptive features of a system to support and integrate
traditional teaching: Test++. The system goals are to provide supplementary
personal self-training sessions and synchronous exercitations/exams to the traditional classroom and laboratory activities. The goal of the project (whose first
part we describe here) is to interleave in a single session personalized testing and
training. Questions are selected according to the performances of the student but
they also lead to supplementary reading material.

In this paper, we focus on the adaptive training policy that is proposed to
the student. We describe the strategy that is followed by the system to propose
the questions, adapting the number of questions in each topic to the results

---

* Current affiliation: Finmatica s.p.a.

P. Brusilovsky, O. Stock, C. Strapparava (Eds.): AH 2000, LNCS 1892, pp. 264–267, 2000.

obtained by the student so that his/her preparation is accurately tested. In a certain way, since testing system is coupled with presentation of support and reading material related to questions/answers, the system will offer two-level adaptivity: a first level, described in this paper, offers a mechanism to adapt questionnaires to students so that they are challenged and (implicitly) shown their weaknesses by reiterating and insisting on some topics. A second level, not described here, will offer, on the basis of the interactions with questions, access to adapted and personalized course material.

2 Adaptivity in Test++

The system is designed to work in two different, complementary modes. The first one is the *self-training* mode that is treated throughout the rest of the paper. The system can only work in a second mode, named *virtual classroom*: students are connected through clients (Java applets or applications) and are synchronously given a whole (static) questionnaire to answer. Questionnaires appear differently to each student and the teacher is able to monitor the behaviour of students by real-time statistics (by single student and collectively).

Test++ architecture is client-server: a "fat" client (a Java applet) implements the adaptive strategy and asks server a new question to present. In this way, first, the system is more efficient than usual server-side systems (one round-trip is avoided for checking correctness of answers); moreover, it is also possible to implement the synchronous mode within the same system and, finally, the XML questions archive is safely stored on the server and not directly accessible (as a whole) by the students.

In *self-training* mode, Test++ offers a personalized questionnaire to the student. The questionnaire is built randomly from a sample of questions contained in an XML archive but according to a set of configuration rules that specify how many questions for each topic are placed into the questionnaire. The objective of the whole system is to interleave questions and material (that will also be adapted in the next phase of the project) so that the student is interactively presented material according to his/her needs.

The system offers to the teacher a wide choice of behaviours ranging from absolutely static (i.e. non adaptive at all) to absolutely "mean" (ask all the questions on the topic that is less known by the student).

We expected that the strategy could be helpful for students: their needs should be addressed and shown implicitly. If they do not study homogenously the topics then it is not possible to get high scores. Moreover, sometimes, it can be difficult for students to recognize what topics are the ones that "the teacher really care about": we expect that, in this case also, the questionnaire can be helpful since adaptive behaviour can be accurately tuned by the teacher. Some experiments (not reported here) show positive feedbacks by students.

Now we describe the adaptive mechanism for the self-training session. The goal of the mechanism is to force the student to a thorough study of all the topics of the course. In fact, the strategy is, in a way, designed to find weaknesses of student's preparation for the exam.

We identify the knowledge domain of the adaptive strategy as consisting of T disjoint *topics*. The mechanism is aimed at ensuring that good scores are associated with a complete preparation of the student. In a way, the system wants to avoid that a student can score $15/20$ (15 right answers over 20 questions) when the five wrong answers all belong to the same topic.

The questionnaire is built interactively according to configuration parameters: each time the student is presented a single question; when the answer is provided by the student the system selects the next topic and asks the server to randomly pick a test in that topic, ensuring, at the same time, that questions are not repeated in the same session.

It is well recognized that one of the problems in adaptive systems is authoring and configuring systems. To provide the teacher with a versatile mechanism, we model the self-training session with a number of *configuration parameters*:

- the total number N of questions (tests) in the session;
- for each topic i of the knowledge domain:
  - D_i the number of tests in the topic that should be presented in the session;
  - MIN_i the minimum number of right answers that the student must provide in order to pass to a different topic;
  - MAX_i the maximum number of tests that can be shown to the student about the topic (regardless of right answers).
- breadth-first round width w (more details follow).

The policy of the mechanism can be seen as a game played by the student against an adversary (Test++) that tries to understand the topics where the student has studied/understood the least. The system starts with a (randomly ordered) breadth-first round of the topics by asking w questions for each topic (w is the *width* parameter). Then, once identified "weak" topics (i.e. topics where student has shown some deficiency) the system keeps asking questions in "weak" topic i until either the student reaches the minimum number of right answers (MIN_i) or the total number of questions in topic i exceeds the maximum allowed MAX_i. Once all the "weak" topics are passed, then questions are picked in the topics whose D_i was not reached. It should be noticed that the role of D_i is simply to ensure that successful questionnaires (i.e. when the student is almost always correct according to the configuration) are well-balanced, anyway. The tie-breaking rule (for the choices above) was to pick topics in the definition order.

It can be seen that, assuming given N, T and w, the parameters are T triplets of integers $(D_i, \text{MIN}_i, \text{MAX}_i)$. The parameters allow a wide variety of behaviours (including a totally static, *a-priori* fixed questionnaire).

For example, assume that there are $T = 4$ topics and $N = 10$ questions. Then a static, non adaptive, random questionnaire Q_1 is built by specifying parameters $(3, 3, 3)$, $(3, 3, 3)$, $(2, 2, 2)$, $(2, 2, 2)$. On the other hand, an adaptive questionnaire Q_2 with configuration parameters $(3, 2, 4)$, $(3, 2, 3)$, $(2, 1, 3)$, $(2, 1, 2)$ shows a behaviour that gives a certain relevance (in this order) to each topic, by differentiating between the first and the second topic, and the third and the fourth topic by the maximum number of questions. Finally, a stronger bias toward the first topic is shown by a questionnaire Q_3 with the following configuration $(3, 2, 6), (3, 2, 3), (2, 1, 3), (2, 1, 2)$ that allows up to the 60% of the total number of questions to be about the first topic if the student does not correctly answer at least 2 questions. Notice that, given the algorithm followed by the system to challenge the student, correct configurations are such that $N = \sum_{i=1}^{T} D_i$.

It is helpful to represent configurations as surfaces in the 3D space by interpolating the points represented by the triplets. In this way static questionnaires (i.e. no adaptive behaviour) are represented by a line since triplets of the form $D_i = \text{MIN}_i = \text{MAX}_i$ adequately describe the static questionnaire[1] while adaptive questionnaires are represented by "large" surfaces that correspond to "stretching" the original (static) line into surfaces.

References

1. T. Berners-Lee, R. Cailliau, and, J.F.Groff. "The World Wide Web". Computer Networks and ISDN Systems, Nov. 1992, vol.25 (no.4-5), 45-49.
2. P. Brusilovsky, J. Eklund and E. Schwarz. "Web-based education for all: A tool for developing adaptive courseware". Computer Networks and ISDN Systems. (Proc. of Seventh International World Wide Web Conference, 14-18 April 1998) 30 (1-7), 291-300.
3. P. Brusilovsky. "Adaptive Educational Systems on the World-Wide-Web: A Review of Available Technologies". In Proc. of Workshop "WWW-Based Tutoring" at 4th International Conference on Intelligent Tutoring Systems (ITS'98), San Antonio, TX, August 16-19, 1998.
4. P. Brusilovsky and P. Miller. "Web-based testing for distance education. In: P. De Bra and J. Leggett (eds.) Proceedings of WebNet'99, World Conference of the WWW and Internet, Honolulu, HI, Oct. 24-30, 1999, AACE, pp. 149-154.
5. Cisco Academy. http://www.ciscoacademy.com
6. Paul De Bra. "Hypermedia Structures and systems" (Course 2L670) Eindhoven University of technology (http://wwwis.win.tue.nl/2L670).
7. D. Dwyer, K. Barbieri, H.M. Doerr. "*Creating a Virtual Classroom for Interactive Education on the Web*". Proc. of WWW 95, Third Int. Conf. on World Wide Web.
8. B. Ibrahim, S.D. Franklin. "*Advanced Educational Uses of the World Wide Web*". Proc. of WWW95, 3rd International Conference on World Wide Web.
9. A.Rios, J.L. Pérez de la Cruz, R.Conejo. "SIETTE: Intelligent evaluation sytem using tests for TeleEducation". Workshop "WWW-Based Tutoring" at 4th Int. Conf. on Intelligent Tutorial Systems (ITS'98).
10. W. A. Bogley, J. Dorbolo, R.O.Robson, J. A. Sechrest. "New Pedagogies and Tools for Web Based Calculus". Proc. of AACE WebNet 96, San Francisco, CA (USA), Oct. 15-19, 1996. See also http://www.peak.org for usage examples of QuestWriter.

---

[1] Of course, the really relevant parameters are $D_i = \text{MAX}_i$ since the MIN_i can be any number less than or equal to D_i.

What Does the User Want to Know About Web Resources? A User Model for Metadata

Diana Bental[1], Alison Cawsey[1], Patrick McAndrew[2], and Bruce Eddy[1]

[1] Dept of Computing and Electrical Engineering, Heriot-Watt University, Edinburgh
EH14 4AS, UK
{diana, alison, ceebde1}@cee.hw.ac.uk
http://www.cee.hw.ac.uk/~mirador/
[2] The Open University, Milton Keynes MK7 6AA, UK
p.mcandrew@open.ac.uk

Abstract. MIRADOR aims to create tailored descriptions which assist users in selecting relevant resources on the Web. In this paper, we distinguish between the processes of *searching* with a query and *selection* among the results of the query, and we describe a user model for metadata which supports selection. We outline how we may combine the user model with aspects of tailoring to the query, so as to produce concise and useful descriptions of resources.

1 Background

An increasing amount of information is available on the Web, and increasing numbers of documents include multimedia material. It is becoming difficult to track down the material most relevant to an individual's needs and it is becoming expensive to download a resource just to see if it is relevant [2]. Some responses to this problem have been in the form of improved tools for search and retrieval [5], but it has also been shown to be beneficial to provide mechanisms through which *users* are supported in assessing for themselves the potential relevance of an interesting resource.

Techniques such as sentence selection [7] and natural language generation [4] are being used to generate summaries of documents for information retrieval. However, they cannot present multimedia content nor information *about* the resource. An alternative is the use of rich *metadata* to describe a resource, i.e. separate information such as the title, topic, author and date of last modification. There is now considerable progress towards standards for the syntax and semantics of metadata to describe resources (e.g. [8]) and increasing numbers of Web-based resources now include metadata. Metadata has primarily been used to enhance search, and we believe it should also be used to support selection.

The MIRADOR project has developed different methods to produce tabular or text descriptions of resources from metadata [1]. We focus on educational resources, for which specialised metadata sets are being developed and used. A simple table is illustrated in Table 1. A text descriptions of (a subset of) that data, produced using language generation techniques, might be:

P. Brusilovsky, O. Stock, C. Strapparava (Eds.): AH 2000, LNCS 1892, pp. 268–271, 2000.
© Springer-Verlag Berlin Heidelberg 2000

Table 1. Simple Educational Metadata for a Resource

Title The Moon and Stars	*Type* Lesson plan
Subject Astronomy	*Age* 10–12
Price Free	*Resources* Star chart, dictionary

"The Moon and Stars" is an astronomy lesson plan for 10–12 year olds.

An alternative description of the same resource, which we can generate by specifying a different set of elements, is:

"The Moon and Stars" is a free astronomy lesson plan which requires the use of a star chart and a dictionary.

In the rest of this paper, we show how user models may be built which help to present information from metadata, information that is tailored to the user's needs and so assist the user in selecting relevant resources. More detailed information about this project is given in [1].

2   A User Model for Resource Selection

We view the process of choosing relevant resources as having two stages. First, the user poses a query to a search engine. A long list of resources may be returned, perhaps with a title and some other summary information, and then the user must (somehow) choose a few of those resources to download. Summaries may usefully be tailored to the user's query [7], but the query is not the whole story. To help with selection we need to distinguish between the user's *search* criteria, which are expressed in the initial query, and the user's *selection* criteria, which are the means by which the user decides which of the resources to download. Users typically do not express all of their selection criteria in the query.

The MIRADOR model allows users to express their selection criteria in terms of the metadata that is of most interest. A user can set up a profile which specifies the user's degree of interest in the contents of different metadata fields. We use a four point scale: for example, the user profile will contain information on whether the metadata element *price* is important to the user, interesting, dull, or of no interest. Such a scale is useful to determine whether information from that metadata field should appear in a description at all. If including all the interesting information would make the description too long, then less important information can be omitted.

Occasional users may find that the effort in specifying a detailed profile is not worth the benefit in more concise or relevant descriptions. We therefore specify a number of stereotypes for typical categories of user (e.g. teacher, student, parent). We first created a basis for our stereotypes by presenting different search scenarios (e.g. a teacher searching for classroom material, or a researcher wishing to do an overview of web-based resources) to a group of users and asking them which items of metadata they found most useful in each scenario. Our group of users was small (six users) but it included teachers, lecturers and university researchers who were able to give detailed comments based on their own experience. These initial stereotypes can easily be refined following actual use of the system [6]. Users may adapt their own profiles, adjusting the elements that interest them (or not). We intend to gather information about the adjusted profiles during testing, so as to create improved stereotypes which are more representative of actual users.

3 Tailoring the Response to the User's Query

We have so far used two sources of information to create summaries: the metadata returned from the search and the user model. We now intend to include a third source of information, tailoring to the query itself. The user model enables us to present information that is generally relevant to the user, while taking the query into account will enable us to highlight how closely a resource matches the user's specific requirements [7] and produce explicit comparisons [3] such as

> *Constellations is broadly aimed at ages 11-18, while you specifically requested material for 14 year olds.*

We have implemented a demonstration query engine to support query tailoring, based on a search engine that supports metadata (such as GEM[1]). An example of such a query and the data gathered for tailoring to it, are shown in Table 2.

Table 2. Information for Tailoring to the Query

Query: any field = astronomy **or** subject = space sciences **and** ages = 8,9,10

Representation 1		
Resource	Matching Metadata Field	Field Value
Resource 1	Title	**Astronomy**
	Subject	**Space Sciences**
	Age	5,6,7,**8,9,10**
Resource 2	Description	**Astronomy** is seldom taught...
	Age	**9,10**

Representation 2	
Query Component	Matching Resources
Any Field = astronomy	Resource 1, 2
Subject = space sciences	Resource 1
Age = 9,10	Resource 1, 2

---

[1] The Gateway to Educational Resources, http://www.thegateway.org/

Table 3. Metadata Table for Multiple Resources with User Model and Query Tailoring

Title	Subject	Description	Age	Price
Astronomy	**space sciences**	This lesson plan shows students...	6 7 **8 9 10**	Free
Constellations	general science	**Astronomy** is seldom taught...	**9 10**	Free

We have used these representations to tailor a tabular metadata display (see Table 3). Values that match the query values are highlighted, and we may also display metadata that is not captured in the user model. If the user model indicates that a metadata field is unimportant to the user (e.g. Description), but this field has matched the user's query, then the field will also be included in the display for this query. We now intend to explore how these representations may produce *text* descriptions that are tailored to the query and include explicit comparisons [3]. We will then evaluate the effects of user– and query–tailored responses. We expect that combining all three information sources — metadata, user model and query — will allow us to provide concise descriptions that enable users to assess quickly which resources are relevant to their needs.

4 Acknowledgments

This work was supported by EPSRC grant GR/M23106.

References

1. Cawsey, A., Bental, D., McAndrew, P.: Generating Resource Descriptions From Metadata to Support Relevance Assessments in Retrieval. *To appear in* The Sixth RIAO Conference, April 12–14, Paris, France (2000)
2. Johnson, C.: What's the Web Worth? The Impact of Retrieval Delays on the Value of Distributed Information. British HCI Group meeting on Time and Web, Staffordshire University, UK, (1997).
3. Milosavljevic, M., Oberlander, J.: Dynamic Hypertext Catalogues: Helping Users to Help Themselves. Proceedings of the 9th ACM Conference on Hypertext and Hypermedia, Pittsburgh, PA, USA (1998) 20–24
4. McKeown, K., Jordan, D., Hatzivassiloglou, V.: Generating Patient Specific Summaries of Online Literature. AAAI Spring Symposium on Intelligent Text Summarisation, (1998) 34–43.
5. Oard, D.: The State of the Art in Text Filtering. User Modeling and User-Adapted Interaction. **7** (1997) 141–178
6. Rich, E.: Users are Individuals: Individualizing User Models. Int. J. Human-Computer-Studies. **51** (1999) 323–338
7. Tombros, A. and Sanderson, M.: The Advantages of Query Biased Summaries in Information Retrieval. Proceedings of the 21st Annual International ACM SIGIR Conference on Research and Development in Information Retrieval, Melbourne, Australia, (1998) 2–10.
8. Weibel, S.: The State of the Dublin Core Metadata Initiative. D-Lib Magazine **5** (1999)

Web Information Retrieval for Designing Distance Hypermedia Courses

Angélique Boitel[1] - Dominique Leclet[2]

University of Picardy - Equip SASO - New Educational Technology Research Group
Pôle Cathédrale - IUP Miage - BP 2716 - 80027 Amiens Cedex 1 - FRANCE
[1]Angelique.Boitel@u-picardie.fr
[2]Dominique.Leclet@u-picardie.fr

Abstract. This paper presents research work in progress that aims to desgin a Web educative information retrieval system in a Distance Education (DE) context. In order to adapt it to trainers features, experimental information searches were performed with trainers involved in a DE course. These experiments allow us to express several assumptions about trainers needs. Thus, we propose a *data model* and a *treatment model* which take into account trainers features in the Web information retrieval process.

1. Introduction

This paper presents research work in progress that aims to conceptualize an information retrieval system in a DE context. This system is dedicated to trainers, who want to design distant hypermedia courses with Web documents. Indeed, the Web represents a privileged environment for trainers who want to obtain information in order to product hypermedia courses for DE [1]. However, it is difficult for the trainers to express their needs, to extract and to select relevant Web documents with the search engines available on the Web, because they aren't adapted to educational context. So, our system seeks to give an assistance for the expression of their specific needs, the extraction and the analysis of Web documents. In order to identify the features of trainers, we performed experimental searches of educative information with trainers, who would like to use educative resources provided by the Web for their courses. These experiments are described in the next paragraph.

2. The Context

The trainers were involved in the DESS Multimedia Information System[1] (MIS), that is a post graduate diploma which provides, via the Web, a 800 hours specialized course in multimedia. Information searches took place in three principal stages. The first stage aims to identify trainers needs. A questionnaire, which was concerned the

---

[1] opened in September 1999 at the University of Picardie in France, http://www. dep.u-picardie.fr

P. Brusilovsky, O. Stock, C. Strapparava (Eds.): AH 2000, LNCS 1892, pp. 272-275, 2000.

description of the trainers features and the DE context (subject, progression of the course, intended use of information,...), was given to the trainers. The second stage intended to extract Web documents according to an experimental information retrieval process described in [2]. Finally, the third stage planed the presentation of the retrieved information to trainers and the evaluation of their relevance.

These experiments have allowed for two different types of search to be distinguished. The first type of search generally occurs when the course plan is precise and unambiguous. Thus, the trainer will search for documents that allow for a notion to be studied in more depth, for a concept to be illustrated, or for a lesson to be made interactive through the inclusion of multimedia elements. The second type of search, takes place when the course plan is imprecise and ambiguous. The trainer will have, at the most, identified the structure of the course by general topic headings and will use searches to gather ideas on the areas about which he or she plans to teach, or to discover how other people have dealt with a particular subject. At the end of this first experiment, it turns out that the trainer uses four types of "indicator" to express the specific information that he or she requires, indicators concerned with : concepts within the course, the media he or she requires, metadata[2], and educational aims. Information concerned with the context of Distance Training and with the structure of the distance training course may also be required and expressed by the trainer.

These reports let us to assume that it necessary to take into account the state of the hypermedia course, the indicators given by the trainers and the features of the DE course, in order to describe trainers needs. So, we present in the paragraph 3 a *data model*, which aims to link the particular needs of a trainer to features of relevant Web documents. In order to organize effectively a method of processing for constituting a corpus of relevant Web documents, we have defined a model called the "*treatment model*". This model describes in the paragraph 3 an information retrieval process that allows documents having properties specified by the *data model* to be taken from the Web.

3.   The Data Model

The *data model* is composed of two distinct levels : the "*description level*" and the "*knowledge level*". The *description level* brings together items pertaining to the trainer's work and to the *search session*[3] that he or she carries out. Thus, we have defined a *Distance Formation* class that is concerned with prerequisites and training objectives. The *Distance Formation* class is linked to a list of *Rules* class, in which limits to be respected by trainers are described. The development of the course is modeled with the help of three other classes : the *General Section* class, the *Section* class and the *Pedagogical Segment* class. These classes are concerned with different parts of the course, from the most general level, for example a chapter, to the most specific, for example a paragraph. Thus, each search can be associated with a part of

---

[2] The type of documents (tutorial, glossary, research article, etc.) or the type of information (historic, news, biography, etc.), are very important for the selection of relevant documents.

[3] A Search Session is represented by the performing of the information retrieval process for a particular trainer.

the course, that is particularly useful in the case of a *Pedagogical Segment*, which could be described by concepts, educational aims and multimedia elements used in that part of the course. Moreover, as has been stated above, the trainer is able to provide specific indicators (of subject, media, educational aims, metadata), which characterize each search session. Thus, we have specified a *Search Session* class, *who_is_decomposed*[4] in a *Conceptual Entity class*, a *Media Entity* class, a *Meta Entity* class and a *Pedagogical Entity* class. The *Conceptual Entity* class is characterized by a label, that describes a concept, and linguistic information, in other words derived forms and semantic related terms. The *Media Entity* class, the *Meta Entity* class and the *Pedagogical Entity* class are respectively characterized by a label deriving form a limited list of terms, and by a Web definition. The latter is a group of features belonging to documents determines each label. The figure 1 presents the description level:

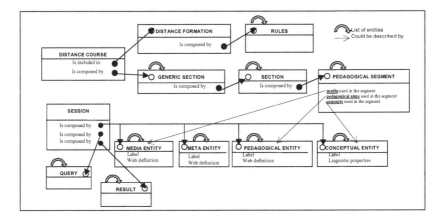

Fig. 1. The description level

The linguistic information of the *Conceptual Entity* class, (the derived forms and the semantic related terms), as well as Web definitions linked respectively to the *Media Entity* class, the *Meta Entity* class and the *Pedagogical Entity* class, are modeled at the second level of the *data model*. Thus, the *knowledge level* is comprised of a lexicon, a thesaurus and a dictionary. The lexicon allows for derived forms of the labels belonging to the *Conceptual Entity* class to be obtained. The thesaurus lets for semantic related terms to be obtained. The dictionary is composed of a collection of Web site or page features that respectively indicate the occurrence of a particular medium, of a specific type of document or a precise educational aims.

The *data model* represents one of the components of our Web Educational information retrieval system. The other one is the *treatment model,* which is described in the next paragraph.

---

[4] *Who_is_decomposed* symbolizes a meronomy. A meronomy is a hierarchical relationship that allows an entity to be defined through its components.

4.   The Treatment Model

The *treatment model* describes our system's information search process and comprises several modules: the *queries generation module*, the *results extraction module*, the *filtering module* the *results presentation module*. The *queries generation module* takes an instance of trainer needs given by the *level description* and produces a set of search queries formulated with the help of Boolean expressions that combine labels from the *Conceptual Entity* class, the *Media Entity* class, the *Meta Entity* class and the *Pedagogical Entity* class. The *results extraction level* takes all the queries generated in the previous stage and produces a corpus of Web page URLs. These are gathered by means of a set of information retrieval tools available on the Web. This module, which currently is implemented in Java language, interfaces with several services, such as Altavista, HotBot, and Lycos. The tools return the first twenty results of each search query. The results are gathered in corpus C_1 and filtered in order to discard clones[5] and invalid URLs[6]. *The filtering module* takes and processes C_1 and delivers a filtered corpus C_2. This filtering process aims to discard all the results that are not " reasonably relevant ". The filtering process constitutes, in fact, the setting of a relevance threshold by imposing a minimum number of conditions elements within the *Rule* class and by the Web definition of the *Conceptual Entity* class, the *Media Entity* class, the *Meta Entity* class and the *Pedagogical Entity* class. Those pages that do not meet these conditions are discarded. *The results presentation module* takes corpus C_2 and produces the results with which the trainer is provided. These results are accompanied by information describing particular features of the pages to which those results refer. Furthermore, it is the Web definition of the *Media Entity* class, the *Meta Entity* class and the *Pedagogical Entity* class.

5.   Areas for Future Research

The trainers needs have been identified by observing and searching for information in an experimental context with DESS MIS trainers. It is now appropriate to apply the *description level* to the informational needs of other trainers in order to confirm or invalidate the original hypotheses. To that end, we are going to perform a series of experiments with another distance training course from the University of Picardy, namely MOCI. Furthermore, it will be necessary to determine how the information retrieval process described in the paragraph 3 could be automated. This work would be reported in future communications.

References

[1] - Owston R. D., *The World Wide Web : A Technology to Enhance Teaching and Learning ?,* Educational Researcher, Vol 26, N°2, 1997, pp 27-33.

[2] – Boitel A., Leclet D., *Information Retrieval on the WWW: A method adapted to trainers' features in Distance Education,* World Conference on the WWW and Internet WebNet 99, Hawaii, USA, 1999.

---

[5] We assume that there is a clone when the corpus contains at least two equal URL.

[6] An invalid URL is a link which returns an error message via HTTP.

Formative Evaluation of Adaptive CALLware: A Case Study

Licia Calvi

Department of Computer Science
Trinity College, Dublin 2, Ireland
Licia.Calvi@cs.tcd.ie

Abstract. The paper presents the results of a formative evaluation concerning an on-line adaptive system to learn Italian. The purpose of this evaluation was to verify the validity of the chosen design methodology and to decide on the system's future development. The design methodology that we have adopted consisted in the use of adaptive disabling of links for a Web-based courseware. This was checked against two alternative versions of the same courseware, i.e., a static version and an adaptive version with removal of links.

1 Introduction

There is an extensive literature reporting empirical studies on the use of link annotation in educational hypermedia, as discussed by Brusilovsky and Eklund [1] and by Eklund and Brusilovsky [6]. There is nonetheless a more general lack of information when it comes to considering alternative methods. One such method is link disabling. Link disabling consists in showing users since the beginning of their interaction session all the links present in the system. Among them, only those links which are appropriate for the learner are enabled. Such an appropriateness feature is determined on the basis of the user's proficiency level in the particular content domain the system covers and on the basis of the user's learning history. In our application [3], the visible (and disabled) links are those which identify main modules within the system and are listed into an index node. Here, they are enabled gradually, as the learner advances in the learning process, from the top until the bottom of the list.

Link disabling, however, poses a number of important questions from the point of view of the interaction modality it fosters: it may indeed cause what Thüring [8] calls a cognitive overload, especially when the system is relatively large, by providing learners with all the existing links in the system; conversely, it seems to help learners orient themselves, as proven by Specht [7], since they immediately have a clear view of the number of links the system contains and can therefore build an adequate mental model of it: much like in a book, where its thickness denotes the probable number of pages, here the amount of links represents the system's structural complexity.

In order to answer these questions, a system was built using link disabling [3]. To evaluate it, different versions of the same applications were developed. In

P. Brusilovsky, O. Stock, C. Strapparava (Eds.): AH 2000, LNCS 1892, pp. 276–279, 2000.
© Springer-Verlag Berlin Heidelberg 2000

particular, we compared the system with an application using link removal and with a static version of it.

2   Rationale and Background

All three versions of the system were developed using a framework to update the information presented to users depending on the knowledge mastery they have gained as described in [2]. This framework assumes the existence of a correlation between every user's knowledge level (which is, in its turn, associated with a knowledge stereotype such as novice, beginner, and advanced), and the information the system progressively supplies. Such a progressive revealing is actually performed by modifying the system link structure: the more the student learns, the more links are revealed. As such, this framework therefore supports link removal because a number of other links are progressively disabled and made invisible, i.e., removed, in order to balance the number of links newly enabled. And in this way, the total number of visible links is maintained within a cognitively manageable size range and the interface has modified itself depending on the user's changing profile.

The above formalism was later improved and extended to support link disabling [4].

3   Formative Evaluation

The evaluation procedure was build following Draper's guidelines as in [5].

Twenty-four students took part in this formative evaluation. They were all university students in Romance languages with Italian as a major. After a pruning based on their number of total hits (as in [1], but in our case the threshold was put at 20 hits), only eighteen log files were retained as valid for this experiment.

Our application [3] is completely written in Italian and aims at providing students with a knowledge of both the Italian economy and the Italian business language. Although our students do speak Italian at a good level, they do not have any knowledge of either the economic notions or the economic language. The application features a set concepts from the economic and financial world, such as the preliminary notions of property, the different types of goods, and the notion of enterprise. Then, it extends to more specialized issues such as the stock market or the economic legislation. The system is structured hierarchically. There is a main starting page, the index page, which mirrors the system organization. It is already at this level that the different interface designs can be perceived. Each item in the list identifies a module of the courseware, each of which can then further branch into several ramifications. Students in the experiment could access all parts of the courseware. They were given a questionnaire at the beginning of the session, consisting of open questions. In order to answer them, they had to navigate, to locate and to retrieve specific data, and ultimately to understand how the system is structured. As final questions, they were asked to evaluate the system qualitatively, on the basis of their impression and of their experience.

Students were randomly assigned to one of the following three groups: one third of them was assigned to a version of the courseware with link disabling, i.e, with links always visible but disabled and only progressively enabled (DIS-students); one third was given a version with link removal, i.e., with links always invisible and disabled but progressively enabled (REM-students); and the last third a version with a static link topology, i.e., links always visible and enabled (STA-students). The results discussed in the next section are drawn from the students' answers in the questionnaire and from the analysis of their log files.

4   Results and Discussion

What emerged from analyzing the students' log files shows that there is no difference between the STA- and the DIS-version students in terms of success rate: in both cases, the same average of correct answers is obtained. Instead, the difference of both versions with the REM-version students is statistically more remarkable. We could also observe that the resort to the initial index page as an orientation device is kept small. This may suggest that most students did use the functionality provided at interface level to browse the material. A more focused analysis revealed the students' navigation behaviour, i.e., which interface functionality was mainly used, in particular, whether the one enabling the three main modalities or others. Since in all versions the presence of two link lists provides learners with a simple and straightforward way to circumvent the navigation guidelines and to access nodes freely, it became necessary to determine what Brusilovsky and Eklund [1] call an "agreement rate", i.e., a value indicating the degree of reliability learners were assigning to the interface design and therefore their degree of acceptance. If students manage to achieve a high success rate in gathering data and answering questions by ignoring the system suggestions, this result can indeed not be used as a positive indicator for the efficiency of the interface design. In our case, because the possible interface functionality is clearly separated (one per system version), the agreement rate is computed by dividing the number of suggested link hits (either removed or disabled) by the total number of hits performed by each student. Clearly, only the performance of those students accepting the interface functionality can be advocated when assessing the ultimate validity of the three interface designs. Students' performance demonstrated a very high agreement rate.

As mentioned above, the analysis of the success rate in retrieving correct information shows that, as average, DIS-version students and STA-version students score similarly and relatively high, whereas REM-version students score lower. This fact may be caused by the default structure given to the information, which exploits a Western culture way of accessing data: from the top to the bottom, from left to right. In the DIS-version system, indeed, the links that are progressively enabled are gradually unveiled by proceeding from the top to the bottom. And the STA-version application mimics the DIS-version one and it is as intuitive. Ultimately, from a usability standpoint, learners seem to experience the DIS- and STA-versions similarly. It is the REM-version which may be perceived as less learnable and user-friendly. It is indeed not consistent, since link visibility changes abruptly (from the learner's point of view, at least) and without any notice. In their qualitative analysis, the learners who were assigned to this version of the system indeed complained about the difficulty in understanding the principle behind this design option.

5   Conclusion

These results are different to what we had expected and are, in a way, disappointing. We had predicted a statistically significant outcome for the DIS-version design compared to the other two. Instead, we found no (statistically relevant) difference at all with the STA-version and students also did not out-perform in comparison with the REM-version.

But if we consider all the various pieces of evidence, it is nevertheless appropriate to conclude that the link disabling option proved to be a good interaction modality since it entails some positive features in the interaction it enables (e.g., lower number of total hits necessity for learners to locate the desired information; high correctness rate; high agreement rate). Still, due to some limitations, the reported evaluation can not inform in general about which interaction modality to adopt at a loss of others.

References

1. P. Brusiliovsky, J. Eklund. A Study of User Model Based Link Annotation in Educational Hypermedia. *Journal of Universal Computer Science*, 4,4:429-448, Springer Science, 1998.
2. L. Calvi, P. De Bra. A Proficiency-Adapted Framework for Information Browsing and Filtering in Educational Hypermedia Systems. *International Journal of User Modelling and User-Adapted Inetractions*, 7:257-277, 1997.
3. L. Calvi. A Proficiency-Adapted CALLware for Business Italian. In: D.P. O' Baoill (ed.) *Special Issue of TEANGA 18*. In press, 1999.
4. P. De Bra, L. Calvi. Towards a Generic Adaptive Hypermedia System. In: P. Brusilovsky, P. De Bra (eds.) *Proceedings of the Second Workshop on Adaptive Hypertext and Hypermedia*. Computing Science Reports, Eindhoven University of Technology, pp 5-10, 1998.
5. S. Draper, M. Brown, F. Henderson, E. McActeer. Integrative Evaluation: An Emerging Role for Classroom Studies of CAL. *Computers and Education*, 26(1-3):17-32, 1996.
6. J. Eklund, P. Brusilovsky. The Value of Adaptivity in Hypermedia learning Environments: A Short Review of Empirical Evidence. In: Brusilovsky P, De Bra P (eds.) *Proceedings of the Second Workshop on Adaptive Hypertext and Hypermedia*. Computing Science Reports, Eindhoven University of Technology, 1998.
7. M. Specht. Adaptive Methoden in computerbasierten Lehr/Lernsystemen. Ph.D. thesis, Unversity of Trier, Germany, 1997.
8. M. Thüring, J. Hannemann, J. Haake. Hypermedia and Cognition: Designing for Comprehension. *Communications of the ACM*, 38(8):57-66, 1995.

How Adaptivity Affects the Development of TANGOW Web-Based Courses

Rosa María Carro, Estrella Pulido, Pilar Rodríguez

Escuela Técnica Superior de Informática, Universidad Autónoma de Madrid,
Campus de Cantoblanco, 28049 Madrid, Spain
{Rosa.Carro, Estrella.Pulido, Pilar.Rodriguez}@ii.uam.es

Abstract. In this paper we describe those aspects a designer has to take into account when designing Web-based adaptive courses with TANGOW. The discussion is specifically focused on the adaptivity issues, which are not covered by any standard design methodology. The first section describes the decisions that need to be made in order to create adaptive courses by using TANGOW. Work done on some approaches to facilitate the design of Web courses is presented next. The paper finishes with some conclusions and work in progress.

1 Adaptivity and the Design Process in TANGOW[1]

TANGOW (*Task-based Adaptive learNer Guidance On the Web*)[1] is a system for Internet-based learning where adaptivity is achieved by establishing a clear distinction between course structure and course contents. The design of a course about „*The HTML Language*" is presented and will be used as example along the paper. A first content schema for this course can be the following: (1) Introduction, (2) How to create HTML pages and (3) Advanced HTML issues.

This structure should be somehow mapped into Web pages that effectively explain the contents associated to each concept. However, there is no need to directly associate a page, or even a set of linked pages to any of the subjects above. The subjects to explain, sequencing among them and associated contents, will be considered at each step of the design process. In TANGOW terms, the subjects to be explained are understood as Teaching Tasks, TTs, which can have a set of HTML fragments associated, whilst the order in which TTs will be presented is implemented as Teaching Rules. From that point of view, the initial course structure can be specified as a rule, rI, with task t0 representing the whole course.

Fig. 1 depicts the set of rules for our example. The information provided for each rule is the following: the name of the rule, the tasks involved, and the selected sequencing mode (the meaning of „AND" and „OR" will be explained below). In some cases, a dependency field is filled in with „*" followed by a task name(s). It means that those rules will not activate and, consequently, the composed task will not be performed, unless the referred task(s) are performed.

---

[1] This paper has been sponsored by the Spanish Interdepartmental Commission of Science and Technology (CICYT), project number TEL97-0306.

P. Brusilovsky, O. Stock, C. Strapparava (Eds.): AH 2000, LNCS 1892, pp. 280-283, 2000.

Composed Task	Tasks	Rule Name & Sequencing	Dependencies
t0	t1: Introduction t2: How to create HTML pages t3: Advanced HTML issues	rI (AND)	
t2	t21: Document Structure t22: Basic HTML Tags	rII (OR)	
t22	t221: Basic Text Formatting ... t224: Images t225: Links	rIII (OR)	*t21
t225	t2251: Text-based Links t2252: Image-based Links t2253: Anchors	rIV (OR)	*t221, *t224

Fig. 1. Some rules of „ The HTML Language,, course.

A Web-based tool to help designers to develop adaptive courses with TANGOW has been implemented. A first version of this tool can be accessed at http://eneas.ii.uam.es/designer/principal.html (see Fig. 2).

In order to establish a structure for a course by using this tool, the designer has to specify the set of tasks the student is required to perform. A good starting point for this is a content schema. Starting from this schema, each concept corresponds, in general, to a task. A task is tagged as atomic if it corresponds to a concept with no subconcepts in the conceptual schema. Otherwise, it is tagged as composed. For each composed task t a rule must be specified. The left-hand-side of this rule is t, and the right-hand-side is composed by the tasks corresponding to t subconcepts in the content schema. Also, for each composed task the following questions must be answered:

- can the task be decomposed in different ways depending on student profiles?
- which subtasks and in which order may be performed by the student to consider the composed task as achieved?
- how the actions performed by the student when performing a task will affect him/her accessing other tasks?

The first issue a designer must consider is whether significant student profiles exist, which make it convenient to present the student with different contents, or with the same concepts in different ways. A special student feature is the language that, if designing multilingual courses, can be used to present the course in the students mother tongue. As for subtask ordering, different options are available, though in this course only two sequencing modes have been used: „AND" and „OR". In the „AND" sequencing cases, the tasks involved have to be achieved consecutively, and students are not required to make any choice. With „OR" sequencing, the achievement of one of the subtasks is enough in order to achieve the composed task.

Finally, it can also be stated that a concept must be assimilated by the student before being presented with others. This is the case of task t225, „Links", that is not accessible unless tasks t221,"Basic Text Formatting", and t224, „Images", have already been achieved. However, the description of the „Links" task, though not accessible, is presented together with the list of all the other „Basic HTML tags". This corresponds to the „dependencies" field in Fig. 1.

Besides the course structure, the designer has also to decide which the proper contents are for each task. In general, this work is simpler than that of deciding on course structure, but some reflections are convenient in order to make a good content distribution.

When a designer is first faced with this task, s/he tends to associate a unique HTML piece to each task, so that the content distribution „copies" the course structure. This approach might be valid, but in most cases it does not take advantage of the system possibilities. For the maintenance tasks to benefit from the facilities offered, it is useful to provide a set of HTML fragments instead of a unique HTML document. Some questions should be answered before deciding on the concrete HTML fragments to include. These questions have to do with the relation among course structure and contents, contents that can be reused in different places of the same course, and the convenience of creating a specific glossary to be used all along the course.

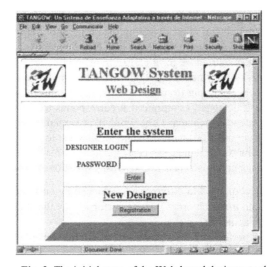

Fig. 2. The initial page of the Web-based designer tool.

2   Approaches to the Design Process of Web-Based Courses

Work has been done on some approaches to facilitate the design of Web courses. In ISIS-Tutor [2], it is suggested to design the main part of the hypermedia network resembling the corresponding domain network, representing each node of the domain network by a node of the hyperspace, and taking the links between domain network as links between hyperspace nodes.

MANIC [3] is a tool for transforming existing multimedia-based courses consisting of a set of slides into one that can be accessed through the Web. In the current version, adaptivity is implemented by allowing students to skip full slides.

In ANATOM-TUTOR [4], a teaching aid for medical students, knowledge is presented in a manner suited to the users' level of knowledge. A hypertext tool is provided although no reference is made to any tool that facilitates the design task.

Web-CT [5] is an easy-to-use environment for creating Web-based courses, that makes use of a Web browser as the interface for the course development. The environment does not include any facility for the development of adaptive courses and the Web pages are the same for every student that accesses to the environment.

3   Conclusions

This paper discusses some issues about the design of adaptive Web-based courses. The analysis is based on the experience gained from developing courses with TANGOW, a system for adaptive Internet-based learning. In TANGOW, adaptivity is achieved by separating course structure and course contents.

Although a variety of tools exist that facilitate the creation of course contents, if adaptiveness is a priority the number of available tools decreases considerably. A designer tool whose aim is to provide support in the specification of the course structure has been implemented. It is our intention to develop other components of this tool, which would assist in the rest of the design process.

References

1. Carro, R.M., Pulido, E., Rodríguez, P.: Designing Adaptive Web-based Courses with TANGOW. Advanced Research in Computers and Communications in Education, Vol. 2. IOS Press (1999) 697-704
2. Brusilovsky, P., Pesin, L.: ISIS-Tutor: An Intelligent Learning Environment for CDS/ISIS Users. CLCE'94, Joensuu, Finland (1994) Available at: http://cs.joensuu.fi/~mtuki/ www_clce.270296/Brusilov.html
3. Stern, M.: The Difficulties in Web-Based Tutoring, and Some Possible Solutions. Workshop on Intelligent Educational Systems on the WWW, Eighth World Conference of the AIED Society, Kobe, Japan. (1997) Available at: http://www.contrib.andrew.cmu.edu/~plb/ AIED97_workshop/Stern.html
4. Beaumont, I.H.: User Modelling in the Interactive Anatomy Tutoring System ANATOM-TUTOR. Adaptive Hypertext and Hypermedia. Kluwer Academic Pub. (1998) 91-116
5. Goldberg, M.W., Salari, S., Swoboda, P.: World Wide Web - Course Tool: An Environment for Building WWW-Based Courses. Fifth International WWW Conference, Paris, France. (1996) Available at: http://www5conf.inria.fr/fich_html/papers/P29/Overview.html

An Adaptive Web Content Delivery System

Jinlin Chen, Yudong Yang, and Hongjiang Zhang

Microsoft Research, China
5F, Beijing Sigma Center, No. 49, Zhichun Road,
Beijing 100080, P.R.China
{i-jlchen, i-ydyang, hjzhang}@microsoft.com

Abstract. The desktop-centric design of most of the current web contents pose many difficulties for pervasive browsing. In this paper, we present our study on the problem to support pervasive browsing in the heterogeneous environment of today's Internet. A system solution – Adaptive Web Content Delivery (AWCD), is presented to overcome the problems existed in present web infrastructure. The system designed is extensible for the further development of Internet. The two major subsystems of AWCD, client profile learning and adaptation, are described in detail. Experiment results of our system are also shown.

1 Introduction

Today, a variety of appliances are emerging into mainstream Internet appliances, which has brought a large variety in users' preferences in browsing even the same web page. In addition, network connections are also quite different. All these variations require that web pages be prepared suitable for the client. However, most of the current Internet servers still provide the same content to all the clients without considering the variations of client environment, which has caused frustration to many users.

Many people have addressed this problem and presented solutions. SpyGlass [1], OnlineAnywhere [2], QuickWeb [3], FastLane [4], TranSend [5], ProxyNet [6], Digestor [7], and Mobiware [8] are commercial products that adapt web content. However, most of them only make adaptation under special conditions due to the lack of structural information of HTML content, and many of them focus on image conversion. Some projects [9] tried to extract structural information from HTML tag. However, this does not work effective because HTML was designed for content presentation.

In this paper, we present a new approach, Adaptive Web Content Delivery (AWCD), to provide a customized and adaptive Web service for clients. With AWCD, a web user can get content most appropriate to one's device and preference. And the bandwidth consumption can also be minimized. AWCD provides an overall solution to the existing problems of web content delivery.

In Section 2, we present the design of our prototype of AWCD system. This is followed by discussions on the client profile learning subsystem and adaptation subsys-

P. Brusilovsky, O. Stock, C. Strapparava (Eds.): AH 2000, LNCS 1892, pp. 284–288, 2000.

tem in Section 3 and Section 4 respectively. In Section 5, we present some experimental results of our system. And conclusions are given in Section 6.

2   System Architecture of AWCD

The basic system architecture of AWCD is shown as Fig. 1.The Client profile learning subsystem discovers the client environment. Adaptation subsystem makes adaptation decisions and generates new web content according to the decision results and various adaptation components.

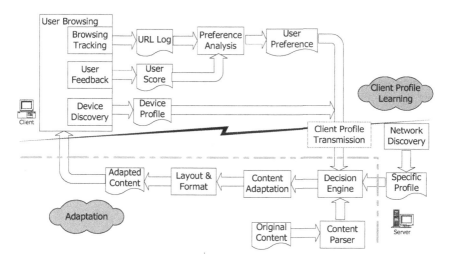

Fig. 1. Basic system architecture of AWCD

Browsing Tracking module tracks users' behavior and obtains user's browsing paths and times. This is realized by embedding a tracking component in the browser. **User Feedback** module gets user preference by implementing an embedded component of the browser. **Preference Analysis** module analyzes users' preferences according to the browsing tracking results and users' feedback. **Device Discovery** module discovers the hardware and software environments of the client device. **Client Profile Transmission** module transmits user preference and device capability to the server by extending the client-specific web services [11]. **Network Discovery** module discovers network-related parameters, including effective bandwidth, latency, error rate, etc. In our system, we have implemented a TCP level network discovery module. **Content Parser** module parses the requested contents and builds the structural representations of them. **Decision Engine** module collects client profile information from discovery module and contents' data from content parser to determine adaptation instructions and layout rules that will generate the most user-satisfying results in most efficient ways. **Content Adaptation** module consists of filters to perform conversion, summarization and substitution of contents according to the instructions given by the decision engine. **Layout & Format** module reorganizes and generates the final contents to be delivered to end-users.

3 Client Profile Learning

Although many papers [5][10] have discussed the variations of client environment, no one can provide an effective and self-contained way in describing the client environments. Concerning this, we have studied the variations of client environment according to the system framework of Internet, and try to give a logic and systematic description, which focuses on the following dimensions:

Network Characteristics include network bandwidth, latency, error rate, and congestion rate. **Processor Module** includes Hardware capability and software type. **User Interface** includes input/output device and browser information. **User Preference** includes accept waiting time, content preference, media preference, delivery preference, presentation preference, accessibility factor.

We transmit client profiles by extending the client-specific web services, which take client properties as "User Agent Attributes". In our approach we extend "User Agent Attributes" to "Client Attributes" which describe client. Client Attributes are sent through the HTTP User-Agent header. They are added to the normal User-Agent header using a comment field.

4 Adaptation

The kernel of adaptation is Decision Engine. It first retrieves and compares content attributes against client profile to decide what possible operations could be done. It then evaluates the cost of an adaptation process. Quality is evaluated by the quality of content and the user waiting time. Let X^m be media object m, X_i^m be the ith version of X^m, $S(X_i^m)$ be the size of X_i^m, the size of the delivered contents is

$$S_T = \sum_{\text{For selected } i,m} S(X_i^m) \tag{1}$$

Currently we define a simple cost function: a service is acceptable when all contents can be delivered within maximum waiting time specified by users or else the service is not acceptable. Let B_A be the average network bandwidth, D_{RTT} be the network roundtrip time. Assume that transcoding processes and fetching contents to the server could be done in negligible time. The user waiting time for the delivered contents is

$$W_T = 2 \cdot D_{RTT} + \frac{S_T}{B_A} \tag{2}$$

The goal of optimization is then

$$W_T \leq T_{MaximumWait} \tag{3}$$

Where $T_{maxWait}$ is the maximum waiting time that a user can accept. We choose a bottom-up approach to do the optimization because the HTML contents could not be well structured.

The optimization starts from a whole collection of detected objects within the document and the first step is to estimate starting W_T. The following step is an iterative checking and trimming procedure and its stop condition is either (3) is satisfied or there does not have any content we can trim.

5 Experimental Results

We have implemented an experimental system to test our ideas. Our client devices include Windows CE based Palm-size PC, Hand-held PC, Laptop, Desktop. Network connections range from 19.2k wire-line modem to 100M LAN. The experimental data are real web pages from popular Web sites such as MSN. Our demonstration results can be accessed at http://www.research.microsoft.com/mcomputing/acd.

In an average, the transferring time consumed by an adapted page is only about 30 percent of that of the original one. And the layout of the new web page is also more suitable to client device.

6 Conclusion

In this paper we have presented AWCD, an overall adaptation system for delivering Web contents. AWCD can effectively overcome the existing problems in Web content delivery. Compared to other systems, our approach is more robust and extensible.

References

1. Spyglass, "White Paper of Prism 2.2", http://www.spyglass.com/images/Prism22.pdf
2. OnLineAnyWhere, FlashMap, http://www.onlineanywhere.com
3. QuickWeb of Intel Crop. http://www.intel.com/quickweb
4. FastLane of Spectrum Information Technologies http://stage.acunet.net/spectrum/index.html
5. Fox A., Gribble S.D., Chawathe Y., Brewer E.A.: Adapting to Network and Client Variation Using Infrastructural Proxies: Lessons and Perspectives. IEEE Personal Communication (1998), Vol 5(4) 10 – 19
6. ProxiNet, ProxiWare, http://www.proxinet.com/products_n_serv/proxiware/
7. BickMore T.W., Schilit B.N.: Digestor: Device-independent access to the World Wide Web, Proc. of the 6th International World Wide Web Conference. (1997) 655–663
8. Angin, O., Campbell, A.T., Kounavis, M. E., Liao, R.-F.: The Mobiware Toolkit: Programmable support for adaptive mobile networking. IEEE Personal Communication (1998), Vol 5(4) 32–43
9. Lim, S. J., Ng, Y. K.: An Automated Approach for Retrieving Hierarchical Data from HTML Tables. In Proceedings of the Eighth International Conference on Information and Knowledge Management (ACM CIKM'99). Kansas City, MO, USA. (1999) 466-474

10. Smith, J.R., Mohan, R., Li, C.S.: Scalable Multimedia Delivery for Pervasive Computing. ACM Multimedia. (1999) 131–140
11. Client-Specific Web Services by Using User Agent Attributes. W3C Note. http://www.w3.org/TR/NOTE-agent-attributes-971230.html

Knowledge Computing Method for Enhancing the Effectiveness of a WWW Distance Education System

Alexandra Cristea and Toshio Okamoto

The Lab. of AI & Knowledge Computing
The Graduate School of Information Systems
The University of Electro-Communications
Chofu, Chofugaoka 1-5-1, Tokyo 182-8585, Japan
{alex,okamoto}@ai.is.uec.ac.jp

Abstract. The ultimate aim of our research is a free, evolutionary, Internet-based, agent-based, long-distance teaching environment for academic English. For this purpose, we are building 2 environments: student learning and teacher courseware design environment. Here we focus on the second research direction, on constructing the teacher authorware environment (courseware management), and especially on a new method of automatic, knowledge computing-based courseware indexing that uses the AI paradigm of Concept Mapping.

1 Introduction

We are building a system to help academicians learn to exchange meaningful information with their peers in English. The system is WWW hypermedia based. The detailed rationale of the research, the system modules and the student environment design were shown in [3]. The system is also a remote authoring system, for teachers designing the courseware. With the growth and spread of the Internet, and at the same time, the constantly increasing transmission bandwidth, many applications are moving towards the net. Benefits are, among others, the wider reach compared to stand-alone applications. For educational applications, another benefit is the extension of the time concept. WWW courses can be accessed at any time, from anywhere, not only when the teacher is in the classroom. However, recently, the rigidity of the existent Web course material has been noticed. The research community generally agrees that knowledge processing and adaptive indexing benefit the end-user. The end goal of this line of research is to design courses which offer the study material in the best way possible for the current student, adapt to his/her needs, knowledge, misunderstandings, representations, and so on. One type of adaptation is via automatic, adaptive courseware indexing. Courseware indexing has been studied by many researchers [2], who have discussed the benefits and dangers of automatic indexing. To decrease system complexity for teacher and student user, and offer correct automatic guidance, we propose indexing as a trade-off between complete automation, and complete teacher input.

P. Brusilovsky, O. Stock, C. Strapparava (Eds.): AH 2000, LNCS 1892, pp. 289-292, 2000.

2   Information, Organization, and Linking

The information exchange from tutor to system contains input of lessons, texts, links between them, etc., but also requests for help in editing. The data from the tutor is stored in 6 different structured databases, including a library of expressions that appear in the text, a Video-on-Demand (VOD) database, a background image database, an audio database of listening examples, a full text database and a link database.

A.   Structuring Information into Knowledge

The information that the teacher inputs is restricted from start to small units of building blocks, called *texts*, that can have a complete audio or video version. These texts can be grouped in *lessons*. Each text/lesson has the following attributes: main text (for text units only), a short title, keywords, explanation, patterns to learn, conclusion, and finally, exercises. We established this structure, as a first step towards efficient indexing, so that we obtain an easy retrieval by a search of information from titles and keywords, as is natural, but also in explanation and conclusion files.

B.   Test Points

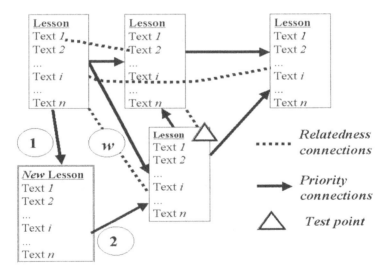

Fig. 1. The subject link database.

The teacher should mark *test points*, at which it is necessary to pass a test in order to proceed with the course. If the student wants to jump one or more subjects, s/he can proceed with only one test, made of a random combination of tests from the previous test points, in a proportional relation. In this way, the teacher can make sure that the student will not pass any level without having actually understood the subject. In this way, aimless searching through the html pages is avoided. Next to these obligatory tests, there can also a number of optional tests.

C. Priority and Relatedness Connections

When introducing one or more subjects (fig.1), the teacher has to specify the *Priority Connections* of the learning order, by building a directed graph (of pointed arrows). When there is no order, subjects will have the same priority, and build a set. Priorities among the texts of a lesson are set implicitly according to the order of the texts, but can be modified, if necessary. The teacher can also add connections between related subjects, with indirect links, called *Relatedness Connections*, for subjects, among which no specific learning order exists, but which are related. These relations are useful, e.g., during tests: if one of the subjects is considered known, the other one should be also tested. The main differences between the priority connections and the relatedness connections is that the first ones are directional, weightless connections, whereas the latter are non-directional, weighted connections.

D. Concept Mapping

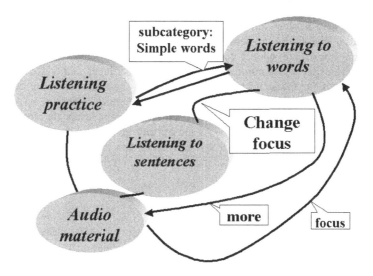

Fig. 2. Labeling example

Concept mapping [1,4] can be applied in two ways in order to improve the connectivity and information content of the subject linking. The teacher inputs more *transversal links* via concept mapping techniques: (1) The system offers a keyword list and a title list, and the teacher can select concepts, and link them in a graphical editing window. In this way, brainstorming and free generation of related concepts is supported. (2) The system *automatically links* concepts, then presents the map(s) to the teacher, for inspection. The teacher can add, delete links, and, more important, can label links. When labeling, the teacher can introduce also labeling directions, as shown in fig.2. The teacher is only responsible to link his/her own course to the existing courses created by him/her or some of the other courseware designers.

E. Subject Relatedness Weight Computation

The relatedness connections have weights that change interactively, reflecting how connected' two subjects are:

$w_{A,B}^0 = \square 1$: teacher selection; **0.5**: system generation; **0**: rest;} .   (1)

$w_{A,B}^{t+tconst} = \square\ w_{A,B}^t + f1$(no. of times connection $_{A,B}$ activated)   +   (2)
  $+ f2$(no. of times connection $_{A,B}$ was accepted, when
        proposed in relation to unknown subject)   +
  $+ f3$(no. of times connection $_{A,B}$ was accepted, when
        proposed in relation to query)   +
  $+ f4$(no. of times tests related to connection $_{A,B}$ were
        solved satisfactorily or not); .

$w_{A,B}^0 = \square 1$: teacher selection; **0.5**: system generation; **0**: rest;} .

where: $\square\square$ (0,1): forgetting rate; f1~f4: linear functions; $w_{A,B}>0$: weight between subjects A and B; t: time; tconst: period for weight update.

3 Conclusion

We showed here in short the adaptive indexing and connection mechanisms of our evolutionary, Web-based, academic English teaching tool, MyEnglishTeacher". We focused on courseware subject connection optimization design, for easy, efficient retrieval of relevant course information, based on teacher input, and on Concept Mapping techniques for the subject-link generator. From system courseware design requirements, we enforce the generation of structured content databases, as a basis to knowledge bases for concept mapping. We showed the weight update function computation for the relatedness links. With the priority graph built by the teacher, the relatedness graph automatically built by the system, and the concept mapping based linking and labeling, student guidance in the multimedia web courseware is possible.

References

1. Beyerbach, B. (1988) Developing a technical vocabulary on teacher planning: preservice teachers' concept maps", Teaching and Teacher Education, Vol. 4.
2. Brusilovsky, P., Schwarz, E. and Weber, G. (1996) ELM-ART: An Intelligent Tutoring System on the World Wide Web", Intelligent Tutoring Systems, Eds.: C. Frasson, G. Gauthier & A.Lesgold, Lecture Notes in Computer Science, Vol. 1086, Springer, 261-269.
3. Cristea, A. and Okamoto, T. (2000) MyEnglishTeacher – An Evolutionary, Web-based, multi-Agent Environment for Academic English Teaching", Proc. of Congress on Evolutionary Computation, San Diego, USA (to appear).
4. Kommers, P.A.M. (1996) Conceptual Support by the New Media for Co-operative Learning in the Next Century", Multimedia, Hypermedia and Virtual Reality; Models, Systems and Applications, Eds.: P. Brusilovsky, P.A.M. Kommers and N. Streitz, Springer.

Interface Adaptation to Style of User-Computer Interaction

Maia Dimitrova[1], Dimcho Boyadjiev[1]and Nikolai Butorin[2]

[1] Institute of Control and System Research, Bulgarian Academy of Sciences
Acad. G. Bonchev Str., Block 2, P.O.Box 79
1113 Sofia, Bulgaria
{dimitrova, boiadjiev}@iusi.bas.bg
[2] Day Center „Van Gogh", Tzar Simeon Str., 13
1000 Sofia, Bulgaria
nik_butorin@hotmail.com

Abstract. The paper presents a framework for interface adaptation to style of user-computer interaction by implicit retrieval of *apriori* defined independent measures of graphical, verbal, procedural and dynamic cognitive characteristics. A neural network is proposed that samples and classifies patterns of style representing data into sets of paired relations among scores for further distinct support. The approach is currently being implemented into a database system for a community mental health center.

1 Introduction

Current interface systems have been mostly oriented towards capturing and employing intentionality-based user-computer interactive behaviors. In the era of the web-based computer systems it may become helpful to view the process of user-computer communication as accounting for more than just the intentional level, but to the „incidental" level of communication, too [2]. Perhaps future interface systems will behave in resemblance to some processes of social support like, for example, computer „empathy" to the current user. This can provide additional help for solutions of problems in the rational domain that is in the end the main goal of any communication – social or with artificial intelligent agents.

„Unintentional „ behaviors as patterns of style can be found in terms of preferences for graphical vs. verbal representation [3], principle-based vs. „anticipative" reasoning and explanation [7], dynamical vs. „rigid" adaptation [6], customization of the interface on one's own or with external help [4], etc.

Recent research has revealed „style-dependent" factors influencing the mathematical modeling of the interaction *itself* [6]. Neural networks have proven to be a flexible and convenient tool for capturing the characteristics and dynamics of the interaction [1], [4]. However, efficient algorithms for feature extraction in neural networks to give fast and correct classification are still under investigation [5]. One promising approach to interface design of widely usable applications is parallel development of feature extraction algorithms suitable to the currently developed application.

P. Brusilovsky, O. Stock, C. Strapparava (Eds.): AH 2000, LNCS 1892, pp. 293-296, 2000.
□ Springer-Verlag Berlin Heidelberg 2000

2 An Approach to User Characterization by a Neural Network

The following „relativity-coding" approach to represent the style of the individual user has been applied – „The current user prefers GRAPHICAL, rather than VERBAL presentation of information; PROCEDURAL, rather than DECLARATIVE coaching, etc." For a set of independent features (represented by normalized values), for example, A, B, C, D, E and F, a class is be defined as a combination of paired relations (e.g. A>B C<D E>F). The number of classes is 2^n where n is the number of pairs of features to be encoded. It has been shown that input-output correlation correspondence influences neural network performance [8]. The prediction here has been that learning and classification can be enhanced if „relativity" correspondence between the input and the output matrices is introduced.

The relativity-coding approach was tested on an empirical sample of data from 16 subjects who had responded to different computer-generated tasks from a standardized job-selection diagnostic tool as well as on simulational data (larger sample) with similar standard deviation. The scores on four uncorrelated tasks from the tool (normalized in the interval [-1, +1]) were selected to form a user profile – dynamic (i.e. multiple-choice) tasks, visual tasks, spatial tasks and verbal tasks. The features were encoded successively – „more/less successful on task A than B and more/less successful on task C than D". Two output matrices were composed. The first is „relational" where any paired relation of the input is associated with plus one for the bigger value and minus one for the smaller value. The second is a standard pattern recognition target matrix of plus ones on the main diagonal and minus ones everywhere else with arbitrary assignment of column vectors to each class (for a hyperbolic tangent as the activation function of the neurons). The network with „relational" output performed faster and with no misclassifications whereas misclassifications were observed in the case of standard (arbitrarily formed) output matrix. The utility of the proposed approach is in that the neural network can be pre-trained on small samples of „real" data plus added simulated samples with similar standard deviation. There is no limitation on the dimensionality of the input samples, the network can be probed with any set of measurements of style, and it gives readily interpretable output.

3 Application

The framework is currently being employed in an interface for users of a mini-database system for clients of a mental health community center (Figure 1). Users of the system are mental health professionals, students or social work trainees, busy with their current work, who use the system in the meantime, very often in a hurry, after work or whenever there is available time. The interface has to be as much as possible simple, self-explanatory and helpful because very often neither the staff nor the students have time to spare on explaining or learning how to use the system.

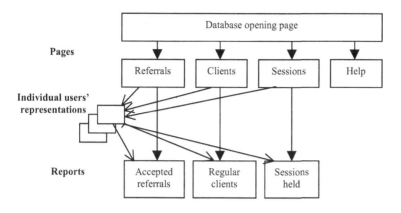

Fig. 1. Structure of the Van Gogh Center database

Table 1. Summary of user comments of the interface

General comments	Style-related comments
About system functionalities: „to collect client data", „produce monthly reports", etc.	*Declarative – procedural dimension:* „would like to have a Help menu" vs. „prefer trial and error"
About system objectives: „feedback on session atten- dance", „recording participation in differ- ent programs", „keeping records of individual progress", etc.	*Graphical – verbal dimension:* „what I like most is the colours/ paintings of Van Gogh" vs. „what I like most is the possibility to keep my own records"
About „fitting in" time for work with the database: „every day/week", „in my computer time", „when my client doesn't turn up", etc.	*Static – dynamic dimension:* „it helps me prepare my monthly re- port" vs. „to see how others are doing and where I am"

At present the interface is being designed to adapt to graphical, verbal, procedural and dynamic cognitive characteristics and serve as a simple „prompt and advise" system. An initial usability assessment of the system was performed via delivering an especially designed questionnaire. It did not direct the attention of the users to the interface but rather oriented them to assessing and expressing opinions on how the newly introduced system helps them work with clients. This was done on purpose for implicit off-line assessment of the interface. Table 1 summarizes the comments that were given by the 8 currently employed members of the staff of the center.

The basic finding is that there are style-related comments supporting in general the initial assumptions of the approach. Currently data is being collected from the frequency of opening respective pages or reports. Features in terms of „more frequently using the STATIC, rather than the DYNAMIC presentation", etc. will be further retrieved automatically to define style and offer support. In general, the introduction of the database helps organize activities of staff and clients of the center and is a convenient platform for testing approaches to incorporating adaptivity in user-computer interfaces.

4 Conclusions

The paper presents a currently developed approach to incorporating adaptivity to style of work in interface systems. The interface can infer style characteristics in relational terms for implicitly monitoring, classification and provision of prompts and advice to users of different background and expert level. A neural network with enhanced „interpretability" of output is employed and revealed simplicity and efficiency of performance. The approach is currently being implemented into a database system for a community mental health center and seems applicable to web based data access systems as well from a user style perspective.

Acknowledgement. This work is partially supported by Grant No 809/98 of the National Research Fund of the Bulgarian Ministry of Education and Science.

References

1. Chen, Q., Norcio, A. F.: Modeling a Users Domain Knowledge with Neural Networks. International Journal of Human-Computer Interaction, 1 (1997) 25-40
2. Gecsei, J.: Adaptation in Distributed Multimedia Systems. IEEE MultiMedia, 2 (1997) 58-66
3. Graesser, A.C, K. Wiemer – Hastings, P. Wiemer – Hastings, R. Krenz.: Autotutor: A Simulation of a Human Tutor. Journal of Cognitive Systems Research, 1 (1999) 21-37
4. http://www.cs.bham.ac.uk/~ipa/work.html
5. Lee, C., Landgrebe D.A.: Decision Boundary Feature Extraction for Neural Networks. IEEE Transactions on Neural Networks, 1, (1997) 75-83
6. Nechyba, M.C., Xu, Y.: Human Control Strategy: Abstraction, Verification and Replication. IEEE Control Systems, 5 (1997) 48-61
7. Renkl, A.: Learning from Worked-out Examples: A Study of Individual Differences. Cognitive Science, 1 (1997) 1-29
8. Yildiz N.: Correlation Structure of Training Data and the Fitting Ability of Back Propagation Networks: Some Experimental Results. Neural Computing & Applications, 1 (1997) 14-19

Adaptation and Generation in a Web-Based Lisp Tutor

Isabel Fernández-Anta, Eva Millán, and José-Luis Pérez-de-la-Cruz

Depto. Lenguajes y Ciencias de la Computación, ETSI Informática,
Universidad de Málaga, E-28080 Málaga, Spain
perez@lcc.uma.es

Abstract. This paper presents an aspect of a tool which will be developed to help teachers in the task of teaching basic Lisp programming. The paper focuses onto the problem generator module.

1   LispTutor2

When teaching programming languages, it is desirable to have (1) a comprehensive and structured collection of problems and (2) an automatic procedure to check inmediatly the solution given by the student (in order to avoid harmful reinforcement effects). Moreover, it is also desirable to have (3) information about students' problem solving activity (in order to improve the elaboration of course materials and organization).

Goals (1) and (2) can be achieved by means of curriculum theory and generative programs. Curriculum theory structures a course in lessons (or items) between which some links are established (prerequisites, for instance). This information is summarized in a graph (*learning strategy*) designed by the teacher and then coded into the system. The learning strategy will give the necessary information for the system to decide which type of problems will be proposed to the student according to his/her current state of knowledge.

Generative programs are based on an educational philosophy [2], [3] in which it is considered that student learning can be improved if he/she faces problems of appropriate difficulty instead of listening to theoretical explanations. Koffman and Blount appleid this method to the problem of teaching machine language programming. The general schema of a generative system is:

1. A suitable problem schema is selected according to the learning strategy and the student model.
2. A problem of this type is generated and presented to the student.
3. The student solves the problem.
4. The solution is compared to the one given by the system. According to the result, the student's model is modified and the next type of problem is selected, that is, we return to step 1.

However, goal (3) demands an additional feature: an easy, decentralized access to the same set of problems. WWW technology can provide this feature. LispTutor2, that can be found in

P. Brusilovsky, O. Stock, C. Strapparava (Eds.): AH 2000, LNCS 1892, pp. 297–300, 2000.

http://alcor.lcc.uma.es/lisptutor2/
is an example of a generative system implemented in the Web. The domain of
LispTutor2 is elementary Lisp programming. Currently only exercises concerning
the evaluation of Lisp expressions are present in the system; in later stages we
hope to implement a more complete set of exercises.

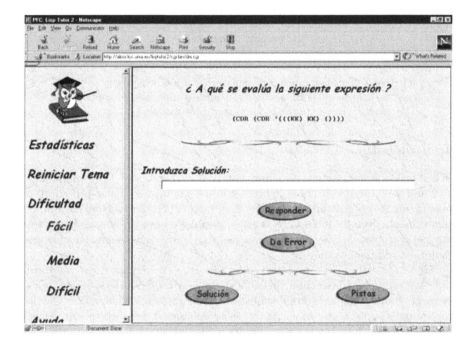

Fig. 1. A screen in LispTutor2

Let us describe the functioning of the system from the student's point of view
(figure 1). When the student starts the session, the system asks for his personal
data (name, surname and identification number). In this way, the system can
create and afterwards handle the student model. If it is the first time that the
pupil uses the tutorial, the course will start from the beginning, and if the system
has already information about the student the course will start from the level
reached in the last session (that information will be in the student model). In
both cases, the system will pose a problem, and then the student can solve it,
ask for a clue or give it up. Every time he/she asks for a clue the system shows
one evaluation rule that has to be used in the resolution of the problem. When
all the available clues have been presented, the system informs the student. After
asking for each clue the student has the opportunity to solve the problem or to
give it up. When the student gives up a problem (either after asking for a clue
or not) the tutorial shows him the solution and proposes a new problem of the

same type. The students are not penalized when they ask for a clue or fail to solve a question. Problems will be posed till the pupil wants to finish the session or completes the course.

2   Problem Generator

When generating a Lisp expression E for tutorial purposes, several issues must be taken into account:

- the evaluation of E will require the application of the evaluation rule which is the current instructional focus.
- the evaluation of E will not require the application of evaluation rules which have not been taught.
- the level of complexity (nesting) of E will be bounded by some "suitable" value.
- some non-evaluable expressions must be generated, since negative examples are at least as useful as positive ones.

On the other hand, the system must be flexible enough to allow modifications and customizations from different instructors or for different classes.

To fulfill these requirements, a generator of Lisp expressions has been implemented based upon the concept of *attribute constrained probabilistic context-free grammar*. The concepts of *attribute grammar* and *probabilistic grammar* are standard in theoretical computer science and compiler construction; the underlying ideas in an attribute grammar are to define a set of attributes and to assign attribute values to every symbol in a given derivation. On the other hand, in a probabilistic grammar every production in the grammar has a certain weight or degree, and the higher the weight of the rule, the most frequent the use of the rule when generating expressions. We call an attributed grammar *constrained* if there are some constraints on the values of the attributes.

The main attribute is the *type* of a grammar symbol. Three types have been considered: (Lisp) symbol, number and list. In fact, the list type is the union of infinite disjoint types given by the length and the type of the elements. These features can be described in our generator. For example, the constraint (L > 3 ((1 S))) expresses that the (grammar) symbol must become finally a list (L) of four or more elements (> 3) whose first element is a (Lisp) symbol (((1 S)))

For example, let us consider the derivation of the CDR form (CDR(CDR'(KK))) (table 1).

In the column *string* we show the (non-)terminal string that the grammar is generating, beginning from the initial symbol *expr*. In the column *production*, the number of the applied production is given. Notice that a special procedure is needed at the last step in order to generate the terminal KK. At each step, several productions have been considered, with probabilities proportional to their weights. For instance, *expr-cdr* could yield with equal probability either *expr-cdr-list* (constraint (L > 0)) or *expr-cdr-sym* (constraint (L = 0)). In this case, the former derivation has been followed.

In the column *constraints*, we show the type constraints imposed to non-terminal symbols occurring in the string. Additional constraints (nesting level, ...) are not shown in the table.

string	constraints	production
expr⇒		
expr-cdr⇒	(L)	86
(CDR expr-cdr-lista)⇒	(L > 0)	88
(CDR (CDR expr))⇒	(L > 0)	90
(CDR (CDR expr-quote))⇒	(L)	8
(CDR (CDR (QUOTE expr-in-quote)))⇒	(L)	9
(CDR (CDR (QUOTE (atom-q))))⇒	(S)	10
(CDR (CDR (QUOTE (atom))))⇒	(S)	13
(CDR (CDR (QUOTE (symbol))))⇒	(S)	21
(CDR (CDR (QUOTE (KK))))		terminal generation

Table 1. A derivation in LispTutor2

Currently 323 productions have been coded to implement the generation of 35 items, ranging from numbers to DO forms. Elementary list functions, conditional and iterative constructs like COND, IF, MAPCAR or DOTIMES, and functional constructs like FUNCALL or lambda expressions are covered by the courseware.

3   Conclusions

In this paper we have described problem generation in LispTutor2, a web-based tool for helping instructors in the task of teaching some aspects of basic Lisp Programming. We think that the generator has successfully met the initial goals fixed: concerning evaluation of Lisp expressions, it provides an unlimited source of problems. Moreover, the design of the generator module has been carried out at an abstraction level such that adaptation to other domains will be possible.

In relation to future work, it is clear that much more is needed in order to achieve a complete Lisp tutor such as ELM-ART [1]: for example, a set of programming design problems, an on line description of the language, etc.

References

1. Brusilovsky, P., Schwarz, E., Weber, G.: ELM-ART: an intelligent tutoring system on the World Wide Web. In Frasson, C. et al. (eds.): Intelligent Tutoring Systems. LNCS 1086, Springer Verlag (1996).
2. Koffman, E. B.: Individualizing Instruction in a Generative CAI Tutor. CACM 15(6) (1972), 472-473
3. Koffman, E. B. and Blount, S. E.: Artificial Intelligence and automatic programming in CAI. Artificial Intelligence 6 (1975), 215-234.

Collaborative Maintenance in ULYSSES

Maria Angela Ferrario, Keith Waters, and Barry Smyth

Smart Media Institute, Department of Computer Science
University College Dublin, Belfield, Dublin 4, IRELAND

{maria.ferrario, barry.smyth}@ucd.ie

Abstract. Maintaining large-scale content repositories is a challenging issue. In this paper we describe collaborative maintenance, a novel framework to intelligently support a distributed user-driven maintenance strategy here implemented in the Ulysses online entertainment planner.

1   Introduction

The World-Wide Web represents a vast and growing information space but suffers from a number of shortcomings in relation to its ability to efficiently service the information needs of individual users [6]. Adaptive hypermedia techniques have been forwarded as a solution to this problem by providing a means to learn automatically [4, 5] about the likes and dislikes of individual users in order to serve these users with relevant and timely information.

In this paper we introduce an adaptive hypermedia project called Ulysses designed to provide a Web-based entertainment planner for Dublin. The system employs user profiling, case-based reasoning, and collaborative filtering technologies to deliver personalised plans that reflect the explicit and implicit preferences of individual users. One of the most difficult issues in relation to systems like Ulysses has to do with the maintenance and update of the back-end content databases. The main focus of this paper is to describe *collaborative maintenance* (CM), a novel solution to this problem. Briefly, collaborative maintenance provides an intelligent support framework to allow users to freely update the Ulysses content repository. It manages the review and acceptance of new content items by selecting trusted and reliable reviewers, and collating and analysing their review results.

2   Collaborative Maintenance in Ulysses

Ulysses is an online, personalised entertainment planner for Dublin (see Fig.1). One of the driving motivations behind Ulysses is the production of a personalised environment for like-minded individuals. As such Ulysses uses automatic user modelling techniques to construct detailed profiles on individual users. This is achieved by tracking their online activity including page requests, click-streams, content rating, and content updates [5]. One of Ulysses' core features is the generation

P. Brusilovsky, O. Stock, C. Strapparava (Eds.): AH 2000, LNCS 1892, pp. 301-304, 2000.
© Springer-Verlag Berlin Heidelberg 2000

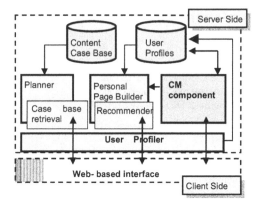

Fig 1. Ulysses Architecture

of a personalised home page for each user to display information items selected by a collaborative filtering recommendation engine [4, 6]. New items are recommended along with links to the personal home pages of similar users and the community that the user belongs to (due to space restrictions the interested reader is referred to [1], http://boffin.ucd.ie/ulysses2000 for more information).

To facilitate content-update Ulysses allows users to add and edit content items, but this introduces problems when it comes to ensuring content correctness and consistency. Collaborative maintenance (CM) helps to address these problems by providing a support framework in which updates are reviewed and analysed by trusted and reliable reviewers [1, 2]. These reviewers are automatically chosen by the CM system, according to their browsing behaviours and profiled expertise [5].

The CM process comprises a number of steps as shown in Fig. 2. When a user adds a content item to the content case-base, the system first selects a set of special users (*information mediators*) which have been found to be reliable and trusted sources of information. Reviewers are chosen from this set according to their suitability to the current content item, and the review request is posted to their personal pages. The review results (submitted by each reviewer) are auto-

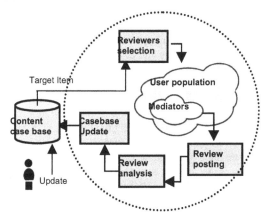

Fig 2. Collaborative Maintenance Cycle

matically collated and a decision is made to either reject of accept (with or without changes) the new content item.

Content Update. To add or update a content item a user fills out an HTML form providing values for each of the fixed features associated with the new content item.

Review Posting and Analysis. Once suitable reviewers have been identified (see last paragraph) the content item is posted to their personal home page on Ulysses and presented in an HTML form similar to the one used to add the content item itself. In this case the fields are instantiated with relevant information. The reviewer can disagree with the content item (*target content item*) by changing any one of the form fields. The result is a modified version of the target content item (*reviewed content* *item*) together with a *review score* for this item. The review score is computed according to equation (1) by calculating the similarity between the target content item and the reviewed content item. The similarity equation used is shown in (2) and is a standard weighted sum similarity metric which computes the similarity between two items, x and y, by calculating the similarity between corresponding features x_i and y_i.

$$RevScore(t', I) = similarity(t' \cdot I, I) \quad (1); \quad similarity(x, y) = \sum_{i=1..n} w_i \cdot sim(x_i, y_i) \quad (2)$$

A typical review cycle for some new items will involve the opinions of a number of reviewers. At any time during the review process a user can view the partial review results collected so far. These results are presented as feature-value histograms for each the descriptive features of the item under review.

Case Base Update. At the end of the review process we use a number of strategies to collate the results and make a decision about the status of the target item. For example we compute an *agreement score* between pairs of reviewers as shown in (3). This metric computes the similarity between the reviewed content items, using the same similarity metric shown in (2), note that $r \cdot I$ refers to the modified version of content item I generated by reviewer r.

$$AgreementScore(r_1, r_2, I) = similarity(r_1 \cdot I, r_2 \cdot I) \quad (3)$$

We then make our reject/accept decision based on a *judgement score*, which is the product of the mean review score and the mean agreement score (4); items that receive a judgement score below a set threshold are rejected.

$$JudgementScore(t, R) = \frac{\sum_{r_i \in R} ReviewScore(r_i, I)}{|R|} \cdot \frac{\sum_{r_i, r_j \in R \wedge R} AgreementScore(r_i, r_j, I)}{|R|^2} \quad (4)$$

An accepted content item may still need to be modified according to the changes suggested by the reviewers. Currently, collaborative maintenance automatically modifies each content item by changing individual features so that they reflect the majority reviewer decision.

Reviewer Selection. Reviewers must be knowledgeable about the target content item, and they must be trusted. Reviewers should be also selected to represent a broad cross-section of opinions. A user is a reliable source of information (an *information mediator*) if there is a general agreement that the information she provide is correct; in other words, we calculate the reliability of a user as the *mean value* of all the judgment scores that a user has received for any content items she has added.

Two techniques are used to select reviewers from the information mediator pool. First, a *collaborative selection* is used to select users (u) that are *related* to the original contributor (c) – related in the sense that there is a significant overlap between their profile items (6). As it stands we select users that have looked at the some of the same items as the target user, but that may have differed in their opinions of these items.

$$Overlap(u, c) = \frac{|u \cap c|}{|u \cup c|} \quad (6)$$

The second selection technique is a *content-based* method. Reviewers are chosen because they have reviewed or rated similar content items to the current target item. This selection is based on the similarity (2) between the target item and the items listed in the profile of an information mediator. The similarity between the contributor and the potential reviewer (u) with respect to the target content item (I) is the maximal similarity between the new content item (added by the target user) and an item in the mediator's profile. We select the top n information mediators with the highest similarity to the contributor's target item.

3   Conclusions

One of the most challenging problems facing Internet and Intranet content applications has to do with managing and maintaining a large content repository. Many traditional strategies have focused on the use of designated editors to oversee the update process. This is often not a practical option. Recent advances in artificial intelligence and adaptive hypermedia make it possible to develop new systems that provide intelligent support for a distributed, user-driven maintenance and update policy. CM is one such approach, which we have described in this paper. We have explained how new content items can be reviewed by specially selected users, and how the resulting data is analysed to inform an accept/reject decision. Furthermore, we have described how high quality reviewers can be identified, and how content items can be adapted after review and before they are added to the content database.

Future work will focus on the large-scale evaluation of the CM technique in Ulysses. We also plan to investigate links between users' behavioural patterns and their motivations to collaborate, in order to better identify the most suitable reward schemes (implicit or explicit) for knowledge-sharing activities.

References

1. M.A. Ferrario and B. Smyth (2000) Collaborative Maintenance – A distributed, Interactive Case-Base Maintenance Strategy. Proceedings of the 5th European Workshop on Case Based Reasoning. Trento, Italy.
2. M.A. Ferrario and B. Smyth (1999) Collaborative Maintenance. Proceedings of the Irish Conference on Artificial Intelligence and Cognitive Science. Cork, Ireland.
3. K. J. Meltsner (1997) Opportunities for AI applications in Knowledge Management, AAAI Spring Symposium Artificial Intelligence in Knowledge Management. Stanford, USA.
4. M. Perkowitz, O. Etzioni (1998) Toward Adaptive Web Sites: Conceptual Framework and Case Study. Proceedings for Second Workshop on Adaptive Hypertext and Hypermedia in Hypertext'98. Pittsburgh, USA.
5. U. Shardanand, P. Maes (1995) Social Information Filtering: Algorithms for Automating "Word of Mouth". Proceeding of CHI 95, Denver, Colorado, USA.
6. B. Smyth & P. Cotter (1999) Surfing the Digital Wave: Generating Personalised Television Guides using Collaborative, Case-based Recommendation. Proceedings of the 3rd International Conference on Case-based Reasoning. Munich, Germany.

Towards an Adaptive Learners' Dictionary

Johann Gamper[1] and Judith Knapp[1]

European Academy Bolzano
Weggensteinstr. 12a, 39100 Bozen, Italy
{jgamper,jknapp}@eurac.edu

Abstract. This paper presents an ongoing research project about the development of an electronic learners' dictionary for the German and the Italian language (ELDIT). Modern psycholinguistic methods for language acquisition will be applied together with technologies for hypermedia and adaptive systems in order to ensure maximum effectiveness.

1 Introduction

Vocabulary acquisition is an important part of foreign language learning. For the learner the main difficulty thereby is the use of the acquired vocabulary in the right way. So-called *learners' dictionaries* [6] have been developed to support this task. They differ from ordinary dictionaries in several ways: The vocabulary coverage is limited, word definitions are simpler and supported by pictures, examples and typical lexico-grammatical patterns, etc. Most learners' dictionaries today are monolingual and are available as textbooks. An exception is the Cobuild English Dictionary which is available on-line as well [8].

Multimedia and hypermedia technologies offer completely new possibilities for the preparation and distribution of teaching/learning material [3, 5, 10]. Even complex information units can be broken down into small units which are linked together yielding a clear and concise presentation. The integration of different media (sound, pictures, etc.) provides a better understanding of the content. Adaptation techniques support an individual and autonomous learning process by providing individually designed pages for each user.

This paper presents a learners' dictionary which is currently being developed at the European Academy Bolzano (2). First ideas for adaptation are discussed in section 3. In section 4 we compare our dictionary to related systems.

2 The ELDIT Project

At the European Academy Bolzano we are currently developing an electronic learners' dictionary called ELDIT (Elektronisches Lern(er)wörterbuch Deutsch ITalienisch). It will contain about 3,000 word entries for both the Italian and the German language.

Figure 1 shows a sample screenshot for the German word "Haus". The information for a word entry is presented in two different frames. The left-hand frame

P. Brusilovsky, O. Stock, C. Strapparava (Eds.): AH 2000, LNCS 1892, pp. 311–314, 2000.

shows the lemma ("Haus") together with morphological information and different word meanings. In figure 1 the first meaning is selected. The loudspeaker-icon activates a sound file with the pronunciation of the word.

Depending on the selected word meaning, the learner gets access to various pieces of information in the right-hand frame: the semantic field (group of semantically related words), collocations, idiomatic expressions, etc. In figure 1 the collocation tab is selected, which presents a list of the most frequently used collocations together with their respective translation and illustrating examples.

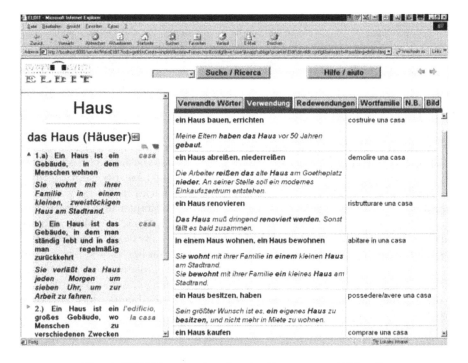

Fig. 1. ELDIT screenshot for the German word "Haus".

In the design of ELDIT several psycho-linguistic theories have been considered. Wittgenstein claims that a word gets its meaning by its use. ELDIT contains a large number of patterns for word usage (collocations, idiomatic expressions) in combination with illustrative examples. According to Aitchinson [2], people not only remember words in a possible context, but group the words in their minds. Two different word groups are distinguished in ELDIT: the semantic field (grouping words by synonymy, hyperonymy, antonymy, etc.) and the associative field (grouping words by topics). For more information on the linguistic part of ELDIT see [1].

The core part of the ELDIT dictionary presented above will be extended in several ways: The vocabulary will be extended to different subject fields; extensive grammar units will provide grammatical background knowledge; text material, exercises, and tests will allow the learner to practice the acquired knowledge and to train both reading and writing skills.

3   Adaptation in ELDIT

This section presents some ideas about adaptation possibilities in the ELDIT dictionary in order to ensure maximum effectiveness in vocabulary learning. Our main focus will be on what aspects of the system can be adapted and which user features can be used as a source for adaptation. In the current stage adaptation is not yet implemented and evaluated.

We identify various user features to which the ELDIT dictionary should adapt. First of all, the user's language skills and knowledge should be considered. Information overflow and the presentation of irrelevant information may have a negative impact on the learning progress. A novice should not be faced with many different word meanings and complex definitions, but with collocations and difficulties with specific words. An advanced learner wishes a more comprehensive picture of the language and, hence, needs more word meanings, precise definitions, free combinations, and lots of idiomatic expressions.

A second class of user features which should be considered for adaptation are user preferences. A learner might be interested to focus on the vocabulary covering specific topics or acts, e.g. traveling, going to a restaurant, etc. While the current version of ELDIT covers standard German and Italian, we plan to extend the dictionary to cover different subject fields. Depending on the user's interest the system could help to systematically acquire the core vocabulary of a given subject field. There might also be users who prefer a monolingual dictionary, while others prefer a bilingual dictionary.

Unlike in other hypermedia systems, in a dictionary predefined paths through the hyperspace are not so obvious. The word entries, which form the core part of the dictionary, act quite autonomously and can be accessed independently. Depending on the user's current needs and preferences, exercises or grammatical units could be proposed and individually linked by the system. A possible and we think meaningful way to come up with paths through the dictionary is to group the words by topics. Accordingly, the dictionary could propose a path for each specific topic, which covers the core vocabulary together with supporting text material and possibly grammatical units.

4   Related Work

A huge number of systems for language learning is available today, but only few systems explore and integrate modern hypermedia technologies in a meaningful way. Rather close to our work are two programs for vocabulary acquisition: PET 2000 [4] for the English language and Alexia [9] for the French language.

Apart from the different languages covered, ELDIT applies a more systematic approach of vocabulary acquisition than PET 2000 and it contains far more dictionary entries than Alexia, which has about 200 entries. Moreover, ELDIT is planned to provide an adaptive component for the adaptation of the system to the individual user.

CASTLE [7] is one of the few adaptive language learning systems. The traditional grammatical approach is combined with a more functional communicative approach. ELDIT mainly differs from other systems in its systematic approach to vocabulary acquisition. Communicative components are provided as short dialogs which are included in the form of illustrative examples.

5   Conclusion

ELDIT is an ongoing research project at the European Academy Bolzano about the development of an electronic learners' dictionary for the standard Italian and German languages. The core part will contain about 3,000 word entries per language. Modern hypermedia and multimedia technologies will be explored in order to provide a clear and concise presentation of the rather complex dictionary entries. Combined with an adaptation component, the dictionary will adapt to the individual user to ensure maximum effectiveness in the learning process.

References

[1] Andrea Abel and Vanessa Weber. ELDIT, prototype of an innovative dictionary. In *Proceedings of EURALEX'00*, 2000. Submitted for publication.

[2] Jean Aitchison. *Words in the Mind: An Introduction to the Mental Lexicon.* Blackwell Publishers Ltd, Oxford, UK, second edition, 1994.

[3] Peter Brusilovsky. Methods and techniques of adaptive hypermedia. In *Adaptive Hypertext and Hypermedia*, pages 1–43. Kluwer Academic Publishers, 1998.

[4] Tom Cobb. Breath and depth of lexical acquisition with hands-on concordancing. *Computer Assisted Language Learning*, 12(4):345–360, October 1999.

[5] John Eklund, Peter Brusilovsky, and Elmar Schwarz. Adaptive textbooks on the world wide web. In *Proceedings of AusWeb97*, 1997.

[6] Thomas Herbst and Kerstin Popp, editors. *The Perfect Learners' Dictionary.* Number 95 in Lexicographica. Max Niemeyer Verlag, Tübingen, 1999.

[7] Maureen Murphy and Michael McTear. Learner modeling for intelligent CALL. In *Proceedings of UM97*, pages 301–312. Springer Wien New York, 1997.

[8] John Sinclair, Gwyneth Fox, and Stephen Bullon, editors. *Cobuild English Dictionary.* HarperCollins Publishers, 1999. On-line version: http://titania.cobuild.collins.co.uk/.

[9] Selva T., Issac F., Chanier T., and Fouqueré C. Lexical comprehension and production in the Alexia system. In *Proceedings of LTLT'97*, April 1997.

[10] Gerhard Weber and Markus Specht. User modeling and adaptive navigation support in WWW-based tutoring systems. In *Proceedings of UM97*, pages 289–300. Springer Wien New York, 1997.

Concept Filtering and Spatial Filtering in an Adaptive Information System

Serge Garlatti and Sébastien Iksal

Laboratoire IASC, ENST Bretagne,
Technopôle de Brest Iroise, BP 832
29285 BREST Cedex, France
{Serge.Garlatti, Sebastien.Iksal}@enst-bretagne.fr

Abstract. Adaptive on-line information systems are able to adapt or to personalize the hyper-document overall structure and content, the navigation help and the layout according to a user's model. SWAN aims at designing an adaptive web server for on-line information systems about nautical publications. According to a task model, concept filtering and spatial filtering are used to select the relevant information space and to sort its content.

1 Introduction

Adaptive on-line information systems are able to adapt or to personalize their content, the navigation help and the layout according to a user's model. Such a model can help in assisting the user for information retrieval by providing navigation help instead of writing queries. The SWAN project aims at designing an adaptive on-line information system about nautical publications. It provides nautical information for different classes of sailors and vessels to prepare a maritime navigation or to navigate on oceans [1]. In this framework, users used to only access a fragment of information space according to their current goal. Then, user's goals can provide navigation help and strategies for information filtering [2], [3], [4], [5].

At present, sailors have to find out the relevant pieces of information in different categories of publications (sailing directions, lists of lights and fog signals, tide and streams publications, radio-signals publications, ...). For some categories, there are dozen of volumes - around five hundred pages per volume - which are geographically organized. It can be found in different publications, volumes and non neighboring pages. For these reasons, they prepare a kind of "road book" consisting of copies of printed pages of publications sorted according to the vessel's route - around twenty pages. In our framework, filtering information and sorting properly the views of information is one of the main issues. In printed publications, information order never fits the user's needs. On the contrary, adaptive hypermedia are able to compute dynamically information views that fit well users's goals and to provide new features.

Free and directed interviews showed that sailors have five common goals which are stable and achieved in a very similar way. They are represented by

P. Brusilovsky, O. Stock, C. Strapparava (Eds.): AH 2000, LNCS 1892, pp. 315–318, 2000.
© Springer-Verlag Berlin Heidelberg 2000

hierarchical task models. We developed a task-based on-line information system to support browsing and to restrict views of information. The task model represents a problem solving method according to a user's goal which determines a relevant information space and arranges dynamically the access to it according to the vessel's route and position. We assume the information space is represented by a domain model. It is composed of information units and nautical objects which are indexed by the domain model. Information views are computed by two different filtering processes: a concept filtering and a spatial filtering. The concept filtering restricts the domain model to relevant concepts according to the current task. The spatial filtering selects all information units or objects present in a geographical area and sorts them according to the current task and concept.

2   User Modeling

Stereotypes, introduced by Rich [6], are an important element of user modeling and it has been extensively used because they give a simple but powerful way for adaptation [7], [8]. The user's model is composed of stereotypes - a user's class and a task model - and an individual model. The user's class consists of a sailor's class and a vessel's class. The former has only one category feature: professional or yachtsman. The vessel's class features are the following: length, breadth, height, tonnage, draught, navigation category, vessel type. The maritime navigation context consists of a set of navigation condition features: tide, time, weather forecast, general inference, GPS position (Lat/Long). The user's individual model enables the sailor to choose an adaptation method for a particular task or to specify its parameters and to choose the minimal depth of a route.

According to Brusilovsky, content-level and link-level, called respectively adaptive presentation and adaptive navigation support, are the two main classes of hypermedia adaptation [4]. Adaptive presentation is computed from the sailor's class. The task model supplies with adaptive navigation support. The task hierarchies are organized with respect to abstraction and aggregation links. We have two kinds of tasks: abstract and atomic. Abstract tasks - or aggregation task - are used to introduce some order in executing its sub-tasks. A control structure using standard operators - the sequence (and) and the selection (or) - determines the sub-tasks ordering. Among atomic tasks, an information retrieval task computes a information view allowing the user to browse freely in a small hyper-space. It determines a filtering process to compute an information view and an adaptive navigation method according to the current task and the user's model.

3   Filtering for Adaptation

The domain model is composed of two looses sub-domains - aids to navigation and the content of the sailing directions. Each one represents a specific information type, the first one describes a set of nautical objects such as buoys and seamarks, and the second concerns a set of multimedia information units - texts, photos, drawing, tables and plans. The filtering is composed of two parts: the concept filtering and the spatial filtering. For concept filtering, the user chooses one of the two sub-domains, then the system displays the graph of annotated relevant concepts related to the current information retrieval task. Two states are used relevant and non-relevant. Concept annotation is based on the weather and time features: fog or not -, day or night. Relevant concepts are computed as follows: fog: fog's signals are relevant; night: lights and lights' alignments are relevant; night and fog: lights, fog's signals and lights' alignments are relevant; day and no fog: these are buoys, seamarks and alignments are relevant.

The information space related to a chosen concept contains lots of irrelevant information units or objects. The system applies a spatial strategy according to the current route section type and the selected concept to compute a spatial view and to sort all data, dynamically - the adaptive method is sorting for each route section. A spatial view is composed of objects and information units present in a geographical area represented by a polygon on a chart. A polygon refers to a paragraph for the sailing direction content and to a nautical area computed according to the vessel position and the route section type - inshore traffic area, landfall or port entry - for the aids to navigation. The computation of the geographical area uses the notion of visibility. It takes into account the range and the angular sector of the navigation's aid - angular sector where the object is visible regardless of its range. We focus on the aids to navigation category to highlight spatial filtering. Aids to navigation are divided into two classes: first class: aids close to the route section, second class: those far from the route section. The first class consists of buoyage, lights on buoys and fog's signals. The second class is composed of seamarks and alignments (with or without lights). The system must consider the three following cases:

1. Port Entry: all first class objects visible from the vessel are selected. They are arranged according to the course section: the nearest is in first, the furthest in last.
2. Landfall: all second class objects visible from the offshore traffic area are selected [1]. They are sorted by direction: North, North-West, North-East, South, South-East, West, East.
3. Inshore traffic area: for first class objects, a polygon around the route section is considered - a rectangle with the length of the section and a user defined width (by default 3 nautical miles). All objects in this polygon are visible from the vessel and they are ordered according to the course section: the nearest is in first, the furthest in last. For second class objects, those visible from the vessel are selected. They are sorted by direction: North, North-West, North-East, South, South-East, West, East.

Comparing to the "road book", the information order is given by the sub-tasks ordering - one per route section - and the corresponding adaptive method

[1] there is a specific chapter in sailing directions for landfall

(sorting). The information views are more relevant and provide more accurate information ordering. The role plays by the sub-task ordering in the task model is very different from that of Hynecosum [2] which focuses on the inclusion of information views of subtasks.

4   Conclusion and Perspectives

We have presented an adaptive on-line information system based on a hierarchical task approach which uses a concept filtering and a spatial filtering. It has been applied successfully on SWAN project. The current version of the system is evaluated. A first step in the evaluation process has been done with some sailors and the french naval hydrographic and oceanographic service. Our approach could be reused and refined to use an electronic chart - ECDIS - to access the sailing direction content according to the sailor's task and maritime navigation context. Our two filtering processes could reused in other domains. For instance, more and more web sites presenting a city guide are available. We could imagine that there is a stereotype task for users wanting to go to a theater, a restaurant and pubs on night. Temporal and spatial constraints could be used to select the relevant theaters, restaurant and pubs according to some user preferences. We could also apply our approach for medical information systems. For example, neurosurgeons need to label cortical structures before a surgery. Then, spatial constraints are accurate to filter the possible anatomical structures which have some specific spatial relationships with a previously labeled structure.

References

[1] S. GARLATTI, S. IKSAL, and P. KERVELLA. Adaptive on-line information system. Orlando, 1999. ISAS'99.

[2] J. VASSILEVA. A task-centered approach for user modeling in a hypermedia office documentation system. In *User Modeling and User-Adapted Interaction*, volume 6, pages 185–224, 1996.

[3] K. HÖÖK, J. KARLGREN, and A. WÆRN. A glass box approach to adaptive hypermedia. *User Modeling and User-Adapted Interaction*, 6:157–184, 1996.

[4] P. BRUSILOVSKY. Methods and techniques of adaptive hypermedia. *User Modeling and User Adapted Interaction*, 6(2-3):87–129, 1996.

[5] S. GARLATTI, S. IKSAL, and P. KERVELLA. Adaptive on-line information system by means of a task model and spatial views. In *Adaptive Hypermedia Workshop 99*. WWW8, http://www.contrib.andrew.cmu.edu/~plb/WWWUM99_workshop/, 1999.

[6] E. RICH. Stereotypes and user modeling. In A. Kobsa and W. Wahlster, editors, *User models in dialog systems*, pages 35–51. Springer-Verlag: Berlin, 1989.

[7] A. KOBSA. User modeling: Recent work, prospects and hazards. In M. Schneider-Hufschmidt, T. Kühme, and U. Malinowski, editors, *Adaptive User Interfaces: Principles and Practice*, North-Holland, Amsterdam, 1993.

[8] J. KAY. Pragmatic user modelling for adaptive interfaces. *Adaptive User Interfaces*, pages 129–147, 1993.

Analysing Web Search Logs to Determine Session Boundaries for User-Oriented Learning

Ayşe Göker and Daqing He

School of Computer and Mathematical Sciences,
The Robert Gordon University
Aberdeen AB25 1HG, Scotland
{asga, dqh}@scms.rgu.ac.uk

Abstract. Incremental learning approaches based on user search activities provide a means of building adaptive information retrieval systems. To develop more effective user-oriented learning techniques for the Web, we need to be able to identify a meaningful session unit from which we can learn. Without this, we run a high risk of grouping together activities that are unrelated or perhaps not from the same user. We are interested in detecting boundaries of sequences between related activities (sessions) that would group the activities for a learning purpose. Session boundaries, in Reuters transaction logs, were detected automatically. The generated boundaries were compared with human judgements. The comparison confirmed that a meaningful session threshold for establishing these session boundaries was confined to a 11-15 minute range.

1 Introduction

Given the increased use of the Web, the amount of information available, and greater variety of regular users, it is imperative to have adaptive techniques for Web-based Information Retrieval Systems (IRSs) which meet individual users' needs more effectively. To this end, research has included work in user profiles, automated browsing and suggesting hyperlinks [1, 5].

Recurring patterns in users' search *activities* (queries, judgements and navigation) can be exploited with learning techniques to enable user-adaptability. This paper focuses on the temporal ordering of activities clustered according to close proximity in time. Although, other forms of activity clustering (i.e., topicality, browsing patterns) are possible, initially we use *time* information, and investigate the extent to which this alone is effective. We group activities and refer to the resulting unit as a **session**. If we view a user with an interest in a specific topic as acting in a particular **role**, then it is not unreasonable to assume that the activities in the same session are likely to correspond to one role. We argue that there are contextual connections between activities if we view the retrieval process as an interactive problem solving task with a goal [3]. Hence, our aim is to specify a session so that it contains data pertaining to one role.

In Web Transaction Log (TL) analyses, studies often group all activities for one user or IP number into a unit referred to as a session [4]. The appropriateness of this grouping is debatable [3], particularly where the time span is large.

P. Brusilovsky, O. Stock, C. Strapparava (Eds.): AH 2000, LNCS 1892, pp. 319–322, 2000.
© Springer-Verlag Berlin Heidelberg 2000

Additionally, the final cut-off point for the TLs is usually arbitrary. This presents us with the risk of grouping together activities that are unrelated. Researchers focusing on Web navigation activities have used the time between two adjacent page accesses to help cut sessions [2]. However, their work focuses on users' navigation behaviour, and does not include activities of using Web search engines. This paper describes an automatic method for detecting session boundaries and then presents the results of the comparison with human judgements.

2   The Method and Data

Due to a lack of adequate information about Web users, our empirical method of detecting session boundaries currently uses only time information. Our aim is to examine the effectiveness of using reliable and easily obtainable information, like time, in detecting session boundaries. A time span called **session interval** could be defined in advance to be used as a threshold. Two adjacent activities are assigned to two different sessions if the time between them exceeds this threshold. The identification of session boundaries then becomes a process of examining the time gap between activities and comparing with the set session interval. Each session has a number of activities in a sequence and within the context of the experiments, we refer to this number as the **iteration** of the session,[1] *e.g.* if a session has three activities, its iteration number is three.

The experiments were based on a set of transaction records of searches by Reuters Intranet users, referred to as the *Reuters logs* (Reuters Ltd.). The search engine used is a local version of *AltaVista*. The time range of the logs extends seven days from 30th March 1999. There are 9,534 activities from 1,440 unique IP addresses. Each record contains: *Time* stamp, *IP address*, and *CGI command*. This command includes information about the query terms, the search method (simple/advanced) and the subsequent page numbers for the same search.

3   The Experiments

Our experiments consisted of two stages: automatically detecting session boundaries then comparing them with human judgements.

3.1   The Automatic Detection of Session Boundaries

We first cut the logs with a large session interval and grouped the sessions with the same iteration number together in order to see the distribution of various sessions. Then, gradually we decreased the session interval and obtained the corresponding distributions, which show the percentage of sessions with a particular iteration in relation to the total number of sessions.

Ideally, a session should contain only those activities from one role. An **optimal session interval** that enables this should not be too large in order to

---

[1] We have chosen this terminology to emphasise the sequence in the activities within the session and their likelihood of being related to the same role.

avoid the risk of grouping activities from different roles together. Also, it should not be too small as there would be less information available on the role.

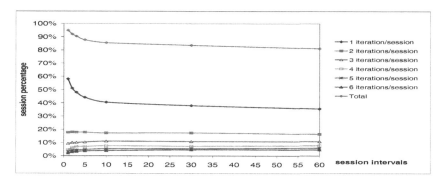

Fig. 1. The frequency of sessions given different session intervals

We monitored distributions of sessions with 6 iterations or less as their total covers the majority (81%) of sessions [3]. The results (Fig. 1) show that most short sessions are not affected when the session interval is larger than 15 mins. When the session interval is shorter than 10 mins, the percentage of sessions with 1 iteration increases dramatically, whereas the percentages of sessions with 3-6 iterations decrease. So, the optimal session interval with regard to the likelihood of grouping activities from the same role together is within 10-15 mins.

3.2   The Human Identification of Session Boundaries

The automatic detection process may result in the following errors: **Type A errors** occur when two adjacent activities for related search statements are allocated into different sessions; **Type B errors** occur when unrelated activities are allocated into the same session. The former is the result of selecting a too tight session interval, whereas the latter is the result of a too loose interval. We view Type B errors as potentially the most damaging to our learning purpose as it could make the role prediction invalid. Hence, we give it a higher weight (nominally twice that of Type A) in this experiment.

Two experts in query formulation worked through the logs and marked the places of a context/role change. Their judgements were compared and anomalies due to oversight or lack of knowledge of domain-specific vocabulary were reduced to a minimum. These judgements were taken as the basis of comparison with the automatic detection method. Resulting types of errors are shown in Fig. 2, which shows that Type A errors decrease sharply until about 15 mins, then continue dropping slowly. Type B errors, on the other hand, increase steadily between 5-15 mins, but do so at a slower rate thereafter. The total percentage of errors (Type A and B) decrease dramatically until about 15 mins. For our learning purpose, we prefer low percentages of total and Type B errors. Hence, the results indicate that the optimal session interval for the logs in this experiment is between 11-15 mins. This confirms the results of Sect. 3.1.

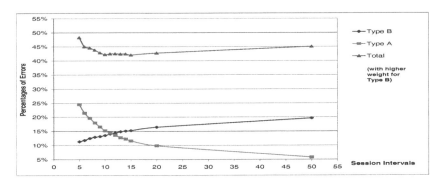

Fig. 2. The frequency of session cut errors given different session intervals

4   Conclusion and Future Work

In this paper, we have presented a method for detecting session boundaries by using a minimal amount of user information that is typically available in Web logs. Our results, after comparing with human judgements, indicate that an optimal session interval should be within the range of 11-15 minutes. In future work, we intend to explore methods of improving automatic session boundary detection by reducing both the percentages of total errors and Type B errors. We envisage using topic information and a statistical model of activity sequence to adjust the automatically generated session boundaries. Additionally, it may be possible to refine the session boundaries by examining the statistical distributions of the intervals between activities within a session.

Acknowledgements We thank Reuters Ltd. for the logs; Jim Jansen, David Harper (especially on future work) and Robin Boswell for their helpful comments.

References

[1] Balabanovic M., Shoham Y., and Yun Y.: An Adaptive Agent for Automated Web Browsing. Tech. Rep. CS-TN-97-52, Dept. of Comp. Sci., Stanford University (1997)
[2] Catledge L. and Pitkow J.: Characterizing Browsing Strategies in the World-Wide Web. In *3rd International World-Wide Web Conference* (1995) http://www.igd.fhg.de/archive/1995_www95/papers/
[3] He D. and Goker A.: Detecting session boundaries from Web user logs. In *22nd Annual Colloquium on IR Research IRSG 2000*, Cambridge, UK (2000) 57–66
[4] Jansen J., Spink A., Bateman J., and Saracevic T.: Real Life Information Retrieval: A Study of User Queries on the Web. *SIGIR Forum*, **32(1)**(1998) 5–17
[5] Joachims T., Freitag D., and Mitchell T.: WebWatcher: A Tour Guide for the World Wide Web. In *Proceedings of IJCAI97* (1997) 770–775

Learning User Profiles in NAUTILUS

Marco Gori, Marco Maggini, Enrico Martinelli, and Franco Scarselli

Dipartimento di Ingegneria dell'Informazione
Università di Siena, Via Roma 56, 53100 Siena (Italy)
{marco,maggini,enrico,franco}@dii.unisi.it
http://nautilus.dii.unisi.it

Abstract. NAUTILUS is a Web recommender system that exploits a new approach to learn user profiles. The novelty consists of using a structured representation of HTML documents that allows us to split the page into logical contexts (lists, headers, paragraphs, ...). The learning algorithm is based on a new neural computational model particularly suited to process structured objects.

1 Introduction

The increase and the rapid changes of the information available on the Internet make it difficult to provide the user with complete and up-to-date indexes to retrieve documents satisfying his/her information needs. For these reasons, recently, new approaches [1, 2, 4, 5] have been studied in order to overcome the limitations of the general purpose search engines. These systems, called Web *recommender systems*, try to model the user's behavior and infer his/her interests to suggest which links may be interesting.

In this article, we describe the architecture and the underlying learning algorithms of a recommender system we called NAUTILUS (NAvigate AUtonomously and Target Interesting Links for USers). It mainly differs from other recommender systems for the novel approaches used both in the representation of the HTML pages and in the page ranking algorithm. The basic idea is to take advantage of the structure of the page defined by the HTML tags, thus going beyond the simple *bag-of-words* representation that is used in most of the other recommender systems.

2 The NAUTILUS Architecture

The NAUTILUS architecture consists of a graphical interface running on the client and a server module. The NAUTILUS server implements the fundamental activities of the system. It keeps a separate profile for each user and it is able to update the profiles with the relevance feedback provided by the users. The user's profiles are employed to perform a focused autonomous navigation by following only the hyperlinks that were evaluated as more promising. Moreover, the server selects the pages to recommend using the stored profiles.

P. Brusilovsky, O. Stock, C. Strapparava (Eds.): AH 2000, LNCS 1892, pp. 323–326, 2000.

The graphical interface is implemented as a JAVA applet or a plug-in which, attached to a browser, allows the user to control the NAUTILUS operation. By this interface the user can ask NAUTILUS to start the autonomous navigation from a given page, he/she can give his/her feedback specifying whether the current page is interesting, and he/she retrieves the NAUTILUS recommendations.

2.1 Representation of HTML Documents as Graphs

NAUTILUS executes two basic tasks: the first task is to search the web for interesting pages; the second one is to select those documents that are more promising for each user. Both of these functionalities require the development of a proper scoring technique. While scoring is obviously needed for the page selection task, it is also useful for defining a good crawling policy, since the scoring of the hyperlinks allows to prune the less promising paths.

In both cases, a *user profile* is employed in order to evaluate both the page and the links it contains. The profile is constructed using a learning algorithm that adapts a set of parameters with the relevance feedback provided by the user on some pages. When a page is retrieved, it is preprocessed in order to extract a set of features to be used as input to the scoring and/or the learning algorithm.

In fact, the representation of a HTML document is obtained by parsing the HTML tags, subdividing consequently the document into smaller contexts. The result of this procedure is a graph whose nodes represent the different contexts. Figure 1 shows an example of an HTML document and its representation. The root of the graph corresponds to the context defined by the tags `<BODY></BODY>`, and stands for the whole page. The two children of the root represent the principal sections which are opened by the two headings `<H1>`, and so on. Thus, each node denotes a context and the arcs represent the inclusion relationship. Moreover, the anchors correspond to arcs that connect the hyperlink location to the referred point (e.g. the hyperlink "Introduction" in Figure 1).

In the proposed graphical representation of the document, each node has a label which "sums up" the text that is contained in the part of the document the node refers to. More precisely, each label is a vector $V = [w_1, w_2, \ldots]$, where w_i is a real value measuring the importance of the i-th word of the user dictionary for the document. NAUTILUS uses a combination of the *TF-IDF* (Term Frequency Inverse Document Frequency) and the *expected information gain* [5] in order to compute w_i. Such a particular combination adds a measure of the importance given to a word by user feedback to the weight provided by TF-IDF. In fact, let TF and IDF be the term frequency and the inverse document frequency, respectively, and let $E(w_i)$ be the information gain of the word w_i given the set of the documents classified by the user. In NAUTILUS, w_i is

$$w_i = \mathrm{TF} \cdot (\mathrm{IDF} + E(w_i)),$$

It must be pointed out that the user's dictionary consists of a small subset of all words which are found in the documents visited by the user. In fact, using too many words usually leads to poor predicting performance since the classification is based on many irrelevant components.

```
<BODY>
<H1>The NAUTILUS Project Home</H1>
This page describes the project.
<OL>
<LI> <A href=''#1''>Introduction</A>
<LI> <A href=''#2''>Architecture</A>
</OL>
<H2 id=''1''>Introduction</H2>
Some introductory stuff.
<A href=''http://nautilus''>Related link</A>
<H2 id=''2''>Architecture</H2>
System architecture.
<IMG src=''nautilus.gif'' alt=''the proxy
connection''>
<H1>The AI group</H1>
<P> Marco Maggini
<P> Marco Gori
</BODY>
```

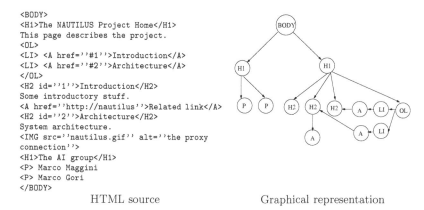

HTML source   Graphical representation

Fig. 1. An example of an HTML page and its representation as a graph.

The reduction of the number of words is done at two different levels. The first level reduction is simply based on a stop-word list and on an elementary stemmer. Finally, words are ordered on the base of the weights and only the t top ranked words for each document are selected. Thus, the set of words considered for a given user dictionary is the union of the all t top ranked words of all the document that were visited and evaluated.

2.2   Adaptive Processing of Graphs

Recursive neural networks (RNNs) [3] are a generalization of recurrent networks particularly suited to process graphs. Fig. 2 shows a recursive network and its computation on a small graph. In order to process a graph G, the recursive network is unfolded through the structure of the graph, yielding the *encoding network*. At each node v of the graph, a *state* $\mathbf{X}_v$ is computed using a parametric function f of the input label $\mathbf{U}_v$ and the state of its children $\mathbf{X}_{\text{ch}[v]}$. Finally, at the root node an output function g is evaluated on the root state $\mathbf{X}_r$, i.e.

$$\mathbf{X}_v = f(\mathbf{X}_{\text{ch}[v]}, \mathbf{U}_v, \theta_f) \tag{1}$$

$$\mathbf{Y}_r = g(\mathbf{X}_r, \theta_g). \tag{2}$$

The nodes of the input graph are processed in an order such that the state of each child of node v has already been computed when the node is being processed. Thus the computation starts from the nodes without descendants. The states of the null children are assumed to be a fixed value $\mathbf{X}_0$. Then, the recursive equation (1) is applied recursively to all the nodes following the ordering obtained by the topological sorting of the nodes. Finally, the state of the root is available, and equation (2) can be applied to calculate the output.

The functions f and g can be realized by any feedforward neural network [3]. The parameters of the recursive network (i.e. θ_f and θ_g) can be learned by examples. According to the classical connectionist learning optimization-based

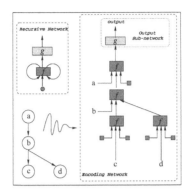

Fig. 2. *Encoding* and *output* network associated to a graph. The *recursive network* is unfolded through the structure of the graph.

approach, the output-target data fitting is measured by means of a cost function. For each graph in the example set a target output can be specified. The parameters that optimize the cost function for the given learning set may be computed using an extension of backpropagation, BackPropagation Through Structure [3].

The proposed recursive model can be used both to compute the score for the links contained in the page, and to score the whole page. These scores can be computed with a two-phase procedure. In the former phase, the states are propagated by a RNN from the leaves to the root following the frontier to root scheme. At the root level the state is used to compute the page score.

In the second phase, a state propagation in a root to frontier direction is performed. Then, the hyperlink scores are computed by applying the output function g to the states of the hyperlink nodes. With such an approach, the leaf nodes corresponding to the hyperlinks will have a state that summarizes the relevant information from all the contexts that contain the link. Thus, the link relevance is computed making use of the context located around it.

References

[1] F. A. Asnicar and C. Tasso. ifweb: a prototype of user model-based intelligent agent for document filtering and navigation in the world wide web. In *Sixth International Conference on User Modeling*, Chia Laguna, Sardinia, 1997.

[2] M. Balabanovic and Y. Shoham. Fab: content-based collaborative recommendation. *Communications of the ACM*, 40(3):66–72, March 1997.

[3] P. Frasconi, M. Gori, and A. Sperduti. A general framework for adaptive processing of data structures. *IEEE Transactions on Neural Networks*, 9(5):768–786, September 1998.

[4] Thorsten Joachims, Dayne Freitag, and Tom Mitchell. WebWatcher: A tour guide for the World Wide Web. In *Proceedings of the 15th International Joint Conference on Artificial Intelligence (IJCAI-97)*, pages 770–777, San Francisco, 1997.

[5] Michael Pazzani and Daniel Billsus. Learning and revising user profiles: The identification of interesting web sites. *Machine Learning*, 27:313–331, 1997.

Lexical Chaining for Web-Based Retrieval of Breaking News

Paula Hatch, Nicola Stokes, Joe Carthy

Department of Computer Science, University College Dublin,
Ireland.
{paula.hatch, nicola.stokes, joe.carthy}@ucd.ie

Abstract. This paper discusses a system for online new event detection in the domain of news articles on the web. This area is related to the Topic Detection and Tracking initiative. We evaluate two benchmark systems: The first like most current web retrieval systems, relies on term repetition to calculate document relatedness. The second attempts to perform conceptual indexing through the use of the WordNet thesaurus software. We propose a novel approach for the identification of breaking news stories, which uses a technique called lexical chaining. We believe that this technique will improve the overall performance of our web retrieval system by allowing us to encapsulate the context surrounding a word and disambiguate its senses.

1   Introduction

This research project aims to develop new techniques to attack the event detection problem based on the use of lexical chains and conceptual indexing. Existing TDT research has focused on the improvement of text-based ranked retrieval techniques previously used for filtering and clustering tasks [1]. We aim to take advantage of these retrieval techniques and to augment them with conceptual indexing. Conceptual indexing requires the identification of the concepts underlying the terms that occur in texts and the construction of a conceptual index of the identified concepts. The conceptual index is made up of lexical chains derived from the documents in the corpus. Lexical chaining has only recently been applied to information retrieval problems with promising results [2, 4]. We aim to investigate whether lexical chaining can be used in the area of TDT specifically for online new event detection of stories within a news domain.

With the boom in the use of the Web and the rapidly-growing amount of electronic information which it provides, new more effective and efficient means of information exploration and organisation are needed. The TDT initiative aims to address these concerns, in particular we are interested in types of electronic information that occur in the form of streams. A stream is a set of time-stamped tokens that arrive in a fixed order, e.g. news corpora and email. In this paper we use the TDT1 corpus containing news sources from CNN and Reuters.

P. Brusilovsky, O. Stock, C. Strapparava (Eds.): AH 2000, LNCS 1892, pp. 327-330, 2000.

The initiative hopes to provide an alternative to traditional query based retrieval, by providing the user with a set of documents stemming from a generic question like, „What has happened in the news today/ this week/ the past month? ". There are several practical Web applications that would benefit from an effective solution to the TDT problem. For example:

☐ A content summary of a corpus in terms of the clusters and topics generated could be given to the user, answering the question „What is this corpus about? ".

☐ The possibility of following the evolution of a news story from the time it was broken to the present time frame.

☐ The automatic retrieval and listing of all breaking news stories within a certain user specified time frame as described in this paper.

2   The Experiment

The domain of the experiment lies in the TDT task of online detection. This involves deciding as each document arrives on the stream of broadcast news (*without* looking at any subsequent documents on the input stream), whether or not the current document discusses some new event. In order to evaluate the effects of using a more sophisticated document representation we have built two benchmark systems, TRAD and SYN [5]. TRAD uses the traditional IR method of representing documents using a 'bag of words' approach where terms are weighted according to their frequency within a document. SYN attempts to improve on this representation by solving the problem of synonymy. This is accomplished through the use of WordNet, an online lexical knowledge database, where synset numbers are used to represent groups of synonymous words, e.g. synset no = 0023432 describes the synonymous set = {automobile, car, auto}. Both systems use a single-pass clustering algorithm to perform detection. So for each incoming document if the story does not exhibit an appropriate degree of similarity to an existing cluster then it is declared to be about a new event and hence a new event is detected. The results for the benchmark systems are presented in Figure 1.

Figure 1 shows a decision error trade-off (DET) graph, which plots misses (the percentage of new events not detected by the system) against false-alarms (the percentage of falsely detected new events). Both the SYN and TRAD systems are evaluated based on this graph, where points closer to the origin indicate better overall performance. Clearly TRAD performs better than SYN even though as stated previously SYN addresses the problem of synonymy. This surprising decline in system performance can be attributed to the fact that the SYN system fails to address the problem of polysemy, where a word has more than one meaning. So in the case of the word 'bank' the WordNet synset numbers for both the 'river' and financial senses of bank are included in the document representation. The effect of this is that documents and clusters that use the same word in a different sense are considered more related than they actually are. This problem however can be overcome by using a method of sense disambiguation, such as lexical chaining which we describe in the following section.

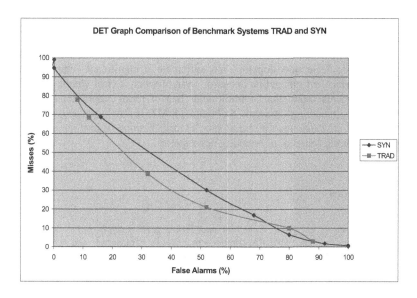

Figure 1. Comparison of Benchmark Systems

3   Lexical Chaining for Improved Story Representation

A lexical chain is a sequence of semantically related words in a text that creates a context and contributes to the continuity of meaning. This method of representing lexical cohesion using lexical chains was first formulated by Hasan [6, 7], and then used by Morris and Hirst [8] who designed an algorithm that automatically built these chains. Our lexical chaining algorithm is described as follows. Using the WordNet thesaurus software [9] each candidate word of a text is expanded to find the synonyms, hypernyms (is-a), hyponyms (kind-of), holonyms (has-part) and meronyms (part-of) of each of its senses. This word, its senses and all its related words are then looked for in each lexical chain of the current document. The word is then added to an appropriate chain if the word is sufficiently related to the words in that chain. If no appropriate chain is found then the word is used to start a new chain.

When a new candidate word is added to a chain the ambiguity of both the candidate word and the chain is resolved. The other senses of the candidate word are rejected and the sense of each word in the chain is clarified. Thus, we have automatically disambiguated the sense of a word and in addition solved both the problem of synonymy, and polysemy. We believe that this is the key to improved classification of stories. So once a document has been represented as above, this new document representation based on lexical chains is then incorporated into the same single-pass clustering algorithm used in the benchmark systems.

4   Summary

In this paper we propose a novel use for lexical chains as document representations within the Topic Detection domain. We anticipate a significant improvement in system performance for our online detection system when lexical chains are used to represent documents rather than a traditional 'bag of terms' representation as was used in both our benchmark systems SYN and TRAD. If this hypothesis proves true we would then envisage incorporating our lexical chaining algorithm into a web-based system for the retrieval of breaking news stories.

5   References

1.   James Allan et al., *Topic Detection and Tracking Pilot Study Final Report*, In the proceedings of the DARPA Broadcasting News Transcript and Understanding Workshop 1998, pp. 194-218.

2.   Mark A. Stairmand, William J. Black, *Conceptual and Contextual Indexing using WordNet-derived Lexical Chains*, Proceedings of BCS IRSG Colloquium 1997, pp. 47-65.

3.   Stephen J Green, *Automatically Generating Hypertext By Comparing Semanitc Similarity*, University of Toronto, Technical Report number 366, October 1997.

4.   D. St-Onge, *Detection and Correcting Malapropisms with Lexical Chains*, Dept. of Computer Science, University of Toronto, M.Sc Thesis, March 1995.

5.   Paula Hatch, Nicola Stokes, Joe Carthy, *Topic Detection, a New Application for Lexical Chaining?*, In the proceedings of BCS-IRSG 2000, Cambridge, pp. 94-103.

6.   R Hasan, *Coherence and Cohesive Harmony*, in J.Flood(ed), Understanding Reading Comprehension, IRA: Newark, Delaware, 1984.

7.   M Halliday, R Hasan, *Cohesion in English*, Longman: 1976.

8.   Jane Morris, Graeme Hirst, *Lexical Cohesion by Thesaural Relations as an Indicator of the Structure of Text*, Computational Linguistics 17(1), March 1991.

9.   George Miller, Special Issue, *WordNet: An On-line Lexical Database*, International Journal of Lexicography, 3(4), 19.

Designing for Social Navigation of Food Recipes

Kristina Höök, Jarmo Laaksolahti, Martin Svensson, Annika Waern

SICS
Box 1263, S-164 29 Kista, Sweden
+46-8-6331500
{kia, jarmo, martins, annika}@sics.se

Abstract. Social navigation has been proposed as a means to aid users to find their way through information spaces. We present an on-line grocery store that implements several different aspects of social navigation. In an initial study, we found that social trails seem to appeal to one group of users while they alienate another group of users. We discuss the implications for design of social navigation.

1   Introduction

In a typical on-line grocery store, there will be 10.000 different products to choose from. Navigating such a space is not only time-consuming but can also be boring and tedious [1]. We have designed an alternative store, based on ideas from social navigation [2]. In a social navigation design other users' actions are visualised in the interface. It can be through direct contact with other users, as in chatting. It can be through trails or footprints, that is, the object bears signs of how it has been used by others. Or, finally, through how the information space is structured, as in recommender systems. Much in the same way as we consult or follow the trails of other people in the real world for solving different tasks, we also try to support this in the virtual world.
But does social navigation 'work'? What are appropriate designs that are not perceived as intrusive or unhelpful? We conducted a small-scale study where we tried to determine whether users are influenced by the actions of others (as visualised in our on-line grocery store), and how they feel about this "intrusion".

2   On-Line Grocery Store

We decided to base our on-line store on recipes rather than having to search for each product separately. Through choosing a set of recipes the user gets all the ingredients from the recipes added to a shopping list. This list can then be edited and new items added prior to the actual purchase.

P. Brusilovsky, O. Stock, C. Strapparava (Eds.): AH 2000, LNCS 1892, pp. 331-334, 2000.

Overview map   **Users**   **Chat Area**

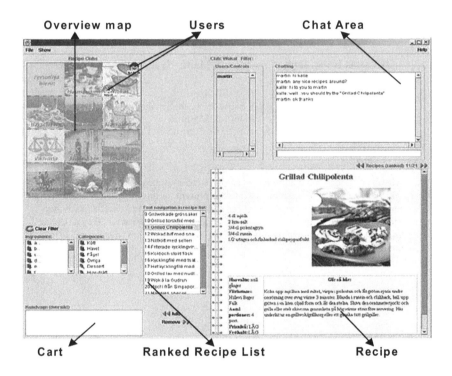

Cart   **Ranked Recipe List**   **Recipe**

Figure 1. A screen dump from the on-line grocery store.

The store has been enriched with a number of different functionalities that enhance social navigation. First and foremost, the recipes themselves are ordered by collaborative filtering methods [3]. Recipes are recommended to customers based on what other customers have chosen. In addition to recommending individual recipes, recipes are grouped into *recipe clubs*. A recipe club is a place with a special theme, for example 'vegetarian food'. Users can move around between clubs to get different recommendations. The selection and ordering of recipes available in a club are also maintained by collaborative filtering methods, and reflect which recipes visitors of the club have liked. On top of the recommendation functionality, users have a virtual presence in the store through avatars representing them in an overview map of the clubs. As the user moves from one club to another, the user's avatar will be shown in the map as moving from one club to another (see fig. 1). Users can also chat with other users who presently are visiting the same recipe club. Finally, we provide social annotations in the recipes themselves: each recipe bears signs of who authored it and how many times it has been downloaded.

3   Study

We believe that social navigation can contribute to the *efficiency* of the interface from the user's point of view, but that is not the only important metric. Social navigation is also useful if it leads to a more pleasurable or entertaining experience, or if it increases users' sense of satisfaction and comfort with the work they have performed.
In a study of our on-line grocery store, we tried to capture some of these issues. Here, we focus on results concerning to what extent users felt that they were influenced by what others did, and whether this was intrusive or not.

Subjects. There were 12 subjects, 5 females and 7 males, between 23 and 30 years old, average 24.5. They were students from computer linguistics and computer science. None of the subjects had any experience of online food shopping.

Task and procedure. The subjects used the system on two different occasions. They were asked to choose five recipes each time. Their actions were logged, and we provided them with a questionnaire on age, gender, education, a set of Likert-scale questions, and a set of open-ended questions on the functionality of the system. They were given a food cheque of 300:- SEK and encouraged to buy the food needed for the recipes.

4   Results

Overall, subjects made use of several of the social navigation indicators. They chatted (in average 6.5 statements per user during the second occasion), and they looked at which recipe clubs other users visited and moved to those clubs. Afterwards they answered the question "Do you think that it adds anything to see what others do in this kind of system? What in such a case? If not, what bothers you?" One subject said: "It think it is positive. One can see what others are doing and the chat functionality makes it more social. One could get new ideas". Not everyone was as positive: "No! I cannot see the point of it, I have never been interested in chat-functions".
In investigating this difference, we found that the subjects could be divided into two groups. 7 subjects claim not to be influenced by what others do, while 5 claim that they are. We asked if the subjects would use the system again. The ones who did not want to use it were the ones who claimed not to be influenced by the actions of others. Thus, it seems to be a correlation between people claiming to be influenced by social navigation and their willingness to use the system again. Interestingly enough, more or less all participants found the system fun to use even the ones claiming they did not want to use it again. One of our participants said: "the system became more alive and fun to use when you could see the other users".
Looking further into how they answered other questions, only 2 subjects were consistently claiming not to be influenced by the social annotations. The larger part of the group, 10 subjects, was positive towards the different social annotations. The logs also backed up their claims: they chatted, and they all moved between clubs without hesitation. In their comments, they also stated that visible activity in recipe clubs

influenced them: they were attracted to clubs where there were other users and they became curious about what the other users were doing in those clubs.

The remaining two subjects were consistently negative towards social trails. They did not chat, they disliked being logged, they did not want more social functions added to the system, and they could not see an added value in being able to see other users in the system.

When investigating subjects' answers to the open-ended questions, certain aspects of social trails in the interface do not seem intrusive at all, while others are more problematic to some users. The fact that the recipes show how many times they have been downloaded is not a problem. Neither is the fact that choosing a recipe will affect the recommender system. Seeing the avatar moving between recipe clubs is more intrusive, and, of course, the chatting is even more so. In general, being logged does not bother users – they know that this happens all the time anyway, and they do not feel very secret about their food choice. It is when their actions are not anonymous and other users can 'see them' that some users react negatively.

5   Discussion

The main result of our study is that many users do in fact appreciate social navigation tools in the shopping scenario. In our study, the majority of subjects liked the social tools, used them, and was influenced by the behaviour of other users.

However, an equally important result is that not everyone was. We need to make the design of Social Navigation interfaces allow for privacy. We must appreciate that there are individual differences between users in this respect, as well as in many others that affect interface design.

References

1. Sjölinder, M., Höök, K., and Nilsson, L-G.: Age differences in the use of an on-line grocery shop – implications for design, In: CHI 2000 Extended Abstracts. ACM, Hague (2000) 135
2. Munro, A.J., Höök, K., Benyon, D. (eds.): Social Navigation of Information Space. Springer Verlag (1999)
3. Svensson, M., Laaksolahti, J., Höök, K., Waern, A.: A Recipe-Based Online Food Store. In: Proceedings of the 2000 International Conference on Intelligent User Interfaces, ACM, New Orleans Louisiana (2000) 260-263

A Study Comparing the Use of Shaded Text and Adaptive Navigational Support in Adaptive Hypermedia

Jatinder Hothi[1], Wendy Hall[2] and Tim Sly[3]

[1]CSC Ltd. Farnborough, U.K.
Jhothi@csc.com,
[2]Electronics and Computer Science,
University of Southampton, Southampton, U.K.
wh@soton.co.uk,
[3]Archaeology Department,
University of Southampton, Southampton, U.K.
tjts@soton.co.uk

Abstract: The experiment discussed in this paper was designed to investigate the usability of combining two adaptive hypermedia (AH) techniques; shading fragments of text and adaptive navigation support (ANS) by means of link annotation, within the educational paradigm. The empirical study required the implementation of three prototype applications, Application A; supported ANS and shading, Application B; supported ANS and Application C; was a non-adaptive version. An in-depth evaluation showed that ANS alone was not as useful as combining it with adaptive presentation i.e. the shading method of AH. It also showed that shading reduced the effects of cognitive overload by reducing the number of highlighted links on documents.

1. Introduction

AH is a new area of research within the field of hypermedia. AH adapts the presentation of content or links, based on the goals and characteristics held in the user model [3]. Adaptive presentation adapts either the content of a document or the style of the text. Stretch-text is a method used in MetaDoc [1] KN-AHS [12] and PUSH [8] where the related text can replace the activated hotword or the text can be collapsed back to a hotword. Shading sections of text is a method used in the work on SaDy [9], where fragments of information are shaded out but left in the document. Shading can be viewed as a form of stretch text without highlighted links i.e. a form of adaptable hypermedia. ANS concentrates on changing the presentation of links. There are various ANS techniques, some examples are, direct guidance, as used by ISIS-Tutor [2], where the next best link may be visually outlined or dynamically added. Pure link hiding, colours the button in the same colour of the text i.e. black, but maintains the functionality of the link as in AHA [7]. Sorting or ordering, presents a list of links with the most relevant first [11]. Link removal, removes the link completely. Link disabling, retains the visible link (one example is by dimming), but its functionality is removed so it cannot be activated as in KN-AHS [12]. Link annotation, annotates the link by changing the colour, font or placing different types of bullet points next to it

P. Brusilovsky, O. Stock, C. Strapparava (Eds.): AH 2000, LNCS 1892, pp. 335-342, 2000.

[4]. This short paper discusses the design, implementation and results of the empirical study. This study also investigated if users were more likely to view the information if it was available on the current screen than to follow links to it. Details of this experiment and other related work can be found in the PhD Thesis.

2. Implementing the Applications

The open hypermedia system, Microcosm [6] was used to develop the applications. The filter architecture provides the ideal mechanism to build AH techniques and experiments. To support the ANS in this experiment a new filter for Microcosm was implemented. Although implemented in Microcosm, the AH techniques used could be applied to any hypermedia system. Another advantage of using Microcosm is that it presents a standard windows style interface for text and image files.

The domain model covered six main topics in Dating Techniques in Archaeology. Each topic was split into four main concepts ranging from an introduction to the topic to more in-depth information or text. To test the usability of combining ANS and shading it was decided to implement and compare 3 different applications, A, B and C.

Fig. 1. Screen shot of Shaded Text Method of Adaptive Presentation

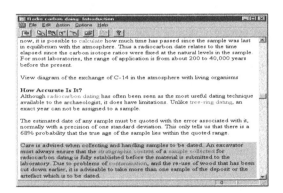

For Application A, the shading of text was implemented statically at design time. Each document had between zero and 3 sections of shaded text, which included information such as formulae and other such details (This information was not the same as the in-depth concepts but was complex text within that particular concept). Expert users were told to read the shaded text as they would be ready to understand the content and the novice users were told to ignore it as it would be too detailed for their current knowledge levels. However, they could read it if they so wished. Figure 1 shows a screen shot of the interface used for each application. In Applications B and C this complex information was presented in separate short documents. Users could reach these documents by following a link, which read, '*More information on concept X can be found by following this link*'. In Application B these links were given the same status as the ready-to-be-learned links and in Application C these links were presented in the default colour i.e. blue. Within Applications B and C each node contained between zero and four of these types of links.

The content in Figure 1 shows a document from the shaded text and ANS application. Users were not required to use the interface functionality as all the navigation was carried out by following the highlighted links. For Applications A and B, ANS was provided in the form of link annotation by dynamically changing the colour of links presented to each user. The method of ANS used within this study was adapted from Brusilovsky's study [3], which used the traffic light metaphor for colouring the links depending on one of four states. Table 1 shows the various annotations used in the study to provide ANS. The ready-to-be-learned highlighted links were links to other documents within the same concept or topic. Generic links (a Microcosm term) were links to reference or glossary terms and to images.

Table 1. Link Annotation Used in Application A and B

Link types	Status of the Link	Colour of the Link
Not visited and relevant link	Ready-to-be-learned	Dark blue
Visited links	Learnt	Dark blue and underlined
Not relevant links	Not-ready-to-be-learnt	Magenta
Not visited generic links	(always ready) Ready	Light blue
Visited generic links	Learnt generic links	Light blue and underlined

The system decided that a user was ready to visit the next concept if they had visited all the documents within the previous concept. In most studies to date, knowledge in AHS is assumed when a document is read (or visited) [5] (or by passing a test) i.e. most authors use the fact that the user has visited a particular page to assume that learning has taken place. Although this method is simplistic it was ideal for experimentation purposes for this study. All visited links were annotated by underling them.

In each application all the hyperlinks within the hypertext network were functional and users could follow any hyperlink. Applications A and B users were advised to traverse only the dark blue links. The idea behind the AH was only to support and aid users, it was entirely down to individual users if they followed the advice provided by the system. For Applications A and B, if a not-ready-to-be-learnt link was followed the system would pop up a dialogue box reminding the user that they are not ready for this particular document and should therefore return to the previous document. Once the user clicked 'OK' on this dialogue box the document would still be displayed and it would be up to the user's discretion if they closed the document and returned to the previous one or continued to read the new document. At this point the ANS was disabled until the user returned to the source document, i.e. the states of the links remain static but the links could still be followed. Each document within each application also contained a hyperlinked contents list, which provided the users with some idea of the domain model.

3. The Evaluation Study

The evaluation techniques used in this study ranged from pre- and post-study questionnaires, observation using video and performance logging. In all, 32 participants took part in the study, all were from the Archaeology or Computer Science Departments at the University of Southampton. Each participant was randomly allocated to one of the three applications. This resulted in 11 of the subjects using Application A, 11 using Application B and 10 using Application C. All the participants were also given a pre-test questionnaire as well as a knowledge test to answer before the start of the session. The questionnaire covered questions on the participants personality characteristics, computing experience and their current knowledge levels on each dating technique. The test was set on paper in a multiple-choice format so that the answers could be assessed easily. Prior to the first session both groups of participants were given a brief introduction to Microcosm and AH.

Each participant arranged a time when they could visit the lab and carry out their individual session, which was carried out in a live working lab environment without any interruptions. It was possible to videotape each subject. At the start of the session the participants were given another set of tasks which were the same for each application. These tasks were the same as the knowledge tasks, however, this time the aim was to use the application to help answer them. At the end of the evaluation session each participant was given a post-test questionnaire (relating to the specific application they used). Some questions were included to test if attitudes had shifted after the evaluation session. The rest of the questions concentrated on the attitudes towards the application itself.

4. Results of User's Subjective Views

These results are presented in percentages as they involve responses from all the evaluators. The participants were asked in the pre- and post-evaluation questionnaire if they felt that AH could be beneficial in supporting CAL (computer assisted learning) applications. Out of the total number of participants 57.6% agreed in the pre test questionnaire and this increased to 66.7% in the post session questionnaire. The percentage who were not sure if AH could be useful was 33%. This percentage decreased to 15.2% in the post test questionnaire. Respondents were also asked if they preferred lectures because they were only exposed to information that they were ready for 21% agreed, 24% were not sure and 54% disagreed.

The following results are presented by the number of users from each application, due to the small number which took part in the study. Users who used Application A were asked if the shading disrupted their flow of reading, only 1 user agreed. All users were asked if the guidance provided by their particular application was useful, 9 Application A users agreed compared to only 4 Application B users and 2 Application

C users. All users were asked if they felt, in control of the application they used 8 Application A, 9 Application B and 6 Application C users felt they had control. Users of Applications A and B were also asked if they could easily understand the adaptability of the system, a high percentage from both Applications agreed. All users were asked if they knew which links to follow next. All of the Application A user's agreed, interestingly only 8 Application B users agreed and only 2 users of Application C agreed but this was expected.

5. Analysis of Performance Logs

Table 2 presents some of the significant results from the study. The Anova test was also used to test the significance of the results are presented at the 5% significance level. Participants were asked if the table of contents was a useful navigation tool, they had a choice from 1 agree to 5 disagree. The ANOVA test (P=0.042) found this result significant. The mean number of tasks answered correctly was found to be similar for each application group, the Anova test also showed that these results were not significant.

Table 2. Results

		Mean	S.D	Min Val	Max Val	P=
Table of contents was useful in navigation	App. A	1.7	0.4			0.04
	App. B	2.6	1.0			
	App. C	2.2	0.6			
Mean number of tasks answered correctly	App. A	13				
	App. B	12.2				
	App. C	12.9				
The mean number of documents re-visited	App. A	4	3	1	11	0.2
	App. B	6.6	5	1	16	
	App. C	5.3	1.5	3	7	
The mean number of 'more information' type links followed	App. B	3.8	-	0	16	0.08
	App. C	2.9	-	0	7	
The mean number of generic type links followed.	App. A	6	5.6	0	21	
	App. B	5.8	3.7	0	11	
	App. C	2.8	1.9	0	6	
Mean number of documents visited	App. A	24	7.2	17	40	0.05
	App. B	33	12.7	18	50	
	App. C	26	4.2	23	37	

Application A users re-visited the least no of documents compared with the other two groups. Application B had the highest mean for users re-visiting documents. The mean was slightly less for Application C, however it had the lowest SD (standard deviation). It is interesting to note that the minimum number of documents re-visited by Application C users was 3 as opposed to 1 each for the other two applications. Also for Application C the highest number of re-visits was 7 as opposed to the much higher values for the AH applications. However, the Anova test (P=0.2) showed that this result was not significant.

For users of Applications B and C the documents were designed to encourage users to follow links to 'more information' type documents. The table shows that the maximum number of 'more information' links followed by Application B users is far greater at 16 than those for Application C. This shows that Application C users were apprehensive in following these links, probably because they could not easily distinguish them. The Anova test (P=0.08) showed that this result was significant at the 10% level.

The table clearly indicates that the Application C user group followed a much lower number of generic links compared with users of Applications A and B, which have a similar mean. The reason for this again, could be due to the fact that Application C users could not distinguish these types of links and therefore users tended not to attempt to follow links by guessing what may lie at the destination. However, Application A and B users who could distinguish the different types of links were more inclined to follow them as and when they required that information. Although, however, the Anova test (P=0.16) showed that this result was not significant. Some of the generic links led to a brief explanation of the current topic on Dating Techniques in Archaeology. The Anova test (P=0.001) showed that the differences were significant. The mean number of documents visited (including glossary type documents) by each application group ranged from 24 for Application A to 33 for Application B. The Anova test (P=0.051) showed that these differences were significant. The time spent viewing reference type documents was also significant with the Anova test (P=0.001).

6. Discussion

The analysis highlights three distinct types of navigational patterns followed by the users. Type 1: Followers, Type 2: Repeaters and Type 3: Roamers. Type 1 users followed the advice most of the time either from the start of the session or soon after realising they were getting lost. Type 2 users, the 'Repeaters'; were users who followed the advice given by the system, they then either repeated this process from the first document or tried random access. The last type 3 the 'Roamers'; did not follow the advice provided by the system and chose random access. This type of user was more prominent within the Application C user group compared with Application A and B users..

It was found that a very high percentage of users tended to run the mouse over the lines that they were reading. A very high percentage of the novice knowledge level group read the shaded text within each topic, even though they were told they were not required to. It was very interesting to find that a very high percentage of Application A users felt that the guidance provided by the application was useful compared with a low percentage of Application B. This illustrates that ANS alone is not beneficial to users compared to combining the two methods of AH. The fact that

Application A users spent a greater amount of time per document could be interpreted as users reading or viewing the shaded text. Again even though Application A users had more to concentrate on they followed more generic links than the users of the other two applications.

It was interesting to find that experts on the subject domain tended to spend a greater amount of time viewing images/ figures compared to novice users. It was also interesting to find that Application C users did not re-visit documents frequently, which could be because they became too cautious.

It was also found that a higher number of novice users read the shaded text in Application A, than the number of novice users who followed the 'more information' type links in Applications B or C. This maybe because the required information was on the current screen/ document and they did not have to search for it. The analysis also showed that a fewer number of Application A users attempted to follow not-ready-to-be-learned links compared to Application B users, to visit a document directly. This may be because they had the shaded text to consider, and they therefore followed the adaptation advice from the system.

7. Conclusion and Future Work

The main problem with this study was the limited number of subjects involved in the evaluation. Also, it would have been beneficial to carry out further investigations into the retention of knowledge, with respect to the various applications over a period of time. The system also lacks support for colour blind users, which can be overcome by using ANS in the form of changing the font of the links. Although it is felt that this experiment brought to light some important and exciting issues, the shading method of AH requires refinement and further experimentation before it can be used in educational applications. The next step would be to experiment with dynamic shading and to investigate the implications of the length of shaded text within documents. It would also be advantageous to apply a more detailed user model incorporating the time variable and on-line tests.

References

1. Boyle, C. and Encarnacion, O., 1994, MetaDoc: An Adaptive Hypertext Reading System, User Modeling and User Adapted Interaction 4 (1).
2. Brusilovsky, P. and Pesin, L, (1995) Visual Annoation of Links in Adaptive Hypermedia, Proc. Of CHI'95 Conference Companion, Denver (eds)Katz, I, Mack, R. and Marks, L. , ACM 222-223
3. Brusilovsky, P., 1999, 'Efficient Techniques For Adaptive Hypermedia', Kluwer Publishers.
4. Brusilovsky, P. and Eklund, J., 1998 (A), A Study of User Model Based Link Annotation in Educational Hypermedia, J.UCS Vol. 4 No. 4.
5. Da Silva, D., 1998, Concepts and Documents for Adaptive Educational Hypermedia: A Model and a Prototype, 2nd Workshop on Adaptive Hypermedia, ACM Hypertext '98.

6. Davis, H., Hall, W., Heath, I. and Hill, G., (1992), Towards an Integrated Information Environment with Open Hypermedia Systems, Proceedings of the ACM conference on Hypertext (eds). D. Lucarella, J. Namard, M. Namard and P. Paolini, ACM Press
7. De Bra, P. and Calvi, L., 1998, AHA: a Generic Hypermedia System, Proceedings of the 2nd Workshop on Adaptive Hypermedia, Hypertext '98.
8. Hook, C., 1997, Evaluating the Utility and Usability of an Adaptive Hypermedia System, Proceedings of IUI Conference.
9. Hothi, J., Using An Open Hypermedia System to Develop New Techniques in Adaptive Hypermedia, 2000, PhD Thesis, University of Southampton.
10. Hothi, J. and Hall, W., 1998, An Evaluation of Adapted Hypermedia Techniques Using Static User Modeling, Proceedings of the 2nd Workshop on Adaptive Hypertext and Hypermedia, Hypertext 1998, Pittsburgh, USA, June 20-24.
11. Kaplan, C., 1993, Adaptive Hypertext Navigation Based on User Goals and Context, User Modeling and User Adapted Interaction 3(3).
12. Kobsa, A., 1994, KN-AHS: An Adaptive Hypertext Klient of the User Modelling System BGP-MS, Proceedings of 4th Conference on User Modeling.

Layered Evaluation of
Adaptive Applications and Services

Charalampos Karagiannidis and Demetrios G. Sampson

Informatics and Telematics Institute (ITI)
Centre for Research and Technology – Hellas (CERTH)
1, Kyvernidou Street, Thessaloniki, GR-54639 Greece
Tel: +30-31-868324, 868785, 868580, internal 105
Fax: +30-31-868324, 868785, 868580, internal 213
karagian@acm.org, sampson@iti.gr

Abstract. In this paper we address the evaluation of adaptive applications and services. We propose a layered evaluation approach, where the *success of adaptation* – the major factor affecting the *acceptability* of adaptive applications – is addressed at two separate layers: (i) interaction assessment and (ii) adaptation decision making. We argue that the proposed framework constitutes an effective means for the evaluation of adaptive applications and services, providing useful information for their improvement, and facilitating generalisation of evaluation results and re-use of successful design practices.

1 Introduction and Background

Evaluation is widely considered as an important and challenging research issue in the area of adaptive applications and services. In fact, the lack of evaluation data, as well as the difficulty in their generalisation, when available, and the resulting difficulty in the re-use of successful design practices constitutes, among others, one of the main barriers for adaptive applications and services to become mainstream technology [1].

The current practice in the evaluation of adaptive applications and services usually adopts a "with or without adaptation" approach, where experiments are conducted between two groups of users, one working with the adaptive application, the other with its "non-adaptive version" – presuming, of course, that an adaptive application can be easily decomposed into its "adaptive" and "non-adaptive" components [2]. In this sense, adaptive applications and services are usually evaluated "as a whole", i.e. the evaluation process focuses on the overall user's performance, according to selected quantitative and/or qualitative criteria, such as task completion time, number of visited nodes, accuracy of tasks, user's satisfaction, etc [3], [4].

While this is reasonable, since the overall criterion for evaluating interactive systems is – or should be – the user's satisfaction, or the user's performance based on selected, measurable criteria, it can be argued that these approaches cannot provide adequate information concerning the improvement of an adaptive system that is *not* found to be satisfactory. This is mainly due to the fact that they do not reflect the fact that the *success of adaptation* is affected by two distinct phases/processes: (i) *interaction assessment*; and (ii) *adaptation decision making* [5]. In this context, when adaptation is found to be successful, one can reasonably conclude that both phases have been successful (except for the unlikely situation when adaptation is successful and both assessment and decision making phases are not – the "minus times minus equals positive" effect!). When adaptation is found to be unsuccessful, however, it is

P. Brusilovsky, O. Stock, C. Strapparava (Eds.): AH 2000, LNCS 1892, pp. 343-346, 2000.
© Springer-Verlag Berlin Heidelberg 2000

not evident whether one, or both of the above phases has been unsuccessful: it could be the case that the adaptation decisions are reasonable, but they are based on incorrect assessment results; or that the assessment results are correct, but the adaptation decisions are not meaningful. In this sense, it can be argued that current approaches do not provide adequate support concerning what, and how to modify adaptive systems in order to improve them. Moreover, they do not support the generalisation of evaluation results, and the re-use of successful design practices.

In this context, the paper presents a *layered evaluation framework*, where the success of adaptation is decomposed into, and evaluated at, different layers, reflecting the main processes/phases of adaptation. It is argued that the proposed framework provides useful insight in the success of each of the phases of adaptation, thus facilitating the improvement of adaptive applications and services, when required, as well as the generalisation and re-use of the evaluation results across different applications and services.

2 Layered Evaluation of the Success of Adaptation

2.1 Layer 1 – Interaction Assessment Evaluation

In this layer, only the assessment process is being evaluated. That is, the question here can be stated as: *"are the conclusions drawn by the system concerning the characteristics of the user-computer interaction valid?"*; or "are the user's characteristics being successfully detected by the system and maintained in the user model?".

low-level monitoring information, e.g.:
- keystrokes
- tasks initiated, completed, or cancelled
- answers to quizzes

interaction assessment

high-level assessment conclusions, e.g.:
- user is disoriented
- user is unable to complete task
- student has not understood the concept

For instance, in the case of adaptive hypermedia systems, and following the classification found in [6], this layer addresses the following issues: does the system detect the real user goals, as they are continuously changing? is the user's actual knowledge of the system being successfully detected? is the user's background actually detected by the system? is the user's experience with respect to the hyperspace structure successfully reflected in the user model? are the user's preferences successfully represented in the user model?

This phase can be evaluated, for example, through user tests, where experts can monitor users as they work with the system, comparing their expert opinion on the user's characteristics versus the assessment conclusions that are maintained in the user model. Additionally, the users can also themselves evaluate whether the conclusions drawn by the system at any particular instance reflect their real needs: "the system detected that my goal, at a particular instance, had been to know more about this subject; was this really the case?". Moreover, this evaluation layer does *not* require that the adaptation decision making phase has been developed, i.e. the adaptive system has been fully developed.

Given that the assessment process has been evaluated separately and found satisfactory, its results can be generalised. That is, we can argue that the conclusions made by the assessment process (usually maintained in a user model) based on the low-level monitoring information, can be re-used in similar contexts, even with different adaptation decision making modules. This facilitates the re-use of successful design practices, i.e. the logic underlying the interaction assessment process.

2.2 Layer 2 – Adaptation Decision Making Evaluation

In this case, only the adaptation decision making is being evaluated. That is, the question here can be stated as: *"are the adaptation decisions valid and meaningful, for selected assessment results?"*. Again, following the classification of [6], the above can be exemplified as: is the selected adaptive presentation technique appropriate for the given user goals? does the selected adaptive navigation technique improve interaction, for specific user's interests, knowledge, etc?

high-level assessment
conclusions, e.g.:

❑ user is disoriented

❑ user is unable to complete
   task

❑ student has not understood
   the concept

**adaptation
decision
making**

selected adaptations, e.g.:

❑ display pop-up window

❑ re-structure hyperspace

❑ provide details on
   educational concept

This phase can, again, be evaluated through user testing, based on specific scenarios, where, for example, the user is given a particular goal, and it is evaluated whether the specific adaptation chosen helps with this goal. Users and experts can evaluate whether specific adaptations contribute to the quality of interaction; e.g. "does the selected adaptation of the presentation of information improve the quality of the system, when the user is disoriented?". Moreover, as in the previous layer, this evaluation layer does *not* require that the interaction assessment phase has been developed, i.e. the adaptive system has been fully developed (i.e. it can be performed using a "dummy" user modelling component).

Similarly, given that the decision making phase has been evaluated separately and found successful, we can generalise its results. That is, we can argue that the design practice adopted in the particular application, as this is reflected in the adaptation logic – e.g. the adaptation rules – can be re-used across similar applications with different assessment modules.

3 Discussion

The proposed evaluation framework is currently being employed for the evaluation of adaptive learning environments in the context of the KOD project (see acknowledgements). The framework does *not* intend to replace current evaluation practices, since the separate evaluation layers can make use of existing evaluation techniques, such as heuristic evaluation, user experiments, etc. The paper addresses the *success of adaptation*, a term that is directly related to the underlying goals of adaptation. In particular, in the context of this paper adaptation is considered to be triggered to "invalidate" specific interaction situations that are "unsatisfactory", when the latter are detected by the interaction assessment process. Since the assessment process is running continuously, it can be tested whether the interaction situation that has triggered a specific adaptation is no longer detected, that is, that the adaptation has met its goal. In this case, adaptation is considered to be successful. If, on the other hand, an interaction situation is still being detected after an adaptation (triggered by this interaction situation) has been implemented, it can be considered that adaptation has not met its goals [7].

On the other hand, it should be noted that the success of adaptation is only one of the issues that may affect the *overall acceptability* of adaptive applications. It has been argued that the acceptability ("overall success") of adaptive applications and services can be affected by a number of additional issues which relate, for example, with the lack of consistency caused by adaptive behaviour, the difficulty of the user in forming a consistent mental model of the application, the security and privacy of the information maintained in the user model, etc [8], which are, however, outside the scope of this paper.

Acknowledgements

Part of the R&D work reported in this paper has been carried out in the context of the IST 12503 KOD "Knowledge on Demand" project (kod.iti.gr), financially supported by the IST Programme of the European Commission. The KOD consortium comprises: Informatics and Telematics Institute-CERTH, Greece (project co-ordinator); xEcomm Advanced Systems, Israel; GIUNTI Interactive Labs S.r.l., Italy; CATAI Centre of Advanced Technology in Image Analysis, Spain; and PROFit Gestion Informatica S.A., Spain.

References

1. Hook, K.: Evaluating the Utility and Usability of an Adaptive Hypermedia System. In: Proc. 3rd ACM Int. Conf. on Intelligent User Interfaces (1997).
2. Hook, K.: Steps to take before Intelligent User Interfaces become Real. Interacting with Computers 12 (2000).
3. Hook, K., Svensson, M.: Evaluating Adaptive Navigation Support. In: Proc. IFIP Workshop on Personalised and Social Navigation in Information Space (1998).
4. Eklund, J., Brusilovsky, P.: The Value of Adaptivity in Hypermedia Learning Environments: A Short Review of Empirical Evidence. In: Proc. Workshop on Adaptive Hypertext and Hypermedia, 9th ACM Int. Conf. on Hypertext and Hypermedia (1998).
5. Karagiannidis, C., Koumpis, A., Stephanidis, C.: Modelling Decisions in Intelligent User Interfaces. Int. J. of Intelligent Systems 12 (1997).
6. Brusilovsky, P.: Methods and Techniques of Adaptive Hypermedia. In: Brusilovsky, P., Kobsa, A., Vassileva, J. (eds.): Adaptive Hypertext and Hypermedia. Kluwer Academic Publishers (1998).
7. Karagiannidis, C., Koumpis, A., Stephanidis, C., Georgiou, A.C.: Employing Queuing Modelling in Intelligent Multimedia User Interfaces. Int. J. of Human-Computer Interaction 10 (1998).
8. Schneiderman, B., Maes, P.: Debate: Direct Manipulation vs. Interface Agents. In: Proc. 3rd ACM International Conference on Intelligent User Interfaces (1997).

Exploratory Activity Support Based on a Semantic Feature Map

Mizue Kayama, Toshio Okamoto, and Alexandra I. Cristea

Graduate School of Information Systems,
The University of Electro-Communications,
Chofugaoka 1-5-1, Chofu, Tokyo, 182-8585, Japan

Abstract. In this paper, we propose a framework based on a sub-symbolic approach for the support of exploratory activities in a hyperspace. By using it, it is possible to express the semantic features of the whole hyperspace and the states of exploratory activities in topological order. This approach is applied to generate the navigation information for the exploratory activity. The space explored is changed automatically by using the semantic similarities of the nodes which constitute that space. An extended self-organizing feature map is used as the semantic feature map of the hyperspace. This map is applied to express the user model and generate the navigation strategy for the user. The exploratory history of the user is mapped on it. Then, the semantic relations between nodes are shown on the map. The result reflects the exploratory state of the user, interpreted with the help of a user model.

1 Introduction

Hypermedia provides an effective activity environment, where users can acquire knowledge by exploring the hyperspace in their own way. Still, users often tend to *"get lost"* in the hyperspace [5]. To improve such undesirable effects on users, many researchers have been working to construct hypermedia systems which can identify the user's interests, preferences and needs, and give some appropriate advice to the students during the exploring activity process [1,2].

We have developed an adaptive navigation system for exploratory activity by using a sub-symbolic approach [3]. This system generates an advice message for a user who is in impasse, and also provides a list of recommended nodes which the system proposes to the user to refer as the next step of exploratory activity. The system shows advice to the user to give the student a chance to escape from undesirable exploratory states. To increase support effect for the learner, the system's navigation function is being improved, to attach semantic knowledge to whole elements in hyperspace. In this study, we use the relations between the concepts, which each node in the hyperspace represents, as the preliminary knowledge, for the process of navigation information generation. By using this knowledge, the system develops a model of the user's exploring activity on a semantic feature map of the hyperspace. The system generates navigation information which ensures that the exploring activity becomes reasonable and continual.

P. Brusilovsky, O. Stock, C. Strapparava (Eds.): AH 2000, LNCS 1892, pp. 347–350, 2000.
© Springer-Verlag Berlin Heidelberg 2000

2   Research Goal

The purpose of this study is to propose a framework to support exploratory learning, based on a-priori knowledge embedded in a semantic feature map of the hyperspace and a user model of the learner's exploratory activity. To support the exploratory learning, our navigation system realizes the following three exploratory learnng sub-goals: to escape from stagnation and deadlock, to clarify the learner's purpose and to guarantee the validity of the result.

3   Semantic Feature Map of the Hyperspace: Hy-SOM

Two extensions of the original SOM [4] (*self-organizing feature map*) are proposed. Firstly, for improving the accuracy of the ability to classify, a new learning function is proposed. With this extension, the features of the input pattern reflect the structure of the output layer more exactly. Concretely, improvements based on the theory of probability are made on the composition of the input pattern and the initial phase of the learning (training) process. Categories for distinguishing each trained pattern (node) are created in the trained network. The configuration of the nodes is based on their semantic topological similarity. Secondly, for improving the robustness of the ability to classify, a method of reconstructing all weights in the trained network is proposed. In this way, some regions are defined on the map. Each region shows distinct topics (semantic cluster). Concretely, in order to represent visually the appearance probability of the value of each element in the input pattern (forming a vector), the trained weights are reconstructed into binary values. The topic configuration, similar to the node configuration, is based on semantic topological similarity. As a result of this structure, semantic similarities between topics, of which the course designers or instructors may not be aware, can appear clearly expressed on the map automatically.

By using our approach, the space explored is reorganized automatically according to the semantic similarities of the nodes which constitute that space. The resulting shape is a kind of map. We call this map the semantic feature map of the hyper-space, in short Hy-SOM. The Hy-SOM is applied to express the user model and navigation strategy for user. The exploratory history of the user is mapped on the Hy-SOM. Then, the semantic relations between nodes are given on the map. The result shows the exploratory state of the user. This is interpreted as a user model.

4   Hy-SOM Based Navigation for Exploratory Activities

The user model assembles information of two kinds. The first type of information is extracted from the exploratory history of the Hy-SOM. The second type of information is gathered from the interpretation of the exploratory history on the semantic network built from the attributes of the nodes and links. From these two types of information, our navigation system creates the user's exploratory activity model. The user exploratory model has three states: reference state, exploratory state and cognition state. The exploratory tendencies of the user are inferred from the above user's exploratory model. Based on the deduction about the user's exploratory tendencies and on the expert knowledge embedded in the navigation system, navigation guidance trying to correct the undesirable patterns is developed. The navigation strategy parameters are instantiated by using the Hy-SOM, the hypermedia node hierarchy and the semantic attributes of both nodes and links.

The result of the instantiation is an ordered list of nodes recommended by the system for reference in the next step of the user's exploration. The system presents this ordered list to the user as navigation guidance information.

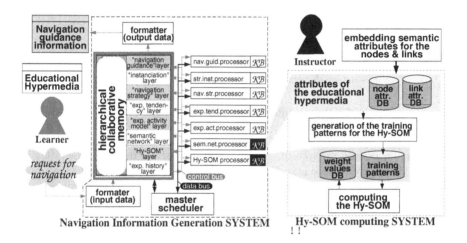

Fig. 1. The architecture of the navigation system.

5   System Architecture and the Interfaces

The entire process, starting from the logging of the exploratory search history, till the navigation guidance information generation, is based on the collaborative problem solving model. This model contains a collaborative memory based on a hierarchic structure, and implements the collaborative-problem-solving's result sharing mechanism.

In Figure 1, the architecture of our navigation system is shown. This system consists of two sub-systems. One is the Hy-SOM computing system. The user of this system is the designers of the educational hypermedia. They have to embed the semantic attributes of whole nodes and links in the hypermedia. Our system also offers an attributes editor. The other sub-system is the navigation

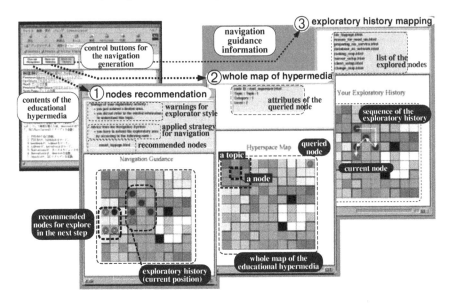

Fig. 2. The interface of the navigation system.

information generation system. The interfaces of this system are shown in Figure 2. Three types of navigation guidance information (recommendation of the appropriate nodes to explore in the next step, the whole map of the educational hypermedia and the learner's exploratory history) are given.

6   Conclusion

In this paper, we have presented an overview of our semantic feature map-based system for exploratory activity support. We have focused especially on the two extensions we proposed for our Hy-SOM, for improving both classification accuracy and robustness. Moreover, we have shown the information types that we use for our user model. Finally, the system architecture was described.

References

1. Brusilovsky, P.: Methods and Techniques of Adaptive Hypermedia. Proc. User Modeling and User-Adapted Interaction. 6 (1996) 87–129.
2. Conklin, J.: Hypertext:An Introduction and Survey. Computer. 20(9) (1988) 17–41.
3. Kayama, M. & Okamoto,T.: Mechanism for Knowledge-Navigation in Hyper-space with Neural Networks. Transaction of JSiSE. 15(2) (1998) 75–84.
4. Kohonen, T.: The Self-organizing Map. Proc. IEEE. 78(9) (1990) 1464–1480.
5. Nielsen, J.: The Art of Navigating Hypertext. Comm.of the ACM. 33(3) (1995) 297–310.

Adaptivity in AHMED

Jaakko Kurhila[1] and Erkki Sutinen[2]

[1] Dept. of Computer Science, Univ. of Helsinki, Finland,
kurhila@@cs.helsinki.fi
[2] Dept. of Computer Science, Univ. of Joensuu, Finland,
sutinen@@cs.joensuu.fi

Abstract. A learning environment based on adaptive hypermedia supports learners with deficits in self-instructability to navigate through a learning material. The schema used in the learning environment allows extending intelligent tutoring to the area of *open learning* where the learner – together with the learning environment and its designer – shares the responsibility of the learning process and actively sets its goals.

1 Introduction

Students with learning difficulties have proven to be a challenge when educational software designers want to use constructivistic learning environments for the benefit of this large and heterogenous group. It is not clear that an unlimited hyperspace with free paths in any direction is the ideal environment for a learner who gets lost even in simple assignments. However, to prevent these people from remaining outside the rest of modern society, where navigation as continuous decisions and choices is needed in everyday life, computer-supported environments are efficient alternatives to reach flexible and useful learning goals.

Not seldom, intelligent tutoring systems are accused of making the student learn by achieving a given learning objective, thus being somewhat closed systems when compared to constructivist learning environments which allow the student to proceed the way he or she likes. In the adaptive hypermedia-based learning environment AHMED, we try to combine these two complementary approaches. AHMED behaves *locally* like a traditional intelligent tutoring system but does not guide the learner towards a given target but rather allows the learner to construct a personally suitable learning path, depending on his or her abilities.

Our primary target group are learners with deficiencies in *mental programming*. According to Korkman [2], mental programming means planning an action, choosing a method of action, the ability to maintain and change the method, searching, fluidity and controlling impulses. A more formal definition is given by Vilkki [5], who states mental programming to be "the subjective optimization of subgoals for the achievement of the overall goal with available skills".

The deficits in mental programming often occur with developmental disabilities. Therefore, children with mental programming deficits often have motorical impairments as well. This also places demands on the learning environment.

P. Brusilovsky, O. Stock, C. Strapparava (Eds.): AH 2000, LNCS 1892, pp. 351–354, 2000.
© Springer-Verlag Berlin Heidelberg 2000

2   Adaptive Learning with AHMED

AHMED employs two properties of benefit: adaptation to an individual learning process and domain-independence. Adaptation is based on the action a learner makes during a learning session in the learning environment. Domain-independence is assured by separating the adaptation mechanism completely from the domain knowledge, and allowing the learning material creation by a generic structured documentation language described with XML.

The key issue in our learning environment is to lead the learner through the hypermedia learning material (which we call a *learning space*) so that the most suitable learning material is exposed to the learner. To activate the learner, the material typically consists of various *tasks*, not just information items.

The learning space in our framework has a certain similarity with an *n*-dimensional hypermedia structure: the learning space has nodes (which we call *learning seeds*) but not necessarily the links between the nodes. The seeds have their position in the learning space, defined by a numerical parameter for every dimension. The seeds can include hypermedia elements, i.e. textual, visual, auditory or interactive elements with temporal aspects, as well as links to URLs.

The learner is represented by a point in the learning space at a given time. Every choice a learner can make in a seed has an effect for the learner's position in the learning space. The effect can pertain to 0 to *n* dimensions, and the strength of the effect can be arbitrary. It should be noted that the choice in a seed can be some other than answering a multiple choice question, such as selecting a subset from the given choices, even specifying their order.

The choice a learner makes in a seed moves the learner to the seed that matches the learner's previous point in the space added with the effect from the last action. The learning material in AHMED, and thus the adaptation mechanism, are completely domain-independent, since the adaptation parameters (dimensions used for each seed, choices in the seeds and the effects of every choice) are freely selectable and described with every seed. As an example, a seed's location is defined as $\langle skill, knowledge \rangle = \langle 1, 1 \rangle$, and the choice a learner has made in that particular seed has an effect $\langle skill, knowledge \rangle = \langle +1, +1 \rangle$ for the learner's position in the learning space, so that the next location for the learner is $\langle skill, knowledge \rangle = \langle 2, 2 \rangle$. It is possible to define the choices to pertain only to some of the dimensions (e.g. $\langle skill \rangle = \langle +1 \rangle$).

During a learning session, the series of learner's choices is recorded. This recorded *profile* of a learner forms the individual learning path through the learning space. The profile also serves as a *learner model* in this environment.

However, the seeds are not necessarily "floating" in the *n*-dimensional learning space. The seeds can be defined to form a *collection of seeds* by linking them with directed absolute links. In such a case, the collection floating in the learning space contains a regular hypermedia structure within itself, i.e., each seed in the collection of seeds has directed links to every other seed in it. To ensure the functionality of the system, a collection of seeds has to be formally equivalent to one seed: the learner cannot be taken to anything but the starting seed in a collection of seeds.

The material itself is *static*, that is, the parameterization of the seeds is conducted beforehand by the person creating the material. This is also the case with the parameterization of the choices in the seeds; the effect on the learner's position is conducted by the learning material author.

To sum up, the expressive power of AHMED's seeds is similar to traditional hypermedia environments. When compared to adaptive educational hypermedia, the learner modelling differs radically from the standard *overlay* (see e.g. [6]) and *stereotype* (see e.g. [1]) modelling approaches. The adaptation system in AHMED is computationally trivial, but the learner model can be inaccurate if the dimensions and the effects in choices are chosen improperly. However, the method employed in AHMED for learner modelling is more expressive, since the modelling does not have to be based on the knowledge level of the learner, as is the case with traditional methods. AHMED suits domain-independent and ill-structured learning materials conveniently [3].

Because of the motorical impairments of the learners, standard intelligent tutoring systems cannot be exploited. Therefore, AHMED employs single-switch input from start to finish. Since every action a learner can make is a form of multiple-choice, a learner can be preferenced to use automatic *scanning* of choices so that every choice is selectable with one-switch input. The use of one switch extends to every function in AHMED, including login with password as well as choosing and correcting an ordered and unordered subset from given choices.

Supporting mental programming by partitioning the tasks. The learning seeds containing a task that supports mental programming should be such that every task can be partitioned into simpler subtasks. The point of this *subtasking* is to find such a set of subtasks that an individual learner can do the task bottom-up from the subtasks. Because of the structure of AHMED, the partition must be made beforehand by the person creating the content. While authoring the material seems laborious, it is the only way to guarantee that the tasks remain pedagogically sound and meaningful.

The partitioning should be made hierarchical, so that the subtasks can be further partitioned to finer subtasks, if needed. The simplest tasks should be such that every learner has enough operational resources to complete them.

To illustrate the concept of subtasking, we use a simple example domain, namely elementary arithmetics. If the learner has to evaluate a sum expression $3 + 2 + 1 + 0$, the first step of subtasking may be $3 + 2$. If the learner is able to accomplish that subtask, the next step in subtasking may be $5 + 1$ and the next after that $6 + 0$ (in Fig. 1, the solid-line arrows).

However, subtasking can be done by another procedure. The example above goes immediately to the finest partitioning, in other words, to the bottom of the partitioning tree. Another method might partition the expression $3 + 2 + 1 + 0$ first to $3 + 2 + 1$, and after that (if the learner does not answer correctly) to the simplest possible partitioning. (in Fig. 1, the dashed-line arrows).

In some cases, it may be beneficial if the learner is allowed to try a "more difficult" level of partitioning after the initial wrong answer. Also, the learner can be raised to the previous level of partitioning after visiting the final level (in

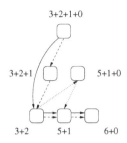

Fig. 1. Three different partitionings of the same exercise.

Fig. 1, the dotted-line arrows). For example, an upper-level partitioning can be presented to the learner after every attempt on the final-level partitioning.

Naturally, the author of the learning material should only choose tasks which *can* be partitioned. This is automatically true in many domains. The partitionings of a task can be different with the same learning seeds, since the seed contents can be the same, and only the linking is different, as in Fig. 1. This helps the preparation of various partitionings.

3   Conclusions

According to the current trends in education, a learner must have an open and flexible learning environment. AHMED fits into this only partially, but the user group to which we aim our system cannot enjoy such a freedom in learning as learners in a regular education classroom. The freedom we can offer is, in fact, the same but much more limited in terms of time: the learner can have a freedom of choice, but not at once.

In addition to the material directly supporting mental programming, AHMED can be used in delivering other types of learning material, such as traditional educational hypermedia, adventure games and simulators [4].

References

1. Brusilovsky, P.: Methods and techniques of adaptive hypermedia. User Modeling and User-Adapted Interaction **2-3** (1996) 87–129
2. Korkman, M.: Applying Luria's method to children: development of NEPSY-tests (in Finnish). In: Ahonen, T., Korhonen, T., Riita, T. et al. (eds.): Brains and learning: clinical child neuropsychology (in Finnish). Atena Publisher (1997) 52–76
3. Kurhila, J., Laine, T.: Individualized Special Education with Cognitive Skill Assessment. British Journal of Educational Technology, **2** (2000) 163–170
4. Kurhila, J., Sutinen, E.: Sharing an open learning space by individualizing agents. Journal of Interactive Learning Research **3-4** (1999) 287–300
5. Vilkki, J.: Neuropsychology of mental programming: an approach for the evaluation of frontal lobe dysfunction. Applied Neuropsychology **2** (1995) 93–106
6. Wenger, E.: Artificial Intelligence and Tutoring Systems. Morgan Kaufmann (1987)

An Adaptive Document Generation Based on Matrix of Contents

Mona Laroussi (1), Pr Mohamed Ben Ahmed(1), Mauro Marinilli (2)

(1)RIADI Laboratory (ENSI Unit) 13 rue slimen Ben slimen 2092 Elmanar II Tunis Tunisie
Mona.laroussi@planet.tn, Mohamed.Benahmed@serst.rnrt.tn
(2)Computer Science and Automation Dept., Roma Tre University, 00146 Rome - Italy
mauro_marinilli@hotmail.com

Abstract. We describe the mechanism used in the CAMELEON system to produce contents adapted to the user. The mechanism is based on matrix products using representations of users and contents by means of boolean vectors.

1 Introduction

One of the goal of the CAMELEON system design was to build a simple but effective way to adapt structured contents to users. After a brief introduction of the system we describe the adaptation mechanism illustrated by an example.

CAMELEON [2] is the English acronym of Computer Adaptive Medium for LEarning On Networks, It's a system running across the Internet / Intranet, helping learners studying the course (presentation of the course material, assessments, etc.) via an adaptive interface. We discuss in this paper the tutoring part and more precisely how the system models student and document and how it uses this data to generate the adaptive presentation on the fly. Adaptive hypermedia is usually related to user/student model and so we generally display pages depending on this user model. In our system we take into account two attributes: level of knowledge and the learning style preferred by this student based on the FELDER learning style model[1]. Via CAMELEON, teachers will be able to split their course material in fragments which can be either composite or elementary (image, video sequence, text, etc.). They can also tag each fragment with values concerning the category of students (visual/verbal, active/reflective, sensitive/intuitive, sequential/global) and knowledge level required for the fragment. These values are attached as a signature to the concepts. All those fragments are stored as objects in an OODBMS. The page generator will then deliver the suitable course to the student.[3].

While CAMELEON has several interesting aspects , like the use of an interlearner distance or exploiting the user feedback in order to assess ill-designed hypergraph fragments, this paper focuses mainly on the adaptation mechanism.

The approach described here is general, anyway, and works in the framework of content dynamically adapted to users. Different attributes also can be added depending on the task, like the level of detail or the browsing style, etc. The hypergraph is repre-

P. Brusilovsky, O. Stock, C. Strapparava (Eds.): AH 2000, LNCS 1892, pp. 355-358, 2000.

sented in an abstract way requiring a page generator module in order to obtain HTML pages to be shown to the user.

The nodes in the hypergraph can be of four types:

- ☐ Concept (classes of objects, kind or documents or tools, categories of events)
- ☐ Procedure (classes of operations actions, kinds of tasks, activities, instructions, algorithms, film or stages of the scenario)
- ☐ Principle (forced integrity, conditions, rules of actions, heuristic)
- ☐ Fact (Example: concrete object representing a concept, Traces: concrete object representing a procedure, Statement: specific declaration of principle)

The arcs in the hypergraph could be of four types:

- ☐ Link of instantiation: connects an abstract knowledge to a fact, can be translated by the relation is derived from.
- ☐ Link of composition: connects a knowledge unit to one of its components or of its constituent parts.
- ☐ Link of specialization: connects two abstract knowledge units in the same way of the "*sort_of*" abstraction.
- ☐ Link of precedence: connects two procedures or principles, the first must be finished or evaluated before the second could begin.

2 System Matrices

The architecture of an adaptive hypermedia system is mainly based on four components: the domain model, the student model, the knowledge database and the page generator.

We represent the knowledge in a domain model with a hypergraph made of $n_{concepts}$ nodes and n_{links} arcs. This knowledge is described by a domain model build on a list of attributes, each with several (finite) possible values. We call $n_{Attribute\ Values}$ the sum of the number of possible values for each attribute. In CAMELEON two attributes are used: (i) a level of knowledge associated to the concept (with three possible values: expert, intermediate, beginner), (ii) a learning strategy associated to the concept (with four possible values: visual/verbal, active/reflective, sensitive/intuitive, sequential/global).

In the following we use the notation: **Matrix**(rows☐columns)=[[row$_1$]..[row$_n$]].

We define the following boolean matrices:

- ☐ $M_{CA}(n_{concepts}$ ☐ $n_{Attribute\ Values})$ (Matrix Concepts-Attributes)
- ☐ $M_{LA}(n_{links}$ ☐ $n_{Attribute\ Values})$ (Matrix Links Attributes)
- ☐ $UM(n_{Attribute\ Values}$ ☐1) a vector that express whether one of the attribute values fits the current User Model.

The hypergraph adapted to the user is obtained from the two matrices, one for the concepts and the other from the links between them:

$$M_{CA}☐ UM , M_{LA}☐ UM .$$

Here and in the following example we used two different matrices ($\mathbf{M}_{CA}$ and $\mathbf{M}_{LA}$) just to illustrates in a clearer way the mechanism; one matrix including the previous two will produce the same result.

For example, a concept having learning strategies of *visual* and *sequential* type only, with an associated   knowledge level of the topic *intermediate*, in the CAMELEON system is tagged with the array:

visual /verbal	induct./ deduct.	sequent. /global	sens./ intuitive	learning level
1 0	1 0	0 0	0 0	1 0

For a matter of clarity, in the following example we use a simplified version (only one attribute) of this tagging scheme.

3 An Example

The aim of this paper is to illustrate the approach chosen rather then explain carefully the details of our system, so the example has been simplified and somehow general-ized from the real system. We have the simple hypergraph shown in Fig.1. We have three concepts (C_0 and C_F describe only dummy initial and final concepts) with one attribute only, for instance the reader's level of knowledge.

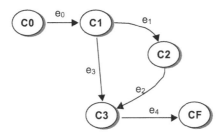

Fig. 1. The complete hypergraph before the adaptation to the user.

We decide also to map this attribute on two values, *good* and *poor* knowledge.

Table 1. Hypergraph tagging

Concept tagging				Link tagging		
	Reader's knowledge				Reader's knowledge	
	Good	*Poor*			*Good*	*Poor*
C_0	1	1		e_0	1	1
C_1	1	1		e_1	0	1
C_2	0	1		e_2	0	1
C_3	1	1		e_3	1	0
C_F	1	1		e_4	1	1

We tag each element with the values shown in table 1. The matrices $\mathbf{M}_{CA}(5\square2)$ and $\mathbf{M}_{LA}(5\square2)$ have the same values as those in the tables. So $\mathbf{M}_{CA}$ = [[11][11][01][11][11]] and $\mathbf{M}_{LA}$ = [[11][01][01][10][11]].Given the only two values for the only one attribute in this example, supposing we have an expert user, her user model is $\mathbf{UM}(2\square1)$=[[0] [1]].

$\mathbf{M}_{CA}\square$ UM gives the concepts to be shown to the user, and $\mathbf{M}_{LA}\square$ UM the relationships that links them, obtaining the hypergraph shown in Fig.2. The hypergraphs adapted to the users can vary greatly one from the other.

After the matrix product we obtain the hypergraph adapted to the given user, that is fed into a representation module to obtain the final usual hypertext structure suitable for browsing from the user.

Fig. 2. The resulting hypergraph adapted to the user.

4 Future Work and Conclusions

In this paper we have presented an adaptive hypermedia system presentation mechanism based on matrix product. We use the matrix notion to model the domain model and the user model. This approach has proven a simple, general purpose adaptive mechanism for the CAMELEON system. While efficient at runtime (when the hypergraph is composed by thousands of nodes and arcs).is also cost-effective on the authoring side. In the near future we plan to enhance several parts of the system and to refine the simple matrix model used here. Also an extensive empirical study is scheduled.

References

1. Felder, R.M.: Matters of Style Principals and applications of four learning style models (Felder-Silverman, Kolb, and models based on the Myers-Briggs Type Indicator and the Herrmann Brain Dominance Instrument). Matters of style, Vol.1(4), Prism, ASEE (1996) 18-23
2. Laroussi, M., Ben Ahmed, M.: CAMELEON: Computer Aided MEdium for LEarning On Networks, In Proceedings of the 10th International Conference ED-MEDIA & ED-TELECOM98, Freibourg Germany (1998)
3. Laroussi, M., Pettenati, M.C., Abou Khaled, C., Vanoirbeek C., Ben Ahmed, M.: A Web Based Authoring and an Adaptive Tutoring, WEBNET99, Honolulu (1999) 1322-1323

Logical Dimensions for the Information Provided by a Virtual Guide

Luisa Marucci, Fabio Paternò

CNUCE-C.N.R., Via V.Alfieri 1, Ghezzano-Pisa, Italy
{luisa.marucci, fabio.paterno}@cnuce.cnr.it

Abstract. If we consider most current applications we can notice a lack of support able to adapt to the different information needs that different users may have regarding a certain topic. In this paper, we present a solution that integrates a virtual assistant, able to implement adaptive support, in an adaptable application and discuss the logical dimensions of the information that can be provided by the virtual guide.

1. Introduction

Adaptive interfaces are flexible because can react in a wide set of modalities depending on the user interactions. This gives adaptive interfaces the possibility of supporting the needs of users in a more tailored way. However, there are two main risks. Wrong deductions can be inferred so that the tailored reaction does not match the user interest or the user does not understand the reasons of the change of behaviour and has a sense of disorientation and frustration. Thus, when designing adaptive support it is important to allow users to clearly understand: when the adaptive support can be activated; how the adaptive support provides information; which criteria determine the generation of information provided by the adaptive support. An application area where adaptive techniques can be particularly suitable is the museum field. A few research prototypes have been developed to use adaptive support in museum applications. This is the application domain where we have applied our approach.

We aim to design an environment where the adaptivity can be easily understood by users and enrich and facilitate navigation through the available information. To this end, users must have full control over when activating adaptive navigation. Then, users should be supported, during their visit, by an agent using a number of techniques. More precisely, we want the information delivered to be adaptive according several logical dimensions [3]:

❑ *Introduction information*, whenever a new topic or aspect is accessed the agent should provide introduction information on that topic;

❑ *Summary information*, the system should be able to provide some summary information concerning the items that have been accessed in the current session;

❑ *Comparison information*, where the purpose is to compare the current information with that previously accessed for some common aspect;

P. Brusilovsky, O. Stock, C. Strapparava (Eds.): AH 2000, LNCS 1892, pp. 359-362, 2000.

❑ *Difference information*, in this case the purpose is to indicate an attribute that was not present in the previous information;
❑ *Curiosity information*, indicating related information that can raise the interest of the user.

Thus, we aim to obtain a wide set of logical dimensions to discuss and present information taking into account also previous works such as that in [1] that focuses on an articulated set of comparisons (illustrative, clarificatory and direct). We have used this approach to design a Web application where there are two main components in the user interface: one part is dedicated to provide the information on works of art in an adaptable manner (the user selects at the beginning one user model and this determines the type of information presented); in the other part, there is the adaptive support that is provided through a virtual assistant that supplements the information presented with additional information belonging to the categories previously introduced. The adaptive support takes into account the current user model because different types of users can be interested in different types of additional information and different ways to group the information that is analysed.

2. The Application

The adaptive support has been designed for an application we developed beforehand, an adaptable virtual museum [2] that was designed following a model-based approach. The original application supported three user models (tourist, student, expert). At the beginning of the session, the user has to select one of them. According to the user model selected, the application provides different support mainly in three aspects: access to the information available, presentation of the information selected, modality of navigation.

To give full control to users on the adaptive support, when the initial choice of the user model appears we have added the possibility of selecting how adaptive support should be activated. Users can choose among three options: activation of the virtual guide, keeping disabled the virtual guide, possibility of activating the virtual guide during the navigation. If the last option is selected, when a work of art is presented there is also an additional button that allows the user to activate the virtual guide at any time.

When the agent is activated, beside the presentation of a work of art, there is a part of the main window dedicated to the comments of the virtual guide. The additional information provided through the virtual guide aims to make the users' visit more interesting and pleasant. Another goal is to provide additional dynamic information that help users link the standard information associated with each work of art, in a manner similar to when a visitor is accompanied by a real museum guide. Thus, at any time we have both standard information that is provided in any case associated with the work of art selected, and the agent-based support that provides additional information taking into account the user model and the interactions performed.

3. The Logical Dimensions of the Information Provided

The virtual guide provides the types of information introduced before with a content tailored for the application considered:

Introduction information. When the user accesses some new aspect (for example a new artist or a new section) then the system provides information useful to introduce it. For example, when the user accesses the work of a new artist, the system provides some information on that artist taking into account the current user model and the works previously accessed. In the case of the tourist user model, the introduction of a new artist highlights how many works of that artist are contained in the museum and where they are located, specifying whether in a single or multiple rooms and the name of such rooms. When the student user model is active, the system generates introductions mainly in terms of definitions, thus helping users to create the association work-definition. Whenever a student accesses a new definition the system provides general concepts, describing materials used to process that definition, the artists that worked for that definition and the historical periods when it is possible to find them. In the case of an expert user model the introduction of a new artist has to take into account that the user is interested in a detailed search among the information contained in the museum, so it is preferable giving additional information concerning chronological motivations, observations, critiques, and historical notions.

Summary information. After having displayed a number of works of art, it can be useful to provide the user with a summary of the most important aspects that have been considered, supplemented by some related information. For example, if the user visits several works from the same historical period this can be interpreted as a strong interest in works belonging to that period. Then, a summary of the most important aspects of that historical period can be provided. The purpose of this information is to highlight the most important aspects common to the works of arts visited. The summary should help a further assimilation of notions already exposed to the user. Summary information is available after a certain number of accesses to the system and it depends on the current user model. Thus, for the tourist the summary will be related to the museum rooms visited whereas in the case of expert and student users will be related to the historic period considered. Additional links to the list of works visited can accompany the summary.

Comparison Information. Comparison is a good tool for supporting learning and can be easily memorised by the user. It allows users to relate works of art or compare them, for example comparing dimensions, chronology. There are different ways to connect a work to those previously seen. More specifically, for every current user model we want to consider aspects concerning artist, historical period, and material used. When there is a change of artist, before comparing two artists, the system controls what are the topics that the user is familiar with considering the works previously accessed and the current user model. Based on this analysis, the system decides whether to apply the comparison, if there are aspects to consider in comparing the two artists, which parameters to use for the comparison. If the comparison between the two artists has already occurred in the session then it is not repeated.

Regarding the aspects to consider in the comparison, the system has to identify the main features of the artist (techniques used, preferred material, ...) by analysing the information contained in the application. The access to a new artist can occur along with the access to a new material, historical period, or definition. Thus, the additional comments have to consider all the changes occurred. If the user goes often back to works previously visited, this is interpreted as a strong interest for comparison information and thus this type of information is provided more frequently.

Difference information. In this case, the purpose is to highlight the difference between a work and those previously accessed. This information is useful for the user to better learn and remember the descriptions of the works of art. It can be triggered for two types of reasons: after the user has accessed some works then, when there is a work of art that completely differs for some aspect from all those previously visited, this is reported by the virtual assistant. For example, when there is a work of art made with a material that was not used for all the previously visited works. Otherwise, when there are works of arts that differ for some aspects that some virtual visitors may not catch then the difference is highlighted. For example, if after having accessed a high-relief the user selects a bas-relief then the virtual guide indicates the difference between these two techniques in order to avoid misunderstanding that can occur as they produce results that are visually similar.

Additional curiosity information. They are additional peculiar information that can increase the involvement of the visitor highlighting the features of the work that can raise the user's interest. This type of information is generated whenever a work that is unique under some aspect is accessed. For example, if the current work of art was made with a material that has not been used for any other work included in the application then the system highlights this feature.

To conclude, we have introduced a solution supporting an integration of a virtual assistant with adaptive behaviour in a previously adaptable application. The adaptive support has been designed following a set of clearly understandable criteria and the information provided makes the users' visits more pleasant, increases their involvement, and better matches their interests.

References

1. M. Milosavljevic, *Augmenting the User's Knowledge via Comparison*, Proceedings of UM'97, Springer Verlag.
2. F. Paternò, C. Mancini, *Developing Adaptable Hypermedia*, Proceedings Intelligent User Interfaces'99, pp. 163-170, ACM Press.
3. F. Paternò, Cristiano Mancini, Effective Levels of Adaptation to Different Types of Users in Interactive Museum Systems, Journal of the American Society for Information Science, Vol.51, N.1, pp.5-13, Wiley, 2000.

Automated Collaborative Filtering Applications for Online Recruitment Services

Rachael Rafter, Keith Bradley, Barry Smyth

Smart Media Institute,
Department of Computer Science, University College Dublin, Belfield, Dublin 4, Ireland

{rachael.rafter, keith.bradley, barry.smyth}@ucd.ie

Abstract. Online recruitment services suffer from shortcomings due to traditional search techniques. Most users fail to construct queries that provide an adequate and accurate description of their (job) requirements, leading to imprecise search results. We investigate one potential solution that combines implicit profiling methods and automated collaborative filtering (ACF) techniques to build personalised query-less job recommendations. Two ACF strategies are implemented and evaluated in the JobFinder domain.

1 Introduction

Online recruitment services have emerged as one of the most successful and popular information services on the Internet, providing job seekers with a comprehensive database of jobs and a dedicated search engine. For example, the award-winning Irish site, JobFinder (www.jobfinder.ie). However, like many similar Internet applications JobFinder suffers from shortcomings, due to its reliance on traditional database technology and the client-pull information access model, which places the burden of representing job requirements (in the form of a query) on the user. Furthermore, most users submit poorly constructed queries, resulting in unfocused search results.

To address these problems the CASPER project seeks to investigate the role of Artificial Intelligence techniques in providing a more proactive, personalised and intelligent model of information access. CASPER focuses on enhancing the existing JobFinder system in two different ways: by improving the existing database search facility using case-based reasoning (CBR) and fuzzy matching capabilities, and, using personalised automated collaborative filtering (ACF) techniques to proactively recommend new jobs to users. For an overview of CASPER as a whole see [5].

In this paper, we focus on the second of these enhancements. Specifically, we investigate the role of ACF within CASPER as the core of its query-less recommendation service. Briefly, ACF is a feature-free recommendation technique that recommends information items to a given user based on what similar users have previously liked (e.g. [2, 6, 7]). The success of ACF is critically dependant on the availability of high-quality user profiles, which contain graded lists of information items, and has been shown to work well when there is a high expected overlap between related profiles. However, JobFinder's dynamic database of jobs, each with a

P. Brusilovsky, O. Stock, C. Strapparava (Eds.): AH 2000, LNCS 1892, pp. 363-368, 2000.

limited life span, means that the expected overlap between related users can be very small (see also [1]). In this paper we will discuss how this is problematic for one common form of ACF, and describe the solution investigated in CASPER.

2   User Profiling in CASPER

User profiles are the primary knowledge source in an ACF system. In CASPER, user profiles are automatically and passively constructed by mining JobFinder's server logs. Therefore, profiles are built without interfering with the user's interaction with JobFinder, unlike related systems that require explicit feedback from users [6].

Fig. 1 shows part of a JobFinder server-log. Each line records a single job access by a user and encodes details like the time and type of access, and the job and user ids. The basic form of a profile is simply a list of jobs that the user has looked at over time. In general though, a user is likely to have different levels of interest in different jobs, and this implicit relevancy information should also be in the profile.

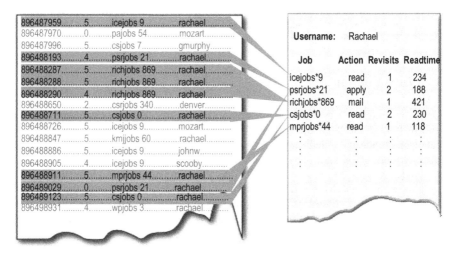

Fig. 1. A partial user profile showing basic and graded profiling information.

CASPER collects three types of relevancy information:

Revisit Data: The amount of times that a user has accessed an information item has been shown to indicate their interest in that item [3]. This information is collected in CASPER and misleading data like "irritation clicks" (repeated clicks on a job description while it is downloading), are removed e.g. job *richjobs*869* in Fig. 1.

ReadTime Data: A more sensitive measure of relevancy gained from read-time data, has also been reported to correlate well with a user's interest [2, 3]. Hence, CASPER also calculates read-time information by noting the time difference between successive requests by the same user, (Fig. 1). Again, a suitable thresholding technique is needed to eliminate spurious read-times, for example a user logging off.

Activity Data: The final and most reliable way to judge user interest in a given job is to avail of JobFinder's online application or email facility. Briefly, a JobFinder user can either email a job description to herself, or apply for the job directly. These actions indicate a more serious interest in a job than a reading of the job description and are recorded in CASPER For example, Fig. 1 shows the jobs that user "Rachael" has read, emailed to herself, and applied for, (5, 4, and 0 respectively in log file).

In our research we have examined each of these factors as measures of relevancy. Obviously, a job will be highly relevant to a user if she applies for it online. However, users tend to do this infrequently, or not at all, resulting in insufficient data to base relevancy predictions on exclusively. It is therefore necessary to consider these other relevancy measures, (readtime, revisits) to supplement this data, and it is interesting as these measures are common to other web-based information filtering domains too.

Although we have found that both revisit and readtime data correlate with the activity data in profiles of users that applied for jobs, this has not resulted in any significant improvements over the simple ungraded profile representation when incorporated into a recommendation task [1]. This was due to a number of reasons, perhaps the most important of which is the nature of CASPER's profile space where the expected overlap (shared jobs) between profiles is very low. We will argue in the next section that this presents a significant problem for one common ACF technique.

3   ACF and the Problem with Relationships

ACF is a recommendation strategy that draws its recommendations from the profiles of similar users in two steps. A set of users related to the *target user* is identified, and profile items from these users that are not in the target profile, are ranked for recommendation to the target user. The success of ACF depends on recognising quality recommendation partners that are genuinely related to a target user. In this section we will introduce two different ACF algorithms (memory-based ACF and cluster-based ACF) that rely on different methods for identifying relevant users. In addition, we will argue that only one of these is likely to be useful in CASPER.

3.1   Memory-Based ACF and Direct Relationships

Memory-based ACF is probably the simplest form of the general ACF approach. Users are related on the basis of a direct similarity between their profiles, for example, by measuring the degree of overlap between their profile items, or by measuring the correlation coefficient between their grading lists [1, 6]. This leads to a lazy form of ACF whereby a *k-nearest neighbour* (K-NN) strategy is used. Currently CASPER uses a simple overlap metric (1) to calculate similarity.

$$Overlap\ (t, p) = \frac{|Items\ (t) \cap Items\ (p)|}{|Items\ (t) \cup Items\ (p)|} \quad for:\ t,\ p\ profiles:\ (t\ being\ the\ target \quad (1)$$
$$profile)$$

---

[1] Relevancy information was used with Pearson's Correlation Coefficient [4, 6] and compared as a similarity measure to a simple overlap metric (1) that had no relevancy information.

Once the k-nearest users (base profiles) have been identified, the jobs not already present in the target profile are ranked, favouring jobs that occur more frequently in the base profiles, and jobs that occur in more similar profiles to the target profile.

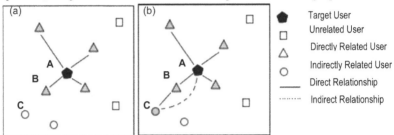

Fig. 2 Direct vs. Indirect User Relationships.

The important thing to note about this form of ACF is its reliance on direct user relationships, for example between A and B in Fig. 2(a), and its ignorance of potential indirect relationships between users. In short, C may have the same job taste as A, but as C has seen a different set of jobs, this will not be recognised in this form of ACF.

In many sparse-profile domains, such as CASPER's, the expected overlap (similarity) between two user profiles is likely to be very small, and the number of other users with significant overlap with a given target user is also likely to be very low [1, 4]. As a result, the target user's recommendations may be based on a small number of profiles with low degrees of similarity. This may compromise the quality of the recommendations, or may even result in no recommendations at all for a user.

3.2   Cluster-Based ACF and Indirect Relationships

Fortunately there is an alternative ACF method that identifies both direct and indirect user relationships. This method uses (eager) clustering techniques to group users prior to recommendation – profiles are clustered into virtual communities such that all of the users in a given community are related, (e.g., [2]).

Fig. 2(b) demonstrates a common scenario where user B is directly related to users A and C. There is no direct relationship between A and C, however there may be an indirect transitive relationship between them through B that should be identified too. Therefore, users A, B, and C should belong to the same virtual community with all other users that are directly or indirectly related to them. In order to specifically exploit this form of indirect relationship the single-link clustering technique can be used with a thresholded version of the similarity metric (1); essentially each community is a maximal set of users such that every user has a similarity value greater than the threshold with at least one other community member.

Once communities of related users are built the recommendation process proceeds in an analogous way to the memory-based approach, except that instead of selecting k neighbours, we select the members of the target profile's community. The benefit then, is the possibility of identifying larger groups of users that are related to the target user and thus provide a richer recommendation base. The disadvantage is that it is no longer possible to judge direct similarities between all pairs of profiles in a community, as there may be no direct relationship between them, and recommendable items are ranked based only on their frequency in the community.

4   Experimental Analysis

In this section, we describe a preliminary evaluation to test the quality of job recommendation produced by each method of ACF described above.

The experimental study is based on the user profiles generated from server logs between 2/6/98 and 22/9/98, which contained 233,011 job accesses by 5132 different users. These profiles spanned 8248 unique jobs with an average profile size of 14.6 jobs, and only 2195 profiles contained 10 or more jobs.

As we had no way of automatically evaluating the recommendations produced by the two ACF versions, the evaluation had to be carried out by hand and was thus restricted to a small set of users. Ten target users were randomly selected, each from a different virtual community. Furthermore, the communities to which these target users belonged covered a range of sizes. Each target user, received two recommendation lists of ten jobs:

□ **Memory-Based ACF (K-NN):** Each target user is associated with its k nearest users (k=10 in this experiment) and a ranked recommendation list is produced.

□ **Cluster-Based ACF (Clustering):** Each target user is recommended the most frequently occurring jobs in its virtual community.

Both sets of results for each target user were then manually graded (by the researchers involved in the project) as good, satisfactory, or poor (mapped on to a numeric value of 3,2, or 1 respectively), based on the similarity between the recommended jobs and the existing jobs in the target profile. Therefore, every target user received a cumulative grading score across the 10 recommended jobs from each ACF technique. Each score was normalised by dividing by the maximum cumulative grade of 30 and presented in Fig. 3 for each target user. Fig. 3 also encodes a measure of cluster size so that we can see how the recommendation quality behaves for different cluster sizes using the cluster-based ACF method.

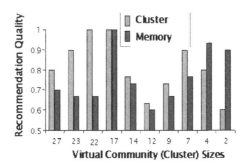

Fig. 3. Recommendation quality for memory-based ACF and cluster-based ACF.

The results clearly show that the cluster-based method outperforms the memory-based version, (except for very small clusters). We believe that this is due to the sparse profile space. As explained in Section 3.1, the expected overlap between users is very small, and therefore many of the 10 nearest users to a target user, chosen by ACF-NN may only overlap with the target profile by 2 or 3 jobs and may not constitute reliable recommendation partners. Thus we can expect some of the recommendations for the ACF-NN method to come from unreliable sources. In contrast, the ACF-Cluster method is basing its recommendation on potentially more reliable measures of indirect relationships between profiles. In this experiment the similarity threshold of the virtual communities was 10, so implicit relationships were based on a transitive overlap of 10 jobs between community members.

5   Discussion

In this paper we have looked at enhancing the JobFinder system with an ACF component. Specifically, we have described how implicit user profiles can be automatically generated from JobFinder server logs to form personalised recommendations using two different ACF approaches, a memory-based method and a clustering-based method. We have argued that the sparseness of CASPER's profile space presents significant problems for the memory-based approach to ACF because of the low expected overlap between profiles in CASPER. The cluster-based approach is presented as a solution, as it can exploit transitive relationships between profiles that otherwise do not overlap, and we argue that this property makes this technique more appropriate in CASPER. This hypothesis is supported by preliminary experimental results and we expect to add a more comprehensive evaluation in the future.

References

1. Billsus, D., Pazzani M.: Learning Collaborative Information Filters. Proceedings of the International Conference on Machine Learning. Morgan Kaufmann, Madison Wisc. (1998)
2. Konstan, J., Miller, B., Maltz, D., Herlocker, J., Gordon, L., Reidl, J.: Applying Collaborative Filtering to Usenet news. Communications of ACM (1997), 40: 3: 77-87
3. Nichols, D.: Implicit Rating and Filtering. Proceedings of 5th DELOS Workshop on Filtering and Collaborative Filtering, Budapest Hungary, November, (1997)
4. Pazzani, M.: A Framework for Collaborative, Content-Based and Demographic Filtering. Artificial Intelligence Review. (in press)
5. Rafter, R., Bradley, K., Smyth, B.: Personalised Retrieval for Online Recruitment Services. Proceedings of the 22nd Annual Colloquium on Information Retrieval, (BCS-IRSG 2000), Cambridge UK, April, (2000)
6. Smyth, B., Cotter. P.: Surfing the Digital Wave: Generating Personalised Television Guides using Collaborative, Case-based Recommendation. Proceedings of the 3rd International Conference on Case-based Reasoning, Munich Germany, (1999)
7. Terveen, L., Hill, W., Amento, B., McDonald, D., Creter, J.: Phoaks: A System for Sharing Recommendations. Communications of the ACM (1997), 40(3), 59 – 65

ConTexts: Adaptable Hypermedia

m.c. schraefel

Department of Computer Science and The Knowledge Media Design Institute,
University of Toronto, Toronto M5S 3G4 Canada
mc@cs.toronto.edu

Abstract. ConTexts is an implementation of and proposed design model for an adaptable hypermedia system. ConTexts provides an easy yet powerful way to author the interactive, adaptable effects of adaptive hypermedia without Natural Language Generation modeling. We present an overview of the architecture and design methodology for ConTexts, its relationship to other technologies, and future research directions for this adaptable hypermedia.

1 Introduction

Adaptive Hypermedia requires an explicit implementation of a user model in order to render versions of a hypermedia document appropriate to the various profiles represented in the model [4]. The user model, while the most critical element of adaptive hypermedia, may also be the most intrigued of the development process. The consequence is that the benefits of adaptable hypermedia are largely out of reach for many hypermedia projects.

In this paper we present an approach to adaptive hypermedia that does not require an explicit user model implementation, but which supports the other significant components of adaptability identified by Brusilovsky [2] such as selective link hiding, page component sorting, link annotation, and stretching and collapsing page components. The result is an *adaptable hypermedia* approach called ConTexts. This approach allows rapid deployment of sites/virtual documents which are either sufficiently adaptive for the type of document they enhance not to warrant an explicit user model implementation, or which can act in concert with user–model–based adaptive hypermedia as the user model becomes available.

1.1 ConTexts' Context: Intensional HTML and IML

The ConTexts project began in the Intensional Programming community independent of work in Adaptive Hypermedia. The points of confluence between these approaches, however, suggest that the models complement each other. ConTexts began in 1997 as part of a project called Intensional HTML [16], [12]. The term "Intensional" refers to intensional semantics in Montague Logic which in part envisions a way to describe a range of possible, multi-dimensional worlds in which certain laws hold true for certain

P. Brusilovsky, O. Stock, C. Strapparava (Eds.): AH 2000, LNCS 1892, pp. 369-374, 2000.

instances of those worlds. An intension refers to the range of possible worlds whereas an extension refers to an instance from that range. Our goal was to create versionable web sites as intensions that could be rendered on demand by users as specific extensions. Our solution was Intensional HTML (IHTML): a set of tags that extended HTML to support multidimensional pages and an engine for processing those dimensional definitions and rendering them as web pages. Within the evolution of IHTML, I developed the ConTexts model as a "rhetoric" or design methodology for intensional web sites, described in section 3, below. Over the past year, IHTML has been developed into a complete language, Intensional System Extensions, or ISE (pronounced "izzy") [14]. The result for intensional web page authorship has been Intensional Markup Language (IML), an evolution in IHTML which makes these versionable web pages more richly functional while improving ease of authorship.

1.2 Related Work

Besides delivering adaptable hypermedia functionality, ConTexts brings to the web some of the not easily available (or authorable) functionality of early hypertext systems like Shneiderman's Hyperties (in Gestures, described below) [10]; Xerox's Notecards [5] (in Tangents, below) and Nelson's Strechtext (in Focus, below) [8]. IML encapsulates these effects in simple tags (see section 2). The simplicity of IML's tags for document rendering separates it from the interesting modeling for dynamic content of the Virtual Document Interpreter [9]. Similarly, ConTexts and IML are distinct from adaptive systems like PEBA-II [6] or ILEX [3] which also render on dimensions like expertise (novice/expert) because IML is *not* a Natural Language Generation, AI-based, system. Indeed, its non-NLG implementation separates ConTexts from most adaptive hypermedia implementations. Further, while ConTexts tracks users' anonymous interactive renderings of the content throughout a session with its Log Roll, it does not seek to use this information, as per Joanna Moore's work on Dialog History [7], to refine the current session interaction with the user. With a ConText, the user, not the system, is always the agent of change. Hence ConTexts is a dynamically adaptable, rather than adaptive system.

2 Architecture and Implementation

The ConText architecture is relatively simple: a source document and any documents referenced by the source's "include" tag are additionally marked up in HTML with IML dot notation version tags. The source is preprocessed by the Intensional Markup Language plug-in for the Apache Web Server. This process converts the version information in the source into standard HTML. This revised HTML source is then sent to the web browser for display. The display page also includes the embedded links which allow users to re-render another version of the page via any available dimension. As well, the version algebra [1], [15] in IML's processor returns at least a best match for a version request. For instance, in a version request where the degree of detail is set to "high" IML will render all components matching "high." If a "high" level component is not available for some part of the site requested, the best available match for the request, "medium" for instance, will be returned. Instrumented with a version request logger, the Log Roll, the log process tracks version requests to indicate which requests have been met exactly and which have not. This allows systems designers to focus on which parts of the site need better version support and which receive fewer requests for particular versions. The log can also act as an aid in cases where developers wish to supplement parts of the site with a user model–based adaptive system. The log makes apparent whether or not users are getting to components of the site which are necessary for some specific task. This can guide designers in determining how to better hide or annotate links and paths in the user modeled components. Users as well can render the log as a record of their session with the site.

2.1 Implementation

Much of the implementation detail for ConTexts has been covered elsewhere [13], [15]. In the following sections, we present only the main aspects to facilitate our discussion of the ConTexts design methodology.

Version Tags. The key attribute of a ConTexts source page is the dimensional information which is embedded in the HTML source with what is referred to as a "version code". For instance, if an author of page `fred` wishes to make a French component available in that web page, the author wraps the French content of that page with named dimension definition markers, such as: `.bdef dimension_name:  +  lang:French` *French Content goes here* `.edef`. To make this version of the content available to a user, a version link (intensional pointer) is written in the source as `.ipt dimension_name + lang:French` `"Select French version of component"`. This appears as a regular link in the rendered web page. If the user clicks "Select French version of component" from the resulting page, the current component will be re-rendered in French. There are several advantages to this tag approach to version management. The version information for the page is stored in the URL, eg `http://www/fred.ise<lang:French>`. The version information, therefore, is *neither stored on the server nor stored as cookies on the client*. Also, these dimensionally encoded URLs can be bookmarked and shared with others, anonymously. Version codes also easily maintain state from one page to the next.

Transversions. Dimensional information can be triggered globally or locally within a site. For example, in a ConTexts prototype available online [13], we present a topic, Sampling, as part of an electronic text on Digital Signal Processing (DSP). The prototype includes the dimension `expertise`, which has two attributes: `plain_language` and `engineering`. By clicking a global expertise link, the user can re-render the entire site as the engineering version. Similarly, the user may select a local, component–level expertise link to re-render *just* that component in `plain_language`. These version controls are referred to as *transversional links.* The user's selection of transversional links re-renders both the content and the navigational links appropriate to that dimension, thus enabling adaptive effects like link annotation, hiding, removing or disabling.

3   ConTexts Rhetoric

Adaptable hypermedia like ConTexts creates specific needs to describe clearly the function and consequence of link actions in order to reduce the *noise* of a link. To that end, we postulate the following link lexicon of *quiet* link signifiers. For the most part, we draw on link techniques that are in practice, but which so far have not been collected to represent a link rhetoric: a consistent way of communicating link intent.

Focus. In ConTexts, focus is a compound (two part) link signifier that indicates the site where information will be expanded into the current point. A **bold faced** term followed by a "[+]" in a document indicates that in clicking the plus, the user will see more information about the emphasized term *at that location in the text*. Once the text is expanded, the "[+]" becomes a "[-]". Clicking on the minus collapses the text at that point. This effect is similar to Nelson's Stretch Text. What we emphasize is the consistent and unambiguous way to indicate what these "+/-" signifiers will actually expand or collapse in the document. Focus links can also be established at the top and bottom of a page to indicate degree of detail can be expanded or collapsed globally (page or site wide) rather than only locally (at that location in the text).

User Level. User level is a link signifier that indicates current user level selected. In the DSP example, there are two user levels: Engineering and Plain Language. A user level link indicator, separate from the text, makes this option apparent and selectable at the header of any component that can be displayed in this way:

Plain Language   Engineering

The taller block is the currently active dimension; the shorter block is the non-active dimension. Clicking the non-active Plain Language block makes it active (tall and light) and the Engineering block non-active (short and dimmed). This dimensional shift can be rendered both globally (site wide) and locally (per component).

Gestures. A gesture is another compound signifier for activating a link. A capitalized, colored term in the document indicates a gesture-enabled link. In the first part of the gesture, the user "rolls over" (also known as "brushes") a term, causing either a definition of the term to appear or specific information about the target to appear. The user may gain enough information from the rollover not to need to click on the term for further information. The second part of the gesture, therefore, is a click to get to the link target. The click on this link opens a new window (a *tangent window*) on the topic specified by the that term and and at the same user level as the originating click.
Tangents. A tangent window described above is a target indicated by the click-through of a gesture link. The tangent window opens off side (at a tangent to) the current window allowing the originating context to remain visible while the user focuses on the tangent. Window placement, in this case, helps demonstrate relations of one point to another, and maintains the context of the given subject.

Light, Medium, and Heavy Weight Clicks. The above link descriptions can also be classified relative to the degree that they change the current document state when activated. Focus and user level clicks are *light* since they indicate the link click only increments the current state of the current page. The click that is the second part of a gesture link is *medium* weight since the user knows from the rollover what *kind* of target will appear, and how it will appear, but the context does shift to a new, related topic/window. ConTexts employ light and medium weight clicks. A *heavy* click refers to a link which does not provide clear information about the kind of target to be invoked. Heavy link signifiers also have a high risk of being noisy. For example, a heavy click is implied by a list of links that give only chapter number information. The user may guess that the link leads to the sixth chapter, but has to click to find out what the chapter topic is. Heavy clicks violate the *quiet signifier* paradigm underlying the ConText document model.

4 Future Work and Conclusions

Relationship to Other Technology. There are many possible ways to implement adaptable/intensional hypermedia. XML may be one; HyperWave may be another. The specific implementation has been incidental to the ConTexts model. IHTML/IML is, however, a robust easy-to-author enabling technology that works well with Java, Javascript and XML, without depending on those technologies or their browsers to create intensional, adaptable hypermedia.

Future Research. Aggregation of ConTexts components is supported by IML but has not been explored fully in terms of possibilities for sorting and presenting loosely structured web components. We are currently investigating this. As well, ConTexts versioning has mainly been applied to hypertext. We are also applying this user-directed adaptable technique to multimedia for video-enabled, versioned, software support.

Conclusions. This paper presents an overview of the architecture, implementation and design of ConTexts, an intensionally modeled, adaptable web-based hypermedia. ConTexts is a low cost system to implement, author and administer. It is a feasible approach to bring adaptable hypermedia even to small scale sites. Its link rhetoric assists communicating the effects of these state change requests. While similar in functionality to adaptive hypermedia systems, as well as to some pre-web hypertext systems, the differences in this user-defined, intensional, adaptable model may complement and expand opportunities for adaptive hypermedia application and research.

Acknowledgements

Graeme Hirst, David Modjeska, Melanie Baljko, U of Toronto; J.H Snyder, AT&T Research Labs. Research in ConTexts is supported by the National Science and Engineering Research Council of Canada, Bell University Labs, Canada and Communication and Information Technology Ontario.

References

1. Brown, G. Intensional HTML, a Practical Approach. Masters Thesis, University of Victoria. (1998)
2. Brusilovsky P. Methods and techniques of adaptive hypermedia. User Modeling and User-Adapted Interaction 6, 2-3, (1996): 87-129
3. Dale, R., J. Oberlander, M. Milosavljevic and A. Knott. Integrating Natural Language Generation and Hype text to Produce Dynamic Documents. Interacting with Computers, (1998) 11(2), 109-135
4. DeBra, Paul. Design Issues in Adaptive Hypermedia Application Development. 2nd Workshop on Adaptive Systems and User Modeling on the WWW. Toronto (1999) 29-39.
5. Halasz, Frank G, Thomas P. Moran and Randall H. Trigg. Notecards in a Nutshell CHI/GI 1987 conference proceedings on Human factors in computing systems and graphics interface (1987) 45 – 52
6. Milosavljevic, M., Tulloch, A., and Dale, R. Text Generation in a Dynamic Hypertext Environment. In Proceedings of the Nineteenth Australasian Computer Science Conference, Melbourne, Australia. (1996) 417-426
7. Moore, Johanna D. Participating in Explanatory Dialogues: Interpreting and Responding to Questions in Context. MIT Press, Cambridge, Mass. (1995)
8. Nelson, T. Dream Machines / Computer Lib. Microsoft Press, Redmond, Washington (1987)
9. Paradis, Franois and Anne-Marie Vercoustre and Brendan Hills, A Virtual Document Interpreter for Reuse of Information. Proceedings of Electronic Publishing '98, Saint-Malo, France. Lecture Notes in Computer Science 1375, 1-3 April (1998) 487-498
10. Schneiderman, Ben. User interface design for the Hyperties Electronic Encyclopedia. *Proceeding of the ACM conference on Hypertext*, (1987) 189 - 194
11. schraefel, m.c. A thousand papers for ISLIP '97, The Tenth International Symposium for Intensional Programming Languages, Victoria, B.C., 1997, 41-45
12. schraefel, m.c. Talking with Antigone. Ph.D. Dissertation, U of Victoria, Canada. (1997)
13. schraefel, m.c., P.F. Driessen. Sampling. A first course in Digital Signal Processing; A ConText Prototype. (1999) http://lucy.uvic.ca/mc/proto/sampling
14. Swaboda, Paul. Intensional Systems Exstensions. Masters Thesis, U of Victoria, 1999
15. Wadge W., G. Brown, m. c. schraefel, T. Yildirim, Intensional HTML, Proc 4th Int. Workshop PODDP '98, Springer Verlag LNCS 1481 (1998) 128-139
16. Yildirim, Taner. *Intensional HTML* Masters Thesis, U of Victoria, Canada. (1997)

Coherence in Modularly Composed Adaptive Learning Documents

Cornelia Seeberg[1,2], Achim Steinacker[1], Ralf Steinmetz[1,2]

[1] Industrial Process and System Communications
Dept. of Electrical Eng. & Information Technology
Darmstadt University of Technology
Merckstr. 25 • 64283 Darmstadt • Germany
{Cornelia.Seeberg,Achim.Steinacker,Ralf.Steinmetz}@kom.tu-darmstadt.de

[2] GMD IPSI
German National Research Center for Information Technology
Dolivostr. 15 • 64293 Darmstadt • Germany

Abstract. In this paper we suggest the Multibook approach how the gap between adaptivity and readability can be diminished. We show how a knowledge base has to be described by metadata (LOM), rhetorical-didactic relations and an underlying ontology to make it possible for the learners to build coherence from the modularly composed document.

1 Introduction

The idea of life long learning makes adaptivity necessary. Adaptivity is best realized using a modular knowledge base where resources can be individually selected according to the special needs of the learner. A disadvantage of modularly composed documents is the missing coherence. The description of the information modules as in the Multibook system (section 2) can help the learner to establish coherence (section 3).

2 Description of the Modules in the Knowledge Base

In order to automatically create dynamic learning documents, Multibook uses the Learning Object Metadata (LOM) approach of the IEEE Working Group P1484.12 [8] as metadata scheme to describe the modules. One of the main prerequisites to accomplish the automatic generation of lessons out of modules, is supporting coherence between the modules. Learners usually tend to distrust working documents which were generated adaptively by computer systems. This will get the worse, the less coherence the system can provide between two subsequent modules in the document.

2.1 Metadata Attributing Single Modules

LOM provides attributes divided in nine categories to describe a learning module. These categories include attributes to represent properties like copyright or utilization

P. Brusilovsky, O. Stock, C. Strapparava (Eds.): AH 2000, LNCS 1892, pp. 375-379, 2000.

aspects of the module and attributes which express the "pedagogical properties" of the module. The problem with these properties is that different authors have different conceptions about the values of these attributes, even if there is a fixed vocabulary for the attribute value. Computer based agents however have to examine exactly these fields if they want to make decisions about the selection of a module from a pedagogical point of view. If the authors of the modules had different meanings about the values for the same property, the generated document will neither be very useful for a learner, nor be a coherent document. To decide whether or not a resource is appropriate for a user in a current situation, more information about the context, where the resource shall be used, is necessary. Furthermore the system needs more information about the background of the learner and also the criteria of the metadata author, who has tagged the resource. These restricts the effective use of algorithms to calculate values like the level of difficulty of a document to closed systems. Additionally more "pedagogical" metadata about a resource can be collected to generate a coherent document. The main disadvantage of a closed system is obvious. The system is not able to use resources generated and described outside of the system. Furthermore not many authors of learning material are willing to provide enough metadata, because describing a resource with metadata can be a time consuming effort. As soon as material, which was built and tagged outside the system, is considered, the coherence of the generated document decreases. More metadata does not necessarily guarantee a better quality of the generated documents. Even if the document was generated of pedagogically fitting modules, the coherence inside the document can still be low. In contrast to metadata schemes used in closed systems, the big advantage of LOM is, that it is very easy to find and (re-)use modular resources generated outside Multibook. As we want to show in chapter 3, we believe that it is possible to select appropriate modules described with LOM and some extensions we are using in Multibook, to generate a coherent document for an individual learner.

2.2 Relations between Modules

The second important aspect for generating coherent documents of modular resources is the possibility to express explicit relationships between modules. The proposed values are:
{isPartOf, HasPart, IsVersionOf,HasVersion, IsFormatOf,HasFormat, References IsReferencedBy, IsBasedOn, IsBasisFor, Requires IsRequiredBy}
Unfortunately, the relations mix content-based and conceptual connections between the modules. The fact that a module is referencing another one, is an indication that the modules contain information about the same topic. It is not enough information to decide, if these connected modules can be presented in a certain order. The relations "isPartOf/hasPart" and "isVersionOf/hasVersion" can be useful for organizing generated lessons. To generate the lesson itself they are not helpful. The relation "Requires/isRequiredBy" is also inappropriate. If a module completely depends on the existence and accessibility of another module, the approach of independent and reusable learning modules gets completely lost. Modules connected with the relation "isBasedOn/IsBasisFor" have the same problem. If this relation expresses a content based connection between two modules, there is no difference between a "isBasedOn" relation and a "isRequired" one. If someone wants to express the fact that a

module is dealing with a concept, which is explained in another module, he or she shouldn't express this fact with connecting two concrete modules or, in other words, representations of the concepts. This kind of connection is independent of the actual modules and should therefore be modeled separately. Multibook uses for this purpose a terminological ontology, where the concepts of the knowledge domain are represented and connected by semantic relations. The modules are connected to the respective concept. Relations between single modules should be restricted to didactic relations. These are for both a computer-based agent and a human learner useful to gain additional, more profound or explaining material. A short characterization of these rhetorical-didactic relations and how they are used to establish coherence is given in the next chapter.

3 Coherence

A criterion of a text is coherence. As Kuhlen remarked in [2] there cannot be (and from our point of view should not be) coherence in a hypertext system as such. It is up to the users to create coherence for their individual path through the system. An educational hypertext system should support the learners at this task.

In the following sections we show how this support can be added to learning systems with a modular knowledge base.

3.1 Local Coherence

Traditionally, the authors assume the job of relating two subsequent sentences or paragraphs. The basic tool is the order of the sections. Phrases like "It follows ..." or "Whereas, ..." etc. state the kind of relation between the sections, the second sentences or paragraph is a conclusion resp. a restriction of the first one. By using a consistent vocabulary and a recognizable style, the authors can support the users at following their train of thoughts and hence at building up coherence by themselves.

With a modular knowledge base – probably originated by several authors – none of these instruments is available. In the following sections we show a possibility to add coherence to such a knowledge base.

Guided Tour

To re-establish clues for coherence, some systems introduce guided tours, especially for beginners. A guided tour is one linear path through the material. By following the path, readers are discharged of the decision making whether two modules are connected at all. They can assume that subsequent modules are related. But adaptivity and guided tour is a contradiction in terms. The "one size fits all" approach does not meet the requirements of life long learning with respect to individuality.

The solution we suggest in the project Multibook are individually generated guided tours [6]. Here, no pre-fixed sections of modules are represented to the learners. The lessons are dynamically composed according to the user profile. The information gained from the user profile is matched to the formal description of the knowledge base. For more details see [4]. The learners are able to visit the neighbor modules which are not included in their guided tour. They can get a natural language list in a natural language with the names of links outgoing from the current module. This way, a deviation of length 1 from the selected path is possible.

Exploiting the Relations

Any link between two modules represents a relation. Untyped links are not really helpful to develop an understanding of the kind of relation. Typed links are fairly widespread and various. Some systems exploit the traffic light metaphor (see for example [1], [7]).

Based on the Rhetorical Structure Theory by Mann and Thompson [3] we have developed a set of relations between modules. We call these relations rhetorical-didactic, examples are "explains" or "deepens" (for a more detailed list see [5]). They can be applied to give clues of coherence. The system adds in the presentation fixed short sentences between two modules according to the relation connecting them. An example of such a sentence is "The following will present deeper aspects." This way, we re-establish the textual clues for coherence. One rhetorical-didactic relation plays an additional role. If a module can be considered as a continuation of another, they can be connected by the relation "continues". It is not necessary that the two modules are deeply semantically related. They may be a continued example: a module being a graphic of an apple might serve as an example for fruit, another module showing a sliced apple might illustrate the structure of a stone fruit. By connecting these modules, the system can – if appropriate – present both to the learner and constitute a thread, else missed in this surrounding.

3.2 Global Coherence

Overview over the Domain

Clues for global coherence of a linear text can often be found in the way the text is presented. Ideally, the users of an adaptive learning system should not be bothered by classifying the context, since they can assume that the information offered to them is adequate.

Normally, authors categorize their books by adding a blurb. Often here is stated the position of this book with respect to the knowledge domain. Articles or conference papers are specified with keywords.

In Multibook, the learners are supported to classify the module or set of modules to a bigger context by showing them a simplified graphical presentation of the ontology where the modules are connected to. Up to about 30 nodes which can be atomic or subsumptions of several nodes are displayed to the learner. The relations between the nodes are not well-defined semantic, but more associative ones. The user can explore this representation by expanding the subsumed nodes. With this tool, the learners can get an overview of the domain.

Table of Contents

The mightiest tool for document-immanent global coherence is a table of contents. Tables of contents offer the readers an overview of the structure of the document. Authors manifest the order and hierarchy, and this way give clues of the position of the single parts in the document. Readers are always able to locate the present piece of information in the context of the whole document.

In Multibook, the documents are composed dynamically from the modules. There is no generally valid table of contents. Therefore, also the tables of content have to be created on the fly. We utilize the underlain ontology; concepts of the ontology serve as entries for the table of content. The selection, order and hierarchy is determined by rules according to the user profile [6]. Which parts the user has already seen and where she or he is at the moment is indicated by colors. The dynamically generated table of contents has the same functionality as in linear documents. Additionally, the learners can navigate on it.

References

[1] Eklund, J. and Brusilovsky, P.: Individualising Interaction in Web-based Instructional Systems in Higher Education. In: Proceedings of the Apple University Consortium's Academic Conference. Melbourne. 1998.

[2] Kuhlen, R.: Hypertext - Ein nicht-lineares Medium zwischen Buch und Wissensbank. Springer-Verlag, Heidelberg. 1991.

[3] Mann, W.C. and Thomson S.A.: Rhetorical Structure Theory: A Theory of Text Organization. Technical Report RS-87-190, Information Science Institute, USC ISI, USA. 1987.

[4] Seeberg, C., El Saddik, A., Steinacker, A., Reichenberger, K., Fischer, S. and Steinmetz, R.: From User's Needs to Adaptive Documents. In: Proceedings of the Integrated Design & Process Technology Conference 1999. To appear in the 2000 proceedings.

[5] Steinacker, A., Seeberg, C., Fischer, S. and Steinmetz, R.: Multibook: Metadata for Webbased Learning Systems. In: Proceedings of the 2nd International Conference on New Learning Technologies. Bern. 1999.

[6] Steinacker, A., Seeberg, C., Reichenberger, K., Fischer, S. and Steinmetz, R.: Dynamically Generated Tables of Contents as Guided Tours in Adaptive Hypermedia Systems. In: Proceedings of the EdMedia. Seattle, WA. 1999.

[7] Weber, G. and Specht, M.: User Modeling and Adaptive Navigation Support in WWW-based Tutoring Systems. In: Proceedings of the Sixth International Conference (UM97). Chia Laguna, Sardinia. 1997.

[8] Draft Standard for Learning Object Metadata; Version 4.0; http://ltsc.ieee.org/doc/wg12/LOM_WD4.htm

ACE - Adaptive Courseware Environment

Marcus Specht

GMD - German National Research Center for Information Technology
Institute for Applied Information Technology (FIT-MMK)
D-53754 Sankt Augustin
email: Marcus.Specht@gmd.de

Abstract: The Adaptive Courseware Environment (ACE) [1] is a WWW-based tutoring framework which combines methods of knowledge representation, instructional planning, and adaptive media generation to deliver individualized courseware over the WWW. In this paper we like to introduce new cooperative components integrated in the ACE framework that support cooperative knowledge/data collection, expert finding and learner group organization. All these new cooperative components are realized with modified components of the BSCW environment [2]. A pedagogical agent in ACE is able to make recommendations for switching between individual and cooperative learning activities and find advanced or expert students in relation to one's own profile.

1. Introduction

The ACE framework utilizes hypermedia technologies and AI methods to deliver individualized hypermedia instruction. The basic ACE components like described in [1] mostly support individualized and goal oriented learning. Therefore we extended these with tools based on the BSCW [2] environment to support cooperative learning in learner groups and collaborative knowledge/data collection. Furthermore awareness information integrated into the ACE learner portal and course interface now support synchronous and asynchronous learning in learner groups. Besides the adaptation of a goal oriented instructional process the integration of cooperative learning components in ACE enables the support of a wider range of learning activities and individual styles of learning. Students can now learn in ACE by discussing with other students and by following the individualized guidance of a pedagogical agent through all available learning materials. The only criteria for a successful learning path are the knowledge test results of a student at the end of a learning unit or even a curriculum.

2. Learning with ACE

When students log into ACE they get an individualized learner portal, where they can book courses, contact courseware authors and other learners, maintain and update their profile, and have a collection of resources linked to that page. Additionally students get some awareness information about current online discussions, teacher's online lessons in their booked courses, and co-learners that are present on the ACE server. From their personal ACE portal they start working on their booked courses.

P. Brusilovsky, O. Stock, C. Strapparava (Eds.): AH 2000, LNCS 1892, pp. 380-383, 2000.

Based on the learner model, the domain model, and the pedagogical model the presentation component of ACE selects appropriate learning units and generates individual hypermedia documents. Throughout the whole course the learner's knowledge is tested so that the system can adapt to the dynamically changing knowledge, interests, and preferences of the learner.

2.1 Adaptive Methods in ACE

In ACE several adaptable and adaptive methods have been implemented and evaluated. The main groups of the implemented adaptive methods are in the field of adaptive navigation support, adaptive sequencing, adaptive recommendation, and pedagogical agent support.

Adaptive navigation support. ACE currently implements two methods of adaptive navigation support: Adaptive annotation and incremental linking of hyperlinks. Adaptive annotation of hyperlinks supplies the user with additional information about the content behind a hyperlink. The annotation is adapted to the individual user by taking the learner's knowledge and relations of the units to be learned into account. Implementations of adaptive annotation can be found in different variants in [5]. Furthermore also several experimental studies [4] have investigated on the effects of these variations. Texts in ACE can contain keywords to related concepts that are not learned by a student yet. If a text is presented to a student first, it will contain no hyperlinks to the related but not yet learned concepts. After working with the system, ACE will present all text keywords with hyperlinks to already mastered concepts and ready-to-learn concepts. Building an individual index in the learner model allows the system to present exactly these links in a text a learner is ready to visit and units that are too complex are presented as plain text. Experimental studies within ACE showed that the successful application of incremental linking is dependent on students' learning style and their prior knowledge [3].

Adaptive sequencing. In ACE the sequence of learning steps is adapted on two main levels, e.g., the system gives proposals for sequencing of whole learning units and the system adapts the sequence of media available for a unit. In tendency the empirical results confirm that the prior knowledge of learners has a strong impact on the learning success with adaptive hypermedia [3]. Furthermore the effects of the explicit warning and recommendation of prerequisite units were confounded by the adaptive navigation support.

Recommendations of a pedagogical agent. In ACE a pedagogical agent was implemented to give individualized recommendations to students dependent from their knowledge, their interests and their media preferences [6]. Beside recommendations of learning material to study the recommendations of the pedagogical agent where extended to propose cooperative activities and contact to other students that are willing to support others. Table 1 shows some type of recommendations given by the agent:

Table 1: Recommendations given by a pedagogical agent in ACE

Student request	Agent's selection and teaching strategy
Anything else?	Find a learning material of the current unit, to complete knowledge about this unit. This proposal draws the student's attention to a learning material of the current unit that has not yet been seen.
Contact advanced student!	Find a student that declared that he/she is willing to support others and has excellent knowledge in the current unit or lesson.
Discuss with other students!	Find students that are willing to cooperate and those have a similar knowledge of the current unit by comparing the overlay model of the current lesson.

The overall results showed that students following the learning material recommendations of the agent gained a better understanding, had more fun, and worked more intense [7].

2.2 Cooperative Knowledge Collection and Co-learner Finding

With the integration of student workspaces into the ACE framework new courses can now consist of a given curriculum structure prepared by a teacher while the contents and learning materials are completely collected by the students. This allows teachers to implement basic courseware that is integrated with the growing knowledge of the learner community and develops towards a living repository of knowledge which includes frequently asked questions, best practice solutions, and open space courseware. Like described in section 2.1 students can ask the assistant for online co-learners and topic experts. Furthermore with every presentation of a learning unit the currently available students that are willing to cooperate are shown to the student. The selection of appropriate co-learners is based on a comparison of the student's knowledge model and the other students' knowledge model. Students that are willing to cooperate with others can get a contact point to very similar students or to very different students in sense of there curriculum expertise. This can lead to very heterogeneous learner groups that consist of topic experts in selected areas or to very homogenous learner groups that consist of experts on the same topic. The expertise of a student on a certain topic is measured with four main criteria: The number of wrong test answers when working on knowledge tests, the time to answer sufficiently enough knowledge tests, the collection of additional learning material in student workspaces that has high request rates by many other students, and the overall score in the curriculum. The learner groups can work in discussion forums, synchronous moderated chat sessions or communicate via integrated email.

3. Perspective

The basic ACE framework like presented in [1] was extended with features for cooperative learning materials and activities, expert finding, and integrated awareness information. This enables the framework to support a wider range of teaching strategies and domains. An ACE course now can range from a goal oriented drill/practice course to a structured collection of arbitrary learning materials by students. In the one case an author prepares a clearly defined curriculum with contents and a highly restricted sequence of individual learning materials. In the other case the author prepares a curriculum structure with an associated target competence definition (knowledge tests) and the students need to build their own knowledge base and collect course contents. The ACE framework will be used in two European projects[1] where the integration with different kinds of learning materials and cooperative software components is planned.

4. References

1. Specht, M. and R. Oppermann, *ACE, Adaptive courseware environment.* New Review of Hypermedia and Multimedia, (1998). **4**: p. 141-161.

2. Bentley, R., *et al.*, *Basic support for cooperative work on the World Wide Web.* Int. J. Human-Computer Studies, (1997). : p. 827-846.

3. Specht, M., *Adaptive Methoden in computerbasierten Lehr/Lernsystemen.* Psychology, ed. G.R. Series. Vol. 1. (1998), Dissertation, Trier: University of Trier. p. 150.

4. Eklund, J. and P. Brusilovsky. *The Value of Adaptivity in Hypermedia Learning Environments: A Short Review of Empirical Evidence.* in *The Ninth ACM Conference on Hypertext and Hypermedia.* 1998. Pittsburgh: Presented at 2nd Workshop on Adaptive Hypertext and Hypermedia with HYPERTEXT '98. http://wwwis.win.tue.nl/ah98

5. Brusilovsky, P., *Efficient Techniques of adaptive hypermedia,* in *intelligent Hypertext,* C. Nicholas and J. Mayfield, Editor. (1997), Springer: Berlin, Heidelberg, New York. p.12-27.

6. Schoech, V., M. Specht, and G. Weber. ADI — An Empirical Evaluation of a Pedagogical Agent. in World Conference on Educational Multimedia ED-MEDIA98. 1998. Freiburg, Germany

---

[1] The WINDS (Web based Intelligent design Tutoring System) Project is supported by the EU in the IST 5th framework programme- Flexible University. The Project Sol-Eu-Net (Data mining and Decision Support for business competitiveness: A European virtual enterprise) is also supported in 5th Framework IST Programme.

The Adaptive University Calendar

Manfred Stede and Stephan Koch

Technische Universität Berlin, FB Informatik, Projektgruppe KIT,
Franklinstr. 28/29, 10587 Berlin/Germany,
{stede|skoch}@cs.tu-berlin.de

Abstract. Each term, university students consult the new calendar for deciding which courses to take in order to advance their studies. At present, university calendars are largely static documents that do not make use of adaptive hypertext technology. We are currently developing a prototypical system that offers course information tailored to the specific student, on the basis of a user profile and the navigation history of the current system session. Documents are thus partly generated dynamically, and hyperlinks into the document space created appropriately. We describe the idea, the user scenario with its roles for adaptivity, and the technical realization, which is currently under way.

1 The Idea: University Calendars and Study Plans

When browsing the web pages of universities, one soon notices that contemporary document presentation technologies are applied only very modestly. Especially the web versions of calendars are designed in very "traditional" ways, ranging from entirely static, long lists of courses to simple search capabilities for keywords in the course descriptions, etc. Yet, putting together the course program for an upcoming term is a highly individual and non-trivial task for the student, and support by appropriate presentation techniques can be of valuable assistance. The extent to which such a personalized, adaptive presentation of course information is useful depends in part on the degree of freedom that students have in choosing their plan of study: When there is not much to choose, there is not much to tailor or to advise, but when the student has a lot of options, the situation changes. We are currently developing a prototype of a highly flexible and adaptive calendar advisory system for the Computer Science Department of Berlin's Technical University. Here, students in the first two years follow a largely prescribed sequence of courses. But for the subsequent three years, there is both more freedom and more complicated regulations. In brief, students are required to attend a minimum number of courses over (typically) three years; they have to cover a range of topic areas; they have to choose one or two 'focus topic areas' and attend classes accordingly; they have to cover a range of course types (i.e., lecture, seminar, project); there are some constraints on the order in which courses can be taken. Trivially, one cannot attend two classes with identical time slots. At the beginning of each term, the student's choices have to respect all these *constraints*; at the same time, there are of course individual

P. Brusilovsky, O. Stock, C. Strapparava (Eds.): AH 2000, LNCS 1892, pp. 384–387, 2000.

preferences for certain topics, certain lecturers, certain course types, or certain time slots. Hence, there is much room for automatically tailoring the information of the university calendar to the user's needs.

2   User's Perspective: Course Listings Tailored to Students

The amount of information given to the user and the mode of presentation are influenced by a *user profile*, which consists of two parts: The static part holds the list of courses the student has already attended and passed, as well as her preferred topics of interest (this list is updated each term). The dynamic part records the navigation history of the current session with the system: Which courses has the student already looked at, for which has she expressed a potential interest to attend, which attributes of course descriptions is she interested in.

A general design strategy of ours is to make each system decision transparent and retractable, based on the belief that students will not accept a system that implicitly makes decisions for them without saying so (even if the decisions are necessary and correct). For instance, if the system determines that some course cannot be taken yet because of a missing prerequisite course, it does not follow that the course becomes invisible to the user. Here, we follow Kobsa [4], who emphasized the need of user control over the system's modeling component. Our system thus makes recommendations and sorts information into particular orders of preference, but does not hide any information.

After the user has registered with the system, the entry page to the calendar for the upcoming term consists of three frames: Views, Courses and Schedule (see Figure 1, which shows an English version of a screendump from our prototype). In the Views-frame, the user can select the general representation of the course listing, mark the items on which she would like to receive system-generated hints, and choose which courses are to be shown in the Courses-frame: all courses, those already selected, or those already dismissed.

The Courses-frame shows the course listing itself, where the amount of information shown depends on the user's settings. Below it there is a menu bar allowing the user to select, preselect, or dismiss a course. Upon selecting or preselecting a course, it appears in the Schedule-frame. Preselection means indicating an initial interest and tentatively reserving the slot in the schedule.

Dynamically filling the schedule can be seen as a first step from an *adaptable* to an *adaptive* system [1]. A second step is taken by offering the user to state individual preferences, which leads to filtering and sorting the information. Specifically, it is possible to exclude from future listings those courses offered by a particular *lecturer*, belonging to a *field of study*, or occupying a *time slot* (which the student may have reserved for other activities). Besides such filtering, course listings are sorted according to the user's preferences for particular *topics*, which are represented as keywords in the user profile.

The last part of the Courses-frame (cf. figure 1) is a section containing hints generated by the system in response to the user's navigational choices; this re-

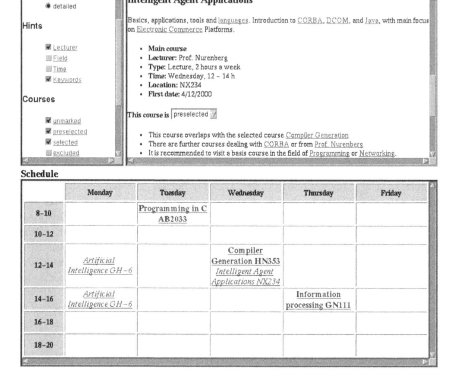

Fig. 1. Translated screenshot

sembles the approach taken in the ILEX [2] and PEBA [6] systems. There can be some advisory information about this course, and a number of hyperlinks to other courses. As for the advisory information, it alerts the user when

- the course has a time slot that is the same as that for a course the user has already (pre-) selected,
- the course takes place in a room far away from an interesting course in a neighbouring time slot,
- the type or topic area of the course is one that the student has already completely covered with previously attended courses,
- the course has a prerequisite course that the student has not taken yet.

If applicable, a list of hyperlinks to other courses is generated for the user, who can now follow one of these (related topic, same lecturer) or continue navigating in other modes.

3 Realization

To implement our prototype, we proceed as follows. The standard ASCII list of courses offered in a term (as created by the department) is semi-automatically converted to an XML document [7]. The different views of the course listing are generated via XSL-T [8] with the Microsoft XML Parser MSXML2 [5], which is integrated in Internet Explorer 5 (IE5). Given the current state of HTML technology, the constraints imposed by the pre-standard XSL portions in IE5 need to be respected, and the target language is currently HTML. The controller is based on Javascript. The dynamic (session-specific) user profile is stored as cookies.

In addition to this approach, we are evaluating (as part of a student's project) various other alternatives, in system design as well as in possible underlying architectures. The online-generated textual information (hints and warnings) currently is produced with straightforward templates that are filled with the appropriate data. For future work, we envisage the generation of text from more abstract representations, and with parameterized communicative goals, similar in spirit to the ADVISOR II system [3], which for instance tailors lexical choice in order to recommend certain actions to the students when deciding on taking courses.

References

1. De Bra, P.: Design Issues in Adaptive Web-Site Development. In: Proceedings of the 2nd Workshop on Adaptive Systems and User Modeling on the WWW, Toronto, http://wwwis.win.tue.nl/asum99/debra/debra.html (1999)
2. Cox, R., O'Donnell, M. and Oberlander, J.: Dynamic versus static hypermedia in museum education: an evaluation of ILEX, the intelligent labelling explorer. In: Proceedings of the 9th International Conference on Artificial Intelligence and Education. Le Mans, France (1999) 181–188
3. Elhadad, M.: Generating adjectives to express the speaker's argumentative intent. In: Proceedings of the Fifth National Conference on Artificial Intelligence (AAAI). Anaheim, CA (1991) 98–104
4. Kobsa, A.: User Modeling in Dialog-Systems: Potentials and Hazards. In: AI & Society 4 (1990) 214–240
5. Microsoft XML Parser Technology, Microsoft Corporation. http://msdn.microsoft.com/downloads/webtechnology/xml/msxml.asp, (2000)
6. Milosavljevic, M., Tulloch, A., and Dale, R.: Text Generation in a Dynamic Hypertext Environment. In: Proceedings of the Nineteenth Australasian Computer Science Conference (ACSC'96). Melbourne, Australia (1996)
7. Extensible Markup Language (XML) 1.0, The World Wide Web Consortium (W3C). http://www.w3.org/TR/REC-xml (1998)
8. Extensible Stylesheet Language Transformations (XSLT), Version 1.0, The World Wide Web Consortium (W3C). http://www.w3.org/TR/xslt (1999)

Sense-Based User Modelling for Web Sites

Carlo Strapparava, Bernardo Magnini, and Anna Stefani

ITC-IRST Istituto per la Ricerca Scientifica e Tecnologica, I-38050 Trento, ITALY,
{strappa | magnini | stefani}@irst.itc.it

Abstract. SiteIF is a personal agent for a news web site that learns user's interests from the requested pages that are analyzed to generate or to update a model of the user. Exploiting this model, the system anticipates which documents in the web site could be interesting for the user. Using MULTIWORDNET, a multilingual extension of WORDNET, a content-based user model is built as a semantic network whose nodes, independent from the language, represent the word sense frequency rather then word frequency.

1 Introduction

The use of user models has been proposed in several tools in order to search and retrieve relevant documents [6,1,7]. However, in these systems the representation of user's interest is built without considering word sense disambiguation, but only taking into account morpho-syntactic properties, such as word frequency and words co-occurrence. This yields a representation that is often not enough accurate from a semantic point of view. The issue is even more important in the Web world, where documents have to do with many different topics and the chance to misinterpret word senses is a real problem.

SiteIF is a personal agent for a news web site that takes into account the user's browsing "watching over the user's shoulder" (see [9] for details about the whole system). It learns user's interests from the requested pages that are analyzed to generate or to update a model of the user. In this paper we present some developments of SiteIF that take advantage of natural language processing (NLP) techniques in building the user model. In particular we describe a module that uses MULTIWORDNET [2] – an "extended" multilingual version, developed at IRST, of the WORDNET [3] lexical database – to make the model more meaningful and accurate. In this perspective the user model is built as a semantic network whose nodes represent not simply the word frequency but the *word sense* in frequency. Furthermore, taking advantage of MULTIWORDNET, the resulting user model is independent from the language of the documents browsed. This is particular valuable with multilingual web sites, that are becoming very common especially in news sites or in electronic commerce domains.

Finally, once the user model network is built, it is important to have a method to estimate how much the user model talks "about the same things". A clusterization of the synset network is described with the purpose to dynamically infer the interest areas of the resulting user model.

P. Brusilovsky, O. Stock, C. Strapparava (Eds.): AH 2000, LNCS 1892, pp. 388–391, 2000.

2   MultiWordNet and Word Sense Disambiguation

MULTIWORDNET [2] is an Italian version of the English WORDNET. It is based on the assumption that a large part of the conceptual relations defined for the English (about 72,000 IS-A relations and 5,600 PART-OF relations) can be shared with Italian. From an architectural point of view, MULTIWORDNET implements an extension of the WORDNET lexical matrix to a "multilingual lexical matrix" through the addition of a third dimension relative to the language. The Italian version of WORDNET currently includes about 30,000 lemmas.

Taking advantage of MULTIWORDNET hierarchies, actually we use two techniques to deal with word sense disambiguation.

Semantic Field Code Annotations. Besides extending WORDNET with the language dimension, MULTIWORDNET synsets are annotated with subject field codes (SFCs) (e.g. MEDICINE, ARCHITECTURE, LITERATURE, etc...) by a semiautomatic procedure which exploits the WORDNET structure. SFCs provide cross-categorial information, which is almost completely absent in WORDNET, and can be considered basically language independent. MULTIWORDNET has about 250 semantic field codes. Given a text (i.e. a news text), a classification algorithm uses the SFC assignement to compute the probability that words in the text belong to a certain subject code. Then, for each SFC an overall score is computed taking into account the SFC hierarchy: at the end, the SFC with highest score is selected as the best text classification.

Semantic Similarity. Following Resnik [8], MULTIWORDNET associates probabilities with synsets using noun frequencies from large corpora. Each synset S is augmented with a probability function $\mathcal{P}r(S)$ that gives the probability of encountering an instance of concept S. The probability function has the following property: *if* S_1 IS-A S_2 *then* $\mathcal{P}r(S_1) \leq \mathcal{P}r(S_2)$. The probability of the root is 1. Following the usual argumentation of information theory, the information content of a concept S can be represented as the negative logarithm of its probability (i.e. $- log \, \mathcal{P}r(S)$). The more abstract is a concept, the lower is its information content. The root of the hierarchy has information content 0. Given two polysemous words and the list of synsets which the words belong to, the algorithm for their sense disambiguation is based on the fact that their most informative subsumer provides information about which sense of each word is the relevant one. This method can be generalized for a group of words, considering the words pairwise. In MULTIWORDNET this approach has been recently extended taking advantage from multilingual corpora and Meronymy/Holonymy relations.

3   Word Sense Based User Modelling

The current domain of SiteIF is news texts supplied by AdnKronos, an important Italian news provider. The news are from different topics (e.g. politics, history, economics, etc ...) and both the Italian and English versions are available.

We refer to the task of building an appropriate model of the user exploiting documents in different languages as Cross-Language User Modeling (CLUM).

This task shares some of the goals with Cross-Lingual Information Retrieval (see for example [4] for a survey), but it is less complex in that it does not require a query disambiguation process. In fact in CLUM the matching is between a fully disambiguated structure, i.e. the user model, and the document content. We have approached this problem with the idea of indexing documents by means of WORDNET synsets. The advantages of synset indexing are that: (*i*) each ambiguous term in the document is fully disambiguated, allowing its correct interpretation and consequently a better precision in the user model construction (e.g. if a user is interested in financial news a document containing the word "bank" in the context of geography will not be relevant); (*ii*) synonym words belonging to the same synset can contribute to the user model definition. For example both "bank" and "bank building" will bring evidences for financial documents, improving the coverage of the indexing; (*iii*) finally, we use a multilingual wordnet, synsets will match with synonyms in various languages, allowing the user model to be defined on a multilingual base.

Document Representation. For every news text in the web site, a classification algorithm uses the SFC assignement to compute the probability that words in the text belong to a certain subject field code. The SFC with highest score is selected as the best text classification. A module to detect proper nouns and relative category is also used, for those proper nouns not included in WORDNET.

A representation of a document takes into account: the semantic field with highest score, an indication of the mean polisemy of the text, a list of proper nouns, a list of synsets belonging to the winner semantic field, a list of non-ambiguous synsets.

Modelling Phase. SiteIF considers the browsed documents during a navigation session. In the modelling phase, the system yields (i.e. builds or augments) the user model as a semantic net whose nodes are synsets or proper nouns and arcs between nodes are the co-occurrence relation of two concepts. Every node and every arc has a weight derived from the frequencies of the synset in the document. As far as the arcs are concerned, an indication of the semantic similiarity between the synsets is also present (see sec. 2). The weights of the net are periodically reconsidered and possibly lowered, depending on the time passed from the last update. Also no longer useful nodes and arcs may be removed from the net. So it is possible to consider changes of the user's interests and to avoid that uninteresting concepts remain in the user model.

Filtering Phase. During the filtering phase, the system compares any document (i.e. any representation of the document in terms of synsets) in the site with the user model. A matching module receives as input the internal representation of a document and the current user model and it produces as output a classification of the document (i.e. it is worth or not the user's attention). The relevance of any single document is estimated using the Semantic Network Value Technique (see for details [9]). The idea behind the SiteIF algorithm consists of checking, for every concept in the representation of the document, whether the context in which it occurs has been already found in previously visited documents (i.e. is already stored in the semantic net). This context is represented by a co-occurrence relationship, i.e. by the couples of terms included in the document which have already co-occurred before in other documents.

UM Clusterization and Interest Areas. Once the user model network is built, it is necessary to have a method to estimate how much the user model talks about the same things in order to dynamically infer the interest areas of the resulting user model (for the moment, in SiteIF, there are a fixed number of interest areas). The idea to introduce a notion of coherence looking for clusters formed by cohesive synsets chains is common to many approaches (see for example [5]). The user model clusterization process, to dynamically identify user's interest areas, includes the detection of particular aggregations of synsets that display particular cohesion both from topological point of view (high connectivity in the network) and from relevance (weights of nodes and arcs). Peculiar UM network configurations can influence the filtering process and in particular the matching phase. For example, a user that shows many interests (i.e. clusters) could enjoy suggestions for documents not strictly related to previous ones. In this case the filtering process will perform a deeper WORDNET hierarchy navigation (e.g. considering more semantic relations) in the computation of the relevant documents.

References

1. R. Armstrong, D. Freitag, T. Joachim, and T. Mitchell. Webwatcher: A learning apprentice for the world wide web. In *Proc. of AAAI Spring Symposium on Information Gathering from Heterogeneous and Distributed Environments*, Stanford, March 1995.
2. A. Artale, B. Magnini, and C. Strapparava. WORDNET for italian and its use for lexical discrimination. In *AI*IA97: Advances in Artificial Intelligence*. Springer Verlag, 1997.
3. C. Fellbaum. *WordNet. An Electronic Lexical Database*. The MIT Press, 1998.
4. G. Grefenstette. *Cross-Language Information Retrieval*. Kluver, Boston, 1998.
5. G. Hirst and D. St-Onge. Lexical chains representations of context for the detection and correction of malapropisms. In C. Fellbaum, editor, *WordNet. An Electronic Lexical Database*. The MIT Press, 1998.
6. H. Lieberman. Letizia: An agent that assists web browsing. In *Proc. of the International Joint Conference on Artificial Intelligent (IJCAI '95)*, Montreal, Quebec, Canada, August 1995.
7. M. Minio and C. Tasso. User modeling for information filtering on internet services: Exploiting an extended version of the UMT shell. In *Proc. of Workshop on User Modeling for Information Filtering on the World Wide Web*, Kailia-Kuna Hawaii, January 1996. held in conjunction with UM'96.
8. P. Resnik. Disambiguating noun groupings with respect to WordNet senses. In *Proc. of third workshop on very large corpora*, MIT, Boston, June 1995.
9. A. Stefani and C. Strapparava. Personaliziong access to web sites: The siteif project. In *Proc. of second Workshop on Adaptive Hypertext and Hypermedia*, Pittsburgh, June 1998. held in conjunction with HYPERTEXT 98.

Generating Personal Travel Guides from Discourse Plans

Ross Wilkinson, Shijian Lu, François Paradis,
Cécile Paris, Stephen Wan, MingFang Wu

CSIRO, Division of Mathematical and Information Sciences, 723 Swanston St,
Carlton 3053, Australia

Abstract. This paper describes a system that delivers travel guides tailored to individual needs. It does so by integrating a discourse planner with a system for querying the web and generating synthesised web pages using document prescriptions. We show by way of example how a user model can lead to a personal travel guide, and show what this might look like in different media. We briefly describe the investigations we are undertaking to determine the utility of such approaches.

1. Tailored Travel Guides

There is an increasing emphasis on the delivery of information that is tailored to individual needs. This paper describes an approach to delivery that assumes a user profile, a discourse model, and a set of web data sources, and delivers information from those sources in a coherent form to a variety of media including paper, Palm Pilots, and the web. The approach requires developing a system that integrates a discourse planner with a web query and document synthesis technology. Information is acquired from a variety of heterogeneous information sources, including internal databases and web sources. Both components need to be informed by the user model, and a model of travel guides.

There are currently several commercial travel information web guides that allow some degree of tailoring. These sites operate by having a user provide answers to a set of questions, and the information is delivered by applying a filter to the information resources held at the site, and then deliver a standard structured web page or pages. The use of user models to adapt delivery of location dependent information has been demonstrated in prototype by Specht et al.[5]

2. Discourse Planning and Document Synthesis

In producing a tailored document, information should be coherent and relevant to the user. To achieve this, the resulting document is planned automatically by resolving goals representing mental states of the user, and coherence relations representing how sections of text meaningfully relate to each other. This planner, modelled on a one

P. Brusilovsky, O. Stock, C. Strapparava (Eds.): AH 2000, LNCS 1892, pp. 392–395, 2000.

described by Moore and Paris [2], produces an intermediate tree structure called a Discourse, which uses nodes and arcs to represent the content of the document and the coherence relations between content parts, respectively. The particular theory of discourse structure used to represent coherency is Rhetorical Structure Theory [1], which lends itself easily to computational planning. By using such a planner, only relevant content is selected and assembled for the user.

Complementary to discourse planning is the problem of pulling out bits of information from various sources and combining them to form a valid document. Several models have been proposed to query data sources and transform them for inclusion in a virtual document [4]. Not surprisingly, the Web community is very active in this domain. The following are elements of a comprehensive solution: script languages, document object models, style sheets and transformation languages, etc.

Perhaps the best examples of tailored document generation at the moment can be seen on the Web. It has been argued that users already perform some level of customisation merely by navigating a site [3]. Good Web sites are designed to facilitate that navigation, and will do it better by taking into account the user community they are designed for. For example, the difference between Internet and Extranet sites is not only about restricting information, but also about providing different information to different people (the public versus the staff). Likewise, most Web portals are designed to suit a particular user community in a particular context. More sophisticated sites try to dynamically adapt their content to the user. An interactive dialogue is established; the system can learn about the user need by presenting forms to be filled out or multiple choice of links, it can then present information according to what it knows about the user (possibly taking into account what it has "said" before), ask for more precision, etc. We claim that to support a meaningful dialogue, a system must keep a current "view" or profile of the user, and have an appropriate model of the discourse.

3. The Personal Travel Guide Approach

The personal travel guide system starts with two things, a user model appropriate to travel, and a general discourse model appropriate to travel guides.

Let us assume that Frank is visiting Melbourne in Australia, from the 15-17th of October 2001. We will assume that Frank wishes to stay in hotels around the $100-150 range, and that he enjoys opera and cycling, and has an interest in exploring an important local historical figure, Major Mitchell. Frank needs information delivered on the web, for initial exploration, and also in Palm Pilot form, which he will take with him on his trip. Frank has no interest in a paper travel guide. This will be the user profile.

Next we need to develop a discourse model. This is derived by an analysis of a corpus of travel guides, including travel books, travel leaflets, and on-line guides. This leads to a model where after a general introduction, there are generally, depending again on the user model, needs to provide information about accommodation, restaurants, and activities.

The discourse model is now used to develop a discourse. This is done in three stages. First, the general discourse plan is created by evaluating various elements of the user model. The second stage creates the presentation by querying databases of information held as web pages or structured databases. We then have the content of the tailored guide. The third step is to generate a particular form of the content that is dependent upon the medium of delivery. Thus a Palm Pilot presentation has lots of navigation, with concise information on any particular page, whereas the Web form will use less navigation, and more layout in generating an interesting set of Web pages. In figure 1, we compare the top page of a Palm Pilot presentation with a web page presentation.

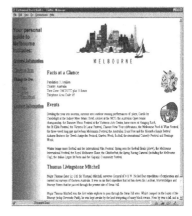

Figure 1 – Delivery modes

The Tiddler System

The architecture of the tailored information delivery system is shown in Figure 2. The core elements of the system are a discourse planner, a presentation planner, and a surface generator. These correspond to the three stages of generation described above. A user dialogue system is also needed to capture the user model and to deliver the information. The discourse planner takes the user model and the prototypical discourse for a travel guide to create a discourse plan, which uses a tree structure. This tree structure is manipulated by a series of RST transformations. The presentation planner then populates this structure with a series of queries against web sources, which are either managed locally, and has a well understood structure, or as general as a list of sources returned from a general web search engine. The Norfolk system [4] is used to create a set of virtual web pages by evaluating document prescriptions lying in the nodes of the tree structure. The answers to these queries are synthesised into a set of HTML answer fragments. The surface generator then takes these fragments and generates a hypertext that is appropriate to the desired medium for delivery. The surface generator again uses RST transformations to take the tree of document fragments and determine a final presentation form.

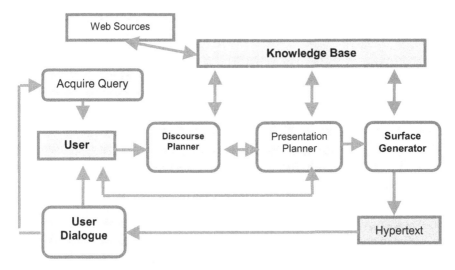

Figure 2 – System

4. Remarks

We have described a system that delivers travel guides tailored to individual needs. By basing this system around a series of transformations of a basic discourse plan, quite different applications, quite different user models, and quite different delivery platforms can be supported by just changing the data and the transforms. There is no need to change the software. While engineering benefits accrue from this approach, the key issue is the level of benefit of a discourse approach to tailored information delivery. This issue is currently being investigated.

References

[1] Mann, W.C., & Thompson, S.A. (1988). Rhetorical structure theory: Towards a functional theory of text organization. In *TEXT*, 8(3), (pp 243- 281).
[2] Moore, J.D. & Paris, C.L. (1993). Planning Text for Advisory Dialogues: Capturing Intentional and Rhetorical Information. In *Computational Linguistics*, Cambridge, MA. Vol 19(4), (pp.651- 694).
[3] Nielsen, J. (1998). Personalization is Over-Rated, in *The Alertbox: Current Issues in Web Usability* (Web bi-weekly), October. URL: http://www.useit.com/alertbox/981004.html
[4] Paradis, F., Vercoustre, A.M., & Hills, B. (1998), A Virtual Document Interpreter for Reuse of Information, in *Lecture Notes in Computer Science 1375*, *Proceedings of Electronic Publishing*, Saint-Malo, France (pp. 487-498).
[5] Specht, M., Oppermann, R. "User Modeling and Adaptivity in Nomadic Information Systems" *Proceedings of the 7th GI-Workshop "Adaptivität und Benutzermodellierung in Interaktiven Softwaresystemen" (ABIS99)*, pp. 325 -328, Universität Magdeburg, 1999.

Distributed Systems for Group Adaptivity on the Web

Maria Barra

Dipartimento di Informatica ed Applicazioni "R.M. Capocelli"
Università di Salerno, Baronissi (Salerno), 84081, Italy
and
IBM Almaden Research Center
650 Harry Rd. San Jose, CA 95120
marbar@dia.unisa.it

Abstract. This paper describes the project of an Adaptive System for Group navigation on the Web. The objective of the project is to provide collaborative and adaptive navigation to users groups sharing a "common interest" on the Web. The goal of the collaborative navigation is to promote the knowledge and information exchange among users having common objectives.

1 Introduction

Internet can be considered the first real global hypermedia network. For the user it is principally an information retrieval system that offers a simple user-interface to retrieve information from everywhere. The Web counts millions of users and for this reason it presents remarkable relevance at social level that has induced a growth of the research activity centered on it. The research is focused on improving Web's performances and overcome the boundaries dictate from its architecture by using new emergent technologies. This paper describes the project of an Adaptive System for Group (GASs) navigation on the Web to provide collaborative and adaptive navigation to users groups sharing a common interest. The goal of the collaborative navigation is to promote the knowledge and information exchange among users. For example, accessing the Web and discovering new resources can be a useful group activity to share and to learn from. Users can take advantage of the other members' activities and save their time to search relevant information on the Web.

The objective hence is to discover what requirements a model for group personalization should have and how a Web-based GAS could implement such model to provide adaptive navigation.

Adapting system's behavior to groups is more complex than user modeling. For example, adapting the system's behavior to a single user has little impact on users' privacy: group adaptation requires to preserve part of the members' behavior with respect to other users while sharing the useful part. Furthermore, GASs require support by typical cooperative tools, e.g., the control of the communication among users as well as the management of the group awareness.

P. Brusilovsky, O. Stock, C. Strapparava (Eds.): AH 2000, LNCS 1892, pp. 396–402, 2000.
© Springer-Verlag Berlin Heidelberg 2000

A challenging issue here is how to get group adaptivity (or even toward single users) when the knowledge base is not fixed and is not under the control of the adaptive system designer/manager.

About the implementation of GASs, it seems that the distributed architecture is dictated by the system's characteristics. In fact, group modeling cannot be easily implemented on client-side, since, of course, it is difficult to catch data from different clients. Moreover, our choice is not to implement GA mechanisms on server-side since the goal is to provide group adaptation on the Web.

A natural solution is offered by proxy programming that could fulfill adaptive and cooperative requirements of GASs, by providing a common (and, in part, transparent) access point to the members' group. Proxy programming infrastructure is offered by a flexible and complete framework like Web Based Intermediaries (WBI) developed by IBM Research Center in Almaden (California USA).

In section 2 we give an overview of the research framework. In section 3 we outline the project directions and the application scenarios.

2 Research Framework

This section presents the related research areas whose experiences and techniques will be useful in the project design. Briefly we introduce CSCW and Adaptive discipline: their issues and basic requirements must be evaluate in order to extrapolate strategies and techniques that can be fruitfully used in group adaptivity.

2.1 Computer Supported Cooperative Work (CSCW)

One of the main emphases of the research in Distributed Systems area is on CSCW discipline, it defines the requirements of a collaborative system. Key issues [12] are group awareness, multi-user interfaces, concurrency control, communication and coordination within the group as well as shared information space and the support of a heterogeneous and open environment which integrates existing single-user applications. A CSCW system offers collaborative characteristics that are useful in several working environments one didactic [1], of tutoring and help desk, commercial services and medical structures.

Groupware technology is used to enable users with different skills and job competence to communicate, cooperate, coordinate and resolve problems.

2.2 Adaptive Systems

Adaptive systems tailor information to the user and may guide the user in the information space. They try to guess the user's needs taking in account a model of the goals, interests and preferences of user. A user model provides a representation of the user's state, it is computed on several aspects related to user (for example, background knowledge, preferences, past interactions and skills).

In News Duke[10] users have no a well-defined need: here a agent (Personal News Agent) allows to respond to the user's questions "What is new and what I should know?".

Generally, an adaptive system keeps a classification of the information domain and associates concepts specified by user model to the contents of the domain. This classification allows to produce on-the-fly dynamic documents according to user model changes.

Adaptive Hypermedia systems guide the user in the information space presenting him/her only relevant material. Adaptive technologies [7] allow to adapt page content and link presentation (link removal, link annotation, link disabling, etc.) as well as to add new navigation paths in the documents proposed to its users. Adaptive features are applied to improve the user's navigation, to research and collect information directly specified by user (or specified by his/her behavior), to address the users' lectures [9] and testing phases, to filter the information avoiding cognitive overload.

3   Group Adaptive Systems

This section offers a more detailed view of the project. The objectives are twofold: study effective and efficient models for modeling groups, as well as develop Group Adaptive Systems for using, surfing and accessing the Web. Hence, we will try to provide a validation to the model developed during the previous part.

3.1   The Overall Project

The overall synthesis of our work is the design and realization of an unobtrusive Group Adaptive System for cooperative navigation of the Web. Often, different users in the same environment share common objectives, common interests and common experiences. An example is the usual teamwork in software development centers: Web navigation is a useful experience to share with colleagues, especially when it is necessary to get quick and prompt updates about software technology. In this case, common adaptive techniques offer tools like for example link annotation, to inform team members about the content and usefulness of a navigation path.

Adaptation is often based on User Modeling technologies. We need a model to represent group characteristics and their evolution in order to tailor Web content presentation to group's members. Of course, it looks like a challenging issue to extend adaptation to a group: a single member has his/her own particular characteristics that should also be recognized and accounted for by the GAS. The right compromise between what a single member of the group likes as an individual and what he/she likes as a group member is an interesting problem. For example, a common view for all participants could appear redundant to users that discovered them.

It looks clear, that the group model can not be the unique resource on which base group adaptivity: a model that characterizes single users could be need to adapt system to different group's member. For example, in [10] two different user model (short-term and long-term model) are used to classify stories to present to users: if the first model fails, the second is used to gain the system's goal.

In this direction, single-user model could be useful both, to extrapolate common paths (a group model) and characterze members inside the group if it needs.

GAS system should be able to learn by the implicit and repeated navigation of some sources. In such a way it is able to offer and suggest the paths and news to each participant as fruitfully experience by others without interfering with the normal navigation of each member. This could be used for example, to rearrange the presentation of popular (among group members) Web sites so that they are presented according to what are the navigation criteria and patterns followed by the group that is, as the product of people's activities in an information space[11].

With Group adaptivity, problems arise also in preserving a part of the behavior from the other users in the same group while, at the same time, the system must be able to share the behavior that is useful for the group. Members should be able to provide explicit indications to the GAS, if desired, but the goal is to provide an implicit adaptation to group's behavior.

3.2   Tools and Techniques

Adapting Web navigation to a group is, indeed, challenging because (1) the system must take into account both group and user characteristics and (2) because of the huge amount of information available on Web. User-adaptive characteristics are usually obtained generating dynamic content, this is accomplished using CGI-BIN (Common Gateway Interface) or other server-side scripts that manipulate contents according to a relationship between knowledge base and user model. But, adaptive groups cannot be implemented on server side: we want deal the information on the Web as the resource available to group, and it is not realistic to implement adaptive group on any Web server on the net. Moreover group's privacy is one of basic requirements for such systems. Group privacy can not be obtained easily if the group data are stored on the servers. Furthermore it is possible that the sources are not interesting in knowing users needs.

Naturally, group modeling cannot be implemented on client-side, because it is difficult to catch data from different clients. Furthermore each client should sustain additional computation and communication load.

As a result, a group-model engine and the information management must be programmed proxy-side. Proxy programming means to put and intermediary program beetwen clients and servers. Proxy program knows the client/server protocol and can manipulate the exchanged information during the transactions. Proxy program is not constrained to run on a specified location, it can be anywhere[4] along the information stream. It can resolves the users' privacy issues, related to information sources, in fact proxy can be located nearby the clients and adaptive group can be obtained on it. Proxy programming also enables synchronous navigation on the Web: in fact, proxy could hold persistent[1] communication among users, by traslating or interpreting new protocols, to enable users to communicate by synchronous systems.

GASs could be implemented using WBI [3] framework developed by IBM. The IBM research team has proposed a new approach to programming Web applications that augments Web's computational power, its flexibility, and the programmers productivity.

Intermediaries are new places for producing and manipulating Web's data[3], that lie along the path of a Web transaction. IBM team has implemented an architecture for building intermediaries, enabling the construction of several applications, for example, personal histories, password management, image distillation, collaborative filtering and so on. It is hence reasonable to use this philosophy to realize systems that offer group adaptive functionality. WBI is an HTTP request processor that receives the users requests and produces or filters the responses to these requests. How it produces these responses is completely under the control of the programmer and system administrator.

3.3   Scenarios and Applications for Group Adaptive Systems

In this section we describe some application fields where the group adaptivity can be applied successful. It is interesting to study how a GA system could be applied in an educational context. We proposed a CSCW system [1] for distance learning. It is a WWW-based multi-user environment that supports synchronous communication among participants to a virtual classroom. Group modeling could be added to this system. The group model could give a representation of the collective knowledge that can be used by teacher to extrapolate evaluations on knowledge level of a class. Furthermore collaborative navigation allows students browsing the course material basing its presentation on the group's knowledge level.

Group adaptive navigation could be useful for research teams that need exchange data about information and news discovered on the net. Team members could be made aware of the browsing activities of group automatically when they navigate sources which group is interested. The annotation of contents anyone discover can provide awareness about their activities and avoid members' team to communicate explicitly where a document can be found or which news are important for each other. Collective navigation can provide a common view of the team environment, save time they spend to search information and increase awareness on their activity.

On one hand Group Adaptive features can be useful in Electronic Commerce. For example, a GAS system could allow collective navigation through an electronic store. Customers could be interested in shop together, watch the same goods at the same time and exchange advice on the purchases, as well as customers could be interested in see (in some way) other shoppers moving in the store or setting agents to "talk to" personnel of the store[14]. Another example

---

[1] HTTP does not allow this

sees an electronic store as a recommender system[14]: pointing customers toward goods that others bought.

From another perspective EC group could allow to keep informed all employees of a business-to-business commercial relationship about purchases they make, or companies would like to find an open and "intelligent" system where to buy and sell.

References

1. Barra M., Cattaneo G., Garofalo V., Ferraro Petrillo U., Rossi C., Scarano V.: "Teach++: A Cooperative Distance Learning and Teaching Environment". In Proc. of ACM Symp. on Applied Computing. March 19-21, 2000. Villa Olmo, Como, Italy.
2. Barra M., Cattaneo G., Negro A., Scarano V.: "Symmetric Adaptive Customer Modeling in an Electronic Store". In Proc. of 3th IEEE Symp. on Computers and Communications (ISCC), Athens (Greece), July 1998.
3. Barrett R., Maglio P.: "Intermediaries: New Places for Producing and Manipulating Web Content". In Proc. of the 7th International WWW Conference.
4. Barrett R., Maglio P.: "WebPlaces: Adding people to the Web." Poster at 8th International WWW Conference.
5. Bentley R., Busbach U., Sikkel K.: "The Architecture of the BSCW Shared Workspace System". In Proc. of ERCIM workshop on CSCW and the Web. Sankt Augustin, Germany, Feb. 1996.
6. Berners-Lee T., Cailliau R., Groff J.F.: "The World Wide Web". Computer Networks and ISDN Systems, Nov. 1992, vol.25 (no.4-5), 45-49.
7. Brusilovsky P., Eklund J., Schwarz E.: "Web-based education for all: A tool for developing adaptive courseware. Computer Networks and ISDN Systems. In Proc. of 7th International WWW Conference, 14-18 April 1998.
8. Brusilovsky P.: "Adaptive Educational Systems on the WWW: A Review of Available Technologies". In Proc. of Workshop "WWW-Based Tutoring" at ITS'98, S. Antonio, TX, August 16-19, 1998.
9. De Bra P., Calvi L.: "AHA: a Generic Adaptive Hypermedia System". In Proc. of HYPERTEXT'98 2nd Workshop on Adaptive Hypertext and Hypermedia. Pittsburgh, USA, June 20-24, 1998.
10. Billsus D., Pazzani M. "A Hybrid User Model for News Story Classification". In Proc of the Seventh International Conference on User Modeling (UM '99), Banff, Canada 1999.
11. Dieberger A. "Social Connotations of space in the Design for Virtual Communities and Social Navigation". In the CSCW. Springer Verlag 1998.
12. Dix A.: "Challenges and Perspectives for Cooperative Work on the Web". In Proc. of the ERCIM workshop on CSCW and the Web. Sankt Augustin, Germany, 1996.
13. Dovgiallo A., Bykov V., Kolos V., Kudrjavtseva S., Tsybenko Y., Vlasenko N.: "WWW based distance course on the Communication and Information Technology".
14. Murno A. J., Hook K., Benyon D.: "Computer Supported Cooperative Work. Social Navigation of Information Space." Springer-Verlag Great Britain 1999.
15. Negro A., Scarano V., Simari R.: "User Adaptivity on WWW through CHEOPS". In Proc. of 2nd Workshop on Adaptive Hypertext and Hypermedia, in conjunction with HYPERTEXT '98 (Pittsburgh, PA, USA, June 20-24, 1998)
16. Streitz N., Haake J., Hannemann J., Lemke A., Schuler W., Schutt H., Thuring M.: "SEPIA: a cooperative hypermedia authoring environment". In Proc. of ECHT '92, 4th ACM European Conference on Hypertext, Milan (Italy), pp. 11-22, 1992.

17. TeamWave Software Ltd.: "Collaborative Education with TeamWave Workplace." http://www.teamwave.com/. Calgary, Alberta Canada 1998.
18. Walther M.: "Supporting Development of Synchronous Collaboration Tools on the Web with GroCo". In Proc. of the ERCIM workshop on CSCW and the Web. Sankt Augustin, Germany, February 1996.
19. Yeh P., Chen B., Lai M., Yuan S.: "Synchronous Navigation Control for Distance Learning on the Web". In Proc. of 5th Intern. WWW Conference, 1996.

Open Multimedia Environment to Retrieve and Organise Documents: An Adaptive Web-Based IR System in the Field of Textile and Clothing Industry

Cristiano Chesi and Francesca Rizzo

University of Siena
chesi@media.unisi.it - francy@media.unisi.it

Abstract. Computer based information repositories are becoming larger and more diverse. In this context the need for an effective information retrieval system is related not only to the efficiency of the retrieval process but also to its compatibility to support information seekers during a typical problem solving activity (Marchionini 1995). OMERO project (national research project, n. 41902) perspective considers information seeking as a problem solving activity (Rumiati 1990) that depends on communication acts.

Introduction

The main purpose of OMERO is to support working people with different roles in the field of textile and clothing industry, making them able to retrieve, modify, and share useful information. The project is specifically aimed at designing, developing and testing an information system to satisfy the textile and clothing operator's needs of knowledge through an usable tool supporting effective and intelligent information searching processes.

The core system is composed by an expert system with a large knowledge base managed by an ontological conceptual network. To retrieve relevant information from the system, the user has to formulate a question with natural verbal expressions (OMERO provides a module to analyse the complex nominal phrases) and the system, using a previously created user-model, starts a dialogue to focus upon the problem by mapping the related data present in the conceptual network with the interests of the user in a semantic way (see fig. 1).

The identification of a relevant node or an area of nodes brings the system to present an editable dossier of text documents, charts, images, which are related to the search space identified.

The most relevant aspects of the project reside in the adaptation to the specific user's information needs, which presents a selective view of the knowledge tree and of the search graph useful to retrieve and share the relevant expert information inside OMERO.

P. Brusilovsky, O. Stock, C. Strapparava (Eds.): AH 2000, LNCS 1892, pp. 403-408, 2000.

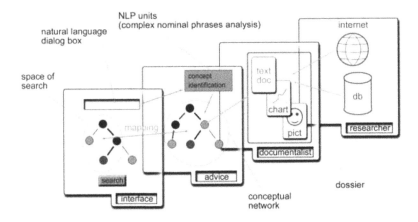

natural language
dialog box

NLP units
(complex nominal phrases analysis)

internet

space of
search

concept
identification

text
doc

db

chart

mapping

pict

researcher

documentalist

search

advice

dossier

interface

conceptual
network

Fig. 1. System architecture

Searching for Information in a Specific Field

It is clear that the complexity and the huge amount of every kind of information in the Internet make useful an adaptation of research systems to the needs of the specific users, to retrieve only the information relevant to them. Dealing with a system oriented to a small and specific domain we have also to solve a similar problem of adaptability: an expert user requires an answer to very precise questions about his work and the answer must be properly related to his own knowledge.

The OMERO system design takes place in the framework of the User Centred Design (UCD) approach. This is a dynamic and iterative method of design-evaluation and redesign that aims to achieve a usable system. The UCD approach consists of four principal phases: definition of user requirement, prototyping, design and evaluation. Currently we are engaged in the first step.

The first strategy that we have applied to design our information retrieval system has been the analysis (by interviews) of information, observing the behaviour of people in the real problem-solving context in which their information needs are created. This technique of inquiry helped us to outline some general guidelines for user requirements. The Emilia Romagna region currently represents one of the major clothing and textile districts in Italy. For this reason public administration has decided to finance an information service centre in this field. The Citer service centre is able to produce and to make available standard information regarding fashion trend, marketing and technologies for T/C working context. In fact Citer's users often know what information they need; in this case users can be helped immediately through the information retrieval process.

There are many cases in which the user does not know what he is searching for. In this case information seeking becomes a problem solving activity. For the users in this field, information seeking is an iterative process of communication developed with a human operator of a service centre. This process can be briefly described as follows:

The first step is characterised for general awareness of the knowledge of problem domain. For this purpose some analysts have listed eight knowledge categories related to the searching process in the textile and clothing industry: planning and strategic control; design, development and research; administration and finance; provisioning; logistics; production; marketing; human resources. But with an initial enquiry we have seen that the user search strategy through these previous categories is chaotic and non-sequential. In addition the user often shows that he is not fully aware of his goal. In this phase, a human operator helps the client to understand his problem through a process of question and answer that supports the identification of possible information source required to satisfy the user's need. The human operator knowledge makes available a better possible solution for typical problems (i.e. information about spring-summer trend for women), contingent problems (i.e. I need information's about behaviour and performance of competitors) or with identification of obscure problems (i.e. how can I improve in my field?).

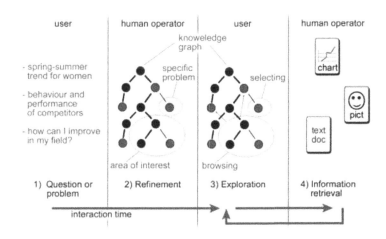

Fig. 2. Dialogue user - human operator

Alternative Approach to Information Retrieval

To support the process of Information Retrieval the most traditional search engines implement two kinds of strategy:
1) keyword-based approach, in which some relevant keywords can be combined with boolean operators and the research works on pre-indexed documents in a database;
2) hierarchical indices approach, in which the user can browse a classification tree to find the information sources pre-classified in the database

The first approach can be improved by the techniques of Information Filtering or Information Extraction (Basili R. and Ciravegna F. 1999) that serve to cover the deficiencies of vagueness and inaccuracy of traditional approach by a linguistic analysis finalised to find particular information in a relevant specified context (i.e. search information about trading on-line in a mailing list).

These techniques, when the template of research is clearly specified, ensure efficient results, despite flexibility or refinability in the definition of special information contexts that differ from the originally template.

Against this weakness of adaptability web agents systems are largely employed; their task is to prevent user moves and understand his undeclared information needs by simply tracking his choices. Agents often work in a parallel and independent way to that of the user, trying to combine the queries of the user in an original manner in order to find new interesting information (Lesnick and Moore 1997, Perkowitz, Dorenbos, Etzioni and Weld 1997).

In the first case (Information Filtering, Information Extraction etc.) we have identified three weak points:

1) the necessity of a robust tool for language processing difficulty adaptable to different domains;

2) the considerable time required to process the texts;

3) the high probability to make mistakes and to restart the interaction when the domain of research is high variable and the typical pattern of information presentation is difficult to define.

For these aspects we have renounced to use only the strongest version of this approach. We believe, anyway, that some techniques employed in Information Extraction, like analysis of complex nominal phrases (we dispose of a exhaustive lexical database rich of terms and phrases specifics of the T/C field), and the possibility to interact overtly with the own knowledge representation tree, may play a crucial role in the process of information seeking and in the refinement of user query.

Otherwise, in the second case (Agents Systems), the obscure way to control the search process and the difficult to interact explicitly with the agents or with a semiautonomous component of the system, have persuaded us to abandon this other way to pursue the adaptability of the system. Fleming and Cohen (1999), in accordance with this conclusion, note that:

1) in ambiguous situations the agents systems do not make clear choices;

2) the user often does not understand the choices of agents owing to a lack of communication between user and agents;

3) the large amount of interactions to be analysed by the agents slowed down the memory-based learning.

We think that the best solution to elicit the user's knowledge in addition to realize overtly the dialogue with the system is to show clearly the knowledge mapping that the system made, tracking the user's interaction and to permit him to modify the search/knowledge representation tree.

Adaptive Approach Used in OMERO

To satisfy heterogeneous needs and to support an efficient interaction with OMERO expert system we have chosen an adaptive design approach based on User Centred

Design (Norman 1988, 1993) guidelines. In our approach adaptability is considered a key characteristic (Shneiderman 1992) of computer technology that allows information seeker to use an electronic environment in a way which emulates the interaction with human sources of information. The communication channel between the user and the system is the interface. Our goal is to design a usable interface (Redmand-Pyle 1995) that facilitates the flow of messages. To implement such an interface a model of information (Jonson-Laird 1983) seeking must be taken as the basis of the design process.

The adaptive features of system are based on the identification of user profiles. These profiles rise from three categories of information collected by the system about the user:

1. Navigation preferences
- preferences about format and position of information in the interface
- history of previous interactions with the system

2. Cognitive map of user's knowledge
- user's specific interests in the field of textile and clothing
- user's information needs (typical Vs contingent)
- user's typical modality of manipulation and sharing information

3. General information about user
- role and position in the enterprise
- working area
- production area of enterprise
- geographic location of enterprise

Using this profile OMERO maps the knowledge tree in different ways for different users to reinforce some connections between areas and inhibit others.

We have chosen to combine natural language processing tools with a direct manipulation interface to facilitate and improve the performance of the user in the refinement of queries and during the editing of dossier given in answer by the system.

The user will start the interaction with an explicit question composed by a combination of complex nominal phrases (i.e. "China's market", " production of wool pullovers") and proceed to a direct browsing of knowledge tree give from the answer of the system.

Conclusion

Until now our work has investigated different interaction styles:

1. direct manipulation of knowledge categories, elicited from information seekers
2. process of searching through a natural language interaction with a system
3. a combination of the two previous strategies

As previous works show (Bagnasco and al. 1999, De Angeli and al. 1998), the third style is a powerful way to solve complex and articulated research problems in very specific fields.

From this way the possibilities to support users in identification of information needs are improved using, in addition to the direct manipulation of categories and a natural language understanding approach, an iterative dialogue starting up from a specific user profile, mapping the user's knowledge with that of expert system.

References

Bagnasco C., Cappelli A., Magnini B., Zamatteo D. (1999) Accesso in linguaggio naturale ai dati della Pubblica Amministrazione: il sistema TAMIC-P. In Proceedings of AIIA-99, Sesto Congresso dell'Associazione Italiana per l'Intelligenza Artificiale, Bologna

Basili R., Ciravegna F. (1999) Introduzione all'estrazione di informazioni da testi Tutorial of AIIA-99. Sesto Congresso della Associazione Italiana per l'Intelligenza Artificiale, Bologna

De Angeli A., Magnini B, Zancanaro M. (1998) Naturally Constraining Natural Language: a Case Study for an Information Access System. ITC-Irst Technical Report, Trento

Fleming M., Cohen R. (1999) User Modelling in the Design of Interactive Interface Agents. UM99 User Modeling, proceedings of the 7th International Conference edited by Judy Kay, Springer Verlag, Udine

Marchionini G. M., (1995) Information Seeking in Electronic Environments. Cambridge University Press, Cambridge, Eng.

Norman D. A. (1988) The psychology of everyday things. Basic Book Publisher, New York

Norman D. A. (1993) Things that make us smart. Addison Wesley, New York

Perkowitz M., Dorenbos R., Etzioni O., Weld D. (1997) Learning to understand Information on the Internet: An example-based Approach. Kluwer Accademic Publisher, Boston

Jonson - Laird P. (1983) Mental models. Harvard University Press, Cambridge, MA

Redmand-Pyle, D. (1995) Graphical user interface design and evaluation (guide): a practical process. Redwood Books, Trowbridge

Rumiati R. (1990) Giudizio e decisione. Il Mulino, Milano

Shneiderman B. (1992) Designing the user interface: strategies for effective human computer interaction. Addison - Wesley Publishing Company, Inc., Reading, MA

Researching Adaptive Instruction

Juan E. Gilbert[1] and Chia Y. Han[2]

[1] Auburn University, Department of Computer Science and Software Engineering,
Auburn, AL 36849-5347 U.S.A.
juan.gilbert@acm.org
[2] University of Cincinnati, Department of ECECS, 814 Rhodes Hall, PO Box 210030,
Cincinnati OH 45221-0030, U.S.A.
chia.han@uc.edu

Abstract. Human tutors have the ability to explain concepts several different ways using multiple instruction methods. Typically, instruction methods are used when students are having difficulty learning a concept. Intelligent tutoring systems are expert systems[5] where the expert is a tutor. Ideally, an intelligent tutoring system should have the ability to explain concepts several different ways using a knowledge base of multiple instruction methods[3,4,6,7]. The technique of providing instruction using multiple instruction methods during a single tutoring session is "Adaptive Instruction". An intelligent tutoring system that provides adaptive instruction has been developed, Arthur[2]. Arthur has been used in a research experiment with human subjects. The results of this experiment are discussed in the section below.

1 Introduction

In a traditional lecture based classroom, there is a one to many (denoted 1-M) relationship between the instructor and students, one instructor and many students. In the tutoring environment, there is a one to one (denoted 1-1) relationship between the instructor/tutor and the student. Arthur's design changes this relationship to a many to one (M-1) relationship. The system provides many instructors, or instruction methods, to each student. Imagine a classroom where there is only one student and several instructors. Each instructor is an expert on the subject matter being taught, yet each instructor teaches the material using a different instruction method. This explanation describes Arthur's pedagogical motivation, which is to provide multiple instruction methods for each learner. These instruction methods are kept in an instruction repository. The instruction repository is a collection of all the instruction methods that Arthur knows. Each instruction method is contributed by an expert in the subject that is to be taught. Arthur defines a set of components that make the M-1 model possible.

Arthur is an intelligent tutoring system that consists of four major software components. Each component may consists of sub-components, but the four major software components clearly define Arthur. The first component is the client interface. The client interface is a Java applet that executes inside the learner's Web browser. The client interface is responsible for delivering instructional content to the learner from

P. Brusilovsky, O. Stock, C. Strapparava (Eds.): AH 2000, LNCS 1892, pp. 409–414, 2000.

the Web server. The client interface also has the responsibility of establishing a network connection with the second component, the server process. The server process is a Java application that is used to establish initial contact with the client interface across a predefined network socket port. Once these two components shake hands, the server process will spawn a new process, which is the third component. The new process is a Java agent-thread process which is created as the primary point of communication with the client interface. All communication with the client interface is passed from the server process to the newly created agent-thread process. The agent-thread process makes all of Arthur's decisions by accessing a database. The database is the final component, which serves as the primary knowledge base for Arthur. The database is a relational database that supports Java database connectivity (JDBC). The JDBC is a Type I - 3 tier approach. This approach is bandwidth friendly. It keeps the client side thin with respect to the size of data that has to be downloaded upon login. Therefore, Arthur can be defined as a Web based intelligent tutoring system that consists of four major software components, client interface, server process, agent-thread process and the database.

Other aspects of the implementation such as IFAQ can be found in [2]. The purpose of this paper is to discuss the research experiment and the data results, which can be found below.

2 Research Experiment

The goal of the research experiment is to evaluate Arthur with respect to learner outcomes. Learner outcomes will provide the main data points for evaluation. Arthur's goal is to accommodate learning style[1] by providing multiple instruction methods. In order for a student to advance through the system, the student must demonstrate concept competency at a level of 80% or better[2]. If a student completes the course, it is understood that the student comprehends the subject matter at a level of 80% or better based upon their quiz performance. The learner outcomes are predetermined based upon this criteria of 80% or better, therefore, success will be observed with respect to completion rate of the course material. Students that complete the course or those that demonstrate significant progress towards the completion of the course, will be successes. This type of experiment has a strong focus on the subjects. Therefore, the demographics of the subjects are extremely important.

2.1 Subjects

There were a total of 89 students that participated in the experiment. The students were all registered for an introductory course in programming using C++ taught in a traditional lab/lecture environment. Their participation in the experiment was strictly voluntary. The students were taking the course for college credit with frequent use of the Web. The first half of the course covered C++ through arrays and functions. After these topics, the students were given an examination over C++ through arrays and functions. As an extra credit assignment, the students were allowed to learn C++

pointers using Arthur via the Web. This portion of the class was the beginning of the experiment. The students were given 23 days to complete the online lesson. The student's were engineering, management information systems and computer science majors ranging from freshmen to seniors. The experiment consisted of several different instruction methods.

2.2 Pedagogy

The experiment consisted of seven different instruction methods. The instruction methods were:

- Text (Explanation First) text and code similar to a book.
- Text (Example First) text and code similar to a book.
- Audio (Explanation First) text, code and streaming audio similar to a lecture.
- Audio (Example First) text, code and streaming audio similar to a lecture.
- Visual (Explanation First) text, code and picture illustrations.
- Visual (Example First) text, code and picture illustrations.
- Hands On (Example First) text, code, audio, pictures and fill in the blank code samples.

Each instruction method covered five different concepts on C++ pointers. The concepts were:

0. Pointers (Introduction)
1. Pointers as Constants and Parameters
2. Pointers and Arrays
3. Pointers and Strings
4. Pointers and Strings (array of pointers and the string library)

These concepts were delivered using Arthur as specified in [2] without the automatic adaptive instruction selection. In other words, the students were given the freedom to choose from one of the seven instruction methods when their evaluation was below 80% as opposed to the system selecting the next instruction method. Under these circumstances, a research experiment was conducted and the data results are reported below.

3 Data Results

The experiment was conducted over the course of 23 days. One student completed the course in 4.2 days, while another student completed the course in 21.3 days. The average days to completion for all students was 11.39 days with a median of 10.1 days. On the last day of the experiment, the distribution of students per concept can be found in Fig. 1. Along the bottom of Fig. 1, each concept is given a number as described in the previous section, (2.2 Pedagogy). The 5 under the red bar represents the students that completed the course. In the end, there were 64 students that completed the course, 72%. Notice that concept 2, "Pointers and Arrays", has no students. With this division in the student distribution, students were classified into three groups. Group C, students that completed the course, Group B, students that ended the course beyond concept 2, "Pointers and Arrays", but did not complete the course, and Group A, students that ended the course before concept 2. Group A contained 16 students and Group B contained 9 students.

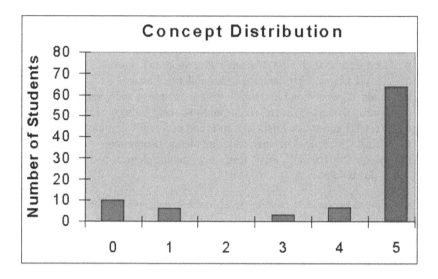

Fig. 1. Student distribution at the end of the course.

Given these groups, the obvious question was asked, "Why didn't the students in Group A and Group B complete the course?" At the end of each concept, the students were given an end of concept quiz as a means of evaluating the student's performance. For the concepts "Pointers and Strings" and "Pointers and Strings (array of pointers and the string library)" the average grades were 81.1% and 80.5%, respectively. Given these scores, it is very likely that if the students in Group B were given more time to complete the course, they would have joined Group C. Under this assumption, the number of students in Group C would increase to 73 yielding a 82% completion rate. The same principal could apply to some students in Group A, but that is not very likely. As a result, other data points were needed to explain their poor performance.

3.1 Performance Tracking

Upon system login, each student was asked to enter their mood and motivation on a scale ranging from good to bad where -2 was bad and 2 was good. Table 1 contains the average mood and motivation for Group A versus Groups B and C combined. Group B was combined with Group C because these students made it pass the concept Pointers and Arrays where Group A did not. The average mood and motivation for Group A in both cases was negative versus a positive mood and motivation for Groups B and C combined. At a first glance, it appears that Group A was obviously less motivated that Groups B and C combined, but when a t-distribution significance test was executed on this data, no significant difference was found. This may be due to the large difference in sample sizes between the two groups.

Table 1. Average mood and motivation.

Group	Mood	Motivation
A	-0.13	-0.03
B & C	0.04	0.10

After further investigation, it was observed that the students in Group A viewed 54.2 pages of material. The students in Groups B and C on the average viewed 59.6 pages of material through the first two concepts. This observation supports the argument that the students in Group A were not motivated as well. Yet again, when a t-distribution significance test was executed, there was no significance difference found. Finally, the students in Group A were surveyed and asked , "Give your best explanation as to WHY you didn't complete the course". The responses were overwhelmingly consistent. The students admitted to one or more of the following:

- Technical difficulties with their home computer.
- Lack of motivation.
- Insufficient effort to review the material.
- Insufficient time allocation due to other classes.

After the survey, the results were confirmed. The students in Group A did not put forth an effort to complete the lesson on pointers. With this result, the experiment was viewed as a success. The experiment also provided interesting data with respect to repetition and instruction methods.

On the average, when students passed any given concept, it took the student 1.72 attempts. This data point illustrates the use of repetition before passing any given concept. Within those 1.72 repetitions, 1.42 different instruction methods were used. In other words, students preferred to have concepts explained using a different instruction method when the concept needed to be repeated. Recall, that in this experiment, the students were given the freedom to choose instruction methods. With this final data point, the experiment was summarized.

4 Conclusion

This experiment was the first phase of a two part experiment. Phase I of this experiment was conducted in the absence of automatic adaptive instruction. The students were given the freedom to select instruction methods. Phase II of the experiment will be conducting using the automatic adaptive instruction. The system will select the instruction methods automatically. Phase I was viewed as a success in that the learner outcomes were successful. Recall that Arthur forces students to perform at a level of 80% or better before those students can advance to the next concept. In this experiment 64 out of 89, 72%, students completed the lesson on pointers within 23 days. It is very likely that the 9 students from Group B would have completed the lesson if given more time. Also, the students were found to use different instruction methods when concepts needed to be repeated. This observation supports the use of adaptive instruction throughout the course of instruction from beginning to end.

Phase II of this experiment will be conducted teaching a lesson on Planck's Constant from Physics. The data findings from Phase II will be compared to Phase I. Success will be determined with respect to learner outcomes and distribution.

References

1. Dunn, K. and Dunn, R. Teaching students through their individual learning styles: A practical approach. Reston, VA: Reston Publishing (1978)
2. Gilbert, J. E. & Han, C. Y. Adapting Instruction in Search of "A Significant Difference". Journal of Network and Computing Applications, 22, 3 (1999)
3. Major, N. REDEEM: Creating Reusable Intelligent Courseware. In Proc. of AI-ED 95, Washington, D.C., August, (1995)
4. Ohlsson, S. Some Principles of Intelligent Tutoring. In Lawler & Yazdani (Eds.), Artificial Intelligence and Education, Volume 1. Ablex: Norwood, NJ (1987)
5. Russell, S., & Norvig, P., Artificial Intelligence A Modern Approach. (p. 151). NJ:Prentice Hall (1995)
6. Spensley, F., Elsom-Cook, M., Byerley, P., Brooks, P., Federici, M. and Scaroni, C. "Using multiple teaching strategies in an ITS," in Frasson, C. and Gauthier, G. (eds.),Intelligent Tutoring Systems: At the crossroads of Artificial Intelligence and Education. Norwood, NJ: Ablex (1990)
7. Van Marcke, K. Instructional Expertise. In Frasson, C., Gauthier, G., & McCalla, G.I. (Eds.) Procs. of Intelligent Tutoring Systems '92. Springer Verlag, Berlin (1992)

A Modular Approach for User Modelling

Ilaria Torre

Dipartimento di Informatica - Università di Torino
Corso Svizzera 185 - 10149 Torino (Italy)
ila.torre@di.unito.it

Abstract. Adaptive hypermedia systems are spreading widely in these last years, but each application uses its own models and techniques. What I am studying is the possibility of developing a framework for user modelling in adaptive systems and in particular of creating a library of stereotypes for representing the different dimensions of the user models.

1   Introduction

Differently from other concepts and labels, *adaptivity* has the peculiarity that it does not pertain a specific type of application but it is rather a modus operandi that may concern any application that interacts with a human or software agent. In fact, if we regard the latter as a system having its own goals and thus some interests that it pursues, then an adaptive application may exploit these interests and goals to satisfy the needs of the software agent.

Providing the "right" service (the "right" pieces of information) in the "right" way and at the "right" time is the main goal of an adaptive system. However, defining what "right" means in these contexts is a difficult task. This difficulty (ambiguity) is the main problem of adaptive systems in general and of adaptive hypermedia in particular. In the latter, in fact, the leverage to infer the model and the goals of a user is limited and also the range of alternative forms of personalization is restricted (as regards what has to be shown and/or hidden and how the user can be guided in the navigation). And even though a "correct" model is available and "correct" strategies for extracting information are used, there are still other fundamental problems such as: how to avoid that the choices of the system, tailored to the needs of the user, block her/his curiosity and stimuli for innovation and discovery? How to involve the user in the personalization process, that is: should all the choices be made without involving her/him or should the user be active in the process of selecting the service to be provided (or the pieces of information to be presented), or finally should adaptation be a co-operative process? How and to what extent should the user be allowed to access/inspect/modify her/his model?

The approach to these problems depends only partially on the technologies that are adopted while it is strictly dependent on the psychological and cognitive choices that impact the various phases of the process: how data are gathered from a user, how the user model is built, how the feedbacks from the user are collected and used to update (revise) her/his model, which features of the user model are related to the type and

P. Brusilovsky, O. Stock, C. Strapparava (Eds.): AH 2000, LNCS 1892, pp. 415-420, 2000.

amount of information to be presented and to the form of the presentation. The various applications in the literature faced these problems using different strategies and formalisms, depending on aspects such as the application task (and domain), the goals of the system, etc.

Goal. The goal of my research work is to study whether it is possible to abstract from specific application tasks and domains in order to build a reference framework for user modelling in adaptive systems. My study will first focus on the attempt to define: (i) a precise classification of application tasks and domain, (ii) a taxonomy of goals and (generic) sub-goals for adaptive systems and (iii) a set of conceptual dimensions for user modelling derived from the previous steps. Then I will concentrate on studying and relating these dimensions to create an ontology for user modelling, separating the dimensions that are general and may be related to different goals, tasks and domains from those that are more specific and task or domain dependent. The framework resulting from this work could have a significant impact on the construction of adaptive systems. On the one hand, it could simplify the analysis that has to be performed when designing a new application, providing guidelines to analyse the goals and the application task and domain and then suggesting the dimensions of user modelling that are most relevant. On the other hand, the modularity of the framework could allow the re-use of user modelling components across different applications.

Methodology. In order to investigate the possibility of building the framework mentioned above, I will start from Brusilovsky's classification of adaptive hypermedia [3] (and the subsequent analysis by De Bra [4]), focusing on the specific topic of the creation and management of the user model and I will perform a systematic analysis of adaptive systems with the aim of building the ontology discussed above. According to the terminology in [3], this will mean focusing on defining a correlation between: (i) "what features of the user are used as a source of adaptation" and (ii) "where adaptive hypermedia can be helpful" and the "adaptation goals". Instead, the criteria concerning the strategies for adapting the presentation ("what can be adapted" in [3]) will not be the focus of this analysis.

The bottom-up approach will start from an analysis of specific adaptive systems, in different tasks. This will involve both the design of adaptive applications and the analysis of systems described in the literature and implemented in the field.

The dimensions that are relevant in user modelling will emerge from such a study and will be progressively refined and aggregated. Each dimension will partition the population of users into classes that will be described using stereotypes [5][6], as it is common in many systems. I will adopt a standard formalism in which each stereotype is formed by a set of slots (corresponding to features of the user) and each slot contains a set of pairs <linguistic value (of the feature), probability (of the linguistic value of the feature given the stereotype)>.

Thus, besides the framework, one of the results of my work will be the creation of a library of stereotypes, grouped into families according to the conceptual dimensions. For each family, a set of metadata will provide information on the stereotypes in the family, about their generality and about the adaptation goals and application tasks/domains for which the family is relevant. It is well known that stereotypes are not sufficient for all aspects of user modelling; therefore, while in the first phase of my work I am concentrating on this formalisms, in a second phase I will also consider other formalisms that are more suitable for capturing dynamic aspects of user modelling (as, for example, rules for updating/refining the user model after tracking the user's behaviour).

2 Conceptual Dimensions in User Modelling

As noticed above, the dimensions that are relevant in a user model are strongly related to the *application task* and to the *specific goals of the adaptive system*. Therefore, it is necessary to analyse more deeply these two aspects to determine the dimensions in a precise way. As regards the former, it is important to isolate specific application domains and features for each task; as regards the latter, it is fundamental to decompose the goal of a system into sub-goals which may be intermediate goals or goals related to a specific functionality of the overall system.

The approach I am experimenting in my research work is that of building some matrices having on one of the axes the goals and sub-goals of the adaptive system and on the other the specific features of the application tasks and domains. Then each entry, corresponding to a specific row and column, describes in a precise way the characteristics of a specific adaptive application, and thus, for each entry, one can isolate the relevant dimensions as regards user modelling.

The most interesting consideration that emerged from a first analysis is that while the high-level goals of a system are related to the application context, the sub-goals are often common to many applications and thus the dimensions of user modelling related to these sub-goals can be re-used for different tasks and applications. An example of a sub-goal (function) that is common to all the application domains that I analysed up to now (and that I will mention later) is that one of offering users the possibility of getting more information about an item. This sub-goal is strictly related to a dimension of user modelling: the level of receptivity of the user, which is thus common to many applications.

An interesting direction for future research is thus the study of the sub-goals mentioned above, in order to analyse them precisely, trying to make them generic and then to isolate a structured library of goals and of the corresponding dimensions for user modelling. As regards the high-level goals and application domains, on the other hand, the analysis up to now does not evidence strict correlations with user modelling dimensions. However, the use of different application domains is important to weigh the contribution of different user modelling dimensions that, although common to a particular task may have different relevance in the different domains.

Let me consider an example. In a recommender system the high level goal could be selling some product or service, providing recommendations (with the aim of selling something) or providing advice or comparative information. At a deeper level the goal of selling can be specialised distinguishing between the goals of leading the user to an "impulsive" purchase or to a "rational" one. In this latter case a sub-goal will be the presentation of detailed information and so forth. As regards the application domain, a first distinction is the one related to the type of product that is sold (e.g., a product of mass market vs. a sophisticated and complex product requiring configuration or special demonstrations and assistance). A second distinction is the one concerning the market to which the product is directed (e.g., business to business or business to consumer).

In a matrix like the one discussed above, for example we could have an entry corresponding to the (sub)goal of leading the user to an "impulse purchase" and to the domain feature "mass market product". The most relevant user modelling dimension associated with such an entry is the one concerning the "life-style" of the users, while other dimensions such as the user expertise or experience are less relevant. Having a matrix providing this information is very useful, allowing the designer to re-use the user modelling knowledge bases in the library for different recommender systems and to decide the specific relevance of each one of the selected dimensions.

In conclusion, I report in the following a first classification of the application tasks that I defined starting from the adaptive hypermedia in the literature (including those that we are designing and that we plan to deign):

- recommender systems (e.g., e-commerce, advertisement systems, etc.);
- access to information sources (e.g., news servers, information retrieval);
- education systems;
- decision support systems (e.g., trading on line);
- applications for co-operative work.

3   Adaptive News Servers

The first task that I considered is that of "adaptive news servers"; this work led to the design and implementation of a prototype personalized newspaper [1][2].

Referring to the previous methodology of classification, the system presents the following *domain features*: the service deals with large amounts of information (news), on different topics (organized in a hierarchy of sections), including very detailed pieces of information and various kinds of links between different pieces. The *goal* of the system is that of providing personalized views of the sections and subsections and of the specific news. This involves selecting and ordering sections and subsections and presenting news items at the detail level which is appropriate for each specific user. These goals distinguish, in my view, adaptive news server from adaptive information retrieval (which are separate sub-tasks in the matrices on which I am working); in the latter, in fact, the user has an active role (searching for some specific information) and the system provides a personalized answer to such a need (selecting the appropriate pieces of information).

Three dimensions emerged as relevant for user modelling in this application: the interests of the user, her/his expertise, her/his receptivity. Dealing with interests is fundamental for the goal of selecting the sections/subsections that are most relevant for the user. Receptivity is critical for deciding the appropriate detail level and for tailoring the presentation to the capability of the user (i.e., for deciding the amount of information that (s)he can read/process). This dimension allows one to decide how many (sub)sections must be presented and how many details should be provided for news items. The second dimension (expertise) is in some sense intermediate between the other two, allowing one to vary the detail level in different sub(sections). For example, if the user is very interested in a topic (corresponding to a (sub)section), has medium receptivity but limited expertise, then the presentation will not be very detailed but the (sub)section will be put in a prominent position among the other ones.

As noticed in the paragraph concerning methodology, the knowledge regarding each dimension is represented using stereotypes which relate classificatory features with predictions concerning the dimension. Thus the news server application is based on the following three families of stereotypes:

Interests: this family of stereotypes classifies the users according to their interests in the topics of the (sub)sections of the news server. Starting from classificatory data such as the age, gender, type and field of work, the scope of the connection (e.g., work or personal reasons), the stereotypes make a prediction on the interest level (which may be "high", "medium", "low" or "null") in the topic of each (sub)section.

Expertise: these stereotypes make use of classificatory data such as the education level (and type), the field of work and make predictions on the users' expertise in a set of domains (which are related to the (sub)sections of the news server).

Receptivity: these stereotypes make predictions on the user's level of receptivity using classificatory data such as the user's age, education level, type of work, frequency of access to the WWW. An example of stereotype in this family (the "Medium receptive adult reader") is reported in the following:

Profile:
age: 14-19: 0.00 | 20-25: 0.10 | 26-35: 0.20 | 36-45: 0.40 | 46-65: 0.20 | >65: 0.10
education level: primary school: 0.10 | secondary school :0.70 | university: 0.20
job: manager: 0.00 | self-trader: 0.10 | self-employed: 0.35 | employee: 0.35, etc.
frequency of access to WWW: less than once a month: 0.00 | about once a week: 0.80, etc.

Prediction:
receptivity level: high: 0.00 | medium: 1.00 | low: 0.00

In conclusions, the designed application seems to suggest (as shown also by the example) that there are dimensions of user modelling that are general and that can be re-used across different tasks and application domains. In this specific case, this holds for all the dimensions, especially as regards the classificatory part of the stereotypes.

Indeed a preliminary study of other application tasks (recommender systems for e-commerce) provides a first confirmation of such a claim (and some of the dimensions above can be re-used also in this different application).

However, a definite answer on which dimensions can be generalized and re-used across multiple tasks and which one are more specific will be possible only after analysing and decomposing all the tasks for various application domains.

References

1. Ardissono, L., Console, L., Torre, I.: Strategies for personalizing the access to news servers. In Proc. AAAI Spring Symposium on Adaptive User Interfaces, Stanford, (March 2000) 7–12
2. Ardissono, L., Console, L., Torre, I.: On the application of personalization techniques to news servers on the WWW. In Lamma, E., Mello, P. (eds.): Advances in Artificial

Intelligence. Lecture Notes in Computer Science, Vol. 1792. Springer Verlag, Berlin Heidelberg New York (2000) 261–271

3. Brusilovsky, P.L.: Methods and Techniques of Adaptive Hypermedia. User Modelling and User-Adapted Interaction 6 (1996) 87–129

4. De Bra, P.: Design issue in adaptive hypermedia application development. In Second International Workshop on Adaptive Systems and User Modelling on the World Wide Web. Banff, Canada (1999) 29–39. Also available at
http://www.contrib.andrew.cmu.edu/~plb/WWWUM99_workshop

5. McTear, M.F.: User modelling for adaptive computer systems: a survey of recent developments. Artificial Intelligence Review 7 (1993) 157–184

6. Rich, E.: Stereotypes and user modelling. In Wahlster, W., Kobsa, A. (eds): User Models in Dialog Systems, Springer Verlag, Berlin Heidelberg New York (1989) 35–51

Author Index

Aerts, A., 250
André, E., 1
Ardissono, L., 5
Arrigo, M., 305

Baena, A., 17
Baggio, D., 202
Bailey, C., 260
Barra, M., 264, 396
Belmonte, M.-V., 17
Ben Ahmed, Pr. M., 355
Bental, D., 27, 268
Boitel, A., 272
Bollen, J., 38
Boticario, J. G., 51
Boyadjiev, D., 293
Bradley, K., 62, 363
Butorin, N., 293

Calvi, L., 276
Carro, R. M., 280
Carthy, J., 327
Cawsey, A., 27, 268
Chen, J., 284
Chesi, C., 403
Cheverst, K., 73
Chittaro, L., 86
Condit, C., 155
Conejo, R., 239
Corrao, R., 305
Cotter, P., 98
Cristea, A. I., 289, 347

Davies, N., 73
De Bra, P., 250
Delahunty, T., 179
Dimitrova, M., 293

Eddy, B., 268

Farrell, S., 144
Fernández-Anta, I., 297
Ferrario, M. A., 301
Fulantelli, G., 305

Gamper, J., 311
Garlatti, S., 315
Gaudioso, E., 51
Gilbert, J. E., 409
Göker, A., 319
Gori, M., 323
Goy, A., 5
Grandbastien, M., 214
Grigoriadou, M., 189
Guzmán, E., 239

Hall, W., 260, 335
Han, C. Y. , 409
Hatch, P., 327
He, D., 319
Henze, N., 109
Hernandez, F., 51
Höök, K., 331
Hothi, J., 335
Houben, G.-J., 250
Hübscher, R., 121

Iksal, S., 315

Jones, R., 27

Karagiannidis, C., 343
Kayama, M., 347
Knapp, J., 311
Koch, S., 384
Kurhila, J., 351
Kushmerick, N., 133

Laaksolahti, J., 331
Laroussi, M., 355
Leclet, D., 272
Lu, S., 392

Maggini, M., 323
Maglio, P. P., 144
Magnini, B., 388
Magoulas, G. D., 189
Mandow, L., 17
Marinilli, M., 355
Martinelli, E., 323
Marucci, L., 359

McAndrew, P., 268
McKee, J., 133
Millán, E., 297
Mitchell, K., 73
Murphy, A., 179
Murray, T., 155

Napolitano, S., 264
Nejdl, W., 109
Not, E., 167

O'Hare, G., 179
Okamoto, T., 289, 347

Palmieri, G., 264
Papanikolaou, K. A., 189
Paradis, F., 392
Paris, C., 392
Paternò, F., 359
Pearson, J., 27
Pérez-de-la-Cruz, J.-L., 297
Petrelli, D., 202
Pezzulo, G., 202
Piemonte, J., 155
Pulido, E., 280

Rafter, R., 62, 363
Ranon, R., 86
Rizzo, F., 403
Rizzo, R., 305
Rodríguez, P., 280

Sampson, D. G., 343
Sanrach, C., 214
Scarano, V., 264
Scarselli, F., 323

schraefel, m. c., 369
Seeberg, C., 375
Sewell, K., 179
Shen, T., 155
Sly, T., 335
Smith, P., 73
Smyth, B., 62, 98, 301, 363
Specht, M., 380
Stede, M., 384
Stefani, A., 388
Steinacker, A., 375
Steinmetz, R., 375
Stern, M. K., 227
Stokes, N., 327
Strapparava, C., 388
Sutinen, E., 351
Svensson, M., 331

Thibedeau, J., 155
Toolan, F., 133
Torre, I., 415
Trella, M., 239

Waern, A., 331
Wan, S., 392
Waters, K, 301
Wilkinson, R., 392
Woolf, B. P., 227
Wu, H., 250
Wu, M., 392

Yang, Y., 284

Zancanaro, M., 167
Zhang, H., 284
Zitarosa, L., 264

Lecture Notes in Computer Science

For information about Vols. 1–1795
please contact your bookseller or Springer-Verlag

Vol. 1796: B. Christianson, B. Crispo, J.A. Malcolm, M. Roe (Eds.), Security Protocols. Proceedings, 1999. XII, 229 pages. 2000.

Vol. 1797: B. Falsafi, M. Lauria (Eds.), Network-Based Parallel Computing. Proceedings, 2000. X, 179 pages. 2000.

Vol. 1798: F. Pichler, R. Moreno-Diaz, P. Kopacek (Eds.), Computer-Aided Systems Theory – EUROCAST'99. Proceedings, 1999. X, 602 pages. 2000.

Vol. 1800: J. Rolim et al. (Eds.), Parallel and Distributed Processing. Proceedings, 2000. XXIII, 1311 pages. 2000.

Vol. 1801: J. Miller, A. Thompson, P. Thomson, T.C. Fogarty (Eds.), Evolvable Systems: From Biology to Hardware. Proceedings, 2000. X, 286 pages. 2000.

Vol. 1802: R. Poli, W. Banzhaf, W.B. Langdon, J. Miller, P. Nordin, T.C. Fogarty (Eds.), Genetic Programming. Proceedings, 2000. X, 361 pages. 2000.

Vol. 1803: S. Cagnoni et al. (Eds.), Real-World Applications and Evolutionary Computing. Proceedings, 2000. XII, 396 pages. 2000.

Vol. 1804: B. Azvine, N. Azarmi, D.D. Nauck (Eds.), Intelligent Systems and Soft Computing. XVII, 359 pages. 2000. (Subseries LNAI).

Vol. 1805: T. Terano, H. Liu, A.L.P. Chen (Eds.), Knowledge Discovery and Data Mining. Proceedings, 2000. XIV, 460 pages. 2000. (Subseries LNAI).

Vol. 1806: W. van der Aalst, J. Desel, A. Oberweis (Eds.), Business Process Management. VIII, 391 pages. 2000.

Vol. 1807: B. Preneel (Ed.), Advances in Cryptology – EUROCRYPT 2000. Proceedings, 2000. XVIII, 608 pages. 2000.

Vol. 1809: S. Biundo, M. Fox (Eds.), Recent Advances in AI Planning. Proceedings, 1999. VIII, 373 pages. 2000. (Subseries LNAI).

Vol. 1810: R.López de Mántaras, E. Plaza (Eds.), Machine Learning: ECML 2000. Proceedings, 2000. XII, 460 pages. 2000. (Subseries LNAI).

Vol. 1811: S.W. Lee, H.. Bülthoff, T. Poggio (Eds.), Biologically Motivated Computer Vision. Proceedings, 2000. XIV, 656 pages. 2000.

Vol. 1813: P.L. Lanzi, W. Stolzmann, S.W. Wilson (Eds.), Learning Classifier Systems. X, 349 pages. 2000. (Subseries LNAI).

Vol. 1815: G. Pujolle, H. Perros, S. Fdida, U. Körner, I. Stavrakakis (Eds.), Networking 2000 – Broadband Communications, High Performance Networking, and Performance of Communication Networks. Proceedings, 2000. XX, 981 pages. 2000.

Vol. 1816: T. Rus (Ed.), Algebraic Methodology and Software Technology. Proceedings, 2000. XI, 545 pages. 2000.

Vol. 1817: A. Bossi (Ed.), Logic-Based Program Synthesis and Transformation. Proceedings, 1999. VIII, 313 pages. 2000.

Vol. 1818: C.G. Omidyar (Ed.), Mobile and Wireless Communications Networks. Proceedings, 2000. VIII, 187 pages. 2000.

Vol. 1819: W. Jonker (Ed.), Databases in Telecommunications. Proceedings, 1999. X, 208 pages. 2000.

Vol. 1821: R. Loganantharaj, G. Palm, M. Ali (Eds.), Intelligent Problem Solving. Proceedings, 2000. XVII, 751 pages. 2000. (Subseries LNAI).

Vol. 1822: H.H. Hamilton, Advances in Artificial Intelligence. Proceedings, 2000. XII, 450 pages. 2000. (Subseries LNAI).

Vol. 1823: M. Bubak, H. Afsarmanesh, R. Williams, B. Hertzberger (Eds.), High Performance Computing and Networking. Proceedings, 2000. XVIII, 719 pages. 2000.

Vol. 1824: J. Palsberg (Ed.), Static Analysis. Proceedings, 2000. VIII, 433 pages. 2000.

Vol. 1825: M. Nielsen, D. Simpson (Eds.), Application and Theory of Petri Nets 2000. Proceedings, 2000. XI, 485 pages. 2000.

Vol. 1826: W. Cazzola, R.J. Stroud, F. Tisato (Eds.), Reflection and Software Engineering. X, 229 pages. 2000.

Vol. 1827: D. Bert, C. Choppy, P. Mosses (Eds.), Recent Trends in Algebraic Development Techniques. Proceedings, 1999. X, 477 pages. 2000.

Vol. 1829: C. Fonlupt, J.-K. Hao, E. Lutton, E. Ronald, M. Schoenauer (Eds.), Artificial Evolution. Proceedings, 1999. X, 293 pages. 2000.

Vol. 1830: P. Kropf, G. Babin, J. Plaice, H. Unger (Eds.), Distributed Communities on the Web. Proceedings, 2000. X, 203 pages. 2000.

Vol. 1831: D. McAllester (Ed.), Automated Deduction – CADE-17. Proceedings, 2000. XIII, 519 pages. 2000. (Subseries LNAI).

Vol. 1832: B. Lings, K. Jeffery (Eds.), Advances in Databases. Proceedings, 2000. X, 227 pages. 2000.

Vol. 1833: L. Bachmair (Ed.), Rewriting Techniques and Applications. Proceedings, 2000. X, 275 pages. 2000.

Vol. 1834: J.-C. Heudin (Ed.), Virtual Worlds. Proceedings, 2000. XI, 314 pages. 2000. (Subseries LNAI).

Vol. 1835: D. N. Christodoulakis (Ed.), Natural Language Processing – NLP 2000. Proceedings, 2000. XII, 438 pages. 2000. (Subseries LNAI).

Vol. 1836: B. Masand, M. Spiliopoulou (Eds.), Web Usage Analysis and User Profiling. Proceedings, 2000, V, 183 pages. 2000. (Subseries LNAI).

Vol. 1837: R. Backhouse, J. Nuno Oliveira (Eds.), Mathematics of Program Construction. Proceedings, 2000. IX, 257 pages. 2000.

Vol. 1838: W. Bosma (Ed.), Algorithmic Number Theory. Proceedings, 2000. IX, 615 pages. 2000.

Vol. 1839: G. Gauthier, C. Frasson, K. VanLehn (Eds.), Intelligent Tutoring Systems. Proceedings, 2000. XIX, 675 pages. 2000.

Vol. 1840: F. Bomarius, M. Oivo (Eds.), Product Focused Software Process Improvement. Proceedings, 2000. XI, 426 pages. 2000.

Vol. 1841: E. Dawson, A. Clark, C. Boyd (Eds.), Information Security and Privacy. Proceedings, 2000. XII, 488 pages. 2000.

Vol. 1842: D. Vernon (Ed.), Computer Vision – ECCV 2000. Part I. Proceedings, 2000. XVIII, 953 pages. 2000.

Vol. 1843: D. Vernon (Ed.), Computer Vision – ECCV 2000. Part II. Proceedings, 2000. XVIII, 881 pages. 2000.

Vol. 1844: W.B. Frakes (Ed.), Software Reuse: Advances in Software Reusability. Proceedings, 2000. XI, 450 pages. 2000.

Vol. 1845: H.B. Keller, E. Plöderer (Eds.), Reliable Software Technologies Ada-Europe 2000. Proceedings, 2000. XIII, 304 pages. 2000.

Vol. 1846: H. Lu, A. Zhou (Eds.), Web-Age Information Management. Proceedings, 2000. XIII, 462 pages. 2000.

Vol. 1847: R. Dyckhoff (Ed.), Automated Reasoning with Analytic Tableaux and Related Methods. Proceedings, 2000. X, 441 pages. 2000. (Subseries LNAI).

Vol. 1848: R. Giancarlo, D. Sankoff (Eds.), Combinatorial Pattern Matching. Proceedings, 2000. XI, 423 pages. 2000.

Vol. 1849: C. Freksa, W. Brauer, C. Habel, K.F. Wender (Eds.), Spatial Cognition II. XI, 420 pages. 2000. (Subseries LNAI).

Vol. 1850: E. Bertino (Ed.), ECOOP 2000 – Object-Oriented Programming. Proceedings, 2000. XIII, 493 pages. 2000.

Vol. 1851: M.M. Halldórsson (Ed.), Algorithm Theory – SWAT 2000. Proceedings, 2000. XI, 564 pages. 2000.

Vol. 1853: U. Montanari, J.D.P. Rolim, E. Welzl (Eds.), Automata, Languages and Programming. Proceedings, 2000. XVI, 941 pages. 2000.

Vol. 1854: G. Lacoste, B. Pfitzmann, M. Steiner, M. Waidner (Eds.), SEMPER — Secure Electronic Marketplace for Europe. XVIII, 350 pages. 2000.

Vol. 1855: E.A. Emerson, A.P. Sistla (Eds.), Computer Aided Verification. Proceedings, 2000. X, 582 pages. 2000.

Vol. 1857: J. Kittler, F. Roli (Eds.), Multiple Classifier Systems. Proceedings, 2000. XII, 404 pages. 2000.

Vol. 1858: D.-Z. Du, P. Eades, V. Estivill-Castro, X. Lin, A. Sharma (Eds.), Computing and Combinatorics. Proceedings, 2000. XII, 478 pages. 2000.

Vol. 1860: M. Klusch, L. Kerschberg (Eds.), Cooperative Information Agents IV. Proceedings, 2000. XI, 285 pages. 2000. (Subseries LNAI).

Vol. 1861: J. Lloyd, V. Dahl, U. Furbach, M. Kerber, K.-K. Lau, C. Palamidessi, L. Moniz Pereira, Y. Sagiv, P.J. Stuckey (Eds.), Computational Logic – CL 2000. Proceedings, 2000. XIX, 1379 pages. (Subseries LNAI).

Vol. 1862: P.G. Clote, H. Schwichtenberg (Eds.), Computer Science Logic. Proceedings, 2000. XIII, 543 pages. 2000.

Vol. 1863: L. Carter, J. Ferrante (Eds.), Languages and Compilers for Parallel Computing. Proceedings, 1999. XII, 500 pages. 2000.

Vol. 1864: B. Y. Choueiry, T. Walsh (Eds.), Abstraction, Reformulation, and Approximation. Proceedings, 2000. XI, 333 pages. 2000. (Subseries LNAI).

Vol. 1865: K.R. Apt, A.C. Kakas, E. Monfroy, F. Rossi (Eds.), New Trends Constraints. Proceedings, 1999. X, 339 pages. 2000. (Subseries LNAI).

Vol. 1866: J. Cussens, A. Frisch (Eds.), Inductive Logic Programming. Proceedings, 2000. X, 265 pages. 2000. (Subseries LNAI).

Vol. 1867: B. Ganter, G.W. Mineau (Eds.), Conceptual Structures: Logical, Linguistic, and Computational Issues. Proceedings, 2000. XI, 569 pages. 2000. (Subseries LNAI).

Vol. 1868: P. Koopman, C. Clack (Eds.), Implementation of Functional Languages. Proceedings, 1999. IX, 199 pages. 2000.

Vol. 1869: M. Aagaard, J. Harrison (Eds.), Theorem Proving in Higher Order Logics. Proceedings, 2000. IX, 535 pages. 2000.

Vol. 1872: J. van Leeuwen, O. Watanabe, M. Hagiya, P.D. Mosses, T. Ito (Eds.), Theoretical Computer Science. Proceedings, 2000. XV, 630 pages. 2000.

Vol. 1876: F. J. Ferri, J. Iñesta, A. Amin, P. Pudil (Eds.), Advances in Pattern Recognition. Proceedings, 2000. XVIII, 901 pages. 2000.

Vol. 1877: C. Palamidessi (Ed.), CONCUR 2000 – Concurrency Theory. Proceedings, 2000. XI, 612 pages. 2000.

Vol. 1880: M. Bellare (Ed.), Advances in Cryptology – CRYPTO 2000. Proceedings, 2000. XI, 545 pages. 2000.

Vol. 1881: C. Zhang, V.-W. Soo (Eds.), Design and Applications of Intelligent Agents. Proceedings, 2000. X, 183 pages. 2000. (Subseries LNAI).

Vol. 1889: M. Anderson, P. Cheng, V. Haarslev (Eds.), Theory and Application of Diagrams. Proceedings, 2000. XII, 504 pages. 2000. (Subseries LNAI).

Vol. 1892: P. Brusilovsky, O. Stock, C. Strapparava (Eds.), Adaptive Hypermedia and Adaptive Web-Based Systems. Proceedings, 2000. XIII, 422 pages. 2000.

Vol. 1893: M. Nielsen, B. Rovan (Eds.), Mathematical Foundations of Computer Science 2000. Proceedings, 2000. XIII, 710 pages. 2000.

Vol. 1896: R. W. Hartenstein, H. Grünbacher (Eds.), Field-Programmable Logic and Applications. Proceedings, 2000. XVII, 856 pages. 2000.

Vol. 1897: J. Gutknecht, W. Weck (Eds.), Modular Programming Languages. Proceedings, 2000. XII, 299 pages. 2000.

Vol. 1900: A. Bode, T. Ludwig, W. Karl, R. Wismüller (Eds.), Euro-Par 2000 Parallel Processing. Proceedings, 2000. XXXV, 1368 pages. 2000.